# A COMPANION TO
# THE ANGLO-NORMAN WORLD

# A COMPANION TO
# THE ANGLO-NORMAN WORLD

EDITED BY

Christopher Harper-Bill and Elisabeth van Houts

THE BOYDELL PRESS

First published 2002
The Boydell Press, Woodbridge
Reprinted in paperback 2007


ISBN 978-184383-341-3


The Boydell Press is an imprint of Boydell & Brewer Ltd
PO Box 9, Woodbridge, Suffolk IP12 3DF, UK
and of Boydell & Brewer Inc.
668 Mt Hope Avenue, Rochester, NY 14620, USA
website: www.boydellandbrewer.com


A CiP catalogue record for this book is available
from the British Library

Library of Congress Catalog Card Number: 2002027997


This publication is printed on acid-free paper


Printed in Great Britain by
Athenaeum Press Ltd, Gateshead, Tyne and Wear

# Contents

# Illustrations

# Abbreviations

| | |
|---|---|
| *AA SS* | *Acta Sanctorum* (of the Bollandists) |
| AD | Archives Départementales |
| *AHR* | *American Historical Review* |
| *Ann. Mon.* | *Annales Monastici*, ed. H.R. Luard, 5 vols, RS XXXVI, 1864–69 |
| *ANS* | *Anglo-Norman Studies* |
| *Antiqs Jnl* | *The Antiquaries Journal* (Society of Antiquaries of London) |
| ANTS | Anglo-Norman Text Society |
| *Arch. Jnl* | *Archaeological Journal* (Royal Archaeological Institute) |
| *ASC* | *Anglo-Saxon Chronicle* (various edns) |
| *ASE* | *Anglo-Saxon England* |
| BAA | British Archaeological Association |
| BAR | British Archaeological Reports |
| Bates, *Regesta* | *Regesta Regum Anglo-Normannorum: the Acta of William I (1066–1087)*, ed. D. Bates, Oxford 1998 |
| *Battle Chronicle* | *The Chronicle of Battle Abbey*, ed. E. Searle, OMT, 1980 |
| *BIHR* | *Bulletin of the Institute of Historical Research* |
| BL | British Library |
| BN | Bibliothèque Nationale |
| *BNJ* | *British Numismatic Journal* |
| *Cal. Docs France* | *Calendar of Documents preserved in France . . .* i, *918–1216*, ed. J.H. Round, HMSO, 1891 |
| *Carmen* | *The Carmen de Hastingae Proelio of Guy, Bishop of Amiens*, ed. C. Morton and H. Munz, OMT, 1972, rev. edn, F. Barlow, OMT, 1998 |
| *CCM* | *Cahiers de Civilisation Médiévale* |
| *Chron. Abingdon* | *Chronicon Monasterii de Abingdon*, ed. J. Stevenson, 2 vols, RS II, 1858 |
| CNRS | Centre National de la Recherche Scientifique |
| *Coggeshall* | *Radulphi de Coggeshall Chronicon Anglicanum*, ed. J. Stevenson, RS LXVI, 1875 |
| *C & S* | *Councils and Synods with other Documents relating to the English Church* i, *A.D. 871–1204*, ed. D. Whitelock, M. Brett and C.N.L. Brooke, 2 vols, Oxford 1964 |
| *DB* | *Domesday Book, seu liber censualis . . .*, ed. A. Farley, 2 vols, 'Record Commission', 1783; iii, iv, ed. H. Ellis, 1816 (also other edns) |
| *De gestis pontificum* | William of Malmesbury, *De gestis pontificum Anglorum*, ed. N.E.S.A. Hamilton, RS LII, 1870 |
| *Dialogus* | Richard Fitz Nigel, *Dialogus de Scaccario*, ed. C. Johnson, rev. edn, F.E.L. Carter and D. Greenway, OMT, 1983 |
| *Diceto* | *Radulphi de Diceto Opera Historica. The Historical Works of* |

|  |  |
|---|---|
|  | *Master Ralph de Diceto, Dean of London*, ed. W. Stubbs, 2 vols, RS LXVIII, 1876 |
| *Domesday People* | K.S.B. Keats-Rohan, *Domesday People: a Prosopography of Persons occurring in English Documents, 1066–1166* i, *Domesday Book*, Woodbridge 1999 |
| *Dudo* | *De moribus et actis primorum Normanniae Ducum auctore Dudone Sancti Quintini Decano*, ed. J. Lair, Société des Antiquaires de Normandie, 1865; *Dudo of St Quentin, History of the Normans*, trans. E. Christiansen, Woodbridge 1998 |
| Eadmer, *HN* | *Historia Novorum in Anglia*, ed. M. Rule, RS LXXXI, 1884 |
| Eadmer, *VA* | *The Life of St Anselm, Archbishop of Canterbury by Eadmer*, ed. R.W. Southern, NMT, 1962 |
| *Ec. HR* | *Economic History Review* |
| *EEA* | *English Episcopal Acta* (British Academy) |
| *EHD* | *English Historical Documents*, 2nd edn, i, *500–1042*, ed. D. Whitelock; ii, *1042–1189*, ed. D.C. Douglas and G.W. Greenaway, London 1979–81 |
| *EHR* | *English Historical Review* |
| *England and Normandy* | *England and Normandy in the Middle Ages*, ed. D. Bates and A. Curry, London 1994 |
| Fauroux | *Recueil des actes des ducs de Normandie (911–1066)*, ed. M. Fauroux, Mémoires de la Société des Antiquaires de Normandie XXXVI, 1961 |
| *GDB* | *Great Domesday Book* |
| GEC | *Complete Peerage of England, Scotland, Ireland, Great Britain and the United Kingdom*, ed. Vicary Gibbs *et al.*, 13 vols, London 1910–59 |
| *Gesta Guillelmi* | *The Gesta Guillelmi of William of Poitiers*, ed. R.H.C. Davis and M. Chibnall, OMT, 1998 |
| *Gesta Regis Henrici* | *Gesta Regis Henrici Secundi Benedicti Abbatis. The Chronicle of the Reigns of Henry II and Richard I, 1169–92*, ed. W. Stubbs, 2 vols, RS XLIX, 1867 |
| *Gesta Regum* | William of Malmesbury, *Gesta Regum Anglorum*, ed. R.A.B. Mynors, R.M. Thomson and M. Winterbottom, 2 vols, OMT, 1998–99 |
| *Gesta Stephani* | ed. K.R. Potter and R.H.C. Davis, OMT, 1976 |
| *Giraldi Cambrensis Opera* | ed. J.S. Brewer, J.F. Dimock and G.F. Warner, 8 vols, RS XXI, 1861–91 |
| Glanvill | *The Treatise on the Laws and Customs of the Realm of England commonly called Glanvill*, ed. G.D.G. Hall, NMT, 1965 |
| *Haskins Soc. Jnl* | *Haskins Society Journal* |
| *Historia Novella* | William of Malmesbury, *Historia Novella*, ed. E. King and K.R. Potter, OMT, 1998 |
| HMSO | Her Majesty's Stationery Office |
| *Howden* | *Chronica Rogeri de Houedene*, ed. W. Stubbs, 4 vols, RS LI, 1868–71 |
| *Huntingdon* | *Henry, Archdeacon of Huntingdon: 'Historia Anglorum'*, ed. D. Greenway, OMT, 1996 |

| | |
|---|---|
| *JBAA* | *Journal of the British Archaeological Association* |
| *JBS* | *Journal of British Studies* |
| *JEH* | *Journal of Ecclesiastical History* |
| *JMH* | *Journal of Medieval History* |
| *Jnl* | *Journal* |
| John of Worcester | *The Chronicle of John of Worcester* ii–iii, ed. R.R. Darlington and P. McGurk, OMT, 1995–98 |
| *Jumièges* | *Gesta Normannorum Ducum of William of Jumièges, Orderic Vitalis and Robert of Torigni*, ed. E.M.C. van Houts, 2 vols, OMT, 1992–95 |
| *Lanfranc's Letters* | *The Letters of Lanfranc, Archbishop of Canterbury*, ed. H. Clover and M. Gibson, OMT, 1979 |
| *Med. Arch.* | *Medieval Archaeology* |
| *MGH SS* | *Monumenta Germaniae Historica, Scriptores* |
| *MRSN* | *Magni Rotuli Scaccarii Normanniæ*, ed. T. Stapleton, 2 vols, London 1840–44 |
| *Newburgh* | *Historia Rerum Anglicarum of William of Newburgh*, in *Chronicles of Stephen, Henry II and Richard I*, ed. R. Howlett, 4 vols, RS LXXXII, 1885–90 |
| NMT | Nelsons Medieval Texts |
| ns | new series |
| OMT | Oxford Medieval Texts |
| *Orderic* | Orderic Vitalis, *Historia Ecclesiastica*, ed. M. Chibnall, 6 vols, OMT, 1969–80 |
| os | old series |
| *PBA* | *Proceedings of the British Academy* |
| *PL* | *Patrologiae cursus completus, series Latina*, ed. J.P. Migne, Paris 1841–64 |
| *PR* | *Pipe Roll* (as published by Pipe Roll Society) |
| PRO | Public Record Office |
| PRS | Pipe Roll Society |
| *Recueil H II* | *Recueil des actes de Henri II, roi d'Angleterre et duc de Normandie . . .*, ed. L. Delisle and E. Berger, 4 vols, Paris 1916–27 |
| *Regesta* | *Regesta Regum Anglo-Normannorum* i, ed. H.W.C. Davis, Oxford 1913; ii, ed. C. Johnson and H.A. Cronne, Oxford 1956; iii, ed. H.A. Cronne and R.H.C. Davis, Oxford 1968 |
| *RHF* | *Recueil des historiens des Gaules et de la France*, Paris 1738–1904 |
| *Rigord* | *Œuvres de Rigord et de Guillaume le Breton*, ed. H.-F. Delaborde, 2 vols, Paris 1882–5 |
| RO | Record Office |
| *Rot. Chart.* | *Rotuli Chartarum in Turri Londinensi Asservati*, ed. T.D. Hardy, Record Commission, London 1837 |
| *Rot. de Lib.* | *Rotuli de Liberate ac de Misis et Praestitis, regnante Iohanne*, ed. T.D. Hardy, Record Commission, London 1844 |
| *Rot. de Obl.* | *Rotuli de Oblatis et Finibus in Turri Londinensi Asservati*, ed. T.D. Hardy, Record Commission, London 1835 |

| | |
|---|---|
| *Rot. Litt. Claus.* | *Rotuli Litterarum Clausarum in Turri Londinensi Asservati,* ed. T.D. Hardy, Record Commission, London 1833–44 |
| *Rot. Litt. Pat.* | *Rotuli Litterarum Patentium in Turri Londinensi Asservati,* ed. T.D. Hardy, Record Commission, London 1835 |
| *Rot. Norm.* | *Rotuli Normanniae in Turri Londinensi Asservati,* ed. T.D. Hardy, Record Commission, London 1835 |
| *Royal Writs* | *Royal Writs in England from the Conquest to Glanvil,* ed. R.C. van Caenegem, Selden Society LXXVII, 1959 |
| RS | Rolls Series |
| S | P.H. Sawyer, *Anglo-Saxon Charters. An Annotated List and Bibliography,* Royal Historical Society Guides and Handbooks 8, London 1968 |
| *s.a.* | *sub anno* |
| *SCH* | *Studies in Church History* |
| ser. | series |
| *Studies . . . to Brown* | *Studies in Medieval History presented to R. Allen Brown,* ed. C. Harper-Bill, C. Holdsworth and J.L. Nelson, Woodbridge 1989 |
| Symeon, *HR* | *Historia Regum,* in *Symeon of Durham: Historical Works,* ed. T. Arnold, 2 vols, RS LXXV, 1882–85 |
| *Torigni* | *Chronique de Robert de Torigni,* ed. L. Delisle, 2 vols, Rouen 1872–73 |
| *Trans.* | *Transactions* |
| *TRHS* | *Transactions of the Royal Historical Society* |
| *VCH* | *Victoria County History* |
| *Vita Aedwardi* | *The Life of King Edward who Rests at Westminster,* ed. F. Barlow, 2nd edn, OMT, 1992 |
| Wace | Wace, *Le Roman de Rou,* ed. A.J. Holden, 3 vols, Société des Anciens Textes Français, Paris 1970–73 |
| *Worcester* | Florence of Worcester, *Chronicon ex Chronicis,* ed. B. Thorpe, English Historical Society, London 1848–49 |

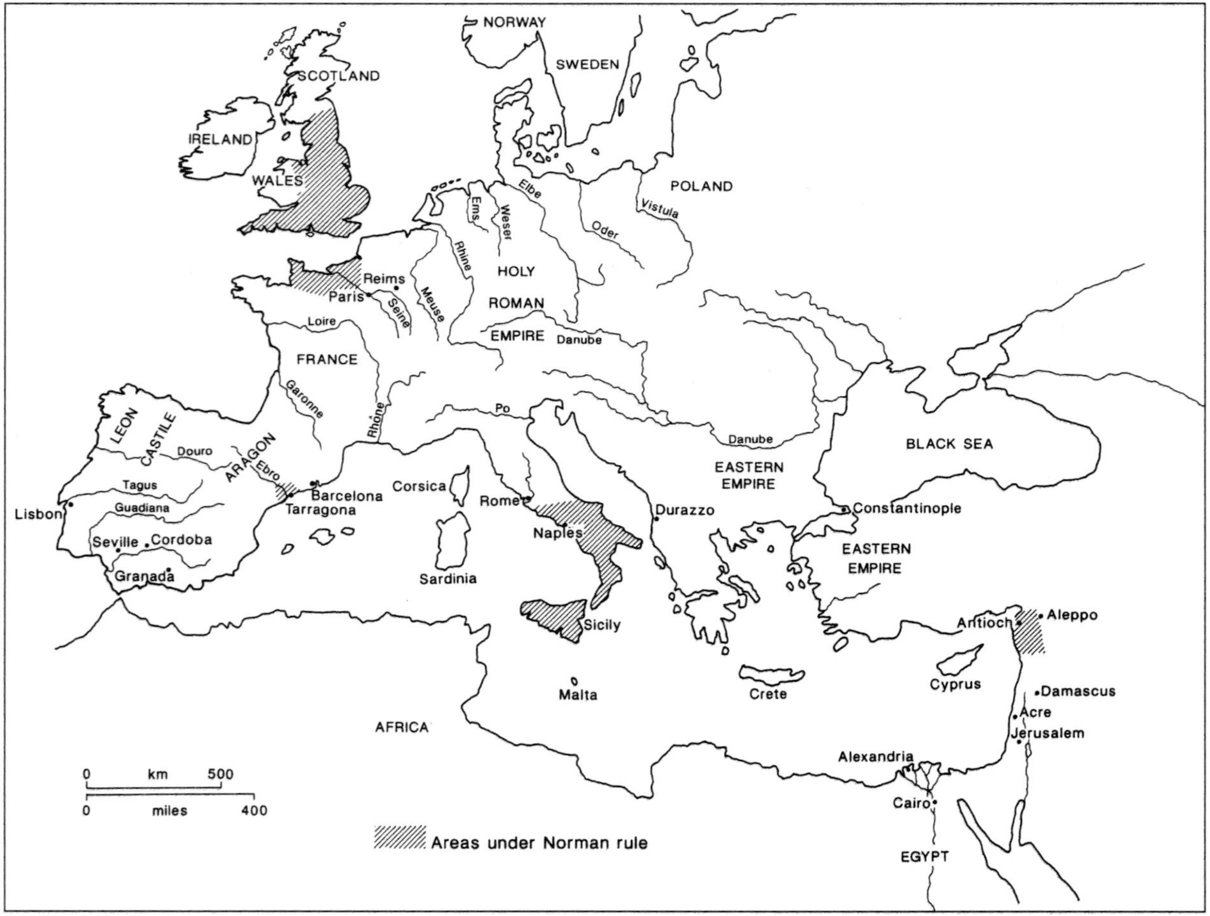

Map 1. Europe c. 1130

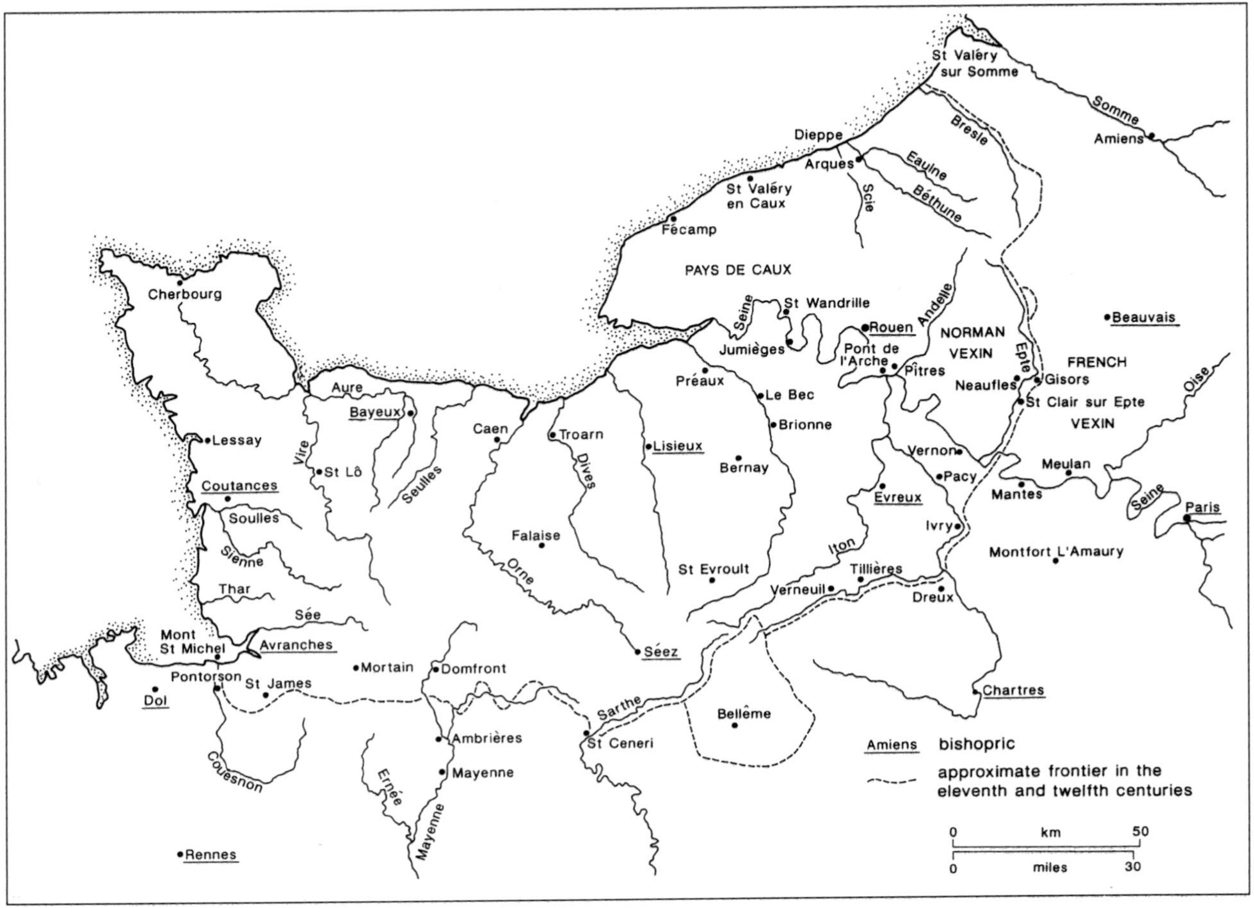

Map 2. Normandy

Map 3. Britain

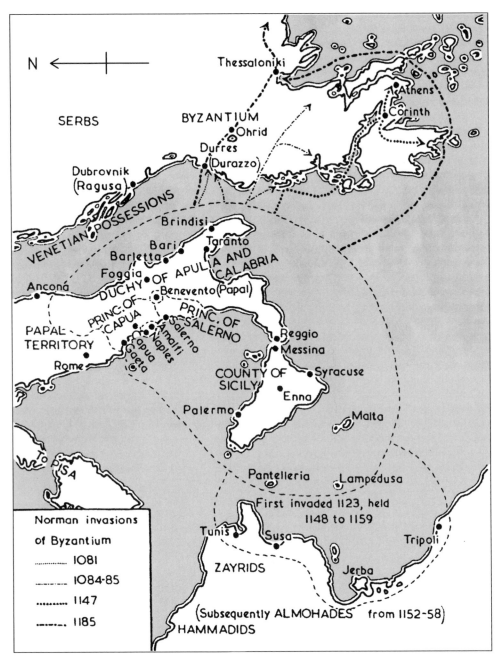

Map 4. The Norman Kingdom of Sicily c. 1150

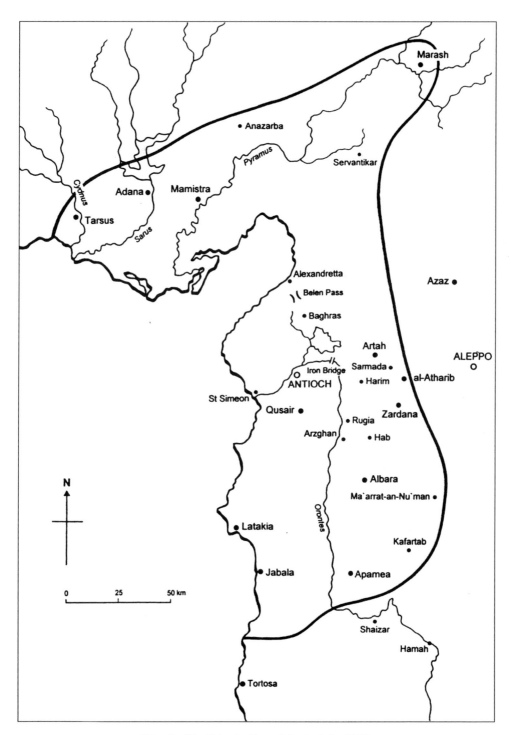

Map 5. The Principality of Antioch in 1112

# Preface

At a time when the relationship of the United Kingdom with the mainland of western Europe is a topic of intense and empassioned debate, the Anglo-Norman period of English history obviously still matters, even if it is so often ignored by those who perceive the distinctive English character to have been forged in the Tudor age by Protestantism and maritime adventure. 1066 remains indeed the most memorable date in English history – the occasion of the last successful invasion of the southern kingdom, the effects of which were extended peaceably, by means of service and marriage, into Scotland. All this was accomplished, too, while Norman adventurers were establishing in the Mediterranean the lordships which were eventually to be united in the kingdom of Sicily, and further east the shorter lived principality of Antioch.

The nature of Anglo-Norman society and government remains as controversial today as it was when in 1966 Sir Richard Southern delivered a famous lecture on 'England's first entry into Europe'. Certainly, as he stated then, 'never before or since has the union of England with the community of Europe been so all embracing, and so thoroughly accepted as part of the nature of things'.[1] In terms of cultural advance, Southern was convinced that the long-term effects of the Conquest had been beneficial: 'the intellectual isolation, which had been so marked a feature of pre-Conquest England, was a thing of the past'[2] – an observation at which many scholars of Old English art and literature might, it must be confessed, demur. Yet Southern also viewed England between the reigns of the Conqueror and King John as a colony, exploited for the benefit of the motherland: 'it is very doubtful if the kings had any policy at all in England; they had only expedients for furthering a policy elsewhere'.[3] His own measured judgement was that 'these were prosperous years for England, but there was not much expression of joy'.[4]

Since the ninth centenary of the Conquest there has been continuous lively debate on every aspect of Anglo-Norman history, from the rituals of kingship to numismatics, from religious sentiment to the nature of tenures. Students of the period writing at the beginning of the twenty-first century may be able to see somewhat further than their predecessors, but this is merely, as Bernard of Chartres famously said of twelfth-century scholars, because they are standing on the shoulders of their eminent predecessors and masters who, from Victorian times onwards, laid the foundations of Anglo-Norman scholarship. In one important aspect the task of the historian of the Conquest and its aftermath is very much easier than it was even thirty years ago. Then, when R. Allen Brown initiated the Norman Conquest special subject in the University of London, there was little primary source material available in

---

[1]   R.W. Southern, 'England's First Entry into Europe', in his *Medieval Humanism and Other Studies*, Oxford 1970, 135–57, at p. 140.
[2]   Ibid., 139.
[3]   Ibid., 139.
[4]   Ibid., 140.

translation beyond the excellent collection of extracts in *English Historical Documents, 1042–1189*. Since then there have appeared critical editions, with translations, of all the major narrative sources relating to the Conquest.[5] As regards archival evidence, the last few years have seen the gradual appearance of a new edition of the corpus of Anglo-Saxon charters,[6] a monumental re-edition of the *acta* of the Conqueror after 1066,[7] and a luxurious and scholarly new edition of Domesday Book.[8] The relative ease of access to the sources is surely one reason why the Norman Conquest is such a popular undergraduate special subject in British universities. While the coverage for the succeeding century and a half is not so even, and there remains the need for new editions of the chronicles of the Angevin kings, much has been achieved too for the twelfth century – for example, the series of English episcopal *acta* which provide the evidence for the administration of the church in times of normality[9] and a new edition of the Becket correspondence which illustrates its greatest crisis.[10] Local record societies have published numerous editions of charters, which are for the Anglo-Norman period in their totality the most fruitful sources for economic and social history – although in this field much remains still to be done.[11] At the apex of political society, an edition of the *acta* of Henry II and Richard I will soon extend our knowledge of the intricacies of royal government.[12] In short, the sources for the years from the Conquest to the loss of Normandy by King John have greatly increased in recent years, so that young historians are increasingly able to test the evidence for themselves.

The multiplication of monographs and articles in learned journals has been even more pronounced. For example, in 1966 the student of King Stephen's reign was still largely dependent on J.H. Round's *Geoffrey de Mandeville: a Study of the Anarchy*, published in 1892. Since 1967 there have been five major studies of the reign, a full-scale treatment of the Empress Matilda, and a plethora of essays.[13] For the period as a whole two major series of conference proceedings have been inaugurated: *Anglo-Norman Studies*, now extending to twenty-four years of the proceedings of the Battle Conference, and across the Atlantic, the *Haskins Society Journal*; but the invention of these specialist outlets does not appear to have diminished the flood of

---

5   See ch. 6 below. There are good selections of sources in R.A. Brown, *The Norman Conquest of England: Sources and Documents*, Woodbridge 1984, and E. van Houts, *The Normans in Europe*, Manchester 2000.

6   The *Anglo-Saxon Charters* series of the British Academy, most recently S. Miller, ed., *Charters of the New Minster, Winchester*, Oxford 2001.

7   Bates, *Regesta*.

8   Published by Alecto Editions as a facsimile, translation and commentary, by county, ed. A. Williams, R.W.H. Erskine and G.H. Martin, London 1986–2000.

9   The *English Episcopal Acta* series of the British Academy; most recently of relevance to Anglo-Norman England is B.R. Kemp, ed., *English Episcopal Acta 18: Salisbury 1078–1217*, Oxford 2000.

10  A. Duggan, ed., *The Correspondence of Thomas Becket, Archbishop of Canterbury*, 2 vols, Oxford 2000.

11  For example, the *Suffolk Charters* series of the Suffolk Records Society, which has since 1979 presented seventeen volumes.

12  To be published by the British Academy.

13  R.H.C. Davis, *King Stephen*, Marlow 1967, 3rd edn 1990; H.A. Cronne, *The Reign of Stephen: Anarchy in England, 1135–54*, London 1970; E. King, ed., *The Anarchy of King Stephen's Reign*, Oxford 1991; D. Crouch, *The Reign of King Stephen*, London 1993; D. Matthew, *King Stephen*, London 2002; M. Chibnall, *The Empress Matilda*, Oxford 1991.

articles on Anglo-Norman history in more general historical periodicals in Britain, continental Europe and the United States.

This multiplication of research and scholarship is, of course, the most obvious indication of the healthy state of Anglo-Norman studies. It is impossible now, however, as it was not thirty years ago, for the most conscientious undergraduate or for the teacher whose own specialisms may lie in another area of medieval scholarship to keep abreast of this torrent of literature. It was this consideration which prompted the editors to approach colleagues with the request that they should provide surveys of the current state of research within their own specialisms.

The scope of this volume is specifically Anglo-Norman. There are thus surveys of the history of the two constituent parts of the 'cross-Channel realm', of the place of kingdom and duchy in the politics and culture of the North Sea, and of the parallel Norman achievement in the Mediterranean. There are overviews both of secular administration and of the church, and a consideration of the vexed question of 'feudalism' and lordship.[14] While the history of the various dominions subject after 1154 to Henry II and his sons has not been treated as a whole, there is a chapter on the somewhat neglected topic of Normandy itself under the Angevin kings. Within the broad field of cultural history, there are discussions of historical writing, language and literature and ecclesiastical architecture, and here the story has been taken beyond 1154 to the end of the century, when the traditions became diluted. The relative neglect of military matters in this volume is deliberate, as it is in a sense a companion to the essays gathered by Matthew Strickland in *Anglo-Norman Warfare* (1992) and to the forthcoming collection of important articles on castles edited by Robert Liddiard.

The editors wish to thank all the contributors, and particularly the foremost amongst them who had to wait for some time for this volume to appear. They are grateful to Manchester University Press for permission to reprint Chapter 7, to Mrs Judith Loades and Headstart History for similar courtesy with regard to Chapter 9, and also to all those who gave permission for the reproduction of illustrations. They are indebted, too, to Alicia Corrêa, who compiled the index. Thanks are also due to the staff of Boydell & Brewer Ltd, and most especially to Caroline Palmer, for their patience and for their customary care in the production of this book.

C.H-B.                                                                                November 2001
E.v.H.

---

[14] For which most recently D. Bates, 'England and the "Feudal Revolution" ', in *Il feudalesimo nell'alto medioevo, 8–12 aprile 1999*, Settimane di studio sull' alto medioevo xlvii, 2 vols, Spoleto 2000, ii, 611–49.

# 1

# England in the Eleventh Century

## ANN WILLIAMS

Twelfth-century historians differed as to which of the Old English kings was most worthy of admiration. For William of Malmesbury, it was Edgar, 'the honour and delight of Englishmen', who experienced 'no treachery from his own people and no destruction from foreigners', and in the chronicles of whose reign 'scarcely a year is passed over . . . without his doing his country some notable and necessary service and without his founding some new monastery'.[1] Eadmer of Canterbury agreed, describing Edgar as 'that most glorious king . . . a devoted servant of God, [who] when foreign invaders surged in on every side fought them, conquered them and kept them at bay'.[2] For Henry of Huntingdon, it was Cnut who held the palm; 'before him there had never been in England a king of such great authority . . . lord of all Denmark, of all England, of all Norway and also of Scotland'.[3] The Ramsey Chronicler was of the same mind: Cnut was 'inferior to none of his royal predecessors in virtue or strength of arms'.[4]

Edgar and Cnut were significant choices for twelfth-century writers. The former had kept invaders at bay, as Edward the Confessor and Harold II had not, and the latter stood, in implicit contrast to William I, for the ideal conqueror king, a foreigner who nevertheless preserved the fabric of the English Church and kingdom. Now this kingdom had fallen, and 'all had been reduced to servitude and lamentation, and it was even disgraceful to be called English'.[5] To contemporaries, the reason was clear: 'such things happen because of the people's sins, in that they will not love God and righteousness'.[6] Later writers have required more specific causes, and have been more accustomed to apportion blame than praise. Some have seen 'a certain built-in obso-lescence' in the Old English kingdom itself, with its 'many weaknesses, in military organisation, in uncertain frontiers, in racial divisions and political instability, in the absence of a unified law and custom, and, not least, in the absence also of the feudal bond'.[7] Others have concentrated on politics rather than institutions. The genesis of the Norman Conquest is traced to that of the Danes, which destroyed the close-knit web of noble kinsmen upon whom the tenth-century kings had depended and replaced

---

1   *Gesta Regum* i, 238–9.
2   Eadmer, *HN*, translated by Geoffrey Bosanquet, *Eadmer's History of Recent Events in England*, London 1964, 3.
3   *Huntingdon*, 366–7.
4   *Chronicon Abbatiae Rameseiensis*, ed. W.D. Macray, RS, London 1886, 125.
5   *Huntingdon*, 402–3.
6   *ASC*, 1087. The writer was speaking of the pestilence and famine of 1087, but the same sentiments are expressed of the Conquest and its aftermath.
7   R.A. Brown, *The Normans and the Norman Conquest*, 2nd edn, Woodbridge 1985, 86, 87.

them with a new aristocracy, whose jockeying for power destabilized the kingdom: 'when this rootless élite lay dead at Stamford Bridge or at Hastings, the fragile structure of eleventh-century secular lordship collapsed'.[8] Earl Godwine and his sons, greedy, self-seeking and endowed with overweening ambition, have been cast as the villains of the piece: 'a cancer on the body politic that had to be cut out'.[9] It is a formidable consensus, but it is possible to suggest another way of looking at the matter.

Contemporary sources for the reign of Edward the Confessor are relatively abundant but patchy in their coverage. The king's latter years are particularly obscure. Few charters survive from the 1050s and the *Anglo-Saxon Chronicle* becomes oddly reticent; the 'C' text has nothing to record for the years 1057–64, and for 1062 and 1064, neither have the 'D' and 'E' texts. The 'D' text is particularly cagey; of Edward Ætheling's death in 1057 it observes that 'we do not know for what reason it was brought about that he was not allowed to see the face of his kinsman King Edward', and the second outlawry and re-instatement of Earl Ælfgar in 1058 is dismissed with the exclamation that 'it is tedious to relate fully how things went'. Perhaps the various chroniclers were overtaken by events, like the 'Life of King Edward' (*Vita Edwardi*), which, having promised to tell the stories of Earl Harold's campaigns in Wales and Earl Tostig's dealings with Scotland, abandons both after the deaths of the earls in 1066.[10] The accounts of continental writers, useful though they may be in other ways, cannot be expected to contribute much to our knowledge of internal English affairs.

Much of our information on Edward's reign comes from material compiled after the Conquest. One of the most important sources is Domesday Book, which, in the expert analysis of Professor Fleming, has revealed the imbalance in wealth between the king and the family of Earl Godwine. Even after the fall of Earl Tostig in 1065, the total value of the *terra regis* was still less than that of the lands held by Godwine's heirs.[11] Such wealth allowed the sons of Godwine to enrich their followers as well as themselves, draw local thegns into their allegiance, form alliances with lay and ecclesiastical magnates and appropriate for themselves comital land set aside for the support of earls and sheriffs.[12]

How had such a situation come about? The precursors of the eleventh-century earls were the ealdormen who had once administered the local divisions of the West Saxon kingdom. From the ninth century, if not earlier, Wessex had been divided into shires (Hampshire, Berkshire, Wiltshire, Dorset, Somerset), and as the kingdom expanded, new shires were created: the old kingdom of Dumnonia, finally conquered by King Ecgberht in 838, became the shires of Devon and Cornwall, while the former king-

---

8   R. Fleming, *Kings and Lords in Conquest England*, Cambridge 1991, 103; for the Danish conquest and its social consequences, see Fleming, loc. cit., 21–52; K. Mack, 'Changing Thegns: Cnut's Conquest and the English Aristocracy', *Albion* xvi, 1984, 375–87.

9   E. John, *Re-assessing Anglo-Saxon England*, Manchester 1996, 168.

10  *Vita Ædwardi*, xxx–xxxi, 64–6.

11  Fleming, *Kings and Lords*, 71; see also the estimate of the holdings of individual earls in P.A. Clarke, *The English Nobility under Edward the Confessor*, Oxford 1994, 13–30, which brings out the dominating position enjoyed by Harold Godwineson. J.L. Grassi, 'The Lands and Revenues of Edward the Confessor', *EHR* cxvii, 2002, 251–83, has questioned the estimates of Edward's wealth vis-à-vis the family of Godwine and suggested that the 'imbalance' favoured the king rather than the earl.

12  Fleming, *Kings and Lords*, 53–104; idem, 'Domesday Estates of the King and the Godwinesons: a Study in Late Saxon Politics', *Speculum* lviii, 1983, 987–1007.

doms of Kent, Surrey, Sussex and Essex, also conquered by Ecgberht and his son Æthelwulf, became in their turn shires of a greater Wessex.[13]

Administrative units (*provinciae*) comparable to the West Saxon shires had existed within the kingdoms of Mercia and East Anglia, but when these kingdoms fell into West Saxon hands during the first half of the tenth century, their *provinciae* were dismembered and replaced by shires based upon towns fortified by the West Saxon rulers. The transformation did not happen overnight. Some of the older *provinciae* survived for a while; the *Pecsæte* and the *Wrocensæte* are recorded in 963 and the *Magonsæte* as late as 1016.[14] The boundaries of the new shires were also subject to change; a territory dependent upon Gloucester was probably created when Worcester was fortified in the 890s, but it was not until the days of Eadric Streona, ealdorman of Mercia from 1007 to 1017, that this territory was amalgamated with the lands dependent upon Winchcombe to form something like the pre-1974 county.[15]

In the ninth century, each shire of Wessex had its own ealdorman, but the great extension of the kingdom made this impractical, and by the time of Æthelstan (924–39) there were probably no more than a dozen ealdormen in office at any one time.[16] Not only were their territories larger than a single shire, but a hierarchy was beginning to develop in their ranks. The best-known of Æthelstan's ealdormen is his namesake, Æthelstan Half-king, who between c. 930 and 956 was responsible for a huge swathe of land, covering not only East Anglia but also the districts of the east midlands whose inhabitants were still known as the 'east Mercians'.[17] By the 960s, Ælfhere (956–83), a royal kinsman who originally held only central Mercia (the old kingdom of the *Hwicce*), supervised the whole of western Mercia from Cheshire to Gloucestershire.[18]

The assimilation of the Scandinavian population in the north must have been one of the major priorities in the 950s and 960s. It was probably in this period that the confederacy of the Five Boroughs (Lincoln, Stamford, Nottingham, Derby and Leicester) was established, as a regional system of defence for the provinces south of York.[19] In the 990s, Æthelred II (978–1016) legislated for this area in his third code (III Æthelred), issued at Wantage, Berks., but by the end of his reign the confederacy had been replaced by shires based on Lincoln, Nottingham, Derby and Leicester. By

[13] There is an admirable study of pre-Conquest Wessex by B. Yorke, *Wessex in the Early Middle Ages*, Leicester 1995; see especially the chapter on 'Wessex and England, 802–1066', 94–148. On the structures of government and administration in tenth- and eleventh-century England, see also A. Williams, *Kingship and Government in Pre-Conquest England, c. 500–1066*, London 1999.

[14] S.677, dated 958, *ASC*, 1016 (the *Magonsæte*); S.723, dated 963 (the *Wrocensæte*); S.712a, also 963 (the *Pecsæte*; see N. Brooks *et al.*, 'A New Charter of King Edgar', *ASE* xiii, 1989, 137–55).

[15] A. Williams, 'An Introduction to the Worcestershire Domesday', in *The Worcestershire Domesday*, ed. A. Williams and R.W.H. Erskine, London 1988, 9–11; idem, 'An Introduction to the Gloucestershire Domesday', in *The Gloucestershire Domesday*, ed. A. Williams and R.W.H. Erskine, London 1989, 12–14.

[16] Twenty-nine named ealdormen attest the surviving charters of Æthelstan, but no more than fifteen appear at the same time (S. Keynes, *An Atlas of Attestations in Anglo-Saxon Charters, c. 670–1066*, Cambridge 1995, table XXXVIII).

[17] For his career, see C.R. Hart, 'Athelstan "Half-king" and his Family', *ASE* ii, 1973, 115–44, reprinted with additions in *The Danelaw*, London 1992, 569–604.

[18] A. Williams, '*Princeps Merciorum gentis*: the Family, Career and Connections of Ælfhere, Ealdorman of Mercia, 956–83', *ASE* x, 1982, 143–72.

[19] D. Roffe, 'The Origins of Derbyshire', *Derbyshire Archaeological Jnl* cvi, 1986, 111–16; 'Hundreds and Wapentakes', in A. Williams and G.H. Martin, eds, *The Lincolnshire Domesday*, London 1992, 135–43.

1086, Lincolnshire included the territories of Kesteven and Holland, which may at first have been dependent upon Stamford; the two were still separate in 1016, when Cnut led his army from Northamptonshire 'along the fen to Stamford *and then* into Lincolnshire'.[20]

Yorkshire is mentioned for the first time in 1065, but similarities of organization show that it was created at the same time as the counties of the 'Five Boroughs'.[21] Danish York (roughly equivalent to the ancient kingdom of Deira) was absorbed into the West Saxon hegemony after the expulsion of Eric Bloodaxe, its last Scandinavian king (killed in 954).[22] It became the southern region of the ealdordom (later earldom) of Northumbria. Ancient Bernicia had fallen apart during the Danish raids of the ninth and tenth centuries. The territory between the Tyne and the Tees became the land of the *Haliwerfolc*, 'the people of the holy man', i.e. St Cuthbert, who was posthumously resident first at Chester-le-Street and, from 998 onwards, at Durham.[23] The remnant of Bernicia beyond the Tyne was ruled by a dynasty based on the ancient royal fortress of Bamburgh.[24] West Saxon kings from Alfred onwards made efforts to draw the north English into their orbit, and during the tenth century both the bishops of Durham and the rulers of Bamburgh came to acknowledge their authority. It was Osulf of Bamburgh (934–63) whom King Eadred appointed as earl of Northumbria after the fall of Danish York.[25] He was succeeded by Oslac, who came from a different family, perhaps native to the Fens.[26] But though men from other kindreds might, from time to time, have overall authority in Northumbria, Osulf's successors retained their authority beyond the Tyne until 1072, when Gospatric, the last of the line to hold power in England, was expelled.[27]

[20] *ASC*, 1016 (my italics); C. Mahany and D. Roffe, 'Stamford: the Development of an Anglo-Scandinavian Borough', *ANS* v, 1983, 211–14. The *Chronicle* is contemporary for this period (S. Keynes, 'The Declining Reputation of Æthelred II', in D. Hill, ed., *Ethelred the Unready: Papers from the Millenary Conference*, BAR British series lix, 1978, 227–53).

[21] *ASC* 'C', 1065, and see the article by D. Roffe cited in note 19 above.

[22] See note 25 below.

[23] Its origins lie in the agreement made between the community and Guthfrith, king of York (883–894/5), see the *Historia de Sancto Cuthberto*, translated in *EHD* i, no. 6, 261–3. For the history of the community and its region, see W.M. Aird, *St Cuthbert and the Normans: the Church of Durham, 1071–1153*, Woodbridge 1998, especially 9–67, which deal with the pre-Conquest period; idem, 'St Cuthbert, the Scots and the Normans', *ANS* xvi, 1993, 1–20.

[24] In the tenth and early eleventh centuries, this included land north of the Tweed (A.P. Smyth, *Warlords and Holy Men*, London 1984, 231–7; B.J. Hudson, 'Cnut and the Scottish Kings', *EHR* cvii, 1992, 358).

[25] *ASC* ('D' and 'E') says that Eric was driven from Northumbria in 954, but the *Historia Regum* (hereafter Symeon, *HR*), which at this point is using a set of tenth-century annals, says that it was in 952 that 'the kings of the Northumbrians came to an end, and henceforward the province was administered by earls', and places the appointment of Osulf as 'earl of the Northumbrians' in 953 (T. Arnold, ed., *Symeonis monachi opera omnia*, RS, London 1885, ii, 94). Roger of Wendover dates the death of Eric (*Eilricus*), in which Osulf was implicated, to 950 (H.O. Coxe, ed., *Rogeri de Wendover Chronica, sive Flores Historiarum*, London 1841, i, 402–3). The chronology of Eadred's dealings with the last Scandinavian kings of York is very confused (P. Sawyer, 'The Last Scandinavian Rulers of York', *Northern History* xxxi, 1995, 39–44).

[26] E.O. Blake, ed., *Liber Eliensis*, Camden Society 3rd ser. XCII, 1962, 106 and note 4.

[27] Osulf was the successor (and probably the son) of Ealdred, lord of Bamburgh (912–933), whose father Eadulf is called 'king of the northern Saxons' in the *Annals of Ulster* (D. Whitelock, 'The Dealings of the Kings of England with Northumbria in the Tenth and Eleventh Centuries', in *The Anglo-Saxons: Studies . . . presented to Bruce Dickins*, ed. P. Clemoes, London 1959, 70–88, reprinted in *History, Law and Literature in Tenth- and Eleventh-Century England*). For the later members of the dynasty, see W.E. Kapelle, *The Norman Conquest of the North*, London 1979.

The division of England north of the Thames into three 'super-ealdordoms' is implied in Edgar's Fourth Code, which makes Oslac (who succeeded Osulf as earl of Northumbria), Ælfhere of Mercia and Æthelwine of East Anglia responsible for the implementation of the royal decrees.[28] There were drawbacks to entrusting such large territories to men already supported by powerful and well-connected families. The ealdormen of East Anglia and Mercia came from West Saxon noble families, related (in Ælfhere's case) to the West Saxon royal house, but they soon put down roots in their localities, and there was a tendency for their offices to become hereditary in fact if not in theory.[29] Ælfhere had succeeded to his father Ealhhelm, ealdorman of central Mercia (940–51), and was himself succeeded by his brother-in-law, Ælfric *cild* (983–85).[30] Æthelstan Half-king was followed as ealdorman of East Anglia by two of his sons, Æthelwold (956–62) and Æthelwine *amicus dei* (962–92); Oslac of Northumbria, banished in 975, was succeeded by his son Thored (979–92).[31] It was not uncommon, moreover, for more than one earldom to be held by members of the same family; three of Æthelstan Half-king's brothers were also ealdormen (Æthelwold I in Kent, Eadric and Æthelsige successively in mid-Wessex) and Ælfhere's brother Ælfheah was ealdorman in Hampshire.

The sudden and probably unexpected death of King Edgar on 8 July 975, in only his thirty-second year, pointed up the dangers of the situation. The kingship was disputed by his two young sons, or rather by those who supported them. Edward, who can have been no more than sixteen, was allegedly a violent and evil-tempered youth who 'inspired in all not only fear but even terror'; nevertheless he had the support of Dunstan, archbishop of Canterbury, Æthelwine, ealdorman of East Anglia, and Oswald, bishop of Worcester and archbishop of York.[32] Æthelred, a boy of eight or nine, had the backing of his mother Ælfthryth, Edgar's queen, Æthelwold, bishop of Winchester, and Ælfhere, ealdorman of Mercia. The participation of the two leading magnates south of the Trent, both of whom were arming their followers, nearly resulted in civil war before the matter was settled in favour of Edward.[33] On 18 March 978, however, he was murdered at Corfe, Dorset, by adherents of his half-brother. The corpse was concealed at Wareham, and only after its discovery and translation to

---

28 IV Edgar, 15.

29 P. Stafford, 'The Reign of Æthelred II: a Study in the Limitations on Royal Policy and Action', in Hill, ed., *Ethelred the Unready*, 15–46, especially 31–2.

30 John of Worcester wrongly states that Ælfric *cild* was Ælfhere's son (*Worcester* ii, 434–5). Ælfric *cild* came from the east midlands (he held land in Huntingdonshire and was a benefactor of Peterborough) and was probably married to Ælfhere's sister, for his son Ælfwine (killed at the battle of Maldon in 991) is remembered in the will of his uncle Ælfheah, Ælfhere's brother (S.1485; M.A.L. Locherbie-Cameron, 'The Men Named in the Poem', in *The Battle of Maldon, AD 991*, ed. D. Scragg, Oxford 1991, 241–2; Williams, '*Princeps Merciorum gentis*', 161 and note 90).

31 Earl Thored, father of Æthelred II's first wife, has been identified with Thored Gunnar's son, for whom see *ASC*, 966 (Whitelock, 'The Dealings of the Kings of England with Northumbria', 78–9), but the fact that Æthelstan, the king's brother-in-law, was killed with the men of Cambridgeshire at the battle of Ringmere (*ASC*, 1010) suggests that his father was Thored Oslac's son, who held land in Cambridgeshire (Blake, *Liber Eliensis*, 106).

32 *Vita Oswaldi*, in J. Raine, ed., *The Historians of the Church of York and its Archbishops*, RS, London 1879–94, i, 448 (translated in *EHD* i, no. 236, 841).

33 D.J.V. Fisher, 'The Anti-Monastic Reaction in the Reign of Edward the Martyr', *Cambridge Historical Jnl* x, 1950–52, pp. 254–70.

Shaftesbury, in February 979, could Æthelred be consecrated and crowned, at Kingston-on-Thames, on 4 May 979.[34]

The disturbances of Edward's brief reign may have sown suspicions of the powerful lay magnates in the mind of Æthelred II. His early years were dominated by the men who had advised his father, but by the time the king came of age (c. 984), they were reaching the end of their lives; Ælfhere died in 983 and Bishop Æthelwold in 984; the death of Dunstan followed in 988, while Ealdorman Æthelwine and his close friend, Archbishop Oswald, survived only until 992. Æthelred seems to have taken advantage of these deaths to reduce the power of their families.[35] Ælfric *cild*, Ælfhere's successor, was exiled in 985 on unspecified charges and no-one was appointed to succeed him.[36] The ealdordom of East Anglia remained vacant after the death of Æthelwine, although he had adult sons. Oslac's son Thored succeeded to Northumbria but Thored's successor, Ælfhelm (993–1006), came from a north Mercian family unrelated to him.[37]

Northumbria apart, the ealdormen of the 990s seem to have had more restricted *sciras* (spheres of authority) than their predecessors. Leofwine (994–1023) is described as *Wicciarum provinciarum dux* (ealdorman of the Hwiccian provinces) in a charter of 997, which also supplies geographical areas for the other ealdorman in office at that time; Æthelweard 'of the Western shires', Ælfric 'of the provinces of Winchester', Ælfhelm 'of the Northumbrian provinces' and Leofsige 'of the East Saxons'.[38] Others seem to have exercised the powers of ealdormen without holding the title. In 1004, Ulfcytel *Snilling* (the Bold), along with the East Anglian *witan*, arranged a truce with the invading host of Swein Forkbeard of Denmark, and continued to lead the East Anglian resistance to the Vikings, but even though he is called Ulfcytel 'of the East Angles' (*of East Englan*) in the annal recording his death at the battle of *Assandune* in 1016, he attests the king's charters simply as thegn (*minister*).[39] Lesser officials known as 'high-reeves' (*heah-gerefan, summus praepositus*) also begin to appear.[40] The earliest reference, from the mid tenth century,

---

34 For the murder of Edward and its ramifications see S. Keynes, *The Diplomas of King Æthelred 'the Unready', 978–1016*, Cambridge 1980, 163–76. The hiding of the corpse was part of the definition of 'murder' (*murdrum*, 'concealment') in this period.

35 It is also noticeable that the king's mother Ælfthryth ceases to attest his charters between 985 and 990x993 (Keynes, *The Diplomas of King Æthelred*, 176).

36 Ælfric *cild*'s son Ælfwine seems to have taken service with Byrhtnoth, ealdorman of Essex, and in the poem on the battle of Maldon, it is his maternal kin he boasts of (*The Battle of Maldon*, ed. D.G. Scragg, Manchester 1984, 64).

37 Earl Thored's last appearance is in 992 and Ælfhelm begins to attest as ealdorman (*dux*) in 993 (*ASC*, 992; Keynes, *An Atlas of Attestations in Anglo-Saxon Charters*, table LXII). Ælfhelm was brother to the wealthy Mercian thegn, Wulfric Spot (S.1536; P.H. Sawyer, *Charters of Burton Abbey*, Oxford 1979, xxii–xxiii, xxxviii–xliii; see also next note).

38 S.891. Such geographical designations are almost unique, but Ælfhelm is called 'ealdorman of the provinces across the Humber' (*dux Transhumbranae gentis*) in S.1380 (996 for 994), a confirmation of his mother Wulfrun's gifts to Wolverhampton, whose witness-list may reflect a genuine document of the 990s (Keynes, *The Diplomas of King Æthelred*, 104, 252 note 62). See also the next note for Ulfcytel 'of the East Angles'.

39 *ASC*, 1004, 1010, 1016; Keynes, *An Atlas of Attestations in Anglo-Saxon Charters*, table LXIII; idem, *The Diplomas of King Æthelred*, 208–9 and note 199.

40 The lords of Bamburgh used the title 'high-reeve', but in their case it is perhaps a translation of the Scottish *mormaer*; both words could be translated as 'great steward' (Smyth, *Warlords and Holy Men*, 235–6).

suggests an urban official, but later high-reeves had military functions.[41] In 1001, two high-reeves were killed while leading the levies of Hampshire against the Danes, and a third suffered defeat at the head of the forces from Devon and Somerset.[42] Commanding the shire-levies was one of the functions of ealdormen, and some friction between them and the high-reeves is suggested by the murder in 1002 of the high-reeve Æfic by Leofsige, ealdorman of Essex, a crime for which the ealdorman was banished.[43]

If Æthelred was deliberately trying to curb the power of his ealdormen, he abandoned the attempt in 1007, when he bestowed the ealdordom of Mercia on Eadric Streona (1007–17).[44] The rise of Eadric, who rapidly became the king's most favoured counsellor, coincided with the fall of Ælfhelm, ealdorman of Northumbria, murdered in 1006. John of Worcester accuses Eadric of encompassing Ælfhelm's death, with the connivance of the king, and the fact that Æthelred celebrated Christmas in Shropshire in 1006 (well outside the limits of his normal itinerary) lends some credibility to the assertion.[45] The ealdordom of Northumbria was entrusted to Uhtred of Bamburgh. It seems that Æthelred attempted to bind these two powerful lords to himself by marriage, for Eadric received the king's daughter Eadgyth as his wife, while Uhtred married her sister Ælfgifu; for a parallel to such alliances we have to look back to the marriage of Alfred's daughter Æthelflæd to Æthelred, Lord of the Mercians in the 880s.[46]

Uhtred of Bamburgh was murdered at Cnut's orders (or at least with his connivance) in 1016. In 1017, after the Danish Conquest, Cnut divided the English kingdom into four: 'Wessex for himself, East Anglia for Thorkell [the Tall], Mercia for Eadric [Streona] and Northumbria for Eric [of Lade]'.[47] Much has been made of this allegedly revolutionary expedient, but in fact it is foreshadowed in Edgar's reign, nor did it last long.[48] Eadric Streona was murdered before the year's end, and it is not clear that anyone was appointed to replace him as earl of all Mercia.[49] Thorkell the Tall fell out with the king and returned to Denmark in 1021, and no earl of East Anglia is recorded between that time and the appointment of Harold Godwineson in 1045. Eric of Lade drops out of sight after 1023, and probably never controlled Northumbria beyond the Tyne, which passed from Earl Uhtred's brother Eadulf to his son Ealdred; the next earl

[41] II Edmund 5; A.J. Robertson, *Laws of the Kings of England from Edmund to Henry I*, Cambridge 1925, 14–15. The clause prohibits trading except in the witness of the high-reeve (*summus praepositus*) or of the priest, treasurer or town-reeve.

[42] *ASC* 'A', 1001.

[43] *ASC*, 1002; S.926, printed and discussed in A. Campbell, *Charters of Rochester*, Oxford 1972, no. 33, 45–7. See also F.M. Stenton, *Latin Charters of the Anglo-Saxon Period*, Oxford 1955, 76–81.

[44] For Eadric, see Keynes, *The Diplomas of King Æthelred*, 212–13; idem, 'A Tale of Two Kings: Alfred the Great and Æthelred the Unready', *TRHS* 5th ser. xxxvi, 1986, 213–17; A. Williams, ' "Cockles amongst the Wheat": Danes and English in England in the First Half of the Eleventh Century', *Midland History* xi, 1986, 3–6.

[45] *ASC*, 1006; *Worcester* ii, 45–6. For Æthelred's itinerary, see D. Hill, *An Atlas of Anglo-Saxon England*, Oxford 1981, 91.

[46] For the marriage of Uhtred and Ælfgifu, see C. Morris, *Marriage and Murder in Eleventh-Century Northumbria: a Study of 'De Obsessione Dunelmi'*, Borthwick Paper 82, York 1992.

[47] *ASC*, 1017.

[48] IV Edgar 15; S. Keynes, 'Cnut's Earls', in A. Rumble, ed., *The Reign of Cnut*, Leicester 1994, 81; M.K. Lawson, *Cnut: the Danes in England in the Early Eleventh Century*, London 1993, 184.

[49] See below, at note 51.

to have authority over southern Northumbria was Siward, who attests for the first time in 1033.

Many of Cnut's earls are little more than names, and in some cases it is not even certain where their spheres of authority lay.[50] The position is clearest in Mercia, where the archives of the church of Worcester provide a fuller picture than is available elsewhere.[51] In 1017, two ealdormen held power there; Eadric Streona as ealdorman of Mercia itself, and Leofwine, ealdorman 'of the Hwiccian provinces' (the Worcester area).[52] Cnut appointed no fewer than three Danish earls in western Mercia; Ranig was perhaps earl of Herefordshire as early as October or November 1016, though there are no charters from the years 1016–17 to confirm this.[53] He attests Cnut's earliest surviving charters from 1018, as does Earl Eilaf, who probably held Gloucestershire, and in 1019, they are joined by Earl Hakon, whose authority lay in Worcestershire. These shires constituted virtually the whole territory of the *Hwicce*, and since Leofwine continues to attest until 1023, it has been assumed that he was promoted to the earldom of all Mercia on Eadric's murder in 1017, but he may simply have been an English colleague of the Scandinavian Earl Hakon.[54] Two of Leofwine's sons, Leofric and Edwin, held positions of authority in the west, perhaps as sheriffs, Leofric in Worcestershire, Edwin in Herefordshire.[55]

Cnut's treatment of Mercia suggests a continuation of the policies of Æthelred's reign when, as we have seen, ealdormen were appointed to spheres more restricted than those of Edgar's time. Mercia after Eadric's murder looks very different from the other earldoms, but if we had the same kind of evidence for Northumbria and East Anglia, we might find that Eric and Thorkell also had 'subordinate' earls within their respective spheres.[56] Earl Siward certainly seems not to have held northern Northumbria until after the murder of Earl Eadulf of Bamburgh in 1041.[57] In Wessex, which Cnut kept at first in his own hands, there seem to have been two (or possibly three) ealdormen, as in the time of the tenth-century kings.[58] If, however, Cnut wished to reduce the authority of the great earls, then like Æthelred he abandoned the attempt, for by the 1030s two men stand out above all the rest: Leofric of Mercia (1023/32–57) and Godwine of Wessex (c. 1022–53).[59]

Lack of material for Cnut's reign (especially the latter half) prevents us from seeing how Leofric and Godwine attained their eminence, nor can we assess their

---

50  After the Danish Conquest, the title of ealdorman was replaced by that of earl. The change, foreshadowed in the tenth century (IV Edgar 15 describes Oslac of Northumbria as 'earl', while Æthelwine of East Anglia and Ælfhere of Mercia are 'ealdormen'), is probably due to the presence of Scandinavians among the ranks of the ealdormen, but it would have to be shown that the change in title was accompanied by a change in function for it to be of real significance, and there is no indication that this was so (Williams, *Kingship and Government*, 131–2).

51  Williams, ' "Cockles amongst the Wheat" ', 6–11; Keynes, 'Cnut's Earls', 54–78.

52  Both attest a Worcester lease of Archbishop Wulfstan *lupus*, dated 1017 (S.1384).

53  T. Hearne, ed., *Hemingi Chartularium Ecclesiæ Wigorniensis*, London 1723, i, 274.

54  Keynes, 'Cnut's Earls', 74–5.

55  Williams, ' "Cockles amongst the Wheat" ', 8.

56  Godric, who attests a charter of 1022 as ealdorman (*dux*), might be one of them, and another possibility is Earl Sihtric, who appears in the late 1020s; Godric is associated with Norfolk and Sihtric with Hertfordshire (Keynes, 'Cnut's Earls', 65, 77–8, 86).

57  *ASC*, 1041; Morris, *Marriage and Murder*, 14 and note 57.

58  Godwine in the east and Æthelweard in the west; an Earl Sired, who attests in 1019 and 1023 (S.954, 960), may have had authority in Kent (Keynes, 'Cnut's Earls', 67–74, 76).

59  For Godwine's appointment to the whole of Wessex, see Keynes, 'Cnut's Earls', 71–3.

relative wealth in respect of each other, or in regard to the king.[60] To describe them as 'new men' is tempting but misleading, for Leofric's father Leofwine had been ealdorman of the *Hwicce* since the 990s, and his daughter-in-law Ælfgifu, the wife of his son Ælfgar, may have been related through her mother to Ælfhelm, ealdorman of Northumbria, and through her father to one of the leading kindreds of the Five Boroughs.[61] Godwine's father Wulfnoth *cild* was perhaps a man of some local importance, possibly connected with the æthelings Æthelstan and Edmund, Æthelred's eldest sons by his first wife.[62]

Whatever their origins, their influence emerges in the succession dispute on Cnut's death in 1035. Harthacnut, his son by Queen Emma, was detained in Denmark by a Norwegian invasion, and Harold, Cnut's son by Ælfgifu of Northampton, made a bid for the kingship. He had the support of 'Earl Leofric and almost all the thegns north of the Thames and the shipmen (*liðsmen*) in London', while Harthacnut's cause was backed by 'Earl Godwine and all the chief men in Wessex', along with Queen Emma, who took possession of Winchester 'with the housecarls of her son the king'.[63] Comparison with the situation on Edgar's death in 975 is irresistible; once again, the rival candidates for the kingship were backed by the two most powerful secular lords, each of them, to judge from the references to the *liðsmen* (the stipendiary fleet) and the royal housecarls, with access to armed force. Yet, as in 975, outright conflict was averted. John of Worcester says that 'the kingdom of England was divided by lot', Harold holding Mercia and the north and Harthacnut the south, an arrangement born out by the numismatic evidence.[64] Eventually, however, 'Harthacnut was deserted because he was too long in Denmark' and only on Harold I's death in 1040 did he regain the kingdom. The only casualty of the affair was Alfred, son of Emma by Æthelred II, who was murdered while making his own bid for the crown; Godwine's part in the death of 'the blameless ætheling' was to have momentous consequences when Alfred's brother Edward eventually succeeded to Harthacnut in 1042.[65]

So far there is little in the careers of Cnut's two premier earls to distinguish them from their tenth-century predecessors. Both survived the accession of Harthacnut (though Godwine had some explaining to do) and the subsequent accession of Edward the Confessor. Thereafter what is striking is the aggrandizement of Godwine and his sons; Swein Godwineson received an earldom based on Hereford in 1043 and in 1045 Edward married Godwine's daughter Edith and bestowed earldoms on her brother Harold and her cousin Beorn Estrithson. Why Edward should so advance Godwine's family has never been satisfactorily explained. He had no need to buy support, for he

---

60 For Godwine, see D. Raraty, 'Earl Godwine of Wessex: the Origins of his Power and his Political Loyalties', *History* lxxiv, 1989, 3–19; F. Barlow, *The Godwins*, Harlow 2002.

61 Sawyer, *Charters of Burton Abbey*, xlii–xliii, suggests that Earl Ælfgar's wife was the daughter of Wulfric Spot's niece Ealdgyth and her husband Morcar, thegn of the 'Seven Boroughs', murdered at Æthelred II's orders (*ASC*, 1015); two of the children of Ælfgar and Ælfgifu were called Ealdgyth and Morcar. If so, Ælfgar's wife was also related to Ælfgifu of Northampton, wife to King Cnut, and daughter of Wulfric's brother, Ealdorman Ælfhelm, killed in 1006 (see above); this may be the reason why Earl Leofric supported the claims of Ælfgifu of Northampton's son, Harold I, in 1035 (see below).

62 A. Williams, 'Land and Power in the Eleventh Century: the Estates of Harold Godwineson', *ANS* iii, 1981, 171–87; idem, *Kingship and Government*, 132–3.

63 *ASC* 'E', 1035.

64 *Worcester* ii, 520–3; T. Talvio, 'Harold I and Harthacnut's *Jewel Cross* Type Reconsidered', in Mark Blackburn, ed., *Anglo-Saxon Monetary History*, Leicester 1986, 273–90.

65 *ASC* 'C', 'D', 1036.

seems to have been a popular choice for the kingship, and he had no rivals; Swein Estrithson, who succeeded Harthacnut in Denmark, was fighting for his life against Magnus of Norway, and more concerned to sue for English support than to bid for the English kingdom. Indeed in this Earl Godwine, Swein Estrithson's uncle by marriage, did not succeed in influencing the king, who turned down Swein's requests for aid.[66] Nor was Godwine able to have his kinsman Ælric elected to the archbishopric of Canterbury in 1050, for the king overturned the choice of the monks, and established his own crony, Robert of Jumièges, in the archiepiscopal see.[67]

It is in the stand-off between king and earl in the years 1051–52 that the malign influence of Godwine and his family has been chiefly discerned. The 'D' and 'E' texts of the *Anglo-Saxon Chronicle* devote some of their longest and most detailed entries to the affair. Other ealdormen and powerful thegns had been (and would be) banished; but for the king to repudiate his wife and to exile and dispossess her whole family was unprecedented.[68] In the event, Godwine forced the king to reinstate him and his sons (though Swein did not return to England with his brothers in 1052).[69] This was personally damaging to Edward, but whether it tarnished the office of kingship is debateable. One of the striking elements in Earl Godwine's defiance is the unwillingness of his own men to follow him in any direct confrontation with the king. They were, to quote the 'E' text of the *Chronicle*, 'reluctant to have to stand against their royal lord (*cynehlaford*)', and when, at a council held at London in late September, 'the king asked for all those thegns that the earls had had . . . they were all handed over to him'. The 'E' text is noticeably partisan to Godwine, and 'D' presents the earls as 'ready to do battle against the king', but in fact they did not, and even 'D' records the dwindling of Godwine's support during the month of September and the transfer of Harold's thegns, at least, to the king's allegiance. The *Vita Edwardi* says that many openly sent messages of support to Godwine, but implies that few were prepared to share his exile. One of Godwine's associates, Ealdred, bishop of Worcester, did allow the escape of Earl Harold from Bristol to Ireland, and seems to have earned the king's disfavour thereby.[70]

The events of 1052 show the limitations of Godwine's influence. Domesday Book reveals a huge concentration of wealth in the family's hands in Wessex.[71] Yet when Harold landed at Porlock, Som., in the summer of 1052, 'there was a great force gathered there to oppose him', and his father met with similar opposition both in the Isle of Wight and at Portland, Dorset.[72] Only when the combined fleets moved into the south-east, the ancestral lands of the family, did the picture change; 'all the men of

66 *ASC* 'D', 1045, 1047, 1048; *Worcester* ii, 544–5.

67 *Vita Ædwardi*, 18–19; N. Brooks, *The Early History of the Church of Canterbury*, Leicester 1984, 295–303.

68 'It would have seemed remarkable to everyone in England if anybody had told them that it could happen' (*ASC* 'D', 1051).

69 He went straight from Bruges on his barefoot pilgrimage to Jerusalem, dying on the return journey in Lycia at Michaelmas (29 September) 1052; he was buried at Constantinople (*ASC* 'C', 1052; *Worcester* ii, 570–1).

70 *ASC* 'D', 1051: 'the king sent Bishop Ealdred from London with a force and they were to intercept [Harold] . . . but they could not – or would not'. Ealdred's activities seem to have been confined to his diocese in 1051–52 (V.J. King, 'Ealdred, Archbishop of York: the Worcester Years', *ANS* xviii, 1996, 127, 134). See Williams, *Kingship and Government*, 139–42.

71 Fleming, *Kings and Lords*, 53–103, especially table 3,1 (59).

72 *ASC*, 'D', E', 1052.

Kent, and all the *butsecarles* from the district of Hastings, and from the region round about there by the sea-coast and all Essex and Surrey and much else beside' declared for the earls.[73] Yet the king still had a force of fifty ships waiting for them at London, and a land-army augmented by the men of Earls Leofric and Siward.[74] Once again, as in 1051, the decisive factor was the unwillingness on either side to push the confrontation to the limit: 'it was hateful to almost all of them to fight against men of their own race, for there was little else that was worth anything apart from Englishmen on either side'.[75] The councillors prevailed upon the king to back down. Godwine was allowed to clear himself of all charges, he and his sons were reinstated and the king took back his repudiated wife. Most of those who had actively opposed the earl were driven into exile.

Godwine died on 15 April 1053, and was succeeded by his eldest surviving son, Harold, whose former earldom of East Anglia went to Earl Leofric's son Ælfgar.[76] The late 1050s saw further advances in the fortunes of Godwine's heirs. In 1055 Earl Siward of Northumbria died, leaving only a minor son, and the earldom went to Godwine's third son Tostig.[77] There seems to have been opposition to the appointment, for at the same council Earl Ælfgar was exiled. There is a revealing disagreement at this point in the various versions of the *Chronicle*: 'C' says that Ælfgar was innocent of any fault, 'D' that he committed 'hardly any' crime, and 'E' that he admitted to 'being a traitor to the king and to all the people . . . though the words escaped him against his will'.[78] Ælfgar's intemperance might have stemmed from the expectations of his own family in Northumbria, for his wife was arguably the grand-niece of a previous ealdorman of the region, and daughter of one of the leading thegns of York.[79] He fled to Ireland, where he gathered a fleet of eighteen ships, and allied with Gruffudd ap Llewelyn, king of Gwynedd, who married Ælfgar's daughter Ealdgyth, either then or a little later.[80]

Gruffudd and Ælfgar launched an attack on Herefordshire. The defence of the region fell upon the Confessor's nephew Ralph, who had been earl of Hereford since the outlawry, or more probably the death, of Swein Godwineson.[81] Ralph met the

---

[73] *ASC* 'C', 'D', 1052. The *butsecarles* ('boatmen') discharged the obligation to provide ships and crews for the royal fleet, laid on some of the south-eastern sea-ports.

[74] We are not told the size of Godwine's fleet but Harold brought nine ships from Ireland.

[75] *ASC* 'E', 1052. In the *Vita Edwardi*, it is Godwine himself who refuses to make any warlike move against the king, even when urged to do so by his followers; see the discussion in T.S. Jones, 'The Outlawry of Earl Godwine from the *Vita Ædwardi regis*', in T.H. Ohlgren, ed., *Medieval Outlaws: Ten Tales in Modern English*, Stroud 1998, 3–4.

[76] Swein predeceased his father, see note 69 above.

[77] Siward's elder son Osbearn was killed in 1054 and the younger, Waltheof, cannot have been above thirteen, for he was the child of Siward's second wife Ælfgifu, whom he married in 1041 (*ASC*, 1041; Symeon, *HR*, 1072).

[78] The 'E' text, which is noticeably pro-Godwine, was probably being compiled at St Augustine's, Canterbury, at this date.

[79] See above, note 61. Ælfgar had three sons living at this date, all probably of age, though Burgheard, who was perhaps the eldest, died in 1061 (Williams, *The English and the Norman Conquest*, 54–5, notes 41, 43).

[80] K. Maund, 'The Welsh Alliances of Earl Ælfgar of Mercia and his Family in the mid Eleventh Century', *ANS* xi, 1989, 186–8.

[81] It is usually assumed that Ralph received Herefordshire on the outlawry of Swein in 1051 (or even earlier). But at least two of the comital manors in the shire were held by Osbern Pentecost 'while Godwine and Harold were exiled', i.e. in 1051–52 (*GDB*, fo. 186); and the castle built in Herefordshire in 1051 is called 'Pentecost's castle' in 1052 (*ASC* 'E', 1051–52). It may be that Osbern was holding

invaders near Hereford but 'before any spear was thrown, the English army fled, because they were on horseback, and many were killed there – about 400 or 500 men – and they killed none in return'.[82] Ralph's incompetence probably cost him his command in the west. It was Earl Harold who saved the day with the levies of Wessex; he also negotiated the peace, whereby Ælfgar was restored to his earldom of East Anglia. The campaign against Gruffudd in 1056 was conducted by Leofgar, bishop of Hereford, one of Earl Harold's clerks, who was killed in the process, and a truce was brokered by Harold, Earl Leofric of Mercia, and Ealdred, bishop of Worcester, with no mention of Ralph's participation.[83] It is not surprising therefore that when Ralph died on 21 December 1057, leaving a son who was still a minor in 1066, Harold added the earldom of Hereford to that of Wessex. Ralph's earldom in the east midlands, which he had held since 1050, was divided, the northern shires going to Earl Tostig, while the southern portion formed an earldom for Godwine's fifth son, Leofwine.[84] The other death in 1057 was that of Earl Leofric, on either 31 August or 30 September. Earl Ælfgar succeeded to Mercia, but East Anglia passed to Godwine's fourth son, Gyrth.[85] By 1066, Gyrth was also holding Oxfordshire, which had been in the hands of Earl Ælfgar and perhaps of Earl Leofric before him; but Mercia itself passed to Edwin on the death of Ælfgar, probably in 1062.[86]

By the early 1060s all the English earldoms save Mercia alone were in the hands of Harold and his brothers, but they were not unassailable. Just after Michaelmas (29 September) 1065, the thegns of Yorkshire (and perhaps Northumbria also) rose against Earl Tostig, killed those of his housecarls who were stationed at York and seized his treasure.[87] In Tostig's place they chose Morcar, brother of Earl Edwin, who led them south to Northampton, where they were joined by Edwin and the Mercians. Morcar has often been regarded as a 'compromise candidate', an outsider acceptable both to the Anglo-Danes of York and the lords of Bamburgh, but as we have seen he

---

Herefordshire during the exile of the earls and that it only passed to Ralph when the news of Swein's death (in Lycia, on 29 September 1052, see note 69 above) reached England.

82  *ASC* 'C', 1055.

83  *ASC* 'C', 1056. It was this Leofgar who 'wore his moustaches all through his priesthood until he became a bishop', a sign of his interest in lay, rather than ecclesiastical affairs.

84  A. Williams, 'The King's Nephew: the Family, Career and Connections of Ralph, Earl of Hereford', in *Studies . . . to Brown*, 327–43, especially 338–40. Leofwine attests as earl from 1059, but no charters survive for the years 1055–58. He certainly held the shires of Hertford, Middlesex and probably Buckingham, but the evidence connecting him with Kent, Sussex and Staffordshire is unreliable. It is not certain whether he was older or younger than his brother Gyrth (see next note).

85  Like Leofwine (see previous note), Gyrth attests as earl from 1059, but he had held Norfolk during Ælfgar's exile in 1055 (*Vita Ædwardi*, 50–1). This suggests that he was older than Leofwine, although he does not, like Leofwine, attest Edward's early charters (Keynes, *An Atlas of Attestations in Anglo-Saxon Charters*, tables lxxiv, lxxv).

86  S.1139. According to Domesday, Ælfgar had held the third penny (the earl's share) of the revenues of Oxford (*GDB*, fo. 154); for Earl Leofric's reeve in Oxford, see S.1423 and S. Keynes, 'A Lost Cartulary of St Albans Abbey', *ASE* xxii, 1993, 266–7; see also S. Baxter, 'The Earls of Mercia and their Commended Men', *ANS* xxiii, 2001, 25–37. For the date of Ælfgar's death, see Maund, 'The Welsh Alliances of Earl Ælfgar', 188.

87  *ASC* 'C', 1065. 'D' includes the men of *Norðymbra lande* (Northumbria beyond the Tyne); 'E' speaks of 'Northumbrians', without distinguishing between the northerners and the men of York. John of Worcester names the leaders as Gamalbearn, Dunstan son of Æthelnoth and Gluniairn son of Eardwulf; Gamalbearn certainly and the others probably can be identified among the pre-Conquest holders of land in Yorkshire (*Worcester* ii, 596–9; M. Faull and M. Stinson, *Domesday Book: York-shire*, Chichester 1986, no. C10 and note, and appendix 3).

may already have had connections with York through his mother's kindred.[88] At first sight, this looks like an attempt by the Mercian brothers to stem the rise of their West Saxon rivals, but the situation may not have been so simple. There is some ambiguity in the role of Tostig's brother, Earl Harold. The author of the *Vita Edwardi* says that Tostig publicly accused Harold of inciting the northerners against him, and though the anonymous writer affects horror at the very suggestion, he tempers his indignation with the remark that 'Harold, rather too generous with oaths (alas!), cleared this charge too with oaths'.[89] In his version, it is the king who defends Tostig, though without success. The *Anglo-Saxon Chronicle* and John of Worcester say merely that Harold acted as Edward's envoy in negotiating with the malcontents, negotiations which ended in the confirmation of Morcar as earl, and Tostig's exile to Flanders.

The testimony of the *Vita Edwardi* deserves respect, for it is not only a nearly contemporary account of events, but also must derive from Queen Edith, who supported Tostig against Harold. Harold is presented as an able and ambitious man. Precisely when he began to think of himself as a possible successor to Edward we cannot know; possibly not until the death of the ætheling Edward in 1057.[90] He did leave a son, but Edgar ætheling was no more than fourteen in 1066.[91] Edward the Confessor's continuing vacillation over the succession, and particularly his re-opening of negotiations with William of Normandy, may have sharpened Harold's perceptions of his own chances. All the machinations detailed by Professor Fleming might suggest not simple greed alone, but the laying of a basis for an attempt at the richest prize of all.[92]

Harold made his reputation as a warrior in the wars against Gruffudd ap Llewelyn, culminating in the joint land- and sea-assault on Gwynedd which led to Gruffudd's murder and the establishment of what amounted to an English client-kingdom in North Wales.[93] This triumph was the result of co-operation between Harold and Tostig, the latter leading the land-army into Gwynedd, while Harold brought the ship-fyrd around the Welsh coast from Bristol to Chester. But Harold may already have taken thought for the future. At some point between 1063 and 1066, he married Gruffudd's widow Ealdgyth, sister of Edwin of Mercia and his brother Morcar.[94] The date of the marriage is not recorded but since Ealdgyth seems to have borne Harold two children it may have taken place as early as 1063–64. This would make Harold Morcar's brother-in-law even before the northerners rose against Tostig.[95] The

---

88 See notes 61, 79 above.

89 *Vita Ædwardi*, 78–81.

90 The ætheling's return from Hungary, whither he had been carried as a child, was negotiated by Ealdred, bishop of Worcester, who was not only one of the king's ablest ambassadors but also a close associate of Harold (*ASC* 'C', 'D', 1054; *Worcester* ii, 575–7; see note 70 above). Harold himself was at Saint-Omer in November 1056, perhaps to meet the ætheling and conduct him to England (P. Grierson, 'A Visit of Earl Harold to Flanders in 1056', *EHR* li, 1936, 90–3).

91 He was of an age with Robert Curthose, who was born about 1052 (N. Hooper, 'Edgar the Ætheling: Anglo-Saxon Prince, Rebel and Crusader', *ASE* xiv, 1985, 29).

92 Fleming, *Kings and Lords*, 71–91, 101–2.

93 *ASC* 'D', 'E', 1063; F. Barlow, *Edward the Confessor*, London 1970, 210–11. Harold's 1063 campaign was recommended by John of Salisbury to Henry II as the epitome of how an assault on the Welsh should be conducted (F.C. Suppe, *Military Institutions on the Welsh March: Shropshire, 1066–1300*, Woodbridge 1994, 17 and note 56).

94 The lands in north Mercia held by Harold may represent Ealdgyth's dower (Barlow, *Edward the Confessor*, 243 and note 6; Williams, 'Land and Power in the Eleventh Century', 176).

95 This is to assume that both Harold the younger and Ulf were the children of Ealdgyth (see E.A.

support of both the Northumbrians and the Mercians would have been vital in any bid for the kingship, and Tostig's alienation of the Yorkshire thegns (and perhaps their northern neighbours also) would be a serious embarrassment. It may be significant that after Tostig's expulsion efforts were made to reconcile not only the men of York but also both the lords of Bamburgh and the heir of Earl Siward; Morcar entrusted the lands beyond the Tees to Earl Osulf, son of Earl Eadulf of Bamburgh, and it was probably at this time that Waltheof received an earldom based on Northamptonshire, a shire particularly associated with Earl Tostig.[96] In short, perhaps Tostig had some basis for the accusation which he flung at his brother.

Edward's childlessness and the immaturity of the only other member in the male line of the West Saxon royal house meant that a change of dynasty was almost inevitable. This does not, in itself, imply any weakness in the English kingdom. The death of Henry I in 1135 also led to a disputed succession and a change of dynasty, preceded by a bitter and prolonged struggle which saw the death and dispossession of men who had been rich and powerful, but we do not therefore consider Henry a failure nor his kingdom weak. Nor was it an independent Wessex at which Harold aimed, but the kingship of the English itself. The nature of the prize may be appreciated by remembering some of the things that earls, however powerful, could not do. They could not mint coinage, though they might receive a share in the profits of the mints in their localities.[97] Edgar's Third Code commands that 'one coinage shall be current throughout all the king's realm, and no-one shall refuse it', and the ability of his successors to control and manipulate the coinage demonstrates the efficiency of at least one aspect of their administration.[98] Earls could not issue charters; Harold's foundation and endowment of Waltham Holy Cross required a royal diploma.[99] Nor could they raise taxes; the various gelds were levied and collected by royal agents at the behest of the king.[100] They could not hold their own courts, though they might preside over the shire-courts within their respective earldoms, and receive a third of the profits (the earl's third penny) from them and from the lesser courts of their constituent hundreds and boroughs.

Earldoms were not provincial governorships. There was no tier of local organiza-

---

Freeman, *The History of the Norman Conquest of England* iv, Oxford 1871, 755–6), though only Harold is specifically described as such in the genealogies appended to John of Worcester's Chronicle (B. Thorpe, ed., *Florentii Wigornensis monachi Chronicon ex Chronicis*, London 1848, i, 276). He is said to have fled (or perhaps he was taken) to Norway, where he eventually found favour with Magnus Bareleg, son of Olaf the Peaceable (*Gesta Regum* i, 480–1, 570–1). Ulf, perhaps the younger of the two, was imprisoned by the Conqueror, but freed in 1087 by Robert Curthose (*Worcester* iii, 48–9). The remaining children of Harold, three sons who fled to Ireland, and two daughters, were the children of Edith Swanneck, but this was presumably a 'hand-fast match' (like that of Cnut and Ælfgifu of Northampton), and therefore no bar to a more regular arrangement.

96 Osulf was nephew to Gospatric, son of Earl Uhtred of Bamburgh, whose murder in 1064 on Edith's orders was alleged as one of the reasons for the rising (*Worcester* ii, 596–9; Symeon, *HR*, 1072; *De primo Saxonum adventu*, in H. Hinde, ed., *Symeonis Dunelmi Opera et Collectanea* i, Surtees Society LI, 1868, 213). For Waltheof, see Williams, 'The King's Nephew', 339 and note 67.

97 Baronial coinages appear for the first time under King Stephen (J. Campbell, *The Anglo-Saxon State*, London 2000, 187 and note).

98 D.M. Metcalf, 'Continuity and Change in English Monetary History, c. 973–1086', *BNJ* l, 1980, 20–49; li, 1981, 52–90.

99 S.1036, the authenticity of which has been defended by S. Keynes, 'Regenbald the Chancellor (*sic*)', *ANS* x, 1988, 200–2.

100 Stenton, *Anglo-Saxon England*, 3rd edn, Oxford 1971, 636–41; H.R. Loyn, *Anglo-Saxon England and the Norman Conquest*, 2nd edn, London 1991, 315–23.

tion higher than the shire. The pre-Conquest kings (like all successful rulers of this period) took care to maintain direct links between themselves and the local communities in various ways. In areas where the royal demesne was extensive (basically the shires of Wessex and southern Mercia) the reeves who managed the royal estates represented the king's interests. Tenth-century injunctions to royal reeves cover various matters, but perhaps the most significant is contained in Edward the Elder's Second Code, which commands each reeve to hold a monthly court in his district for the settlement of legal disputes.[101] By the mid tenth century, these meetings had grown into the hundred courts, held monthly in each of the smaller districts into which the shires were divided.[102] The earliest sheriffs (*scir[es]man*, *scirgerefa*) appear in the late tenth century, and by the mid eleventh they had authority over all lesser reeves.[103] Sheriffs were, in theory at least, king's men, not earls' men, responsible for the royal estates, and accountable to the king for his share (the king's two pennies) of the profits of the shire and hundred courts.

Sheriffs were, by their nature, essentially local officials, often perhaps quite literally, in the sense that they came from the local shire community.[104] They were not, however, the only link between that community and the circle around the king, for royal agents (*ærendracan*) could be despatched from time to time to look after the king's interests. By 1066, the duty to assist and provision such agents (*legati regis*, *missatici regis*) had been laid on some English towns.[105] Bishops, abbots and lay nobles are all found acting as royal envoys. The tenth-century *pedisequi*, men 'in close personal relations with the king', may have been used as royal messengers; the best-recorded of them is Wulfstan of Dalham, who, in King Edgar's reign, attended a royal council at London, acted as the king's agent in his native Cambridgeshire, and assisted St Æthelwold to expel the clerks from the Old Minster at Winchester.[106] Both in status and function, such men resemble the eleventh-century stallers. There is some question whether this term is derived from Scandinavian or French models, but the office itself seems to be indigenous; the word 'staller' recalls the higher grade of thegn in the writings of Archbishop Wulfstan *lupus*, who had 'a seat and a special office in the king's hall'.[107]

---

101  II Edward 8; S. Keynes, 'Royal Government and the Written Word in Late Anglo-Saxon England', in R. McKitterick, ed., *The Uses of Literacy in Early Medieval Europe*, Cambridge 1990, 226–57, especially 234–7.

102  I Edgar (*The Hundred Ordinance*), which may belong either to the latter years of Eadred, or the opening years of Edgar's reign; H.R. Loyn, 'The Hundred in England in the Tenth and Eleventh Centuries', in *Society and Peoples: Studies in the History of England and Wales, c. 600–1200*, London 1992, 111–34.

103  Sheriffs and *portgerefan* (borough-reeves) are distinguished from *tunesgerefan* (reeves of individual vills and estates) in IV Æthelred 3, VII Æthelred 2,5; the earliest named sheriff is Wulfsige the priest, sheriff of Kent in the 980s (S.1458). For the eleventh-century reeves, see J. Campbell, 'Some Agents and Agencies of the Late Anglo-Saxon State', in J.C. Holt, ed., *Domesday Studies: Papers from the Novocentenary Conference*, Woodbridge 1987, 210–18; Williams, *Kingship and Government*, 108–9.

104  It is very difficult to identify individual sheriffs in the pre-Conquest period, but for one example see A. Williams, 'A Vicecomital Family in pre-Conquest Warwickshire', *ANS* xi, 1989, 279–95.

105  Dover, Wallingford and Torksey (*GDB*, fos 1, 56, 337).

106  D. Whitelock, 'Introduction', in Blake, ed., *Liber Eliensis*, xxi–xxiv; *Chron. Abingdon* ii, 260.

107  *Geþyncðo*, in F. Liebermann, *Die Gesetze der Angelsachsen*, Halle 1903, 456; *EHD* i, no. 52A, 432. L.M. Larson argued that the English 'staller' is derived from ON *stallari*, one with a seat in the king's hall (*The King's Household in England before the Norman Conquest*, Madison, Wisconsin, 1904, 146–52). R.H.C. Davis, on the other hand, connected it with 'the Franco-Norman constable or *comes*

The form in which the royal commands were transmitted has been a matter of some controversy. In the 990s, Ælfhere, abbot of Bath, brought the king's *insegel* (seal, token) to the shire-court of Berkshire and commanded it in the king's name to settle a legal dispute fairly between two parties. Whether this order was delivered in written form or by word of mouth is unclear.[108] At about the same time a royal writ and seal (*gewrit and insegl*) ordered the shire-court of Kent to hear another case; in this instance, the message was certainly in writing (*gewrit* cannot mean an oral message), but whether the seal in question was attached to the writ, or carried separately as a sign of authority is still disputed.[109] Only from the reign of Edward the Confessor do we have copies of writs which still bear (or are known once to have borne) impressions of the double-sided royal seal.[110]

Surviving royal writs are addressed to the bishop, earl, sheriff and king's thegns in the shire (or shires) to which they are directed. These thegns, the suitors of the shire-court, were the major local worthies, the 'better men' (*meliores*) of the neighbourhood. Like the sheriffs, they are difficult to discern as individuals, but some areas are better-documented than others. In Kent, for instance, the chief landholders are actually listed in Domesday Book, and the relative abundance of vernacular memoranda for the region allows their identification and gives some idea of their activities.[111] Most were local men, some from families which can be traced back to the early eleventh and even the late tenth centuries.[112] Beside them appear men of more substantial wealth, whose estates spread into several shires, including Æthelnoth *cild* of Canterbury, who may have been port-reeve of the city, and Wulfweard white, a man in the service first of Queen Emma and subsequently Queen Edith.[113] All, however, were king's thegns, though some were clearly associated with Earl Harold as well.[114] Outside Kent, identification of the local thegns is more difficult, but a vernacular

---

        *stabuli*' ('Did the Anglo-Saxons have Warhorses?', in S. Hawkes, ed., *Weapons and Warfare in Anglo-Saxon England*, Oxford 1989, 143; see also K. Mack, 'The Staller: Administrative Innovation in the Reign of Edward the Confessor', *JMH* xii, 1986, 123–34). Whatever the origin of the name, the position has English precedents (Williams, *Kingship and Government*, 126–7).

108    S.1454.

109    S.1456.

110    T.A. Heslop, 'English Seals from the mid Ninth to the Eleventh Century', *JBAA* cxxxiii, 1980, 1–16. All surviving examples (there are only three) were sealed open ('patent'), with the seal attached on a strip of parchment partially cut from the bottom of the writ, so that it could be opened without destroying the seal.

111    *GDB*, fos 1, 1v; A. Williams, 'Lost Worlds: Kentish Society in the Eleventh Century', *Medieval Prosopography* xx, 1999, 51–74.

112    Sired, the Domesday tenant of Chilham, can be associated with the brothers Siweard of Chilham and Sired the Old, who attest charters of Æthelred II at the turn of the tenth and eleventh centuries (Keynes, *The Diplomas of King Æthelred*, 132–6), while the father of Godwine and Godric, sons of Karl, was probably Karl the king's *cniht*, who witnessed a Kentish marriage-agreement between 1016 and 1020 (S.1461; A.J. Robertson, *Anglo-Saxon Charters*, 2nd edn, Cambridge 1955, 150–1).

113    They appear in seventh and eighth place respectively on Dr Clarke's table of the ninety major thegns below the rank of earl in Edward the Confessor's day; Æthelnoth held land to the value of £260 and Wulfweard and his family land to the value of £223 (Clarke, *The English Nobility under Edward the Confessor*, 38–9, 237–8, 366–8).

114    For Æthelnoth's connection with Harold, see *GDB*, fo. 1 (*Merclesham* and Hawkhurst, Kent). Professor Fleming (*Kings and Lords*, 73 and note 69) identifies him with the Alnod who held Wilmington, Sussex, of Earl Godwine, but the name is a common one, and the Alnod (which can also in Domesday represent the name Ælfnoth) who held Wilmington is not distinguished by any of Æthelnoth *cild*'s distinctive bynames (*cild*, 'the Kentishman', 'of Canterbury').

memorandum of the early 1050s names some of the members of the Devon shire-court.[115] The most prominent are Odda of Deerhurst and Ordgar, patron of Tavistock Abbey, both royal kinsmen and rich men.[116] Beside them appear others of more modest standing, some of whom are nevertheless found (like Odda and Ordgar) among the witnesses to King Edward's charters. The presence of such men in the western shires (where Odda was earl in 1051–52) goes far to explain the lack of enthusiasm displayed by the locals when Godwine and Harold staged their return in 1052.

The bonds between king and community were obviously strongest in those areas most frequently visited by the itinerant court, effectively Wessex, southern Mercia, and the London area.[117] North of these regions, the king was a remote figure, rarely if ever seen, and few of the northern thegns regularly attest royal charters. The direct influence of the West Saxon kings petered out at the Tees. The shires of Northumberland and County Durham are post-Conquest creations; before 1066, the regions were governed by the lords of Bamburgh and the bishops of Durham respectively. This circumstance helps to explain why the north-east was not surveyed in 1085–86; the Domesday survey used the pre-Conquest institutions of shire and hundred (or in the north, shire and wapentake) which did not exist there. West of the Pennines, a similar situation existed. Earl Siward re-established some control over 'the lands which were Cumbrian' (*þam landan þeo weoron Combres*) in the 1040s and 1050s, but there was little attempt to impose West Saxon custom in the region.[118] Only a very few estates which lay in the later counties of Cumberland and Westmorland are surveyed in Domesday Book, and those that are appear, like the northern parts of the post-Conquest county of Lancashire, in the Yorkshire folios. Southern Lancashire ('the land between Ribble and Mersey') was appended to Cheshire, and apparently had been since the early tenth century.[119]

All these northerly regions had idiosyncratic customs of their own, unlike the more tightly controlled regions of the West Saxon heartlands. The same was true of York. The region dependent on the tenth-century Danish kingdom had been shired by the early eleventh century, but its legal particularities had been recognised by Edgar, whose Fourth Code allows the Danes 'such good laws as they best decide on', in recognition of their loyalty.[120] The laws of Cnut, as codified by Wulfstan *lupus*, archbishop of York, which sum up the legislation of the tenth-century kings, allow some

---

[115] S.1474.

[116] Both were dead by 1066 (Odda died in 1056), and do not appear in Dr Clarke's lists, but Ordgar's son Ordulf held land worth £67 in Somerset, Devon and Cornwall, putting him fifty-fourth on the list of major non-earlish thegns (Clarke, *The English Nobility under Edward the Confessor*, 38–9, 326), while the known estates of Odda of Deerhurst, which can only represent a minimum of his lands, amount to 167 hides in four shires, worth perhaps £143, which would put him equal twentieth (A. Williams, *Land, Power and Politics: the Family and Career of Odda of Deerhurst*, Deerhurst 1997, 7). For Ordgar, see H.P.R. Finberg, 'The House of Ordgar and the Foundation of Tavistock Abbey', *EHR* liii, 1943, 190–201; idem, 'Childe's Tomb', *Lucerna*, London 1964, 186–203.

[117] See the royal itineraries in Hill, *An Atlas of Anglo-Saxon England*, 84–91, 94–5.

[118] S.1243; F.E. Harmer, *Anglo-Saxon Writs*, Manchester 1952, no. 121, 423–4. For a recent revision of the date of this document, see C. Phythian-Adams, *Land of the Cumbrians*, Aldershot 1996, 132–49, 173–81.

[119] C.P. Lewis, 'An Introduction to the Lancashire Domesday', in A. Williams and G.H. Martin, eds, *The Lancashire Domesday*, London 1991, 1–41; M.A. Atkin, ' "The Land between Ribble and Mersey" in the Early Tenth Century', in A.R. Rumble and A.D. Mills, eds, *Names, Places and People: an Onomastic Miscellany in Memory of John McNeal Dodgson*, Stamford 1997, 8–18.

[120] IV Edgar 12.

regional variation both to the 'Danelaw' and (to a lesser degree) to the Mercians, though (as Stenton remarked) 'the recorded points of difference between Mercian and West Saxon law are few and technical'.[121] The 'separatism' of the north must not be exaggerated; Edgar's Fourth Code limited its recognition of local variation by asserting the king's right to legislate 'for all the nation, whether Englishmen, Danes or Britons, in every province of my dominions', and in 1065, it was the 'law of King Cnut' whose recognition was demanded by the disgruntled men of Yorkshire.[122] Given the exigencies of the time, it was a comparatively united kingdom over which the Old English kings held sway, and whatever their personal failings, they had, as their Norman supplanters were to discover, considerable resources to hand.

When Harold II succeeded to Edward the Confessor on 6 January 1066, he inherited the rights and powers of his predecessor. He appears to have been a popular choice, and there is no sign of the loss of nerve which characterized the final years of Æthelred II.[123] Harold was not unmindful of the comparatively independent northerners and took care to allay any reservations they might have, using Wulfstan, bishop of Worcester, as his envoy, and employing one of their number as his representative in York.[124] His success in establishing control of the kingdom may be judged by the sequel. When Tostig descended upon the south-east in the spring of the year, he met with at best grudging support from the men of the region; some did accompany him north but abandoned him after he was driven from the Humber by Earl Edwin.[125] In contrast, Harold was able to raise a land-fyrd and a fleet 'larger than any king had assembled before in this country' and maintain both in arms for close on four months, twice the normal period, a formidable feat for a medieval commander.[126] His spectacular victory over the Norwegian force of King Harald Hardrada at Stamford Bridge won him the support of any remaining waverers in the north; the 'D' version of the *Anglo-Saxon Chronicle* calls him 'Harold our king' in its account of the engagement. It should also be remembered that as king, Harold could add to the royal lands his own personal estate, effectively almost doubling the wealth at the king's disposal. The imbalance between king and earls was now in the former's favour. It was this prize which, on the 14 October 1066, fell into the grasping hands of the duke of Normandy.

---

[121] II Cnut 14; 15; 15,1a; 15,3; 62; 71a; 83; Stenton, *Anglo-Saxon England*, 3rd edn, 506. The post-Conquest division of England into 'the provinces of Wessex, Mercia and the Danelaw' seems to be a later rationalization (L.J. Downer, ed., *Leges Henrici Primi*, Oxford 1972, 94–5). For the problems of defining the 'Danelaw', see D. Hadley, ' "And they proceeded to plough and support themselves": the Scandinavian Settlement of England', *ANS* xix, 1997, 69–96, especially pp. 84–6.

[122] IV Edgar 2,2; *ASC* 'D', 'E', 1065.

[123] For a favourable survey of Harold as king, emanating admittedly from a source biased towards him, see *Worcester* ii, 600–1.

[124] For St Wulfstan's mission, see R.R. Darlington, ed., *The Vita Wulfstani of William of Malmesbury*, Camden Society 3rd ser. XL, 1928, 22–3; E. Mason, *St Wulfstan of Worcester*, Oxford 1990, 102–4. For Mærle-Sveinn, Harold's 'man in the north', see *GDB*, fo. 376; T.D. Hardy and C.T. Martin, eds, *Lestorie des Engles solum la translacion Maistre Geffre Gaimar*, RS, London 1885, 222, line 5255. Mærle-Sveinn's lands were concentrated in Yorkshire and Lincolnshire, though he also held in the western shires (Somerset, Devon and Cornwall), see Clarke, *The English Nobility under Edward the Confessor*, 322–4. He ranks ninth on Dr Clarke's table of pre-Conquest nobles.

[125] *ASC* 'C' tells of the enforced participation of the south-eastern *butsecarles* (for whom see note 73 above), and *ASC* 'E' of their subsequent desertion of the earl.

[126] *ASC* 'C', 1066: 'all that summer and autumn'. For the normal period of two months, see *ASC*, 1006; *GDB*, fo. 56v.

# 2

# Normandy, 911–1144

## CASSANDRA POTTS

In the early tenth century, a band of Vikings settled along the Seine River in north-western France and laid the foundation for the duchy of Normandy. The term 'Viking' was rarely used in medieval Europe: instead, these unwelcome seafarers from Scandinavia were called by the Franks 'Northmen' (*northmanni*), a word which evoked fear and distrust in the minds of Europeans. Northmen were those who plundered churches, burned villages and captured Christians to be slaves. Consequently, when a sizable group of Northmen or, as they came to be called, Normans, decided to make their home down-river from Paris, they were viewed by their neighbors with alarm and suspicion. Generations after the settlement of Normandy (*Northmannia*), Frankish writers continued to describe the Normans as untrustworthy and violent.[1] Despite the hostility of their neighbors, however, the Normans assumed Frankish ways: they accepted the religion, the language and the women of the Franks. Through this process of assimilation, Normandy gradually came to be accepted as a new principality in France. By the eleventh and twelfth centuries, Norman churches and schools stood at the forefront of European civilization, and within two centuries of their initial settlement along the Seine River, the Normans had conquered England, carved out a new kingdom in southern Italy and Sicily, campaigned against the Byzantines, and charged off on crusade to the Holy Land.[2]

While seeking acceptance, the Normans encouraged the view that their unique heritage set them apart from other Europeans. This pride in their origins is reflected in the legend about the foundation of Normandy which was preserved in writing by Dudo, a churchman at Saint-Quentin in the early eleventh century. Dudo's history of the Normans is notoriously inaccurate in its facts, yet nevertheless valuable in its perspective.[3] In his account, the Normans' first ruler, the Viking Rollo, met with the

---

1  O. Guillot, 'La Conversion des normands peu après 911: des reflets contemporains à l'historiographie ultérieure (Xe–XIe s.)', *CCM* xxiv, 1981, 101–116, 181–219.

2  D. Bates explores the dynamics of Norman expansion in 'The Rise and Fall of Normandy, c. 911–1204', in *England and Normandy*, 19–35. General works on medieval Normandy and the Normans in other lands include M. de Boüard, ed., *Histoire de la Normandie*, Toulouse 1970; F. Neveux, *La Normandie des ducs aux rois, Xe–XIIe siècle*, Rennes 1998; J. Lindsay, *The Normans and their World*, New York 1974; R.H.C. Davis, *The Normans and their Myth*, London 1976; D. Douglas, *The Norman Achievement*, London 1969, and Douglas, *The Norman Fate*, Berkeley 1976. Dated but still useful are: C. Homer Haskins, *The Normans in European History*, New York 1915, and Haskins, *Norman Institutions*, Cambridge, Mass., 1918. A collection of primary sources translated from Latin into French is available in M. de Boüard, ed., *Documents de l'histoire de la Normandie*, Toulouse 1972.

3  *Dudo*, ed. Christiansen. For relevant scholarship on Dudo, see Christiansen's introduction. In addition to the works he cites, see E. Albu, *The Normans in their Histories*, Woodbridge 2001; E. van Houts, ed., *The Normans in Europe*, Manchester 2000, 13–101.

Frankish king Charles the Simple in the year 911 at Saint-Clair-sur-Epte. Dudo describes King Charles as desperate to establish peaceful terms with Rollo and his companions, offering his daughter Gisla to Rollo in marriage, along with the 'territory from the river Epte to the sea as an allod and property; and the whole of Brittany to live off'.[4] In exchange, Rollo was to cease his attacks on the Franks, accept baptism, and swear homage to the king. In Dudo's story, Rollo agreed to these terms and even performed the traditional gesture of homage by placing 'his hands between the hands of the king, which neither his father, nor his grandfather, nor his great-grandfather had done for any man'. But when he was told that the next step was to kiss the king's foot, Rollo balked: 'I will never bow my knees at the knees of any man, and no man's foot will I kiss.' Instead, Rollo ordered one of his comrades to perform this act for him:

> And the man immediately grasped the king's foot and raised it to his mouth and planted a kiss on it while he remained standing, and laid the king flat on his back.[5]

Although Frankish sources confirm that a Viking named Rollo received a grant of land along the Seine from the Frankish king, neither Dudo's story of Rollo's homage nor the so-called treaty of Saint-Clair-sur-Epte find corroboration outside the duchy.[6] The Normans, however, preferred to remember their past in these colorful terms, highlighting the martial valor of their Viking ancestors and celebrating their insubordination toward the king. While the details of Dudo's story are no doubt fictitious, the attitude it reflects was very real.

### Viking Settlements before 1000

To place Dudo's story of Normandy's origins in proper perspective, it should be seen against the broader backdrop of Viking settlements and tenth-century Frankish politics.[7] With the disintegration of the Carolingian empire in the previous century, the tenth century was a chaotic period across western Europe. In the kingdom of the west Franks, which roughly approximated modern France, royal government was weak, and the realm was a patchwork of regional principalities. Local warlords vied with each other and with the king to expand their power and domains. Although the king was technically the feudal overlord of the whole region, this relationship had little practical significance. More often than not, the king appeared as just one of many participants in a ruthless free-for-all for land and power. The Vikings saw this instability within the Frankish realm as an opportunity, and their raids contributed to the breakdown of central authority. In this context, Charles the Simple's grant to Rollo

---

[4]   *Dudo*, ed. Christiansen, 49. On the meaning of 'allod and property' (*in alodo et in fundo*), see S. Reynolds, *Fiefs and Vassals: the Medieval Evidence Reinterpreted*, Oxford 1994, 136–140.

[5]   *Dudo*, ed. Christiansen, 49. For a discussion of Rollo's alleged homage, see J.-F. Lemarignier, *Recherches sur l'hommage en marche et les frontières féodales*, Lille 1945, 74–85.

[6]   D. Douglas, 'Rollo of Normandy', *EHR* lvii, 1942, 427–429.

[7]   D. Bates, 'West Francia: the Northern Principalities', in *The New Cambridge Medieval History*, iii, ed. T. Reuter, Cambridge 1999, and Bates, *Normandy Before 1066*, London 1982, 2–43; E. Searle, *Predatory Kinship and the Creation of Norman Power, 840–1066*, Berkeley 1988, 15–58; S. Coupland, 'From Poachers to Gamekeepers: Scandinavian Warlords and Carolingian Kings', *Early Medieval Europe* vii, 1998, 85–114; R. McKitterick, *The Frankish Kingdoms under the Carolingians, 751–987*, New York 1983, 228–257; N. Lund, 'Allies of God or Man? The Viking Expansion in a European Perspective', *Viator* xx, 1989, 45–59.

and his followers was simply a concession to reality: Northmen had already overrun the Seine River region north-west of Paris, and Charles was not in a position to stop them.

Although certain churchmen objected to alliances with pagans, Frankish lords were often willing to use one set of Vikings as a buffer against other Vikings, or even to enlist Vikings in their wars against their neighbors.[8] These alliances between Christians and Vikings, however, rarely ended well. A Viking leader known as Godefrid, for example, settled near the mouth of the Scheldt River in the late 800s with his warband. Godefrid was called 'the king of the Norsemen' by the Christian sources, and the emperor Charles the Fat made a formal concession of Frisia to him in 882.[9] In addition to the province, Godefrid received baptism and the emperor's daughter Gisla as his bride, an arrangement which clearly set the blueprint for Dudo's later description of the treaty of Saint-Clair-sur-Epte. A few years later Godefrid was ambushed and murdered. There is every reason to believe that Godefrid's history was known in Normandy, especially since Dudo invented a Scheldt episode for Rollo and gave his princess-bride the same name as Godefrid's.[10]

In addition to Viking settlements along the Seine and the Scheldt Rivers, there was also a group of Vikings who attempted to stake a claim along the Loire: Robert of Neustria offered the city of Nantes to them in 921. Although the details are not clear, this effort to create a *Northmannia* along the Loire was overthrown within two decades of Robert's grant.[11] Still other Vikings sought entry into Frankish society by selling their swords, such as Weland, who led a group of Vikings based on the Somme River. Like Godefrid, Weland converted to Christianity and rendered homage to the king. He waged war for the king against other Vikings on the Seine, until he was killed by one of his own followers.[12] When considered in the context of these unsuccessful efforts by *Northmanni* to find permanent homes in Christian lands, it becomes clear that Rollo's group was unique mainly because it survived.

The Seine Vikings also faced rival Norse settlements within the region that eventually became Normandy. Dudo was wrong – Rollo did not receive all of future Normandy in a single grant from Charles the Simple. Rollo's original claim was probably restricted to upper Normandy, a triangle of land bordered by the Epte and Seine Rivers and the sea.[13] Possibly his control extended as far west as the Risle River. Later grants included the Bessin and the Hiémois in 924, and the Cotentin and the Avranchin in 933, but these concessions were similar to the first in that they involved

---

8   The most recent discussion of this practice is by Coupland, 'Poachers to Gamekeepers'.

9   Searle, *Predatory Kinship*, 17–22; Coupland, 'Poachers to Gamekeepers', 108–112.

10  *Dudo*, ed. Christiansen, 32–34. See E. Searle, 'Frankish Rivalries and Norse Warriors', *ANS* viii, 1986, 198–213, at 204.

11  McKitterick, *Frankish Kingdoms*, 232–245.

12  *The Annals of St-Bertin*, trans. J.L. Nelson, Manchester 1991, 95–99, 110–111; Coupland, 'Poachers to Gamekeepers', 104–107; G. Jones, *A History of the Vikings*, Oxford 1984, 215–216.

13  On the boundaries of early Normandy, see L. Musset 'Considerations sur la genèse et le trace des frontières de la Normandie', in *Media in Francia . . . Recueil de mélanges offert à Karl Ferdinand Werner à l'occasion de son 65 anniversaire par ses amis et collègues français*, Maulévrier 1989, 309–318, reprinted in L. Musset, *Nordica et Normannica: Recueil d'études sur la Scandinavie ancienne et médiévale, les expéditions des Vikings et la fondation de la Normandie*, Paris 1997, 403–413; Bates, *Normandy*, 8–11, and map 2; J. Le Patourel, *The Norman Empire*, Oxford 1976, 3–15; K.F. Werner, 'Quelques observations au sujet des débuts du "duché" de Normandie', in *Droit privé et institutions régionales: Etudes historiques offertes à Jean Yver*, Paris 1976, 691–709.

lands which the king no longer controlled. It was up to Rollo's descendants to make these grants meaningful. As they expanded their authority west from the Seine region, Rollo's successors incorporated other Viking groups which had taken up residence in the Bessin and Cotentin. These appear to have been primarily Danish, some of whom had come to France via England, where King Alfred had made a treaty with Danish settlers a generation earlier.[14] Rollo and his group, on the other hand, had come from Norway, where Rollo was remembered in the sagas as Rolf the Ganger: 'a great Viking: he was so big that no steed could bear him, and he therefore walked wherever he went'.[15] An eleventh-century Norman charter indicates that Rollo was known as 'Rolphus' in Normandy as well.[16]

### Origins of the Norman Duchy

In addition to absorbing other Viking bands, the Normans of the Seine incorporated native Franks within their growing community, so that Normans of the eleventh and twelfth centuries were sometimes described as a mixed race of Vikings and Franks. Dudo once again provides the central image that demonstrates this viewpoint. As he tells it, Rollo had a dream on the eve of his departure to France in which he saw a mountain to which birds of many types and colors came to bathe and build their nests. Lest we miss the symbolism, Dudo has a Christian interpret Rollo's dream for him: the birds represent all the different peoples who will be unified under Rollo's rule and washed in the waters of baptism.[17] A later writer makes the same point more directly by describing Rollo as a ruler who 'united in a short time men of all origins and different occupations . . . and from the different races he made one people'.[18] In contrast to most medieval origin-myths which stress a single common descent, Dudo's version acknowledges that the Normans had become a 'people' despite their mixed ancestry – Danish, Norwegian, Frankish, and in the west, Breton.[19]

    To appreciate this achievement, it is important to underline that the *Northmanni* who settled in this region never constituted more than an aristocratic minority. Later writers claimed that the Vikings had depopulated the region, destroying town and countryside. But it is clear by the degree to which French customs, place names, administration, and geographical boundaries survived that the impact of the raids was much less dramatic.[20] Ecclesiastical life suffered during the invasion period, since

---

[14] Bates, *Normandy*, 7; L. Musset, 'Participation de Vikings venus des pays celtes à la colonisation scandinave de la Normandie', *Cahiers du Centre de recherches sur les pas du Nord et du Nord-Ouest* i, 1979, 107–117, reprinted in *Nordica et Normannica*, 279–296.

[15] Douglas, 'Rollo', 419.

[16] Fauroux, no. 53.

[17] *Dudo*, ed. Christiansen, 29–30.

[18] *Inventio et miracula Sancti Vulfranni*, ed. J. Laporte, Rouen 1938, 21. See C. Potts, '*Atque unum ex diversis gentibus populum effecit*: Historical Tradition and the Norman Identity', *ANS* xviii, 1996, 139–152.

[19] On medieval origin-myths, see S. Reynolds, 'Medieval *origines gentium* and the Community of the Realm', *History* lxviii, 1983, 375–390.

[20] Bates, *Normandy*, 2–43; L. Musset, 'Origines et nature du pouvoir ducal en Normandie jusqu'au milieu du XIe siècle', in *Les Principautés au moyen-âge: communications du congrès de Bordeaux en 1973*, Bordeaux 1979, 47–59, reprinted in *Nordica et Normannica*, 263–277; J. Yver, 'Les Premières institutions du duché de Normandie', in *I Normanni e la loro espansione in Europa nell'alto medioevo*,

Vikings targeted churches as repositories of wealth and treasure, but the effects of these raids on the broader population were much less significant. The majority of people in this region was still Frankish, and a key challenge facing Rollo and his descendants was to convince the earlier inhabitants of these lands to accept them as their new lords. We can imagine that many of the more obvious gestures of accommodation by the Normans were aimed at this Frankish audience – such as the staging of parades to celebrate the return of saints whose bodies had been taken out of the region for safe-keeping during the Viking invasions.[21] The success of these efforts is clear from the fact that eleventh-century Normans were perceived as a single people, rather than Franks with Viking overlords.[22]

Yet in Rollo's time, none of this could have been predicted. Indeed, a contemporary observer would have probably considered it more likely that Rollo's community would meet the same end as the Vikings on the Scheldt, the Somme and the Loire. Certainly, no one could have foreseen that one of the most powerful and forward-looking principalities of the next century would emerge from this settlement of Vikings on the Seine. Unfortunately, however, the dynamics of the early duchy are difficult to discern. We have very little evidence for the tenth century, and much of it is suspect. Dudo's stories offer insight into eleventh-century perceptions of the early settlement of the Normans, but he is not a reliable source for the tenth century. Historians continue to argue over fundamental questions, such as the extent of disruption caused by the Viking raids, the percentage and the distribution of Northerners to Franks in early Normandy, and the degree to which the newcomers deliberately conformed to Frankish customs.[23] Was there a Frankish count in Rouen when Rollo and his men arrived? Was the Carolingian political administration still functioning? And if so, did the Northmen take over these functions intact? Because of the paucity of evidence, these questions will probably never find definitive answers, but historians continue to comb the limited sources to try to gain more insight into this formative era of the duchy.

If we put aside for a moment the later legends, the first concrete evidence of the Seine Vikings dates from 918: Charles the Simple refers in a charter to a portion of

Spoleto 1969, 299–366; L. Musset, 'Les Domaines de l'époque franque et les destinées du régime domanial du IXe au XIe siècle', *Bulletin de la société des antiquaires de Normandie* xlix, 1946, 7–97; L. Musset, 'Monachisme d'époque franque et monachisme d'époque ducale en Normandie: le problème de la continuité', in *Aspects du monachisme en Normandie (IVe–XVIIIe siècles): Actes du Colloque Scientifique de l'Année des abbayes Normandes*, ed. L. Musset, Paris 1982, 55–74.

21  C. Potts, 'When the Saints Go Marching: Religious Connections and the Political Culture of Early Normandy', in *Anglo-Norman Political Culture and the Twelfth-Century Renaissance*, ed. C. Warren Hollister, Woodbridge 1997, 17–31. For an alternative interpretation of the hagiographical evidence, see F. Lifshitz, 'The Migration of Neustrian Relics in the Viking Age: the Myth of Voluntary Exodus, the Reality of Coercion and Theft', *Early Medieval Europe* iv, 1995, 175–192.

22  For example, consider the statement by Ralph Glaber in the early eleventh century: 'The whole of the province subject to [Norman] might lived as one clan or family united in unbroken faith.' *Rodulfus Glaber Opera*, ed. J. France, N. Bulst and P. Reynolds, Oxford 1989, 36–37.

23  M. de Boüard discusses this historiographical debate in his article, 'De la Neustrie carolingienne à la Normandie féodale: continuité ou discontinuité?' *BIHR* xxviii, 1955, 1–14. More recently, compare E. Searle, *Predatory Kinship*, and 'Frankish Rivalries', with Yver, 'Premières institutions'; Musset, 'Domaines'; Bates, *Normandy*; E.Z. Tabuteau, *Transfers of Property in Eleventh-Century Norman Law*, Chapel Hill 1988; F. Lifshitz, *The Norman Conquest of Pious Neustria: Historiographic Discourse and Saintly Relics, 684–1090*, Toronto 1995.

land which 'we have granted to the Normans of the Seine, that is to say Rollo and his companions, for the safety of the kingdom'.[24] The tenth-century Frankish historian Flodoard confirms that the city of Rouen and other areas along the Seine were granted to Rollo and his Normans.[25] In 923 Rollo and his warband accompanied Charles the Simple's army on a military campaign near Beauvais. After Charles was defeated in battle at Soissons, the new king, Ralph of Burgundy (923–936), bought Norman support by granting them Bayeux and Maine in 924.[26] This concession is usually interpreted as a reference to the region that became central Normandy, and it essentially meant that the Normans had *carte blanche* from the king to expand west from the Seine. Ralph may have hoped thereby to divert their attentions away from the central theater of Frankish politics. If this was the plan, it failed, as Rollo's alliance with King Ralph broke down the following year: according to Flodoard, the Normans of Rouen lashed out to the north, raiding and sacking Amiens, invading Flanders and attacking Arras.[27] In retaliation, the counts of Flanders and Vermandois, who were allies of King Ralph, defeated Rollo in battle at Eu, on the Bresle River. After this setback, we hear no more about Rollo from contemporary sources, although later stories say that he named his son William Longsword as his successor and died a few years later.[28]

This brief account of Rollo's career in Francia should dispel any notions that Rollo and his companions merely sought a quiet corner in which to live. Rollo flung himself into Frankish politics, and he played at the highest level. He sent his daughter to marry the duke of Aquitaine, where she was known by the Frankish name Adele, and his son William was probably married to the daughter of the count of Vermandois.[29] But the Franks were reluctant to consider Normans equal partners. Part of the problem was religious. Tenth-century Frankish writers complained that the Normans reverted to their pagan practices 'like dogs to their own vomit', despite their reported conversion to Christianity.[30] Churchmen who lived among the Normans were viewed with great sympathy by those in more civilized regions – one letter of encouragement to the archbishop of Rouen during Rollo's time recommended patience in his efforts to convert the Normans and not to expect a complete break with the past, citing Pope Gregory the Great's advice to the early missionaries in England.[31] Later Norman sources claim that Rollo respected the saints of the province, donated generously to the monasteries and churches, and arranged to be buried in the cathedral of Rouen. But tenth-century sources called him a pagan. It was said that as he lay dying, Rollo hedged his bets and ordered that Christian slaves be sacrificed to Odin and Thor.[32] As long as rumors like this circulated, the Normans would be viewed with hostility and suspicion, as

[24]  Bates, *Normandy*, 9; *Recueil des actes de Charles III le Simple, roi de France*, ed. P. Lauer, Paris 1949, i, no. 92; van Houts, *The Normans*, 25.
[25]  Flodoard, *Les Annales de Flodoard*, ed. P. Lauer, Paris 1906, 30–31; van Houts, *The Normans*, 42–51.
[26]  Flodoard, 17–24.
[27]  Flodoard, 30–33.
[28]  Douglas, 'Rollo', 433–435.
[29]  Searle, *Predatory Kinship*, 54, 281, note 74.
[30]  *PL* cxxxii, col. 663.
[31]  *PL* cxxxii, col. 665.
[32]  Adémar de Chabannes, *Chronique*, ed. J. Chavanon, Paris 1897, 139–140; *Complainte de Guillaume Longue-Épée*, in J. Lair, *Étude sur la vie et la mort de Guillaume Longue-épée, Duc de Normandie*, Paris 1893, 66; van Houts, *The Normans*, 41, 51–2.

outsiders to Frankish society. And indeed, throughout the tenth century, the Norman rulers were called 'leaders of pirates', and Rouen was known as 'the city of the Danes'.[33]

### Assimilation: William Longsword and Richard I

The reign of Rollo's son, William Longsword, underscores the tension between Viking and Frankish traditions within the growing province. In certain respects, William clung to Scandinavian ways: he spoke Norse, took a concubine according to the custom of the Danes (*ex more Danico*) and recognized her son as his heir, despite his marriage to a Christian wife. William's chief advisor was a Dane, and he continued to welcome Vikings who came to trade in his towns or settle in his province. In other ways, however, William Longsword followed Frankish customs. For instance, he revived the mint at Rouen and modeled his money on Carolingian coinage.[34] Unlike his father, William Longsword was widely known as a Christian: a poem that was written within a decade or two of his death contrasts William's Christian piety to Rollo's paganism.[35]

Looking back from the early eleventh century, Dudo of Saint-Quentin presented the conflict between the Viking and Frankish sides of Norman identity as a central theme of William Longsword's reign. Dudo told the story of a local lord named Riulf who challenged William Longsword's control over the province, demanding treasure and lands from him.[36] Riulf accused William Longsword of becoming soft and betraying the Normans to the Franks. And indeed, William's first impulse was to appease Riulf with soft words, offering to share the realm with him. When this tactic failed, William planned to seek aid from his Frankish kinsmen, in particular his uncle Bernard of Senlis. But Dudo placed a warning in the mouths of William's followers that if he hid behind the swords of the Franks, they would return to Scandinavia in disgust. Mindful once again of his Viking heritage, William destroyed all his enemies in a rage.

Leaving the question of its historical accuracy aside, Dudo's tale of Riulf's rebellion had significance for his eleventh-century audience: it reminded them that their Norman ancestors had faced the challenge of fitting into the Frankish world without losing touch with their Viking roots. This reminder was particularly significant for Dudo's audience, since the early eleventh century witnessed a conflict within Norman society between 'old and new loyalties' as the duchy's relationships with Scandinavia, France and England were shifting.[37] Dudo's account of William Longsword's reign underlines this central conflict between the Viking and Frankish sides of the Norman identity.

Like his father, William Longsword participated in Frankish politics. As the royal

33 On Normans as *pirati*, see Richer, *Histoire de France*, ed. R. Latouche, Paris 1930. On Rouen, see A. Poncelet, 'Vita Sancti Gildardi, episcopi Rothomagnesis et ejusdem translatio Suessiones, anno 838–840 facta', *Analecta Bollandiana* viii, 1889, 389–405, at 396–397.

34 Bates, *Normandy*, 12. On the existence of mints and the evidence of coinage in early Normandy, also see: F. Dumas, *Le Trésor de Fécamp et le monnayage en Francie occidentale pendant la seconde moitié du Xe siècle*, Paris 1971; L. Abrams, 'England, Normandy and Scandinavia', ch. 3 below.

35 *Complainte de Guillaume Longue-Épée*, 61–70. On the date of this poem, see *Jumièges* i, xxviii–xxix.

36 *Dudo*, ed. Christiansen, 64–68.

37 Abrams, 'England, Normandy and Scandinavia', ch. 3 below.

crown alternated between various contenders, he rendered homage to three kings in succession.[38] Flanders remained a target of Norman aggression as William sought to expand the boundaries of his region to the north.[39] He also led raids against the Bretons – a coin or medallion found at the monastery of Mont Saint-Michel suggests that he may have attempted to assert lordship over Brittany.[40] In this pattern of politics and predation, William was acting much like his fellow Frankish princes, but a late tenth-century historian offers a Frankish perspective on this Norman lord.[41] According to Richer, King Louis IV summoned his vassals to attend a meeting with the emperor Otto the Great. William Longsword arrived with the others, but when the conference was convened, he alone was locked out of the room. In fury, he broke down the door by force and demanded a place: 'Why shouldn't I be present at these proceedings?' Forceful and rash, William Longsword demanded to be included in the sphere of Frankish politics, even after he had been rather pointedly excluded.

But within a year, William Longsword was permanently eliminated from Frankish affairs: the count of Flanders arranged an ambush similar to the one that had destroyed Godefrid a half century earlier. Lured to a parley on an island in the Somme River, William was attacked and murdered in 942. A poem written at a monastery near Rouen lamented the death of this Christian prince of the Normans.[42] The author clearly exaggerated – William Longsword was no innocent – but it is a testament to how far the Normans had assimilated that their leader could be presented as pious and peace-loving. At the same time, however, the harsh reality remained: the Franks had disposed of William Longsword with the same brutal contempt they reserved for Vikings in a Frankish world.[43] And the future of the Norman settlement on the Seine hung in the balance as William Longsword's ten-year-old illegitimate heir Richard faced rebellion from within and invasion from without.

In 944 King Louis IV and Hugh the Great formed an alliance and attacked the region of the Normans from two directions.[44] The royal forces invaded from the north, defeating the Normans in the Pays de Caux and forcing their way into Rouen. Meanwhile, Hugh the Great led his armies against lower Normandy, concentrating on Bayeux. What saved young Richard and the Normans in this period of crisis was the inability of King Louis and Hugh to remain in alliance for long. They quarreled, turned on each other, and by 945 Hugh the Great had captured the king and was helping Richard regain Rouen. To strengthen this new alliance, Hugh offered his daughter Emma to Richard as a bride, creating a marriage bond that linked Rollo's house with the Capetians. Although Emma died without children before her brother assumed the throne in 987, this marriage brought considerable status to the Norman line.[45] Hugh the Great also provided fighting men to help Richard in his wars. By 965

[38]  Flodoard, 39, 55, 75.
[39]  Searle, *Predatory Kinship*, 52–58.
[40]  M. Dolley and J. Yvon, 'A Group of Tenth-Century Coins Found at Mont-Saint-Michel', *BNJ* xl, 1971, 1–16.
[41]  Richer, *Histoire de France (888–995)*, ed. and trans. R. Latouche, Paris 1930, reprinted 1967, i, 172. Also see Potts, *'Atque unum'*, 145–146.
[42]  Above, note 35.
[43]  Searle, 'Frankish Rivalries'.
[44]  Searle, *Predatory Kinship*, 79–90; Bates, *Normandy*, 12–15.
[45]  It has been suggested that Richard I's wife Emma, rather than his second wife Gunnor, was the mother of Emma of Normandy who married Ethelred of England. While this might seem a reasonable supposition, it is nevertheless unlikely. The Capetian Emma was dead by 968, which would make Emma of

Richard I's authority was relatively secure, at least in upper Normandy, and he spent the next three decades broadening the base of his support.

Richard strengthened his position in a number of ways. On one hand, he scaled back his involvement in Frankish politics and disputes.[46] After the 960s, Richard avoided being pulled into the petty wars that continually embroiled neighboring princes. At the same time, he organized his government along Frankish models. He began using Frankish titles, such as 'marquis' and 'count' in his documents, and he carefully regulated the coinage.[47] Richard also supported the efforts of churchmen to restore churches and monasteries with gifts of land and protection.[48] He even attempted to recruit Mayeul of Cluny to reform the monastery of Fécamp, but the famous abbot declined. An eleventh-century writer explained that Mayeul still considered the Normans 'barbaric and savage men, who destroy rather then build holy temples'.[49] Perhaps to improve this image, Richard made pious donations to religious houses outside, as well as inside, his realm.[50]

Marriage was a strategic tool in Richard I's hands.[51] Through his own marriage to Emma, Richard attached his house to the rising star of the Capetians. After Emma died, Richard regularized through Christian marriage his relationship with a Danish concubine named Gunnor. Since she came from a rival Viking clan which had settled in western Normandy, Gunnor's union with Richard helped consolidate his position, especially in the Cotentin where Gunnor's family were valuable allies. According to later sources, Gunnor had several sisters who found husbands among Richard's men, and from these unions were descended the most powerful families of the eleventh and twelfth-century Norman aristocracy.[52] Richard's daughters were married carefully to weave peace with the neighboring princes of Blois-Chartres, Brittany and the king of England.[53] Gunnor also gave Richard I several sons, including his heir Richard II, who continued his father's policies and ruled the duchy for another thirty years.

Richard I's reign witnessed a dramatic turn-around in the fortunes of this region. In 942 when his father William Longsword was murdered, it must have appeared to contemporaries that the Vikings on the Seine would soon meet the same fate as their cousins on the Loire or the Scheldt. But by Richard I's death in 996, his realm was firmly set on a different path. Through a process of consolidation, assimilation and intermarriage, *Northmannia* was no longer a patchwork of unwelcome Viking settlements. It was a functioning realm with an active church, its own currency, and a count who ruled according to Frankish forms of authority. But the Norse connection was not

Normandy almost fifty years old when, in 1017, she married Cnut, with whom she subsequently had two more children. I am grateful to E.M.C. van Houts for bringing this issue to my attention. For further discussion, see Pauline Stafford, *Queen Emma and Queen Edith: Queenship and Women's Power in Eleventh-Century England*, Oxford 1997, 210–211 and note 1.

46 Searle, *Predatory Kinship*, 87.
47 Bates, *Normandy*, 25–27.
48 C. Potts, *Monastic Revival and Regional Identity in Early Normandy*, Woodbridge 1997, 24–28.
49 A. du Monstier, ed., *Neustria Pia*, Rouen 1663, 212.
50 Fauroux, 21–23, and no. 3.
51 On this subject, see Searle, *Predatory Kinship*, 87–140.
52 G.H. White, 'The Sisters and Nieces of Gunnor, Duchess of Normandy', *The Genealogist* xxxvii, 1921, 57–65, 128–132. Most recently, see E.M.C. van Houts, 'Robert of Torigni as Genealogist', in *Studies . . . to Brown*, 215–233.
53 See Searle, *Predatory Kinship*, 136–140. Matilda married Odo of Blois-Chartres, Hadvis married Geoffrey of Rennes and Emma married King Ethelred, and later King Cnut.

lost or forgotten.[54] Rouen had a Viking slave market late into the tenth century. Richard I spoke Norse as well as Frankish, and he allowed Vikings to use Norman harbors, despite a promise in 991 to King Ethelred of England that they would not aid each others' enemies.[55] The number of Norman coins found in Scandinavian hoards also suggests that economic ties still linked Normandy with the north. In the late tenth century it appears that the Normans presented two faces to the world: Frankish when they looked toward England and the continent and Viking when they looked north.[56]

This double-faced aspect of early Normandy has led modern historians to disagree sharply over the character of the duchy in the tenth and eleventh centuries. For over forty years, historians of Normandy have been divided into two main camps: those who emphasize the Viking heritage of the early Normans and those who stress the Normans' ability to assimilate, to absorb Frankish qualities, ways of life and methods of governance.[57] This historiographical division has generated much lively debate, but it tends to obscure the very process by which Normans came to reconcile their conflicting impulses of Viking heritage and Frankish acculturation. The fact is that the transformation of Norsemen into Normans was an uneven and gradual process that required close to a century.

## Consolidation and Expansion: the Reign of Richard II

Good relations continued between Normandy and Scandinavia into the early eleventh century. Richard II allowed Danes to use Norman harbors, and the later eleventh-century historian William of Jumièges records that the Norman ruler made a peace treaty with King Svein of Denmark on the eve of the Danish invasion of England in 1013.[58] The same source also records that Olaf of Norway 'with a host of heathens' assisted Normans against Blois-Chartres around the same time; after the campaign, Olaf agreed to receive baptism from Archbishop Robert of Rouen, Richard II's brother.[59] This appears to have been the last time the Normans called on their Viking cousins for help against the Franks. Contacts between Normandy and the Scandinavian world faded by the second quarter of the eleventh century.

The growing separation between Normandy and Scandinavia is attested at the economic level by the disappearance of Norman coins from Scandinavian hoards in the early eleventh century. It is also reflected in the writings of Franks outside of Normandy, who contrasted the bad *Northmanni* who destroyed churches and towns to the good *Northmanni* who had settled around Rouen and 'made generous gifts to the churches of almost the whole world'.[60] And Richard II worked hard to emphasize that contrast. He continued his father's search for an abbot to rule the ducal monastery of Fécamp, eventually recruiting the well-known reformer William of Dijon in 1001. He entrusted several other monasteries to William, and encouraged the abbot to use

---

[54] See Abrams, 'England, Normandy and Scandinavia', ch. 3 below.

[55] Bates, *Normandy*, 7, 37–38. The record of the 991 agreement is published in Fauroux, 22, note 15.

[56] Musset was the first to describe Normandy as a 'Janus-state', in 'Origines et nature du pouvoir ducal', 50.

[57] See above, note 23.

[58] *Jumièges* ii, 16–17.

[59] *Jumièges* ii, 25–29. This Olaf later became St Olaf, king of Norway, 1014–1030.

[60] Glaber, 36–37.

Fécamp as a training ground for monks throughout the region.[61] Richard II was generous to other monasteries and churches, both within his duchy and beyond his borders. He assumed the expenses of pilgrims, participated in the Peace of God movement, and even sent gifts of treasure to churches as far away as the Holy Land.[62] Through his generous patronage of the church, Richard II helped revise the image of the Normans from the children of pirates to pious members of Christendom.

Richard I had generally withdrawn from Frankish politics after the 960s, but Richard II reentered the fray in the first decades of the eleventh century. He fought more like a Frank than a Viking, however, in that he did not attempt lightning raids deep into another lord's territory, but went to war when diplomacy broke down along his borders, or to support the king in his military campaigns. The marriage ties of his siblings also influenced the direction of Richard II's policies. When his sister died without children, Richard successfully waged war against his brother-in-law, the count of Blois-Chartres, to regain property from her dowry. The peace treaty that resulted helped secure Normandy's southern boundary.[63] When the count of Brittany, another brother-in-law, failed to return from a pilgrimage to Rome, Richard II raised the count's young sons at Rouen.[64] Norman expansion to the west could thereby proceed without threat from Brittany, at least while his nephews were children. And when Svein of Denmark conquered England in 1013, Richard II welcomed his sister Emma home to Rouen, along with her children, the heirs of King Ethelred.[65] Even after Emma returned to England to marry Cnut, Svein's son and successor, her two sons and daughter by Ethelred stayed behind to be raised in the Norman court. Perhaps it was this connection to the Anglo-Saxon royal family, which later embroiled Normandy in the politics of the English succession, that led Richard II to turn away finally from Scandinavian ties.

There is little known about the social structure of early Normandy. The continuity of estate boundaries from Carolingian to Norman times suggests that the majority of disruption occurred at the upper levels of society: the Normans replaced the Frankish aristocracy without dismantling the underlying social infrastructure.[66] But it would be naive to assume that this transition occurred without tensions. A peasant revolt which occurred toward the beginning of Richard II's reign indicates the potential for deep-seated internal conflict.[67] According to William of Jumièges, the peasants had formed assemblies and sent representatives to a central assembly to seek legal free-

---

61 Potts, *Monastic Revival*, 28–35.
62 J.-F. Lemarignier, 'Paix et réforme monastique en Flandre et en Normandie autour de l'année 1023: quelques observations', in *Droit privé et institutions régionales*, 443–468; H. Prentout, 'Le Règne de Richard II duc de Normandie, 996–1027: son importance dans l'histoire', *Academie nationale des sciences arts et belles-lettres de Caen* v, 1929, 57–104; H. Dauphin, *Le Bienheureux Richard: Abbé de Saint-Vanne de Verdun*, Louvain 1946, 262–263; Glaber, 36–37; A. Poncelet, 'Sanctae Catharinae virginis et martyris translatio et miracula rotomagensia saec. XI', *Analecta Bollandiana* xxii, 1903, 423–38, at 426–431.
63 The sister who died was Matilda, wife of Odo of Blois-Chartres. See *Jumièges* ii, 22–23.
64 Geoffrey count of Rennes had married Richard II's sister Hadvis, and Richard II had married Geoffrey's sister Judith. See *Jumièges* ii, 6–7, 28–29. After Geoffrey's departure to Rome, his sons Alan and Odo were 'in the care of' Richard II.
65 Stafford, *Queen Emma*, 209–236; S. Keynes, 'The Æthelings in Normandy', *ANS* xiii, 1991, 173–205; Abrams, 'England, Normandy and Scandinavia', ch. 3 below.
66 Musset, 'Domaines de l'époque franque', especially 42–53; R. Carabie, *Propriété foncière très ancien droit normand (XIe–XIIIe siècles)*, Caen 1943, 122–123.
67 *Jumièges* ii, 8–9.

doms from their overlords. The Normans reacted with swift brutality: they cut off the hands and feet of the peasants' representatives, and sent them home to their communities.[68] While this example indicates the ruthlessness of the Norman aristocracy, the reign of Richard II also witnessed gentler efforts to assure the loyalty of the people. Thus, Richard II honored the region's traditional saints by rebuilding monasteries that had fallen into disrepair and by participating in their cults.[69] In doing so, he associated his authority with that of the spiritual heroes indigenous to the land. Richard II's reign also witnessed the rise of a literary circle in Rouen, centered around Richard's brother Archbishop Robert.[70] And finally, it was during Richard II's reign that Dudo of Saint-Quentin crafted his story of Normandy's past.[71]

### Normans in the South

Some historians have suggested that the Vikings took to the sea in reaction to the consolidation of the Scandinavian kingdoms in the late ninth and tenth centuries.[72] A similar process is discernable in Normandy during the reign of Richard II. As Duke Richard was expanding and tightening his authority in the duchy, ambitious sons of Norman lords began leaving the duchy in pursuit of adventure and wealth. Some went to Spain to participate in the early stages of the *Reconquista*, but many more went to Italy, where they served first as mercenaries for rival powers and then as conquerors themselves. The expansion of the Normans into Southern Italy and Sicily highlights Norman ambition, opportunism and resourcefulness. It also demonstrates the restless energy that characterized this aristocracy.[73] The new kingdom of Southern Italy and Sicily forged from these conquests demonstrates the Normans' ability to blend their institutions with those of the people they conquered: Norman, Lombard, Byzantine

---

68  See M. Arnoux, 'Classe agricole, pouvoir seigneurial et autorité ducale: l'évolution de la Normandie féodale d'après le témoignage des chroniqueurs (Xe–XIIe siècles)', *Le Moyen Age* xcviii, 1992, 35–60, at 45–51.

69  Potts, *Monastic Revival*, 40–41.

70  On the literary circle of Archbishop Robert, see L. Musset, 'Le Satiriste Garnier de Rouen et son milieu (début du XIe siècle)' *Revue du Moyen Age Latin* x, 1956, 237–266; Warner of Rouen, *Moriuht: a Norman Latin Poem from the Early Eleventh Century*, ed. and trans. C. McDonough, Toronto 1995, 4–15; *Jezebel: a Norman Latin Poem from the Early Eleventh Century*, J. Ziolkowski, New York 1989, 37–61.

71  *Dudo*, ed. Christiansen, introduction, especially xxvi–xxix. On Dudo as the beginning of the Norman historiographical tradition, see E.M.C. van Houts, 'The *Gesta Normannorum Ducum*: a History without an End', *ANS* iii, 1980, 106–118, and her introduction, *Jumièges* i, xix–xxxix; L. Shopkow, *History and Community: Norman Historical Writing in the Eleventh and Twelfth Centuries*, Washington DC 1997, especially 68–95, and Shopkow, 'The Carolingian World of Dudo of Saint-Quentin', *JMH* xv, 1989, 19–38; E. Searle, 'Fact and Pattern in Heroic History', *Viator* xv, 1984, 119–137; E. Albu, 'Dudo of Saint-Quentin: the Heroic Past Imagined', *Haskins Soc. Jnl* vi, 1994, 111–118, and Albu, *Normans*; see also ch. 6 below.

72  For example, see Jones, *Vikings*, 87–90.

73  See M. Bennett, 'The Normans in the Mediterranean', ch. 5 below. For a general overview, see Davis, *Normans and their Myth*, 71–100. More detailed studies include: K.B. Wolf, *Making History: the Normans and their Historians in Eleventh-Century Italy*, Philadelphia 1995; H.E.J. Cowdrey, *The Age of Abbot Desiderius: Montecassino, the Papacy, and the Normans in the Eleventh and Twelfth Centuries*, Oxford 1983; G. Loud, *Church and Society in the Norman Principality of Capua, 1058–1197*, Oxford 1985, and Loud, 'How "Norman" was the Norman Conquest of Southern Italy?' *Nottingham Medieval Studies* xxv, 1981, 13–34.

and even Muslim components contributed to the cultural and political environment of this Mediterranean realm. The conquest of Southern Italy and Sicily, however, had little effect on the Normans in Normandy, except perhaps in perpetuating their reputations as warriors and conquerors.[74]

## The Eve of the Conquest: Normandy before 1066

Normandy was very fortunate in the long reigns of Richard I and Richard II. During the half century that Richard I ruled, an insecure Viking settlement evolved into a principality that gained acceptance in the Frankish world. Richard II built upon the foundation his father had established and spent three decades strengthening his resources and winning respect, both within the region and beyond its borders. Towns grew and flourished, and a rising aristocracy directed considerable wealth toward the enrichment of religious establishments.[75] After Richard II's death in 1026, however, internal strife undermined stability. Richard II's heir was Richard III, but his younger brother Robert rebelled against the young duke within a year of their father's death. Richard III defeated Robert at Falaise and demanded homage from his brother. In theory they were reconciled, but Richard III died a year later – the rumor was of poisoning, and later writers suggested that Robert was to blame for his brother's death.[76] Richard III's young son and heir was conveniently committed to monastic life.

Although posterity added the sobriquet 'the Magnificent' to his name, Robert's own reign was troubled. At the outset he attacked his uncle, the archbishop of Rouen, and forced him into exile. The archbishop placed the duchy under ecclesiastical anathema and sought help from the French king. The young duke capitulated, blamed his actions on evil advisers, and welcomed his uncle back to Rouen.[77] Following this incident, Duke Robert faced opposition along the southern frontier, where the powerful Bellême family maintained an independent lordship, and in the west, where Robert's cousin Alan III of Brittany attacked the Avranchin and gained control of Mont Saint Michel.[78] Robert resolved these conflicts, at least for the short term, with the help of his uncle. According to William of Jumièges, Duke Robert even attempted an invasion of England on behalf of Emma's children, Edward and Alfred, who were still living at the Norman court.[79] Strong winds were said to have thwarted this invasion. Shortly thereafter, Robert decided to embark on a pilgrimage to Jerusalem. Since he had no wife and no legitimate issue, Robert presented his young illegitimate son William to his magnates as his heir. After that, Robert the Magnificent departed on a pious journey from which he never returned.

At his father's death in 1035, William II was only seven or eight years old. He

---

[74] Davis, *Normans and their Myth*, 87–90.

[75] On the aristocracy and economic life, see Bates, *Normandy*, 94–146; L. Musset, 'Foires et marchés en Normandie à l'époque ducale', *Annales de Normandie* xxvi, 1976, 3–23, and Musset, 'A-t-il existé en Normandie au XIe siècle une aristocratie d'argent?' *Annales de Normandie* ix, 1959, 285–99. On Richard II, see note 62 above .

[76] *Jumièges* ii, 44–49. On the rumor of poison, see *Jumièges* ii, 47, note 3.

[77] *Jumièges* ii, 49.

[78] Bates, *Normandy*, 68–71; *Jumièges* ii, 48–59. On the Bellêmes, see G. Louise, *La Seigneurie de Bellême Xe–XIIe siècles*, Flers 1992–1993; K. Thompson, 'Family and Influence to the South of Normandy in the Eleventh Century: the Lordship of Bellême', *JMH* xi, 1985, 216–226.

[79] *Jumièges* ii, 76–79.

barely survived the next ten years, and the decade and a half that followed those years were likewise filled with peril. William II's position as duke of Normandy was not finally secure until he was in his thirties, at which point he tempted fortune by crossing the channel in a reckless bid for the English crown. His success should not lead us to underestimate the odds William faced, both initially as the illegitimate heir to a troubled duchy, and later, as a foreign invader with an uncertain claim. More has been written about William II, and the consequences of his conquest of England in 1066, than any other duke of Normandy, and his story is a remarkable tale of a man who succeeded in the face of nearly overwhelming odds.[80] His mark on the history of England and France was profound. But however much historians praise the courage, intelligence and military leadership of William the Conqueror, they must also ac-knowledge the role that sheer luck played in his accomplishments.

William II's reign did not start out lucky. Internal wars rocked the duchy during the first two decades of his rule. As the duke passed from childhood to adolescence, enemies attacked his household and supporters – William of Jumièges reports that the young duke's guardian, his teacher and his steward were all killed by rebels.[81] Feuds broke out as members of William's extended family attempted to unseat him. In 1046, one of William's cousins, Guy of Burgundy, led a full-scale rebellion against the duke in lower Normandy. It was King Henry I of France (1031–1060) who saved the day for William at the Battle of Val-ès-Dunes in 1047. But within five years, the same French king reversed his position, gave military support to a rebellion within Normandy, and led an alliance of French magnates against William.[82] Henry I's decision to oppose William in 1052 was occasioned by the king's alliance with the count of Anjou, Geoffrey Martel. Anjou was a powerful county in northern France, a challenge to both Normandy and the monarchy.[83] When King Henry decided to ally with Anjou at the expense of Normandy, he placed the Norman duchy on a new political track: from this point on, the rulers of Normandy appeared as adversaries more often than supporters of the French crown.[84] The insubordination of the Normans toward the king, which Dudo had celebrated, hardened into distrust and open rivalry.

The offensive alliance that challenged William II in 1052 included the duke's paternal uncles, William of Arques and Mauger archbishop of Rouen (1037–1055), as well as the king and the counts of Anjou and Ponthieu. After two years of warfare, the duke's forces were victorious at the battle of Mortemer in 1054.[85] The count of Arques was exiled, the archbishop of Rouen was deposed, and the French and Angevin forces withdrew. But 1057 witnessed another joint invasion of Normandy by King Henry and Geoffrey Martel, perhaps to avenge their losses at Mortemer.[86] Duke William again defeated the French at the battle of Varaville, and the king withdrew with his allies. Hostilities continued for the next two years, mainly along Normandy's

---

80  There are several biographies of William the Conqueror in which different perspectives are offered. Compare D. Douglas, *William the Conqueror: the Norman Impact on England*, London and Berkeley 1964; D. Bates, *William the Conqueror*, London 1989; Michel de Boüard, *Guillaume le Conquérant*, Paris 1984; F. Barlow, *William I and the Norman Conquest*, London 1965.

81  *Jumièges* ii, 90–95; Douglas, *William*, 31–52.

82  For a closer narrative of William's minority and the challenges he faced, see Douglas, *William*, 47–69.

83  For Anjou, see O. Guillot, *Le Comte d'Anjou et son entourage au XIe siècle*, Paris 1972; L. Halphen, *Le Comté d'Anjou au XIe siècle*, Geneva 1906, reprinted 1974.

84  Douglas, *William*, 62.

85  *Jumièges* ii, 142–145.

86  *Jumièges* ii, 150–153.

borders as Duke William endeavored to expand his realm at the expense of his neighbors. Tensions eased, however, in 1060 with the deaths of both King Henry I of France and Count Geoffrey of Anjou.

The death of King Henry was particularly fortunate for William II, since the king's son and heir, Philip, was a child under the guardianship of William's father-in-law, Baldwin count of Flanders. William had married Baldwin's daughter Matilda around 1050, despite papal opposition. Various reasons have been suggested to explain the pope's objection to this match, but political factors probably outweighed later rumors of consanguinity: a Norman-Flemish-French alliance was probably perceived as a threat to the pope's ally, the Holy Roman Emperor.[87] In any event, by 1060 the French monarchy was under the control of a friend of Normandy, while Anjou was embroiled in a civil war following Geoffrey Martel's death. Duke William was in his early thirties, surrounded by a circle of battle-hardened veterans and supporters. His successful suppression of the rebellions of the past two decades had allowed William to enrich his vassals with property confiscated from his opponents. And by 1064, he had gained the county of Maine for his son Robert, who was engaged to the sister of the deceased count of Maine.[88] In 1066, when succession to the English crown was in dispute, William was in an excellent position to press his claim.

### Opportunity and Challenge: the Conquest of England

Norman sources of this period, such as William of Jumièges and William of Poitiers, would have us believe that William II of Normandy was the only rightful contender for the English crown in 1066, but in fact his claim was fairly tenuous.[89] By blood William's link to the English throne descended from Emma, his great-aunt, who had married King Ethelred and whose son Edward gained the crown in 1042, after having grown up in exile in Normandy.[90] The Norman sources tell us that King Edward, who was childless, named his cousin William as his heir, and sent Harold Godwinson to Normandy in 1064 or 1065 to swear fealty and confirm William's right to be the next king of England. But the English sources before 1066 do not corroborate this claim.[91] It is true that Edward preferred the company of Normans, having spent twenty-five years in the duchy. There was a backlash in England against the Normans whom King Edward had appointed to high office early in his reign. Most notably, King Edward chose Robert of Jumièges to be archbishop of Canterbury in 1051, but the Anglo-Saxon earls Godwin and Harold Godwinson led a revolt that forced the archbishop and several other Norman favorites into exile across the channel.[92] Even if it

---

[87] Douglas, *William*, 78.

[88] *Gesta Guillelmi*, 61–63.

[89] Historians have different opinions of William's claim to the English throne. For example, compare R.A. Brown, *The Normans and the Norman Conquest*, London 1969, 121–133, and F. Barlow, *Edward the Confessor*, London and Berkeley 1970, 220–229.

[90] On Emma, see Stafford, *Queen Emma*. On Edward in Normandy, see Keynes, 'Æthelings', and Barlow, *Edward*, 28–53.

[91] For the primary sources, see *EHD* ii, especially 142–150. For analysis, see D. Douglas, 'Edward the Confessor, Duke William of Normandy and the English Succession', *EHR* lxviii, 1953, 526–545; E. John, 'Edward the Confessor and the Norman Succession', *EHR* xciv, 1979, 241–267. See above, note 89.

[92] For a fuller account and discussion of sources, see Barlow, *Edward*, 104–126; see also ch. 1 above.

was Edward the Confessor's wish when he died in January 1066 that William of Normandy succeed him as king, the most powerful lords of the kingdom clearly opposed foreign rule.

English sources tell us that it was Harold Godwinson, the earl of Wessex, whom King Edward appointed as his successor.[93] But King Harold faced challenges to his rule from both William of Normandy and Harold Hardrada, king of Norway, who had been encouraged by Godwinson's brother Tostig to invade England. In the summer of 1066, King Harold prepared for two invasions, but he had no way of knowing which would strike first.[94] As it turned out, the northerly winds which carried Hardrada's ships to the Yorkshire coast delayed William's departure from Normandy. The English king rushed north to meet Hardrada, defeating him at the battle of Stamford Bridge on 25 September. Three days later the winds shifted, allowing William's fleet to cross the channel and land on the southern coast, near Hastings. The Normans spent the next couple of weeks establishing a fortified position at Hastings. King Harold hurried south after hearing that the Normans had landed, and the two armies met on 14 October. The English were defeated, and King Harold was killed on the battlefield. Two months later, William of Normandy was crowned king of England on Christmas Day.

The long-term significance of the Norman conquest of England has led historians to speculate for centuries over the key to the success of the Normans. Some have attributed Norman military prowess to the Viking blood that flowed in their veins, clearly an argument which the Normans themselves favored. Others have lauded the Normans for superior military discipline and administrative organization.[95] More recent historians have pointed to the church and the rise in eleventh-century Normandy of a new aristocracy that was linked by marriage and kinship to the ducal house.[96] All of these explanations for the rise of Normandy have generated considerable debate among historians. Discussion of Norman military organization has raised the question of feudalism, with its attendant features of knight-service, private justice, fiefs, and castles.[97] And much ink has been spilt by historians attempting to determine whether or not the Normans introduced feudalism to England. These scholarly arguments have brought many aspects of the Conquest into clearer focus, as historians

---

[93] *EHD* ii, 143; *Vita Ædwardi*, 79. Although he insists on the righteousness of William of Normandy's claim to England, William of Poitiers, *Gesta Guillelmi*, 140–141, also remarks that Harold Godwinson received the throne as 'the death-bed gift of Edward'.

[94] For primary sources on the battles of Stamford Bridge and Hastings, see *EHD* ii; R.A. Brown, *The Norman Conquest of England: Sources and Documents*, Woodbridge 1984; Stephen Morillo, ed., *The Battle of Hastings: Sources and Interpretations*, Woodbridge 1996.

[95] Haskins, *Norman Institutions*, 3–44; Davis, *Normans and their Myth*, 7–8; Brown, *Normans*, 141–202. On Norman legal procedures, see Tabuteau, *Transfers of Property*.

[96] See especially Douglas, *William*, 83–104.

[97] Haskins, *Norman Institutions*, 5–24; E.Z. Tabuteau, 'Definitions of Feudal Military Obligations in Eleventh-Century Normandy', in *On the Laws and Customs of England: Essays in Honour of S.E. Thorne*, ed. M.S. Arnold, T.A. Green, S.A. Scully and S.D. White, Chapel Hill 1981, 18–59; F.M. Stenton, *The First Century of English Feudalism 1066–1166*, Oxford 1971; C.W. Hollister, '1066: "the Feudal Revolution"', *AHR* lxii, 1968, 708–723, reprinted in *Monarchy, Magnates and Institutions in the Anglo-Norman World*, London 1986, 2–16. Also see Hollister's edition of sources and essays, *The Impact of the Norman Conquest*, New York 1969, which takes up the question of feudalism; J. Gillingham, 'The Introduction of Knight Service into England', *ANS* iv, 1981, 53–64. On the problem of feudalism in general, see E.A.R. Brown, 'The Tyranny of a Construct: Feudalism and Historians of Medieval Europe', *AHR* lxxix, 1974, 1063–1088, and more recently, Reynolds, *Fiefs*, 1–14.

have scoured the sources to compare England and Normandy both before and after 1066, but many issues remain unresolved.

Despite the controversies, certain general points are widely accepted. Normandy in the second half of the eleventh century was a well-ordered society. The economy was strong, and the church was led by men who commanded respect in other lands. An ambitious and closely-knit aristocracy, trained for war and hardened in battle, was eager for new lands to conquer. While Spain and Italy provided an outlet for the restless energy of some of these men, many of those remaining in Normandy were keen for adventure. And tensions had been rising between England and Normandy since the early 1050s. For William, 1066 was a good year to strike: with his rivals on the continent dead and the duchy firmly in hand, he could exploit the opportunity which Edward the Confessor's death offered. Even the winds conspired to help the duke, timing his invasion to follow closely on Hardrada's. Thus, the Normans could disembark unopposed on the shore near Hastings, without facing the full brunt of the Anglo-Saxon force in battle. These advantages must be acknowledged, however much we admire William's leadership and his men's courage on the battlefield. Moreover, in hindsight William enjoyed one other key advantage over his opponents in 1066: the victor's prerogative to have his version of events dominate the historical narratives.

### *Perspectives on the Norman Conquests*

Having won the battle, William and his followers could assert that their victory was ordained by God. Writing shortly after 1066, Norman historians elaborated on this theme, adding a moral and religious component to William's claim to the English throne. William of Jumièges, William of Poitiers, and the *Carmen de Hastingae Proelio* all agree that Harold Godwinson committed perjury when he took the crown of England, violating the oath he had allegedly sworn to William in 1064/65.[98] The Bayeux Tapestry, embroidered within a decade or so of the Conquest, offers pictorial testimony of Harold's oath-taking and breaking.[99] William of Poitiers also includes a description of Pope Alexander II's support for William's invasion, claiming that 'the duke received a banner with [the pope's] blessing, to signify the approval of St Peter, by following which he might attack the enemy with greater confidence and safety'.[100] William of Poitiers even has the duke place 'around his neck in humility the relics whose protection Harold had forfeited by breaking the oath that he had sworn on them'.[101] Later narratives of the Norman conquest retained these dramatic details and perpetuated the idea of the Norman Conquest as holy cause.[102]

Contemporary historians also described the aggression of the Normans in Italy as favored by God. Writing in the same decade as William of Poitiers, Amatus of Montecassino places the following warning in the mouth of St Matthew, who appears before the archbishop of Salerno in a vision:

98   *Jumièges* ii, 88–89, 158–161; *Gesta Guillelmi*, 70–71, 76–77, 100–101; *Carmen*, 16–17, 20–21.
99   *EHD* ii, 267.
100  *Gesta Guillelmi*, 104–105.
101  *Gesta Guillelmi*, 125–125.
102  For example, see *Orderic* ii, 142–143.

For it has been ordained in the presence of God that whosoever shall oppose the Normans will be put to flight by them . . . For this land has been given to the Normans by God. Because of the perversity of those who used to hold it and the paternal ties that God has with the Normans, the just will of God turned the land over to them.[103]

Divine favor was somewhat trickier for Amatus to assert when describing Norman campaigns against the papacy, but he nevertheless held his ground, maintaining that the Normans 'took no joy' from trouncing the pope.[104] From the perspective of historians writing in the last quarter of the eleventh century, it appeared that the Normans were everywhere triumphant, and to some their success presupposed heaven's help. Others, however, such as the Byzantine princess Anna Komnena, described the Normans as rapacious, untrustworthy, war-loving barbarians.[105] For better *and* for worse, the reputation of the Normans increased with their conquests in England and southern Italy, their campaigns in Greece and Asia Minor, their participation in the First Crusade, and the creation of the Norman principality of Antioch under Bohemond in 1098.[106]

The range of their activities has contributed in some quarters to the view of the Normans as a race of conquerors, and the relatively narrow time frame in which the Norman conquests occurred has also tempted some historians to view these enterprises as connected elements of Norman empire-building. David Douglas, for example, suggests that 'all the enterprises undertaken by the Normans between 1050 and 1100 can be regarded as forming part of a single movement that was everywhere marked by common modes of actions and co-ordinating principles of policy'.[107] Similarly, R. Allen Brown asserts, 'By the end of the eleventh century, there was a kind of Norman commonwealth of states and settlements, of which England was one item only, stretching from the marches of Wales to Antioch.'[108] More recent historians, however, have challenged this view of a 'single Norman endeavor'.[109] Most notably, David Bates rejects the notion of the Normans as a 'dominant people' with an 'exceptional aptitude for war', and instead places Norman expansion within the context of social changes taking place throughout northern France during the eleventh century.[110] These developments include the organization of families from extended kin-groups into lineages, the use of toponyms, and the rise of primogeniture which ensured that the patrimonial inheritance – which in the eleventh century increasingly meant the family's chief castle – would pass down to the next generation intact. As Bates points out, moreover, the view of the Normans as a special race of conquerors fades when it is acknowledged that chroniclers from England to Palestine often used the terms 'Norman' and 'French' interchangeably.[111]

Where David Bates emphasizes continuity of Norman institutions, Eleanor Searle on the other hand sees discontinuity, and she argues against associating the Normans

---

103    Wolf (as n. 73), 100.
104    Wolf, 101.
105    *The Alexiad of Anna Comnena*, ed. and trans. E.R.A. Sewter, Harmondsworth 1969, 438–440. Also see Albu, *Normans*.
106    For a comparative chronology of Norman enterprises in the north and south, see Douglas, *Achievement*, 4–6.
107    Douglas, *Achievement*, 110.
108    Brown, *Sources*, xvi.
109    Douglas, *Fate*, 3.
110    Bates, *Normandy*, xv, 49–56, 242–247.
111    Bates, *Normandy*, xvii, 111–121, 245–251.

with the French. In her view, Normandy emerged in the eleventh century through a process of 'slow unification based upon more Scandinavian predatory, expanding kin-groups'.[112] And Searle suggests that it was this tradition of predation which sent the Normans to invade England once Normandy itself became too small for their ambitions: 'Thus it was that in the fateful spring of 1066 William could . . . put to his great warriors a plan that no ruler but a Scandinavian would have considered, and no state in Christendom but theirs could have accomplished with such efficiency.'[113] Continuity or discontinuity, French or Scandinavian: these historiographical debates have in turn generated more inquiry into the nature of the Norman identity.[114] How were the Normans perceived by their neighbors, how did they perceive themselves, and to what extent did they and the lands they conquered exhibit distinctively Norman qualities? These were the central questions that R.H.C. Davis asked in his work *The Normans and their Myth* over twenty years ago; they continue to occupy historians today.

### The Consequences of Conquest: Normandy after 1066

Although eleventh-century historians in Normandy sometimes boasted about the exploits of Normans in Italy, their contemporaries in the south did not describe the creation of the Norman kingdom of Southern Italy and Sicily as part of a wider movement of Norman expansion.[115] Nor did the establishment of Norman kingdoms in the Mediterranean have much effect on Normandy itself. The consequences for Normandy of the conquest of England, on the other hand, deserve more attention. On the face of it, there were many reasons for the Normans to rejoice over their victory at Hastings. Their duke became a king who rewarded his vassals with the spoils of a rich kingdom: Norman knights replaced the Anglo-Saxon aristocracy in England after 1066, gaining huge estates, lordships and offices.[116] Ecclesiastical communities in Normandy were likewise enriched with English lands, while Norman prelates found high positions in the English church.[117] On the other hand, however, administrative resources were stretched thin over the lands under Norman control. The same ruler governed England and Normandy for sixty-two of the seventy-seven years that separated Duke William's Christmas coronation in 1066 and Geoffrey of Anjou's conquest of Normandy in 1144.[118] During these years, a single household and a single

---

112 Searle, *Predatory Kinship*, 238.
113 Searle, *Predatory Kinship*, 232.
114 In addition to the works already cited, see G.A. Loud, 'The *"Gens Normannorum"* – Myth or Reality?', *ANS* iv, 1982, 104–116, 204–209.
115 Davis, *Normans and their Myth*, 89.
116 The literature on this subject is enormous. For an overview, see *EHD* ii, 21–28, and sources; M. Chibnall, *Anglo-Norman England, 1066–1166*, Oxford 1986; Le Patourel, *Norman Empire*, especially 28–88; R. Fleming, *Kings and Lords in Conquest England*, Cambridge 1991, especially 107–144; see also ch. 7 below.
117 For an introduction to this subject, see F. Barlow, *The English Church, 1066–1154*, London 1970; D.J.A. Matthew, *The Norman Monasteries and their English Possessions*, Oxford 1962; D. Spear, 'The Norman Empire and the Secular Clergy, 1066–1204', *JBS* xx, 1982, 1–10; E. Cownie, *Religious Patronage in Anglo-Norman England, 1066–1135*, London 1998; and ch. 9 below.
118 See J. Le Patourel, 'Normandy and England 1066–1144', in *Feudal Empires: Norman and Plantagenet*, London 1984, ch. vii, 3–38, at 4.

court faced the challenges of government on both sides of the channel.[119] The result, as we hear contemporary chroniclers frequently complain, was that Normandy was too often left to her own devices and torn by private war.

Succession crises in 1087, 1100 and 1135 divided the aristocracy as the children and grandchildren of the Conqueror vied with each other over his inheritance. Noble families with cross-channel estates were forced to choose sides as brothers, sons and cousins fomented rebellions and waged the wars that eventually dismantled the constellation of territories that William the Conqueror had assembled.[120] William had designated his oldest son Robert Curthose to be his heir in Normandy and Maine, and perhaps in England as well, but Robert's revolt at the time of his father's death in 1087 defeated hopes of a unitary succession.[121] Orderic Vitalis, a monk and historian at the Norman monastery of Saint-Evroul writing in the first half of the twelfth century, tells us that the dying king spoke harshly of Robert Curthose at the end, warning that 'any province subjected to his rule will be most wretched'.[122] No doubt the Conqueror was disappointed with his eldest son – during the last ten years of his life, William faced two serious rebellions in Normandy, both led by Robert Curthose. At the Battle of Gerberoy in 1079, Robert Curthose actually met and defeated his father in the field.[123] A brief reconciliation was followed by another bitter quarrel which lasted until William's death.

Contemporary sources suggest that William the Conqueror would have preferred to have disinherited Robert entirely for his treason and rebellion, but such an act would have plunged Normandy deeper into civil war.[124] He therefore confirmed Robert Curthose's inheritance of Normandy and Maine, but designated William Rufus, his second son, heir to the kingdom of England.[125] Young Henry, the third son, received a sum of money. Private warfare ravaged Normandy during the reign of Robert Curthose, inspiring Orderic's characterization of the Normans as a people who, if not disciplined by a firm ruler, would 'tear each other to pieces and destroy themselves, for they hanker after rebellion, cherish sedition, and are ready for any treachery'.[126] In Orderic's view, these violent and unruly qualities were unleashed after William the Conqueror's death, since 'all men knew that Duke Robert was weak and indolent . . . he exercised no discipline over either himself or his men'.[127]

To reward his circle of knights with treasure, Robert Curthose sold the Cotentin to his youngest brother in 1088, thus relinquishing approximately a third of Normandy to Henry.[128] Robert then attempted to dethrone William Rufus and reunite England

[119]  Le Patourel, *Feudal Empires*, ch. vii, 10–12.
[120]  Le Patourel, *Norman Empire*, 89–117; J. Green, *The Aristocracy of Norman England*, Cambridge 1997, 274–326.
[121]  On the question of succession, see J. Le Patourel, 'The Norman Succession, 996–1135', *EHR* lxxxvi, 1971, 225–250, and Le Patourel, *Norman Empire*, 181–184, especially 183, note 1; B. English, 'William the Conqueror and the Anglo-Norman Succession', *Historical Research* lxiv, 1991, 221–236; J.A. Green, 'Unity and Disunity in the Anglo-Norman State', *Historical Research* lxiii, 1989, 115–134.
[122]  *Orderic* iv, 92–93.
[123]  C.W. David, *Robert Curthose, Duke of Normandy*, Cambridge 1920, 19–27.
[124]  *Orderic* iv, 92–93.
[125]  On Rufus, see F. Barlow, *William Rufus*, London and Berkeley 1983.
[126]  *Orderic* iv, 82–83.
[127]  *Orderic* iv, 114–115.
[128]  *Orderic* iv, 120–121.

and Normandy under his authority. This plan, organized by Odo of Bayeux, backfired entirely, and in 1091 Robert Curthose found himself forced to appeal to King Philip of France for help when William Rufus invaded Normandy with the same plan of bringing the duchy and kingdom under a single rule.[129] The two older brothers agreed to peace at the expense of the youngest: they invaded the Cotentin and drove Henry into exile. All this fraternal strife exacerbated the breakdown of central authority in Normandy. In 1091 Robert Curthose and William Rufus attempted to reestablish public order in the duchy, issuing a reassertion of ducal rights as they had been exercised during the reign of William the Conqueror.[130] The two brothers also agreed that if one should die without an heir the other would inherit his lands.[131] However, the détente between William Rufus and Robert Curthose broke down again, and the king and duke were at war in 1095 when Pope Urban II preached the sermon that inspired Curthose, like so many knights of Christendom, to join the First Crusade.[132]

To pay for his expedition, the duke borrowed 10,000 marks of silver from William Rufus, with Normandy as collateral. Thus Robert Curthose was far away when William Rufus suddenly died in early August of 1100, leaving the throne of England vacant.[133] His brother Henry, however, was on the scene, and he acted quickly to gain the crown. Curthose returned home later that summer, resumed his position as duke and demonstrated his incompetence as a ruler repeatedly over the next six years. Helias of La Flèche stripped Curthose of the county of Maine, and his brother Henry suppressed the conspiracy Curthose organized to claim the throne of England.[134] Anarchy reigned in the duchy as bands of marauding soldiers terrorized the countryside: Robert of Bellême attacked the Hiémois, and Eustace of Breteuil waged war in the Evrecin. Curthose proved weak and ineffectual in the face of all these disorders. He also alienated the church through highhanded carelessness and corrupt appointments. Meanwhile, Henry I was preparing his own invasion, carefully building up a network of allies in France and Normandy.

In 1105 Henry invaded Normandy with the support of many lay and ecclesiastical lords in the duchy. At the Battle of Tinchebrai in 1106, Robert Curthose was captured and imprisoned.[135] He died twenty-eight years later, still a prisoner of his youngest brother. Historians on occasion refer to Henry's victory at Tinchebrai as the Norman invasion in reverse: duchy and kingdom were reunited under a single rule, but this time the king of England had defeated the Norman duke. In general, Normandy enjoyed better government under Henry I than it had under the feckless Robert Curthose. Peace was enforced, adulterine castles were destroyed or surrendered to

---

[129] David, *Curthose*, 44–69; Barlow, *Rufus*, 69–85, 273–284. On Odo of Bayeux, see D. Bates, 'The Character and Career of Odo Bishop of Bayeux (1049/50–1097)', *Speculum* l, 1975, 1–20.

[130] *Consuetudines et Justicie*, in Haskins, *Norman Institutions*, 277–284. For a partial translation, see Brown, *Sources*, 152–153.

[131] Le Patourel, *Norman Empire*, 184–185; Barlow, *Rufus*, 281.

[132] For Robert's role in the First Crusade, see S. Runciman, *A History of the Crusades*, i, Cambridge 1951, 164–168, 291–301. On the effect of the First Crusade on Jewish communities in Normandy, see Norman Golb, *The Jews in Medieval Normandy: a Social and Intellectual History*, Cambridge 1998, 115–135, 171–176.

[133] On the hunting accident that killed William Rufus, see Barlow, *Rufus*, 420–430; C.W. Hollister, 'The Strange Death of William Rufus', *Speculum* xlviii, 1973, 637–653, reprinted in *Monarchy*, 59–75.

[134] David, *Curthose*, 125–126; C.W. Hollister, 'The Anglo-Norman Civil War: 1101', *EHR* lxxxviii, 1973, 315–334, reprinted in *Monarchy*, 77–96.

[135] For contemporary accounts, see *Orderic* vi, 88–93; *EHD* ii, 329–330; *Huntingdon*, 453–457; Robert of Torigny in *Jumièges* ii, 222–223; William of Malmesbury, *Gesta Regum*, 721–725.

Henry, and ecclesiastical properties were restored.[136] Financial and judicial systems of governance clearly functioned in Normandy during Henry's reign, and obligations of knight-service were formalized.[137] Henry's triumph over the king of France in 1119 at the Battle of Brémule was a high point in his reign.[138] When it became known in 1120, however, that Henry I's only legitimate son had drowned in the sinking of the White Ship, dissension once again undermined stable government in the duchy.

For the next eight years, the rallying point for rebellions against Henry in Normandy was William Clito, the son of Robert Curthose.[139] King Louis VI of France supported Clito's claim to the duchy – it was in the French king's interest to break the union between England and Normandy. And Norman nobles with little at stake in England likewise backed Clito's right to inherit his father's duchy. Henry put down a rebellion in 1124, but the problem of succession still haunted him.[140] He demanded that his barons swear oaths to his daughter Matilda in 1127, and he married her to Geoffrey Plantagenet of Anjou the following year to neutralize a potential rival: the marriage of Matilda and Geoffrey of Anjou ensured that Anjou and the king of France would not ally again against Normandy, as they had in the 1050s.[141] The death of Clito in 1128 and the birth of Henry, Geoffrey's and Matilda's son and Henry I's grandson, in 1133 raised hopes for a unified succession, but the old king quarreled with his daughter and son-in-law over some border castles included in Matilda's dowry.[142] At the time of Henry's death in 1135 this conflict was unresolved, and the situation deteriorated further after his death.

Whatever Henry I's intentions for succession, it was Matilda's cousin Stephen of Blois who seized the moment, crossing the channel with the claim that he was the rightful ruler of both England and Normandy.[143] Stephen was a grandson of William the Conqueror: his mother Adela had been the sister of Robert Curthose, William Rufus and Henry I. The Norman lords had initially looked toward Stephen's older brother Theobald of Blois to rule Normandy after Henry I's death. The majority decided, however, to accept Stephen after he had secured the English throne 'on account of the honors which they held in both provinces'.[144] But Matilda and Geoffrey did not surrender their claim, and civil war destroyed the peace in both

---

136	*Orderic* vi, 92–101. Also see C.W. Hollister, *Henry I*, New Haven 2001; C.W. Hollister, 'Henry I and the Invisible Transformation of Medieval England', in *Studies in Medieval History Presented to R.H.C. Davis*, ed. H. Mayr-Harting and R.I. Moore, London 1985, 303–316, reprinted in *Monarchy*, 303–315.

137	Haskins, *Norman Institutions*, 85–122.

138	Le Patourel, *Norman Empire*, 81–82; *Orderic* vi, 234–243; *Huntingdon*, 462–467.

139	S. Hicks, 'The Impact of William Clito on the Continental Policies of Henry I of England', *Viator* x, 1979, 1–21. Also see C. Newman, *The Anglo-Norman Nobility in the Reign of Henry I: the Second Generation*, Philadelphia 1988, 66, note 115; M. Chibnall, *The Empress Matilda: Queen Consort, Queen Mother and Lady of the English*, Oxford 1991, 37–39.

140	C.W. Hollister, 'The Anglo-Norman Succession Debate of 1126: Prelude to Stephen's Anarchy', *JMH* i, 1975, 19–39, reprinted in *Monarchy*, 145–169.

141	Chibnall, *Empress*, 50–63. For Anjou, see J. Chartrou, *L'Anjou de 1109 à 1151: Foulque de Jerusalem et Geoffroi Plantagenet*, Paris 1928.

142	M. Chibnall, 'Normandy', in *The Anarchy of Stephen's Reign*, ed. Edmund King, Oxford 1994, 93–115.

143	On Stephen, see R.H.C. Davis, *King Stephen*, 3rd edition, London 1990, and Davis, 'What Happened in Stephen's Reign', *History* xlix, 1964, 1–12; J. Le Patourel, 'What Did Not Happen in Stephen's Reign', *History* lviii, 1973, 1–17.

144	*Orderic* vi, 454–455.

England and Normandy. Concentrating at first on the southern marches, Matilda and Geoffrey used the border castle of Argentan, which had been included in Matilda's dowry, as a base for their efforts to seize the duchy by force.

Geoffrey's Angevin troops undermined Stephen's defenses through a series of invasions, while Stephen himself remained occupied with establishing his rule in England.[145] Orderic complained repeatedly that Normandy was left without a protector in this period.[146] Many of Stephen's supporters in Normandy crossed the channel to help his cause in England, while English lords unhappy with Stephen increasingly saw the duchy as a place of refuge and resistance.[147] In 1138, Robert of Gloucester defected from Stephen's side and joined his half-sister Matilda in Normandy. Three years later, Waleran count of Meulan joined the Angevins after Stephen's capture at the Battle of Lincoln in February 1141.[148] The support of these two men, Robert of Gloucester and Waleran of Meulan, was a decisive factor in the Angevin conquest of Normandy, as they brought lower and central Normandy to Geoffrey and Matilda's side. It also helped their cause that Theobald of Blois turned down the offer of kingdom and duchy after Stephen's capture, and instead recommended that the Normans accept Geoffrey as their lord.[149]

Although Matilda's fortunes in England suffered grievously with the rout at Winchester and Stephen's release from prison in November 1141, Geoffrey steadily hammered away at resistance in Normandy.[150] After a brutal campaign that ravaged the countryside and suburbs around the city, Geoffrey took possession of Rouen in January 1144 and assumed the title of duke. Once in command of Rouen, Geoffrey overcame remaining opposition and suppressed private wars. For the next six years, Geoffrey ruled the duchy with a firm hand, restoring Norman institutions of government that had fallen into abeyance during the anarchy of Stephen's reign.[151] Around 1150, Geoffrey of Anjou transferred Normandy to his eldest son Henry, who used it once again as a base from which to conquer England.

## Conclusion

Between 1066 and 1144 the fortunes of Normandy and England were clearly linked, but what was the precise nature of this relationship? Some historians have argued that the lands ruled by the Normans in this time period comprised 'two parts of a single political unit', and that 'the barons of England and Normandy formed a single aristocratic community'.[152] According to one scholar, this trend toward a unified Anglo-Norman realm continued through the reign of Henry I, so that, 'Normandy was

---

145 *Orderic* vi, 466–475; C.W. Hollister, 'The Aristocracy', in *Anarchy of Stephen's Reign*, 37–66, at 62–63. For a recent survey of the civil war, see J. Bradbury, *Stephen and Matilda: the Civil War of 1139–53*, Stroud 1996. In addition to Orderic, important contemporary sources include William of Malmesbury's *Historia Novella*; *Gesta Stephani*; *Worcester* iii; *ASC*; *Huntingdon*.

146 *Orderic* vi, 454–455, 456–457, 458–459; David Crouch, *The Beaumont Twins: the Roots and Branches of Power in the Twelfth Century*, Cambridge 1986, 31.

147 Chibnall, 'Normandy', 101.

148 Crouch, *Beaumont Twins*, 50–51.

149 *Orderic* vi, 548–549.

150 Chibnall, *Empress*, 114, 118; Bradbury, 152–156.

151 Haskins, 123–155; Bradbury, 154–156.

152 C.W. Hollister, 'Normandy, France and the Anglo-Norman *Regnum*', *Speculum* li, 1976, 202–242, at

governed as if it were the southern part of a trans-Channel kingdom'.[153] But the aristocracy was not so unified, and the situation was more complicated than this.[154] Even when they were under the same ruler, England and Normandy had two separate bodies of justice and two separate exchequers during this period.[155] Moreover, many Norman lords did not participate in the conquest of England. While some of the wealthiest Conquest families held lands on both sides of the channel, there were numerous Norman magnates, especially in the lesser ranks of the aristocracy, with little or no interest in England and less incentive to keep England and Normandy under a single ruler.[156] Families with trans-channel estates frequently split into Norman and English branches after the Conquest generation died.[157] And the king of France, repeatedly, encouraged factions within Normandy to undermine the Anglo-Norman connection. Thus, it is more correct to speak of a tension between centrifugal and centripetal forces than a unified Anglo-Norman realm between 1066 and 1144.[158] The conquest of Normandy by Geoffrey of Anjou, however, tilted the balance permanently toward France rather than England.

209; Le Patourel, 'France and England in the Middle Ages', in *Feudal Empires*, ch. xviii, 1–14, at 3, and Le Patourel, *The Norman Empire*, 319–354.

[153]  Hollister, 'Anglo-Norman *Regnum*', 216.

[154]  For a critical reappraisal of the evidence for a unified, cross-channel aristocracy, see D. Crouch, 'Normans and Anglo-Normans: a Divided Aristocracy?' in *England and Normandy*, 51–67.

[155]  J. Green, 'Unity and Disunity', 119–123; D. Bates, 'Normandy and England after 1066', *EHR* civ, 1989, 851–880, at 870–871.

[156]  Crouch, 'Divided Aristocracy?' 59–64; Bates, 'After 1066', 854–855; Crouch, *The Beaumont Twins*, 13–28; Green, 'Unity and Disunity', 129–132.

[157]  Newman, *The Anglo-Norman Nobility*, 20–21; Green, 'Unity and Disunity', 128. Also see Green, *Aristocracy*, 126–140.

[158]  This point is made by Bates, 'After 1066', 859–860.

# 3

# England, Normandy and Scandinavia

## LESLEY ABRAMS

Normandy's origins lie in the context of Frankish politics of the ninth century, when competing Carolingian kings and princes struggled for power, and Viking armies preyed on centres of wealth in uncoordinated, irregular, but disabling attacks, from northern Britain to the Mediterranean. Hoping to employ poachers as gamekeepers, if only temporarily, embattled native rulers granted land and some kind of authority to Viking leaders in Frisia, Francia, and the British Isles, but only Rollo's early tenth-century settlement on the Seine survived; it was transformed by his descendants into the mighty political player which, from the second half of the eleventh century, drastically altered the balance of power and redrew the political map of western Europe. For years the issue of Normandy's origins has divided historians.[1] Some have seen little of Scandinavian character in the political inheritance of the first settlers and have argued for continuity, supposing that Rollo was handed a Carolingian political and cultural package on his arrival in 911. Supporters of continuity have seen the later workings of ducal power as the visible end of a continuum which began in unfortunate obscurity as Rollo took over the exercise of public authority from his Carolingian predecessors. A contrary view has characterised the first stages of Viking control as insecure and makeshift; but, it is argued, when the Vikings proceeded to dig themselves in they fashioned a new social order drawing more fundamentally on their own native customs and institutions in law, social regulations, and agrarian and maritime practice. Some subscribers to this view would see Frankish institutions as only late grafted onto an enduringly Scandinavian stem. Crucial to the question is the issue of numbers: a large complement of immigrants (of all social levels) would presumably have been required to produce a society with a strong Scandinavian flavour, while a small aristocratic minority might have made less of an impression on native Frankish culture (though neither of these assumptions has gone unchallenged). The difficulty in deciding between these two options consists in reconciling the two faces of continuity – Scandinavian and Carolingian – presented by the Norman evidence. In the absence of a reliable historical narrative or informative local annalistic material, and without helpful early documentary evidence (especially dated administrative records)

---

[1] The bibliography on this subject is vast. Some of the main contributions to the debate are M. de Bouard, 'De la Neustrie carolingienne à la Normandie féodale: continuité ou discontinuité?', *BIHR* xxviii, 1955, 1–14; L. Musset, 'Origines et nature de la pouvoir ducale en Normandie jusqu'au milieu du XIe siècle', *Les principautés au moyen âge. Communications du congrès de Bordeaux*, Bordeaux 1979, 47–59, reprinted in *Nordica et Normannica*, Paris 1997, 263–77, with other relevant articles; J. Yver, 'Les premières institutions du duché de Normandie', *Settimane di studio del centro italiano di studi sull'alto medioevo* xvi, 1968, 299–366 and 589–98; D. Bates, *Normandy before 1066*, London 1982, 2–24; E. Searle, *Predatory Kinship and the Creation of Norman Power, 840–1066*, Berkeley and Los Angeles 1988; D.C. Douglas, *William the Conqueror*, London 1964, 19–30.

or identifiable archaeological remains,[2] the blank tenth-century canvas has been sketched in with linguistic and place-name analysis and the study of later institutions. Results are chronologically elusive, with the consequence that how and when Scandinavian settlers in Normandy accommodated to Frankish institutions remain questions on which scholars disagree. It is worth remembering, however, that what little we know of the history of Normandy in the tenth century suggests regional variation – in the density and date of settlement and in the origins and identity of incoming groups – sufficient to produce Scandinavian affinity in different degrees in the various areas settled. Although opinion on the Scandinavian contribution to Normandy remains divided, there is at least general agreement that, at some point in its development, the 'creative use of existing resources'[3] by Normandy's rulers involved the amalgamation of Carolingian institutions and a characteristically dynamic Scandinavian economic energy. Normandy, however, was not the only West Frankish political unit to be reconstructed in the tenth century by means of a combination of old and new, although only in Normandy was the new element Scandinavian.

In the early eleventh century the triangle of relationships between England, Normandy, and Scandinavia begins to emerge from the obscurity which envelops Normandy's early history. This triangle is actually a rectangle, 'Scandinavia' being not one entity but several, though only two points – Norway and Denmark – make a significant impression in the relevant sources for the period. We are very much in the dark about England's relations with Normandy before the marriage which brought the two ruling houses together in 1002. The continental interests and involvement of King Æthelstan (924–39) are exemplified by his distribution of sisters among continental royal families in marriage alliances during the 920s; he also offered refuge and military support to Breton rulers who had been forced to flee by Vikings on the Loire. Any English dealings with those Vikings recently established as Brittany's neighbours, however, have left no trace.[4] Æthelstan's successors are less known for their continental interests, and relations between Scandinavians settled in England and the Norman colony are very obscure.[5] We have no context, for example, for an intriguing twelfth-century reference by Hugh of Fleury to assistance rendered to Duke Richard I (943–96) by 'Deiri' (men from Deira, i.e. York) in c. 963.[6] Lucien Musset, while acknowledging that surviving sources are silent on the subject, has proposed that

---

2   See P. Perin, 'Les objets vikings du musée des antiquités de la Seine-Maritime à Rouen', *Recueil d'études en homage à Lucien Musset*, Caen 1990, 161–88, on the few finds and the problem of identifying the Viking and Scandinavian presence in Normandy. On the archaeology of early Rouen, see D. Bates, 'Rouen from 900 to 1204: from Scandinavian Settlement to Angevin "Capital" ', in *Medieval Art, Architecture, and Archaeology in Rouen*, ed. J. Stratford, BAA Conference Transactions, 1993, 1–11, and references there.

3   The phrase is Bates's: 'The Rise and Fall of Normandy, c. 911–1204', in *England and Normandy*, 19–35, at 25.

4   F.M. Stenton, *Anglo-Saxon England*, 3rd edn, London 1971, 344–8.

5   A coin probably of Olaf Sihtricsson, king of York, two coins of King Æthelstan, two Æthelstan imitations, and a coin of William Longsword (c. 928–42) were deposited c. 942, possibly together, at Mont Saint-Michel; see M. Dolley and J. Yvon, 'A Group of Tenth-Century Coins Found at Mont Saint-Michel', *BNJ* xl, 1971, 1–16. Dolley and Yvon (at 11) suggested that the Viking Sihtric active on the continent in 943 was the man of that name who had briefly ruled and issued coins at York c. 942, an identification which rests on the coincidence of names and dates. For two coins found in England at Berkhamsted (Herts.), possibly issued by William Longsword, see F. Dumas, 'Nouvelles découvertes de monnaies normandes', *Bulletin de la société française de numismatique* xxv, 1984, 502–4.

6   Hugh of Fleury, 'Hugonis liber qui modernorum regum Francorum continet actus', ed. D.G. Waitz, *MGH SS* ix, ed. G.H. Pertz, Hanover 1851, 376–95, at 384.

throughout the first half of the tenth century there was a regular exchange of people and ideas between Scandinavian York and Rouen. Certainly, writers on both sides of the Channel offer evidence of intellectual exchange between the clergy of Anglo-Saxon England and Normandy in the late tenth century and early eleventh.[7] A letter from the abbot of St Ouen in Rouen to King Edgar (959–75), asking for financial support,[8] survives to attest to more mundane business, evidence for most of which is inevitably lost.

We can assume, however, that the resumption of Viking raids in the 980s, directed most intensely at England, would have impinged on England's neighbours in some way; as James Campbell has put it, 'involved with Æthelred's troubles with the Danes may be a complex relationship with Normandy the details of which may be lost, but whose course could have been significant in the determination of events'.[9] The surviving agreement of 991 between King Æthelred and Duke Richard I, mediated by Pope John XV, where the two parties agreed to be at peace and not to shelter one another's enemies, suggests that Normandy had played a role, if only a passive one, in facilitating the raids on England.[10] This Norman assistance seems to have continued despite the pope's intervention: the Anglo-Saxon Chronicler states that in the summer of the year 1000 'the enemy fleet had gone to Richard's kingdom'.[11] The marriage in 1002 of King Æthelred and Emma, daughter of Richard I and Gunnor, belongs to the diplomacy surrounding this renewal of Scandinavian aggression. The marriage was presumably intended by the English to bring Normandy more firmly in line with Anglo-Saxon interests, and they must at least have hoped for some degree of co-operation thereafter. Whether we think they got it depends in part on what we make of William of Jumièges's description of an English invasion of the Cotentin not long after the marriage, with the ultimate goal of capturing Duke Richard, a goal which failed.[12] William alone also tells us that Svein Forkbeard took a break from harrying Yorkshire and visited Normandy (in 1003 or in 1013) 'in order to seek peace with Richard', that the duke offered magnificent hospitality to Æthelred's enemy, and that the two concluded a peace treaty and an agreement whereby the Danes would sell their booty in Normandy, which they would also be allowed to use as a safe haven for their wounded.[13] This would hardly have constituted Norman co-operation with

7   L. Musset, 'Les apports anglais en Normandie de Rollon à Guillaume le Conquérant (911–1066)', in *Nordica et Normannica*, 447–66, at 465 (originally published in *Les liens entre l'Angleterre et la France de l'Ouest. Actes du colloque de Poitiers 1976*, Poitiers 1977, 59–72); M. Lapidge, 'Three Latin Poems from Æthelwold's School at Winchester', *ASE* i, 1972, 85–137, and 'Schools, Learning and Literature in Tenth-Century England', *Settimane di studio del centro italiano di studi sull'alto medioevo* xxxviii, 1991, 951–98 (reprinted in his *Anglo-Latin Literature 900–1066*, London and Rio Grande 1993, 225–77 and 1–48).

8   *Memorials of Saint Dunstan*, ed. W. Stubbs, RS LXIII, 1874, 363–4.

9   J. Campbell, 'England, France, Flanders and Germany in the Reign of Ethelred II: Some Comparisons and Connections', in *Essays in Anglo-Saxon History*, London 1986, 191–207, at 201.

10  *EHD* i, 894–5 (no. 230).

11  *ASC*, s.a. 1000.

12  *Jumièges* ii, 12–14; Alistair Campbell argued that this incident preceded the marriage: *Encomium Emmae reginae*, ed. A. Campbell, 2nd edn, Cambridge 1998, xlii [cxxiv]; see also J. Campbell, 'England', 199–200.

13  *Jumièges* ii, 16–19; on the disputed date, see 17, n. 4, and Keynes, 'The Historical Context of the Battle of Maldon', in *The Battle of Maldon AD 991*, ed. D. Scragg, Oxford 1991, 81–113, at 94–5. William of Jumièges's information on the relationship between William Longsword, Richard's father, and the Viking Harald may provide a parallel: Harald's army sold their booty (from continental raids) to the Normans; *Jumièges* i, 88–90 and 126.

England, and if it was true it cannot have pleased the English. A more constructive relationship, however, is suggested by Henry of Huntingdon's (late) claim that in 1009 the English king sent messengers to Duke Richard, asking for advice and help.[14] Anglo-Saxon relations with Normandy were clearly complicated during England's Danish wars, and attempting to rationalise the confusions in the sources may be trying to improve on reality. Help *was* definitely applied for and received in 1013, however, when London submitted to the Danish king, Svein Forkbeard, and Emma and members of her Anglo-Saxon royal family made their separate ways to Normandy. Svein's death not long after allowed them to return to England, but when first Æthelred and then his son Edmund Ironside died in 1016, and the Dane Cnut Sveinsson succeeded to the throne, the Norman court once again offered refuge to three of Æthelred's children – Edward, Alfred, and Godgifu – but not, necessarily, to his widow, Emma. Different versions of Emma's fate immediately after the death of Æthelred do not obscure the fact that within a year she had married Cnut and was again queen of England. Emma's motives of self-interest have earned her criticism from many historians, who have been less condemning of, though more at variance about, the motives of her second husband.[15] The author of the tract the *Encomium Emmae*, writing in 1041–42, presented the union as a reconciliation between the English and the Danes; however, his statement that Emma had been fetched from Normandy (in contrast with William of Jumièges's account, where Emma appears to have remained in England) helps to suggest that the marriage was a continuation of the Anglo-Norman alliance.[16] Rodulfus Glaber, writing probably before 1030 at Dijon, presented the marriage explicitly in this light, stating that Cnut 'made a peace with Richard by which he married the duke's sister'.[17] William of Malmesbury, on the other hand, saw it (a century later) as a deliberate deterrent to the ambitions of the sons of Æthelred and their protector, Duke Richard. Modern historians likewise have had different views. Alistair Campbell argued that the object of Cnut's marriage was a reconciliation with Normandy;[18] Simon Keynes has emphasised instead the domestic, English, context and the significant practical and psychological advantages which the marriage offered to the immigrant king. Keynes has suggested that with this marriage Emma could in fact be seen as abandoning her Norman connections, and thereby abandoning the interests of her sons by Æthelred to the sole protection of her brother the duke.[19]

King Æthelred's Viking Age had a Norwegian as well as a Danish aspect. Although the career of Olaf Haraldsson 'has given an astonishing amount of trouble to English historians', one rationalised version of the confusing evidence is that Olaf

14  *Huntingdon*, 344–6; Henry wrote and revised his *Historia* from the 1120s to the 1150s.
15  For an extensive list of references, see Simon Keynes's supplementary introduction to *Encomium*, ed. Campbell, [xxiii], n. 7; see also P. Stafford, *Queen Emma and Queen Edith: Queenship and Women's Power in Eleventh-Century England*, Oxford 1997, 225–36.
16  *Encomium*, ed. Campbell, 32; *Jumièges* ii, 20; see S. Keynes, 'The Æthelings in Normandy', *ANS* xiii, 1990, 173–205, at 183–4.
17  *Rodulfus Glabri: Historiarum libri quinque*, ed. J. France, Oxford 1989, 54–6; the *Inventio et miracula sancti Vulfranni*, composed c. 1053–54, took a similar view (*Mélanges publiés par la société de l'histoire de Normandie*, 14th ser., ed. J. Laporte, Rouen and Paris 1938, 30).
18  *Encomium*, ed. Campbell, xxi, xlv–vi [ciii, cxxvi–cxxvii], and [xxii–xxiv]; see also E.M.C. van Houts, 'The Political Relations between Normandy and England before 1066 according to the "*Gesta Normannorum ducum*"', in *Les mutations socio-culturelles au tournant des XIe–XIIe siècles*, ed. R. Foreville, Paris 1984, 85–97, at 87–8.
19  'The Æthelings', 183–6; see also L. Musset, 'Relations et échanges d'influences dans l'Europe du Nord-Ouest (Xe–XIe siècles)', *CCM* i, 1958, 63–82, at 76.

fought against the English with the Danish chieftain Thorkell in the campaigns of 1009–12 and continued his career as a hired hand in Normandy in 1013 or 1014, when he helped Duke Richard against a local enemy;[20] after this Olaf was baptised in Rouen by Robert, archbishop of Rouen and brother of the duke.[21] When Æthelred returned to England in 1014 from his exile in Rouen, Olaf Haraldsson accompanied and supported him against the Danes. In *Hǫfuðlausn*, a praise-poem said to have been composed by Ótarr the Black, one of Olaf's skalds, the Norwegian is explicitly credited with restoring the Anglo-Saxon king to his throne: 'You brought back to his land Æthelred, and gave him his realm. That close friend of warriors, strengthened in power, had there your help. Harsh was the strife when you brought Edmund's kinsman to his heritage. Of old that king of noble race had ruled the region there.'[22] Olaf soon returned to Norway to pursue his own royal ambitions, which would clash seriously with Danish interests there for the next fifteen years, as Cnut attempted to extend and strengthen his Northern hegemony. Cnut's principal agents in Norway, the jarls of Hlaðir, were tied to him by marriage and political office in England.[23] After Olaf returned to Norway, Hákon of Hlaðir came to England and served as earl in Worcestershire. When Olaf was expelled from Norway in 1028, Hákon was installed as ruler there by Cnut.[24]

A few fragments may support the existence of a widening gulf between Cnut's Anglo-Danish regime and Normandy. There is some evidence that during Cnut's reign the duke's Norman enemies saw England as a potentially friendly place of refuge;[25] charter evidence attests to the fact that the æthelings' royal status was not

[20] *Encomium*, ed. Campbell, 76; Campbell summarised the Scandinavian evidence (76–82) and argued that Olaf's campaign with Thorkell in 1009–12 was confused with participation in the Danish conquests of 1013–16: hence the story in William of Jumièges (*Jumièges* ii, 20) and Adam of Bremen (Adam of Bremen, *Gesta Hammaburgensis ecclesiae pontificum*, ii.51, ed. B. Schmeidler, Hanover and Leipzig 1917, 112; *History of the Archbishops of Hamburg-Bremen*, trans. F. Tschan, New York 1959, 90) that Olaf (and, in William's account, an otherwise unkown *Lacman*, a king of the Swedes) helped Cnut invade England: Campbell rejected this story (*Encomium*, 79–80). See also *Jumièges* ii, 24–5, n. 3. The contemporary poem *Víkingarvísur* by the skald Sigvatr Þórðarson (*Den norsk-islandske skjaldedigtning*, ed. F. Jónsson, Copenhagen 1912–15, 2 vols in 4, Ai, 223–8; Bi, 213–16; *EHD* i, 332–3, no. 12) tells of Olaf's battles; see A. Campbell, *Skaldic Verse and Anglo-Saxon History*, London 1971, 8–12, Stenton, *Anglo-Saxon England*, 402–5, and R.G. Poole, *Viking Poems on War and Peace*, Toronto 1991, 86–102.

[21] *Jumièges* ii, 24–8. The *Historia de antiquitate regum Norwagiensium*, written in Norway 1177x1188 by the monk Theodoric, mentions several traditions about Olaf's baptism, but prefers the Norman one, setting it in the context of military help offered by Olaf (ch. 13; *Monumenta historica Norvegiae*, ed. G. Storm, Christiania 1880, 21–3; *The Ancient History of the Norwegian Kings*, trans. D. and I. McDougall, London 1998, 16–17).

[22] This verse of the poem translated in R.I. Page, *Chronicles of the Vikings: Records, Memorials and Myths*, London 1995, 156.

[23] Erik of Hlaðir, married to Cnut's sister Gytha, became earl of the Northumbrians in 1016, and he retained his position as Cnut's principal earl until dislodged by Godwine in 1022; S. Keynes, 'Cnut's Earls', in *The Reign of Cnut: King of England, Denmark and Norway*, ed. A.R. Rumble, London 1994, 43–88, at 57–8. On Cnut's reign as reflected in poetic sources, see R.G. Poole, 'Skaldic Verse and Anglo-Saxon History: Some Aspects of the Period 1009–1016', *Speculum* lxii, 1987, 265–98, at 280–95.

[24] He died in 1030; Keynes, 'Cnut's Earls', 61–2; see also *Encomium*, ed. Campbell, 71–2.

[25] Musset, 'Relations et échanges', 76; Richard, count of Avranches, fled 'across the sea' after an attempt on the life of Duke Richard II (*André de Fleury: Vie de Gauzlin, abbé de Fleury*, ed. Robert-Henri Bautier and Gillette Labory, Paris 1969, 48–50 (ch. 16)); according to Orderic Vitalis, Osmund Drengot, one of the first Normans to settle in Apulia, fleeing from Duke Robert after a killing went first to Brittany and then to England with all his family (*Orderic* ii, 56).

forgotten in the Norman court,[26] and Norman sources tell us that the duke raised his English nephews as though they were his sons and sent envoys to England to plead for their rights.[27] However, according to Glaber (whose authority in this matter is not necessarily impressive), during Cnut's reign, 'whenever the necessity of war pressed upon the duke of Rouen, he was able to call to his aid a great army from the islands across the sea'.[28] Cnut's generosity to churches included at least one in Normandy – a charter, possibly issued early in his reign, records a grant of land to Fécamp, the ducal monastery par excellence.[29] On the other hand, the claim by the Danish historian Svein Aggesen (writing c. 1188) that Cnut translated relics of St Martin to Rouen and loved the Norman city has been rejected as 'nonsensical' by Eric Christiansen.[30] Glaber (and later Adam of Bremen and Scandinavian historical writers) also claimed that Cnut sought to establish further ties with Normandy by offering one of his sisters to Duke Robert (or, in Adam and the northern sources, to Richard II, a more likely story), who repudiated her.[31] According to William of Jumièges, an invasion of England ordered on behalf of the exiled æthelings by Duke Robert, probably in 1033, went badly wrong (the fleet, blown off course, contented itself with ravaging Brittany). No contemporary English source preserves mention of this incident, but Simon Keynes has shown how charters may support this otherwise doubtfully attested story.[32] William of Jumièges also tells us that soon afterwards, Cnut, seriously ill, offered to restore half of England to the sons of Æthelred[33] – a transaction which did not then take place but which prefigured the actual division six or seven years later between Cnut's son Harthacnut and Æthelred's son Edward. Before this, however, when Emma fled England in 1037 as her political fortunes (temporarily) collapsed, she chose to go to Flanders, not Normandy; the latter, admittedly, would have been a

26  Keynes, 'The Æthelings', 186–94.
27  *Inventio et miracula sancti Vulfranni* (ed. Laporte, 30), and *Jumièges* ii, 76–7. For a literal interpretation, making Edward, Alfred, and Duke Robert 'artificial brothers', see van Houts, 'Political Relations', 90–3; also E.M.C. van Houts, 'Scandinavian Influence in Norman Literature of the Eleventh Century', *ANS* vi, 1983, 107–21, at 119, and E.M.C. van Houts, 'Historiography and Hagiography at Saint-Wandrille: the Inventio et miracula sancti Vulfranni', *ANS* xii, 1989, 233–51, at 247–9.
28  *Historiarum* 54–7. This statement follows discussion of Cnut's wars and subsequent alliance with the king of the Scots; the Scandinavian communities of the Northern and Western Isles of Scotland or of Ireland, rather than the English, could perhaps have been intended.
29  C.H. Haskins, 'A Charter of Canute for Fécamp', *EHR* xxxiii, 1918, 342–4. The surviving copy records three transactions from two different documents; see P.H. Sawyer, *Anglo-Saxon Charters: an Annotated List and Bibliography*, London 1968, nos 949 (AD 1017) and 982 (AD 1028x1035). Edward the Confessor amplified this grant (Sawyer, *Anglo-Saxon Charters*, no. 1054 (AD 1042x1047)), and Fécamp held the land in 1066.
30  *Scriptores minores historiae Danicae medii aevi*, ed. M.C. Gertz, 2 vols, Copenhagen 1917–22, i, 122–3; *The Works of Sven Aggesen, Twelfth-Century Danish Historian*, trans. E. Christiansen, London 1992, 125. See further below, 51.
31  Glaber, *Historiarum* 204–5; Adam of Bremen, *Gesta*, ii.54 (ed. Schmeidler, 114–15; trans. Tschan, 92). See D.C. Douglas, 'Some Problems of Early Norman Chronology', *EHR* lxv, 1950, 289–303, at 292–5, on the contradictory aspects of this story. Douglas had doubts about this marriage, thanks to chronological problems and evident confusion in the transmission. If there had been a failed Norman marriage, however, it may later have coloured the attitude of Estrith's son from another union, Svein, king of Denmark from 1047 to 1074.
32  Keynes, 'The Æthelings', 186–94; William of Malmesbury later supplemented the tendentious William of Jumièges: *Jumièges* ii, 76–7; William of Malmesbury, *Gesta Regum* i, 318–19). The latter commented that 'the remains of the ships [of the expedition] . . . were still to be seen at Rouen in our own day' (321).
33  *Jumièges* ii, 78–9.

perilous place of refuge, due to the turmoil during the minority of William the Bastard, and Emma had relations in Flanders as well. The choice may have been politically significant, however. Flanders's role in political relations of the later tenth and the eleventh century was crucial (though complex), the counts harbouring exiles from England, being generally supportive of Danish interests, but not always unfriendly to the Norman dukes.[34] After Edward became sole king in 1042, Anglo-Scandinavian and Norman elements competed for power within England, while Denmark retracted its foreign ambitions, at least temporarily, in the face of trouble nearer home stirred up by Magnus Olafsson (the Good), king of Norway (1035–47). If there was any truth to the rumour that Emma offered the English throne to Magnus in 1043,[35] she was clearly unable to deliver. A possible invasion of England from Norway in 1045 came to naught.[36] The Anglo-Saxon Chronicle tells us that Svein Estrithsen (1047–74) asked for King Edward's help to defend Denmark against Magnus in 1047, but was refused – this although one of Svein's brothers, Björn, was one of Edward's earls.[37] The Anglo-Saxon king (and most of his advisors) apparently had no wish to get too involved in Denmark's problems at this time.[38] A fleet from Norway led by the king's son, Magnus Haraldsson, who was accompanied by the Welsh king Gruffydd ap Llywelyn and the Anglo-Saxon exile, Ælfgar, raided England in 1058 – intent on conquest, according to an Irish chronicler.[39] Disinformation and strategic political posturing deriving from England's succession crisis obscure our view of external relations thereafter; it is difficult to judge what credence should be given to Adam of Bremen's claim (transmitted doubtless through Svein himself) that the Danish king had been designated as his heir by Edward the Confessor.[40] According to William of Poitiers, Svein pledged to support William the Bastard's attempt to conquer England, but broke the promise, and Danes fought at Hastings on the English side.[41]

It could therefore be construed that Normandy in the eleventh century experienced a conflict between what might be seen as old and new loyalties. Gunnor, the mother of Emma and Duke Richard II, was 'sprung from the most famous stock of Dacian [i.e.,

---

34 Keynes, 'The Æthelings', 196, and Stafford, *Queen Emma*, 246. For background, see P. Grierson, 'The Relations between England and Flanders before the Norman Conquest', *TRHS* 4th ser. xxiii, 1941, 71–112, at 95–104, and D. Nicholas, *Medieval Flanders*, London 1992, 45–55. Musset ('Relations et échanges', 78) suggested that Flanders's rivalry with Normandy led the count to support Emma and her Danish interests in the 1030s; but Nicholas (57) has pointed out that Baldwin V (1035–67), unlike earlier and later counts, had peaceful relations with Normandy (which led to the marriage of his daughter to William the Bastard). Flemings played a major role on William's side in the Norman Conquest of England. See also R. Nip, 'The Political Relations between England and Flanders (1066–1128)', *ANS* xxi, 1998, 145–67, at 145–53.

35 Goscelin, *Translatio S. Mildrethe*, ch. 18; D.W. Rollason, 'Goscelin of Canterbury's Account of the Translation and Miracles of St Mildrith (*BHL* 5961/4): an Edition with Notes', *Mediaeval Studies* xlviii, 1986, 139–210, at 176–7; quoted in *Encomium Emmae*, ed. Campbell, [lxxii–lxiii]; see Stafford, *Queen Emma*, 249–51.

36 *ASC* 'D', *s.a.* 1046 (*recte* 1045).

37 *ASC* 'D', *s.a.* 1048 (*recte* 1047); Magnus was victorious and was recognised as king of Denmark in 1047, but died later that year. On Björn, see *Encomium Emmae*, ed. Campbell, 85.

38 According to John of Worcester, Godwine supported sending fifty ships: *John of Worcester* ii, 544–5.

39 *ASC* 'D', *s.a.* 1058; see also A.O. Anderson, *Early Sources of Scottish History AD 500 to 1286*, 2 vols, Stamford 1990, ii, 1.

40 Adam of Bremen, *Gesta*, ii.78 and iii.12 (ed. Schmeidler, 136 and 152; trans. Tschan, 108 and 123).

41 *Gesta Guillelmi*, 104–6 and 126.

Danish] nobles',[42] according to Dudo of St Quentin, the ducal historian, and her children could have had close relatives in Denmark or in England after 1016. David Douglas considered Gunnor's kindred to have been an important factor in the growth of the Norman aristocracy.[43] Doubtless other Normans had family ties in Denmark or England of which we know nothing. Such relationships may have helped Svein Forkbeard and others to assume that in this second Viking Age the inhabitants of Normandy would be friends; and friends of the Danes and Norwegians they apparently were, until, that is, other factors of a more immediate nature – such as exiled Anglo-Saxon æthelings – intervened. The 991 agreement of Æthelred and Richard I and the subsequent marriage of Emma sowed the seeds of an alliance that would set the Norman dynasty on a course opposed to Danish interests. Warmth towards fellow Northmen and a feeling of community with the homelands seem to have cooled in the face of Cnut's worrying success just across the water. Developments in England must surely have stimulated Normandy's instinct for self-preservation, not to mention ducal envy and ambition.[44] Lucien Musset argued as long ago as the 1950s that Normandy passed a crucial point of no return when it undertook to protect Cnut's enemies, and that after the death of Duke Richard II in 1026, opposition to Anglo-Danish England hardened in Normandy under Robert the Magnificent, who had grown up with the Anglo-Saxon princes. Musset reasoned that in the process of supporting their cause the duchy turned its face from north to south and detached itself from the Scandinavian world ('l'espace scandinave').[45]

While Norman hostility to Danish interests in England may have led to a *froideur* between Normans and Danes, it does not explain Normandy's apparently simultaneous detachment from Norway, with which Denmark was very often at war. Nor can the absence of Norwegian kings from Normandy after Olaf's visit in 1014 be attributable to preoccupation with domestic politics or to a new Norwegian insularity, as the subsequent activities of Harald Hardrada (1047–66) (in the East and in England), Magnus Barelegs (1095–1103), and Sigurd the Crusader (1103–30) make clear. Harald Hardrada's support of Tostig, exiled from Northumbria in 1065, and his assault on England the following year reveal the extent to which Norway continued to look beyond the homelands.[46]

Norway's attempt to seize power in England may have failed in 1066 with Harald's death at Stamford Bridge, but it did not necessarily end there: according to William of Malmesbury, King Magnus Barelegs – best known for his ambitions in the Irish Sea – was attempting to invade England in 1098 in association with Harold, son of Harold

---

[42] 'Ex famosissima nobilium Dacorum prosapia exorta': *Dudo*, iv.125 (ed. Lair, 289; *Dudo*, trans. Christiansen, 163–4). On Denmark as Dacia, see *Jumièges* i, xxxvi.

[43] One brother and three sisters are mentioned in Robert of Torigni's additions to William of Jumièges (*Jumièges* ii, 266–74); kinship with Gunnor (who did not die until 1031) was a favourite claim of the Norman aristocracy, a claim which Douglas did not entirely discount; see D.C. Douglas, 'The Earliest Norman Counts', *EHR* lxi, 1946, 129–56, at 147; also E.M.C. van Houts, 'Robert of Torigni as Genealogist', *Studies . . . to Brown*, 215–33, and Stafford, *Queen Emma*, 212–14, on Gunnor's 'Danishness'. See also below, n. 54.

[44] Keynes has suggested that 'Cnut may have been rather less secure from Norman intervention than might have been supposed': 'The Æthelings', 199–200.

[45] Musset, 'Relations et échanges', 76–7; see also L. Musset, 'Les relations extérieures de la Normandie du IXme au XIme siècle, d'après quelques trouvailles monétaires récentes', *Annales de Normandie* iv, 1954, 31–8, esp. 37–8 (reprinted in *Nordica et Normannica*, 297–306).

[46] See S. Körner, *The Battle of Hastings, England, and Europe, 1035–1066*, Lund 1964, 145–54, on Harald and the English.

Godwineson, when he was defeated by the earls of Shrewsbury and Chester.[47] Meanwhile, Danish royal initiatives against England continued under Kings Svein Estrithsen (1047–74) and Cnut the Holy (1080–86). According to Ælnoth, biographer of the latter, the English sought Danish help in throwing off Norman rule.[48] Svein's unsuccessful assaults on England in 1069–70 and Cnut's abandoned invasion of 1085 demonstrate the persistence of Danish efforts to re-establish their hegemony in the North Sea zone, efforts which also enlisted the services of Flanders.[49] Unfortunately, we have only remote echoes of the diplomatic activity and political negotiations which probably enlivened relations between Denmark, Norway, and William's England.[50]

It seems, therefore, that England was the prize for which Norway and Denmark were willing to oppose their erstwhile fellow Northmen now established in Normandy. The fight for England between the three competitors – Denmark, Normandy, *and* Norway – produced a major realignment of allegiances in the eleventh century. If Cnut's love of Normandy was a construction of twelfth-century Danish historiography,[51] we cannot tell whether any sense of solidarity between native Normans and Danes survived in his day. Rival ambitions over England nonetheless appear to have helped to dissolve whatever sense of brotherhood remained between Northmen and descendants of Northmen in Francia, setting Norman interests firmly against those of both Norway and Denmark. On the other hand, it has also been argued that the pursuit of entente with the Capetians, which brought significant political and military advantages to the duchy, was the principal cause of the shifting of orientation from Scandinavia; good relations with different Frankish parties were achieved through military and marriage alliances, especially during the time of the first two Richards.[52] Normandy's detachment from 'l'espace scandinave', in this

47  *Gesta Regum* i, 570.
48  Ælnoth, *Gesta Swenomagni regis et filiorum eius et passio gloriosissimi Canuti regis et martyris*, ch. 11, in *Vitae sanctorum Danorum*, ed. M.C. Gertz, Copenhagen 1908–12, 96–7; see Körner, *The Battle*, 138–45, on Svein's English ambitions.
49  Although William the Conqueror was married to his sister, Robert 'the Frisian', count of Flanders (1071–93), gave asylum to William's rebellious son Robert Curthose in 1078 and assembled troops in support of the 1085 Danish assault on England which never took place; see Nicholas, *Medieval Flanders*, 56–7, and Nip, 'The Political Relations', 153–9. Robert's daughter, Adela, married Cnut the Holy, king of Denmark (*Gesta Regum* i, 474).
50  See, for example, the tale (known later in England and Scandinavia) of Abbot Aelsi of Ramsey, said to have been an envoy of William the Conqueror: 'Lectiones de legatione Helsini abbatis in Daniam', *Scriptores rerum Danicarum*, ed. J. Langebek, Copenhagen 1772–92, 7 vols, iii, 252–8; E.A. Freeman, *The History of the Norman Conquest of England*, 6 vols, Oxford 1867–79, iv, 749–52. The abbot's absence is attested by reference in Domesday Book to a time 'cum abbas esset in Danemarka'; he is also said to have been *utlage* (*Domesday Book, Huntingdon*, fo. 208a; ed. and trans. J. Morris, Chichester 1975, D.8; *Berkshire*, fo. 62d; ed. and trans. P. Morgan and A. Hawkins, 46.4). For what it is worth, Symeon of Durham's account of the adventures of the churchman Turgot says that he left England on a ship bound for Norway with *legati Willelmi regis* on board: *Symeonis monachi opera omnia*, ed. T. Arnold, 2 vols, RS LXXV, London 1882–85, ii, 202–3. Adam of Bremen adds the detail that the archbishop of Hamburg-Bremen, 'persuaded by William's gifts, wished to make peace' between the kings of Denmark and England (Svein Estrithsen and William the Conqueror): *Gesta*, iii.54 (ed. Schmeidler, 198; trans. Tschan, 160).
51  L. Musset, 'Pour l'étude des relations entre les colonies scandinaves d'Angleterre et de Normandie', *Nordica et Normannica*, Paris 1997, 145–56, at 146. See above, 48, on Sven Aggesen.
52  L.W. Breese, 'The Persistence of Scandinavian Connections in Normandy in the Tenth and Early Eleventh Centuries', *Viator* viii, 1977, 47–61, at 54; D.C. Douglas, 'The Rise of Normandy', *PBA* xxxiii, 1947, 101–31, at 110. See *Dudo*, trans. Christiansen, 234–5, for charts of tenth- and early eleventh-century relations established through military and marriage alliances.

view, took place after 965, as the region assimilated with the Frankish world.[53] The Frankish names of the children of Gunnor and Richard I may reflect a deliberate decision among the elite not to perpetuate their Scandinavian heritage (as opposed to the use of Scandinavian names beyond AD 1000 lower down the social scale).[54]

Lauren Breese has taken this argument further and judged that once 'the emancipation of the mixed Franco-Scandinavian nobility from military and political dependence on the northern powers' took place, Normandy ceased to be a 'Scandinavian outpost' and a 'satellite of Scandinavia' and acquired a 'separate European identity'.[55] Breese was influenced by the identification of Harald, a Viking ally of William Longsword against the Franks in the 940s, with the king of Denmark of the same name – an identification now rejected[56] – and therefore saw the activities of 'Viking' colonies as closely linked to those in power in Scandinavia. Our sources are not very informative on relations with the homelands, but most tenth-century Viking bands appear to have been autonomous and independent,[57] and settlements, once established, were primarily players in their regions rather than sub-units of Scandinavian power. It is therefore difficult to see Normandy and the other Scandinavian settlements abroad as ever having been dependent on or 'satellites' of the homelands, politically, militarily, or economically, although political, military, and economic contact existed.

In what ways, then, *did* Normandy continue to be a part of the Scandinavian world? And when did contemporary Scandinavian culture stop influencing Norman society? These questions would be easier to consider if we knew when the majority of settlers became Christian and when the Norse language died out.[58] In the absence of conclusive evidence on these points, we can instead ask when the Normans stopped thinking of themselves as akin to the people of the homelands, or in community with the Scandinavian populations elsewhere in Europe, and created their own identity.[59] Although Dudo's history, written probably in the first quarter of the eleventh century,

---

[53] Musset, 'Les relations extérieures', 37–8; Yver, 'Premières institutions', 323; Breese, 'The Persistence', 61.

[54] E.M.C. van Houts, 'Countess Gunnor of Normandy (c. 950–1031)', *Collegium medievale* xii, 1999, 7–24. I should like to thank Liesbeth van Houts for a copy of this article before its publication.

[55] Breese, 'The Persistence', esp. 47–8 and 61. Breese dated the achievement of this separate identity c. 1010.

[56] *Jumièges* i, 89–90.

[57] J. Nelson, 'The Frankish Empire', in *The Oxford Illustrated History of the Vikings*, ed. P. Sawyer, Oxford 1997, 19–47, at 35–8.

[58] In *Dudo*, iv.68 (ed. Lair, 221–2; trans. Christiansen, 97) we are told that in Rouen they preferred *Romana lingua* to *Dacisca lingua*, and that the young Richard I (perhaps in the 940s) was put in the care of Botho, leader of the army at Bayeux, in order to learn Danish more thoroughly. According to William of Jumièges, the aim of Richard's language training was 'suis exterisque hominibus sciret apte responsa' (so that he could reply fittingly to his own men and those from overseas): *Jumièges* i, 88. What this means about the language habits of the elite, let alone the rest of the Scandinavian population, is not clear; it is highly doubtful that it meant that no one in Rouen spoke Norse at this time, as some have assumed. F. Amory has suggested that it was rhetorical training, not simple language teaching, that was available in Bayeux: 'The *dönsk tunga* in Early Medieval Normandy: a Note', in *American, Indian, and Indoeuropean Studies*, ed. K. Klar, The Hague 1980, 279–89. Emily Albu Hanawalt has interpreted the story in terms of politics, not language: 'Scandinavians in Byzantium and Normandy', in *Peace and War in Byzantium: Essays in Honor of George T. Dennis, S.J.*, ed. T.S. Miller and J. Nesbitt, Washington DC 1995, 114–22.

[59] On Norman identity, see (among others) L. Musset, 'L'image de la Scandinavie dans les oeuvres normandes de la période ducale (911–1204)', in *Les relations littéraires franco-scandinaves au moyen âge*, Paris 1975, 193–215, at 194–9 (reprinted in *Nordica et Normannica*, 213–31); R.H.C. Davis, *The Normans and their Myth*, London 1976, 49–69; G. Loud, 'The "Gens Normannorum" – Myth or

portrayed the Normans as distinct from their Viking antecedents as well as from their Frankish neighbours, the description of Roger of Montgommery as *ex Northmannis Northmannus* in a charter of c. 1082 reminds us that identity is a complex web of elements.[60] Musset argued that Normandy developed an identity which evoked its Scandinavian background in order to insist on its difference from France, its political rival.[61] Danishness in this construct was a totemic legacy, however, not a real contemporary force with an actual location elsewhere. When Stephen of Rouen's *Draco Normannicus* of c. 1168 referred to William the Conqueror as *Danus*,[62] it was not because the author intended to evoke a link between William and his contemporaries on the Danish throne, but rather with Rollo and Normandy's Viking founders (actually Norwegians and Hiberno-Scandinavians as well as Danes).

Scholars have attempted in a number of different ways to address the issue of when Scandinavians ceased to have direct contact with Normandy and when Normans last appeared on the Scandinavian scene. The year 1014 has been proposed as one answer to both these questions, Olaf Haraldsson's campaigns and subsequent baptism marking the last appearance of a Norwegian king (or king-to-be) in Normandy, and the participation of Normans at the battle of Clontarf on the side of Sihtric Silkenbeard, king of Dublin, being the last time Normans joined a Scandinavian cause.[63] It has to be said, however, that Sigurd the Crusader, king of Norway from 1103–30, stopped off in England for an entire winter with the permission of the Anglo-Norman Henry I before continuing on to Jerusalem (perhaps even via Normandy).[64] The Normans at Clontarf, on the other hand, may have been extrapolated from a reference in Ademar of Chabannes's *Chronicon*, which described the participation of *Normanni* (at about the right date) in a three-day battle in Ireland at a place not named. These *Normanni*, however, are the *supradicti . . . ex Danamarcha et Iresca regione* who had invaded Aquitaine, not the *Normanni* governed by the count of Rouen, mentioned later in the chapter.[65] There are four or five Norman-sounding names in a Clontarf death-list in the *Cogadh Gaedhel re Gallaibh*, an Irish vernacular account of the Viking wars; this (extremely unreliable) retrospective source was not written until 1103x1113, however, and the later chapters (including the death-list) occur only in a seventeenth-century paper manuscript.[66] 'The *Danair* of western

Reality?', *ANS* iv, 1981, 104–16 and 204–9; and C. Potts, '*Atque unum ex diversis gentibus populum effecit*: Tradition, Perception and Identity in Normandy before 1100', *ANS* xviii, 1996, 139–52.

60  R.N. Sauvage, *L'abbaye de Saint-Martin de Troarn*, Caen 1911, 352–3 (no. 3); Musset, 'Relations et échanges', 73. The charter exists only in much later cartulary-copies, however.

61  Musset, 'L'image', 194.

62  Musset, 'L'image', 194; H. Ormont, ed., *Le dragon normand et autres poèmes d'Etienne de Rouen*, Rouen 1884, 57–8, esp. ch. 30.

63  Musset, 'Les relations extérieures', 31; Breese, 'The Persistence', 60; Bates, *Normandy*, 7.

64  William of Malmesbury (*Gesta Regum* i, 740–1) stated that he travelled by sea along the coast. In saga tradition, Sigurd sailed 'west to Valland' (France) on his way to Santiago, a route later (c. 1150) followed by men from Norway in company with the earl and bishop of Orkney: 'Saga of the Sons of Magnus', ch. 4, and 'Saga of the Sons of Harald', ch. 17 (Snorri Sturluson, *Heimskringla*, ed. B. Aðalbjarnarson, 3 vols, Íslenzk Fornrit XXVI–VIII, Reykjavík 1941–51, iii, 240 and 324; *Heimskringla: History of the Kings of Norway*, trans. L.M. Hollander, Austin TX 1991, 689 and 751).

65  *Adémar de Chabannes. Chronique*, ed. J. Chavanon, Paris 1897, 176–8 (chs 53–5). Ademar used *Normanni* to mean Northmen of all kinds, including (but never exclusively) those under the rule of Rouen.

66  *Cogadh Gaedhel Re Gallaibh. The War of the Gaedhil with the Gaill*, ch. 117 (ed. and trans. J.H. Todd, RS XLVIII, London 1867, 207); see also *Cogadh*, ix–xiv and cxci, and A.J. Goedheer, *Irish and Norse Traditions about the Battle of Clontarf*, Haarlem 1938, esp. 29–30. For background, see M. Ní

Europe' are also said to have taken part in the battle, but as kings of Ireland are referred to as 'emperors of western Europe' in this text and in the Annals of Ulster, by analogy these *Danair* should be Danes from Ireland, not abroad.[67] Unless better sources attest to their presence, Clontarf's Normans, fighting for their Scandinavian brethren, may therefore be phantoms. What of other contacts? Olaf Haraldsson's skald Sigvatr Þorðarson visited Rouen c. 1024,[68] and there were Vikings, possibly Norwegian, in the Channel in 1048, according to the Anglo-Saxon Chronicle;[69] this time, however, they sold their booty in Flanders, not Normandy. Osgod Clapa, an old colleague of Cnut now exiled from England, also used Flanders as his base for a raid against England the following year, before returning to Denmark.[70]

The evidence therefore seems generally to substantiate the idea of a growing political distance between Normandy and its Scandinavian cousins. Elisabeth van Houts has argued, however, on the basis of eleventh-century Norman literature, that whatever rupture there was in political and economic relations was not matched by a cultural break – but she also argued that Normandy received its Scandinavian traditions through the British Isles, not directly from the homelands.[71] Van Houts and Graham Loud have both pointed to Scandinavian elements in eleventh- and twelfth-century Norman accounts of the duchy's history.[72] The source of these Scandinavian elements is a matter of debate. Some attribute them to a legacy from the early settlers, handed down through the medium of an enduring Northern culture and nurtured by Scandinavian contacts during the tenth and eleventh centuries; others prefer to see any similarities as a result of borrowing and cultural contact at a later stage, most probably through England, given the scarcity of known direct contacts. Specific knowledge of Scandinavia in Norman historians has been judged distinctly thin and formulaic, relying heavily on the classical and fantastical collection of clichés assembled by Dudo of St Quentin in his *De moribus et actis primorum Normanniae ducum*. The cultural context of Dudo's work has inspired much disagreement. In Christiansen's opinion, 'there is not a theme, verse, or episode in this history which is inconsistent with, if not evidently derived from, the literary culture of Carolingian Francia'.[73] Leah Shopkow has demonstrated the extent to which Dudo

---

Mhaonaigh, '*Cogad Gáedel Re Gallaib* and the Annals: a Comparison', *Ériu* xlvii, 1996, 101–26. As the authors (above, n. 63) who have cited the presence of Normans at Clontarf gave no references to any primary sources, I have assumed that Ademar or the *Cogadh* comprises the evidence behind the assertion; there may, however, be better evidence in other works which I have not identified.

[67] *Cogadh*, chs 87 and 118 (ed. Todd, 150–3 and 208–9); *The Annals of Ulster*, ed. S. Mac Airt and G. Mac Niocaill, Dublin 1983, *s.a.* 1014. Thanks are due to Máire Ní Mhaonaigh and Erin Moran for help with the *Cogadh* and to David Dumville and Alex Woolf for elucidation of its *Danair*.

[68] Sigvatr's *Vestrfararvísur* refers to mooring his ship in the west bay of Rouen: *Den norsk-islandske skjaldedigtning*, ed. Jónsson, Ai, 241–3, Bi, 226–8; *EHD* i, 338, no. 17. Christiansen has emphasised that this need not mean that there was an audience for skaldic poetry in Rouen at the time (*Dudo*, xvii, n. 24).

[69] *ASC* 'E', *s.a.* 1046 (*recte* 1048).

[70] *ASC* 'C', *s.a.* 1049, 'D', *s.a.* 1050 (*recte* 1049).

[71] Van Houts, 'Scandinavian Influence', 106 and 120.

[72] Loud, 'The "Gens" ', 115; van Houts, 'Scandinavian Influence', 119–20.

[73] *Dudo*, ed. Christiansen, xviii. See also Musset: 'Jusqu'ici on n'a pu déceler en Normandie rien qui présente une saveur nordique, rien qui rapelle, même de loin, sous un travestissement latin, les sagas ou les poésies scaldiques' ('Le satiriste Garnier de Rouen et son milieu', *Revue du moyen âge latin* x, 1954, 236–66, at 236–7).

modelled his history on Frankish hagiography.[74] Mathieu Arnoux, however, pointing out that no Scandinavian source has been found for Dudo's story of the peasant from Longpaon, for example, has proposed that it was 'un thème original'.[75] Other scholars see in Dudo's Latin text disguised memories and traditions of Scandinavia.[76] Whatever the nature of Dudo's sources, Musset has argued that his history erected a screen of false knowledge which hid the real Scandinavia from Normandy.[77] Comparison of historical traditions may support this. The founder of Normandy in West Norse tradition, for example, was 'Rolf the Ganger', son of Rognvald, earl of More, and therefore a Norwegian, rather than Dudo's Dane; in the thirteenth-century Saga of Saint Olaf, Snorri Sturluson traced the genealogy of Olaf's contemporary, Richard II, back to Norwegian ancestors, describing the Normans as kin of Norwegian chieftains and great friends of Northmen.[78] Olaf Tryggvason, so central in Norway's Kings' Sagas, was apparently not known in Normandy.[79] Musset suggested that what Orderic Vitalis knew about Norway – more detailed than his contemporaries, but not always accurate – reached him from England.[80]

Musset also argued that knowledge of Normandy in Scandinavia was unimpressive. In the West Norse tradition represented by the thirteenth-century Saga of Harald Fairhair, Normandy was seen as of a piece with the Scandinavian settlements such as Iceland and Ireland forty to fifty years earlier, motivated like them by the tyranny of King Harald (c. 860x880–930x940), who expelled Rollo from Norway.[81] A different, East Norse, historical tradition is represented in Books X and XI of Saxo Grammaticus's *Gesta Danorum*, a work completed before 1223. Given the gusto with which Saxo shaped his raw material, it is difficult to judge whether his distinctive eleventh-century facts (Cnut died in Normandy in the course of his second war against the duke; Harold Godwineson killed Edward the Confessor) are an indication of ignorance in thirteenth-century Denmark of real events, a sign of sources at several removes from their historical contexts, or simply a historically regrettable preference for the colourful.[82] The Norwegian monk Theodoric, however, knew a *historia*

---

74 L. Shopkow, 'The Carolingian World of Dudo of Saint-Quentin', *JMH* xv, 1989, 19–37.

75 The point was to illustrate and praise ducal authority: 'Classe agricole, pouvoir seigneurial et autorité ducale: l'évolution de la Normandie féodale d'après le témoignage des chroniqueurs (Xe–XIIe siécles)', *Le moyen âge* 5th ser. vi, 1992, 35–60, at 38–45.

76 E. Searle, 'Fact and Pattern in Heroic History: Dudo of St Quentin', *Viator* xv, 1984, 119–37, esp. 123; Amory, 'The *dönsk tunga*', 284–6.

77 'Malgré ses rares accès d'authenticité, [Dudon] est finalement surtout l'inventeur d'un écran de fausse érudition qui a masqué durablement la Scandinavie aux Normands': Musset, 'L'image', 197–8.

78 'Saint Olafs Saga', ch. 20 (*Heimskringla*, ed. Aðalbjarnarson, ii, 26–7; trans. Hollander, 259). The Icelandic history *Landnámabók*, extant in a thirteenth-century text, tells us that a son of Rognvald of More, Ganger-Hrolf, conquered Normandy (*Nordmandi*). 'From him came the earls of Rouen and the kings of the English': *Íslendingabók. Landnámabók*, ed. J. Benediktsson, Reykjavík 1968, Íslenzk Fornrit I, 314 (*The Book of the Settlements. Landnámabók*, trans. H. Pálsson and H. Edwards [Winnipeg] 1972, 119–20 (ch. 309)); also in 'The Saga of Harald Fairhair', ch. 24 (*Heimskringla*, ed. Aðalbjarnarson, i, 124–5; trans. Hollander, 79).

79 On Olaf, see Musset, 'L'image', 215.

80 *Orderic* v, 218–23; Musset, 'L'image', 201–6. Marjorie Chibnall has suggested that Orderic's description of Norway was derived not from Adam of Bremen or the source of the *Historia Norvegiae* but from a now lost Latin source (221, n. 5).

81 'The Saga of Harald Fairhair', ch. 24 (*Heimskringla*, ed. Aðalbjarnarson, i, 123–5; trans. Hollander, 78–9).

82 *Saxo Grammaticus, 'Danorum regum heroumque historia', Books X–XVI*, trans. E. Christiansen, 3 vols in 2, BAR int. ser. 84 and 118, 1980–81, i, 2–88, esp. 44–5 and 49; see also i, 210 (n. 163). Books

*Normannorum*, probably that of William of Jumièges, when he wrote his *Historia de antiquitate regum Norwagiensium* in the later twelfth century.[83]

In Scandinavian colonies elsewhere, the study of sculpture and art has contributed to the question of the cultural contribution of the immigrants to their new environments. In tenth-century England, for example, settlement was followed by a creative mix of Scandinavian and Anglian sculptural traditions. Maylis Baylé's studies of Norman ecclesiastical architecture, however, have found little to indicate an early or direct Scandinavian impact.[84] The importance of wooden churches (more likely to have been early and, because of their material, to have demonstrated Scandinavian features) cannot be determined, as none have been preserved. What late tenth-century and early eleventh-century sculpture survives in Normandy mostly belongs to a continental tradition, but at Evrecy (Calvados) fragments in a Scandinavian idiom survive from a church now destroyed. These were not, in Baylé's opinion, produced by a Scandinavian, but perhaps by a local Norman sculptor working with a Scandinavian – or Anglo-Scandinavian – model.[85] Other sculptural parallels are later and probably came through England: Baylé has identified the years 1080x1140 as a period when Scandinavian influence on English architecture was particularly productive.[86] The architecture therefore supports the literary evidence, again directing us away from the homelands towards influences from Britain.

The Norman Church reinforces this picture. In the early eleventh century the Church in Normandy was experiencing a dynamic revival, led by the ducal house, which rebuilt in new forms on Frankish foundations. Cassandra Potts has demonstrated how the newly Christian ducal family exercised patronage to legitimise and enhance its status, using reformed monasticism as an instrument of settlement and a means of establishing its authority within the duchy.[87] In Scandinavia, by contrast, the Church was still in its infancy, and information on the conversion period and early stages of development is very sparse.[88] English and German churchmen are, however, the most visible in the obscure drama whereby Germanic paganism's last major stronghold was formally converted to Christianity, a process which begins to appear in the written record from the late tenth century. One possibly Norman cleric, Rodolf, has been tentatively identified in the Scandinavian mission-field, first in Norway and then in Iceland, though the sources linking him with Normandy are not contemporary and are far from conclusive.[89] He became abbot of Abingdon in 1050 or 1051, and the

X and XI deal with the period 925–1066. See A. Campbell, 'Saxo Grammaticus and Scandinavian Historical Tradition', *Saga-Book of the Viking Society* xiii, 1946–53, 1–22, esp. 16–18.

83  *Monumenta*, ch. 13 (ed. Storm, 22; *The Ancient History*, trans. McDougall and McDougall, 17).

84  M. Baylé, *Les origines et les premiers développements de la sculpture romane en Normandie*, [Caen] n.d., 24–5. I should like to thank Dr Baylé for providing me with a copy of her book and for help with the question of Scandinavian influence. For England, see R.N. Bailey, *Viking Age Sculpture in Northern England*, London 1980.

85  Baylé, *Les origines*, 49 and 52; see also M. Baylé, 'Interlace Patterns in Norman Romanesque Sculpture: Regional Groups and their Historical Background', *ANS* v, 1982, 1–20.

86  M. Baylé, 'Réminiscences anglo-scandinaves dans la sculpture romane de Normandie', *ANS* xiii, 1990, 35–48, at 45–8.

87  C. Potts, *Monastic Revival and Regional Identity in Early Normandy*, Woodbridge 1997.

88  *The Christianization of Scandinavia*, ed. B. Sawyer *et al.*, Alingsås 1987.

89  See Abrams, 'The Anglo-Saxons and the Christianization of Scandinavia', *ASE* xxiv, 1995, 213–49, at 223–4 (n. 52). The Anglo-Saxon Chronicle records the appointment of a Bishop Roðulf who had worked *apud Norweiam gentem* (*ASC* 'E', *s.a.* 1048 (*recte* 1051), 'C', *s.a.* 1050); according to ch. 8 of the Icelandic history *Íslendingabók* (c. 1120s), a Bishop Hróðólfr spent nineteen years in Iceland (*The Book of the Icelanders (Íslendingabók)*, ed. and trans. H. Hermannsson, Ithaca NY and London

Anglo-Saxon Chronicle identified him as a relative of Edward the Confessor; as Frank Stenton suggested, his relationship may have been through Edward's mother Emma. It is perfectly sensible to suggest that when Olaf Haraldsson left Normandy after his baptism, he was accompanied by churchmen, and a minor member of the ducal house may have chosen or been selected to accompany the royal convert. If Rodolf was a Norman, he did not return home on retirement; but there were other Norman churchmen in England in 1050.[90]

Ecclesiastical contact of any kind with Norway and Denmark is difficult to trace, and few Scandinavian clerics are known within, let alone outside, Scandinavia in the eleventh century. One Danish churchman, Odinkar the Younger, who became bishop of Ribe, was apparently educated in England thanks to Cnut's patronage. Consecrated bishop in Bremen, he had also sought learning in *Gallia* – this could be anywhere in 'Gaul', not necessarily Normandy, but it may be the closest that our sources can get us to the duchy.[91] Later in the eleventh century, churchmen from *Gallia* worried the pope. Concerned for his authority in the North, Alexander II wrote to Harald Hardrada in 1061x1066, criticising the Norwegian king's bishops who *in Anglia uel in Gallia pessime sunt ordinati*.[92] Not long after, in 1080, Pope Gregory VII chided Inge, king of the Swedes, for listening to evangelisers from the *ecclesia Gallicana*.[93] Whether Normans may have been among them is unclear. Musset maintained that Normandy did not entirely abstain from the enterprise of converting Scandinavia, referring to *episcopi uagantes* (bishops with no known see) who are mentioned in late tenth-century Norman charters as suitable candidates for involvement.[94] Our knowledge of contemporary Norman churchmen, however, is not good enough to rule these three stray bishops out of local ecclesiastical affairs. The predominantly monastic orientation of the revived Norman Church in the eleventh century may argue against any connection with the Church in Scandinavia, the latter being exclusively secular, it seems, until the very end of the century. Normandy's reform movement under William of Volpiano looked to Italy and eastern France for guidance and personnel, and it may have been preoccupied with its new directions. There are apparently no dedications in Normandy to Olaf Haraldsson, Scandinavia's first native saint, and, despite the historical association of the real Olaf with Rouen, no other evidence of a cult in Normandy (except for a relic – Olaf's baptismal cloak – recorded at Mont Saint-Michel in a fourteenth-century inventory). By contrast, Olaf's sanctity left its mark on written records in England within very few years of his death in 1030.[95] The

1930, 54 and 67). Later Icelandic sources such as *Hungrvaka* identify Bishop Rúðólfr with *Ruða* (Rouen; but note the names' similarities); see J. Stefánsson, 'Rúðólf of Boe and Rudolf of Rouen', *Saga-Book of the Viking Society* xiii, 1946–53, 174–82, and Stenton, *Anglo-Saxon England*, 463.

90  Stenton, *Anglo-Saxon England*, 464–5.

91  Adam of Bremen, *Gesta*, ii.26, and scholium (ed. Schmeidler, 96–7; trans. Tschan, 79).

92  Adam of Bremen, *Gesta*, iii.17 (ed. Schmeidler, 160–1; trans. Tschan, 128–9); see Abrams, 'The Anglo-Saxons', 232, n. 96.

93  *The Register of Pope Gregory VII, 1073–1085*, trans. H.E.J. Cowdrey, Oxford 2002, 376–7; Abrams, 'The Anglo-Saxons', 238.

94  L. Musset, 'La pénétration chrétienne dans l'Europe du nord et son influence sur la civilisation scandinave', *Settimane di studio del centro italiano di studi sull'alto medioevo* xiv, 1967, 263–325, at 291; Fauroux, 70, 77 (nos 3, 7) (AD 968 and 996–1006).

95  J. Dubois, 'Le trésor des reliques du Mont-Saint-Michel', in *Millénaire monastique du Mont-Saint-Michel*, 5 vols, Paris 1967–93, i, 501–93, at 531–2. William of Jumièges knew of Olaf's sanctity, but implied that he was culted only in Scandinavia (*Jumièges* ii, 26–8); Musset knew of no dedications in Normandy ('L'image', 198). For England, see B. Dickins, 'The Cult of Saint Olave in the

cult of St Clement, which Barbara Crawford has tentatively associated with the Danish presence in England and Scotland in the early eleventh century, is attested in a reference to a chapel and *mansus* attached to the 'gate' of St Clement at Rouen in 1025; Clement's association with the sea, however, had ensured his popularity in maritime and riverine societies before this putative Scandinavian adoption of his cult.[96]

The interests of the Norman Church, strongly oriented towards monasticism and the Continental reform movement, contrast with the obscure but undoubted connections of the fledgling Church in Scandinavia with the English and German Churches.[97] This divergence, if not caused by a rift between Normandy and the North, doubtless strengthened it. On the other hand, after 1150, as Peter Foote has pointed out, direct influence from 'central and western France' was exerted in Scandinavia, especially Norway, through the Cistercians and Victorines.[98]

Trade was clearly a crucial element in linking Normandy with the external world, but the extent of Normandy's economic activity outside its borders is difficult to identify. Rouen's position had long made it a natural centre for trade, a status which it retained when power was transferred to Viking hands. This is confirmed by random references to merchants or commercial activity from the ninth, tenth, and eleventh centuries.[99] Musset has argued that while Charles the Bald's bridge-building policy stifled trade on the Seine, the takeover of Rouen by Vikings in 911 re-opened the river to commerce.[100] There had been Carolingian mints at Rouen, Bayeux, Évreux, Lisieux, Coutances, and at one or two monastic houses; minting is attested at Rouen from the time of William Longsword (c. 928–942), possibly inspired by the example of Scandinavian York, and much later in the eleventh century at Bayeux.[101] The drafter of the law-collection II Æthelred envisaged a situation where English

---

British Isles', *Saga-Book of the Viking Society* xii, 1937–45, 53–80; also Abrams, 'The Anglo-Saxons', 248, n. 190.

[96] The chapel existed in 1006, when it was granted to Fécamp, but no dedication is mentioned in the original charter of that date. It is identified in 1025 in a charter of confirmation which is extant in a 'pseudo-original in a late eleventh-century script'; see Fauroux, 80, 125 (nos 9, 34). For the chapel's location, see B. Gauthiez, 'Hypothèses sur la fortification de Rouen au onzième siècle: le donjon, la tour de Richard II et l'enceinte de Guillaume', *ANS* xiv, 1991, 61–76, esp. 61 and 65. On Clement's cult, see B.E. Crawford, 'The Dedication to St Clement at Rodil, Harris', in *Church, Chronicle and Learning in Medieval and Early Renaissance Scotland*, ed. B.E. Crawford, Edinburgh 1999, 105–18.

[97] P. Foote, 'Aachen, Lund, Hólar', in *Aurvandilstá. Norse Studies*, Odense 1984, 101–20; Abrams, 'The Anglo-Saxons'.

[98] Foote, 'Aachen', 118.

[99] L. Musset, 'La Seine normande et le commerce maritime du IIIe au XIe siècle', *Revue des sociétés savantes de Haute-Normandie* liii, 1969, 3–14 (reprinted in *Nordica et Normannica*, 337–50); L. Musset, 'Rouen au temps des francs et sous les ducs (Ve siècle–1204)', in *Histoire de Rouen*, ed. M. Mollat, Toulouse 1979, 31–74; Bates, 'Rouen from 900 to 1204'.

[100] Musset, 'La Seine normande', 344.

[101] Musset, 'Rouen au temps des francs', 49; on earlier Norman coins, see F. Dumas and J. Pilet-Lemière, 'La monnaie normande – Xe–XXe siècle: le point de la recherche en 1987', in *Les mondes normands (VIIIe–XIIe s.)*, ed. H. Galinié, Caen 1989, 125–31, at 125. Jens Christian Moesgaard has recently pointed out that hoard evidence attests to minting at Bayeux just before the Scandinavian takeover of middle Normandy (usually dated c. 924). He has also drawn attention to several Carolingian imitations which could be candidates for early Scandinavian issues in Normandy ('The Vikings on the Western European Continent', forthcoming in the series Nordiske Fortidsminder, Det kongelige nordiske oldskriftsselskab, ed. Iben Skipsted Klæsøe, Copenhagen). I should like to thank Jens Christian Moesgaard for allowing me to cite his paper in advance of publication.

merchant ships entered 'towns within the peace' (*friðburig*) and territories 'outside the peace' (*unfriðland*);[102] Rouen in the 990s may have qualified for either status, given the (failed) 991 agreement between King Æthelred and Duke Richard. It may have been there that Svein Forkbeard agreed to sell his English booty.[103] We know from other legislation of Æthelred that *homines Rotomagi*, 'men of Rouen', brought wine and blubber-fish (*craspiscis*) to the port of London.[104] The tolls on these commodities mentioned in Æthelred's code were still in place c. 1150, when Rouen merchants were assigned the special harbour (*portum de Dauegate*) which they had held in the time of King Edward.[105]

The effect on trade of the political rift between Normandy and England is difficult to gauge, especially as the volume of direct trade between Normandy and Scandinavia at any time is unknown. Archaeological evidence for Normandy's external trading connections in the tenth and eleventh centuries is sparse. It is unfortunate that more is not known about the slave trade with which Rouen is credited, for a decrease in local supply (slaves were doubtless prominent among the 'booty' of Viking raids) may have led to a need to look elsewhere for commodities to trade.[106] By the mid-eleventh century, commerce with Ireland is attested by Norman pottery in Dublin, but earlier imports await analysis. Coins from the Scandinavian homelands, first minted in the late tenth century, have not been found in Normandy; Anglo-Saxon coins, on the other hand, occur in the Fécamp hoard (buried 960x985), but the only identified eleventh-century find has been a Harthacnut penny from Saint-Martin-de-Boscherville.[107] Re-cycling of external coinages naturally skews these figures.

Cnut, when in Rome in 1027, negotiated for better security and fewer tolls for his English and Danish subjects on the route to Italy; unfortunately only the emperor and Rodulf of Burgundy are mentioned by name in Cnut's report to the English people, so we cannot say whether the duke of Normandy was among the 'other princes through whose lands our road to Rome lay' and therefore part of the agreement at this time.[108] A small number of tenth-century Norman coins have been found in Ireland and

---

102  II Æthelred 2.1 and 3.1 (*The Laws of the Kings of England from Edmund to Henry I*, ed. and trans. A.J. Robertson, Cambridge 1925, 56–61); see N. Lund, 'Peace and Non-Peace in the Viking Age – Ottar in Biarmaland, the Rus in Byzantium, and Danes and Norwegians in England', in *Proceedings of the Tenth Viking Congress*, ed. J.E. Knirk, Oslo 1987, 255–70; Lund argued that the law's provisions were for England only.

103  *Jumièges* ii, 18.

104  IV Æthelred, 2.6 (ed. and trans. Robertson, 72).

105  *Regesta* iii, 269 (no. 729) (*recte Danegate*?).

106  See D. Pelteret, *Slavery in Early Medieval England*, Woodbridge 1995, esp. 70–9, on the sources of slaves and the slave trade. Pelteret has pointed out that Scandinavians were prominent in the trade, that there is good evidence for it in England still in the late eleventh century, and that it was not outlawed there until 1102. Scandinavian slavers and slave-markets in Normandy and the Insular world play a crucial role in 'Moriuht', the satirical poem of c. 1000 by Garnier of Rouen; see van Houts, 'Scandinavian Influence', 107–9, and D.N. Dumville, 'Images of the Viking in Eleventh-Century Latin Literature' (*Proceedings of the Third International Medieval Latin Congress*, ed. M.W. Herren, Turnhout, forthcoming (Publications of the Journal of Medieval Latin)). I should like to thank David Dumville for a copy of this paper in typescript.

107  Musset, 'Les relations extérieures', 38; Dumas and Pilet-Lemière, 'La monnaie', 128. I am indebted to Mark Blackburn and Jens Christian Moesgaard for more up-to-date information on the coins, and to Pat Wallace for information on Dublin's pottery. See also n. 120 below. For the Harthacnut coin, see *Boscherville. Du temple païen à l'abbaye bénédictine*, Rouen 1986, no. 44a.

108  *John of Worcester, s.a.* 1031 (512–18); *EHD* i, 476–8, at 477 (no. 53).

western Scotland but only two possible candidates in England.[109] The discovery of a number of coins of Richard II or III in southern and northern England, in the Hebrides, and at two unprovenanced Scottish and Irish sites, however, as well as in Denmark, Sweden, Poland, and Pomerania may suggest that Norman goods, if not Norman traders, travelled these routes.[110] The coin evidence was used by Musset to argue that, as a result of the Danish conquest of England and the associated political fallout, Normandy withdrew from northern trade in preference for a new commercial route, via Italy.[111] Pottery could usefully be brought into the discussion: new evidence from Irish excavations would be relevant. Repetition has given Musset's conclusions the force of doctrine. Bates, for example, citing Musset, has stated that the mapping of coin hoards means that 'the ending of connections can be charted with some accuracy', the final rupture taking place c. 1020.[112] The argument relies on the observation that 'after the first years of the eleventh century, Norman coins cease to appear in northern hoards. Instead, they begin to occur in some numbers on very different routes, most especially in France and in Italy. This suggests a fairly abrupt rupture . . . [and] a conscious redirection of Norman [economic] activity.'[113] That may indeed be what happened; but the coin evidence does not demonstrate it as conclusively as is implied. For one thing, the dating of Norman coinage is a very loose affair. Instead of the precise dates attributable to contemporary Anglo-Saxon coins, Norman numismatists work in very broad and very flexible date bands. The categories established by Françoise Dumas group all tenth-century coins together; her next category, Group A, runs roughly from 996 to 1027; Group B is mid-eleventh-century (possibly associated with William the Conqueror); Group B/C is similar and may span the third quarter of the eleventh century; Group C is influenced by Anglo-Saxon coins and belongs to the late eleventh century and first half of the twelfth; and Group D has a similar range.[114] The dates are explicitly approximate. Part of the difficulty is that, like other contemporary feudal coinages, Norman deniers exhibit immobilised legends and designs – that is to say, these do not change from one duke to another – and they therefore resist close dating. Furthermore, the date proposed for the rupture, c. 1020, comes towards the end of Dumas's Group A (996–1027), the next group being described as mid-century. The crucial period after 1027 is therefore only vaguely identifiable numismatically, and 1020 is indistinguishable from the late 990s. Furthermore, while all the 'Northern' coins Bates mentioned are in Group A, so are a number of finds from Italy, which must therefore be contemporary, at least according to Dumas's dating scheme. There are, in addition, Group B and B/C coins in England, Ireland, and

---

[109]  Dumas, 'Nouvelles découvertes'.

[110]  J. Lafaurie, 'Le trésor monétaire du Puy (Haute Loire)', *Revue numismatique* 5th ser. xiii, 1951, 59–169, at 93–4 (with map); F. Dumas, 'Les monnaies normandes (Xe–XIIe siècles) avec un répertoire de trouvailles', *Revue numismatique* 6th ser. xxi, 1979, 84–140, at 110–16; M. Blackburn, 'Two Norman Deniers from the Stornoway Hoard', *Numismatic Chronicle* clv, 1995, 334–7.

[111]  Musset, 'Les relations extérieures', 37, quoting Lafaurie, 'Le trésor', 94–5. Musset actually used three somewhat different dates for this break ('Les relations extérieures', 35, 37, and 38): 'vers le règne de Robert le Magnifique' (i.e. beginning 1027); between 1005 and 1025; and 1014–15. In his view, only after the Norman Conquest, however – or rather, after 1070 and the Norman Harrying of the (Scandinavian) North of England – was the break between the two sides of the North Sea complete: 'Relations et échanges', 80–2.

[112]  Bates, *Normandy*, 23 and 36.

[113]  Bates, *Normandy*, 36.

[114]  Dumas, 'Les monnaies'; the dates are set out at 87–96 and 103.

the Isle of Man (though not Scandinavia), as well as in Italy.[115] The 'North'-'South' sequence therefore collapses, and there seems to be no tidy division between coins found exclusively in one region before 1020/1030 and in another after that date.

Since some scholars have focussed on the disappearance of Norman coins from the Scandinavian North after 1020/1030, we should also consider their importance before that date: but only eighteen Norman deniers have been recorded in Sweden, one in Denmark, and none in Norway, compared with over 100,000 coins from the Insular world and Germany. It seems therefore that Norman coins were never statistically significant in late Viking-Age Scandinavia. Kenneth Jonsson has pointed out that the dates of the hoards suggest two (small) phases of import, one in the early 990s and another in the 1020s.[116] It is not clear what route they took. However, as there are large numbers of Hiberno-Norse coins in Scandinavia before 1030 and few thereafter, Mark Blackburn has suggested that a trickle of Norman deniers could have reached Scandinavia via the Irish Sea, and that the cessation of this Hiberno-Norse coin traffic after c. 1030 could account for the scarcity or absence of Norman coins thereafter.[117] The number of English coins drops dramatically as well. As no political break between the Hiberno-Scandinavian world and the Scandinavian homelands (or between England and Scandinavia) can be responsible for the drying-up of coin flow after 1030, other explanations need to be found; these might interpret the absence of Norman coins after 1020/1030 in terms quite different from those of Musset. Political instability after the death of Richard II and the power vacuum in southern Italy, which drew Normans into southern affairs in a military capacity from the 1020s,[118] clearly turned attention to the south and doubtless produced an impact on economic configurations, but explanations of Normandy's new directions should also take into account the logic of trade in Scandinavia itself. Norman trade with the Scandinavian world did not cease entirely, however. Trade links may account for Irish knowledge of hardship in Rouen as recorded in the Annals of Tigernach; an Exchequer account for 1198 mentioned a ship from Iceland in Rouen with a cargo of cloth,[119] while trade with Irish ports is attested at Rouen and Cherbourg in 1150–51 by a charter of liberties as well as by pottery exports.[120]

115  Dumas, 'Les monnaies', 110–25.

116  Nine certain hoards in Sweden contained thirteen Norman coins, with hoards of unknown provenance providing another five. I should like to thank Kenneth Jonsson for supplying me with these figures and details of the relevant specimens; Musset ('Les relations extérieures', 32) cited forty-five Frankish coins dating from 800 to 1000 in Denmark, fifteen in Sweden, and twenty-five in Norway, but gave no figures specifically for coins originating in Normandy. On Swedish finds, see V. Hatz, 'Die französischen Münzen des 10./11. Jahrhunderts in den schwedischen Funden der Wikingerzeit', in *Festskrift till O. Lagerqvist*, ed. U. Ehrensvärd et al., Stockholm 1989, 115–29.

117  Dumas suggested that they arrived via Germany: 'Les monnaies', 128. Many thanks are due to Mark Blackburn for discussing the coin evidence with me.

118  G.A. Loud, *The Age of Robert Guiscard*, Harlow 2000; J. France, 'The Occasion of the Coming of the Normans to Southern Italy', *JMH* xvii, 1991, 185–205. The coin hoards on the route south may in fact be evidence of military, as well as economic, activity.

119  *Magni rotuli scaccarii Normanniae sub regibus Angliae*, ed. T. Stapleton, 2 vols, London 1840–44, ii, 306. For the annals of Tigernach, see *Revue Celtique* xvi, 1895, 374–420.

120  *Regesta* iii, 268–9 (no. 729). P. Wallace, 'Northern European Pottery Imported into Dublin, 1200–1500', in *Ceramics and Trade. The Production and Distribution of Later Medieval Pottery in Northwest Europe*, ed. P. Davey and R. Hodges, Sheffield 1983, 225–30, at 226.

The coin evidence clearly awaits re-evaluation by qualified experts. Such analysis may, with further archaeological discoveries, increase our understanding of the complex triangular relationship between England, the Scandinavian homelands, and Normandy – the most enduring of the Scandinavian settlements in western Europe.[121]

[121] I am grateful to the Arts and Humanities Research Board, thanks to whose grant of leave this paper was written in the autumn of 1999. Delay in publication has meant that research and publications appearing after that date are unfortunately unrepresented here.

# 4

# Angevin Normandy

## DANIEL POWER

The years in which the 'Plantagenet' counts of Anjou ruled Normandy (1144–1204) are usually regarded as a period of Norman decline.[1] In 1144 the Angevin conquest of Normandy deprived the duchy of the dominant place which it had hitherto enjoyed within the Anglo-Norman *regnum*, and in 1204 the dukes of Normandy were ousted from the province completely. Thereafter the leaderless duchy became a supine dominion of the Capetian kings of France. The Normans retained a strong sense of provincial identity after 1204 and occasionally asserted their political weight, securing their famous charter of liberties, the *Chartes aux Normands*, during the revolt of the provincial leagues in 1314–15, but they never recovered the preponderant role they had enjoyed in the eleventh and early twelfth centuries.[2] Nor did a new ducal family emerge, not even from the Capetian dynasty, although the Valois kings were later to make their eldest sons dukes of Normandy from time to time. In part, the province's decline reflected the more general eclipse of territorial principalities in France in the face of the rising Capetian monarchy.[3] However, the history of Normandy after 1144 should not be seen merely as an appendix to a story of Norman greatness that ended in 1135. These six decades of Angevin rule were crucial to the establishment of enduring Norman customs and institutions, many of which lasted until the French Revolution – and in the Channel Islands survive even today.

Angevin Normandy has been curiously neglected by historians, but the reasons are not hard to find.[4] Geoffrey of Anjou's subjugation of the duchy in 1144 was narrowly preceded by the death of Orderic Vitalis, and no narrative from the Angevin period matches his *Ecclesiastical History* as a source for Norman history. Most that survive are short annals; the only significant chronicler in Normandy was Robert of Torigny, abbot of Mont Saint-Michel (1154–86), whose chronicle is both laconic and prosaic. Torigny had previously added to the *Gesta Normannorum Ducum*, the text which had been rewritten to legitimise the reigning prince in almost every generation since Dudo of Saint-Quentin, but despite Torigny's initial plans he did not continue this work past

1   E.g. J.C. Holt, 'The End of the Anglo-Norman Realm', *PBA* lxi, 1975, 223–65, at 250, 252, 258–60; L. Musset, 'Quelques problèmes de l'annexation de la Normandie au domaine royal français', in *La France de Philippe Auguste: le temps des mutations*, ed. R.H. Bautier, Paris 1982, 291–307, at 291–4; D. Bates, 'The Rise and Fall of Normandy, c. 911–1204', *England and Normandy*, 19–35.

2   P. Contamine, 'The Norman "Nation" and the French "Nation" in the Fourteenth and Fifteenth Centuries', *England and Normandy*, 215–34.

3   Bates, 'Rise and Fall of Normandy', 20–9, 35.

4   The chief surveys remain C.H. Haskins, *Norman Institutions*, Cambridge, Mass., 1918, 123–95, and F.M. Powicke, *The Loss of Normandy 1189–1204: Studies in the History of the Angevin Empire*, 2nd edn, Manchester 1961. Many of the issues discussed here are considered in my forthcoming monograph, *The Norman Frontier in the Twelfth and Early Thirteenth Centuries*.

the death of Henry I; nor did Gervase, prior of Saint-Cénery on the border of Normandy and Maine, whom Torigny urged to perform this task in his stead.[5] In the reign of Henry II two authors, Wace and Benoît de Sainte-Maure, both adapted the *Gesta Normannorum Ducum* into vernacular poetry, and in the thirteenth century a number of vernacular prose chronicles and histories of the dukes of Normandy made extensive use of passages from the narratives of Dudo and William of Jumièges, showing that the history of the Norman dukes still had strong appeal to lay audiences;[6] but the Latin version of the *Gesta* had ceased to be a 'living text' even as the native dynasty of Norman dukes was replaced by a new dynasty from Anjou.[7]

Even before Torigny's death, then, far more may be gleaned about Angevin Normandy from sources written elsewhere, especially the authors of the 'golden age' of English historiography such as Roger of Howden and William of Newburgh. Yet the immense increase in other forms of written evidence in Normandy compensates for the poverty of narratives. Perhaps the most important documentary sources are the products of ducal government itself, especially the Angevins' charters and writs concerning the duchy.[8] The reign of John Lackland as duke of Normandy (1199–1204), though brief, is exceptionally well documented because his clerks kept copies of the voluminous royal correspondence.[9] Account rolls from the Norman exchequer survive to varying degrees for six years between 1180 and 1203,[10] together with a miscellaneous collection of documents from the ducal exchequer at Caen.[11] These fiscal records yield a great deal of information about ducal government on the eve of its overthrow. In addition, vast numbers of charters, mostly for religious houses, represent another rich source for Norman history under the Angevins. This evidence means that we can actually discover far more about the governance and people of Normandy in the last decades of ducal rule than at any previous time in Norman history.[12]

5   *Jumièges* i, xci–xciv; E.M.C. van Houts, 'The *Gesta Normannorum Ducum*, a History without an End', *ANS* iii, 1989, 106–15, 215–19, at 114–15.

6   The best-known, but by no means the only text, is *Histoire des ducs de Normandie et rois d'Angleterre*, ed. F. Michel, Paris 1840; see also F. Michel, *Chroniques de Normandie*, Paris 1839.

7   Van Houts, 'The *Gesta Normannorum Ducum*', 115.

8   Until the publication of the acts of Henry II and Richard I by Professors Sir James Holt and N.C. Vincent, see *Recueil des actes de Henri II*, ed. L. Delisle and E. Berger, 3 vols and intro., Paris 1909–27; L. Landon, *The Itinerary of Richard I*, PRS ns xiii, London 1935. For Geoffrey and Matilda, see *Regesta* iii.

9   *Rot. Norm.*, 1–122; there are many items concerning Normandy up to 1204 in *Rot. Litt. Pat.*, 1–43; *Rot. Chart.*, 1–128; *Rot. de Lib.*, 1–108; *Rot. de Obl.*, 1–196.

10   *MRSN* (1180, 1195, 1198, and fragments for 1184, 1201, 1203); *Recueil H II*, intro., 334–44 (1184); H. Legras, 'Un fragment de rôle normand inédit de Jean sans Terre', *Bulletin de la Société des Antiquaires de Normandie* xxix, 1914, 21–31 (1201).

11   S. Packard, *Miscellaneous Records of the Norman Exchequer, 1199–1204*, Northampton, Mass., 1927.

12   Haskins, *Norman Institutions*, 193–4; his negative view of this evidence is challenged by V. Moss, 'The Norman Fiscal Revolution, 1193–98', in *Crises, Revolutions and Self-Sustained Fiscal Growth: Essays in European Fiscal History 1130–1830*, ed. W.M. Ormrod, R. Bonney and M. Bonney, Stamford 2000, 38–57, at 38–40.

*Political History*

Four members of the Angevin dynasty were acknowledged as dukes of Normandy, namely Geoffrey of Anjou, his son Henry II, and Henry's two sons Richard I and John; two others, Henry the Young King and Arthur of Brittany, briefly aspired to rule the province, and the Empress Matilda, as erstwhile heiress of Normandy and wife and widow of Geoffrey of Anjou, was an influential figure in the duchy until her death in 1167.[13]

With such a paucity of narrative sources the political history of Angevin Normandy is quickly told. The opening phase was the establishment of Angevin rule between 1135 and 1151. Almost immediately after the death of Henry I in December 1135, the Empress Matilda and her husband Geoffrey, count of Anjou, gained a foothold in the southern marches of the duchy, and although most Norman lords initially accepted Stephen of Blois as their duke, Count Geoffrey gradually wore down their resistance.[14] Stephen's one attempt to establish his authority in the duchy (1137), although initially successful, degenerated into a shambolic failure.[15] Early in 1144 Geoffrey captured Rouen and most of Upper Normandy, although he had to cede the important fortress of Gisors, and subsequently the entire Norman Vexin, to Louis VII of France as the price of his acceptance as duke. Geoffrey then adopted the ducal title and began to reestablish order in the duchy, and a year or two before his premature death in 1151 he handed over a pacified duchy to his eldest son Henry.

The long reign of Henry of Anjou as duke of Normandy (1149/50–1189) was to be one of the most important in the history of the duchy; but at its outset he faced a series of dangerous challenges both from within his duchy and from his neighbours. The deterioration of Angevin-Capetian relations from 1149, Henry's hasty but spectacular marriage to Eleanor of Aquitaine in 1152, and the young duke's overriding ambition to make good his claims to the English throne arrayed a formidable host of enemies against him, mainly on the borders of Normandy. They soon attracted some support from several Norman barons, including the frontier lords Richer de l'Aigle and Hugh de Gournay and Richard fitzCount in the heart of Normandy; the greatest and most brilliant nobleman in Normandy, Count Waleran of Meulan, was also implicated.[16] By 1154, Henry had defeated his enemies both within Normandy and without, and his position in the duchy from then on was secure. It is likely, however, that he did not forget his first taste of Norman resistance; perhaps he was never wholly at ease with his Norman subjects again.[17]

For the rest of the Angevin period, the Normans rarely appear in chronicles except

---

13  M. Chibnall, *The Empress Matilda: Queen Consort, Queen Mother and Lady of the English*, Oxford 1991, 149–90. For an introduction to Anjou and the Angevin dynasty, see J. Dunbabin, *France in the Making 843–1180*, 2nd edn, Oxford 2000, 184–90, 333–40.

14  For the period 1135–54 see Haskins, *Norman Institutions*, 123–55; J. Chartrou, *L'Anjou de 1109 à 1151: Foulque de Jérsualem et Geoffroi Plantegenêt*, Paris 1928, 36–76; M. Chibnall, 'Normandy', in *The Anarchy of King Stephen's Reign*, ed. E. King, Oxford 1994, 93–115; D. Crouch, *The Reign of King Stephen 1135–1154*, London 2000, 59–71, 147–53, 190–9, 247–53, 280–5.

15  *Orderic* vi, 480–94; *Torigni* i, 206–7. R. Helmerichs, 'King Stephen's Norman Itinerary, 1137', *Haskins Soc. Jnl* v, 1993, 89–97, and Crouch, *Reign of King Stephen*, 59–71, pass less damning judgments upon Stephen's expedition.

16  *Torigni* i, 253–5, 260–70, 286–7; D. Crouch, *The Beaumont Twins: the Roots and Branches of Power in the Twelfth Century*, Cambridge 1986, 71–6.

17  I owe this suggestion to the late Professor Thomas Keefe.

in moments of crisis. There were further border conflicts with the king of France in 1159–60 and 1160–61, during which Henry II recovered the Norman Vexin and Gisors, and in 1167–68.[18] Within his duchy Henry missed no opportunity to recover lands and rights which he believed to be his by right. Noble discontent at his actions soon materialised: when his eldest son Henry 'the Young King' rebelled against him in 1173, he won the support of many Norman nobles, although others rallied to the side of their duke.[19] The insurrection led to fighting in a number of districts of Normandy, mostly near the duchy's borders. In the north-east the counts of Flanders and Boulogne took Gournay, Aumale, Eu and Drincourt, helped by the collusion of the counts of Eu and Aumale. In south-eastern Normandy a Flemish attack near Pacy was repelled with heavy loss, but Louis VII of France burned part of the great fortress of Verneuil. The earl of Chester, who had extensive lands in Normandy and was hereditary *vicomte* of Avranches, joined forces on the borders of Normandy and Brittany with Hasculf de Saint-Hilaire, one of the chief instigators of the revolt,[20] and the Breton magnate Ralph de Fougères; but they were routed by the king's forces and, after taking refuge in the Breton town of Dol, soon surrendered to Henry II himself. In 1174 the rebels and their French allies made an abortive raid upon the city of Sées in January, and in the summer Louis VII besieged Rouen equally fruitlessly, just as the revolt was collapsing. The strength and luck of Henry II's forces and the loyalty of many Normans to their reigning duke had prevented the revolt spreading deep into the duchy from marcher regions, where the insurgents were sustained by external aid. It is a significant indication of the Old King's power within the duchy that rebels with castles in central Normandy made little or no attempt to base their rebellion on these fortresses.[21]

The period 1193–1204 forms a final, turbulent phase in the history of Angevin Normandy. In 1193, the captivity of Richard the Lionheart in Germany encouraged King Philip Augustus of France to invade the duchy, where he was assisted by several leading Anglo-Norman nobles, including King Richard's brother, Count John of Mortain, and Hugh de Gournay, Richard de Vernon, and the count of Meulan.[22] Most of the Norman nobility, however, remained conspicuously loyal to their captive prince and rejected John's attempt to woo them.[23] After the return of Richard I to Normandy in May 1194, most Norman rebels returned to his ranks with speed. However, the province suffered greatly at King Philip's hands from 1193 onwards. As in 1173–74, the length of the Franco-Norman marches from Verneuil to the county of Eu was devastated; war also spread to the borders with Brittany in 1196. In contrast to 1173–74, however, the king of France set out to win Norman territory for himself rather than merely supporting a dissident Angevin prince. In 1193 Gisors was surren-

[18] *Torigni* i, 326, 365–7; ii, 7–8; *Diceto* i, 330–1; Crouch, *Beaumont Twins*, 77–8; idem, *William Marshal: Court, Career and Chivalry in the Angevin Empire, 1147–1219*, London 1990, 30–2.

[19] W.L. Warren, *Henry II*, London 1973, 117–36, gives a fine if 'royalist' account of the revolt. The Norman rebels' names are known mainly from *Gesta Regis Henrici* i, 45–8, 57–8; *Torigni* ii, 35–46; *Diceto* i, 371; see J. Boussard, *Le Gouvernement d'Henri II Plantegenêt*, Paris 1956, 476–88, especially 477–9; T.K. Keefe, *Feudal Assessments and the Political Community under Henry II and his Sons*, Univ. California 1983, 236–7.

[20] For Hasculf's part in the rebellion, see *Torigni* ii, 35.

[21] E.g. the earl of Leicester and the count of Meulan: *Gesta Regis Henrici* i, 51; *Torigni* i, 36.

[22] D. Power, 'King John and the Norman Aristocracy', in *King John: New Interpretations*, ed. S.D. Church, Woodbridge 1999, 117–36, at 123.

[23] *Howden* iii, 204.

dered to King Philip by its constable, Gilbert de Vascœuil;[24] the king of France soon also acquired almost all the castles of the Epte, Eure and Avre valleys, including Château-sur-Epte, Pacy and Nonancourt; many of these fortresses were still in French hands at the death of Richard the Lionheart.[25] Beyond these border strongholds the king of France established a lasting foothold along the Seine valley as far as Gaillon, but was less successful elsewhere: for a time he held Évreux, Vaudreuil, Eu, Arques and Drincourt, but all were restored to Norman control by 1196.[26] Nevertheless, the duke's grip upon the eastern Norman marches remained insecure as well, despite Richard's breathtakingly rapid construction of several fortresses at Andely, above all La Roche-d'Andely, known to history as 'Château-Gaillard', in 1197–98. When Richard died suddenly from a wound in Poitou in April 1199, King Philip seized the city of Évreux and the surrounding district and recovered most of the Norman Vexin with ease, before Count John of Mortain could replace his brother Richard as duke as Normandy and king of England.[27]

Despite this revival in French power, few would have predicted that the king of France would conquer the entire province within five years. The history of the final years of ducal rule in Normandy is a sorry story of renewed war and suffering, which for the first time since 1154 afflicted central Normandy as well as the marches.[28] The duchy's fate was in part determined by events elsewhere in the Angevin lands in France, especially the claims of King John's nephew, Arthur of Brittany, and John's alienation of his mightiest subjects in Poitou and Anjou. Responding to the complaints of the Poitevins, King Philip declared forfeit the Angevin lands in France in April 1202, and subdued north-eastern Normandy as far as Arques. Nevertheless, John retained a reasonably secure hold upon the duchy until January 1203, when one of the greatest Norman magnates, the count of Sées, surrendered Alençon to the king of France. In the spring and summer of 1203 other magnates joined this new Norman revolt, notably Peter de Meulan, Hugh de Gournay and Richard de Vernon. Philip Augustus, confident of his success in the Loire provinces, returned to the attack in Normandy after nearly a year's respite: his capture of the fortresses of Vaudreuil and Radepont allowed him to close in around Andely with impunity. John's attempts to recapture Alençon in August and to relieve Château-Gaillard in October were lamentable failures. These defeats were the last straw for John; in December he left for England to rally more support, but he never returned to the duchy. On 6 March 1204 Château-Gaillard succumbed to a French assault; in May the king of France marched

---

24 Powicke, *Loss of Normandy*, 96. For Gilbert, see *T[rès] A[ncien] C[outumier]*, in *Coutumiers de Normandie*, ed. E.-J. Tardif, 2 vols in 3, Rouen and Paris 1881–1903, i, I, 108–9; D.J. Power, 'Between the Angevin and Capetian Courts: John de Rouvray and the Knights of the Pays de Bray, 1180–1225', in *Family Trees and the Roots of Politics*, ed. K.S.B. Keats-Rohan, Woodbridge 1997, 361–84, at 375–6, 378–9.

25 *Howden* iii, 205–8, 217–20, 252–60; *Newburgh* i, 389–90, 403; *Coggeshall*, 61–2; *Rigord*, 123–7; Powicke, *Loss of Normandy*, 96–8.

26 Powicke, *Loss of Normandy*, 107–8; J. Gillingham, *Richard I*, New Haven, Conn., and London 1999, 239–45, 283–97.

27 Power, 'King John', 123–6.

28 For the end of Angevin Normandy, see Powicke, *Loss of Normandy*, especially 127–69, 251–64; J.C. Holt, 'The Loss of Normandy and Royal Finance', in *War and Government in the Middle Ages*, ed. J. Gillingham and J.C. Holt, London 1984, 92–105; Power, 'King John'; idem, 'The End of Angevin Normandy: the Revolt at Alençon (1203)', *Historical Research* lxxii, 2001, 444–64; V. Moss, 'The Norman Exchequer Rolls of King John', in *King John*, ed. Church, 101–16; N. Barratt, 'The Revenues of John and Philip Augustus Revisited', ibid., 75–99.

to Argentan, Falaise and Caen, meeting little opposition, while his Breton allies breached the Norman defences in the south-west. King Philip then turned eastwards to Lisieux and Bec, before storming the barbican commanding the bridge at Rouen. It was enough to force the garrison to seek terms. On 24 June the surrender of Rouen, Arques and Verneuil ended sixty years of Angevin rule in Normandy.[29]

### Norman Government

By and large, the few chronicles for the period depict the history of Angevin Normandy as a dreary tale of Capetian sieges of Norman border castles, occasionally punctuated by Norman revolts but with the majority of Norman barons remaining loyal to their duke. The reasons for rebellion varied: longstanding rivalries between the dukes and some of their great subjects, particularly over castles, tended to flare up at times of ducal weakness, and French pressure on the eastern borders could have repercussions deeper into the duchy.[30] Yet most of the duchy enjoyed long periods of peace; that was why the rapacity of King John's mercenaries in central Normandy so shocked the Norman aristocracy. For the history of Angevin Normandy consists of far more than a laconic list of sieges and rebellions; the twelfth century was characterised by the development of what has been dubbed 'administrative rulership' in Western Europe, and Normandy provided one of the leading examples. Ducal administration was as rapacious and predatory as any other medieval government, as the spiralling costs of Richard I's campaigns recorded in the Norman exchequer rolls testify; but it also established procedures which endured when the Angevin dukes were but a memory.

### The ducal fisc

The evidence for the Norman exchequer in the reign of Henry I is very thin, and it may have been too embryonic to survive the disruptions of Stephen's reign. However, the ducal treasury at Rouen was functioning as a centre of fiscal organisation soon after the accession of Henry I's grandson Henry of Anjou (the future Henry II of England).[31] Repeatedly attempting to extract more revenue from Normandy, in 1171 Henry II ordered an inquest into the alienation of ducal lands which allegedly doubled his revenues.[32] Under his aegis a more formalised exchequer comparable to the English Exchequer was established not at Rouen but at Caen, perhaps by Richard of Ilchester in 1176 but more probably during the 1160s, a period of great reforms in Angevin administration.[33] Norman fiscal practice developed rapidly, with the exchequer as just one element in a complex and diverse financial system;[34] and in 1198,

---

[29] Powicke, *Loss of Normandy*, 256–63; for the three-week siege and the barbican, see William the Breton, *Rigord* i, 221; *RHF* xxiii, 358 (chronicle of Rouen).

[30] Cf. D.J. Power, 'What did the Frontier of Angevin Normandy Comprise?', *ANS* xvii, 1994, 181–201, at 186–9, 193–5.

[31] J.A. Green, 'Unity and Disunity in the Anglo-Norman State', *Historical Research* lxiii, 1989, 114–34, at 117–22; M. Chibnall, 'L'avènement au pouvoir d'Henri II', *CCM* xxxvii, 1994, 41–8.

[32] *Torigni* ii, 28.

[33] Green, 'Unity and Disunity', 121 and n. 34, 122; V. Moss, 'England and Normandy in 1180: the Pipe Roll Evidence', *England and Normandy*, 185–95, at 187–8.

[34] Packard, *Miscellaneous Records*, *passim*; V. Moss, 'Normandy and the Angevin Empire: a Study of

Robert, abbot of Saint-Étienne de Caen, was even sent over to England to reform the English exchequer. Although the abbot died soon after his arrival – unmourned, it was said, by the English justices and sheriffs who had dreaded his coming – his mission indicates how much the Norman practices of revenue-raising had impressed Richard I.[35]

In fact, Vincent Moss has argued that King Richard's reign saw a veritable 'fiscal revolution' in Normandy. The driving forces for this development, not surprisingly, were the exigencies of war: the costs of fortifications, garrisons and mercenaries to meet the repeated assaults from the king of France encouraged the régime to develop new ways of raising finance, with commendable success. Hitherto the system had relied heavily upon fixed farms paid by *prévôts* (local revenue-collectors) and *vicomtes* (local administrative and judicial officials); but by 1195 there had been a striking increase in the number of *ad hoc* levies such as tallages, forced loans and the ransom to free King Richard from his German captivity.[36] This increase was accompanied by an expansion in the number and extent of the *bailliages*, so that tallages and other exactions were now levied in areas which had hitherto paid little into the ducal coffers.[37] Moreover, unlike the traditional methods of revenue-raising, these innovations took account of the distribution of wealth by milking the flourishing Norman towns for all they were worth.[38] In 1180, ducal revenue in Normandy amounted to about 27,000 *livres angevines* (*l.a.*); in 1198, it comprised at least 97,000 *l.a.*, perhaps even as much as 150,000 *l.a.*[39]

It is less clear, though, how long Normandy could sustain such demands. What was the political price of such remorseless taxation when the wars showed few signs of abating? After 1204 King John increased his fiscal demands in England year after year; he vastly expanded his war finances but the political reaction to these demands contributed heavily to the Magna Carta crisis at the end of his reign.[40] The exactions of the 1190s and early 1200s may well have placed a similar strain upon the Normans before 1204. If so, the Norman 'fiscal revolution' helps to explain the unwillingness or inability of the Norman aristocracy to defend the duchy by 1204.

## Justice

The Angevin rulers are renowned for reforming and systematising the judicial systems of England; and their régime also had a significant impact upon the organisation of Norman justice.[41] Under Angevin rule the legal cases pertaining to the duke on account of their gravity, such as murder, maiming, theft, arson and rape, start to be described as the 'pleas of the sword', comparable to the English 'pleas of the

---

the Norman Exchequer Rolls 1180–1204', unpubl. Ph.D dissertation, University of Wales 1996, 127–46.

[35] *Howden* iv, 5; *Newburgh* ii, 464–5; Moss, 'Angevin Empire', 189–92.

[36] Moss, 'Norman Fiscal Revolution', 46–56.

[37] Moss, 'Angevin Empire', 133–8.

[38] Moss, 'Angevin Empire', 138–43, 193–4. See below, 82.

[39] Moss, 'Angevin Empire', 36–54, 63–4 (97,100–100,400 *l.a.*); Holt, 'Loss of Normandy', 96 (153,131 *l.a.*).

[40] N. Barratt, 'The Revenue of King John', *EHR* cxi, 1996, 835–55.

[41] Haskins, *Norman Institutions*, 158–95, remains fundamental. See also the works of Jean Yver cited below. For the extensive debates concerning Angevin justice in England the most significant recent work is J. Hudson, *Land, Law, and Lordship in Anglo-Norman England*, Oxford 1994, especially 253–81.

crown'.[42] Standardised writs emerged in Normandy before 1200, similar to those which had developed in England in a slightly earlier period.[43] As in England, the coronation of Richard I (1189) became a date from which legal memory in Normandy was calculated in the thirteenth century.[44] Also strikingly similar to English practices were the itinerant justices who regularly toured the duchy to hold assizes; the earliest Norman custumal (c. 1200) stated that judicial circuits took place twice a year in each *vicomté*.[45] We have little other evidence of these visitations,[46] but a charter of King John reveals the system operating in the *bailliage* of Falaise: the duke's *vicomte* or one of the ducal sergeants would normally summon the men of the *bailliage* to pleas in Falaise, where the itinerant justices would then preside over assizes dealing with all the cases from the *bailliage*.[47]

Another important development in the late twelfth century was the rise of the court of the Norman exchequer at Caen.[48] Although cases and agreements from as far away as the county of Mortain and the district of Nonancourt were heard there, its judicial importance was largely restricted to central and north-western Normandy.[49] Nevertheless, the exchequer was where the seneschal of Normandy is most often recorded, presiding there over the barons of Norman exchequer – administrators such as Abbot Samson of Caen or Ralph l'Abbé, the influential burgess of Sées and Argentan.[50] In addition the duke's officials held local courts which, wherever they were held, were regarded as the *curia regis* or 'court of the king' (of England); examples are found as far apart as Mortain in 1162–63, the Channel Islands in 1179, or Moulins-la-Marche on the southern Norman border in the 1190s.[51]

Half a century of Angevin justice and administration left its mark upon Norman customary law. The notion that Normandy had distinctive customs was well estab-

42 *TAC* (as n. 24) i, I, 43–4, 64–5; Haskins, *Norman Institutions*, 160–1, 187–8; D. Bates, *Normandy before 1066*, London 1982, 163.

43 *TAC* i, I, 95–6, 97, 99; Rouen, Bibl. Mun., Y 200 (cartulary of St-Gilles de Pont-Audemer), fos 44v–45r (six writs); J. Yver, 'Le bref anglo-normand', *Tijdschrift voor Rechtsgeschiedenis* xxix, 1961, 313–30.

44 *Recueil des Jugements de l'Échiquier de Normandie au XIIIe siècle*, ed. L. Delisle, Paris 1864, nos 325 (1222), 451 (1229). For the use of this date, see P. Brand, ' "Multis vigiliis excogitatam et inventam": Henry II and the Creation of the English Common Law', *Haskins Soc. Jnl* ii, 1990, 197–222, at 197–8.

45 *TAC* (as n. 24) i, I, 44.

46 Haskins, *Norman Institutions*, 165–9 (1155–65), 335–6 (1176–93); for other assizes, see BN, MS lat. 17759, fo. 78r–v (Rouen, 1155); MS lat. nouv. acq. 2231, no. 1 (Montfort-sur-Risle, 1171); MS lat. 10079, fo. 121r, no. 52 (Troarn, 1200); AD Orne, H 770 (Falaise, 1199x1200); AD Seine-Maritime, 14 HP 18 (Rouen, 1199), 20 HP 5 (Bernay, 1201); Archives Nationales, L 969, no. 340 (St-Lô, 1199x1204); *Rot. Norm.*, 42 (Bernay, c. 1200–1201); Moss, 'Angevin Empire', 64, following *MRSN* i, 272 (Bayeux, 1195); *Cartulaire de l'abbaye de la Luzerne*, ed. P.M. Dubosc, St-Lô 1878, no. XXXIV (St-Lô, 1196x1204).

47 *Rot. Norm.*, 20 (1200–1201); cf. Powicke, *Loss of Normandy*, 46n., 64n., 76–7.

48 Moss, 'Angevin Empire', 114–23.

49 D.J. Power, 'The Norman Frontier in the Twelfth and Early Thirteenth Centuries', unpubl. Ph.D. dissertation, University of Cambridge 1994, 199–200; Power, *Norman Frontier*, ch. 3. For cases from the county of Mortain, see Archives Nationales, L 976, no. 1143 (Le Teilleul, 1202); *The Charters of the Anglo-Norman Earls of Chester, c. 1071–1237*, ed. G. Barraclough, Chester 1988, no. 318 (Vale of Mortain, also concerning lands in Brittany and England, 1200); for a case from Illiers-l'Évêque near Nonancourt, see AD Eure, G 6, p. 17, no. 10 (*Cal. Docs France*, no. 309).

50 Moss, 'Angevin Empire', 114–23. For Ralph see Power, 'John de Rouvray', 383; AD Calvados, H 5637, describes him as 'Ralph l'Abbé of Argentan' (1196).

51 Rouen, Bibl. Mun., Coll. Leber 5636, MS 3122, no. 4; Haskins, *Norman Institutions*, 185; *Cartulaire de l'abbaye de Notre-Dame de la Trappe*, ed. le Comte de Charencey, Alençon 1889, 225.

lished long before 1144;[52] yet the resemblance of Norman customs to those of other Angevin provinces led the most prolific historian of Norman law, Jean Yver, to argue that a 'Plantagenet' zone of customary law developed under Henry II and his sons in western France.[53] Although this surely exaggerates the influence of the ruling dynasty upon the legal development of its different dominions, the importance of the Angevin rulers for Norman law was made plain in the first Norman custumal, written between 1200 and 1204. Many chapters of this treatise, the first part of the so-called *Très Ancien Coutumier*, closely resembled ducal proclamations. We should not look to the dukes alone for the source of these decrees, however, since most were issued at great court gatherings when the dukes sought the counsel and consent of their magnates.[54] The Norman aristocracy retained a sense of the distinctiveness of their provincial customs to the end of Angevin rule, for when Philip Augustus conquered Normandy, he prudently emphasised that the lands which he distributed were to be held 'according to the uses and customs of Normandy'.[55]

## Personnel

After the duke and the archbishop of Rouen, the most important figure in Angevin Normandy by 1200 was the seneschal. There had been seneschals or stewards in Normandy before 1144, but these household officials lacked the great judicial, fiscal and territorial power that the Seneschal of Normandy came to enjoy under the Angevins, and the office probably mirrored that of the seneschals of Anjou.[56] Up until 1180 we find sometimes one, sometimes several men at the head of Norman administration and justice. Henry of Anjou had conferred the stewardship (*dapiferatus*) of England and Normandy upon Robert, son of the earl of Leicester, in 1153, although this was primarily an honorary title.[57] Real power in Normandy, though, was wielded by the earl's cousin Robert du Neubourg, who had been a steward (*dapifer*) under Geoffrey of Anjou and who was described as 'steward and justice of all Normandy' at his death in 1159.[58] Bishops Arnulf of Lisieux (1141–81) and Rotrou of Évreux (1139–65) and Renaud de Saint-Valéry also acted as the chief justices in Normandy at times in the 1150s and 1160s. In the early 1170s William de Saint-Jean was variously described as 'governor' (*procurator*) and 'seneschal' of Normandy.[59] William de Courcy, head of the 'Norman' branch of that family, was 'justice' of Normandy soon afterwards, and after his death he was replaced in this post in 1176 by Richard of

52  E.Z. Tabuteau, *Transfers of Property in Eleventh-Century Norman Law*, Chapel Hill 1988, 224–5. For territorial aspects of Norman custom see also Power, 'Frontier of Angevin Normandy', 191–3.

53  J. Yver, 'Les caractères originaux des coutumes de l'Ouest', *Revue Historique du Droit Français et Étranger* 4 sér. xxx, 1952, 18–79, especially 21–7, 76–9.

54  J. Yver, 'Le *Très Ancien Coutumier* de Normandie, miroir de la législation ducale? Contribution à l'étude de l'ordre public normand à la fin du XIIe siècle', *Tijdschrift voor Rechtsgeschiedenis* xxxix, 1971, 333–74.

55  *Recueil des actes de Philippe Auguste, roi de France*, ed. H. Delaborde *et al.*, 4 vols, Paris 1916–79, ii, no. 845 (Oct. 1204) is the first example of this henceforth ubiquitous formula.

56  Boussard, *Gouvernement*, 364–70, traces the mingling of the posts of *dapifer, senescallus* and *justicia* under Henry II. For the chief office-holders in Normandy, see *Regesta* iii, xxx–xxxi, xxxv–xxxvii (1144–59); Haskins, *Norman Institutions*, 164–7.

57  *Recueil H II* i, no. XLVII*; Crouch, *Beaumont Twins*, 87.

58  *Torigni* i, 322: 'dapifer et justicia totius Normannie'.

59  *Torigni* ii, 31 (1171); P. Langlois, *Histoire du Prieuré du Mont-aux-Malades-lès-Rouen*, Rouen 1851, 429–30 (act of William l'Aiguillon, witnessed by 'Willelmo de Sancto Johanne senescallo Normannie').

Ilchester, bishop of Winchester (1173–88).[60] It is difficult to discern how permanent these positions were and how far their duties overlapped with one another. Under Richard's successor, William FitzRalph, however, the seneschal of Normandy became a permanent and pivotal figure in Norman administration, fulfilling much the same function in Normandy as the Justiciar in England.

William fitzRalph oversaw the duchy in all matters from about 1178 until his death in 1200.[61] A native of Derbyshire, he contrasted strongly with most of his predecessors because he was not a Norman magnate. Although mocked at the French court for his lack of martial skills,[62] he appears to have been trusted by the Norman barons, who, in the absence of Richard I on crusade, gathered behind the seneschal to rebut the French king's unacceptable demands in 1192.[63] Nevertheless, William fitzRalph is found chiefly at Caen in the judicial sessions of the Exchequer, and his legal decisions figure prominently in the *Très Ancien Coutumier*;[64] it was surely he who was remembered long afterwards in the great mid-thirteenth-century Norman custumal, the *Grand Coutumier*:

> In days of old a certain justiciar called the prince's seneschal, superior to the other justices, used to travel around Normandy. He would correct what the lesser justices omitted to do, would guard the prince's territory, would ensure that the laws and customs of Normandy were properly maintained, and whatever the *baillis* did unjustly he would correct.[65]

After the stable régime of William fitzRalph the office of seneschal passed through a far more turbulent phase, being rotated almost every year, before being suppressed entirely by Philip Augustus. King John first gave the office to Guérin de Glapion, who haled from Sainte-Scolasse on the southern border of Normandy with Perche; his time as seneschal was brief, although he remained high in King John's favour until 1203, when he joined Philip Augustus.[66] In 1201 Ralph Taisson, lord of Thury near Falaise and Saint-Sauveur in the Cotentin, became seneschal.[67] Perhaps by choosing a powerful Norman magnate King John was hoping to appease the Norman nobility; if so, his final candidate for seneschal, in May 1203, appears intended to incense them. William le Gras (*Crassus*) was from an Anglo-Norman baronial family long established in central Normandy and was a kinsman of William Marshal and Ralph Taisson;[68] nevertheless, he tended to favour John's detested mercenaries and was

60  *Gesta Regis Henrici* i, 124, 125; *Receuil H II*, intro., 476–8, which, however, confuses the Norman and English William de Courcy. AD Calvados, H 7076, an act of Gervase de Fresnay for St-Pierre-sur-Dives, was performed 'coram domino Will(elm)o de Curceio senescallo Normann(ie)'.

61  For William fitzRalph, see Haskins, *Norman Institutions*, 183–4; Powicke, *Loss of Normandy*, 51–2, 65; J. Le Patourel, 'Guillaume fils Raoul, sénéchal de Normandie, 1178–1200', *Annales de Normandie* xxx, 1980, 321–2.

62  *H[istoire de] G[uillaume le] M[aréchal]*, ed. P. Meyer, 3 vols, Paris 1891–94, i, lines 7517–28, 7596–604 (iii, 88–90): a French courtier jestingly proposed that the seneschal should be one of King Henry's champions. William Marshal replied that the seneschal was brave and wise but too old to fight.

63  *Gesta Regis Henrici* ii, 236; *Howden* iii, 182.

64  *TAC* (as n. 24) i, I, e.g. 52–3, 55–6; cf. Haskins, *Norman Institutions*, 183–4.

65  *Summa de legibus in curia laicali*, in *Coutumiers de Normandie*, ed. Tardif, ii, 12, c. IV *bis*.

66  *MRSN* i, 244–5; Powicke, *Loss of Normandy*, 173–4; Power, 'King John', 133n.

67  Powicke, *Loss of Normandy*, 173, 352–3.

68  N.C. Vincent, 'The Borough of Chipping Sodbury and the Fat Men of France', *Transactions of the Bristol and Gloucestershire Record Society* cxvi, 1998, 42–59, at 44–6.

afterwards credited with turning the Norman barons against John in 1203.[69] A generation later he was remembered with loathing in the region around Falaise for using his
power as seneschal to extort lands from his neighbours; hence the king of France
confiscated the lands of William le Gras as he marched through this district in 1204,
and loudly excluded him from his amnesty to the Normans.[70] Yet despite their
different backgrounds and deeds, all three of John's seneschals continued the
adminstrative activities of William fitzRalph, presiding over the Exchequer and
assizes and assisting in the financing of John's wars.

Compared to the seneschals, the other main Norman 'household' officials were far
less important and their offices tended to be hereditary. Under Duke Geoffrey the
constableship came to rest with Richard du Hommet (d. 1178x1180), whose son
William (d. c. 1204) received the office as a hereditary fief from Henry II; it was more
than an honorary function, for Richard du Hommet led the army of Normandy into
Brittany in 1164 and against the king of France in 1173, while in 1180 William du
Hommet was constable of the border fortress of Pontorson.[71] By the end of the twelfth
century the constable's title was being territorialised, so that William du Hommet
began to describe himself as 'constable of Normandy' rather than the previous style,
'the lord king's constable'. The position of chamberlain had been held by the lords of
Tancarville since the eleventh century, but in contrast to the constables, they rarely if
ever called themselves 'chamberlain of Normandy', even after 1204.[72] While the
office was largely honorific by the Angevin period, William de Tancarville famously
insisted upon his hereditary right to wash the duke's hands at the Christmas feast of
1182;[73] the forcefulness with which he made his symbolic request reflected his
strained relationship with Henry II, for his chamberlainship had not prevented
William de Tancarville joining the revolt of the Young King in 1173.[74]

Apart from the seneschal the main figures of Angevin administration came to be
the bailiffs or *baillis*. As the earliest use of the terms *baillivus* and *baillia* dates from
the reign of Geoffrey of Anjou, these officials seem to have been installed as a remedy
for the chaos afflicting Normandy after the death of Henry I.[75] In both fiscal and judicial affairs the *baillis* gradually replaced the *vicomtes* as the main agents of ducal
power, although this transition was by no means complete in 1204. By 1180 there
were about twenty-five *baillis*, presiding over defined *bailliages*: at least six more
appeared between 1180 and 1195, but others disappeared,[76] as the dukes gave away
the domains and fortresses which formed the basis of these *bailliages*.[77] More signifi-

---

69 *Diplomatic Documents* i, ed. P. Chaplais, London 1964, no. 206.

70 Power, 'King John', 133–4; *Actes de Philippe Auguste* ii, nos 792–6; *Layettes du Trésor des Chartes*,
ed. A. Teulet *et al.*, 5 vols, Paris 1863–1909, i, no. 716.

71 *Recueil H II* ii, no. DXLIX (c. 1180); *Torigni* i, 353; *Gesta Regis Henrici* i, 45; cf. Boussard,
*Gouvernement*, 363–4; *MRSN* i, 40.

72 Cf. J. Green, *The Government of Henry I*, Cambridge 1986, 275; GEC x, app. F, 47–54.

73 Walter Map, *De Nugis Curialium*, ed. and trans. M.R. James, rev. C.N.L. Brooke and R.A.B. Mynors,
Oxford 1983, 488–94.

74 *Torigni* ii, 39; *Gesta Regis Henrici* i, 45.

75 Haskins, *Norman Institutions*, 151–2; Boussard, *Gouvernement*, 335–6.

76 Powicke, *Loss of Normandy*, 52–4, 68–76; Moss, 'Angevin Empire', 42, 133–8.

77 Cf. Power, 'Frontier of Angevin Normandy', 189 and n. 35 (Moulins); idem, 'King John', 125
(Drincourt).

cantly, the *bailliages* became the main channels through which the dukes extorted tall-ages and forced loans during the crippling wars at the end of the century.[78]

### Coinage and fouage

A striking development under Angevin rule was the introduction of the money of Angers as the main coinage in Normandy.[79] Like all French provinces Normandy was accustomed to coins minted elsewhere: the coinage of Le Mans, for instance, had been regularly used in southern Normandy since the eleventh century and was still widespread until the 1220s, while by 1200 trade and war were bringing immense quantities of English silver into Normandy. However, from the 1140s onwards, the mint of Rouen was in Angevin hands and the *denier angevin* (Angers penny) began to oust the indigenous Norman coin, the Rouen penny, as the standard currency in the duchy. The *denier angevin* remained the main unit of account there until 1204, when Philip Augustus replaced it with the money of Tours, which had the same value. Since the moneys of Angers, Le Mans and England were all being minted for the Angevin dynasty from 1154 to 1204, they developed a simple ratio of 4:2:1 for exchange purposes: the penny sterling, which contained an unusually high proportion of silver, was worth four *deniers angevins* or two *deniers mançais*.

By the middle of the Angevin period the duke was levying a 'hearth-tax' (Latin *focagium*, Fr. *fouage*) from each household in the duchy, and in return he remitted his notional right to remint all coins every three years. Knights, clergy and some other privileged groups, notably millers, were exempt, as were those widows who were too poor to pay; the names of all those obliged to pay were to be written down whenever the tax was collected.[80] It is generally assumed that this tax was of eleventh-century origin; nevertheless, the earliest concrete evidence for its existence comes from the reign of Henry II.[81] Whatever its date of origin, the tax symbolised the pervasive influence of ducal power in most of Normandy, and the fact that the southernmost lord-ships of Normandy were mostly exempt from the tax accords with the late twelfth-century view that the duke's control over coinage did not extend to the marches of his duchy.[82]

In general, ducal government was built upon longstanding Norman traditions but was significantly regularised and strengthened in the Angevin period. The seneschal of Normandy, the *baillis*, the adoption of the money of Angers and various aspects of customary law all reflected the impact of Angevin rule. The history of Norman ad-ministration between 1144 and 1204 also shows the continuing importance of the duchy's connection with England, where many of the chief agents of ducal power had cut their administrative teeth. Yet it simultaneously demonstrated that the indigenous creativity which had characterised Norman rule in the eleventh century was by no

---

[78] See above, 69.

[79] For coinage, see F. Dumas, 'Les monnaies normandes', *Revue Numismatique* 6e sér. xxi, 1979, 84–140, especially 96–101; Power, 'The Norman Frontier', 275–312.

[80] T.N. Bisson, *The Conservation of Coinage: Monetary Exploitation and its Restraint in France, Catalonia and Aragon c. 1000–1225 AD*, Oxford 1979, 14–28, 204–5; *Les Registres de Philippe Auguste*, ed. J.W. Baldwin, i (*texte*), Paris 1992, 556–7. I discuss *fouage* in detail in my forthcoming monograph.

[81] Bisson, *Conservation of Coinage*, 19–20, suggests a date of c. 1078.

[82] *TAC* (as n. 24) i, I, 65.

means spent; the kings of England relied heavily upon native expertise and initiatives in governing Normandy until 1204, and the kings of France did the same thereafter.

## The Norman Aristocracy

The three pillars of Norman political society were the aristocracy, the Church and the towns. One of the striking factors in the eleventh-century Norman expansion had been the cooperation of an aggressive, close-knit military élite; but this harmony of interests had dwindled by the time of Henry I, largely because some families retained extensive lands in England whereas for others the island colony had ceased to be of importance.[83] In the Angevin period most of the greatest families in Normandy also had important possessions elsewhere; many had far more lands in England (and sometimes also Wales and Ireland) than in Normandy, including the earls of Leicester, Chester, Gloucester, Striguil, Essex and Warenne, and the counts of Aumale and Mortain.[84] The Talvas dynasty, later known as the counts of Sées or Alençon, had a sizeable lordship across the border in north-east Maine, and William Talvas (d. 1171) was also count of Ponthieu. Until 1181 the counts of Évreux were lords of Montfort-l'Amaury in *Francia*; thereafter they no longer had French lands but became coheirs of the earldom of Gloucester.[85] The counts of Eu and Aumale had great estates in England as well as lands in *Francia*; moreover, Richard I gave Alice, countess of Eu, in marriage to the Poitevin lord Ralph de Lusignan, and married Countess Hawise of Aumale – already the widow of the earl of Essex – to another Poitevin, William de Fors (d. 1195), and then to the Flemish knight Baldwin de Béthune.[86] In sum, hardly any of the greatest nobles in the duchy would have regarded their Norman lands as their most important possessions; they belonged to a much wider Anglo-French world, and in 1204, many chose to leave the duchy for the sake of their English lands.

Below this handful of great lineages, however, there was a second tier of families whose landed wealth was concentrated in Normandy; notable families included Neubourg, Hommet, Taisson, Harcourt, Tancarville, Bertram, Gournay, l'Aigle, Vernon and Tillières. Since 1066 a considerable number of lineages had divided into branches based predominantly on one side of the Channel, but these often retained some interests in the other country. In the late twelfth century, the more 'English' branch of the Courcy family was based at Stogursey (Stoke Courcy) in Somerset but

---

83 J.A. Green, 'King Henry I and the Aristocracy of Normandy', *La France Anglaise: 111e Congrès National des Sociétés Savantes (Poitiers 1986), Histoire Médiévale I*, Poitiers 1988, 161–73; idem, 'Unity and Disunity', 128–33; D. Crouch, 'Normans and Anglo-Normans: a Divided Aristocracy?', *England and Normandy*, 51–67.

84 Powicke, *Loss of Normandy*, 328–58, although neither comprehensive nor accurate in every detail, remains an indispensable guide to the aristocracy of Angevin Normandy, whereas Boussard, *Gouvernement*, 87–99, is full of errors. For the Norman counts and the frontier lineages, see my forthcoming monograph. The only counts of Mortain in this period were William of Blois (1153–59), younger son of King Stephen, and John (1189–99), the future king of England.

85 K. Thompson, 'William Talvas, Count of Ponthieu, and the Politics of the Anglo-Norman Realm', *England and Normandy*, 169–84; Power, 'Frontier of Angevin Normandy', 197–8.

86 GEC v, 160–6; i, 353–5; B. English, *The Lordship of Holderness 1086–1260*, Oxford 1979, 27–37. For Baldwin's Flemish lands see *Layettes* v, nos 126, 140.

had lands near Falaise and Bonneville,[87] whereas the senior, more 'Norman' branch held Courcy itself but retained lands in Kent, Oxfordshire and Hampshire until 1204.[88] Of three branches into which the Pantulf family had divided by 1166, one was exclusively based in England,[89] one endowed mostly or entirely in Normandy,[90] and the third retained lands in both countries until 1204, when its head chose to dwell in England.[91] The family of Étouteville or Stuteville had split into essentially 'English' and 'Norman' branches in the reign of Henry I, but the 'Norman' (Valmont) branch retained English lands and substantially augmented its interests on both sides of the Channel through the marriage of Robert de Stuteville of Valmont to Leonia de Rames.[92] The Norman baronage was a relatively stable group: despite disruptions caused by rebellion or lack of sons, a great many families in 1200 held the same lordships as a century earlier. Even the 'newer' families could be deceptively 'old': Richard du Hommet, described by Davis and Cronne as one of Henry II's 'new men',[93] was probably a great-grandson of Bishop Odo of Bayeux, half-brother of William the Conqueror.[94] With the retreat of the English earls and other Anglo-Norman magnates to England in 1204, most members of this second tier of barons chose to stay in Normandy and became the leading families of the duchy from then on.

As well as the great nobles the Norman aristocracy included a notional total of over two thousand knights in Normandy,[95] many of whom emerge from obscurity for the first time during the Angevin period because they begin to issue their own charters for monasteries on a regular basis. For example, Landry d'Orbec, who joined the rebellion of the Young King in 1173, perhaps in the retinue of his lord Robert de Montfort, was very probably descended from an earlier Landry d'Orbec (d. c. 1090), *vicomte* and 'pleader in courts' (*causidicus*) of Orbec, but only from the late twelfth century do the religious benefactions of the Orbec family enable us to reconstruct a continuous genealogy.[96] This example suggests that these knightly families had often played a significant role in Norman society long before the more abundant documents of the Angevin period bring them out of obscurity; but in the second half of the twelfth century they began to acquire a more prominent position still. Outwardly most of them followed the great nobles: an inquest which Henry II ordered to be executed in

[87] AD Calvados, H 6694, and AD Orne, H 2009 (*Cal. Docs France*, nos 1199, 1200): lands at Villy and Pomerville near Falaise, and Saint-Arnoult (near Bonneville?). For this branch see W. Farrer, *Honors and Knights' Fees*, 3 vols, London and Manchester 1923–25, i, 103–8.

[88] Powicke, *Loss of Normandy*, 337; *VCH Oxon.* i, 209, and *The Book of Fees commonly called Testa de Nevill*, 3 vols, HMSO 1920–31, i, 614 (William, brother of the 'Norman' Robert de Courcy).

[89] J. Meisel, *Barons of the Welsh Frontier: the Corbet, Pantulf, and Fitz Warin Families, 1066–1272*, Lincoln, Nebraska, 1980, 23–33, 77–85 (Wem, Shrops.).

[90] AD Calvados, H 6679: nine acts of the Pantulfs and their successors, the Bouquetots, concerning Samesle (Orne, cant. Vimoutiers, cne. Le Sap).

[91] AD Calvados, H 6679 (two acts, including *Cal. Docs France*, no. 597, also Samesle); *Early Yorkshire Charters IX*, ed. C.T. Clay, Yorkshire Archaeological Society 1952, 25–7 (Breedon, Leics.).

[92] *Early Yorkshire Charters IX*, 1–17, 41–55.

[93] *Regesta* iii, p. xxxv.

[94] D. Bates, 'Notes sur l'aristocratie normande', *Annales de Normandie* xxiii, 1973, 7–38, at 33–7.

[95] Boussard, 'L'enquête de 1172', 207–8, estimates 2,800 knights' fees in Normandy in 1172; Keefe, *Feudal Assessments*, 73–4, 225–6, calculates c. 2,500.

[96] *Gesta Regis Henrici* i, 45–6; *Orderic* iv, 242; AD Seine-Maritime, 56 HP 1 (abbey of Camp-Souverain); AD Eure, H 548, H 550, H 571 (Lyre Abbey acts); AD Calvados, H. Suppl. 484 (II. A. 6) (Hôtel-Dieu de Lisieux).

1172, the *Infeudationes Militum*, recorded the knight-service which the bishops, counts, barons and some lesser landowners owed to the duke of Normandy, and usually services owed to themselves as well.[97] The following entries are typical. 'The bishop of Bayeux, the service of twenty knights and 120 in his own service.' 'William de Briouze, three knights for the honour of Briouze, and the service of one knight for Couvert.' Yet few of these knights would serve their lord unquestioningly, simply because they held a knight's fee from him. During the revolt of the count of Sées against King John in 1203 some, perhaps the majority, of the count's knights in central Normandy did not join his rebellion; a number were still in arms against him when Rouen surrendered.[98] Magnates relied upon a variety of means to build up their power. As early as the 1140s the power of Waleran, count of Meulan in 'France' and lord of Beaumont, Brionne and Pont-Audemer in Normandy, was founded not only upon formal ties defined by land tenure and military service, but also upon a sizeable but unstable affinity of kinsmen and cronies who greatly increased his influence in and around the Seine valley.[99]

Even the most loyal honorial baron in Angevin Normandy might have multiple obligations. Hugh de Bacquepuis came from a family which had been associated with the counts of Évreux since the eleventh century, and he was one of the most frequent testators of the acts of Counts Simon (d. 1181), whose seneschal he was for a time, and Amaury III (d. c. 1191).[100] Yet Hugh had connections with another magnate from the Évrecin, Roger de Tosny, and also served as a ducal justice in the Norman Vexin.[101] So it would be misleading to describe Hugh de Bacquepuis merely as the man of the counts of Évreux; his activities were clearly much more diverse. Many other members of the lesser aristocracy in Angevin Normandy had a close association with a magnate, but were independent enough to enter ducal service. In central and southern Normandy Kathleen Thompson has identified at least four associates of Count William Talvas whom the dukes lured into their administration.[102] For some, ducal service brought great power and status indeed. John de Préaux, a minor baron from near Rouen, had joined the Young King's revolt in 1173, but like many other former rebels he and his four brothers became favoured 'royal companions' of Richard I, especially during the Third Crusade; during the expedition the third brother, Roger, acted as the king's steward in the early stages and the fourth, William, fell into Saracen hands in order to save the king from capture.[103] Of them the *History of William the Marshal* said, 'Never between Rouen and Le Mans were there five better brothers, and no king or count was finer than they.'[104] In 1204 Peter de Préaux

97   *The Red Book of the Exchequer*, ed. H. Hall, 3 vols, RS 1896, ii, 624–47 (*Registres de Philippe Auguste*, 267–76); J. Boussard, 'L'enquête de 1172 sur les services de chevalier en Normandie', in *Recueil de travaux offerts à M. Clovis Brunel*, 2 vols, Paris 1955, i, 193–207; Keefe, *Feudal Assessments*, 4–6, 141–53.

98   Power, 'King John', 131; idem, 'The revolt at Alençon', 447–8.

99   Crouch, *Beaumont Twins*, e.g. 35–7, 51–4, 59–60, 76–7, 214–15.

100  *Chartes de l'abbaye de Jumièges*, ed. J.J. Vernier, 2 vols, Rouen and Paris 1916, i, no. LXXI.

101  BN, MS lat. 17048, p. 432; A. Le Prévost, *Mémoires et notes pour servir à l'histoire du département de l'Eure*, 3 vols, Évreux 1862–69, i, 148.

102  Thompson, 'William Talvas', 179–80.

103  *Gesta Regis Henrici* i, 46–7; Landon, *Itinerary of Richard I, passim* (including Roger as steward until the king's stay at Messina); Ambroise, *Estoire de la Guerre Sainte*, ed. G. Paris, Paris 1897, e.g. lines 4729–30 ('des compaignons reials'), 7121–6, 12264–70 (capture and ransom of William de Préaux).

104  *HGM* (as n. 62) i, lines 4662–74; cf. iii, 59 n. 1. I am grateful to Catherine Hanley for discussing this passage with me.

commanded the garrison of Rouen for King John, whereas John de Préaux helped to organise the surrender of Norman castles for Philip Augustus – while simultaneously giving his son as hostage for Peter's good faith.[105] Most knights found no such fortune, but their services in arms, rents and administrative activities continued to form one of the bases of both ducal and baronial power.

### The Norman Church

The history of the Church in Angevin Normandy was far from untroubled. The dukes repeatedly clashed with cathedral chapters over episcopal elections, affecting at least five of the seven Norman bishoprics between 1144 and 1204.[106] In the diocese of Sées, part of which lay outside the duchy in the county of Perche, Bishop Gerard (1144–57) was persecuted and perhaps even castrated by the followers of Geoffrey of Anjou, a crime which Gerald of Wales repeatedly linked with the murder of Thomas Becket as the greatest of the Angevins' enormities.[107] Henry II famously drove Bishop Arnulf of Lisieux into exile at Paris, although the bishop had been compromised by his support for the Young King's rebellion.[108] In 1196 Archbishop Walter of Rouen (1184–1207) clashed bitterly with Richard I over the manor of Andely, fled to Paris and placed Normandy under an interdict.[109] In 1202–1203, King John refused to accept the election of a new bishop by the chapter of Sées, and Normandy incurred a papal interdict as a result; Innocent III also believed that John was harming the chapter of Coutances.[110] In the remaining Norman dioceses, Évreux, Bayeux and Avranches, the kings of England certainly secured the election of their *familiares*.[111]

On the basis of these assorted quarrels, Sidney Packard maintained that the Norman episcopal hierarchy came to regard the king of France as a potential liberator from Angevin oppression, while John Baldwin has argued that Philip Augustus cultivated the Norman church with lavish gifts before 1204. Yet the evidence is too sparse to support the view that there was an Angevin 'tyranny' against the Norman Church, still less that the Capetians appeared as its saviours.[112] Each dispute seems to have had

105  *Layettes* i, no. 716; Power, 'King John', 135. The fifth brother, Enguerrand, was closely associated with King John before he became king (S.D. Church, *The Household Knights of King John*, Cambridge 1999, 21–2), and is not recorded on the Crusade.

106  For the Angevins and episcopal elections in general see I.P. Shaw, 'The Ecclesiastical Policy of Henry II on the Continent', *Church Quarterly Review* cli, 1951, 137–55; R.V. Turner, 'Richard Lionheart and the Episcopate in his French Domains', *French Historical Studies* xxi, 1998, 517–42.

107  *Giraldi Cambrensis Opera* viii, 160, 301, 309; cf. *The Letters of Arnulf Bishop of Lisieux*, ed. F. Barlow, Camden Soc. 3rd ser. lxi, London 1939, xxxiv and no. 3; *Diceto* i, 256.

108  *Letters of Arnulf of Lisieux*, l–lix; G. Teske, 'Ein unerkanntes Zeugnis zum Sturz des Bischofs Arnulf von Lisieux?', *Francia* xvi, 1989, 185–206.

109  *Diceto* ii, 141–2, 148–50; Powicke, *Loss of Normandy*, 113–16.

110  *Selected Letters of Innocent III concerning England (1198–1216)*, ed. C.R. Cheney and W.H. Semple, London 1953, 51, no. 17; for the Sées dispute, see below, 79.

111  Turner, 'Richard Lionheart and the Episcopate', 523–5.

112  S.R. Packard, 'King John and the Norman Church', *Harvard Theological Review* xv, 1922, 15–31; J.W. Baldwin, 'Philip Augustus and the Norman Church', *French Historical Studies* vi, 1969, 1–30, at 1–6; idem, *The Government of Philip Augustus*, Berkeley, California, 1986, 179–83, 186–8; cf. *Letters of Arnulf of Lisieux*, li. For criticism, see W.B. Stevenson, 'England and Normandy, 1204–59', unpublished Ph.D. dissertation, 2 vols, University of Leeds 1974, 29–52, 113–36; Power, 'Frontier of Angevin Normandy', 196 n. 68. I discuss this problem in detail in my forthcoming paper, 'The

a very specific context. For most of its course the Sées election conflict of 1202–1203 was a very localised affair, and apart from levelling scurrilous accusations against the chapter's candidate, the archdeacon Silvester, King John's letters appear dignified and restrained, appealing to the dukes' traditional rights over the Norman Church. Moreover, John gave way soon after the interdict was imposed.[113] Richard the Lionheart's quarrel with the archbishop of Rouen certainly caused a great rift between them, but Archbishop Walter had previously come to blows with the king of France over the same manor; in any case, once Richard I had generously compensated the archbishop with the port of Dieppe and two rich manors in 1197 and King John had resolved the difficulties which this exchange caused in 1200, the dispute may be treated as resolved.[114] After 1204 Walter made no attempt to recover Andely from Philip Augustus, whose scribes instead copied the charters of Richard and John into the Capetian registers.[115] During the Andely dispute Richard I had been supported by the bishops of Évreux and Lisieux, and King John confirmed the judicial privileges of the bishop of Lisieux soon afterwards.[116]

There are many signs of a warmer relationship between the Norman Church and Angevin dukes. The frequency with which ecclesiastics witnessed ducal charters and participated in the administration of the duchy needs no retelling here. The ducal family also contributed generously to the new religious orders that had been gaining footholds in the duchy since the early twelfth century. The sixty years of Angevin rule witnessed the establishment of numerous Cistercian houses, mainly in Upper Normandy, and in 1147 the Order of Cîteaux absorbed Normandy's only native order, the Order of Savigny, including numerous houses in Lower Normandy.[117] The three main orders of canons all founded houses in Normandy in the twelfth century, mostly after 1135: the Premonstratensians established abbeys at Lucerne and Blanchelande in the west, Île-Dieu and Bellozanne in the east, and Ardenne, Mondaye and Silly-en-Gouffern in central Normandy; Augustinian canons appeared at Montmorel and Saint-Lô in western Normandy and Plessis-Grimoult, Sainte-Barbe, Le Val and Corneville in the centre; and Victorine canons were established at Cherbourg (Le Vœu) and took over the abbey of Eu. Most often religious houses of the reformed orders were founded by a magnate family and patronised by the lesser aristocracy of the district, but the abbeys of Le Valasse, La Noë, Silly-en-Gouffern and Cherbourg all owed their foundation wholly or in part to Empress Matilda, and her son and grandsons encouraged the Orders of Cîteaux, Grandmont, Prémontré and Saint-Victor as well as the military orders.[118] So far as orders of women are concerned

Norman Church and the Angevin and Capetian Kings', *The Plantagenets and the Church*, ed. N.C. Vincent.

113 *Rot. Litt. Pat.*, 8, 16 (accusing Silvester of adultery); *Rot. de Lib.*, 72.

114 Landon, *Itinerary of Richard I*, frontispiece (facsimile); *Diceto* ii, 154–6; *Rot. Norm.*, 1–3; *Rot. Chart.*, 59, 69.

115 *Registres de Philippe Auguste*, 477–9, 483–5.

116 *Diceto* ii, 149; *RHF* xviii, 358; Gillingham, *Richard I*, 302n., 344; *Rot. Chart.*, 19 (*Registres de Philippe Auguste*, 481–2).

117 L. Grant, 'The Architecture of the Early Savignacs and Cistercians in Normandy', *ANS* x, 1987, 111–43.

118 E.M. Hallam, 'Henry II, Richard I and the Order of Grandmont', *JMH* i, 1975, 165–86, e.g. 179; *Actes de Henri II* ii, no. DCXXVI (cf. intro., 298, 301–2); Chibnall, *Empress Matilda*, 179–81; acts for the Templars include *Recueil H II* ii, no. DXXIII; Rouen, Bibl. Mun., Y 201, fos 19v–20r (Richard I); for the Hospitallers, *Cartulaire Normand de Philippe Auguste, Louis VIII, Saint Louis et Philippe-le-Hardi*, ed. L. Delisle, Caen 1852, no. 27 (Richard I). A full study of Norman knightly

the chief development was the spread into Upper Normandy of the Order of Fontevraud, with which the Angevin dynasty had particularly close links.[119] In monastic chronicles the dukes frequently appear as conventional patrons, protectors, and benefactors; but reactions to the death of Henry the Young King in 1183 provides a more convincing illustration of the importance of the ruling dynasty to the Norman Church. The dying prince had allegedly expressed a wish to be buried at Rouen Cathedral,[120] and so the canons of Rouen and their Norman compatriots fought tooth-and-nail against the canons of Le Mans and men of Maine, with success but without dignity, to have the Young King's body buried in their cathedral rather than at Le Mans; furthermore, miracles were soon occurring at the young Henry's tomb.[121] A warm relationship extended into more overtly political matters. In 1173, all the bishops of Normandy except Arnulf of Lisieux supported Henry II;[122] in 1203 churchmen such as the archdeacon of Lisieux actively supported King John's war effort, and John is said to have given Archbishop Walter an important say in the defence of Rouen in 1203–1204.[123]

So the Norman Church should be seen as at worst indifferent to the Angevins rather than in a state of incurable hostility. In a dispute between the citizens and canons of Rouen over ecclesiastical privilege in 1207, the French king's officials sought to placate the canons by offering to observe the customs of Henry II and Richard I; but the canons refused to abide by anything other than the proclamations of the eleventh-century Council of Lillebonne – the period of Angevin rule, it seems, was best forgotten.[124] Yet this does not mean that the Capetians appeared preferable to Normandy's former rulers. The king of France had proved no friend of the Norman Church in 1194, when he sacked and destroyed Évreux Cathedral and the abbey of Saint-Taurin; did the canons of Évreux recall this, perhaps, when six years later he ostentatiously granted them the right of free election? King Philip gave almost no gifts to the Norman Church after 1204; almost all his acts and payments on its behalf merely confirmed earlier gifts made by the local aristocracy.[125] Even after the fall of Rouen the Norman bishops had enough qualms about the disinheritance of their duke to seek papal guidance as to whether they should accept King Philip, rather than welcoming him as a liberator.[126]

Certain other characteristics of the Norman Church in this period merit consideration. Despite the Angevin conquest of Normandy the Norman Church continued in many respects to form part of a single Anglo-Norman Church rather than being integrated into a broader 'Angevin' ecclesiastical system. Hence Henry II made the Englishman Walter de Coutances archbishop of Rouen (1184–1207), while Richard I

religious patronage of the new orders remains to be written, but see Thompson, 'William Talvas', 178 (Gouffern); Power, 'End of Angevin Normandy', 449–58 (La Noë).

119  J.M. Bienvenu, 'L'ordre de Fontevraud et la Normandie au XIIe siècle', *Annales de Normandie* xxxv, 1985, 3–15.

120  *Cal. Docs France*, nos 35–8.

121  *Torigni* ii, 120–2; *Gesta Regis Henrici* i, 303–4; *Howden* ii, 280; Thomas Agnellus, 'Sermo de morte et sepultura Henrici regis junioris', *Coggeshall*, 263–73; *Newburgh* i, 234.

122  *Gesta Regis Henrici* i, 51 n. 4; Teske, 'Ein unerkanntes Zeugnis', 185–206.

123  *Rot. Norm.*, 101–3; *Histoire des ducs de Normandie*, 97–8.

124  *Antiquus Cartularius Ecclesiæ Baiocensis*, ed. V.A. Bourrienne, Rouen and Paris 1902–1903, ii, no. CCCIV (*RHF* xxiv, I, *preuves*, no. 16). Henry II himself had ordered the prelates and barons of Normandy to observe the canons of Lillebonne in 1162 (*Torigni* i, 336).

125  Power, 'Frontier of Angevin Normandy', 196 n. 68; idem, 'Norman Church'.

126  Baldwin, 'Norman Church', 1–2; Stevenson, 'England and Normandy', 48–52.

appointed Normans to the sees of Ely and London, respectively William de Longchamps (1189–97) and William de Sainte-Mère-Église (1198–1221). These bishops often brought armies of clerics in their wake who were soon granted prebends in their new cathedral chapters: Archbishop Rotrou of Rouen (1165–83) filled the chapter of Rouen Cathedral with clerks associated with the great Beaumont-Meulan kin-group to which he belonged, whereas his English successor Walter de Coutances (1184–1207) displaced this clique and introduced many canons from Lincoln where he had briefly been bishop.[127] Although such irruptions disturbed the harmony of these great establishments, they also demonstrate the ease with which the higher clergy moved between England and Normandy. The Norman Church does not seem to have been integrated with the other Angevin lands in France to anything like the same extent; so far as the higher clergy were concerned there was an 'Anglo-Norman realm' rather than an 'Angevin empire'.[128] The same was true in its ecclesiastical architecture, for in the opinion of Lindy Grant Normandy was 'hermetically sealed against the distinctive architectural forms of Maine and Anjou'.[129] In any case it was not a period of great cathedral building in Normandy.[130] In many respects the Norman Church remained fiercely traditional, even archaic.

*Towns*

In contrast, perhaps, to the magnates and the Church, the Norman towns flourished as never before under Angevin rule. In Lower Normandy several towns vied for dominance: Caen, Argentan and Falaise stand out, for by 1180, as we have seen, they supplied an immense proportion of ducal revenue.[131] In Upper Normandy the same was true of Dieppe, but by far the most important in this region was Rouen. In 1144 the city covered about fifty hectares, a greater area than contemporary Paris (a mere forty hectares), yet it continued to expand so much that some years later a new city wall was built, enclosing an area half as great again. The enlargement of the market hall in 1192 symbolises the city's growing prosperity, and Rouen probably still surpassed Paris in size and population in 1204.[132] Geoffrey of Anjou and Matilda constructed a new bridge, encouraging suburbs to spring up on the left (south) bank of the Seine, and the main streets had probably been paved before 1200.[133] The burgesses flaunted their prosperity by constructing larger stone houses, and English nobles and prelates as well as lords from the remotest parts of Normandy acquired

---

[127] D. Spear, 'Power, Patronage, and Personality in the Norman Cathedral Chapters, 911–1204', *ANS* xx, 1998, 205–21, at 214–16, 219–21.

[128] For one exception, the Angevin William de Chemillé who became bishop of Avranches in 1196, see Turner, 'Richard Lionheart and the Episcopate', 524–5.

[129] Grant, 'Savignacs and Cistercians', 136–7.

[130] L. Grant, 'Architectural Relationships between England and Normandy, 1100–1204', *England and Normandy*, 117–29, at 119.

[131] Moss, 'England and Normandy', 194; above, 69.

[132] B. Gauthiez, 'Paris, un Rouen capétien? (Développements comparés de Rouen et Paris sous les règnes de Henri II et Philippe Auguste)', *ANS* xvi, 1993, 117–36, at 123, 133–5. See in general D. Bates, 'Rouen from 900 to 1204: from Scandinavian Settlement to Angevin "Capital"', *Medieval Art, Architecture, and Archaeology at Rouen (British Archaeological Association Conference Transactions XII)*, ed. J. Stratford, Leeds 1993, 1–11, at 4–8.

[133] Chibnall, *Empress Matilda*, 151–3; Gauthiez, 'Paris, un Rouen capétien?', 117–22.

property in the city.[134] The city's thriving Jewish community, one of the largest north of the Alps, also deserves mention.[135] The merchants who formed the city oligarchy took an ever-increasing part in the affairs of the duchy. They included Emma, *vicomtesse* of Rouen, one of the most remarkable women in the Anglo-Norman realm, whose commercial and administrative activities ranged from Southampton, where she administered the royal revenues (1158–63), to Paris, where she imported salt and herrings and was a benefactor of the lazarhouse (lepers' hospital). As *vicomtesse* she farmed the ducal revenues of Rouen.[136] The economic activities of the citizens of Rouen helps to explain why the city's customs became a model for town communes as far away as Poitiers, Niort and Saint-Jean-d'Angely in Aquitaine, and Philip Augustus granted versions of the customs of Rouen to the burgesses of Falaise and Pont-Audemer when they surrendered to him in 1204.[137] Yet Rouen's economic influence appears to have extended mainly over eastern Normandy, as well as south-east England, rather than over the duchy as a whole: almost all the identifiable citizens came from Upper Normandy.[138]

As the wars with the king of France intensified the burgesses of Normandy were called upon to provide more and more cash for war through tallages and 'loans'.[139] Not surprisingly, the political influence of the towns increased as well as their contributions. A significant development under Angevin rule was the adoption of the commune, often termed a 'sworn commune', as the main form of urban organisation. Most were formed either early in the reign of Henry II or during the short Norman reign of King John; nearly twenty communes had appeared by 1204, including all the main Norman towns except Lisieux, and some smaller communities such as Montivilliers and Fécamp. In some cases the dukes created communes for financial advantage, in others undoubtedly for military reasons; but in every case the urban oligarchies acquired greater control of their own affairs.[140] The grant of a measure of self-governance to the towns did not free them from urban strife: when the Archbishop Walter of Rouen fled to France in 1196 he complained not only of King

---

[134] B. Gauthiez, 'Les maisons de Rouen XIIe–XVIIIe siècles', *Archéologie Médiévale* xxiii, 1993, 131–217, at 132–44; idem, 'Paris, un Rouen capétien?', 123–7; *Cartulaire de l'abbaye de Notre-Dame de Vaux-de-Cernay*, ed. L. Merlet and A. Moutié, Paris 1857, no. CXVVII (fief of Simon d'Anet at Rouen).

[135] N. Golb, *Les juifs de Rouen au moyen âge: portrait d'une culture oubliée*, Rouen 1985, 129–41, 259–88; idem, *The Jews in Medieval Normandy: a Social and Intellectual Study*, Cambridge 1998, 137–69, 208–377.

[136] For Emma and her sons, see *Recueil H II*, intro., 214–18, 364; L. Musset, 'Y eut-t-il une aristocratie d'affaires commune aux grandes villes de Normandie et d'Angleterre de 1066 à 1204?', *Etudes Normandes* iii, 1986, 7–19, at 10–12.

[137] *Registres de Philippe Auguste*, 336 (also naming Caen and Verneuil); A. Giry, *Les établissements de Rouen*, Paris 1883, 47–53; *Actes de Philippe Auguste* ii, nos 789, 809.

[138] Gauthiez, 'Rouen, un Paris capétien?', 127, 129 (map).

[139] See above, 69.

[140] *Cartulaire Normand*, xv–xviii, xl; S.R. Packard, 'The Norman Communes under Richard and John, 1189–1204', *Anniversary Essays in Mediaeval History by Students of Charles Homer Haskins*, ed. G.H. Taylor, Boston and New York 1927, 231–54; S. Deck, 'Formation des communes en Haute-Normandie et communes éphémères', *Annales de Normandie* x, 1960, 207–27, 317–29. Moss, 'Angevin Empire', 138–43, counts eighteen communes, but Sées, Bibl. de l'Évêché, *Livre Blanc de St-Martin de Sées*, fo. 13v, furnishes another, at Sées (1195).

Richard's oppression but also of discord between the clergy and citizens of Rouen, and this flared up afresh just before his death in 1207.[141]

What, meanwhile, of the rest of the Norman population? In 1221, the hearth-tax or *fouage* raised 15,384 *li. 9 s. tournois*, which at a shilling a hearth implies that there were then 307,689 taxpaying households in Normandy.[142] Without more information about family structure it is impossible to calculate the population of the duchy directly from this figure, and in any case, as we have seen, knights, clergy, millers and certain others were excluded along with the inhabitants of several exempted districts in southern Normandy.[143] Nevertheless, even the most conservative estimate would imply there were more than a million people in Normandy at the end of Angevin rule – a considerable number for a province of only modest size. The true figure is likely to have been significantly higher. Moreover, in 1328 the number of taxable hearths had increased only slightly, to 320,030; if the population of Normandy had barely grown in the century or so following the end of Angevin rule, the province was already relatively densely populated in the late twelfth century.[144] For Philip Augustus it was a rich prize indeed.

## *The End of Angevin Normandy*

Why, then, did this wealthy and well-fortified province fall so easily into King Philip's hands? Most answers to this question have concentrated either upon the balance in wealth between the Angevins and the Capetians or upon the misrule of King John.[145] The Norman aristocracy also failed to defend the duchy as successfully as they had in the past. A satisfactory explanation for their passivity continues to elude historians. It has been suggested that there was a crisis of Norman identity. By the late twelfth century, it has been argued, the cultural superiority of the Île-de-France was putting the rest of western Europe in the shade; hence the superiority of French to Norman culture was 'written in stone' at the chapter house of Saint-Georges-de-Boscherville near Rouen, for it was designed by French architects and sculptors.[146] Yet perhaps this interpretation prematurely anticipates the triumph of Paris over Rouen and of the Île-de-France over Normandy, by no means foregone conclusions in 1204. Another interpretation emphasises the shift of political gravity in the Anglo-Norman realm to England: Lucien Musset has seen the prominence of English officials, clergy and nobles in the duchy by 1200 as a reversal of the Norman conquest, since the Normans were no longer in charge of their own affairs.[147] At the same time, the ruling dynasty's interests lay further south, in the Loire valley, Poitou and Gascony, but few Normans shared their concern for these distant regions.

---

141 *Diceto* ii, 144; for the dispute in 1207, see above, n. 124.
142 M. Nortier and J.W. Baldwin, 'Contributions à l'étude des finances de Philippe Auguste', *Bibliothèque de l'École des Chartes* cxxxviii, 1980, 5–33, at 14.
143 Above, 74.
144 Nortier and Baldwin, 'Contributions', 14: Nortier assumes an average of five people per hearth. It should be remembered that the early fourteenth century saw widespread population crises in western Europe.
145 See above, n. 28; Gillingham, *Richard I*, 335–48.
146 R.W. Southern, 'England's First Entry into Europe', in *Medieval Humanism and Other Studies*, Oxford 1970, 135–57; Grant, 'Architectural Relationships', 129.
147 Musset, 'Quelques problèmes', 292–4.

There is a danger here, however, of exaggerating the foreign character of the dukes and nobles of Normandy. Henry the Young King and Richard the Lionheart were afterwards remembered even in England as the epitome of Norman chivalric leadership;[148] the first was buried in Rouen Cathedral at his own request, the second bequeathed that church his heart. Indeed, in the last years of his life Richard developed an affection for eastern Normandy which must have been due to more than mere military necessity: John Gillingham has described the series of ducal castles and residences along the Seine valley between Rouen and Andely as the closest that the Angevin lands had to a capital under Richard I and John, and it was Richard who was mainly responsible for this transformation.[149] After 1204 the notion that Normandy should be ruled by dukes remained strong, and was stridently expressed in the *Grand Coutumier* (c. 1250):

> The duke of Normandy or the prince is the one who holds sovereignty over the entire duchy. This dignity the lord king of France holds together with the same honours to which, with the aid of the Lord, he has been raised.[150]

Persisting enthusiasm for the concept of the duke found a bizarre manifestation in the reconstruction of the choir of Rouen Cathedral in the 1220s as if it were a ducal coronation church and mausoleum.[151] In this period the Normans also did much to preserve their distinctive past: many Norman cartularies were compiled and histories were copied, sometimes even by the same person, such as the monk of Saint-Pierre de Préaux who transcribed the *Gesta Normannorum Ducum* and composed the abbey's cartulary (c. 1227).[152] Thus the dead continued to inspire the living; but in the 1220s the living man who claimed to be duke of Normandy, King Henry III of England, offered no inspiration to the barons of the province, and with a few exceptions they remained conspicuously loyal to the Capetians.[153]

Despite the relative unity of Normandy, it may have been too incoherent to withstand the strain of a dozen years of damaging and costly warfare. There were many fault-lines within the duchy. Its nobles certainly had a sense of their Norman identity; but they were also castellans with their own, more local and sometimes conflicting concerns of lineage and inheritance. Too many Norman landowners did not share the interest of Anglo-Norman lords in their island possessions. In a large part of southern Normandy the border lords nursed traditions of hostility towards the dukes, often focussed upon castles, which re-emerged as bones of contention between 1193 and 1204; and for the whole length of the land frontier the aristocracy enjoyed connections with their neighbours that were sometimes of greater importance to them than their associations with central Normandy.[154] Despite its sophistication the Norman system of government still admitted great judicial and fiscal immunities, especially

---

148  *HGM* (as n. 62) ii, lines 4645–52.

149  J. Gillingham, *The Angevin Empire*, 2nd edn, London 2001, 73–5.

150  *Summa de legibus*, 37, c. XI: 'Dux autem Normannie sive princeps dicitur qui tocius ducatus obtinet principatum; quam sibi dignitatem retinet dominus rex Francie cum ceteris honoribus ad quos provectus est, ipsum Domino promovente.'

151  L. Grant, 'Rouen Cathedral 1200–1237', *Medieval Art, Architecture and Archaeology at Rouen*, BAA Conference Transactions xii, 1993, 60–8, at 66.

152  *Jumièges* i, cxi.

153  Stevenson, 'England and Normandy' ii, 226–34, 326–34. Holt, 'Anglo-Norman Realm', 264–5, notes pro-Angevin sentiment in Caen in the mid-1220s.

154  Power, 'Frontier of Angevin Normandy', 186–9, 193–5.

the counties and the lands of some ancient abbeys;[155] the advances in the collection of ducal finances did not embrace the south-west of the duchy, which retained older, less efficient or productive methods of raising revenue;[156] while many southern districts did not pay *fouage*, and the exchequer court served mainly central and western Normandy. In ecclesiastical terms, the differences between the duchy and the metropolitan province of Rouen were not insignificant.[157] In its economy and culture eastern Normandy benefited from close contacts with the Paris Basin whereas the west had more in common with Brittany and the Loire provinces.

Most important of all, the avowed aim of the king of France to supplant Angevin lordship in eastern Normandy from 1193 onwards threatened the territorial integrity of the duchy. Norman identity and Norman power had always been far more insecure than the constant use of the names 'Norman' and 'Normandy' implies; they provided a convenient umbrella for a patchwork of castelries and local concerns, which in the early thirteenth century simply slipped from Angevin to Capetian lordship. That was how Roger of Wendover portrayed King Philip's triumphal march through the leaderless duchy in May 1204:

> He pointed out that he was the chief lord of those regions, and that he wished to preserve unharmed what was rightfully his, namely his lordship over those regions, even if the king of England had already deserted them out of cowardice; hence with words of friendship he requested that they should receive him as their lord, since they had no other.[158]

Hence although the Norman administrative system, aristocracy, Church and towns were all affected by the events of 1204, the legacies of ducal rule survived. Wendover's account supports the verdict of Sir James Holt: ultimately the end of the Angevin regime in Normandy was 'not annexation but supersession', the substitution of one dynasty for another.[159]

---

155  E.g. the county of Évreux: see Power, 'Norman Frontier', 190–6.
156  Moss, 'Norman Exchequer Rolls of King John', 111–12.
157  Power, 'Frontier of Angevin Normandy', 191.
158  Matthew Paris, *Chronica Majora*, ed. H.R. Luard, RS, 7 vols, 1872–73, ii, 483: 'Proposuit etiam se principalem esse dominum illarum regionum, quas si jam rex Anglorum per ignaviam deseruit, ipse quod suum erat, videlicet principale dominium, sibi indemne voluit reservari. Unde amicabiliter supplicavit, ut ipsum in dominum reciperent, dum alium non haberent.' Wendover's tone here is very ironic, for he also claims that the king of France threatened to hang or flay alive anyone who refused his 'request'.
159  Holt, 'Anglo-Norman Realm', 225.

# 5

# The Normans in the Mediterranean[1]

## MATTHEW BENNETT

At Christmas 1099, Bohemond, Prince of Antioch, completed the pilgrimage upon which he had set out four years earlier by praying in the church of the Holy Sepulchre at Jerusalem. The city had been captured by the First Crusaders nine months earlier while Bohemond was still securing control over his new territories in northern Syria. Up to the time of the capture of Antioch he had been one of the main leaders of the crusade. He was by descent a Norman, his grandfather Tancred of Hauteville having a quiver-full of sons who sought their fortunes outside the duchy. Bohemond's father, Robert Guiscard, had made himself master of southern Italy in a series of campaigns from the early 1050s into the 1070s.[2] In 1081, Guiscard had even invaded the Byzantine territory of what is now Albania and northern Greece and defeated its emperor in battle.[3] Bohemond (his unusual name stemming from a legendary giant) continued his father's policies of expansion at the expense of the Christian Greeks both before and after the First Crusade, but it was that expedition against the Muslims that gave him opportunity to seize one of the greatest cities of the Levant and create his principality.

He was not the only significant Norman to play a part in the dramatic events which followed upon Pope Urban II's sermon at Clermont in November 1095. Robert, duke of Normandy (the eldest surviving son of William the Conqueror) also proved himself a fine soldier in the holy war. It was claimed that he had been offered the throne of Jerusalem itself following the city's capture, but that he had declined the offer. Arnulf de Chocques, the Patriarch responsible for restoring the structure of the Church in a region long under Muslim control, was formerly a ducal chaplain in Normandy. Several contemporary Latin chronicles stressed the importance of the Norman contribution to the great adventure, the pilgrimage in arms, which established Christian rule over the Holy Land for the first time since its conquest by the armies of Islam some five centuries earlier. The popular, vernacular literature represented by twelfth-

---

1  R.A. Brown, *The Normans*, Woodbridge 1984, contains a brief introductory synopsis of the subject in chs 5 and 6, 93–169. J.J. Norwich, *The Normans in the South*, London 1967, and *The Kingdom in the Sun*, London 1970, have been reprinted as *The Normans in Sicily*, Harmondsworth 1992, and provide a lively and extensive narrative. Lord Norwich's approach has been rather overtaken by the last generation of research, notably by G.A. Loud's numerous works (cited in detail below) and D. Matthew, *The Norman Kingdom of Sicily*, Cambridge 1992. E. van Houts, *The Normans in Europe*, Manchester 2000, provides a selection of translated sources at 223–78. P. Bouet and F. Neveux, eds, *Les Normands en Méditerranée dans le sillage des Tancrède (Colloque de Cerisy-la-Salle 24–27 septembre 1992)*, presents both an introductory survey and a useful selection of recent research into specialist areas.

2  See G.A. Loud, *The Age of Robert Guiscard: Southern Italy and the Norman Conquest*, London 2000, 104–45.

3  Ibid., 209–23.

century *chansons de geste* (songs of great deeds) fêted Duke Robert's heroism for generations afterwards.[4] Seen from a Norman perspective, indeed, the First Crusade looked like a Norman expedition. This view has certainly proved attractive to historians stemming from the English-speaking tradition, although continental European commentators have sought to redress the balance in favour of the southern French and German contributions. For to the Christian and Muslim inhabitants of the eastern Mediterranean the invaders were all 'Franks', a generic term for westerners, as even the very pro-Norman *Gesta Francorum* recognised in its title.[5] Yet people who were self-consciously Norman and aware of their historical tradition did play an important role in the history of the eleventh- and twelfth-century Mediterranean lands and left their mark in the creation of ideologies, states, and institutions.

*Arrivals*

The first appearance of Normans in the Italian peninsula is often ascribed to a group of pilgrims visiting St Michael's at Monte Gargano in 999, who displayed their military virtue by driving off Muslims who threatened the shrine. But this may be no more than legend, and Norman involvement in the revolt of the Lombard count Melo against his Byzantine overlords in 1017 is a more certain event.[6] Chief among them was Ralph II of Tosny, an exile from ducal justice, which was to prove a rich source of recruitment of Norman adventurers. This first group, numbering perhaps 250, shared Melo's crushing defeat by the Greeks at Cannae (1018); but this did not prevent others from coming south. The fractured nature of southern Italian politics meant that there were plenty of opportunities for mercenaries, first to find employment and then to establish their own rule. By 1030, Ranulph 'Drengot' had made himself master of Aversa. He was confirmed in his lordship by Emperor Conrad II in 1038, and on his death in 1045 was succeeded by his nephew. The famous Hauteville family – possibly stemming from Hauteville-le-Guichard (Manche) – made their appearance in the mid-1030s. Of Tancred of Hauteville's twelve sons, the first to arrive were William, Drogo, and Humphrey. Gaimar, the Lombard count of Capua, sent them as part of a contingent of 'three hundred' Frankish knights to join the ill-fated Byzantine expedition to recover Sicily in 1038. They had more luck in the service of Arduin, a Lombard rebel against the Greeks, helping him to secure a territory around Melfi in 1041. But an outbreak of peace in the following year persuaded all the northerners in the region to gather together and seek to supplant their employers. William Hauteville 'Iron-Arm' proclaimed himself count of Apulia, although (like Ranulph of Aversa) he was still subject to Duke Gaimar, whose niece he married. He was succeeded by his brother Drogo, who was confirmed by Emperor Henry III as leader of all the Normans in Apulia and Calabria (1047). Richard I was similarly elevated to become prince of Capua in 1058. He had arrived with Robert Hauteville ('Guiscard', or the wily, as he later became known) in 1046, and between them they dominated southern Italy for a

---

[4]   For poetic representations of the Normans see M. Bennett, 'Poetry as History? The *Roman de Rou* as a Source for the Norman Conquest', *ANS* v, 1982, 21–39, and 'Stereotype Normans in Old French Material', *ANS* ix, 1986, 7–19.

[5]   *Gesta Francorum et Aliorum Hierosolimitanorum*, ed. and trans. R. Hill, London 1962.

[6]   See J. France, 'The Occasion of the Coming of the Normans to Southern Italy', *JMH* xvii, 1991, 185–205; cf. Loud, *Robert Guiscard*, 59–91.

generation. Robert married Alberada, the daughter of an established Norman lord, who brought with her the dowry of two hundred knights with which to conquer Calabria. She also bore him a son, Mark 'Bohemond', before, in 1058, Guiscard traded her in for an even more advantageous match: Sichelgaita, sister of the ruling Lombard prince of Salerno.[7]

In 1053 came a defining moment in the establishment of Norman rule. The reforming Pope Leo IX was persuaded that he needed to establish his authority over the unruly northerners, but his Lombard army, even stiffened as it was by German troops, was scattered at the battle of Civitate. This changed the political map and, in 1059, Nicholas II acknowledged the new realities by awarding Guiscard a papal banner to represent his elevation as duke of Apulia and Calabria. The oppressors had become the protectors. There was no stopping the Hautevilles now. In 1061, Robert's younger brother Roger began the conquest of Sicily with an amphibious assault across the Straits of Messina. Yet a North African Muslim fleet prevented the capture of Palermo in 1064. It was not until Robert had made himself master of crucial mainland ports, culminating in a three-year siege of Bari (August 1068 – April 1071) that the brothers possessed the naval capacity to take the city which was the key to the island. Palermo fell in January 1072, after a six-month siege, and from then on Roger's success seemed assured, although it took another two decades to secure Sicily, which was swiftly followed by the capture of Malta (1090).[8]

Meanwhile, in 1081, Guiscard launched an attack on the Byzantine Empire (on the pretext of a failed marriage alliance for his daughter) which shows how powerful he had grown. His target was the well-defended bridgehead port of Durazzo (modern Durres, Albania). Anna Komnena, the historian daughter of Emperor Alexios I, whom he opposed, claims that Robert's fleet numbered 150 vessels, while his land forces may have included 1,300 knights. Initially, Alexios's Venetian allies surprised Guiscard's fleet, and scattering and largely destroying it. Nonetheless, the Normans began a siege and their horse and foot combined well to drive off Alexios's relief attempt, so that Durazzo fell after nine months. It proved too difficult to hold, though, and was lost in 1083. So, in 1084, Robert launched an expedition of '120' ships which successfully overwhelmed the Veneto-Byzantines off Corfu. Then, aged seventy, he caught typhoid and died in the following summer. His son, Bohemond, was not able to revive his ambitions until the First Crusade offered the possibility a decade later.

Until recently, historians have characterised expeditions against the Muslims in Spain as proto-crusades. The conquest in 1064 of Barbastro (just south of the Pyrenees on the border of the county of Barcelona), which involved contingents from several regions of France, was presented as the prime example. This is important in the context of Normans adventuring in the Mediterranean because one of the leaders was Roger of Tosny. Another Norman, Robert Crispin, is credited by the contemporary monastic chronicler Amatus of Montecassino with heroic deeds of legendary proportions. This is scarcely surprising since this Crispin also played a part in the conquest of southern Italy and progressed from there into Byzantine service. Along with Roussel of Bailleul, another Norman, he took part in the Emperor Romanus

---

7   For the significance of Sichelgaita and the Lombard connection to Guiscard see Loud, *Robert Guiscard*, 125–7.

8   M. Bennett, 'Norman Naval Activity in the Mediterranean c. 1060 – c. 1108', *ANS* xv, 1992, 41–58. N. Hooper and M. Bennett, *Cambridge Illustrated Atlas of Warfare: the Middle Ages 768–1487*, Cambridge 1996, provides maps of the conquests on pp. 82–3.

Diogenes's campaign against the Turks in eastern Anatolia in 1071. They managed to avoid the disastrous battle of Manzikert (near Lake Van) in which the Byzantine army was scattered and the emperor made prisoner. The Normans then took advantage of the civil war which broke out amongst the Greeks to establish short-lived independent lordships in the region. They were eventually overcome by the energy of Alexios Komnenos (emperor 1081–1118).[9]

So, it is easy to see why historians could believe that the Normans were in the forefront of the developing ideology of Holy War (although this was only articulated by Pope Urban II, at Clermont, in November 1095). After all, Normans had borne papal banners in Italy and in the invasion of England (for which one justification was the reform of its church), and they had fought the Muslims in Spain. Unfortunately for this theory, there is nothing in the language of papal documents prior to the First Crusade to suggest that the remission of sin for military activity preceded Urban's pronouncements. According to the anonymous *Gesta Francorum*, when Bohemond heard the pope's message during a siege of Amalfi, he immediately had his most valuable cloak cut up to provide crosses for his enthusiastic followers.[10] This source is far from impartial, though, and actually represents a rewritten account probably circulated in France to support Bohemond's recruiting trip of 1106.[11] His intention then was to repeat his father's invasion of northern Greece. Small surprise that the emperor Alexios suspected him, and all the other leaders of the First Crusade, of territorial ambitions in the East when they arrived at Constantinople in 1096. The emperor had only been looking for volunteers to join his foreign legions to fight the Turks, who had overrun most of Anatolia in the first fifteen years of his reign. What he got was described by his historian daughter as barbarian migration. Accordingly, Alexios tried to bind the crusaders to him with oaths, especially concerning cities and territories previously part of the Byzantine Empire.[12]

## The First Crusade[13]

It is difficult to know exactly how important a part the Normans played on the First Crusade. Accounts favourable to them emphasise their role and criticise other leaders and their contingents, with especial opprobrium reserved for Raymond de St-Gilles and the southern French. No king accompanied the first crusaders and so there was no obvious single leader, rather several prominent players with claims to authority. The

---

[9]  J. Shepard, 'The Uses of Franks in Eleventh-Century Byzantium', *ANS* xv, 1992, 275–305.

[10] *Gesta Francorum*, 7–8.

[11] A.C. Krey, 'A Neglected Passage in the *Gesta* and its Bearing on the Literature of the First Crusade', in *The Crusades and Other Historical Essays presented to D.C. Munro*, ed. L.J. Paetow, New York 1928, 57–79. K.B. Wolf, 'Bohemond and the *Gesta Francorum*', *JMH* xvii, 1991, 207–16.

[12] J. France, *Victory in the East: a Military History of the First Crusade*, Cambridge 1994, 19–21. *The Alexiad of Anna Comnena*, trans. E.R.A. Sewter, Harmondsworth 1969, 322–6. J. Shepard, 'When Greek Meets Greek: Alexius Comnenus and Bohemond in 1097–98', *Byzantine and Modern Greek Studies* xii, 1988, 185–277.

[13] S. Runciman, *The First Crusade* (vol. 1 of 3), Cambridge 1951, is still a good starting point for crusade studies, but it is pro-Byzantist and so anti-Frankish and anti-Norman in tone. J. Riley-Smith, *The First Crusade and the Idea of Crusading*, London 1986, and many other works, has pro-crusader bias. J. Phillips, ed., *The First Crusade: Origins and Impact*, Manchester 1997, is a useful collection of essays reflecting the current state of research.

first real crisis of the expedition befell it three days' march from the newly captured city of Nicaea (in north-western Anatolia) when the Seljuk sultan ambushed the vanguard at a river crossing (1 July 1097). Bohemond is credited with holding the troops together until the other columns came to their rescue, routing the Turks. The crusaders' next target was the great city of Antioch, which they reached after a difficult march over the Amanus mountain range. Meanwhile, another Norman, Tancred, who was Bohemond's nephew, had made a name for himself by taking a different route onto the rich Cilician Plain where he seized the city of Tarsus.

The siege of Antioch, which began in October 1097, and lasted for ten months, almost destroyed the crusade. The city was too large and too well defended by its walls and a citadel high above the town on a steep ridge. It would have to be starved out. The risk was that it would be the besiegers who starved, or that relief forces would drive them off. Again the *Gesta Francorum* credits Bohemond with exceptional powers of leadership and determination. For example, he led a crucial foraging expedition against the nearby town of Harim in December 1097.[14] This was vital both to maintain supplies and keep up the morale of the crusaders. In February 1098, it was Bohemond's generalship which utterly routed a relief force under Ridwan, the ruler of Aleppo, as the Muslims were ambushed south of Lake Antioch. Finally, to Bohemond goes the credit for the taking of Antioch, by the bribery of an Armenian tower captain, just a few days before the arrival of the huge army of Kerbogha, *atabeg* of Mosul. He also commanded the reserve in the great battle outside the city on 28 June in which the crusaders shattered the greatly superior Muslim forces and finally secured the city.[15] This was, of course, Bohemond's intention, and sources favourable to him necessarily stress his crucial role by way of justifying his next action: his seizure of Antioch for himself. This was exactly what Emperor Alexios had feared and why he had extracted an oath from the crusaders two years earlier; but now a Norman dynasty was established which would last nearly two centuries.

Despite his superior status, Robert of Normandy almost disappears from the narrative during the siege of Antioch, only to reappear as one of the victors of the siege of Jerusalem (7 June – 15 July 1099). Tancred, who had obviously run out of funds, had only been able to continue on the expedition by serving in the contingent of Raymond de St Gilles. So, when the crusaders broke into the city, Tancred led his contingent to the Dome of the Rock mosque, seeking its fabled wealth. Finding many Muslims had rushed for shelter upon its roof, he and a southern French lord set up their banners, claiming the prisoners as their own. The next day other crusaders massacred these unfortunates in cold blood. Tancred was recorded to be very angry, although whether this was due to the loss of ransoms or the betrayal of his protection is unclear. He certainly did very well out of the sack, becoming a wealthy man and the inheritor of his uncle's territory of Antioch (in 1111).[16]

---

14  *Gesta Francorum*, 30–1. France, *Victory in the East*, 228–9, places a less positive gloss on the outcome of the raid.

15  Once again *Gesta Francorum*, 67–71, gives Bohemond much credit for the victory. France, *Victory in the East*, ch. 9, 269–96, has produced a re-interpretation of the battle outside Antioch, which must replace that of R.C. Smail, *Crusading Warfare*, Cambridge 1956, 172–4, in an otherwise excellent survey which has stood the test of time well.

16  The biographies of the first two rulers of crusader Antioch (R. Yewdale, *Bohemond I Prince of Antioch*, Princeton 1924, and R.L. Nicholson, *Tancred: a Study in his Career and Work in their Relation to the First Crusade and the Establishment of the Latin States in Syria and Palestine*, Chicago

The arrival of Norman rulers in Syria and Palestine represents the furthest expansion of men with ancestral roots in the duchy. What followed was the establishment of new regimes across the Mediterranean: in Sicily and southern Italy, in Antioch and its territories, even briefly in North Africa. With the Normans came their ideas of how these new territories should be governed. Just how far they brought their own traditions and how much they adapted to local conditions will be the subject of the rest of this essay.

*New Realms*

Anyone coming from northern France in the eleventh century had certain characteristics readily identified by outsiders. Their first distinguishing feature, clearly recognisable even before the crusaders' cross provided the logo for it, was their affiliation to the Latin Church. This meant that almost wherever they went, the Normans brought with them a different form of religion from the people over whom they ruled. While this might seem obvious for the former Muslim territories it was also an issue in southern Italy, where many still followed the Orthodox rite, and even in the Holy Land and Syria where most Christians belonged to the Armenian or Nestorian Church, or the syncretist faith of the Druze. And Latin Christianity was not in a very tolerant phase during the period of Norman expansion. The papal reform movement, which began around the middle of the eleventh century and became increasingly strident under Pope Gregory VII (1073–85) in setting out its objectives, managed to alienate many secular rulers in the West. Even the Normans, who were often the standard-bearers of reform (both physically and metaphorically), often found papal demands excessive. William the Conqueror, extremely pious though he was, fell out with Rome over the issue of the fealty demanded by Gregory (if not to the extent of the German emperors' resort to violence and resulting civil wars which scarred their realms for almost half a century until 1122). Yet Norman rulers were keen to support papal condemnations of simony and pluralism, and especially the pope's insistence on clerical celibacy, the last being an innovation alien to the Eastern churches. The breakdown of communication, dating from 1054, between the Latin and Orthodox Churches (usually known as the Great Schism), also created a divide between Norman lords and their new Eastern Christian subjects. But the Normans were to enforce the Latin rite, whatever the cost, and if this meant replacing native bishops with new men, so be it. As William the Conqueror was to do in England, Mediterranean Normans enforced reform and uniformity in their own dominions. Not that all the change was necessarily confrontational or oppressive; certainly the Church flourished from the great wealth acquired by the conquerors. For many new subjects of the Normans, though, they came imposing an alien faith.

During the period of Norman expansion, a population group was identified as belonging to a certain *lex* (meaning law but with the wider implication of faith as well) and *gens* (meaning people as identified by customs, social organisation, dress and behaviour). There has been a great deal of scholarly debate as to whether the idea of a

---

1940) are now very dated. The tendency in crusader studies is to move away from the biographical approach to regional studies: see, for example, T.S. Asbridge, *The Creation of the Principality of Antioch 1098–1130*, Woodbridge 2000.

*gens Normannorum* ('Norman Race') actually meant anything.[17] Nineteenth-century historians, and twentieth-century historians prior to 1945, were quite happy to use such labels. They saw terms such as 'race' as positive and confirming terms, implying pride in shared blood, customs and assumptions. In the second half of the twentieth century such a comfortable interpretation seemed no more than a fantasy, and a potentially very dangerous one at that. But the question does remain as to whether there was a particularly 'Norman' way of doing things: of managing inheritance and land transfers, of raising troops and taxation, of governing and even of creating a state. To the early-twentieth-century doyen of Norman studies, Charles Homer Haskins, there was no doubt that the Normans took their 'institutions' with them wherever they went and imposed them upon new lands and subject populations.[18] The post-war generation of historians is far less certain, W.L. Warren and Donald Matthew, for example, preferring to see flexibility, accommodation and downright *laissez-faire* as more characteristic of 'Norman governance'.[19] These were common characteristics of *ancien régime* governments, of course, but earlier historians' views of state-building and centralisation as being essential parts of the creation of a 'nation' (another nineteenth-century obsession) have perhaps obscured the more pragmatic aspects of princely rule in the period under discussion.

## *The Principality of Antioch*[20]

Although Antioch survived as a Christian enclave in northern Syria until 1268, its Norman inheritance lasted only a generation from the conquest. In 1130, Bohemond II died in battle at Mamistra, in Cilicia, the last of the Hauteville line. The first few years of the principality's existence had proved to be precarious. Antioch faced threats from three main directions, although they also presented opportunities for expansion. To the north lay Cilician Armenia, disputed with the Byzantines; to the east Aleppo and its Muslim rulers was its most determined rival; while the southern border was contested with the Banu-Munquidh, ruling Shaizir on the Orontes. In addition, players from further afield, both Muslim and Christian, had influential roles on occasion.

In June 1100, Bohemond again defeated Ridwan of Aleppo (1095–1113) at Kella, south-east of Antioch. But later that year, attempting to relieve the siege of the Armenian city of Melitene, the prince was himself made prisoner by the Danishmend Turk, Gumushtigin. Luckily for the Latins, his nephew, Tancred, proved an able regent (1101–1103), capturing Latakia (after an eighteen month siege) in 1102 and

17 This isssue is considered by R.H.C. Davis, *The Normans and their Myth*, London 1976, and G. Loud, 'How Norman was the Norman Conquest of Southern Italy', *Nottingham Medieval Studies* xxv, 1981, 13–34; G. Loud, 'The *Gens Normannorum*, Myth or Reality', *ANS* iv, 1981, 104–16. L.-R. Ménager, 'Inventaire des familles normandes et francques émigrées en Italie méridionale et en Sicile (XIe et XIIe siècles)', in *Roberto il Guiscardo e il suo tempo (realzione e commuicazioni delle Prime Giornate normanno-sveve, Bari, mai 1973)*, Rome 1975, 259–360 provides the prosopographical detail.

18 C.H. Haskins, *The Normans in European History*, New York 1915; C.H. Haskins, *Norman Institutions*, Cambridge, Mass., 1918.

19 W.L. Warren, 'The Myth of Norman Adminstrative Efficiency', *TRHS* 5th ser. xxxiv, 1984, 113–32; D. Matthew, *Norman Kingdom of Sicily*, chs 7 and 8.

20 The following section owes much to the valuable research of T. Asbridge, *Principality of Antioch* (n. 16 above).

re-establishing Antiochene authority over Cilician Armenia. This increased the size of the principality to its greatest extent, from Tarsus in the west, through Adana and Mamistra, to Servantikar in the north, past Artah, Harim and Hab in the east, and down to Kafartab in the south. After his release, Bohemond campaigned north-east around Marash, in conjunction with Baldwin of Edessa. This provoked a response from the Muslim rulers of Mosul and Mardin who combined their forces to inflict a serious defeat upon the Franks at Harran, in May 1104. As a result, most of the gains were lost, only Rugia (Chastel Rouge) and Hab being retained east of the Orontes, while a Greek fleet seized Latakia. Bohemond then departed for the West to pursue his ambitions in leading a 'crusade' against the Greeks, leaving Tancred to repair the damage. This he proved most able to do, raising a large force to attack and rout another attempted invasion by Ridwan at Artah in April 1105.

Tancred proved to be the most energetic and successful early ruler of Antioch. His seizure of Apamea in 1106 served to defend the principality's southern frontier against Muslim attacks based on Shaizar. The Byzantines had regained possession of Cilicia in the wake of the Harran, in 1104. Tancred recovered the territory in 1107–1108, undoubtedly helped by Bohemond's simultaneous attack on Durazzo, even though the prince was forced into a humiliating treaty with Emperor Alexios. Latakia was also recovered from the Greeks by 1108, and Tancred advanced along the Syrian coast to within a few miles of Latin-held (but rival) Tortosa. Against Aleppo, all the important fortresses were recovered, and strategically-placed al-Atharib added to strengthen Antioch's eastern frontier. As a result of these successes, in 1111 Tancred was able to demand a 20,000 dinar tribute from Aleppo, and 10,000 from Shaizar. His successor Roger of Salerno (1113–19) continued the policy, although it is not clear if the sums were collected annually. This closely parallels the Iberian system of *parias*, by which aggressive Christian rulers weakened their rival Muslim city-states' ability to resist, the wealth which should have paid for military forces being siphoned-off as protection money.[21]

Antioch's position was strengthened in relation to Aleppo in 1113 when Ridwan died, leaving a minor as his heir. In 1115, the rulers of Mardin and Damascus combined to seize the city, and, when threatened by the Baghdad caliph's general Bursuq, offered an alliance to Roger. Bursuq was first rebuffed (in a stand-off) by combined Latin forces at Apamea and later defeated by Roger, as he retired north, at Tell Danith. Antiochene pressure on Aleppo seemed to be telling as Roger surrounded the city, taking Azaz to the north (1118) and Buza'ah to the east (1119). Then came disaster. Over-confidently Roger offered battle to Il-ghazi of Mardin, and on the 'Field of Blood', near al-Atharib, he was killed, along with most of his force (28 June 1119).[22] That Antioch did not fall owed much to Il-ghazi's caution and Baldwin II of Jerusalem's rapid response. He marched north in August and initiated a recovery that by 1126 had restored the borders of the principality (despite almost a year spent in captivity: June 1123 – May 1124). In 1126, Bohemond II arrived from the West to take up his inheritance. Aged 16, he was to be the last of the brief Norman dynasty. After some initial successes on the eastern border, in 1130 he was defeated and killed fighting the Armenians at Mamistra, in Cilicia. The principality survived Saladin's

[21] This important point about the processes of managing a frontier state comes from Asbridge, *Principality of Antioch*, 48–9, 60, 66.

[22] T. Asbridge, 'The Significance and the Causes of the Field of Blood', *JMH* xxiii, 1997, 301–16, provides a detailed study of the campaign.

conquests of 1187–88, although in much shrunken form, and continued in Christian hands until 1268.

There is the question of just how Norman was the 'Norman Principality of Antioch'? Of course, it could only be so at one remove, for it was founded by a man born in Italy (although both parents were of Norman stock).[23] Certainly Bohemond thought of himself as a prince of the French overseas, for he returned to France to marry Constance, the king's daughter. As in his own son's case, the crusading states continued to find heirs and heiresses from the 'old country' for generations yet. In all their cases, however, they did not need to be from the region of the state's founder. The very fact that members of the comital family of Boulogne had become kings meant that they could chose to marry into other ruling dynasties. To remain attached to their origins would have been an expression of failure. Deriving from this is the issue of just how far the Frankish colonists brought with them their own institutions and how far they adapted those which they found already in existence in the East.

Essentially there was a contrast between how they tackled ecclesiastical and secular organisation. For all the implications of the Haskins view of the introduction of 'Norman Institutions', it is precious difficult to see them in the Antiochene state. True, the prince had vassals who provided him with his primary military strength and these were mostly incomers (although Armenian Christians could be recruited too). But when it came to law and administration the approach was pragmatic. Medieval rulers were content to allow peoples to live under their own laws as long as these did not contradict the lord's authority. Government was based upon the household, which provided both military and other officers. Although it is likely that the great city of Antioch preserved some of the structures of Byzantine rule, these are also difficult to discern. The outlying regions are occasionally described as having a *dux* set over them, and there may have been a similar officer in the city itself. Any metropolitan institutions representative of the citizenry are invisible in the Norman period. There is evidence for officers of the household. The constable appears on several occasions (sometimes more than one), responsible for the direction of military effort in the absence of the prince. The marshal's task was to support and manage the troops on campaign, and, as his name suggests, to deploy them in battle. No seneschal is mentioned by name before 1149, although this was a crucial position. He was responsible for the management of finances, administration, the judicial system and the control of castles. One problem with these household offices is that unless they became hereditary they could be temporary appointments or subsumed by the authority of the lord. They were not institutional posts in the modern sense of the word. One important post which was certainly filled, though, is that of chancellor. He oversaw a chancery responsible for the production of documents of command, communication and administration. The only detailed history of early Antioch was written by Walter the Chancellor, who is estimated to have held the office c. 1114–22. In 1127, a charter issued by Bohemond II was witnessed as chancellor by a Ralph. Finally, a chamberlain is mentioned on the eve of the 'Field of Blood', although only in connection with ensuring that the valuables in the baggage train were escorted back to Antioch.[24]

---

23 Asbridge (163–8) is inclined to allow a certain *Normannitas* to the settlers of Antioch, although this is based upon only a handful of examples.
24 This paragraph is based upon Asbridge, *Principality of Antioch*, ch. 7.

In contrast, and unsurprisingly, the development of ecclesiastical structures is well-recorded. This is because the existing organisation could not serve its new masters. Although the Greek Orthodox patriarch intially retained some authority, the result of the 1054 schism was that the Latins considered Orthodoxy heretical. So when Bohemond visited Jerusalem in December 1099, the cost for his support of Daimbert of Pisa as patriarch of the city was the consecration of three Latin bishops. The most important appointment was Bernard of Valence as patriarch of Antioch. Initially, there were five other bishops; but by 1130 their number had risen to fourteen. Their responsibilities were as much military as spiritual. For example, Peter of Narbonne played a crucial role as bishop of Albara and also (simultaneously and, of course, uncanonically) archbishop of Apamea from 1110. Patriarch Bernard of Valence (1100–35) proved adroit at establishing authority across political boundaries: to Edessa in the east and even south along the Syrian coast as far as Tripoli. Cilician Armenia was a more problematic area, the bishops appointed spending time in exile from their sees as the region was regained by the Byzantines. Antioch had a substantial Christian tradition, of course, since St Peter had established the Church there before that of Rome. But the political realities ensured that Jerusalem was pre-eminent. When Tyre was captured in 1124, it was patriarch Warmund who chose its new bishop, and not Bernard. There can be no doubt, though, that the ecclesiastical structure which he created contributed importantly to the wealth and organisation of the principality in the first generation of its existence.[25]

For all its relative success in surviving in an exposed position close to the Muslim hinterland, Antioch could not compare with the glittering achievement of the Kingdom of Sicily; a study of which Norman-founded state takes us almost to the end of the twelfth century.

## The Creation of the Kingdom of Sicily[26]

The largest state to be created under Norman supervision comprised territories in southern Italy, Sicily, Malta and temporarily in North Africa.[27] On Robert Guiscard's death in 1085, he was succeeded as duke of Apulia by Roger, the eldest son of his second wife. Bohemond had been suffering an untimely illness, and, although he later claimed rights over Taranto and Bari, as we have seen, his ambitions lay elsewhere. Roger 'Borsa' (his nickname meaning 'purse' and suggesting an ignoble interest in money) ruled until 1111 and was succeeded by his son William, who died in 1127, aged only thirty. Ruling in parallel, and often in competition, in Sicily, was Roger 'Great Count', Guiscard's youngest brother, who died in 1101. He was succeeded briefly by Simon (1101–1105), and then followed by Roger II (but as a minor until 1112).

To Roger II fell all the spoils of the Norman conquests in the region. He achieved

---

25  For further details see Asbridge, *Principality of Antioch*, ch. 8.

26  For a detailed narrative of events in the twelfth century see Norwich, *Normans in Sicily*, 303–752, and Matthew, *Norman Kingdom of Sicily*, 33–67 and 262–306. Matthew takes the history of the kingdom up to 1266, with good reason, for thirteenth-century evidence helps to interpret the earlier structure of the kingdom, 307–380; but there are equally good reasons for no longer considering Sicily part of the Norman orbit after its conquest by the German emperor in 1196.

27  D. Abulafia, 'The Norman Kingdom of Africa', *ANS* vii, 1984, 195–216.

this not without effort, the barons of Calabria resisting attempts to enforce his authority in the early 1120s. Roger enjoyed several strokes of good fortune, however, which enabled him to consolidate his position. In 1126 Bohemond II left to take up his inheritance at Antioch, and the following year his cousin William died. Although he was initially opposed by his overlord the pope, in 1128 Honorius II accepted Roger's homage in return for military help in recovering Benevento. When he was succeeded in February 1130 by Anacletus II, the new pope faced a rival (Innocent II) and the cost of Roger's support was a crown. Roger's new kingdom, based at Palermo (where his coronation took place towards the end of that year), comprised Sicily, Calabria and Apulia, to which were quickly added Capua and Naples. Not that these territories immediately came to hand, as Roger faced rebellions in the early 1130s. In 1137, supporting Innocent II, King Lothar II invaded his kingdom, advancing as far as Bari, which he took, receiving a general submission from the Apulian lords. Lothar was the first German ruler to be seen in the region for almost a century and he soon returned north. Anacletus died in January 1138, and Innocent II became the undisputed pope, this leading to Roger's excommunication at the Second Lateran Council in April 1139. In the summer Innocent attempted to impose his will by the use of military force. His army was surprised whilst engaged in siege and scattered, leaving the pope in Roger's hands. The king then forced Innocent to grant him written title to his kingdom, symbolised by the donation of a papal banner at Benevento in July.

Displaying great harshness, Roger re-established his authority in southern Italy. At Bari, for example, after a brief siege and a negotiated surrender which safeguarded the life and limb of its defenders, the king nevertheless had the ruler and his counsellors executed, and inflicted many other mutilations and imprisonments. By the end of 1143, the last vestiges of papal influence in the region had been swept away. The following year the new pope, Lucius II, was able to obtain a truce but only at the cost of conceding to Roger control of territories almost as far north as Rieti, in Marsia. The declaration of the 'Second' Crusade did threaten to undermine his position in southern Italy, as it would bring south the emperor Conrad as well as Louis VII of France. Roger was quick to offer his fleet to transport the crusaders; but they suspiciously refused. This freed the king to launch seaborne attacks on the Byzantines and to occupy Cephalonia and Corfu in the Ionian Islands, so reviving Guiscard's strategy of expansion. Roger also set about creating a colony in North Africa. He had been sending expeditions there since the 1120s, in response to Muslim raids on the Sicilian coast. Initially he had established a tributary relationship with individual ports and then, in the early 1140s with al-Hassan, the ruler of Mahdia. In 1146 Tripoli was taken and made formally part of the kingdom under the governorship of Roger's admiral, George of Antioch, until his death in 1152. It became truly a colony, with Sicilians being encouraged to settle there, and the territories were expanded to include Susa and Sfax. Unlike the leaders of the disastrous crusade of 1147–48 in the East, Roger had proved himself a victor in the holy war, although his interests were clearly more to do with trade and finance than ideology.

Not that this helped his relationship with the papacy. Eugenius III was unwilling to confirm the status and privileges accorded to Roger by the anti-pope Anacletus II. In a meeting at Ceprano, in July 1150, the pope agreed to legitimise the status of Archbishop Hugh of Palermo and the other bishops of the kingdom. Hugh was granted no metropolitan rights, however, and it was only his authority that consecrated Roger's surviving son William as co-ruler at Palermo, Easter 1151. In 1154, Roger died, leaving a kingdom seemingly strong but still faced by many enemies. William I suspected his cousin Robert, count of Loritello, of treachery, leading the count to flee. He appealed for help to Emperor Frederick Barbarossa and then the Byzantine emperor Manuel, while Pope Adrian IV was also keen to regain territory recently lost to Roger. 1155–56 were crisis years as rebellion spread and the Greeks re-occupied Apulia. William fell ill, and his chief minister Maio was distrusted by his barons. The new king proved his metal, though, recovering and leading a reconquest of his territories in 1156. He negotiated a treaty which gave the pope rights in southern Italy, but none in Sicily. William made peace with Emperor Manuel in 1158. He also showed a firm hand with rebels, but abandoned his father's harshness. Even Robert of Loritello, who led another revolt in 1161–62, was accepted back into his lands (during the regency), in 1169.

For William had died in 1166, to be succeeded by William II. Just how strongly the kingdom was now established is apparent from the ambitious nature of his strategic projects. Initially he tried to form a dynastic alliance with the Byzantine emperor. This turned from expected triumph to humiliation in April 1172, when William's expected bride did not arrive in Italy. (In 1177, he married Joanna, daughter of King Henry II of England.) The reason that Manuel had courted a Sicilian alliance in the first place was that he had in 1171 expelled the Venetians and cancelled their extensive trading privileges. By insulting William, he ensured that the king was thrown into the camp of the Italian maritime cities. William made an alliance with Genoa in 1174 and in the next year concluded a pact, intended to last for twenty years, with Venice. Manuel's defeat by the Seljuk Turks at Myriocephalon in 1176 left the empire as weak as it had been after Manzikert a century earlier. His death and the succession of Alexios II as a minor, in 1180, encouraged William to exploit the situation several years later.

William's ambition and strategic reach was well-illustrated by Sicilian attacks on Egypt in the 1170s. In 1174 a fleet carrying a large army and siege engines was sent to attack Alexandria. The intention was to link up with King Almaric of Jerusalem, but he died before he could launch his land invasion. The Sicilian fleet arrived at the end of July, but was driven off with heavy loss. Despite this there were regular raids on Muslim shipping and two more serious attacks on the Delta. In 1185 the king's ambitions once again extended to invading the Byzantine Empire, despite the depressing precedents of over a century of failure in such expeditions. Durazzo was taken in June, and the army advanced upon Salonika while the fleet sailed around the Peloponnese to attack the city by sea. The combined assault carried the place quickly and prospects looked good for the Sicilians. Yet they were defeated by a Byzantine policy of refusing battle and harrying foragers and the enemy lines of communication. The invaders were first forced into retreat and then attacked and dispersed, leaving only Durazzo in their hands. The city surrendered a year later.

William does not seem to have been disheartened by this disaster. His fleet was engaged supporting the ruler of Cyprus, Isaac Komnenos, against imperial attack in 1187. In the same year, Saladin overthrew the Latin Kingdom of Jerusalem and captured the city. In 1188 a Sicilian fleet sailed once more under its admiral Margaritone to support the remaining crusader outposts in Syria. In November 1189, William died. His only heir was his aunt Constance, who had married Henry, the German emperor's son, in 1184. The Sicilians preferred another grandson of Roger II, Tancred of Lecce, who unfortunately was illegitimate. This did not prevent his coronation in January 1190, but it did legitimise opposition to his rule. Tancred survived the confusion of the arrival of Richard the Lionheart, Philip II of France and their crusaders in the autumn. The death of Frederick Barbarossa on crusade meant that

Henry VI became king of Germany and now had the power to enforce his wife's claim. Henry arrived in Rome for his imperial coronation, which took place in April 1191. He conducted a brief siege of Naples before returning north. This enabled Tancred to reassert his authority over his mainland possessions. He also received papal recognition from Clement III. It was by no means apparent that the Norman Kingdom was about to be subsumed into the western empire. But this is precisely what happened in 1194, when Tancred died in February, shortly pre-deceased by his son and heir Roger, and leaving only a child to succeed him. Henry VI seized the opportunity presented. Supported by the maritime cities of Pisa and Genoa he swiftly subdued the island and was crowned on Christmas Day. Within two years he, too, was dead, leaving Empress Constance to rule in her stead. Her three-year-old son Frederick II was crowned king of Sicily in May 1197. Less than two years later Constance herself died. It was only after two decades of civil war that Frederick came fully into his inheritance, and by then the territories could only be seen as one of the Hohenstauffen realms rather than a Norman kingdom.

## The Government of the Norman Kingdom

Although the Kingdom of Sicily survived for another six hundred years, there was no particular reason why, in the eleventh and twelfth centuries, its territories should have been held together. Before the conquests of Robert Guiscard, his competitors and successors, the Lombard principalities on the mainland, under loose Byzantine hegemony, and Muslim Sicily, were distinctly different in nature. Unlike William the Conqueror, who inherited an ancient, if regionalised kingdom, fully part of western Christendom, the Norman rulers in the south had to create a new state from local materials. For Haskins and his imitators this was done through the establishment of a feudal regime which brought the disparate elements of the area under royal control. Recent work has been revisionist in nature, though, suggesting that Norman rule was pragmatic and eclectic, depending not just upon local expertise but old families and old structures as much as on the rulers' fellow immigrants. Certainly, the kingdom was a remarkable synthesis of societies and cultures, incorporating Latin and Greek Christianity as well as the largely Islamic population of Sicily. The incoming Frankish nobility has been estimated at no more than two to three thousand, so this is hardly surprising; but it was also a normal part of colonisation in the period.[28]

The Norman kingdom is also often seen in the light of its later unity. Although Robert Guiscard eventually succeeded in subjecting its territories to his rule, as duke of Apulia he was faced with a continuous series of revolts in his lifetime. This was despite his determined efforts to emphasise his legitimacy. His marriage to Sichelgaita at Melfi in 1058 was followed in the next year by papal investiture as duke, and in 1060 by acclamation by his troops after the capture of Reggio. These three events represented his appeal to the three political constituencies whose support he required to remain in power: the Lombard aristocracy, the Church and his own barons. The last group particularly required convincing that he was their lord, for a generation

---

28 Loud and Matthew are foremost of the revisionists. Loud, *Robert Guiscard*, 278–90, in a section entitled 'Native and Norman', provides a concise analysis of the issue; my generalised statistic is based on his comments on p. 279.

earlier the Hautevilles had been only two counts amongst twelve. The cost of Robert's expeditions against the Byzantine Empire also caused opposition and led to revolt. By the time of his death in 1085, though, Guiscard had established ducal lordship over most of the important towns in the region: in Apulia, the important ports of Trani, Bari, Brindisi, Otranto (all on the Adriatic) and Taranto; on the west coast, Salerno and Amalfi (overlordship alone); in Sicily, Palermo and half of Messina, together with control over numerous places inland. He had also made himself rich through war, especially the plunder of the Byzantine camp at Durazzo, in 1081.[29]

Not that this inheritance fell easily to his heirs. Graham Loud has identified five important Norman kin-groups in the region, together with other important comital dynasties whom any ruler had to manage.[30] Robert's choice as duke was his son by Sichelgaita, Roger, leaving the elder Bohemond effectively landless, so that he revolted in 1088. Although reconciled two years later, he remained a threat to the duchy's stability until he left on crusade in 1096. The process by which the mainland and Sicily were united under Roger II has already been explained, and thereby the kingdom of Sicily only came into being seven decades after Robert became duke. Just how 'Norman' this realm was has been questioned by the current generation of scholars. Although Roger II referred to *nostri Normanni* (in the context of a legal case) in 1130, detailed research has revealed the names of only 375 incomers of noble rank, one third of whom came from other regions of France.[31] In one sense, this does not matter, for the conquerors were Frankish in origin and culture; but when attempts are made to parallel too closely developments in England and Sicily, 'Norman' becomes an unhelpful attribution.

Roger's kingdom was not quite as large as his contemporary Henry I's, and much more disparate geographically and ethnically.[32] In part this was its strength, of course, and Sicily's position in the central Mediterranean meant that its rulers were well-placed to exploit its potential for trade and conquest. The kingdom was also wealthy from the traditional agricultural resources of the region, especially grain, but also many other exportable products. Roger II was the only king in western Europe to mint a gold currency (the *tari*, worth ¼ of an Arabic *dinar*), establishing a royal monopoly over its production. This was of high purity, and in 1140, Roger reformed the currency, with 60 copper *follari* and a silver ducat at 2½ to the *tari*.[33] To the Arabic influence on the administration of the realm has been attributed an anachronistic level of governmental efficiency. For example, the *diwan*, staffed by Latins, Greeks and Muslims appeared to earlier commentators to be a precocious treasury department.[34] To Donald Matthew, though, its work was focused 'on managing the royal "estate" rather than the control, collection and audit of royal finances in general'.[35] The king did possess an active and multi-lingual writing office, but this was essential to manage the diverse population under his rule.

Nor was the administration of the kingdom quite the modern marvel that Miss

---

[29] Loud, *Robert Guiscard*, 236, 245–6.

[30] Ibid., 246–52.

[31] Matthew, *Kingdom of Sicily*, 170 (legal case) and 140 (numbers taken from L.-R. Ménager, cited in n. 17 above).

[32] See Matthew, *Kingdom of Sicily*, ch. 3, 71–85.

[33] Matthew, *Kingdom of Sicily*, 240–1.

[34] Matthew, *Kingdom of Sicily*, 219–228.

[35] Matthew, *Kingdom of Sicily*, 224.

Jamison and others have made of it.[36] It was an extremely regionalised realm, and Professor Matthew has been unable to find any evidence of its division into the *comestabulia* units which she identified.[37] Local administration seems to have been carried on very much along traditional lines. Roger was happy to be seen to be supporting ancient custom at comital and communal level, as long as their representatives accepted his rule and paid their dues. These were a miscellaneous collection of tolls and tariffs ranging from harbour dues to levies on agricultural practices and production. There is no evidence that the annual *collecta*, imposed by Frederick II in 1235, was a regular royal tax a century earlier. Rather the government appealed for traditional 'aids' for a specific purpose, such as William II's *collecta* of 1185, raised to fund his attack on Durazzo.[38] There is evidence of the use of *bauli*, who were directed to supervise tax collection in 1171, but much of the local administration was left under the control of the counts. This was largely true of the law, too. The appearance of justiciars, a term found equally in the Anglo-Norman realm, is suggestive of government intervention in the legal process. Yet these seem to have been local men, selected to represent the king's interests in court, rather than the itinerant justices of the English system. They included Greek and Muslim individuals with the responsibility for running the legal structures of their own communities.[39]

The numerous barons of the kingdom had rights of jurisdiction as well as military obligations. They are recorded in the *Catalogus Baronum* of 1130 as providing 8,620 knights and over 11,000 less well-equipped *servientes*. Many estates and communities clearly owed military service long before the institution of the survey. It can be directly paralleled with other information-gathering exercises (such as the Bayeux Inquisition of the same decade) designed to discover the extent of military obligation available to the monarch. The easy assumption that the introduction of Frankish warriors into Italy resulted in an increase in vassalic commendation has been challenged by Loud and Matthew alike. The term homage first appeared in 1110, and the practice of enfeofment was not common.[40] Only on particular occasions, such as when Roger II finally gained control of Naples in 1140, was the king able to specify military obligation. So, every existing Neapolitan knight was supposedly provided with five *modia* of land with five *villani* to work it. This sounds very like the 'five hide' entry requirement of Anglo-Norman England.[41] Also, just as in Domesday Book, it transpires that in the *Catologus Baronum*, in over half of the cases where *villani* are mentioned (only 160 examples), they number less than five. So were there 'poor knights' in Italy as well as England? Well, only forty-seven were described as very poor, and another eighty-seven as having no land at all. Donald Matthew considers these *milites* as composing a 'kind of gentry group' of lower standing than in contemporary England.[42] This may be because the greater economic importance of the

---

[36] E. Jamison, 'The Norman Adminstration of Apulia and Capua', *Papers of the British School at Rome* vi, 1913, 211–481.

[37] Matthew, *Kingdom of Sicily*, 231–3.

[38] Matthew, *Kingdom of Sicily*, 237.

[39] Matthew, *Kingdom of Sicily*, 247–51.

[40] Loud, *Robert Guiscard*, 289; Matthew, *Kingdom of Sicily*, 144–5.

[41] C. Warren Hollister, *The Military Organization of Norman England*, Oxford 1965, 'hides, unit of five' p. 311 and *passim*. Hollister points out how just unsystematic this supposed organisation was.

[42] S. Harvey, 'The Knight and the Knight's Fee in England', *Past and Present* xlix, 1970, 3–43; Donald F. Fleming, 'Landholding in Domesday Book: a Revision', *ANS* xiii, 1990, 83–98; Matthew, *Kingdom of Sicily*, 146.

monasteries and the towns meant that they contributed more to the military, and naval, strength of the kingdom. The maritime nature of much of the realm (nowhere was more than fifty miles from the sea) resulted in the maintenance of substantial fleets. Obligations to provide naval service – ships and men – seem to have been both ancient and heavy.[43] Sicilian fleets, especially under the direction of George of Antioch (the first man to bear the title of admiral) gave the kings a powerful offensive weapon in war and diplomacy, as well as assuring the safety of long exposed coastlines. Generally, they performed well except in times of domestic political crisis, as in the mid-1150s when the emperor Manuel's forces were able to operate unchecked in Italy.

When Roger set about his coronation he, like William of Normandy, insisted upon establishing legitimacy. Unlike the duke, he had to do so in the face of papal opposition. He was able to ensure a *pallium* for the archbishop of Palermo, though, before his coronation in 1130. He also had his successor, William I, crowned as co-king in 1151, both to emphasise his regality and to secure the succession. This was entirely in keeping with Capetian and general Frankish practice at the time.[44] The Norman monarchs also spent enormously on celebrating their kingship, in the creation of lavish palaces, huge monasteries and beautiful churches. It was in the field of art and architecture that the blend of cultural influences found at the crossing point of the Mediterranean left an enduring mark. The cathedral at Cefalu still contains a magnificent Christ Pantokrator head, while the church of the monastery of Monreale is laden with mosaics. This is built in the western style, a nave and aisled building, allowing the artists ample room to demonstrate their craft in a series of long displays of biblical tales. Begun in 1174, it is an almost excessive display of the wealth of the patron, William II, intended as a royal mausoleum, into which he transferred his father's body and where he buried his mother. In addition, the palace chapel and the Martorana (an Orthodox nunnery) at Palermo demonstrated the dynasty's self-confidence and self-assertiveness through religious art.[45]

The foundation of the Norman kingdom was a remarkable achievement in a region which had been divided on political, cultural and religious grounds for centuries. It is not to decry this achievement to point out that the kingdom was rather less Norman than had been confidently asserted by an earlier generation of scholars. For the northerners, who first infiltrated and then conquered southern Italy and Sicily in the period before 1100, were essentially pragmatic and flexible rulers. Although Latin Christianity did not know tolerance at this period, its practitioners, in this kingdom at least, were prepared to allow other forms of Christian worship and not to persecute non-believers. The Normans did not arrive with a 'feudal blueprint' for the societies which they conquered, although their rulers did operate in a thoroughly conventional, Frankish, manner in establishing the monarchy. If it looked (and sounded in its administrative titles) Byzantine and oriental, this was due to the Latin immigrants taking on the forms and representations of authority long understood in their new domains. There was never truly a fusion of cultures, but the Norman kings created an edifice that long outlasted their dynasty and survived, with mutations, until the revolutionary era of the nineteenth century.

---

[43] Matthew, *Kingdom of Sicily*, 260–2.
[44] Matthew, *Kingdom of Sicily*, 170–1.
[45] Matthew, *Kingdom of Sicily*, 197–206.

# 6

# Historical Writing

## ELISABETH VAN HOUTS

Normandy and England in the central Middle Ages are exceptionally well provided with chronicles, even though their composition, as we shall see, tended to occur in clusters, leaving gaps for periods of great upheaval and trauma.[1] For example, there are few contemporary indigenous reports on the settlement of the vikings in Normandy c. 900 or on the conquest of England in 1066 or on the 'loss of Normandy' in 1204. Conquests are usually reported by the conquerors and not by the victims, while defeats are usually digested over a long time and the victims' views do not emerge until the second or third generation afterwards. Moreover, as this chapter will show, historians' comments are not static but change over time, sometimes frequently. Hence, as we shall see, many narratives were revised, updated, and altered by their authors as they went along, illustrating the changing perspectives on the (recent) past. The chronicles of Normandy and England also illustrate the interesting change of balance between the two nations. Normandy rose from a small, relatively insignificant, principality to become the dominant political force in France (and England), but then fell out of the English orbit in 1204. England in contrast, having suffered two successive submissions to foreign forces (Danes in 1016 and Normans in 1066), emerged as the dominant partner of the Anglo-Norman alliance before, in 1204, it 'lost' Normandy. Conquest and defeat led to the migration of people across national boundaries, with the consequence of Normandy and, especially, England becoming multi-ethnic communities. What political upheaval and social change meant for these countries can be charted through the comments of their historians. This chapter is concerned with the Latin historiography of the eleventh and twelfth centuries in the Anglo-Norman realm. In England the vernacular Old English was replaced by Latin on a large scale by the end of the eleventh century, while from that time onwards, as Ian Short describes in Chapter 10, vernacular French begins to rival Latin as a language for literature and historiography.

The viking settlement of Normandy and the rise of the house of Rollo, founding father of the principality, was first related by Dudo of Saint-Quentin, himself a Vermandois clerk, who served the dukes Richard I (943–96) and Richard II

---

[1] Helpful introductions are L. Shopkow, *History and Community: Norman Historical Writing in the Eleventh and Twelfth Centuries*, Washington 1997; A. Gransden, *Historical Writing in England c. 550 to c. 1307*, London 1974; and E.M.C. van Houts, *History and Family Traditions in England and the Continent 1000–1200*, Aldershot 1999. An interesting study, emphasizing national identity in the historical writing of the Anglo-Norman realm, can be found in N. Kersken, *Geschichtsschreibung im Europa der 'Nationen': National geschichtliche Gesamtdarstellungen im Mittelalter*, Münstersche Historische Forschungen 8, Cologne 1995, esp. 78–125 (Normandy) and 126–367 (England).

(996–1026).[2] Having started before 996 he may have made good progress by 1001, the year in which a foundation history of Fécamp, probably composed by Dudo himself, was included in the 'Deeds of the Normans'.[3] As chancellor, Dudo found himself at the heart of the ducal administration and in an ideal position to take up the request from father and son to write a history of their people. The chronicle is a curious mixture of oral tradition, learned Latin literature and ecclesiastical historiography. The oral tales derived from Duke Richard I's illegitimate son, Count Rodulf of Ivry, and his widow Countess Gunnor, whose memory is praised and who presumably filled in some details on the family background.[4] The sophisticated style of Dudo's writing owes much to his education in the late Carolingian schools of upper Lotharingia where Vergil's Aeneid has been shown to have inspired his grammar and vocabulary.[5] The form of his work, divided into four books each of which devoted to one Norman leader, Hasting, Rollo, William Longsword and Richard I, was modelled on the so-called '*gesta*' genre used thusfar exclusively for the serial biographies of popes, bishops and abbots. It was Dudo's innovation to apply this technique to the succession of secular princes in the same, ducal, office.[6] As a result his chronicle projected backwards into Norman history the norms and values of Duke Richard I's reign. The dukes' struggle for independance in France was based on the argument that the duchy had been given as allodial land to Rollo in 911 by King Charles the Simple, who allowed Rollo to pass on this possession freely to his sons and grandsons in perpetuity. We now know that this was never the case. The scanty documentary evidence reveals that the French king gave Rouen and its immediate area to Rollo to provide him with a temporary base from which to assist the king in his fight against (other) viking intruders. By Dudo's time, however, this was conveniently forgotten and the *de facto* power of the Norman princes was such that the kings of France were in no position to challenge their version of events. In the eleventh and twelfth centuries Dudo's version became the official Norman evidence for semi-independence and was repeatedly quoted in support of Norman refusals to perform homage, and even sometimes, military service.

Although Dudo can legitimately be identified as Normandy's first dynastic historian, his view of pre-Rollo Normandy as a waste land and of the tenth century as shaped exclusively by Rollo's successors is extremely misleading. Recent research on the state of hagiography in tenth-century Normandy has shown that the principality was home to lively communities of monks and canons aware of their privileges, estates and saints.[7] These monks and canons knew their history, but faced with a new ruling family after an unsettled time, they needed to renegotiate whatever rights and

2    *Dudo*, trans. Christiansen. For Dudo in a historiographical context, see also *Dudone di S. Quintini*, ed. P.G. A Degli'Innocenti, Trent 1995.
3    M. Arnoux, 'Before the *Gesta Normannorum* and beyond Dudo: Some Evidence on Early Norman Historiography', *ANS* xxii, 1999, 29–48 at 31–2.
4    E. Searle, 'Fiction and Pattern in Heroic History: Dudo of Saint-Quentin', *Viator* xv, 1984, 75–86.
5    L. Shopkow, 'The Carolingian World of Dudo of St Quentin', *JMH* xv, 1989, 19–37; P. Bouet, 'Dudon de Saint-Quentin et Virgile: "L'Enéide" au service de la cause normande', in *Recueil d'études en hommage à Lucien Musset*, Cahiers des Annales de Normandie xxiii, Caen 1990, 215–36.
6    M. Sot, *Gesta episcoporum, gesta abbatum*, Typologie des sources du moyen âge occidental, 37, Turnhout 1981; and E.M.C. van Houts, 'The Gesta Normannorum ducum: a History without an End', *ANS* iii, 1980, 106–118 at 107.
7    F. Lifshitz, *The Norman Conquest of Pious Neustria: Historiographic Discourse and Saintly Relics, 684–1000*, Toronto 1995; and Arnoux, 'Before the *Gesta Normannorum*', 38–42.

lands they had with the newcomers. At Rouen's cathedral, as at Saint-Ouen and at Fécamp, they used their knowledge of the past to argue with dukes Richard I and Richard II for the exercise of authority over their churches. The tenth-century Reform movement, so well known from Anglo-Saxon England and Flanders, had certainly infiltrated the duchy, whether the dukes liked it or not. Around the first millennium we witness not a revival of the Norman Church (implying near death and waste land), but instead a new relationship between on the one hand the secular church as represented by bishops (from 989 at Rouen and Bayeux members of the ducal family) and the autonomous monasteries, and on the other hand the new ruling family.

Dudo's history of the Norman dukes became the starting point for all later Norman historiography, whether it be saints' lives and miracles describing the devastation caused by the vikings, or more elaborate annals or chronicles. The 'Discovery and Miracles of Saint Vulfran', a history of the re-foundation of the Merovingian monastery of Saint-Wandrille, written in c. 1053–54, illustrates Dudo's influence very well.[8] The first few chapters describe the viking settlement of Normandy in virtually identical terms to Dudo, including his dating of events. The author of the 'Discovery' pictured the dukes, and in particular Richard I, as defenders of the Christian faith by restoring the monastic lands lost during the viking raids to the monks of Saint-Wandrille. Other historical writing at Jumièges,[9] Fécamp[10] and Mont-Saint-Michel shows a similar tendency.[11] The rise of Normandy is inextricably linked with the refoundation, or rebirth, of its own monasteries due to the dukes themselves.[12] Dudo had propagated the theme of transformation from pagan robbers to Christian princes as justification of Rollo's rightful occupancy of Normandy, a historical fiction that became the canon for Norman historical writing for generations to come.

This is nowhere more clear than in William of Jumièges's work. As a monk of Jumièges, another house that owed its refoundation to ducal involvement, he was active from the 1050s to just before 1070.[13] During the reign of William the Conqueror, but well before 1066, it had become clear that an update of Dudo's chronicle was desirable. Unlike Dudo, William was not prompted by either the duke himself or other members of the ducal house, even though he hints (and Orderic Vitalis later repeated this claim) that the update on the Norman Conquest took place as the result of a request from King William.[14] In the late 1050s or early 1060s William of Jumièges took Dudo's chronicle, revised it and added three more books covering the reigns of Richard II (Book V), Richard III (1026–27) and Robert the Magnificent (1027–35)

---

8   *Inventio et miracula sancti Vulfranni*, ed. Dom Laporte, Mélanges publiés par la Société de l'Histoire de Normandie, 14e série, Rouen and Paris 1938; and E. van Houts, 'Historiography and Hagiography at Saint-Wandrille: the *Inventio et miracula sancti Vulfranni*', *ANS* xii 1989, 233–51, and reprinted in Van Houts, *History and Family Traditions*, no. iv.

9   *Jumièges* i, xxviii–xxx.

10  Arnoux, 'Before the *Gesta Normannorum*'; and M. Arnoux, 'La fortune du *Libellus de reuelatione, edificatione et auctoritate Fiscannensis monasterii*: note sur la production historiographique d'une abbaye bénédictine normande', *Revue d'Histoire des Textes* xxi, 1991, 135–58; and 'Les premières chroniques de Fécamp: de l'hagiographie à l'histoire', in *Les saints dans la Normandie médiévale*, ed. P. Bouet and F. Neveux, Caen 2000, 71–82.

11  C. Potts, 'Normandy or Brittany? A Conflict of Interests at Mont-Saint-Michel (996–1035)', *ANS* xii, 1989, 135–56.

12  C. Potts, *Monastic Revival and Regional Identity in Normandy*, Woodbridge 1997, and also Chapter 2 in the present volume.

13  *Jumièges* i, xxxii–xxxv.

14  *Jumièges* i, xxxi, 4–5, and *Orderic* ii, 2–4, 78, and iii, 304.

(Book VI), and William the Conqueror in Book VII. William's revision of Dudo's work is remarkable because he removed the chapters on Hasting and Rollo as pagan leaders and replaced them with an account of the viking settlement taken from hagiographic sources from his own monastery and from Saint-Benoît-sur-Loire (Fleury) and interlaced them with stories containing Scandinavian saga motifs. The result was a sober account emphasizing a joint venture of anonymous vikings, from whom Rollo was chosen as a leader by lot, rather than an epic adventure centered on the pagan heroes, Hasting and Rollo. In developing Dudo's portrayal of the dukes as Christian princes, William removed all sections which in his opinion were pure entertainment and not instructive (in a Christian moralistic sense) at all. The effectiveness of the serial biography was beyond doubt. The normally precarious succession of leaders in the French principalities is portrayed here as a legitimate inheritance of an office from father to son after proper designation ceremonies.[15] William's identical language for virtually all designation ceremonies helped to enhance this fiction. In reality, the ducal successions were not at all the peaceful transfers of authority which William's carefully drafted discourse suggests. From the perspective of William the Conqueror's time, however, it was sheer necessity to pretend that each duke had succeeded the previous one without apparent effort, if only to underline that William's own succession had ultimately confounded those who were against it on the grounds of his illegitimacy.

The history of the Norman Conquest of England, covered in the last seven chapters of Book VII, rapidly outgrew its treatment as part of the *Gesta Normannorum Ducum*. In epic terms it called for a biographical approach that could centre more freely on William's personality than the *gesta* genre, with its focus on the ducal office, allowed. Also a secular clerk or chaplain was in a better position than a monk to provide such a portrait. In c. 1077 William of Poitiers, one-time ducal chaplain, portrayed the duke/king as a second Caesar who as potential emperor attained leadership of the Christian world.[16] This theme had already been introduced by Bishop Guy of Amiens, chaplain of William's wife Matilda, who in 1067 had composed his *Carmen de Hastingae Proelio* (Song of the Battle of Hastings).[17] The duke's half-brother, Bishop Odo of Bayeux, commissioned a eulogy of another kind in the form of the Bayeux Tapestry.[18] Moreover, several other French prelates joined this trio by offering shorter poems which celebrated the most famous victory in the western world to date.[19] All these Latin texts were products of writers schooled in classical tradition, educated in the early cathedral schools and far more sophisticated in their language than William of Jumièges or the other monastic chroniclers mentioned. The result was a propaganda

[15] G. Garnett, ' "Ducal" Succession in Early Normandy', in *Law and Government in Medieval England and Normandy: Essays in honour of Sir James Holt*, ed. G. Garnett and J. Hudson, Cambridge 1994, 80–110.

[16] *Gesta Guillelmi*, and R.H.C. Davis, 'William of Poitiers and his History of William the Conqueror', in *The Writing of History in the Middle Ages: Essays presented to Richard William Southern*, ed. R.H.C. Davis and J.M. Wallace-Hadrill, Oxford 1981, 71–100.

[17] *Carmen*, and G. Orlandi, 'Some Afterthoughts on the *Carmen de Hastingae Proelio*', in *Media Latinitas: a Collection of Essays to Mark the Occasion of the Retirement of L. J. Engels*, Instrumenta Patristica xxviii, ed. R. Nip *et al.*, Turnhout 1996, 117–28.

[18] *The Bayeux Tapestry*, ed. D. Wilson, London 1985, and *La Tapisserie de Bayeux*, ed. B. Levy and F. Neveux (forthcoming).

[19] E.M.C. van Houts, 'Latin Poetry and the Anglo-Norman Court 1066–1135: the *Carmen de Hastingae Proelio*', *JMH* xv, 1989, 39–62, reprinted in Van Houts, *History and Family Traditions*, no. ix.

campaign on a scale that easily matched that launched by the learned entourage of the Carolingian and Ottonian kings.[20] They had trumpeted the legitimization of conquest in terms of missionary achievement and Christianisation, while the Norman and French propagandists of William the Conqueror whitewashed a terrible bloodbath by stressing his legal revenge against perjury. It had been William's Christian duty to kill the tyrant king (Harold) who had committed this perjury. However, this legalistic excuse was received mostly with scepticism throughout Europe, where it was claimed that the Conqueror, with papal approval, had gone too far in his pursuit of a foreign crown.[21]

What strikes the modern historian of this material most, however, is the transient nature of the propaganda materials produced by the Norman court, none of which has survived in large numbers of manuscripts, except for the *Gesta Normannorum ducum*, or, as we shall see below, the later Anglo-Norman histories. William of Poitiers' biography circulated in a few copies, perhaps less than three or four, none of which survived beyond the seventeenth century. Bishop Guy's *Carmen* was known to William of Poitiers, Orderic Vitalis and Robert of Torigni but no Norman copy has survived. Only two early twelfth-century manuscript fragments from the north-east of France are extant. As is well known, the Bayeux Tapestry is unique, and there is little evidence to support the idea that many such pictorial histories of the Conquest existed.[22] It is equally interesting that these three contemporary documents are incomplete. William of Poitiers's biography lacks the beginning and the end, though Orderic knew it in its complete state. The text of Bishop Guy's *Carmen* breaks off, coincidentally like William of Poitiers' book, during the coronation ceremony of William the Conqueror on Christmas Day 1066. And this is exactly the event one might have expected as the grand finale of the Bayeux Tapestry, except that we do not have it. The present final scene, badly frayed, shows fugitive soldiers racing for their lives away from the battlefield. The conclusion, therefore, is that the fame and eulogies following 1066 were relatively shortlived and the texts got mutilated.

In contrast to eleventh-century Normandy, very little historiographical activity can be discerned in pre-Conquest England, a situation seemingly confirmed by William of Malmesbury who was in no doubt about the dearth of historical writing after Bede:

> The history of the English, from their arrival in Britain to his own time has been told with straightforward charm by Bede, most learned and least proud of men. After Bede you will not easily, I think, find anyone who has devoted himself to writing English history in Latin . . . for my own part I have kept continual watch, but hitherto my labours in the quest have been a waste of time.[23]

20  M. Innes and R. McKitterick, 'The Writing of History', in *Carolingian Culture: Emulation and Innovation*, ed. R. McKitterick, Cambridge 1994, 193–220; and P. Corbet, *Les saints ottoniens: sainteté dynastique, sainteté royale et sainteté féminine autour de l'an mil*, Beihefte der Francia 15, Sigmaringen 1986.

21  E.M.C. van Houts, 'The Norman Conquest through European Eyes', *EHR* cx, 1995, 832–53, reprinted in Van Houts, *History and Family Traditions*, no. viii.

22  The only parallel exists in an imaginative poem written by Baudri of Bourgueil, who describes a tapestry hanging in Countess Adela of Blois's chamber: see M. Herren, 'Baudri de Bourgueil, Adelae comitissae', in *The Bayeux Tapestry: History and Bibliography*, ed. S.A. Brown, Woodbridge 1988, 167–77; and G.A. Bond, *The Loving Subject: Desire, Eloquence and Power in Romanesque France*, Philadelphia 1995.

23  *Gesta Regum*, 14–15.

Although William immediately afterwards acknowledged the existence of the Anglo-Saxon chronicle as 'some records in the form of annals in the mother tongue', the general picture he sketched is true enough. The *Anglo-Saxon Chronicle* is the generic name of a series of annals going back to one original, but branching out in different directions. Its various versions, each of which is known by a letter from the alphabet, provide no more than a rather bare framework of dates with brief entries for each year.[24] The original, composed under the direction of King Alfred (d. 899), is now lost, but it was copied and continued at other monasteries in England. We know for certain that A was at Winchester and Christ Church, Canterbury, that a now lost one was at Abingdon and from it B and C derive, and that E is a Peterborough copy made from an exemplar at St Augustine's Canterbury. Each redactor entered material that was particularly relevant for his locality, hence the variations in the text. The *Anglo-Saxon Chronicle* was sparsely updated throughout the later 1060s and 1070s. The entries are short, though only marginally shorter than the pre-1066 ones. Of the surviving versions, only D and E warrant discussion, even though in both cases it is virtually impossible to decide what was written as a contemporary account and what is due to later revision or interpolation dating from a time when England was firmly under Norman authority. The only copy of D available was written after 1100, and therefore the extent of the copyist's rewriting may never be known. E survives in a twelfth-century copy kept up-to-date till the mid-1150s at Peterborough. Here too the difference between contemporary annal, Canterbury revision and Peterborough text is difficult to assess. Despite the problematic transmission of the text, the codicological problems of the manuscripts and the sparsity of its contents, the *Anglo-Saxon Chronicle* is the prime example of historical writing in eleventh-century England.

Two other historical works are known, both written at the request of English queens. The first, the *Encomium Emmae reginae*, was commissioned by King Edward's mother, Emma, queen of king Aethelred (d. 1016) and then of his successor the Danish King Cnut (d. 1035).[25] It is ostensibly a biography of her second husband Cnut, but is in fact an apology for their son Hartacnut at the expense of Emma's sons by Aethelred, Edward and his brother Alfred. Thus the praise is for the Danish settlers in England and the work is indirectly an apology for Scandinavian occupation. On the grounds of her Norman origin (she was a daughter of Duke Richard I and Gunnor), one could argue that the inspiration behind the *Encomium* might have been Norman rather than English. This argument loses some of its force once one takes into account that its author was neither English nor Norman, but Flemish. He was a monk of St Bertin at Saint-Omer who was engaged by Emma during her years in exile in Flanders (1037–40). Thus her choice of a Flemish writer rather than an English one might have been dictated by her absence abroad rather than by an absence of skilled historians in England.[26] No such excuse can explain the Flemish authorship of the other historical work written at a queen's behest, *The Life of King Edward*, commissioned by Emma's daughter-in-law Queen Edith. Edith was in England when during her husband's last illness in 1065, she asked another monk of St Bertin at Saint-Omer to make a begin-

---

[24] *ASC*. A collaborative edition is in progress under the general editorship of D. Dumville and S. Keynes, Woodbridge 1983– .

[25] *Encomium Emmae Reginae*, ed. A. Campbell with a supplementary introduction by S. Keynes, Camden Classic Reprints iv, Cambridge 1998.

[26] *Encomium*, introduction by Keynes, p. xxxviii, suggests that her choice was dictated by the fact that no Englishman might have wished to associate himself with her.

ning of Edward's biography.[27] Here too we find the woman behind the throne setting out her agenda. Edith was concerned, however, as much as with her husband, with her father Earl Godwin and her brothers Earl (later King) Harold and Earl Tostig. As Frank Barlow has noted, half way through the text the tone dramatically changes, arguably as the result of the Conquest.[28] Here is a good example of a historical narrative in progress, begun in the autumn of 1065, its production being overtaken by events, the drama of 1066, and finished in 1067. King Edward's death had been anticipated, but not the quarrel between Harold and Tostig leading to the battle of Stamford Bridge where Tostig (Edith's favourite brother) lost his life, nor the calamitous invasion by William the Conqueror leading to the death of Edith's other brother. In this case the biographical account or life-story of one important figure helped literally to bridge the gap in a calamitous period in history.[29]

As there is no hint of xenophobia in William of Malmesbury's complaint about the absence of recent historical writing England, there is no reason to think that he glossed over the two works commissioned by queens on account of their foreign authorship. But the presence of Flemish historians and hagiographers in eleventh-century England is as remarkable as it is puzzling. Perhaps these monks spotted the same gap in the market that William of Malmesbury later identified and were attracted by the patronage available in England. The number of continental, especially Lotharingian, bishops in England was growing during the reign of King Edward and they provided for eager clerks an approachable group of patrons. Conversely, instead of an English pull it might have been a case of a Flemish push. Flanders may not have appreciated its scholars despite a proven audience for monastic hagiography there.[30] Whatever the reason behind this domination of the historiographical scene may have been, one of the Flemings, Goscelin of Saint-Bertin, stood out even in the opinion of William of Malmesbury.[31] He came to England in the late 1050s or early 1060s, perhaps with Bishop Herman of Wiltshire, and trekked from one church to the next, in great demand for his literary skills. He recorded the lives and miracles of Anglo-Saxon saints and by so doing documented the history of many monastic communities. After the Norman Conquest his skills were in particular demand as far afield as Wilton, Ramsey and Canterbury. Although there was a clear tradition of hagiographical writing in pre-Conquest England, there is no doubt that the Norman Conquest accelerated the process and gave it an urgency it would not otherwise have had. Other compatriots came to England and were likewise fêted as skilled hagiographers: Folcard of Saint-Bertin worked at Thorney Abbey, while Herman (or Bertran) of Flanders was active at Bury St Edmunds.[32] If there is any continuity here with

---

27  *Vita Aedwardi.*

28  *Vita Aedwardi,* xxix–xxxiii.

29  M. Otter, '1066: the Moment of Transition in Two Narratives of the Norman Conquest', *Speculum* lxxiv, 1999, 565–86.

30  B. de Gaiffier, 'L'hagiographie dans le marquisat de Flandre et le duché de Basse-Lotharingie au XIe siècle', in *Etudes critiques d'hagiographie et d'iconologie*, Subsidia hagiographica 43, Brussels 1967, 415–507.

31  For Goscelin, see F. Barlow, 'Goscelin of Saint-Bertin and his Works', in *Vita Aedwardi*, appendix C, 132–49.

32  For Folcuin, see *Vita Aedwardi*, lii–lvii. For Herman (or Bertran), see A. Gransden, 'The Composition and Authorship of the *De miraculis sancti Eadmundi* Attributed to "Hermann the Archdeacon" ', *Journal of Medieval Latin* v, 1995, 1–52.

pre-Conquest tradition, then the Flemish nationality of the hagiographers stands out. This again begs the question of where were the English authors?

Apart from the *Anglo-Saxon Chronicle* the evidence for historical writing in Old English, as opposed to Latin, is tantalizingly vague, due to the fact that several works have been lost and knowledge about them comes only from later sources. Whether the handful of works mentioned form the tip of an iceberg or whether they were the only ones that were written is difficult to determine. Two narrative texts can be identified with confidence. At Worcester between 1095 and 1113 the monk Coleman wrote a now lost biography of Bishop Wulfstan (1062–95) in Old English. Its existence is known from William of Malmesbury, who reworked the original and translated it into Latin.[33] At Ely there existed an Old English life of the Anglo-Saxon resistance fighter Hereward, composed by his one time chaplain Leofric, which was adapted and translated into Latin by someone called Richard.[34] Three other texts in Old English, moreover, were replaced by Latin versions, two of which, interestingly, come from Worcester and Ely where the now lost Old English biographies were kept. In Worcester Coleman's contemporary, Hemming, at the behest of Bishop Wulfstan and therefore before the bishop's death in 1095, copied a wide variety of Old English and Latin charters and other documents. He was not simply a compiler but acted as historian/archivist by providing a narrative that gave cohesion to his own collection, which he added to an early eleventh-century cartulary.[35] A similar project was undertaken in Ely, where Bishop Hervey (1109–31) commissioned a Latin translation of Bishop Aethelwold's book of grants to Ely. This version was subsequently included in the *Liber Eliensis*, the cartulary-chronicle of Ely compiled in the 1170s.[36] We also have evidence for (Latin) historical compilation at Christ Church, Canterbury, where too, within two decades of the Norman Conquest, the monks produced a collection of charters with historical commentary.[37] These are some of the most important examples of monastic historical compilations assembled to provide the English monasteries with the written evidence to defend their rights and claims against predatory newcomers.

One of the most interesting sources for historical consciousness in England is the information about the past contained in the law codes. After the Norman Conquest

[33] *The Vita Wulfstani of William of Malmesbury*, ed. R.R. Darlington, London 1928, and trans. M. Swanton in *Three Lives of the Last Englishmen*, Garland Library of Medieval Literature series B, x, New York and London 1984, 91–148. Otter, '1066', 565–86, argues that his work together with *The Life of King Edward* acted as a literary bridge between the good old days and the uncertain future.

[34] *Gesta Herwardi incliti exulis et militis*, ed. Th.D. Hardy and C.T. Martin in *Lestorie des Engles solum la translacion maistre Geffrei Gaimar*, RS, London 1888, 339–404, and trans. M. Swanton, in *Three Lives*, 45–88, and revised in *Medieval Outlaws. Ten Tales in Modern English*, ed. T.H. Ohlgren, Stroud 1998, 12–60.

[35] *Hemingi Chartularium ecclesiae Wigorniensis*, ed. T. Hearne, 2 vols, Oxford 1723, and N.R. Ker, 'Hemming's Cartulary: a Description of the Two Worcester Cartularies in Cotton Tiberius A. XIII', in his *Books, Collectors and Libraries*, ed. A.G. Watson, London 1985, 31–59. This and other contemporary documents are discussed in J. Barrow, 'How the Twelfth-Century Monks of Worcester Preserved their Past', in *The Perception of the Past in Twelfth-Century Europe*, ed. P. Magdalino, London 1992, 53–74.

[36] *Liber Eliensis*, ed. E.O. Blake, London 1962; the *Libellus quorundam insignium operum beati Aethelwoldi*, the early-eleventh-century cartulary, can be found in book II c. 1–49 on pp. 65–117.

[37] R. Fleming, 'Christ Church Canterbury's Anglo-Norman Cartulary', in *Anglo-Norman Political Culture and the Twelfth-Century Renaissance: Proceedings of the Borchard Conference on Anglo-Norman History, 1995*, ed. C.W. Hollister, Woodbridge 1997, 83–156.

William the Conqueror and his sons promised to respect the laws of their English predecessors and to govern England according to the laws of Edward. What this meant in practice for the many continental newcomers and their successors is less clear. There is no evidence of a centralised royal rescue operation for the compilation of one corpus of laws. What has survived dates predominantly from the reign of Henry I, when many of the English laws were either copied into new collections or translated from Old English into Latin to make them available to the Norman rulers. The most important are the *Textus Roffensis* from Rochester (1120s),[38] the *Quadripartitus*, or 'Law in Four Parts' (c. 1100–1108),[39] the *Leges Henrici Primi*[40] and the *Laws of Edward the Confessor* probably from Lincoln (c. 1136).[41] With the exception of the *Leges Henrici*, they are *ad hoc* compilations of whatever legal material was available locally, especially in episcopal centres. They were practical handbooks for clerks and bishops, many of whom were foreign and had a desperate need for knowledge about the workings of English law in a country beset with disputes about land, rights and the interpretation of customs.[42] These legal encyclopaedias, to use Patrick Wormald's phrase, were presented, however, as legislation produced by kings, with long introductions praising the Anglo-Saxon and Norman rulers for the peace they brought through these laws. It is in this context that we find mini-surveys of eleventh-century history, the succession of kings and the impact of the Conquest that throw light on the compilers' views of that past. These historiographical sections remain virtually unexplored but merit fresh scrutiny.[43]

The same need for knowledge about the past can be detected in local histories that were produced all over England. One of the first was Simeon of Durham's Latin history of Durham which now constitutes our major source for the post-Conquest history of northern England.[44] On the basis of his distinctive handwriting he has been identified as a continental clerk from north-western France (perhaps a Norman) who came to Durham probably with William of St Carilef (d. 1096) after the bishop's temporary exile on the continent in the 1080s.[45] Simeon became chanter, librarian/archivist and head of the *scriptorium* at Durham. He used his historical talent for the production of the 'Tract on the Origins and Progress of this the Church of Durham', written between 1104–1107 and 1115, to provide the evidence that Durham

---

[38] *Textus Roffensis*, ed. P. Sawyer, Early English Manuscripts in Facsimile vii and xi, Copenhagen 1957 and 1962; the legal texts can be found on fos 1r–118r and the charters on 119r–234r. The collection is discussed by P. Wormald, '*Laga Eadwardi*: the *Textus Roffensis* and its Context', *ANS* xvii, 1994, 243–66, and *The Making of English Law: King Alfred to the Twelfth Century, volume 1: Legislation and its Limits*, Oxford 1999, 244–52.

[39] F. Liebermann, *Quadripartitus: Ein englisches Rechtsbuch von 1114*, Halle 1892; P. Wormald, ' "*Quadripartitus*" ', in *Law and Government in Medieval England and Normandy: Essays in Honour of Sir James Holt*, ed. G. Garnett and J. Hudson, Cambridge 1994, 111–48; and R. Sharpe, 'The Prefaces of "*Quadripartitus*" ', in ibid., 148–72; see also Wormald, *The Making of English Law*, 236–44.

[40] *Leges Henrici Primi*, ed. and trans. J.J. Downer, Oxford 1972.

[41] B.R. O'Brien, *God's Peace and King's Peace: the Laws of Edward the Confessor*, Philadelphia 1999.

[42] Wormald, '*Quadripartitus*', 144–5; Wormald, '*Laga Eadwardi*', 264–6; and O'Brien, *God's Peace*, 44–63.

[43] Particularly interesting are Sharpe, 'The Prefaces' and O'Brien, *God's Peace*, 158–9 and 192–7.

[44] *Symeon of Durham, Libellus de exordio atque procursu istius hoc est Dunhelmensis ecclesie; Tract on the Origins and Progress of this the Church of Durham*, ed. and trans. D. Rollason, Oxford 2000; and *Symeon of Durham, Historian of Durham and the North*, ed. D. Rollason, Stamford 1998.

[45] M. Gullick, 'The Hand of Symeon of Durham: Further Observations on the Durham Martyrology Scribe', in *Symeon of Durham, Historian*, ed. Rollason, 14–31.

had rights over the ancient monasteries of Jarrow and Lindesfarne. What makes Simeon's achievement so remarkable is that he had to acquire mastery of the English language in order to access the source material on which so much of his (Latin) chronicle is based. Within two decades of the Conquest Christ Church at Canterbury had in its precentor Osbern an avid propagandist of its saints, whose lives he wrote down, albeit with less care than his younger contemporary Eadmer wished.[46] Perhaps to set the record straight Eadmer began his *History of Recent Events*, the first attempt by a full-blooded Englishman to digest the impact of the Norman Conquest. Despite its brief introductory section from King Edgar to the Conquest, it is primarily an account of the affairs of the Church of Canterbury. Eadmer had intimate knowledge of the local archives in Canterbury, which he exploited also for his hagiographical work. To his local expertise he added, as right-hand man of Archbishop Anselm, whose biography he wrote, a wider European perspective.[47] Eadmer's work on the primacy of Canterbury did not remain unchallenged, for at its rival archiepiscopal see of York, in c. 1127 Hugh the Chanter produced a counter-attack in a failed attempt to prove York's allegations of parity.[48] At Rochester, as at Christ Church, Canterbury and York, historical writing served a clear political agenda. For example, the *Life of Gundulf* was written in an attempt to protect the institution's monastic ideal against those who wished to give priority to its role as a bishop's see.[49] While Simeon of Durham and the anonymous hagiographer of Rochester were apologists for the monastic cathedrals, two of their colleagues put their skills at the disposal of monasteries near to each other: Battle and St Pancras at Lewes.[50] Since both were post-Conquest foundations they had virtually no archives and therefore there was no need for skilled archivists. Instead they produced propagandistic literature centered on the founding families of the monasteries. The Battle author eulogized William the Conqueror and his son Henry I, while the 'Hyde' Chronicler praised the Warenne family.

Besides the local historical work produced in many of the cathedrals (Canterbury, Durham, York and Rochester) larger scale historical enterprises were undertaken. At Worcester, where, as we have seen, Coleman had written the vernacular Life of Wulfstan and Hemming had put the archives in order, John began his adaptation of the *Anglo-Saxon Chronicle*.[51] He translated the text from Old English into Latin and

---

[46]  J. Rubenstein, 'The Life and Writings of Osbern of Canterbury', in *Canterbury and the Conquest: Churches, Saints and Scholars 1066–1109*, ed. R. Eales and R. Sharpe, London 1995, 27–40.

[47]  Eadmer, *HN*, and *Eadmer's History of Recent Events in England: Historia Novorum in Anglia*, trans. G. Bosanquet, London 1964; *The Life of St Anselm Archbishop of Canterbury by Eadmer*, ed. and trans. R. Southern, Oxford 1979; and R.W. Southern, *Saint Anselm: a Portrait in a Landscape*, Cambridge 1990, 404–36.

[48]  *Hugh the Chanter, the History of the Church of York 1066–1127*, ed. and trans. C. Johnson, revised by M. Brett, C.N.L. Brooke and M. Winterbottom, Oxford 1990.

[49]  *The Life of Gundulf, Bishop of Rochester*, ed. R. Thomson, Toronto 1977; M. Brett, 'Gundulf and the Cathedral Communities of Canterbury and Rochester', in *Canterbury and the Norman Conquest*, 15–26; and J. Potts, 'The Vita Gundulfi in its Historical Context', *Haskins Soc. Jnl* vii, 1995, 89–100; see also C. Harper-Bill in ch. 9 of this volume.

[50]  *The Brevis Relatio de Guillelmo nobilisissimo comite Normannorum Written by a Monk of Battle Abbey*, ed. and trans. E.M.C. van Houts in idem, *History and Family Traditions*, no. vii; the 'Hyde' chronicle (*Chronica monasterii de Hida juxta Wintoniam ab anno 1035 ad annum 1121*, ed. E. Edwards in *Liber monasterii de Hyde*, ed. E. Edwards, RS, 1866, 284–321) is briefly discussed by me in *ANS* xix, 1996, 177–8.

[51]  *Worcester*, and M. Brett, 'John of Worcester and his Contemporaries', in *The Writing of History in the Middle Ages*, ed. Davis and Wallace-Hadrill, 101–26. For Eadmer's correspondence with Prior Nicholas of Worcester about the origins of King Edgar, see ibid., 113 n. 1.

updated it to the mid-twelfth century. His choice of the chronicle as the main frame-work of his narrative reveals his effort to link the Anglo-Saxon past with the Norman present. His pre-Conquest interpolations amount to explanations of events in the Church as a whole, especially under the influence of the World Chronicle of Marianus Scotus that had been introduced at nearby Hereford a few decades previously.[52] The late eleventh- and twelfth-century material is invaluable for two reasons: first as a source for hagiographical traditions at Worcester, and secondly as a source for the settlement of the Normans in Britain. John of Worcester, like Eadmer at Canterbury, was as far as we know of English parentage. There is little criticism of the Normans in his work, though here and there some regret about the loss of Anglo-Saxon rulership can be detected. John, like Eadmer, was working in a monastery under non-English leaders. Eadmer was an intimate of Archbishop Anselm (d. 1109) at Canterbury and John was a monk under the priors Nicholas (d. 1124) and Warin (d. c. 1142). But, as Martin Brett has observed, there is no doubt who of the two was the more interesting historian: Eadmer as a lively observer of his own times wins it from John's 'resolute if blinkered interest in the dates of men's deaths and the succession to ecclesiastical offices'.[53]

Like John of Worcester, Henry, archdeacon of Huntingdon (d. c. 1157) also took the *Anglo-Saxon Chronicle* as his point of departure.[54] He maintained the annalistic lay-out but added to it a division of his narrative into books and chapters, perhaps in imitation of Bede's *Ecclesiastical History*. Several versions of his work survive and they illustrate how continuously Henry revised, altered and changed his text. From minor stylistical changes to major revision of whole chapters we learn how Henry, during a career spanning four decades, viewed the past through the prism of the present. Friends became rivals, patrons turned into enemies and colleagues achieved promotion while he never got a bishopric. Diana Greenway has recently revealed that Henry came from a mixed Anglo-Norman background: his father Nicholas was a member of the Glanville family from Normandy, whereas his mother was English, presumably of East Anglian origin. Such background meant that he was bilingual and, presumably, indebted to his mother for his knowledge of English which enabled him to read and translate Old English into Latin. As with the other bilingual historians with 'dual nationality', William of Malmesbury and (in Normandy) Orderic Vitalis, it is likely that he received from his mother some of the earliest impressions of knowl-edge of the past. Family history must have been first amongst these memories.[55] It is also reasonable to suppose that as an historian he was conscious of his family's past stretching back into Normandy and England, though yet again the precise ways in which this dual heritage helped him the shape the history of the past remains unknown. His account of the Norman Conquest, for example, is markedly more down to earth and rational than that of William of Malmesbury or John of Worcester. Since the latter were monks, it is tempting to see their difference in attitude in terms of his standing in the world. As an archdeacon he was in charge of the administration of that

---

52   *Worcester*, ii, xviii–xix; M. Brett, 'The Use of the Universal Chronicle at Worcester', in *L'Historiographie médiévale en Europe*, ed. J.P. Genet, Paris 1991, 277–86.

53   Brett, 'John of Worcester', 125.

54   *Huntingdon*.

55   For his paternal and maternal background, see *Huntingdon*, xxix–xl. See also D. Greenway, 'Henry of Huntingdon and Bede', in *L'Historiographie médiévale*, ed. Genet, 43–50; and 'Authority, Convention and Observation in Henry of Huntingdon's *Historia Anglorum*', *ANS* xviii, 1995, 105–22.

part of the bishopric of Lincoln in the Huntingdon area. Yet this archdeaconry was situated close to East Anglia where resistance to the Normans lasted longest. A telling example is a (Henry's own?) correction made to his entry on Hereward who is said to have been killed in 1071 together with Morcar and Bishop Aethelwine by King William.[56]

If Henry can be called a pragmatic historian and an annalist (though never as dull as John of Worcester), William of Malmesbury is commonly hailed as the most outstanding and reflective of the Anglo-Norman historians.[57] His work is founded on a wide variety of Anglo-Saxon sources, some of which we only know through his work. William took his job seriously and he travelled round collecting Old English texts, copying manuscripts and gathering oral information with the express purpose of writing it down and preserving it for posterity. As a preserver of the Anglo-Saxon past he did for national history what Goscelin had done on a much more local scale for hagiography. Like Henry of Huntingdon, William had his enemies, who forced him occasionally to alter his texts, but his reworkings, as far as we can establish, are not nearly as elaborate or frequent as those of Henry. Whereas Henry wrote and revised one narrative and reshaped it constantly, William wrote several works of different genres: a biography (of Bishop Wulfstan), a history of the kings of the English, a chronicle of the bishops of the English and of a monastery (Glastonbury), and an account of his own time (*Historia Novella*). Eadmer, John of Worcester, William of Malmesbury and Henry of Huntingdon wrote general or national histories of England for a multi-ethnic public of English, Norman, Anglo-Norman and Anglo-Continental families. Satisfying the needs of the various constituencies was not easy. The national histories linked the pre-Conquest past with the Norman present. The four historians variously explained the change in government and the defeat of the English on the battlefield of Hastings, issues that were as real in the early twelfth century as they were in the traumatic late 1060s.[58] Blame was approportioned to the English for their sinfulness, unholy behaviour and lack of attention to God, while praise for the Normans was expressed in terms of military prowess, efficient logistics, and architectural achievement. Of the four general histories William of Malmesbury's *History of the Kings*, whose quality we may rate highest, survived in more than thirty manuscripts. In terms of surviving copies, however, it was not as popular as Henry of Huntingdon's *History*, which is known in all its versions in more than forty-five complete manuscripts. Compared with their popularity, the spread of Eadmer's *History of Recent Events* or John of Worcester's *Chronicle*, each surviving in only a handful of copies, pales into insignificance.

However, the most popular history of England at this time was the 'historical novel' written by Geoffrey of Monmouth.[59] Surviving in more than two hundred

---

56  *Huntingdon*, 396n. e and 397 n. 188.

57  *Gesta Regum*; Brett, 'John of Worcester', 102; and R.W. Southern, 'Aspects of the European Tradition of Historical Writing', *TRHS* 5th ser. xxiii, 1973, 246–56. R.M. Thomson, *William of Malmesbury*, Woodbridge 1987, esp. 11–38.

58  For trauma as an explanation for the relatively long silence in England before the first substantial accounts of the Conquest were written down, see E. van Houts, 'The Trauma of 1066', *History Today* xlvi, 1996, 9–15; and *Memory and Gender in Medieval Europe*, London 1999, ch. 6.

59  A multi-volume edition of this bizarre Latin history is in preparation: *The Historia Regum Britannie of Geoffrey of Monmouth, I: Bern Burgerbibliothek, MS 568, II: The First Variant Version: a Critical Edition* and *V: Gesta Regum Britannie*, ed. N. Wright, Cambridge 1985, 1988 and 1991; *IV: Dissemination and Reception in the Later Middle Ages* by J. Crick, Cambridge 1991. An excellent translation

medieval manuscripts, this bestseller purports to be based on a now lost Celtic book from the library of Canon Walter of Oxford. Mostly fictitious in content, it was clearly meant to fill in the substantial gaps left by the *Anglo-Saxon Chronicle* and William of Malmesbury's royal chronicle for the early history of Britain in the post-Roman period. If the Latin language was to give the *History* a semblance of authority that its stories did not deserve, Geoffrey failed in the eyes of his learned colleagues, even though aristocratic audiences loved it, particularly in the vernacular translations.[60] Yet there was scope to present the past in a seemingly authentic fashion, as is illustrated by the work of Gaimar, an enigmatic figure of unknown background. In c. 1137 at the request of Constance, the wife of a Lincolnshire nobleman, he wrote a vernacular adaptation of the *Anglo-Saxon Chronicle* that provides in places a brilliant evocation of court life, in particular in the time of William Rufus. The emphasis on secular life for a female patron of French ancestry, who clearly did not know Old English, makes the *L'Estoire des Engleis* a fascinating exercise in historical writing for a mixed ethnic audience.[61]

To a great extent Geoffrey of Monmouth and Gaimar produced escapist historical writing, which did not satisfy those readers who longed for the blow by blow account of contemporary reportage. They had to turn to the more journalistic accounts of King Stephen's reign, such as the *Gesta Stephani* and the *Historia Novella*. As the title of the former implies, the 'Deeds of King Stephen' is concerned with one king.[62] Written by a Frenchman, the *Gesta* starts as an apology for King Stephen but gradually turns into an account that accepts the inevitable succession of the Empress's son Henry. William of Malmesbury's *Historia Novella*, is its nearest rival.[63] Both authors therefore act as journalist-commentators who deliver snap commentaries on a constantly changing political scene. Because neither author had to fit the eyewitness accounts into any specific narrative framework like a series of annals or successive deeds of kings, there were no constraints on what they could report. Neither the national chronicles nor the contemporary shorter histories could be said to be sources of practical information about the past that could help settle disputes at a local level; and it is to that kind of historical writing that we now return.

The local thirst for detailed historical records was the main motor for the production of historical-legal compilations. As we have seen, already at the end of the eleventh century the first collections of charter material were put together, and this trend was continued on an impressive scale from the first quarter of the twelfth century onwards. Most of the old Anglo-Saxon foundations began seriously to put their archives in order to protect themselves against encroachment on their lands and rights. Episcopal churches and monasteries had the same urgent need for written evidence for their titles, and both types of institution produced cartulary-chronicles.[64]

---

of the standard Latin edition by Acton Griscom, London 1929, is *Geoffrey of Monmouth, The History of the Kings of Britain*, trans. L. Thorpe, Harmondsworth 1966. For a recent reassessment of Geoffrey's work as hovering between historical and fictional literature, see M. Otter, *Inventiones: Fiction and Referentiality in Twelfth-Century English Historical Writing*, Chapel Hill and London 1996, 69–84.

60 For Wace's vernacular translation, see Ian Short in ch. 10 of this volume.

61 J. Gillingham, *The English in the Twelfth Century*, Woodbridge 2000, chs 7 and 13; see also Ian Short in ch. 10 of this volume.

62 *Gesta Stephani*.

63 *Historia Novella*.

64 J.Ph. Genet, 'Cartulaires, registres et histoire: l'exemple anglais', in *Le métier d'historien au Moyen*

We have already seen how this had led to the compilations of law codes, but during the course of the twelfth century these were accompanied by other documents as well. The *Textus Roffensis*, for example, was not only a law compilation, it also contained a cartulary chronicle of Rochester cathedral.[65] Ely followed in two stages under Bishop Hervey (1109–31) and Bishop Geoffrey Ridel (1173–89), with the impressive result of the *Liber Eliensis* or Book of Ely.[66] As for the monasteries, Battle produced its cartulary-chronicle in the 1160s and Abingdon in 1170.[67] Among the Fenland abbeys, Peterborough had its *Liber Niger* or Black Book by the mid-1130s and at Ramsey the cartulary-chronicle was well underway in c. 1170.[68] The production of such documentary histories was encouraged by the insistence of King Henry II's judges on written evidence for legitimate tenure. Claims based on oral testimony were, however, still being made well into the early thirteenth century, and this evidence through word of mouth was often transmitted through the female line.[69] Scarcely less significant than continued reliance on oral evidence, passed from one generation to another, is the role of women in this transmission as significant guardians of knowledge of the past.[70]

Behind the hunger for information about the past, however, lurked the threat posed by forgery. For at the same time that genuine efforts were being made to collect material from the past and to write it down, wishful thinking led many a monk or clerk to produce written evidence from scratch. In a time of customary law that depended on oral transmission of information, the lack of written evidence did not mean that oral claims were false. But with the passage of time and particularly after a hostile take-over of government, some oral claims were increasingly difficult to substantiate. Hence the production of new evidence. This could take the form of the entirely legal method of producing written documentation based on sworn testimonies; for example most of the *Domesday Book* evidence was collected in this way.[71] More suspicious is the written charter that is clearly interpolated. The bulk of the text may have been copied from an entirely proper legal document but extra passages could be added to justify a new claim. Much the most serious form of 'creative' historical documentation is the forgery of the sort produced by various mid-twelfth-century scribes who

*Age: Etudes sur l'historiographie médiévale*, ed. B. Guenée, Paris 1977, 95–138; *Les cartulaires. Actes de la Table Ronde . . . Paris 5–7 Décembre 1991*, ed. O. Guyotjeannin, L. Morelle and M. Parisse, Mémoires et documents de l'Ecole des chartes 39, Paris 1993; J.A. Paxton, 'Charter and Chronicle in Twelfth-Century England: the House-Histories of the Fenland Abbeys', unpublished Doctoral Thesis, Harvard University 1999. I am most grateful to the author for allowing me to consult her work.

65  See above, n. 38.
66  See above, n. 36.
67  *Battle Chronicle*, and N. Vincent, 'King Henry II and the Monks of Battle: the Battle Chronicle Unmasked', *Belief and Culture in the Middle Ages: Studies presented to Henry Mayr-Harting*, ed. R. Gameson and H. Leyser, Oxford 2002, 264–86, where it is argued that most of the Battle charters and its Chronicle are blatant fabrications; *Chron. Abingdon*, and J. Hudson, 'The Abbey of Abingdon, its *Chronicle* and the Norman Conquest', *ANS* xix, 1996, 181–202.
68  J. Martin, *The Cartularies and Registers of Peterborough Abbey*, Northamptonshire Record Society xxviii, Peterborough 1978, 1–7; Society of Antiquaries of London, MS 60, and Paxton, 'Charter and Chronicle', 71 and 85. For Ramsey, see *Chronicon abbatiae Rameseiensis*, ed. W.D. Macray, RS, London 1886; and Paxton, 'Charter and Chronicle', 105–56.
69  P. Brand, 'Time Out of Mind: the Knowledge and the Use of the Eleventh-Century and Twelfth-Century Past in Thirteenth-Century Litigation', *ANS* xvi, 1993, 37–54.
70  E. van Houts, *Memory and Gender in Medieval Europe 900–1200*, London 1999, 65–92 and 137–50.
71  R. Fleming, 'Oral Testimony and the Domesday Inquest', *ANS* xvii, 1994, 101–122; and *Domesday Book and the Law: Society and Legal Custom in Early Medieval England*, Cambridge 1998, 11–36.

manufactured 'authentic' charters of William the Conqueror on an impressive scale for Westminster, Durham and Battle. None of them were fools, all of them knew the history of their institutions. Yet, all of them were concerned by the lack of charters of the sort the old Anglo-Saxon institutions had in large quantities. Thus the monks produced new documents that had every pretence of having been drawn up at a particular time, with a witness list and sealed with a royal seal.[72]

In some ways, as David Bates has shown, the mid-twelfth-century English forgeries are similar to the entirely genuine Norman *pancarte*, a narrative of successive grants to a particular monastery drawn up in order to be presented for confirmation by the ruler.[73] The *pancartes* were common in Normandy from the early eleventh century onwards.[74] The documents were normally produced by the monastic *scriptoria*, and not by the ducal or later royal chancery. Their contents were based on individual charters of grants if they were available, on the memory of oral grants or on other documentation, such as written reports after disputes. Though usually discussed in the context of administrative history rather than historiography, the *pancartes* are significant sources for our understanding of historical consciousness. For example, the great *pancartes* composed during the later part of the Conqueror's reign contain narrative passages sketching the history of a monastery, or linking various grants in a not dissimilar way to the late English cartularies such as Hemming's collection. The most significant conclusion based on recent research, published in editions that reveal not only original texts but the afterlife as well, underlines the similarity in production of *pancartes* and chronicles. Both chronicle and charter provide the evidence for the history of the monastery, its monks (or nuns) and endowment, written over a long period. Neither chronicle nor charter was a static spotlight account of the past. Instead both were narratives that were revised and updated over decades, illustrating shifting alliances with donors' families, where younger generations may have disputed grants given by ancestors, or changes to landholdings following disputes with neighbours. The manuscripts in which the chronicles and charters have survived bear vivid testimony to the ongoing scribal activity in the monastic *scriptoria*. Erasures, interlinear additions, marginalia and additional information inserted on scraps of parchments illustrate that information about the past had to be changed continuously so as to keep up with present day developments. This was not forgery in the sense that a document was created *ex nihilo* to support a new claim, but a desperate attempt to catch in writing the fleeting nature of the memory of promises of gifts, or to replace existing fragile evidence in more permanent form.

In Normandy the initial flurry of propagandistic Conquest writing died with the Conqueror in 1087. A short history of his deathbed was written, probably at Rouen, and inserted into the *Gesta Normannorum Ducum* after 1100.[75] Although the *gesta* formula of the history of the dukes had been made popular by Dudo of Saint-Quentin and William of Jumièges, it proved not so versatile as to cope with dukes who added other offices like that of king. William of Jumièges had said as much when he promised to write about Robert Curthose but preferred to leave it to others to write about William as king, a hint perhaps that he knew about William of Poitiers's plan for a

---

72  Bates, *Regesta*, 74–5, where further references can be found.
73  Bates, *Regesta*, 874.
74  Bates, *Regesta*, 22–7.
75  *Jumièges* ii, 184–91.

biography.[76] The disputed succession to William by his sons precluded any definitive sequel to the *Gesta Normannorum Ducum* with an account of a new duke. In fact it was not written until well after Henry I's death in 1135. Meanwhile an interpolated version was produced by Orderic Vitalis.[77] He turned the original cumbersome Latin into a more attractive style and he added crucial information necessary for a new generation of readers for the early history of William the Conqueror's reign. He was also the first historian to draw attention to the substantial Norman migration to southern Italy.[78] Orderic's apprenticeship as reviser of William of Jumièges's text prepared him for his *magnum opus*, the *Ecclesiastical History*, written over a period of four decades (c. 1110–42).[79] Taking Bede as his example, Orderic used the framework of a history of the Christian Church, that is the Christian people of England and France, to write a history of his time. Like William of Malmesbury, who also used Bede as his role model, Orderic reflected on the events of his time and his task as historian to a far greater extent than did, for example, John of Worcester and Henry of Huntingdon. He also offers us a glimpse of his own emotions when a the age of sixty-seven he finally put down his pen, having written one of the most moving chronicle epilogues of the Middle Ages.[80]

Other historiographical activity took place in Normandy during Orderic's lifetime, most of which consisted of local historiography and hagiography. The only account written by a woman is Abbess Marsilia's eyewitness account of a miracle at the nunnery of St Amand at Rouen in 1107, where a young woman's life was saved after an attempted suicide.[81] Of slightly later date is the biography of Bishop Geoffrey of Coutances by John of Coutances, who also wrote a collection of miracles.[82] At Rouen the monks of Saint-Ouen produced a history of their archbishops as well as several hagiographical tracts.[83] Otherwise local historiography, such as the chronicle of Sainte-Barbe-en-Auge,[84] as well as various miracle collections, illustrate the Normans' continuing fascination with the past.[85] The main twelfth-century historian to emerge from Orderic's shadow is his younger contemporary Robert of Torigni,

---

[76] *Jumièges* ii, 182–5.

[77] *Jumièges*, version E, see introduction.

[78] The Norman migration to the Mediterranean prompted historical writing centred on the Normans in Italy, see K.B. Wolf, *Making History: the Normans and their Historians in Eleventh-Century Italy*, Philadelphia 1995.

[79] *Orderic*, and M. Chibnall, *The World of Orderic Vitalis*, Oxford 1984.

[80] *Orderic* vi, 550–7.

[81] 'Marsilia of Saint-Amand, Letter to Abbot Bovo II of Saint-Amand (Elnone)', in *The Normans in Europe*, ed. and trans. E. van Houts, Manchester 2000, no. 23, pp. 80–4; and H. Platelle, 'Les relations entre l'abbaye Saint-Amand de Rouen et l'abbaye Saint-Amand d'Elnone', in *La Normandie bénédictine au temps de Guillaume le Conquérant (XIe siècle)*, Lille 1967, 83–106.

[82] 'De statu huius ecclesiae ab anno 836 ad 1093', *Gallia Christiana* xi, instrumenta, cols 217–24, and partial translation as 'The Miracles of Coutances', *The Normans in Europe*, ed. and trans. Van Houts, no. 8, pp. 38–41.

[83] M. Chibnall, 'Charter and Chronicle: the Use of Archive Sources by Norman Historians', in *Church and Government in the Middle Ages: Essays Presented to C.R. Cheney*, ed. C.N.L. Brooke *et al.*, Cambridge 1976, 1–17, reprinted in *Piety, Power and History in Medieval England and Normandy*, Aldershot 2000, no. xix.

[84] *Des clercs au service de la réforme: Etudes et documents sur les chanoines réguliers de la province de Rouen*, ed. M. Arnoux, Bibliotheca Victoriana 11, Turnhout 2000, 275–93.

[85] For the perception of the past in the Norman miracles, see K. Quirk, 'Men, Women and Miracles in Normandy 1050–1150', in *Medieval Memories: Men, Women and the Past 700–1300*, ed. E. van Houts, Harlow 2001, 53–71.

monk and prior of Le Bec and later abbot of Mont-Saint-Michel.[86] At Le Bec Robert had learned the art of historical writing, a tradition that had started with Gilbert Crispin, later abbot of Westminster (d. 1118), who wrote a biography of Herluin, first abbot of Bec.[87] Slightly later Gilbert's cousin Milo recorded the history of the Crispin family in the shape of a 'Miracle of the Virgin Mary'.[88] In the late 1130s Robert, prompted by Empress Matilda, King Henry I's daughter, revised Orderic's version of the *Gesta Normannorum Ducum* to which he added a biography of Henry I.[89] As part of the same project he planned to incorporate the lives of Queen Margaret and Queen Matilda II, respectively grandmother and mother of Empress Matilda.[90] Although the plan was never executed, it throws interesting light on the importance Robert attached to the women of the royal dynasty and their place within the ducal/royal historiography. After he had become abbot of Mont-Saint-Michel he obviously became too busy to engage in any extensive historical writing, for he asked Abbot Gervase of Saint-Céneri to continue the *Gesta Normannorum Ducum* with a book on Empress Matilda's husband Geoffrey of Anjou as duke of Normandy (1144–51).[91] This project, too, collapsed. Meanwhile Robert produced a continuation of Sigebert of Gembloux's *World Chronicle*, which he interpolated with Norman sections for the pre-1112 period and which he extended, year by year, until his death in 1186.[92] Robert did not update the *Gesta Normannorum Ducum* beyond the death of King Henry I. Perhaps he expected that his contemporary Wace, the vernacular historian from Jersey, would do so, for had not Wace written the *Roman de Rou*?[93] Wace had used primarily Orderic's version of the *Gesta Normannorum Ducum* and extended the story up to the battle of Tinchebrai in 1106. He may have been thought to have been too pro-Robert Curthose in his rendition of the past, and he was forced to give up his work. Apparently Henry II then asked his rival and successor Benoît of Saint-Maur for a new vernacular version based on Robert of Torigni's adaptation of the *Gesta*. Benoît obliged, but like his predecessor he did not extend his narrative beyond Henry I's death. Clearly, Latin and vernacular historians alike felt it impossible to continue what was in effect a dynastic history centered on the duke of Normandy for a ruler who had added to that office the titles of count of Anjou, duke of Aquitaine and king of England. The only exception was Stephen of Rouen, a monk of Le Bec and admirer

86  R. Foreville, 'Robert de Torigni et Clio', in *Millénaire monastique de Mont Saint-Michel*, 4 vols, Paris 1967, ii, 141–53.

87  *The Works of Gilbert Crispin*, ed. A.S. Abulafia and G.R. Evans, Auctores Britannici Medii Aevi viii, Oxford 1986, 183–212, and trans. S. Vaughn, *The Abbey of Bec and the Anglo-Norman State*, Woodbridge 1981, 67–86. See also M. Gibson, 'History at Bec in the Twelfth Century', in *The Writing of History in the Middle Ages*, ed. Davis and Wallace-Hadrill, 167–86. For Gilbert as biographer of Herluin the fundamental study remains C. Harper-Bill, 'Herluin of Bec and his Biographer', *SCH* xv, 1978, 15–26.

88  *Miraculum quo b. Mariae subvenit Guillelmo Crispino seniori; ubi de nobilie Crispinorum genere agitur*, ed. J.P. Migne, *PL* cl, cols 735–44; partial translation in *The Normans in Europe*, ed. and trans. Van Houts, no. 24, pp. 84–9.

89  *Jumièges* ii, 196–289.

90  *Jumièges* ii, 242–3, and M. Chibnall, 'The Empress Matilda and Bec-Hellouin', *ANS* x, 1987, 35–48, and reprinted in *Piety, Power and History*, no. xi.

91  *Jumièges* i, p. lxxxviii.

92  *Torigni*; for Robert of Torigni's relationship with Henry of Huntingdon, see *Huntingdon*, lxxii–lxxiii, cl–cliii.

93  For Wace, see Ian Short, ch. 10 in the present volume; *Wace, The Roman de Rou*, trans. G. Burgess, ed. A. Holden, annot. G. Burgess and E. van Houts, Société Jersiaise 2002.

of Empress Matilda. Shortly after her death in 1169/70 he composed a Latin dynastic poem, mysteriously called *Draco normannicus*, the Norman dragon.[94] Divided into three books, the first part is a compilation based on Dudo and the *Gesta Normannorum Ducum*, while the second half is devoted to Norman and Breton affairs at the start of Henry II's reign. There is scope for new research into the historical value of this mixture of fact, fiction and fanciful verse that would throw light on the Normans' perceptions of their past in the context of the ambitions of their ruler. Henry II's relationship with the emperor and the pope as portrayed here merits further study.

In England, despite the number of historians working at Henry II's court and receiving his patronage, no biography of him was written nor were any of the previously successful genres continued. So, for example, we do not have a continuation of the *Anglo-Saxon Chronicle* for his reign, nor do we have sequels to Henry of Huntingdon's or William of Malmesbury's work. The reign of Henry II saw the appearance of new chronicles, collectively characterized by Antonia Gransden as the 'administrative chronicles'.[95] The authors, 'Benedict' of Peterborough, Roger of Howden and Ralph Diceto, used for the start of their chronicles known material published by others. For their own time, that is the second half of Henry II's reign and the reign of Richard, they compiled their account by inserting administrative documents in the text which were linked together with narrative passages. The technique is not dissimilar to that of the cartulary-chronicles or *pancartes*, except that the narrative structure is more elaborate. Also these authors are far less focused on the king and his family and have far greater interest in the machinery of government, the itinerant judges, court sessions and the making of laws. The overwhelming interest in law and government is as much a result of Henry II's administrative reforms as it is of a new educational system that relied on the use of Roman law, the written word and a rational organisation of material.[96]

As this survey has shown, the wealth of historical narrative produced in Normandy and England between 1000 and 1200 is clearly impressive. The rise of Rollo's dynasty prompted the dukes to have their history recorded. In Normandy their heirs continued with this tradition, as we have seen, for the next one hundred and fifty years. Their political importance in France, the urge to legitimize their position at Rouen and the dreadful pagan past that needed exorcising, created powerful impulses for historical writing. The past could be purged and the present justified by chronicles, a propagandistic tool that was recognized as well by Richard I, his son Richard II and Ralph of Ivry around c. 1000 as it was by William the Conqueror more than sixty years later. The contrast with England cannot be stressed enough. There the Anglo-Saxon royal dynasty was defeated on various fronts by the Danes in 1016, at court by the childlessness of Edward and Edith, and at Hastings by the Normans. The English may be forgiven for concluding that God was not on their side. The trauma of defeat and loss culminating in 1066 remained unrecorded during the first post-Conquest generation

[94] *Le dragon normand et d'autres poèmes d'Etienne de Rouen*, ed. H. Omont, Rouen 1884; and *Draco normannicus*, ed. R. Howlett, *Chronicles of the Reigns of Stephen, Henry II and Richard I*, RS, 1885, ii. See also Chibnall, 'The Empress Matilda', 38 and 46–7; and Shopkow, *History and Community*, 112–16.

[95] Gransden, *Historical Writing* i, 220–1.

[96] M. Clanchy, *From Memory to Written Record: England 1066–1307*, 2nd edn, Oxford 1993, 44–80; and J. Hudson, 'Administration, Family and Perceptions of the Past in Late Twelfth-Century England: Richard FitzNigel and the Dialogue of the Exchequer', in *The Perception of the Past*, ed. Magdalino, 75–98.

before it was unleashed in an outpouring of historical writing. The chronicles, however, were not as in Normandy centered on a dynasty, even though Queen Matilda II (d. 1118), perhaps consciously following in the footsteps of her predecessors Emma and Edith, requested William of Malmesbury to produce a chronicle of kings, her appetite having been whetted by a list of rulers he had produced for her in the first place. After Matilda's death he re-dedicated it to her daughter the Empress Matilda in an unambiguous bid to help her in her struggle for the throne:

> In it you can also discover that none of those chronicled in this present book, whether king or queen, has more royal or more glorious claim to the hereditary crown of England than yourself. May your imperial Majesty therefore deign to accept our humble gift, and by our gift the right to rule over us.[97]

Apart from William of Malmesbury, most of the English writing centered on annals (the versions of the Anglo-Saxon Chronicle), saints (hagiography) and sinners (the English who by their behaviour had deserved the miseries that had befallen them). It focused on the valiant British (the Bretons),[98] who had laid the foundation for England in escapist literature produced by Geoffrey of Monmouth and Gaimar. In the true spirit of salvation, however, the English also put their house in order, hence the almost manic surge of compilation designed to salvage their past in cartularies, chronicles and saints'lives.[99] The emphasis on local history is surely striking. The systematic reorganization of archives and knowledge of the past at a local level resulted in a collective drive intended to ensure that never again would the English be caught out by collective amnesia. After Stephen's reign, another calamity that added to the sense of corporate sin but helpfully produced a breathing space, historians became archivists rather than biographers. As administrators they knew that as long as they kept records of what happened around them, in law and according to custom, at the court and in the localities, no conqueror would be able to take away their past. The rise of administrative history, too, was fuelled, no doubt, by the multi-ethnicity of England's people. How could coexistence and cooperation be set into motion if there were no guidelines, in the form of laws and customs, according to which the races had to live? At the same time, paradoxically when Latin became the global language for law and custom, the vernacular (Old French rather than English) became the vehicle for expressions of nationality and multi-ethnicity. In England a vibrant and reborn community came to terms with its past by embracing record keeping, law giving and vernacular writing to prevent the past from slipping away into oblivion, as it had before. In Normandy, on the other hand, no such vibrance can be detected in the twelfth century. There the future was to be annexation by France, a situation that after 1204 led the Normans to rescue their records in an operation similar to the one on which the English had embarked after 1066, but that is another story.

---

97  *Gesta Regum*, i, 8–9.
98  For this proposition, see Kersken, *Geschichtsschreibung*, 358–67.
99  The 'salvation of knowledge of the past' argument is propounded by Southern, 'Aspects', as well as by J. Campbell, 'Some Twelfth-Century Views of the Anglo-Saxon Past', *Peritia* iii, 1984, 131–50, and reprinted in his *Essays in Anglo-Saxon History*, London 1986, 209–28.

# 7

# Feudalism and Lordship

## MARJORIE CHIBNALL

The recent trend in Anglo-Norman studies to avoid using 1066 as a sharp dividing line has made possible a much broader and more historical treatment of eleventh-century social change.[1] This has involved a refreshing new look at feudal institutions. A long tradition dating from at least the work of Spelman in the seventeenth century to that of J.H. Round in the nineteenth has led to the dominance, first of the legal, then of the military aspect, of 'feudalism'. This view still held the field when both Pocock and Douglas, in discussing Spelman's definitions of 'feudal custom' and 'feudal law' (Spelman never used the word 'feudalism'), hailed him as almost modern in his approach. Pocock wrote in 1957 of eighteenth-century historiography:

> It could be said . . . the heirs of Spelman died beaten and broken men, perishing among the spears of triumphant Whiggery. With their defeat ended the first serious attempt to give feudalism its proper place in English history, and there was not another until the nineteenth century, when the task was successfully accomplished by historians whom we may feel to be still our contemporaries.[2]

In fact the undermining of the whole feudal interpretation of the Norman Conquest became apparent soon after Pocock wrote.

In the first place, historians were looking critically at the actual course of the conquest itself, and at the condition of Normandy before 1066. R.H.C. Davis, in a short and perceptive summing up of the Norman Conquest in 1966, pointed out on the military side that 'for some time the Normans lived as an "army of occupation" based on their castles with their household knights. The date at which it would have been safe for the household knights to be enfeoffed and live on their own lands would have varied.'[3] D.C. Douglas, in 1964, challenged the view of Haskins that 'Norman society in 1066 is a feudal society, and one of the most fully developed feudal societies in Europe.' On the contrary, he argued that 'such definition as was attained in the duchy during the Conqueror's reign is recorded for the most part in Norman charters after the conquest of England.'[4] Jean Yver was even more explicit in his address to the Spoleto conference in 1968 when, citing Douglas, he suggested that perhaps the Norman feudal and military system was developed only after the conquest of England, in imitation of the more logical order that William had been able to impose in a

1  This chapter is a slightly adapted version of ch. 6 in M. Chibnall, *The Debate on the Norman Conquest*, Manchester 1999, reprinted by kind permission of Manchester University Press.
2  J.G.A. Pocock, *The Ancient Constitution and the Feudal Law*, Cambridge 1957, 2nd edn, 1987, 228. For Spelman's views see Chibnall, *The Debate on the Norman Conquest*, 36–7.
3  R.H.C. Davis, 'The Norman Conquest', *History* li, 1966, 279–86.
4  D.C. Douglas, *William the Conqueror*, London 1964, 96–8.

conquered country.[5] The terms 'feudalism' and 'feudal system' continued to be used, even by those historians who questioned their wholesale importation from one country to another; but the meaning of the terms themselves was coming more and more under direct attack.

J. C. Holt expressed the feelings of many historians when he wrote in 1986, 'We seem no longer to believe in feudalism, let alone the notion that it was established at a single stroke.'[6] Historians writing of different countries and periods usually found it necessary to explain just what they meant when using the term. Chris Wickham, writing of Europe generally, argued that the 'feudal mode' 'did not require the extinction of all political power; Normandy and Norman England, as "feudo-vassalic" as any society, show an undiminished political power that certainly had Carolingian (and Anglo-Saxon) roots, though the mode of expression had changed'.[7] His definition treated political units as feudal if they were 'based on the politics and economics of landowning'. This was a far looser definition of 'feudal' than Spelman, or those who wrote in the tradition derived from Spelman, would have allowed.

One unexpected consequence of the cross-fertilisation of disciplines in the twentieth century was that technical terms such as 'concept', 'model', or 'construct', proper to philosophy, economics, sociology, or even literary criticism, slipped into the vocabulary of historians, to be used by them in ways that were neither rigorous nor consistent. When applied to such generalisations as 'feudalism' or 'imperialism' they helped to generate misunderstanding. In his 1941 Cambridge lectures, Postan described the manor as 'a concept'. A few years later the word 'model' had crept into seminar discussions of both manorialism and feudalism. When in 1974 E.A.R. Brown denounced the dominance of feudalism in historical writing, she described it as 'the tyranny of a construct',[8] so replacing philosophical and economic terms by one more familiar in literary criticism. It invited the immediate 'deconstruction' of feudalism. This came from several directions, notably from Susan Reynolds, who launched a comprehensive frontal attack in 1994 on the blinkered discussion resulting from the feudal approach to medieval studies.

In *Fiefs and Vassals* (1994), Reynolds set out to determine 'how far vassalage and the fief as they are generally understood, constituted institutions which are definable, comprehensible, and helpful to the understanding of medieval history', and argued that 'in so far as they are definable and comprehensible, they are not helpful'.[9] Her book looked at the subject across medieval western Europe (excluding Catalonia), and whereas some of its general assertions have been questioned, the section on eleventh- and twelfth-century England has made a useful contribution to the debate on the effects of the Norman Conquest. Starting from the view of seventeenth-century pamphleteers and lawyers that (in different ways) 'the Normans had subverted Anglo-Saxon liberties', she pointed out that, especially since Round's essay on the

---

5   J. Yver, 'Les premières institutions du duché de Normandie', *I normanni e la loro espansione in Europa nell'alto medioevo*, Centro italiano di studi sull' alto medioevo, Settimane 16, Spoleto, 1969, 299–366, at 334–7.

6   J.C. Holt, '1086', in *Domesday Studies*, ed. J.C. Holt, Woodbridge 1987, 41–64, at 42–3.

7   C. Wickham, 'The Other Transition: From the Ancient World to Feudalism', *Past and Present* cxiii, 1984, 3–36; repr. C. Wickham, *Land and Power*, British School at Rome, London 1994, 7–42, at 33.

8   E.A.R. Brown, 'The Tyranny of a Construct: Feudalism and Historians of Medieval Europe', *AHR* lxxiv, 1974, 1063–88.

9   S. Reynolds, *Fiefs and Vassals*, Oxford 1994, 2.

introduction of knight service, the debate had 'been conducted on rather a narrow front'. Many historians had focused on military service and 'a hierarchy of tenure or property rights'.[10] Looking at the evidence of Domesday Book, she noted that although the king undoubtedly gave out properties wholesale, 'not all properties were given out as tidily as the myth requires'; also that 'fief' or 'fee' was not synonymous with 'knight's fee'.[11] Many holdings '*in feodo*' or '*ad feodum*' in Domesday Book were small, and some paid rent. There was no evidence that a precise definition of service formed an automatic part of each grant. Much of this was not new, but it needed to be said. Her arguments provided a comprehensive rebuttal of the assertion (still occasionally made) that William established 'a perfect feudal pyramid' in England. Such a statement shows the malign influence of feudal 'models' at their very worst, and the rebuttal is salutary.

A book of such wide content and combative assertions was bound to provoke discussions and controversy. Frederick L. Cheyette, in a searching review in *Speculum*,[12] questioned some of Reynolds's assumptions, and found some of her interpretations strange and even misguided; but at the same time he welcomed the book for the thoroughgoing critique of the conventional concept of feudalism that would force historians to reconsider their views on fundamental questions about the middle ages. Further discussion of some of the main issues appeared almost at once in a debate on 'the feudal revolution' in *Past and Present*.[13] Much of this debate was, naturally, concerned with the continental background which had made up a large part of Reynolds's book. It brought out the newer methods of looking at the social and institutional changes of the middle ages, which had already gone a long way to undermine the older conception of feudalism. T.N. Bisson was particularly concerned with power and lordship, suggesting a new acceptance of noble lordship as the basis of social order.[14] Timothy Reuter, though finding the stress on lordship helpful, criticised the way European history had been written from the point of view of France and the breakdown of public order there. Looking at the effect of the Norman Conquest in England, he pointed out (though questioning the 'maximalist' view of the Old English State) that the royal grip on the polity was tight enough to be taken over simply by capturing its central apparatus.[15] Chris Wickham raised the fundamental question of how far a given society, in contrast with another, is more usefully described in terms of one ideal type (e.g. Carolingian) rather than another (e.g. feudal). In considering the debate about 1066, he suggested that there were two changes which were important at the time. The first was the changing relationship between local aristocratic power and wider political forces, such as those controlled by kings, dukes or bishops (which had been discussed by Bisson). The second was the development of increasingly explicit and formal personal relationships.[16]

Indeed, much of the work of serious historians in the two decades before the appearance of Reynolds's book had already been concerned with questions of this kind, rather than with the older controversies concealed under the arid word,

---

10  Reynolds, *Fiefs and Vassals*, 342–3.

11  Reynolds, *Fiefs and Vassals*, 348–9.

12  *Speculum* lxxi, 1996, 998–1006.

13  'The Feudal Revolution', *Past and Present* clii, 1996, 6–42, 196–223, and cliii, 1997, 177–208.

14  T.N. Bisson, *Past and Present* clii, 1996, 6–42.

15  T. Reuter, *Past and Present* cliii, 1997, 177–95.

16  C. Wickham, *Past and Present* cliii, 1997, 196–208.

feudalism. As Maitland had said long before of feudalism, it 'covers a multitude of ignorances'. As for the changes produced by the Norman Conquest, Reynolds herself granted that recent work (for instance that of J.C. Holt and John Gillingham) had shown that the existence of immediate and systematic change looks weaker than Round had maintained.[17] Perhaps the persistence of theories long after they had been undermined in serious scholarship was due to the over-simplification of work directed to answering examination questions, of which Keith Thomas had complained.[18] Much of the historical writing generated in part by the 1066 and 1086 centenaries was concerned with a much deeper and more critical examination of the gradual changes over the divide of the conquest. This includes much research which focuses on 'individuals in their particular, complex network of relationships and . . . the systematic practices and transactions in which they are engaged'.[19]

The rejection of 'feudalism' has not involved the rejection of the adjective 'feudal'. Lordship and tenure were of immense importance; they influenced almost every aspect of law and society after the conquest. Writing of the Salisbury oaths and the Domesday Survey, J.C. Holt drew attention to Martin Wright's *Introduction to the Law of Tenures* (1730), where he suggested that 'Domesday and the Salisbury oath marked the introduction of feudal tenures'; an idea developed by Blackstone in his *Commentaries*.[20] On 1 August 1086, William the Conqueror, as one version of the Anglo-Saxon Chronicle relates,

> came to Salisbury, and his council came to him, and all the landholding men of any account throughout England, whosesoever men they were, and they all bowed down to him and became his men, and swore oaths of fealty to him that they would be faithful to him against all other men.[21]

To the question 'for what did they perform homage?' Holt, arguing that by this date the survey on which Domesday Book was based had already been completed, and that homage was then 'part of a reciprocal act . . . not performed *in vacuo* or for the promise of good lordship, but in return for something material and real',[22] proposed that the oaths secured the tenures of both tenants-in-chief and undertenants in the lands granted to them at various times and in various ways in England.[23] The book was used to determine tenure throughout the next two centuries.[24] This is not to imply that William introduced that historical chimera, a 'perfect feudal pyramid'. The oaths 'against all other men' on which William insisted were directed, Holt proposes, particularly against the king of France. The suggestion that the Domesday survey

---

[17] Reynolds, *Fiefs and Vassals*, 350.

[18] K. Thomas, 'History and Anthropology', *Past and Present* xxiv, 1963, 3–24, at 5, referred to 'the rhetoric and impressionism which is so frequently encountered in the work of leading practitioners of modern history (and whose origin may well lie in the educational tradition of encouraging history undergraduates to produce dogmatic and personal interpretations on the basis of rapid reading in secondary sources)'.

[19] F. Cheyette, Review of Reynolds, *Fiefs and Vassals* in *Speculum* lxxi, 1996, 1006.

[20] Holt, '1086', 41. For Martin Wright and Blackstone see Chibnall, *Debate on the Norman Conquest*, 49–50.

[21] Quoted from F.M. Stenton, *The First Century of English Feudalism 1066–1166*, 2nd edn, Oxford 1961, 112.

[22] Holt, '1086', 55–7.

[23] Holt, '1086', 57–9.

[24] E.M. Hallam, *Domesday Book through Nine Centuries*, London 1986, 32–5; V.H. Galbraith, *Domesday Book: its Place in Administrative History*, Oxford 1974, 100–23.

might have been made before the oaths were taken is also considered by Elizabeth Hallam and H.B. Clarke, and there is still an active debate on the subject.[25] The discussion has gained by the reintroduction of the 'Salisbury oaths' as a topic for consideration. It could be added that there were lateral no less than vertical ties; undertenants sometimes had more than one lord to whom they had obligations. Judith Green has given illustrations of some multiple dependencies, as well as of obligations arising from affinity rather than tenure.[26] As late as the fourteenth century any tenant of Lilleshall Abbey, taking an oath to the abbot his lord for admission to his lands, would swear fealty to him 'saving only the fealty which I owe to my lord the king and to my other lords'.[27] As Lindy Grant pointed out in demolishing Lemarignier's suggestion that Abbot Suger of St-Denis invented a feudal hierarchy in France, his approach was political and pragmatic.[28] The Normans in England too were essentially pragmatic. Lordship was only one of the bonds of society, even when tied to land; there were also ducal rights and royal rights, which were part of the ruler's power. It had, however, an important place in many social and legal relationships.

The military side of the conquest was not, and could not have been, neglected, for military power made the conquest possible, and continued to sustain the Anglo-Norman kingdom in its early years. It was, however, looked at in the wider context of social history, and with a clearer understanding of the condition of Normandy before 1066. The appearance of a critical edition of the charters of the Norman dukes in 1961 made possible a re-evaluation of the evidence that has misled Haskins half a century earlier. A wealth of new charter evidence showed that no uniform system of *servicium debitum* had been imposed by the Norman dukes; there was no system that could have been introduced into England. The military duties of vassalage were being worked out; the practical need to maintain a substantial army ready at all times to take the field hastened the imposition of more precise demands for service on the greatest lords who had been enriched with huge estates in England, and on the ecclesiastical tenants-in-chief as well. But the king recognised very soon after the conquest that demands made in terms of knights could when convenient be converted into money; and commutation, in the form of scutage, was calculated on the basis of the knight's fee. Indeed, as J.O. Prestwich had shown as early as 1954, military service was never confined within the limits of the *servicium debitum* and the older English *fyrd*.[29] Paid troops were at least equally important; the military households of the Norman kings contained the most highly-trained units in their armies. They were essential for manning castles and providing the core of resistance to attack in the rare battles and frequent sieges. In times of crisis the royal armies were augmented by the military households of the leading barons. These men relied on regular wages, as did the large contingents of mercenaries, often Breton or Flemish, recruited by the kings in special emergencies. Richard Fitz Nigel, writing the

25 Hallam, *Domesday Book*, 24; H.B. Clarke, 'The Domesday Satellites', in *Domesday Book: a Reassessment*, ed. P. Sawyer, London 1985, 50–70, at 56.

26 J.A. Green, *The Aristocracy of Norman England*, Cambridge 1997, 217–18.

27 *The Cartulary of Lilleshall Abbey*, ed. U. Rees, Shropshire Archaeological and Historical Society, 1997, 165, no. 324.

28 L. Grant, *Abbot Suger of St Denis*, London and New York 1998, 14.

29 Fauroux; J.O. Prestwich, 'War and Finance in the Anglo-Norman State', *TRHS* 5th ser. iv, 1954, 19–43, repr. in *Anglo-Norman Warfare*, ed. M. Strickland, Woodbridge 1992, 59–83. See also M. Chibnall, 'Mercenaries and the *familia regis* under Henry I', *History* lxii, 1977, 15–23, repr. in *Anglo-Norman Warfare*, ed. Strickland, 84–92.

*Dialogue of the Exchequer* in the reign of Henry II, asserted that 'the wealth that accrues to kings by virtue of their position gives power'.[30] The security of the realm, he pointed out, depended upon its wealth, for money was indispensable in both peace and war. 'In war it is lavished on fortifying castles, paying soldiers' wages, and innumerable other expenses.' He did not need to dwell on the economic conditions necessary to produce the wealth. As Prestwich clearly showed, the royal household, which contained the king's chief administrative officers as well as the commanders of his knights, was linked to the provision of men and money for war.[31]

One aspect of the military household was given prominence by Georges Duby, in his seminal 1964 article on 'youth in aristocratic society'.[32] He brought out the importance of the household in aristocratic society, both as a training ground for knights and as a career for younger sons. Mounted warfare depended on long and continuous training of men and horses, best provided in a permanent military force. So household troops included the eldest sons of barons waiting to succeed to their inheritance, as well as the younger sons (both legitimate and illegitimate) who hoped by good service to be given estate of their own or the hand of an heiress. All came from families able to provide the essential equipment of horse and armour, even though some were from relatively poor families. So there was an element of social standing among knights, although essentially they were professional in their skills.[33]

Published work on the military aspects of the Norman Conquest has been concerned with many aspects of war and its place in society. Inevitably, the influence of the Norman Conquest has been one element in this work. But the heat has gone out of the debate; the historical paper battles of Round's day have given way to a calmer (if sometimes acerbic) attempt to assess the nature of the changes in the light of new material published, or older sources made more accessible in new editions and translations. On the military side, some fifteen recent articles were brought together with a useful introduction by Matthew Strickland in *Anglo-Norman Warfare*;[34] and many more on a wide variety of topics have appeared in the published proceedings of conferences. The Battle conferences in Anglo-Norman Studies were initiated and inspired by R.A. Brown in 1978,[35] and have since their inception provided a forum for debate, amicable disagreement, and often consensus for scholars from different disciplines. They have been followed by an American series of conferences held by the Haskins Society.[36] The French have not been backward; a series of *colloques* organ-

[30] Richard Fitz Nigel, *Dialogus de Scaccario*, ed. C. Johnson, corr. F.E.L. Carter and D.E. Greenway, OMT, Oxford 1983, 1–2.

[31] J.O. Prestwich, 'The Military Household of the Norman Kings', *EHR* xcvi, 1981, 1–37, repr. in *Anglo-Norman Warfare*, ed. Strickland, 93–127.

[32] G. Duby, 'Au XIIe siècle: les jeunes dans la société aristocratique dans la France du nord-ouest', *Annales. Economies, sociétés, civilisations* xix, 1964, 835–46, trans. C. Postan, 'Youth in Aristocratic Society', in Duby, *The Chivalrous Society*, London 1977, 112–22.

[33] R.A. Brown, 'The Status of the Norman Knight', in *War and Government in the Middle Ages*, ed. J. Gillingham and J.C. Holt, Woodbridge 1984, 18–32, repr. in *Anglo-Norman Warfare*, ed. Strickland, 128–42, which questions the interpretation of S. Harvey in 'The Knight and the Knight's Fee in England', *Past and Present* xlix, 1970, 15.

[34] Strickland, ed., *Anglo-Norman Warfare* (as in n. 29).

[35] The Proceedings of the Conferences were published by Boydell, first as *Proceedings of the Battle Conference on Anglo-Norman Studies* from 1979–1982, and since 1983 as *Anglo-Norman Studies*.

[36] The *Haskins Society Journal* publishes selected papers from these conferences.

ised by the University of Caen have taken place at Cerisy.[37] Military tactics, the logistics of the conquest, and the character of fortifications before and after 1066 have been discussed in much greater detail.[38] Much of the work of historians is now focused on the effect of the conquest on other topics.

In all the various studies, lordship remains a central issue. It is bound up with power and law enforcement as well as with household organisation and administrative development. It also involves the question of the fate of the English at all levels of society after the conquest. There has been broad general agreement on the disastrous losses of the English aristocracy after their defeat at Hastings; the questions are how far the changes were affected by due process of law, and what happened in the lower ranks of society. Within twenty years the change at the highest level had been so sweeping that, in the part of the country south of Mersey and Humber at least, only a handful of the pre-1066 landholders with estates worth more than £100 remained in possession.[39] Stenton named Colswein of Lincoln and Turchil of Warwick;[40] other men possibly of mixed blood, like Edward of Salisbury (whose mother may have been the noble Wulfwyn) and William Malet have been suggested.[41] The daughters of some Saxon lords gave a formal legitimation to the transfer of land to their Norman husbands, as did Eadgyth, daughter of Wigod of Wallingford. She married Robert d'Oilly and their daughter, Matilda of Wallingford married Miles Crispin from an important Norman family well-endowed in England.[42] A few Normans who had accompanied Edward the Confessor to England and had settled in the Welsh marches remained.

The change, however, took some time to complete, and this affected the way in which estates were distributed among the invaders. Here refinements have been introduced, and different interpretations have emerged. Among recent books, a full-length study by Ann Williams on *The English and the Norman Conquest* has described in detail the stages by which the transfer of great English estates was brought about after successive rebellions. King William's claim was, as the lawful successor of Edward the Confessor, to preserve ancient laws and to take nothing except by due process of law. In the first wave of redistribution he handed out some lands from the royal

---

[37] Papers (in French), read at these conferences, are published by the University of Caen and edited by P. Bouet and F. Neveux.

[38] The view of C.W.C. Oman on the very primitive tactics of the Norman armies has been demolished by numerous studies of the tactical skill of the armies; see R.A. Brown, 'The Battle of Hastings', *ANS* iii, 1981, 1–21, repr. in *Anglo-Norman Warfare*, ed. Strickland, 161–81; J. Gillingham, 'William the Bastard at War', in *Studies . . . to Brown*, 141–58, repr. in *Anglo-Norman Warfare*, ed. Strickland, 143–60; I. Peirce, 'Arms, Armour and Warfare in the Eleventh Century', *ANS* x, 1987, 237–58; and in general, Morillo, *Warfare under the Anglo-Norman Kings 1066–1135*, Woodbridge 1994, esp. 136–79. On fortifications and the purpose of castles being both military and residential, see R.A. Brown, 'The Castles of the Conquest', in *Domesday Book Studies*, ed. A. Williams and R.W.H. Erskine, London 1987, 65–74; R.A. Brown, *English Castles*, 2nd edn, London 1976; N.J.G. Pounds, *The Medieval Castle in England and Wales: a Social and Political History*, Cambridge 1990. On logistics, see B.S. Bachrach, 'Some Observations on the Military Administration of the Norman Conquest', *ANS* viii, 1985, 1–26; E.M.C. van Houts, 'The Ship List of William the Conqueror', *ANS* x, 1987, 159–84; C. Gillmor, 'Naval Logistics and the Cross-Channel Operation', *ANS* vii, 1984, 105–31.

[39] Green, *Aristocracy*, 96–7.

[40] F.M. Stenton, 'English Families and the Norman Conquest', *TRHS* 4th ser. xxvi, 1944, 1–12.

[41] Green, *Aristocracy*, 96–7; A. Williams, *The English and the Norman Conquest*, Woodbridge 1995, ch. 4.

[42] Green, *Aristocracy*, 61, 77; E. Searle, 'Women and the Legitimisation of Succession at the Norman Conquest', *ANS* iii, 1981, 159–70.

demesne, together with the confiscated estates of the Godwine family and the other men who had fought against the Normans at Hastings. The revolts of the earls Edwin and Morcar, a succession of risings in the north, and finally the revolt of Roger, earl of Hereford, the Anglo-Breton Ralph, earl of East Anglia, and Waltheof, earl of the east Midlands and Bamburgh, made further great properties available for distribution.[43] By the time Domesday Book was compiled the massive replacement of the 'English' in the upper ranks of the aristocracy had been completed.[44] Ann Williams shows, however, that in some regions such as Shropshire 'Englishmen were not so much dispossessed as depressed in tenurial status', and that some survived as holders of a portion of their ancestral estates. Some held lands at farm, like Aethelric, who held his manor at Marsh Gibbon from William Fitz Ansculf 'in heaviness and misery'.[45] The highest rate of survival of the better men was in the western shires and the north. There was survival with suppressed status in most regions, though the extent is difficult to quantify. And among the most debatable of remaining problems are the fate of the English in the lower ranks of society, and the changes in the condition of the peasantry.

Recent work based on an analysis of Domesday Book has discussed the method by which estates were built up. So rapid a change in lordship inevitably led to confusion and uncertainty over rights. There is general agreement that two methods were used: the first antecessorial, the handing over of the land of one or more English previous holders to a Norman baron; the second territorial, when fees were made up from lands in a particular region, granted out partly by the local divisions of hundred and wapentake within counties.[46] Such lordships were commonly based on castles; some, like the rapes of Sussex, were established very quickly on the southern coast, others were built up within a few years in the marches of Wales and the north, in the frontier regions of advancing Norman conquest and settlement. These involved much more drastic dispossession of English landholders. The major controversy that has largely replaced the old 'English versus Norman' debate is the extent and nature of the territorial revolution. Historians with different views have supported their assertions by analysis of sections of Domesday Book. Owing to the great diversity of tenures, and the different types of material available in the various circuits of the Domesday commissioners, the different conclusions reached are hardly surprising. Among those stressing continuity, Peter Sawyer claimed that the antecessorial method of transfer was most prevalent. From the examples cited he argued that 'pre-Conquest England had fiefs very much like those of 1086'.[47] Robin Fleming, however, in a much more comprehensive analysis of the whole Domesday Book, maintained that this was only true of certain places. Her conclusion was that, after several changes of lordship in the period 1066–86, 'from Domesday Book's four or five thousand secular landlords TRE, little more than 100 significant *antecessores* can be identified', though in some shires and certain fees, particularly in Eastern England, the organisation of pre-conquest landholding and lordship survived the first twenty years of Norman

---

[43]  Williams, *The English*, chs 2, 3.
[44]  Williams, *The English*, 98.
[45]  Williams, *The English*, 89, 79.
[46]  R. Fleming, *Kings and Lords in Conquest England*, Cambridge 1991, 122–58.
[47]  P. Sawyer, '1066–1086: a Tenurial Revolution?', in his *Domesday Book: a Reassessment*, London 1985, 75–85, at 76–8.

rule.[48] In spite of some continuity, particularly on Church lands, she argues in favour of a general tenurial revolution.

A recent study of the aristocracy of Norman England by Judith Green underlines the intention of the Conqueror to make the transition orderly.[49] She examines the country by regions showing a considerable number of English survivors in the frontier districts, particularly the north, which was 'a patchwork of regions with different histories, ethnic composition and political alignments'. Her conclusion is that the new regime was 'only a thin veneer, so that distinctive features in northern society were better able to survive'.[50]

The incompleteness of the Domesday evidence, particularly in the north of England, leaves the way open for different interpretations. David Roffe has questioned some of Fleming's conclusions about antecessorial holdings, pointing out that Domesday Book does not fully record pre-conquest patterns of overlordship. A number of Anglo-Scandinavian thanes were often tenants of a single lord, so that some of the compact lordships often regarded as Norman creations may already have existed before 1066.[51] Paul Dalton, in his regional study of Yorkshire extending over nearly a century, has argued for a greater and more rapid establishment of Norman power in Yorkshire than has usually been recognised.[52] He describes the systematic way in which William the Conqueror had set about establishing lordships based on castles that were carefully situated at strategic points. At the same time, Dalton modestly points out, his approach 'is only one of many possible approaches . . . intended as a contribution to an on-going debate rather than the last word on the subject'.[53] This, indeed, admirably sums up the present-day state of many conquest studies.

Institutional change, which had a bearing on the changing nature of lordship, was a topic of fierce controversy in the middle years of the twentieth century, as defenders of Anglo-Saxon or Norman institutions hunted for early signs of a chancery, the use of seals, the origin of the jury, the early borough customs, various types of fortifications, the financial system and the currency. The efficiency of the Old English state was compared with that of the duchy of Normandy. Fortunately an understanding has been reached between the contestants, with the recognition that both countries were strongly centralised and exceptionally efficient, though in different ways.[54] James Campbell and Patrick Wormald in particular did much to illuminate the workings of the English government and administration;[55] David Douglas and R.A. Brown, with cross-Channel support from Lucien Musset and Jean Yver, showed that Normandy

---

[48] Fleming, *Kings and Lords*, 109–14.

[49] Green, *Aristocracy*, 49–50.

[50] Green, *Aristocracy*, 124–5.

[51] D. Roffe, 'From Thegnage to Barony: Sake and Soke, Title and Tenants-in-Chief', *ANS* xii, 1990, 157–76, at 169; idem, *Domesday, the Inquest and the Book*, Oxford 2000.

[52] P. Dalton, *Conquest, Anarchy and Lordship: Yorkshire 1066–1154*, Cambridge 1994, 72–3.

[53] Dalton, *Conquest, Anarchy and Lordship*, 22.

[54] See D. Bates, *Normandy before 1066*, London and New York 1982; M. Chibnall, *Anglo-Norman England 1066–1166*, Oxford 1986, esp. 105–6; J. Le Patourel, *The Norman Empire*, Oxford 1976.

[55] J. Campbell, *Essays in Anglo-Saxon History*, London 1986; J. Campbell, 'The Late Anglo-Saxon State: a Maximum View', *PBA* lxxxvii, 1995, 39–65; J. Campbell, *The Anglo-Saxon State*, London 2000; P. Wormald, '*Laga Eadwardi*: the *Textus Roffensis* and its Context', *ANS* xvii, 1995, 243–66; P. Wormald, *The Making of the English Law: King Alfred to the Norman Conquest*, Oxford 1999.

too was wealthy and by no means backward.[56] Many historians now are open to more flexible interpretations; as James Campbell wrote in considering some agents and agencies in the late Old English state, ' "probably", "perhaps" and "there are indications that" are the leitmotifs of this speculative paper'.[57]

Some of the early controversies were due to the difficulty of interpreting scanty sources. The debate on the use of seals and the existence of a chancery is one example of the way new evidence broke down old theories. As long as the only attempt at a published collection of William I's charters was the calendar in the first volume of *Regesta regum Anglo-Normannorum*, eked out with publications of individual charters in scattered sources,[58] the early ducal administration could not be studied adequately, and even the early work of French scholars was insufficiently used in English universities. After an edition of ducal charters up to 1066 appeared in 1961, Douglas was able to attack the view that the ducal administration was primitive; he calculated that up to 1066 Duke William issued or subscribed nearly the same number of writs and charters as Edward the Confessor (1042–66).[59] R.A. Brown insisted that, even allowing for the fact that (as Pierre Chaplais had shown) many charters were already authenticated by the duke, William had at least the nucleus of a chancery organisation on the eve of the conquest.[60] Marie Fauroux suggested that the equestrian seal that William used after 1066 argues for an earlier Norman seal, since no English seal showed the king as a mounted warrior.[61] Simon Keynes, on the basis of charter references to sealing, made a case for the sealing of pre-1066 English diplomas.[62]

All this was tentative and suggestive. The publication of David Bates's edition of the charters of the Conqueror has at last provided the material for a much more precise evaluation of the evidence.[63] The collection includes many previously unknown charters; many, however, have survived only in later copies which may have been tampered with. No new examples of seals have come to light, so the subject still 'does not admit of an easy answer'.[64] After carefully examining the form and language of royal diplomas and writs in both England and Normandy after 1066, Bates decided that there could be no doubt that 'the practice of sealing diplomas continued in England over 1066', and spread in Normandy whatever previous practice there may have been. On the question of whether anything that could properly be called a chancery existed in either dominion before 1066 he is equally cautious. But he notes the marked increase in central control in England after about 1070. From 1066 to 1070 some documents were produced in Old English, and some of the staff of the English royal writing office were employed until new scribes could become more familiar

---

56  Douglas, *William the Conqueror*; R.A. Brown, *The Normans and the Norman Conquest*, 2nd edn, Woodbridge 1985; J. Yver, 'Les premières institutions'; L. Musset, 'Gouvernés et gouvernants dans le monde scandinave et dans le monde normand', *Recueils de la Société Jean Bodin* xxiii, Brussels 1968.

57  J. Campbell, 'Some Agents and Agencies of the Late Anglo-Saxon State', in *Domesday Studies*, ed. Holt, 201–18, at 218.

58  *Regesta* i.

59  Douglas, *William the Conqueror*, 11.

60  R.A. Brown, 'Some Observations on Norman and Anglo-Norman Charters', in *Tradition and Change*, ed. D. Greenway, C. Holdsworth and J. Sayers, Cambridge 1985, 145–63.

61  Fauroux, 46–7.

62  S. Keynes, 'Regenbald the Chancellor (sic)', *ANS* x, 1988, 185–222, at 216.

63  Bates, *Regesta*.

64  Bates, *Regesta*, 103.

with the agents and agencies already existing in the conquered country. After 1070 there was a sharp change: Latin became the normal language of writs, and the witnesses increasingly included individuals 'closely associated with the enactment of the king's will'.[65] His final conclusion was that, although in 1087 the time when the royal chancery would normally write the majority of writs and diplomas was in the far future, the chancery was already a significant organisation. In formal terms, he considered that its origins were primarily English. Yet 'it was staffed by men both well versed in the technicalities of writing and using literate means of government, qualities which are abundantly evident in pre-1066 Norman charters'.[66]

Some of Bates's conclusions about changes in royal government deduced from a study of the charters are reinforced by the conclusions of a number of scholars analysing Domesday Book. These too show a significant change after about 1070. In particular, Robin Fleming has examined all the hundreds of references to legal proceedings about property rights which took place as a result of the survey. They form the climax to a number of great land pleas that had taken place earlier in the reign, largely because of disputes already begun on the estates of the greatest ecclesiastical lords. Some were complaints of spoliation dating from before the conquest, others resulted from violent seizures by the Normans. King William had used traditional methods of initiating pleas by royal writ and the use of sworn inquisitions in the local shire courts, sometimes in joint sessions of several shires.[67] Because the property of church lords was respected, in principle at least, these pleas provided continuity with pre-conquest practice. By 1085 it was clear that complaints of violent dispossession on smaller lay estates could be heard all over the country. The king, claiming to be the lawful successor of King Edward and therefore pledged to uphold Edward's laws, set in motion by his writs a far wider inquest into property in every part of the kingdom. It involved numerous hearings in local hundred and wapentake as well as shire courts, and the summoning of local juries to give sworn testimony. About half the jurors were Englishmen from the ranks of thegns and greater freemen, who were familiar with English customs.[68] So oral testimony was brought into contact with the ideas of lordship and knightly inheritance familiar to the invaders, and oral testimony was blended with the written records provided by the greater lords through their stewards. What emerged from the melting pot of the years of intense activity was a blend of English and Norman custom, enforceable in both the traditional local courts and in the courts of the lords of the land. It was still far from the common law of the late twelfth century, but the methods and characteristics of a common law were beginning to emerge. Moreover, the great guarantee against social disintegration was in the effective power of the king at the centre. From about 1070, when the worst of the revolts had been suppressed, and his officers had learnt how to take over the older institutions, King William began to extend the use of the royal writ in significant ways. The Anglo-Danish kings had used it chiefly to initiate proceedings which directly affected royal estates or royal rights; the new Norman king began to us it regularly to bring disputes between other individuals into the shire courts.[69] This practice

---

[65] Bates, *Regesta*, 106–8.

[66] Bates, *Regesta*, 108.

[67] R. Fleming, 'Oral Testimony and the Domesday Inquest', *ANS* xvii, 1995, 101–22.

[68] R. Fleming, *Domesday Book and the Law*, Cambridge 1998; this important study prints and analyses all the disputes. C.P. Lewis, 'The Domesday Jurors', *Haskins Soc. Jnl* v, 1993, 17–29.

[69] Fleming, 'Oral Testimony', 112–17.

did not attack the honorial courts of the greater barons where they were competent to deal with a case; Henry I made this clear early in his reign.[70] But writs were available for suits between vassals of different lords, or even to hear complaints of defect of justice. In time the honour courts withered away, but for over a century they played a significant part in the handling of claims to property. It will be interesting to see how the debate develops in the light of the most recent work. Much recent historical discussion has been about such topics as the speed of change, the contribution made by royal and seignorial courts, and the nature of property rights. Interpretations are sufficiently different for the question, 'Was there a tenurial revolution?' to be a real one. It is likely that in future discussions of tenurial change historians will give more emphasis to lordship than to feudalism. This will involve greater consideration of peasant society and seignorial authority, topics which English, unlike French, historians, have not normally treated as feudal.

---

[70] *Regesta* ii, no. 892.

# 8

# Administration and Government

## EMMA MASON

John Le Patourel, in a classic survey of the governance and administration of the Anglo-Norman *regnum*, published in 1979, argued that, between 1066 and 1154, Norman practices were introduced into England to a considerable extent, but that this gradually tailed off, more especially after 1154. The 'Norman Empire', which collapsed in the 1140s, and its Angevin successor, were two distinct political constructions. The Angevin territorial complex, besides being much the larger, was ruled by a different dynasty, and its distinctive government was based on different principles. In the time of the 'Norman Empire', England and Normandy were usually governed jointly by one man. In the short periods when this was not the case, the brothers each had claims on the other's authority. Normally, though, the same authority was exercised in both territories. There was one royal household; one set of household officers; one *curia regis*, and even one nobility with estates in both countries. Government was effected by the king, constantly on the move with his household. Some adaptations occurred, such as the adoption of the Old English seal and writ, and provision was gradually made for the operation of one judicial system throughout both lands. In Normandy, this Normano-English judicial system provided the forum, and most of the substance, of the *Coutume de Normandie*. In contrast, Le Patourel argued, the English legal system was largely Norman-inspired. The Normans at first tried to take over the organisation of shires and hundreds, and to treat it as they did their Norman *comtés*, *vicomtés* and *prévôtés*, but Heny I saw an advantage in preventing total assimilation. While the shire units remained untouched, as did variations in the conditions of the peasantry, in other areas the process of assimilation continued down to 1135.

During the 1140s, it appeared for several years as though there would be a clean break, until the Angevin dynasty triumphed. From 1154 onwards, the Normanisation of England declined, and the introduction of further innovations in government and administration was much more of a two-way process. However, each segment of the 'Empire' had its own Law or Customs, and these were not introduced elsewhere, except to a very limited extent. Further innovations in this period included the emergence of the non-royal viceroy, and of an embryo system of record-keeping for the king's lands overall. The need for the Angevin kings to be continually on the move, and therefore absent from any one territory for long periods, led to an increasing delegation of their authority. The success of the king and his advisors in making such arrangements, which stood the test of time, stemmed from frequent contact with a varied range of systems of law and administration.[1] Le Patourel's overview of devel-

---

[1]   J. Le Patourel, 'The Norman Conquest, 1066, 1106, 1154?', *ANS* i, 1979, 103–20.

opments sets the scene for a survey of more recent work in all the key areas which he outlined in this article.

The 'tenurial revolution' which followed the Norman Conquest resulted in a substantial increase in the extent of crown land, so that after 1066, Peter Clarke concluded, the wealth of the greatest magnates, the 'earlish' families, was lower in proportion to that of the king than it had been before 1066, which accounts for royal ability to overcome rebellions.[2]

These great magnates, as Robin Fleming commented, simultaneously supported the king in war and peace and, on their own behalf, practised 'an extravagant and self-interested hooliganism' to enhance their own stature. They were capable of cooperating with the king to great effect, but if their interests no longer coincided with his, or if some individuals began to overtake him in wealth, royal power was rapidly undermined. This uneasy balance, therefore, resulted in the erratic development of English institutions. The personal associations and private values of individual magnates often had a greater impact on the realm than did the machinery of government. If traditional associations and values disintegrated, then political collapse followed.[3]

The participation of these great magnates in government, as witnesses to royal *acta*, has been elucidated by David Bates, in his monumental edition of the charters of William I.[4] In his earlier work, Professor Bates investigated the arrangements for the government of constituent parts of the extended realm. He observed that in the earlier eleventh century, rulers depended on their near kin to act as their representatives, and cited the arrangements which Cnut made for the government of Denmark and of Norway, as well as the status of some members of the ducal house in Normandy.[5] After the Norman conquest of England, William's half-brother, Bishop Odo, was empowered to act on his behalf in England, while Queen Matilda represented his interests in Normandy. Either might act, in effect, as regent, even though major roles in delegated government were played by Lanfranc, archbishop of Canterbury, John, archbishop of Rouen, and William Fitz Osbern. Although Orderic Vitalis used the term *comes palatii* to describe the position of Bishop Odo, it is unlikely that his role stemmed directly from this Carolingian precedent. In England, subsequent prominent clerics, notably Ranulf Flambard and Roger of Salisbury, headed the administration of finance and justice. Neither was a regent, although Roger was styled *procurator.* In the twelfth century, the office of regent continued to be exercised by the queen-consort, down to the earlier part of Henry II's reign, but by the 1170s, Henry II probably no longer trusted any member of his family to maintain his interests. By the time Queen Eleanor resumed the role of regent in the reign of Richard I, the position of justiciar had become well established, combining oversight of legal and financial business.[6]

While Queen Eleanor's successors as queen-consort did not exercise authority to the extent that she did, her own role echoed that of her predecessors. Already in tenth-century England, some queens-consort were prominent among the king's advi-

---

2  P.A. Clarke, *The English Nobility under Edward the Confessor,* Oxford 1994, 153–6, 162.

3  R. Fleming, *Kings and Lords in Conquest England,* Cambridge 1991, xiii–xiv.

4  D. Bates, ed., *Regesta Regum Anglo-Normannorum. The Acta of William I (1066–1087),* Oxford 1998.

5  D. Bates, 'The Origins of the Justiciarship', *ANS* iv, 1981, 1–12. See also C. Potts, 'The Earliest Norman Counts Revised', *Haskins Soc. Jnl* iv, 1992, 23–35.

6  Bates, 'Origins of the Justiciarship', 1–12.

sors. The position of any one woman might fluctuate over the course of her adult life-time, while the records of her activity are often incomplete, owing to the varying extent to which diplomas were edited. In the eleventh century, though, it is clear that both Queen Emma and Queen Edith exercised considerable influence, as Pauline Stafford has demonstrated.[7] Throughout the eleventh century, on both sides of the 1066 divide, the queen-consort's position was personal, flexible and informal, as Laura Wertheimer observed. Those women who became involved in administration early in a reign, such as Matilda, wife of William I, Edith-Matilda, the first wife of Henry I, or Matilda, the wife of Stephen, were active viceregents. Queen Adeliza, however, never played a commensurate role in public life, perhaps in part because she was required to travel with the king, in the hope that she would bear the urgently needed heir. Her election as Lady of the English, prior to her marriage, indicates that she did have a symbolic role in the royal administration, although the ability to exercise this role would depend on the strength of her personality, and was perhaps also constrained by her inability to bear the king an heir.[8]

The Empress Matilda exercised considerable authority in that part of the war-torn kingdom which she controlled during Stephen's reign, issuing charters in which her style was 'empress, daughter of King Henry and Lady of the English'.[9] Despite the fluctuations in her power due to the fortunes of war, she certainly ruled in a substantial part of England, even though she never reigned, and later in life exercised a more limited but still real authority in Normandy, securing and upholding the position of her son, as Marjorie Chibnall has demonstrated.[10]

The governance of England over the eleventh and twelfth centuries was furthered by continuing innovation, tempered by the retention of any traditional practice which enhanced the position of the ruler, and particularly of those who came as conquerors. This can be clearly seen in the policies of Cnut, as argued by M.K. Lawson.[11]

The assertion of a claim to be the legitimate successor to the throne reinforced the position of a conqueror, strengthening his hand against his incoming natural supporters as well as helping in some measure to render him acceptable to the conquered population. The assertion of William I that he was the legitimate successor of King Edward was underlined by his adoption of the style 'king of the English'. George Garnett demonstrated that William's provision of the communal murder-fine as a deterrent to assaults on those Frenchmen who had taken part in the Conquest stemmed from English precedents which protected those of kinless status. Initially the French were afforded some procedural advantages in litigation, but the English were also granted recourse to advantageous procedures. Whatever was perceived as traditional English practice was defined as what was right, so that it became necessary for incomers, whether clerics or laymen, to learn English customs, particularly in matters of land tenure. This legal merging of the peoples developed over several decades, but

7   P. Stafford, *Queen Emma and Queen Edith*, Oxford 1997, 193–206.
8   L. Wertheimer, 'Adeliza of Louvain and the Anglo-Norman Kingship', *Haskins Soc. Jnl* vii, 1995, 101–15. On the last point, see also Stafford, *Queen Emma and Queen Edith*, 193.
9   For instance, *Regesta* iii, nos 791–4.
10  M. Chibnall, *The Empress Matilda: Queen Consort, Queen Mother and Lady of the English*, Oxford 1991, 118–76.
11  M.K. Lawson, *Cnut: the Danes in England in the Early Eleventh Century*, London 1993, 117–210.

was clearly under way by the accession of Henry I, whose coronation charter of liberties repeatedly cites the 'law of King Edward'.[12]

The machinery of government to which William I succeeded owed much, as James Campbell has argued, to a long series of creative and experimental innovations, which in turn partly stemmed from Carolingian practice.[13] When Norman administrators succeeded the last of the English clerks, this highly sophisticated administrative machine was allowed to run down over the Anglo-Norman period, when government became 'a matter of shifts and contrivances', in the view of W.L. Warren.[14] Problems experienced in exercising control over the local courts, or in maintaining the quality of the coinage, were symptomatic of this breakdown, in his view. Professor Warren concluded that the government of Henry I did not address the underlying cause of administrative collapse, which arose from the fact that the Norman clerks were hampered both by a language barrier and by a failure to understand the mechanisms which were designed to ensure the smooth running of the royal government. An indication of efforts to remedy the damage can be seen, he argued, in the treatises, in Latin, on the workings of government, compiled for use by middle-ranking officials. Following his acquisition of the throne by dubious means Henry I's failure to grasp control over the means of efficient government resulted from his having to make great efforts to demonstrate that he was worthy to rule, although the energy which he put into this ensured his posthumous reputation as an exceptionally effective ruler.[15] This scenario of near-disaster countered by frenetic activity contrasts with the more measured approach taken to this reign by Judith Green, although she also concludes that royal initiatives were prompted as much by crisis management as by forward planning. Developments in government, she found, resulted from periodic bursts of activity which became more frequent as the reign progressed, and peaked around the years 1128–31. Administrative changes, when they occurred, can sometimes be seen to correspond to particular problems facing the government.[16]

But even if England really was in so precarious a condition, the right to control its government was still strongly asserted. David Bates has demonstrated that, both in the reign of William Rufus, and again in the first year of Henry I's reign, Robert Curthose, duke of Normandy, issued a charter of his own for a beneficiary in England to confirm a grant made by the king.[17] Even though Robert was in no sense a co-ruler, he was staking a claim to have an authoritative voice in the governing of the kingdom.

Bernard Bachrach argued that the long Norman tradition of family hostility led in time to the emergence of highly integrated administrative structures, which did not depend on harmony among members of the ruling dynasty. In contrast, Henry II's 'empire' comprised lands and lordships which were very loosely grouped together. Their successful management depended upon family harmony and cooperation, a style of government which had suited the house of Anjou for some two hundred years,

[12]  G. Garnett, '*Franci et Angli*: the Legal Distinctions between Peoples after the Norman Conquest', *ANS* viii, 1986, 109–37. See also W. Stubbs, ed., *Select Charters and Other Illustrations of English Constitutional History*, 9th edn, revised H.W.C. Davis, reprinted Oxford 1966, 117–19.

[13]  J. Campbell, 'Observations on English Government from the Tenth to the Twelfth Century', *TRHS* 5th ser. xxv, 1975, 39–54.

[14]  W.L. Warren, 'The Myth of Norman Administrative Efficiency', *TRHS* 5th ser. xxxiv, 1984, 113–32.

[15]  W.L. Warren, *The Governance of Norman and Angevin England 1086–1272*, London 1987, 71–3.

[16]  J. Green, *The Government of England under Henry I*, Cambridge 1986, 215–16.

[17]  D. Bates, 'A Neglected English Charter of Robert Curthose, Duke of Normandy', *BIHR* lix, 1986, 122–4.

but ironically Henry's own family relations deteriorated into the same state of mutual hostility which had been prevalent among the Anglo-Norman kin-group.[18] The reputation of Henry II as a ruler has been questioned by John Gillingham, who argues that he was in fact more bellicose and aggressive than Richard I, while Richard was probably at least as much interested in justice as his father was reputed to be.[19]

Before Professor Gillingham's paper was published, a measured reappraisal of the government of the Anglo-Norman realm during the reign of Richard I had already been made by Sir James Holt. He remarked that notions touching the sovereignty of the king were becoming more clearly defined in this reign, when use of the royal 'We' was first made. Since Richard's *acta*, in contrast to those of his father, were dated both in time and place, Richard's itinerary can largely be correlated with surviving acts of his government. The king's long absences from his realm created administrative difficulties, as contemporary writers noted. Ralph of Coggeshall implied that, whereas Henry II had simply governed energetically, both Richard and John needed to persistently engage in an uphill struggle. An increasing volume of documentation has survived from this later period, including the *Cartae Antiquae Rolls*, with their outline record of royal charters. The relative proportions of *acta* surviving in relation to England and to Normandy suggest that Normans were less likely to enlist the intervention of the king-duke than were his English subjects. Bargains over the cost to the recipient of some royal grant were occasionally made by Richard in person, but more often by the justiciar or some other authorised deputy. No real comparison can be made of governmental activity in England and in Normandy, since Norman Pipe Rolls drawn up in this reign survive only for 1195 and 1198. In particular, it is not possible to know whether there was in Normandy the same extensive sale of offices and privileges which occurred in England at the outset of this reign. Since the Norman rolls were drafted differently from the English Pipe Rolls, it is not clear who authorised the making of particular grants, and probably both fines and proffers were simply agreed in the sessions of the Norman Exchequer.

What was similar, and perhaps identical, in the practice of the respective Exchequers was that in both the accounting officials presented royal writs as authorisations of expenditure. Many writs were not issued by the Chancery but by the Exchequer, and authorised by the Exchequer seal. The justiciars, and notably Hubert Walter, occasionally authorised writs under their own seals, when they were not operating from the Exchequer. Writs issued in the king's name may equally have been directly authorised by him, or by the viceroy using the Exchequer seal. Writs in the king's name, sent to England from Normandy, were chiefly designed to correlate the decisions and actions of the king, and of his administrators in Normandy, with the accounting procedures of the Exchequer in England. Such writs also authorised the movement and transshipment of bullion, and other things needed by the king. The formula *teste me ipso* ('witnessed by me personally') is rarely found in genuine documents before Richard's accession, and was perhaps applied to those documents which were read to the king in final draft, before they were sealed. This practice certainly indicates Richard's personal intervention into matters being administered in his name,

---

18  B.S. Bachrach, 'Henry II and the Angevin Tradition of Family Hostility', *Albion* xvi, 1984, 111–30. See esp. p. 130.
19  J. Gillingham, 'Conquering Kings: Some Twelfth-Century Reflections on Henry II and Richard I', in *Warriors and Churchmen in the High Middle Ages: Essays Presented to Karl Leyser*, ed. T. Reuter, London and Rio Grande 1992, 163–78.

but such direct interest was usually reserved for those which related to warfare and to the organisation of war. So far as legal matters were concerned, Richard very largely responded to litigants, rather than initiating actions. Certainly he left no record of initiating lawsuits on a scale in any way comparable to John's activity, but it was Richard's priorities which were admired by his contemporaries.[20]

Richard's government was not compartmentalised at its higher levels. Both senior clerks and lay officers could be transferred from one province to another, while men with influence at court were able to accumulate lands in several provinces. Provincial autonomy was threatened by the continuous movement of the itinerant court, and resentment was generated against intrusive outsiders. On the other hand, John Gillingham argues, there was never a period when it was obvious that the whole of the Angevin empire was being run for the benefit of one regional group, in the way that the Norman empire was run in the generation after 1066. When the Angevin empire did collapse in 1203–1204, the causes of its downfall owed little either to provincial solidarity or to provincial resentment at outsiders.[21]

Contrasts between the priorities of Richard and John are beyond the chronological scope of this chapter. The re-evaluation of John's rule, which was initiated by Lady Stenton and by Sir James Holt, is now widely accepted, but as Ralph V. Turner has pointed out, John's legal and administrative activities were not such as to excite his contemporaries. Government was predatory, its prime purpose being to exploit the populace for the benefit of the royal family, the magnates and their associates. Far more effort went into raising revenues from the population than into offering any kind of public services. The administrative innovations which rendered royal government more efficient were therefore unlikely to generate enthusiasm among contemporaries. Richard, who is now admired for his skill in raising war finance, was also renowned for his generosity, but this was most likely to be bestowed on those who furthered his interests. The magnates expected to be in the receiving line, and active *curiales* had to be recompensed for their services. To be perceived as a successful ruler, a king had to find some way of balancing his patronage without creating over-mighty subjects. By the later twelfth century, Turner argues, the reforms of Henry II's reign had tipped the balance of power away from the magnates towards the king and the royal government. Yet there was beginning to emerge some idea of 'the public power', which was equated with the king's obligation to rule for the common good, and which arose from the revival of the Roman Law, with its concept of *utilitas reipublicae*, reflected in the work of Ralph Diceto and Roger Howden.[22]

Discussion of specific areas of government includes the long debate over the extent and impact of levies of the geld, which was waged between M.K. Lawson and John Gillingham. Lawson questioned whether, despite the heavy levies of geld in the early eleventh century, the raiders and mercenaries extracted more than a fraction of the wealth of England. Gelds were perceived as oppressive throughout the eleventh century, but in fact the rate at which they were levied gradually declined. The highest was levied by Cnut in 1018. That levied by Harthacnut, although still onerous, was lower, while successive gelds were lower still. Even so, they were a heavy burden on

---

[20] J.C. Holt, '*Ricardus Rex Anglorum et Dux Normannorum*', *Academia Nazionale dei Lincei* ccliii, 1981, 17–33.

[21] J. Gillingham, *Richard Coeur de Lion*, London 1994, 64.

[22] R.V. Turner, 'King John in his Context: a Comparison with his Contemporaries', *Haskins Soc. Jnl* iii, 1991, 183–95; *King John: New Interpretations*, ed. S. Church, Woodbridge 1999.

the taxpayer, and the inducement to pay up seems to have been the threat of forfeiture of the land on which the geld was due. Anyone else who then paid this geld assessment to the sheriff then acquired the land. Many estates, including monastic lands, appear to have changed hands in consequence of this ruling, a process which is documented in Cnut's reign. Lawson deduced that, given the speed with which gelds were raised in the reign of Ethelred, a similar sanction may have been in operation then. The threat of confiscation led to the mortgaging of lands and the melting down of church plate, although some monasteries were probably affected more than others. Even peasants probably came under pressure, giving rise to the danger of a revolt. But the impact of the successive gelds was uneven across the shires as a whole. Some were assessed more lightly than others, irrespective of their ability to pay. Exemptions were perhaps granted to some monasteries, and also to supporters of the king, just as some individuals were later granted exemptions by the Anglo-Norman kings. The efficient collection of geld from the non-exempt majority was perhaps encouraged by permitting collectors to retain a fraction of the proceeds. The existence of the Anglo-Saxon taxation system enabled Cnut to make non-territorial handouts, and to send home the bulk of his followers, while still retaining a mercenary force. Throughout the crisis, the strength and complexity of the coinage system was retained, enabling the king to raise fleets and armies. As late as 1012, Aethelred raised a hidage tax with which to pay mercenaries, although the unequal impact of taxation probably lay behind complaints of his unjust rule, and of a lack of will to resist the invaders.[23]

This scenario was challenged by John Gillingham, who argued that figures in the *Anglo-Saxon Chronicle* for sums raised in Danegeld are generally far too high. He thought it probable that there were accounting and auditing mechanisms capable of raising such large sums, but doubted whether the economy could support such high levies. The actual amounts allegedly raised in taxation over these crisis years were matched again only in the mid and late thirteenth century, after the country had undergone considerable economic and demographic expansion. Even the constraints of land loss, he believed, could not raise the heavy Danegelds reported in the *Anglo-Saxon Chronicle*. On the other hand, he thought that the figures for heregeld may be credible, besides indicating that Harthacnut's unpopularity stemmed from unprecedently high taxation.[24]

Lawson responded by reiterating that the account in the *Anglo-Saxon Chronicle*, with its heavy tribute figures, is basically correct in describing a worsening situation which led to the payment of ever higher sums. Even if the chronicler made the most of his dismal tale, and even if his figures were not always reliable, it would be hard to refute the outline of his narrative. Lawson therefore accepted the traditional view of Aethelred's reign as a time of disaster, and one which included the levying of high taxation. Since the political situation was without parallel, it is not surprising that it resulted in an unprecedented level of taxation.[25]

John Gillingham again returned to the fray, arguing that the chronicler's ascending scale of tributes should be set aside, and with it the overall interpretation of the last

[23] M.K. Lawson, 'The Collection of Danegeld and Heregeld in the Reigns of Aethelred and Cnut', *EHR* xcix, 1984, 721–38.

[24] J. Gillingham, ' "The Most Precious Jewel in the English Crown": Levels of Danegeld and Heregeld in the Early Eleventh Century', *EHR* civ, 1989, 373–84.

[25] M.K. Lawson, ' "Those Stories Look True": Levels of Taxation in the Reigns of Aethelred II and Cnut', *EHR* civ, 1989, 385–406.

twenty-five years of Aethelred's reign as a time when 'ever things got worse and worse'. While the numismatic evidence is difficult to interpret in detail, it does not confirm the chronicler's picture of tribute levels ascending in huge steps over the course of the reign. His interpretation, presented in a highly rhetorical style, is not matched by other sources. Gillingham argues that we should take an alternative view of Aethelred's reign as one of fluctuating fortunes, with disaster striking only in the last few years of the old king's life. If fortunes fluctuated, then levels of tribute probably fluctuated too. As for the exceptional levy reportedly taken by Cnut at the outset of his reign, Gillingham believes that this may well have been matched by sums taken by Harthacnut and William I.[26] This riposte was discounted by Lawson, maintaining that his own arguments had not been addressed, and reiterating his views on the general order of magnitude of the *Chronicle* figures.[27]

Accepting that the figures given by the *Anglo-Saxon Chronicle* for Cnut's geld are essentially correct, N.A.M. Rodger has considered the possible correlations of geld with the size of Danish ships and their crews, but finds that firm conclusions cannot be drawn.[28]

The impact of taxation in the late eleventh century was examined by Sally Harvey, who found a similar inequitable distribution of the taxation burden at this period as Lawson deduced in the opening years of the century. Dr Harvey concluded that tenants-in-chief and royal lessees were exacting much higher returns from small tenants in William I's reign than previously, although they themselves paid very much less tax. Either a much-reduced geld, or no geld at all, was levied on the lands of those who held directly from the king. They themselves may have been levying and consuming the geld, so that the minor agriculturalists and the tenants of small manors bore the burden. Dr Harvey considered that the Domesday Survey's enquiry into estate values was in part intended to gather information useful when administering vacancies and wardships, but at the same time, it indicated where the surpluses formerly produced by freeholders and sokemen were now going, and how much untaxed revenue the tenants-in-chief were receiving. This, she believed, was the reason for requiring the values of estates in the reign of King Edward. These values could be verified by obtaining the information on demesne ploughs and livestock, and it was also possible to verify the actual extent of the demesne in relation to the exemption claimed. Problems in tax collection arose less from the Edwardian hidage being out of date, and more from the extensive exemptions obtained by tenants-in-chief. Diminishing returns in taxation were exacerbated by the effects of rebellion and devastation early in William's reign. The impact of these, coupled with that of the long series of bad harvests which quickly followed on from the making of the Survey, meant that England could not sustain taxation on the scale of the early eleventh-century levies. The Domesday Survey revealed the results of a lax attitude towards tenants-in-chief which distorted the incidence of geld. But initial attempts to correct this situation proved over-ambitious, since demesne production had already peaked by 1086. In the course of William II's reign, adjustments were made towards a more realistic handling of the problem. In the twelfth century, geld assessments reverted to the figures for King Edward's reign. Certain tenants-in-chief received

[26]  J. Gillingham, 'Chronicles and Coins as Evidence for Levels of Tribute and Taxation in Late Tenth-Century England', *EHR* cv, 1990, 939–50.

[27]  M.K. Lawson, 'Danegeld and Heregeld Once More', *EHR* cv, 1990, 951–61.

[28]  N.A.M. Rodger, 'Cnut's Geld and the Size of Danish Ships', *EHR* cx, 1995, 392–403.

pardons, but only for specific yields, and the levy demanded from landed estates was probably more realistic than previously.[29]

This economic interpretation of the causes of the changes in taxation differs from that proposed by Judith Green, who suggested that the decline in the levying of Danegeld, as the geld was termed in the twelfth century, was due to its having become impolitic to make it a regular feature of royal finance, since its name now recalled its origin as a tax to meet threatened invasion. New methods of raising money were consequently devised, including the exploitation of military obligations to the crown, and the exaction of 'aids' or 'gifts' from various groups in the community, and notably from those who represented the growing wealth of the towns. The 1160s marked a real shift in the organisation of royal taxation. The last receipts from Danegeld resulted from the levy of 1161–62, while efforts were then concentrated further on feudal obligations and aids. The inquest of 1166 tried to establish the number of knights' fees which had been created. The figures which were then produced provided the basis for the aid levied in 1168 for the marriage of the king's daughter. Simultaneously aids were first taken from the king's demesne manors, the origin of the payment later known as tallage. The 1160s also witnessed the experimental taxing of revenues and movable property, on this occasion simply to raise funds for the relief of the Holy Land, although taxation of these sources of revenue later played a major part in the levying of royal finance. Professor Green deduced expediency, rather than forward planning, as prompting the new initiatives.[30]

The ninth centenary of the making of the Domesday Survey occasioned considerable research, much of it published in the transactions of the commemorative conference.[31] Sir James Holt, the editor of the volume, examined in his own paper the making of the Survey in the context of the Salisbury Oath of 1086, and the projected campaign in France, which took place in 1087. He suggested that cooperation by the tenants-in-chief in the compiling of the Survey resulted from their recognition that there were advantages to be gained from it by themselves as well as by the king. For the tenants-in-chief, there was a very detailed record of their tenurial gains, both those made in the immediate post-Conquest period and later. They in return would cooperate in the making of the Survey, and would render homage as required. The Salisbury Oath in fact put an obligation on those feudal tenants who were non-Norman to cooperate in the attack to be made on the king of France. In turn, links may be seen between this commitment and the subsequent recognition by the baronage that they owed service in Normandy in respect of their English fees.[32]

The massive enterprise of making the Survey derived some expertise from earlier analogous compilations. Professor R.H.C. Davis drew attention to continental parallels to Domesday Book, both those written before 1086, which may have influenced its structure, and others, written after 1086, which were perhaps influenced by the Survey. The earliest Carolingian forerunners date from the eighth century, and many more from the later ninth. Professor Davis suggested that the underlying motive for the Survey was to value the estates, and so to make a realistic assessment of income to be gained from the feudal incidents. Such income would be managed by the sheriffs,

[29] S. Harvey, 'Taxation and the Economy', in *Domesday Studies*, ed. J.C. Holt, Woodbridge 1987, 249–64.

[30] J. Green, 'The Last Century of Danegeld', *EHR* xcvi, 1981, 241–58.

[31] Holt, ed., *Domesday Studies*.

[32] J.C. Holt, '1086', in *Domesday Studies*, ed. Holt, 41–64.

hence the arrangement of data by shire, rather than nationwide, by fief. He depicted Domesday Book as the title deed of all those who received land in the wake of the Conquest. When these men were first granted their lands, they were given writs to show to the relevant shire courts. None of these writs has survived, which suggests that they were surrendered to the king by the new landholders as part of their Domesday returns. From then on, their title deed was Domesday Book.[33] English influences, as well as continental ones, lay behind the making of the Survey, and H.R. Loyn considered the contribution of a series of these. Carolingian influences included the use of the sworn jury for administrative purposes. The intellectual input and administrative experience of William I's bishops also made a contribution, and Professor Loyn also detected influences derived from Roman Law.[34]

He has argued elsewhere that the purposes behind the making of the Survey included a financial interest, even though Domesday Book is inefficient as a geld-book; secondly he deduced a judicial purpose, the resolution of the *clamores*, which in turn might be expected to secure the cooperation of the tenants-in-chief in the making of the Survey; thirdly there was a political purpose, given the ongoing threat of invasion by the Danes. Above all, though, was the need for the king to discover who were his richest tenants; where their lands were located, and by what tenures they were held.[35]

A variation on this last interpretation came from A.R. Bridbury, who argued that the king wanted to discover what their individual manors were worth to each of his tenants-in-chief. This information was needed because the current system of taxation imposed an income tax on his tenants-in-chief on the basis of the annual value to them of the manors on their estates. Commissioners had therefore to find out not only how much the tenants-in-chief received from their manors, but also the details of how that income was made up. Bridbury argued that the king was suspicious that there were reserves of wealth in the hands of his tenants-in-chief which he could exploit. There is a verifiable link between the manorial income, which was the income of the tenant-in-chief, and hidage, which Bridbury suggested was the tax coding corresponding to that income.[36]

A series of studies on the practicalities of the making of Domesday Book include an investigation by C.P. Lewis on the period over which its compilation was in progress, and maintained that writing was still under way well into 1088.[37] Examining the lists of jurors who produced the evidence required from each hundred, half of them Frenchmen and half English, Dr Lewis concluded that these highlight the incompleteness of Domesday Book's record of land ownership in 1086. The Domesday compilers were interested in recording names only down to that of the undertenant, so that the tenants of these men, together with other small landholders, went unrecorded. Consequently both the intensity of Norman settlement and also the extent of English survival in local society were greater than has previously been deduced.[38]

The facts and figures in the Domesday Survey had often undergone translation

[33] R.H.C. Davis, 'Domesday Book: Continental Parallels', in *Domesday Studies*, ed. Holt, 15–39.

[34] H.R. Loyn, 'The Beyond of Domesday Book', in *Domesday Studies*, ed. Holt, 1–13.

[35] H.R. Loyn, 'Domesday Book', *ANS* i, 1979, 128–30.

[36] A.R. Bridbury, 'Domesday Book: a Reinterpretation', *EHR* cv, 1990, 284–309.

[37] C.P. Lewis, 'The Earldom of Surrey and the Date of Domesday Book', *Historical Research* lxiii, 1990, 329–36.

[38] C.P. Lewis, 'The Domesday Jurors', *Haskins Soc. Jnl* v, 1993, 17–44.

before being recorded. Interpreters were employed both by the Domesday commissioners themselves, and also by members of more localised enquiries held over ensuing decades. Several of the men who translated information which was incorporated in the Survey, or in one or another of its satellites, have been identified by H. Tsurushima, who suggested that men styled *latimer* or *interpres* were also employed in the various courts. The king, bishops, abbots and perhaps also feudal magnates employed such men, who were often drawn from the ranks of small landholders.[39]

The gatherings in which these interpreters worked would be noisy, and often acrimonious. Robin Fleming points to the late Anglo-Saxon assemblies which set precedents for those of the post-Conquest era, but reminds us that the Domesday assemblies and juries reflect a rapid and immediate expansion of royal power, which made real gains over local interests in the first generation of Norman rule. Since the Survey was compiled in the interests of the royal government, only a fraction of the information gleaned from the collective memories of these large juries was organised into a record intended for preservation.[40]

Subsequently Professor Fleming developed these ideas in a major study, in which she emphasised the dependence of the Domesday Inquest on the institution of the Anglo-Saxon joint-assembly. She saw in the assemblies and juries of the Domesday Inquest evidence of the rapid and immediate expansion of royal power in regional assemblies after the Norman Conquest. The oral testimony provided the means through which neighbours of all social classes recognised the permanence of the Norman settlement and the tenurial revolution. The differing views voiced in these noisy gatherings were, though, largely blurred in the written text, the voice of the royal administration. Like David Bates and David Roffe, but arguing from a different perspective than either, Professor Fleming saw Domesday Book as a separate enterprise from the inquest itself. In theory, at least, it freed royal administrators from a reliance on their own memories of the proceedings, or on the memories of the multitude of sworn jurors. This distilled information could now be applied in the processes of government, but she saw this end-use as an entirely different accomplishment from that of the inquest.[41]

Enumerating the varying forms taken by valid evidence of title to land – writs or diplomas; relics, *vitae* of the saints; the testimony of the 'older and better men of the shire'; the oaths of compurgators and trial by battle – Professor Fleming concluded that these varying strategies suggest that in the late eleventh century there was no rigid definition of law which required a close adherence to set legal procedures and written forms.[42] Yet despite the disappearance of the English aristocracy, insular ideas about the law and landholding persisted, reinforcing the interests of the king, and of the long-established ecclesiastical communities, mostly, in 1086, now governed by Frenchmen. Overlapping and conflicting sets of customs were asserted by litigants in the decades leading up to the inquest, but in 1086, in the course of hearing repeated disputed claims, those responsible for making and enforcing the law began forming a consensus about the legal norms which determined rights to land – with emphasis on title derived through inheritance, or through the king's writ. Gradually the regional

---

[39]  H. Tsurushima, 'Domesday Interpreters', *ANS* xviii, 1996, 201–22.

[40]  R. Fleming, 'Oral Testimony and the Domesday Inquest', *ANS* xvii, 1995, 101–22.

[41]  R. Fleming, *Domesday Book and the Law: Society and Legal Custom in Early Medieval England*, Cambridge 1998, 34–5.

[42]  Fleming, *Domesday Book and the Law*, 66–7.

courts came to accept a common set of very broad legal assumptions, derived variously from English, Anglo-Scandinavian and continental sources.[43]

The lawsuits which, over time, gave rise to these commonly held assumptions stemmed from the devastating impact which the Norman Conquest had on the shape of Anglo-Saxon lordships, as Professor Fleming has demonstrated by drawing on the Domesday Book database. She has shown that there was a radical restructuring of pre-Conquest patterns of landholding and lordships, including the shattering of the great pre-Conquest comital lordships, and those of some other exceptional figures, such as Archbishop Stigand.[44]

Paul Hyams has reconsidered Maitland's classic evaluation of the purposes of the Domesday Survey, in which he had argued that Domesday Book was 'no register of title'. Hyams believes that one purpose of the Survey was to assess and increase royal resources, probably through reforms intended to widen the fiscal base, but that these reforms were halted by the sudden death of William I. Consequently, it cannot be argued that because no geld reform resulted from the Survey, none was initially intended. However, Hyams continues, land adjudication was probably also intended, so that the tenurial record of 1086 would constitute a base for future property transactions. In this respect, he believed that it was intended to constitute a limit to legal memory, such as the Common Law later established at 1189. This function of the Survey, he argued, would explain the support of the magnates for the project. Simultaneously the king derived a major advantage from the Survey in that the exercise afforded a nationwide demonstration of royal authority, in addition to its usefulness in tracing and recovering royal rights and revenues.[45]

The function of the Survey as a land register has been challenged by Patrick Wormald, in the light of the variable distribution of *clamores*, or disputes over land-ownership, which are recorded in the findings from the various circuits, and even from shire to shire within particular circuits. In part, this imbalance may indicate that the commissioners did not set out to resolve disputes, but were confronted by them on their travels. Additionally, some areas may have generated more suits because they had experienced more recent troubles, although the distribution of *clamores* does not support this explanation altogether. Perhaps the chief explanation for the discrepancies is that they reflect the extent to which the commissioners on different circuits were interested in settling disputes. When claims were brought to their attention, some were prepared to make a more thorough investigation than were others. On these grounds, Wormald believes that it is doubtful whether registration of title to land was a primary purpose of the Survey. It was no part of a sustained campaign to clarify the tenurial confusion left by the Norman Conquest. If the barons were induced to cooperate by the promise that their land rights would be indisputably registered, then they were deceived. The king, on the other hand, had a financial interest in authorising extensive enquiries into title to land because, at least since the reign of Edgar, defeated claimants in property suits had been heavily amerced by the crown. Even so, investi-

---

[43] Fleming, *Domesday Book and the Law*, 82–4.
[44] R. Fleming, 'Domesday Book and the Tenurial Revolution', *ANS* ix, 1987, 87–101.
[45] P. Hyams, ' "No Register of Title": the Domesday Inquest and Land Adjudication', *ANS* ix, 1987, 127–41.

gations into the *clamores* were conducted spasmodically, and Wormald agrees with Maitland that Domesday Book was 'no register of title'.[46]

David Roffe also argued that the resolution of disputes was only a minor function of the Survey, the principal one in his view being to enquire into royal rights and dues in every shire, and also in the royal boroughs. Roffe believes that a geld assessment was part of the Survey and that the main purpose of summoning jurors of hundred and vill was the audit of geld payment. The views of these jurors on land title really mattered only where the king's interests were concerned.[47]

Limitations to the quality of the information contained in Domesday Book stem from inconsistent practice by the commissioners as they progressed. David Roffe, after studying the returns of Circuit VI, argued that comparisons and general conclusions drawn from these are of little value in themselves, since the scribe seems to have altered his practices during the course of compilation. There are changes in diplomatic and in plan, and in the range of sources employed. There is also a frequent absence of relevant information. This all makes for an inconsistent picture of northern society, which needs to be reinforced by recourse to earlier sources, both pre-Conquest ones and also those from the years immediately following the Conquest.[48] In contrast, as Roffe points out, valuable evidence can turn up in an unlikely context. Although the *Historia Croylandensis*, as a whole, is a highly suspect text, its writer incorporates valuable material drawn from a geographically arranged Domesday Book satellite.[49]

In a subsequent major study, David Roffe argued strongly that the inquest held in 1086 was not initially intended to lead to the making of Domesday Book. Inquests already had a long history, and would continue to be held well through the thirteenth century. The inquest, he argues, was about the geld, and about knight service. Behind the inquest lay a report of an imminent invasion, necessitating the billeting of mercenaries recruited to counter it. The inquest of 1086, like earlier and later ones, established a body of accepted fact, on the basis of which an agreed course of action could be decided. The inquest can be seen as a communal exercise which provided the grounds on which a political relationship was defined at a time of crisis. Although the purpose of the inquest cannot be demonstrated, through lack of any record of the negotiations which lay behind its implementation, the chief focus of interest seems to have been the extent of exempt demesne. The figures made a case for the reimposition of geld, and in return the personal service owed by landholders was probably redefined, after consultation.[50] Roffe argued that the making of Domesday Book was unrelated to these issues. He believes that it was compiled from the records of the inquest, after 1089, most probably under the supervision of Ranulf Flambard. It was intended as a work of reference for the convenience of the central government, produced in response to the tenurial chaos which ensued from the revolt of 1088. It

---

46 P. Wormald, 'Domesday Lawsuits: a Provisional List and Preliminary Comment', in *England in the Eleventh Century*, ed. C. Hicks, Stamford 1992, 61–102.

47 D. Roffe, 'The Making of Domesday Book Reconsidered', *Haskins Soc. Jnl* vi, 1994, 153–66.

48 D. Roffe, 'Domesday Book and Northern Society: a Reassessment', *EHR* cv, 1990, 310–36. See also D. Roffe, 'The *Descriptio Terrarum* of Peterborough Abbey', *Historical Research* lxv, 1992, 1–16.

49 D. Roffe, 'The *Historia Croylandensis*: a Plea for Reassessment', *EHR* cx, 1995, 93–108.

50 D. Roffe, *Domesday: the Inquest and the Book*, Oxford 2000, viii–ix.

was a land register made and used for specifically administrative purposes, and was in no sense a public record.[51]

David Bates has also shown that the administrative process initiated by the making of Domesday Book continued into the early part of the reign of William II, when the management team which had controlled the production of Domesday Book was still at work, and lawsuits initiated by the Survey were still in progress.[52] The making of further, more limited surveys, continued into the twelfth century. Trevor Foulds has suggested that the Lindsey Survey, which he dates mid July 1115 x April–May 1116, may be an assessment made in preparation for the levying of a geld in the latter year.[53]

Various aspects of the organisation of royal finance in the twelfth century which have received attention include Warren Hollister's reappraisal of the origins of the Treasury. He argued that the Treasurership, discussed in the *Constitutio Domus Regis*, was newly established in the mid 1120s. At about the same time, the Exchequer process was coming into being as a semi-annual audit of the sheriffs' accounts. The staff and records were those of the Treasury, and the receipts went straight into the Treasury. During the reign of Henry I, Exchequer audits were conducted concurrently in England, probably at Winchester, and in Normandy, either at Rouen or at Caen. As fiscal administration became more complex by the mid 1120s, the office of Treasurer was created to supervise the entire cross-Channel system. Yet the formal lines of communication, through Treasurer and chamberlains of the Treasury, was shadowed by an informal *ad hoc* line of command, which Professor Hollister illustrated by the episode in which Robert, earl of Gloucester, conveyed much of the royal treasure from Winchester to Falaise, rather than to the Norman Treasury at Rouen, shortly before the death of Henry I.[54]

Judith Green's examination of the Pipe Roll of 1129–30 indicated to her that in the later years of Henry I, government was vigorous and even predatory. There was a drive to keep up revenue from land, even though the stock of land had diminished since the Conqueror's reign. Adjustments were being made to the old system of taxation, but above all, justice and jurisdiction were being exploited for their financial potential. There was selective application of financial pressure; a Forest Eyre was imposed, and indebted sheriffs were dismissed. On the evidence of this Pipe Roll, she believes that financial government had become increasingly confident and progressive throughout the preceding decade, with the provisor that caution needs to be exercised when drawing conclusions from any single Pipe Roll.[55]

The predatory and unpredictable nature of royal financial exactions has also been emphasised by Stephanie Mooers Christelow, when examining the grants – most often concessions or remissions – made by kings from William I to Stephen *pro amore* (for love of) some influential intermediary. While the exercise of the royal *benevolentia* and *malevolentia* has generally been associated with the rule of Angevin kings, it can also be demonstrated in those of their Norman predecessors. Evidence is clearest from the 1130 Pipe Roll, where their frequency demonstrates that *pro amore*

[51] Roffe, *Domesday: the Inquest and the Book*, 250–1.

[52] D. Bates, 'Two Ramsey Abbey Writs and the Domesday Survey', *Historical Research* lxiii, 1990, 337–9.

[53] T. Foulds, 'The Lindsey Survey and an Unknown Precept of King Henry I', *BIHR* lix, 1986, 212–15.

[54] C.W. Hollister, 'The Origins of the English Treasury', *EHR* xciii, 1978, 262–75.

[55] J. Green, '*Praeclarum et Magnificum Antiquitatis Monumentum*: the Earliest Surviving Pipe Roll', *BIHR* lv, 1982, 1–17.

pardons, mediated by influential royal favourites, were institutionalised. The pardon, granted to a client of this favourite, was a mark of the favourite's own high status. By 1135, the royal love, as a fiscal concept resting on extraordinary affection, was formalised in legal documents, chronicles and administrative accounts. Professor Christelow deduced that its exercise peaked about this time, since although the concept of the king's *amor* persisted in literature of the Angevin period, the phrase *pro amore* is not found in the Pipe Rolls of Henry II. The implication is that, by this reign, government was less personal and more clearly regulated than in the time of Henry I.[56]

Kenji Yoshitake suggested that, even during the widespread unrest of Stephen's reign, Exchequer audits continued to be held for those counties where the shire farms were subsequently paid by tale in the early years of Henry II's reign, and audits were perhaps also held in further shires in Stephen's time. He noted that those paying by tale, together with others paying blanch in 1154–55, formed a compact block in eastern England, while another compact block of shires paying blanch was recorded in western England in 1155–57. Both regions, he suggested, had suffered less from disorders than had other parts of the country in the previous decade, while these blocks coincide fairly well with the two areas which, as Edmund King has demonstrated, were under the effective control of Stephen and Matilda, respectively, during the hostilities. A contrast can be made between these two regions and others for which there are no records in the Pipe Roll of 1154–55.[57]

The extent, and limitations, of the exercise of royal government in Stephen's reign have been examined from various angles. Edmund King discussed the role of the negotiated agreement throughout this reign, not only as regards the succession to the throne, but also as a strategy employed by members of landed society for maintaining the peace, whether at national, regional or local level.[58] Royal government, however, did not break down entirely throughout England, and Judith Green demonstrated that Stephen, by his creation of earls who were able to dominate the sheriffs in their respective regions, succeeded in ensuring a steady supply of shire revenues from the area under his control, and particularly from the south-east. The coinage was of a good standard both at the beginning and end of the reign, despite a bad patch in its difficult middle years, and possibly he was in receipt of geld from some areas. Loans were forthcoming from several sources, including the Templars; from William Cade and also from other Flemings and probably also from mercantile interests in London and several other major cities, making it possible to finance the king's campaigns. Within the area under Stephen's military control, the royal administration was effective, and in the course of the 1140s, it is arguable that the centre of the royal financial administration shifted from Winchester to the south-east, since there are indications that at an uncertain date before 1154 the Exchequer operations had already moved to London, or more precisely, to Westminster.[59] Nicholas Vincent supports these conclusions, arguing from a series of previously unknown charters of the king, which

56 S. Mooers Christelow, 'The Royal Love in Anglo-Norman England: Fiscal or Courtly Concept?', *Haskins Soc. Jnl* viii, 1999, 27–41.
57 K. Yoshitake, 'The Exchequer in the Reign of Stephen', *EHR* ciii, 1988, 950–9.
58 E. King, 'Dispute Settlement in Anglo-Norman England', *ANS* xiv, 1992, 115–30.
59 J. Green, 'Financing Stephen's War', *ANS* xiv, 1992, 91–114.

demonstrate his ability to manage the royal forests as a source of revenue, even at the height of the so-called 'anarchy'.[60]

David Crouch, however, argues for distinct limitations to the extent of Stephen's rule. He sees the subordination of the sheriffs to the earls as an imaginative and innovative policy which tied the loyal magnates into the governmental structure. This experiment in decentralisation was a brief one, however, since a revised strategy of regional military governors was introduced after the battle of Lincoln. While there is evidence for the survival of the Exchequer down to 1141, and of its existence at the end of the reign, he is uncertain about its activities, if any, over much of the 1140s, arguing that at best it was a case of survival, rather than of being operational at full strength. While conceding that within areas under the king's military control the forest administration was 'surprisingly vital'; and that minting continued, as did the administration of justice, he argued that the levying of geld was largely, if not entirely, in abeyance during the period of hostilities.[61] In the first years of the new reign, however, Emilie Amt argues that the royal administration was very quickly fully operational again.[62]

Financial administration in Normandy, meanwhile, experienced problems of its own. Judith Green, drawing on the evidence of the Norman Pipe Roll of 1180, suggested that it was possibly only from 1176 that there was a fully restored Exchequer in Normandy, meeting each year to hear the accounts of financial agents. She suggests that the year 1176 marked, not simply a reorganisation, but in fact the refoundation of a fully functional Norman Exchequer.[63]

A comparison of the Norman Pipe Roll of 1180 with its English counterpart has been made by Vincent Moss, who considers Judith Green's argument about the refoundation of the Norman Exchequer. He points out that the incomplete Norman Pipe Roll for 1180 was still longer and more detailed than its English counterpart, even with up to 30% of the Norman Roll missing. In his opinion, a refoundation of the Norman Exchequer is more likely to have occurred in the 1160s, when Henry II first turned his attention to the government of Normandy. In 1180, the income recorded on the Norman Pipe Roll was far smaller than that of 1195 and 1198. However, he found no evidence of large-scale infusions of English money to finance Norman expenditure in 1180. The first serious evidence of this occurs on the Norman Pipe Roll of 1184, and by 1195 this infusion of English money had become systematic. Moss suggests that slightly wider circles were involved in administration in Normandy than in England, but that Norman and English Pipe Rolls show a broad similarity of farming and accounting methods. Sources of revenue in both territories were broadly similar, although there were some distinct types of Norman farm, including the *vicomté* farm, a kind of land tax. He suggests that some differentiation of practice occurred as Henry II recovered lands lost in Stephen's reign. In Normandy, recovered land was absorbed into the farm, while in England such land was accounted for separately in the Pipe Roll. Forest income in both regions had some similarity, but administration of this income differed, and there was no Norman equivalent of the complex English Forest Eyre system. English Forest income arose from infringement of royal rights, while in

60  N. Vincent, 'New Charters of King Stephen with Some Reflections upon the Royal Forests during the Anarchy', *EHR* cxiv, 1999, 899–928, at pp. 899–200.
61  D. Crouch, *The Reign of King Stephen, 1135–1154*, Harlow 2000, 325–6, 328, 330–5, 338–9.
62  E. Amt, *The Accession of Henry II in England: Royal Government Restored*, Woodbridge 1993, 187.
63  J. Green, 'Unity and Disunity in the Anglo-Norman State', *Historical Research* lxii, 1989, 122–3.

Normandy income tended to be generated by the sale of Forest produce. So far as other sources of income were concerned, Norman public rights probably stemmed from Carolingian practices. In England, there was the murder fine, arising from the circumstances of conquest, and also the profitable exercise of regalian right. The profits of justice generated more revenue in Normandy than in England, for the reason that more of each sum due was actually paid in Normandy. In England, there was a powerful monarchical structure, armed with a series of distinct royal rights, which were ruthlessly exploited, as were farms and wardships. In Normandy, the political structure was based on ducal power, although the justice system produced high yields, as did public rights and a relatively advanced commercial economy.[64]

Our inside information on the workings of the English Exchequer in this period owes much to the *Dialogus* of Richard Fitz Nigel, the Treasurer. John Hudson discussed the strands of tradition which lay behind Richard's account of Exchequer practice, and pointed out that there were various collective memories among those who were employed in the royal administration. Richard's strongest tradition, inevitably, was that of his own family, so that Roger of Salisbury and Nigel of Ely were effectively his authorities. Their lives helped to structure his view of the past, as seen from the perspective of an administrator.[65] In the *Dialogus*, it was said that, after the Treasurer, the most heavily worked officer of the Exchequer was the Chancellor's clerk, who deputised for the Chancellor at the Exchequer of Account. Nicholas Vincent has elucidated this clerk's responsibilities, which gradually evolved into those of the Chancellor of the Exchequer.[66]

Considerable income derived from the profits of minting. Michael Metcalf estimated that William I tried to extract an annual sum in excess of £750 a year, and perhaps as much as £1000, from this one source. There is no evidence to indicate how the moneyers were enabled to recoup their outgoings, but they did not try to do so by tampering with the quality of the coins.[67] In fact, the Norman kings took over *en bloc* the late Anglo-Saxon system of coinage, which had been introduced by King Edgar, and which was the most sophisticated in Europe. Production was highly regulated, and the coinage itself was used as a means of taxation, since it was changed regularly, and moneyers were charged a fee for reminting. William I replaced the annual payment due from the moneyers, and also that due on the change of coin-type, with a single tax (*de moneta*), levied on each of the boroughs which had a mint. This new payment amounted to three or four times the value of previous payments by moneyers. In addition to stabilising the weight of the penny, he also introduced the *monetagium commune*, which was possibly a general tax imposed in exchange for stabilising the weight of the penny and reducing the fee charged for minting.

Under Aethelred and Cnut, changes of coin type occurred about every six years, while under later kings they occurred at three-yearly intervals. Recoinages on each change of type were not comprehensive, but for certain transactions only coins of the

---

64  V. Moss, 'Normandy and England in 1180: the Pipe Roll Evidence', in *England and Normandy in the Middle Ages*, ed. D. Bates and A. Curry, London and Rio Grande 1994, 185–95.

65  J. Hudson, 'Administration, Family and Perceptions of the Past in Late Twelfth-Century England: Richard FitzNigel and the Dialogue of the Exchequer', in *The Perception of the Past in Twelfth-Century Europe*, ed. P. Magdalino, London 1992, 75–93.

66  N. Vincent, 'The Origins of the Chancellorship of the Exchequer', *EHR* cviii, 1993, 105–21.

67  D.M. Metcalf, 'The Taxation of Moneyers under Edward the Confessor and in 1086', in *Domesday Studies*, ed. Holt, 279–93.

current issue could be used, and people were obliged to change some of their money into new coins on every change of type. Mark Blackburn surveyed innovations in monetary policy in the reign of Henry I. At his coronation, the king promised to abandon the *monetagium*. Round halfpennies were introduced c. 1107, and about a year later came the order to snick or cut every coin before it left the mint, probably to prevent the circulation of plated forgeries. Major changes came in 1125, when more than half the moneyers were removed from office. The mint network was rationalised, and the periodic recoinages were abandoned in favour of a coinage of an immobilised type. These changes coincided with a period of intensive administrative reform which started in 1123, but was concentrated in 1128–31. In an attempt to increase the royal revenues, the office of sheriff was overhauled, and the methods of accounting for payments were tightened. Much of this activity took place in the years 1123–26, while the king was in Normandy, which indicates his trust in Roger of Salisbury.[68]

Developments in local government have attracted considerable discussion. Simon Keynes pointed out that Aethelred could rely only on the loyalty of his West Saxons, and the force of his presence and personality. Further afield, problems were likely to arise from the entrenched local dynasties with their mutual rivalries. The network of reeves continued to be difficult to control, as in previous reigns, and inevitably there were clashes between individual reeves and ealdormen. The aristocracy monopolised the high offices of state, and it was perhaps to combat this that Aethelred elevated Eadric Streona.[69] The older aristocracy disappeared at Cnut's accession, and was replaced by a new one which owed its wealth and status to the king. But these men did not attest royal charters, and Katharine Mack has argued that local feelings and interests were not taken into account at the centre. Under a weaker king, this would be destabilising.[70]

However, at a lower level in the localities, several networks served to further the interests of eleventh-century kings, as James Campbell has indicated. He suggested that village reeves had obligations not only to their immediate lords but also to the king, as geld collectors. In towns, administration was controlled by local patriciates, many of which still survived well after the Norman Conquest. Much administration was performed on a part-time basis, and Campbell suggested that some of the sergeanties of the Anglo-Norman period were remnants of the Anglo-Saxon system of government which operated in the localities. He suggested that strong links can be traced between thegns and later sergeanties, and that the thegns of Domesday Book were in royal service. At the king's command, thegns might represent him at court hearings, and like the occupants of other administrative posts, they would have opportunities for enrichment. Links between the court and the landholders were maintained, he suggests, by the housecarls, who may have performed duties in the royal household on a rota basis. Campbell deduced that King Edward maintained a considerable administrative machine, and suggests that this was headed by Stigand, which in turn would account for his exceptional wealth. Campbell believed that the late

---

[68] M. Blackburn, 'Coinage and Currency under Henry I: a Review', *ANS* xiii, 1991, 49–76.

[69] S. Keynes, 'A Tale of Two Kings: Alfred the Great and Aethelred the Unready', *TRHS* 5th ser. xxxvi, 1986, 195–217.

[70] K. Mack, 'Changing Thegns: Cnut's Conquest and the English Aristocracy', *Albion* xvi, 1984, 375–87.

Anglo-Saxon kings enjoyed real sovereignty, and points out that, in contrast to continental practice, their earls did pay geld, and did not issue charters.[71]

The stallers, though, did have a close working relationship with the king. This office was introduced by Cnut, but was better recorded in the reign of King Edward, by which time there were English and French in their ranks, in addition to the men of Scandinavian origin. Katharine Mack has shown from figures in Domesday Book that the stallers were among the richest men at Edward's court, and controlled great landed estates, components of which were often spread among several shires. The stallers are shown from writs of King Edward to have carried out his orders in the shires, but usually not in those in which they held their lands. Instructions related to lands which the king had assigned to Westminster Abbey, which he had refounded. Activities of the stallers normally related to matters of personal interest to the king, and their attestations on his charters suggest that they played an increasingly dominant role as Edward's reign progressed. The pattern of their landholding, together with their appearances in charters, suggests that Edward used them to try to incorporate the non-Wessex regions under royal control. But, Katharine Mack suggests, royal policies actually fostered tensions between the aristocracy and the king. In any event, the use of stallers was discontinued by the Norman kings.[72]

One alleged Anglo-Norman administrative experiment owes more to tradition than to hard evidence, in the view of J.W. Alexander. Examining the supposed Anglo-Norman palatinates, he concluded that local traditions and local patriotism, rather than record evidence, are the sources of a belief in their existence in Anglo-Norman times. These great liberties, he argued, can be traced only from the late thirteenth century onwards.[73]

The powers of the sheriffs, in the post-Conquest era, have also attracted attention. Richard Abels, concentrating on the evidence of Domesday Circuit III, and especially entries relating to the sheriffs of Bedfordshire and Buckinghamshire, Buckinghamshire (alone), Cambridgeshire and Hertfordshire, concluded that these officials performed the same duties as their Anglo-Saxon predecessors, but in a radically different social and legal climate. Their preeminent position in the hundred-courts gave them a regular opportunity to confirm their status through the exercise of patronage, and they were among the most successful of interested parties in placing their own men on juries. The sheriff also embodied royal authority, in the eyes of the sokemen, through his duties of managing and farming the royal demesne, and supervising the payment of dues and renders owed to the crown. Like the pre-Conquest earls, stallers and sheriffs, these post-Conquest sheriffs attached royal sokemen *en bloc* to royal demesne manors in order to increase the king's revenues and their own profits, but now there was no earl to restrain them, and in fact they assumed many of the duties of the pre-Conquest earls. Using the mechanisms and powers of office which had been exercised by their Anglo-Saxon predecessors, they built up substantial estates.[74]

---

71  J. Campbell, 'Some Agents and Agencies of the Late Anglo-Saxon State', in *Domesday Studies*, ed. Holt, 201–18.

72  K. Mack, 'The Stallers: Administrative Innovation in the Reign of Edward the Confessor', *JMH* xii, 1986, 123–34. On the stallers in Edward's reign, see also P. Nightingale, 'The Origin of the Court of Husting and Danish Influence on London's Development into a Capital City', *EHR* cii, 1987, 559–78.

73  J.W. Alexander, 'The Alleged Palatinates of Norman England', *Speculum* lvi, 1981, 17–27.

74  R. Abels, 'Sheriffs, Lord-Seeking and the Norman Settlement of the South-East Midlands', *ANS* xix, 1997, 19–50.

A rather different and nationwide view of the post-Conquest sheriffs is given by Judith Green. The Normans, as she observed, were accustomed to the *vicecomes*, and equated his office with that of the shire-reeve. But the Norman *vicecomites* were powerful men, and potential troublemakers. She believed that William I would not want to appoint as sheriffs men who combined territorial wealth with control of shire administration to the extent that they themselves became capable of offering a threat. There was a transitional period during which the shrievalties were handed over to Frenchmen, but subsequently there were relatively frequent changes in personnel. Several sheriffs were key men, and some had links with such powerful figures as Bishop Odo or William Fitz Osbern, but on the whole, their landed status was very mixed. All of these features became more pronounced by the reign of Henry I.[75]

W.L. Warren, however, argued that by this reign there was a possibility that royal control over the shire and hundred courts would be lost to the sheriffs. He believed that this danger prompted the issue of the writ ordering that these courts were to convene at the locations, and at the regular intervals, which were formerly prescribed. Sheriffs were not to take matters into their own hands by convening them at other times, although the king reserved the right to convene other meetings if these were necessitated by royal business. This writ also attempted to increase the drawing power of the royal courts, by insisting that pleas between the men of two different lords should be heard in them, rather than in the defendant's court, as had been customary.[76]

In Stephen's reign, central control over local officials weakened as a result of the grants of *totus comitatus* to powerful earls, which have been discussed by Paul Latimer. For a time, the shire as an administrative unit was weakened in consequence of such a grant, but under the strong government of Henry II the position was reversed. Most earldoms then retained only the 'third penny of the pleas of the shire', and in some cases the 'third penny' of certain boroughs.[77]

The activities of the sheriffs have been scrutinised from several aspects. Emilie Amt raised the question whether the traditional bad (oppressive) sheriff was already a problem in English government during the twelfth century. She also considered whether the royal government recognised oppressive sheriffs as bad ones, or whether it was concerned only that the sheriff's performance of his job came up to the expectations of the king and his ministers, particularly in the collection of the shire farm. Complaints about oppressive sheriffs, it is argued, increased from the reign of Henry II onwards. Public perceptions are seen in that the inquest of 1170, which covered a wide agenda, was termed by contemporaries the Inquest of Sheriffs. In fact this inquest highlighted not only the oppression of the king's subjects by various sheriffs, but also their failure to fulfil their obligations towards the king. The public message of the articles of inquiry, and the dismissals of wrongdoers, demonstrated that the interests of the king and his subjects were the same. An oppressive royal officer wronged the king, whose duty it was to ensure that his subjects were treated rightly. The exercise was beneficial to the king from a public relations standpoint, while he and his ministers continued to enforce the competence, efficiency and loyalty of the sheriffs. The chroniclers' accounts of the inquest reflect public perceptions of the shortcomings of the sheriffs, perceptions which in turn reflected changes both in royal

[75] J. Green, 'The Sheriffs of William the Conqueror', *ANS* v, 1983, 129–45.
[76] Warren, *The Governance of Norman and Angevin England*, 69–70.
[77] P. Latimer, 'Grants of *Totus Comitatus* in Twelfth-Century England: their Origins and Meaning', *BIHR* lix, 1986, 137–45.

government and in the law. An increasingly interventionist government resulted in the legitimate activities of the sheriffs seeming more burdensome, while simultaneously providing the sheriffs with increased opportunities for acting oppressively in their own interests. Further inquiries into the activities of sheriffs in the reigns of Richard and John, culminating in Magna Carta, again highlighted belief in their misconduct. However, while royal government was itself arbitrary, the sheriffs, as its agents, were the objects of popular resentment.[78]

Julia Boorman argues that although the inquest of 1170 has generally been seen as a watershed, it needs to be examined within a wider, and specifically retrospective context. She concludes that replacements of sheriffs in 1170 were not so sweeping as might be inferred, and there were considerable elements of continuity. Additionally, changes of personnel in the period between 1159–60 and 1163–64 produced a total comparable with that of 1170.[79]

In the late twelfth century, the question of appointments to shrievalties carried considerable political significance. Richard Heiser argued that William Longchamps preferred to appoint men who were personally dependent upon him. In his efforts to hold the realm for King Richard, he drew the kingdom's allegiance into himself, making extensive use of members of his family and of other personal dependants. These sheriffs, owing their position and power to Longchamps, were bound to promote his interests. Walter of Coutances, on the other hand, achieved stability by appointing sheriffs who had been trained under Henry II, and who made the king and kingdom their first priority. Their hope of receiving patronage gave them a stake in the kingdom and a concern for its security. Although there was unrest in the time of both justiciars, Walter's policies were better equipped to deal with it. His men, like those of Longchamps, were closely associated with his household, despite their independent political base, so that the household of the justiciar, rather than the *domus regis* as formerly, was the main source of recruits to this office, which both justiciars viewed as being of vital importance to the stability of the realm.[80]

In a further study, Richard Heiser argued that the repeated military crises of Richard I's reign prevented the close management of the shrievalties later exercised by John. Yet, with only two exceptions, the sheriffs appointed in Richard's reign served him well and loyally, even during periods of unrest. He argued that Richard's direct involvement in appointments, whenever possible, his shrewd selection and deployment of these men, and his wisdom in knowing how to turn resources into revenues, indicates that he was a much abler ruler than has traditionally been believed.[81]

The end of Walter de Coutances's period in office marked the arrival of a new development. David Carpenter argued that, from the appointment of Hubert Walter as justiciar, Exchequer officials, being eager to extract more money from the shires, were increasingly appointing as sheriffs men of lower social status and less independent power than their predecessors had enjoyed.[82]

Work on aspects of legal administration covers a wide range. M.K. Lawson

---

78  E. Amt, 'The Reputation of the Sheriff, 1100–1216', *Haskins Soc. Jnl* viii, 1999, 91–8.

79  J. Boorman, 'The Sheriffs of Henry II and the Significance of 1170', in *Law and Government in England and Normandy*, ed. G. Garnett and J. Hudson, Cambridge 1994, 255–75.

80  R. Heiser, 'The Sheriffs of Richard I: Trends of Management as Seen in the Shrieval Appointments from 1189 to 1194', *Haskins Soc. Jnl* iv, 1992, 109–19.

81  R.R. Heiser, 'Richard I and his Appointments to English Shrievalties', *EHR* cxii, 1997, 1–19.

82  D. Carpenter, 'The Decline of the Curial Sheriff in England 1194–1258', *EHR* xci, 1976, 1–32.

suggests that Archbishop Wulfstan's legal texts tell us less about English government in the early eleventh century than they do about clerical attempts to set the ruler on the right spiritual course. The priority given to this indicates that the regimes of Aethelred and Cnut were far from benevolent in practice.[83]

Henry Loyn, on the other hand, has drawn parallels between the *Laws of Cnut* and the *Leges Henrici Primi*, pointing to comparable theocratic notions of peace guaranteed by the king and buttressed by the Church. In both instances, these guarantees were combined with the specific and practical formulation of royal rights and the close association of royal authority with the preservation of peace. However, Professor Loyn perceives a development from the homiletic approach of Archbishop Wulfstan to the analytic one of the author of the *Leges Henrici Primi*.[84] Interest in the workings of the land law can be traced from David Bates's discussion of the Penenden plea which was initiated in 1072. It was pleaded in the context of the beginning of a recovery and reorganisation of property and rights, the end of a period of decline and lay encroachment on Church lands, and the beginning of a period of restoration and definition.[85]

Marjorie Chibnall, drawing on the narratives of the Anglo-Norman period, has demonstrated how law and custom were often threatened, or manipulated, but were never entirely overturned by the powerful.[86] Yet, simultaneously with these pressures on the law, Patrick Wormald argues that the writer or compiler of the *Quadripartitus*, in attempting to express the 'Laws of Edward', reflected the claim of the Norman regime to be founded on respect for the ancient values and procedures of the English kingdom, a mission which continued to influence succeeding generations.[87]

In his study of the law relating to landholding, John Hudson concentrated on the evolvement of measures to ensure security of tenure, heritability and alienability. His examination of legal procedures in the Anglo-Norman period threw light on the workings of seignorial power, as expressed through the land-law, and also on the question of regional and honorial variations.[88] In a subsequent study, Hudson emphasised the importance of the English legacy in the formulation of the Common Law, born of a welding together of customs and procedures, as suitors attended both courts which survived from the pre-Conquest era and others subsequently introduced. The king's oversight, and his transfer of cases from one court to another, further assisted the process of integration.[89] Legal developments in England followed a distinctive path, in part due to the merging of English and Norman customs, and the unifying influence of royal authority. A major contribution was made by the knights and the free men of

---

[83]  M.K. Lawson, 'Archbishop Wulfstan and the Homiletic Element in the Laws of Aethelred and Cnut', *EHR* cvii, 1992, 565–86.

[84]  H.R. Loyn, '*De Iure Domini Regis*: a Comment on Royal Authority in Eleventh-Century England', in *England in the Eleventh Century*, ed. Hicks, 17–24.

[85]  D. Bates, 'The Land Pleas of William I's Reign: Penenden Heath Revisited', *BIHR* li, 1978, 1–19.

[86]  M. Chibnall, ' "Clio's Legal Cosmetics": Law and Custom in the Work of Medieval Historians', *ANS* xx, 1998, 31–43.

[87]  P. Wormald, '*Quadripartitus*', in *Law and Government in Medieval England and Normandy*, ed. Garnett and Hudson, 111–47, at pp. 146–7.

[88]  J. Hudson, *Land, Law and Lordship in Anglo-Norman England*, Oxford 1994. See also his 'Anglo-Norman Land Law and the Origins of Property', in *Law and Government in Medieval England and Normandy*, ed. Garnett and Hudson, 198–222.

[89]  J. Hudson, *The Formation of the English Common Law: Law and Society in England from the Norman Conquest to Magna Carta*, Harlow 1996, 50–1.

the localities involved in self-government at the king's command. The emergence of a fairly coherent and consistent body of custom, over the reigns of the strong Norman kings, paved the way for the further developments in legal procedures of the Angevin period.[90] These extended studies followed earlier work in which Hudson observed that Church lordships were perhaps at the forefront of the development of the Common Law, as ecclesiastical landlords turned to Henry I for help. This often came in forms which foreshadowed those of Henry II's reign. Lay landholders also began to look to the king, although royal justice was not yet as regularly applied as it was to be in the reign of Henry II. The trend continued into Stephen's reign and beyond, as those of knightly status grew less willing to accept the decision of the honorial court as final. Landholders also looked increasingly to the king when confronted by tenants more powerful than themselves. On Church honours, in particular, there was a growing resistance to life-grants. Litigants appealed to the king, and by 1135 progress had been made towards a strictly defined inheritance. Hudson suggests that differences in legal practice between Henry I's reign and that of Henry II were less dramatic than has been suggested.[91]

The legal developments of Henry I's reign were examined by Judith Green commenting on both the activities of locally based justices and also those of panels of justices sent out into the localities, commissioned to hear the king's pleas. She concluded that the first eyres of which there is clear evidence began in 1124.[92] Stephanie Mooers, commenting on the administration of justice in this reign from the standpoint of evidence contained in the Pipe Roll of 1130, deduced that the administration of justice was rarely harsh, either in terms of physical or of fiscal penalties, while officials were kept in check. By 1130, the growing recourse to the royal courts led to a flourishing, though not always lucrative, business in royal writs.[93] In addition to its financial potential for the crown, the growing recourse to the law had the additional benefit of helping to reinforce political stability, by discouraging the feuding over territorial rights which Paul Hyams has shown to have continued well into the twelfth century.[94] Even though court verdicts often contained an element of compromise in disputes over land, skilled arbitration played comparatively little part on this level, although Christopher Holdsworth has deduced the existence of experienced negotiators on the international scene.[95]

The reign of Henry II is conventionally seen as that in which the English Common Law made its real appearance. Paul Hyams has argued, though, that this law embodied a good deal of French noble custom, which in turn probably made it the more acceptable in the higher reaches of society.[96]

Further possible continental influences on the practices of the Common Law have been examined by Ralph V. Turner. He suggests that the presenting jury may have its origins either in earlier Scandinavian practice or in Anglo-Saxon procedures. The

90　Hudson, *The Formation of the English Common Law*, 237–9.
91　J. Hudson, 'Life-Grants of Land and the Development of Inheritance in Anglo-Norman England', *ANS* xii, 1990, 67–80. On the question of inheritance, see also R. DeAragon, 'The Growth of Secure Inheritance in Anglo-Norman England', *JMH* viii, 1982, 381–91.
92　Green, *Government of England under Henry I*, 217.
93　S.L. Mooers, 'A Re-evaluation of Royal Justice under Henry I of England', *AHR* xciii, 1988, 340–58.
94　P.R. Hyams, 'Feud in Medieval England', *Haskins Soc. Jnl* iii, 1991, 1–21.
95　C. Holdsworth, 'Peacemaking in the Twelfth Century', *ANS* xix, 1997, 1–17.
96　P. Hyams, 'The Common Law and the French Connection', *ANS* iv, 1982, 77–92.

Grand Assize, on the other hand, may derive either from Frankish inquests into royal rights, continued by the dukes of Normandy, or from popular recognitions held in Anglo-Saxon times. However, it was Henry II who converted both juries into regular instruments of justice.[97]

Henry II and his advisors, in the opinion of S.C.F. Milsom, addressed the problem of lords abusing their control over the routine of inheritance. This led in turn to their devising the series of assizes which could be used by aggrieved tenants. In the writ of novel disseisin, as much as in the Assize of Northampton, they were dealing with a system of landholding which turned on the relationship between a lord and his tenants.[98]

Paul Brand has also discussed the ways in which seignorial courts were integrated into a common legal system as a result of deliberate changes made by Henry II and his advisors. By integrating all kinds of courts into a single nationwide legal system, they were deliberately creating a structure which was radically different from the localised and inefficient system which they had inherited.[99]

This view has been challenged by Cary L. Dier, who took exception to the alleged inefficiency of Anglo-Norman practice. Emphasis in this earlier era was on the obligations of a tenant to his lord. This encouraged communal decision-making, which promoted the unity of the homage-group. A good lord acted with the advice of his men, and discretionary judgements took account of the special facts of each case, rather than proceeding by strict application of rigid rules of law. The 'best' outcome would not be a judgement, but a consensus which brought the disputants together and promoted harmony among members of the homage group. This was preferable in an age when the only response to an unfavourable verdict was recourse to self-help. In fact, it is concluded, such compromises can still be seen operating at a high level in the reign of Henry II, as instanced by the resolution of the dispute between the bishop of Chichester and the abbot of Battle.[100]

Since much of the English Common Law grew out of native administrative traditions, Ralph V. Turner argued, judges found a practical training of more use than an academic one. Consequently, although Roman legal studies flourished in late twelfth-century England, they had little impact on the shaping of the Common Law. Among clerics, a course of canon or civil law was not considered necessary for advancement in royal service, while in any case half of the justices overall were laymen, who would have had no reason to be deeply learned in the principles of the Roman Law.[101]

The growing use of documentation of acts of government throughout this period has attracted growing discussion. Michael Clanchy, in his masterly work *From Memory to Written Record*, discusses in detail both the proliferation of records and

---

[97]  R.V. Turner, 'The Origins of the Medieval English Jury: Frankish, English or Scandinavian?', *JBS* vii, 1968, 1–10.

[98]  S.C.F. Milsom, 'Maitland and the Grand Assize', *Haskins Soc. Jnl* vii, 1995, 151–77.

[99]  P. Brand, '*Multis Vigiliis Excogitatam et Inventam*: Henry II and the Creation of the English Common Law', *Haskins Soc. Jnl* ii, 1990, 197–222.

[100]  C.L. Dier, 'The Proper Relationship between Lord and Vassal: Toward a Rationale for Anglo-Norman Litigation', *Haskins Soc. Jnl* vi, 1994, 1–12.

[101]  R.V. Turner, 'Roman Law in England before the Time of Bracton', *JBS* xv, 1975, 1–25.

also the changing attitudes which this fostered, both to the processes of government, and also to the processes of memory.[102]

Charter production has attracted much attention. Cassandra Potts has considered the evolution of Norman charters from the time of Duke Richard II to the Conquest era, noting the political and other circumstances which affected both the output of charters and also their quality. She does not believe that Norman charters of the 1060s were modelled on Capetian charters, nor that they were influenced by the formulae of the public acts of the late Roman empire. While Norman and Anglo-Saxon charters differed in many respects at the time of the Conquest, they yet shared certain characteristics which both owed to early private *acta*. The Conquest brought together diplomatic traditions in England and Normandy which were not incompatible.[103]

Technical differences between Norman and Anglo-Saxon royal charters, and the impact of the Conquest on the appearance of post-Conquest official documents, were discussed by the late R. Allen Brown.[104] Some of his conclusions can be questioned in the light of recent work by David Bates and Simon Keynes. At an early stage of the research which culminated in the *Acta of William I*, David Bates's study of early Norman writs led him to consider it possible that a ducal chancery was developing after 1066. Large differences persisted, both in volume of output and in content, between English and Norman writs over the period 1066–1135. He suggests that there was an explosion of output of documents produced in England after 1087, and that Normandy did not altogether share this development, perhaps because English government penetrated feudal society much more deeply than its Norman equivalent. At the same time, he believes that the earliest Norman writs demonstrate a steady centralisation of ducal government between 1066 and 1135. The Norman chancery began to expand its activity under William I, and continued in the time of Duke Robert Curthose. A greater expansion can be seen in the time of Henry I, in part due to growing judicial activity. Norman writs suggest that the *vicomte*, in contrast to the English sheriff, was not an official through whom mandates relating to the men of his *vicomté* could be communicated, and the *vicomte*'s court was never so much a popular court as was the English shire court. Over the whole twelfth century, probably the deployment of new local officials, who took on new functions within existing jurisdictions, created the structure which appears in the late twelfth-century Exchequer Rolls and the *Très Ancien Coutumier.* Probably there was a different balance between ducal authority and seigneurial lordship in the duchy than there was in the kingdom, and to a late date there is little evidence of intervention in Norman property disputes. While *Glanvill* makes a basic distinction between the courts of the king and his justices, and the lesser courts of shire and hundred, the *Très Ancien Coutumier* drew the line between ducal and baronial courts. Administrative developments in England stemmed from the redistribution of property after 1066, a situation which did not

[102]  M.T. Clanchy, *From Memory to Written Record: England 1066–1307*, 2nd edn, Oxford 1993, part i, 23–196.

[103]  C. Potts, 'The Early Norman Charters: a New Perspective on an Old Debate', in *England in the Eleventh Century*, ed. Hicks, 25–36.

[104]  R.A. Brown, 'Some Observations on Norman and Anglo-Norman Charters', in *Tradition and Change: Essays in Honour of Marjorie Chibnall*, ed. D. Greenway, C. Holdsworth and J. Sayers, Cambridge 1985, 145–63.

pertain to Normandy. Differences between English and Norman practice overall were significant and long-lasting.[105]

An examination of English writs and charters of the late eleventh century, which marked a further stage on the way to the publication of the *Regesta of William I*, indicated to David Bates that there was a basic continuity of content and usage between those of Edward and those of William I. He followed James Campbell's earlier argument that royal writs would be received in the hundred courts, and also supported the suggestion of R.H.C. Davis that special writs, drawn up for the original allocation of lands following the Conquest, were returned in 1086. Usage of the writ increased from the time of the Domesday Survey, and even more so from the early years of Henry I. From 1086 onwards, the growing use of documentation far exceeds that in any other country in western Europe at that time. His editing of the charters of William I has revealed that far more were issued on the Continent than was formerly believed to have been the case. Norman documents are longer and more explicit than English ones, while the brevity of English writs may indicate the power of the state, and the fact that there was no need to explain details which could be handled by officers and courts.[106] Subsequently the appearance of *The Acta of William I* has made available both the texts, and a full discussion by David Bates, of all known documents authorised by William I. This magisterial edition has thrown much new light on the detail of government, including the royal itinerary throughout the reign; the ducal style; and the workings and staffing of the chancery, although attention is drawn to the strong indications that most documents were produced by their beneficiaries in this reign. Professor Bates dates to c. 1070 the sharp change from Old English to Latin as the language of writs, together with the change in diplomatic form which is subsequently found in many writs. In both instances, these were clearly decisions reached at the centre. Comparisons can now also be drawn between the manner of documentation and of record-keeping in England and in Normandy.[107]

The surviving charters of Henry I have been used by Stephanie Mooers Christelow in a computer-assisted statistical study of their dates and places of issue. She compares the itinerations of William I, William II and Henry I, and traces the fluctuation in volume of government business throughout the reign of Henry I. By investigating the places from which the king issued *acta*, she found that in England, while Westminster/London/Windsor formed an important grouping, Winchester was of growing importance, notably in the later part of the reign, since it was the home of the Exchequer court. Professor Christelow questions how far (the Tower of) London was a separate centre of government distinct from Westminster. Henry I's administrative business, she concluded, was conducted at three main centres: Westminster, Winchester and Rouen, and three subsidiary centres: London, Windsor and Woodstock, a pattern similar to, if more pronounced than, those followed by William I and William II.[108]

The debate about the authenticity of charters, and hence about the significance of their content for wider studies, hinges on a number of factors. Richard Mortimer, having studied in depth the charters of Henry II, discussed the various criteria of

---

105   D. Bates, 'The Earliest Norman Writs', *EHR* c, 1985, 266–82.

106   D. Bates, 'The Conqueror's Charters', in *England in the Eleventh Century*, ed. Hicks, 1–15.

107   Bates, *Regesta*, 1–138.

108   S. Mooers Christelow, 'A Moveable Feast? Itineration and the Centralisation of Government under Henry I', *Albion* xxviii, 1996, 187–228.

authenticity.[109] Bruce O'Brien also discussed the problem of authenticity, particularly from the standpoint of the twelfth-century lawcourts.[110]

Many scholars have turned their attention to the personnel of government, and to the significance of certain individuals for the development of the royal administration. Simon Keynes's study of Regenbald considered his role, and that of other royal priests, in the reign of Edward and the first year of William I. He concluded that Regenbald presided over an Anglo-Saxon royal chancery, although this did not have the monopoly of issuing royal charters. This study also includes a discussion of the functions of writs in these reigns.[111] In another study, focused on Giso, bishop of Wells, Simon Keynes again discusses the royal priests, and particularly the Lotharingian element among them.[112] The administrative role of bishops in the late eleventh century has been examined by Henry Loyn.[113]

Stephanie Mooers Christelow has examined the career patterns of clerics at the court of the Anglo-Norman kings, both those who never rose beyond the rank of chaplain, and others who became chancellor, and perhaps obtained a bishopric. Those who did become bishops continued to serve as chancellors and curiales. Professor Christelow deduced that the improvements in the chancery and the expansion of the roles of bishops in secular government were practical responses to the necessity of governing an enlarged realm. She suggests that an intensive training was given to those engaged in such activities, and in particular to those who eventually doubled as bishops and financial experts. The curial responsibilities of bishops now enhanced the clerical responsibilities of priors and archdeacons, for whom bishops established prebends to enable them to fulfil their diocesan responsibilities. While continental bishops, often drawn from long-established families, were more intellectually focused, Anglo-Norman curial bishops were often drawn from obscure families, and their training focused on law and finance – skills necessary to reinforce the political stability of the realm.[114]

Much work has been done on those who were active in the royal administration under Henry I, who was formerly believed to have operated largely through 'new men', whose family origins were fairly modest. Charlotte A. Newman has pointed out that the curial families were quick to blend with those of higher rank.[115] Intermarriage between curial and aristocratic families has also been discussed by RaGena DeAragon.[116]

Barbara McDonald Walker pointed out that the participation of *curiales* as administrators of radical policies was balanced by the use of magnates to help ensure political stability.[117] This argument was later developed by Professor C. Warren Hollister,

109  R. Mortimer, 'The Charters of Henry II: What are the Criteria for Authenticity?', *ANS* xii, 1990, 119–34.
110  B. O'Brien, 'Forgery and the Literacy of the Early Common Law', *Albion* xxvii, 1995, 1–18.
111  S. Keynes, 'Regenbald the Chancellor (*sic*)', *ANS* x, 1988, 185–222.
112  S. Keynes, 'Giso, Bishop of Wells', *ANS* xix, 1997, 203–71.
113  H. Loyn, 'William's Bishops: Some Further Thoughts', *ANS* x, 1988, 223–35. See also D. Walker, 'Crown and Episcopacy under the Normans and Angevins', *ANS* v, 1983, 220–33.
114  S. Mooers Christelow, 'Chancellors and Curial Bishops: Ecclesiastical Promotions and Power in Anglo-Norman England', *ANS* xxii, 2000, 49–69, at pp. 68–9.
115  C.A. Newman, 'Family and Royal Favour in Henry I's England', *Albion* xiv, 1982, 268–91.
116  R. DeAragon, 'In Pursuit of Aristocratic Women: a Key to Success in Norman England', *Albion* xiv, 1982, 258–67.
117  B. McDonald Walker, 'King Henry I's "Old Men" ', *JBS* viii, 1968, 1–21.

in a series of articles in which he argued strongly for the participation of magnates in government, and for the contribution which this made towards political stability.[118] The rewards of office can be deduced to a large extent from the Pipe Rolls. Stephanie Mooers Christelow has made detailed use of the Pipe Roll of Michaelmas 1130, the sole survivor from the reign of Henry I, to evaluate the distribution of royal patronage in the latter part of his reign.[119]

Jostling for position among the administrators continued throughout the twelfth century. As J.E. Lally showed, each leading member of the royal court had his own circle of dependants, who hoped to obtain patronage through him.[120] But no one, however fast his rise, was entirely secure, and David Crouch demonstrated how even the high-flying Geoffrey de Clinton was demoted when this helped Henry I to maintain a political balance in the Midlands.[121]

The Pipe Rolls of the later twelfth century have been extensively used by Thomas K. Keefe to deduce the pecking order in the struggle among the *curiales* to enhance their status and increase their chances of obtaining patronage.[122]

Ralph V. Turner's consideration of criticisms of late twelfth-century upwardly mobile administrators drew attention to the fears and resentments of conservative clerics, of aristocrats, and of impoverished lesser knights, which they voiced against those who, by the end of the century, were emerging as virtually professional administrators, whose courtly values were sapping the traditional strength of the warrior class.[123] On the other hand, Professor Turner found that the royal justices were apparently held to conduct themselves in an acceptable manner, and that belief in their competence was demonstrated by the growing numbers of litigants flocking to the royal courts.[124]

Several recent studies have been made of the administrators of the later twelfth

---

118  C.W. Hollister, 'Magnates and *Curiales* in Early Norman England', *Viator* iv, 1973, 115–22; 'The Rise of Administrative Kingship: Henry I', *AHR* lxxxiii, 1978, 262–75; 'Henry I and the Invisible Transformation of Medieval England', in *Studies in Medieval History Presented to R.H.C. Davis*, ed. H. Mayr Harting and R.I. Moore, London 1985, 303–16.

119  S.L. Mooers, 'Familial Clout and Financial Gain in Henry I's Later Reign', *Albion* xiv, 1982, 268–91; 'Patronage in the Pipe Roll of 1130', *Speculum* lix, 1984, 282–307; and S.L. Mooers Christelow, *Royal Patronage and Social Rank in Anglo-Norman England* (forthcoming).

120  J.E. Lally, 'Secular Patronage at the Court of King Henry II', *BIHR* xlix, 1976, 159–84.

121  D. Crouch, 'Geoffrey de Clinton and Roger Earl of Warwick: New Men and Magnates in the Reign of Henry I', *BIHR* lv, 1982, 113–23.

122  T.K. Keefe, 'King Henry II and the Earls: the Pipe Roll Evidence', *Albion* xiii, 1981, 191–222; 'Counting Those Who Count: a Computer-Assisted Analysis of Charter Witness-Lists and the Itinerant Court in the First Year of the Reign of King Richard I', *Haskins Soc. Jnl* i, 1989, 135–45; 'Place-Date Distribution of Royal Charters and the Historical Geography of Patronage Strategies at the Court of Henry II Plantagenet', *Haskins Soc. Jnl* ii, 1990, 179–88; 'Proffers for Heirs and Heiresses in the Pipe Rolls: Some Observations on Indebtedness in the Years before Magna Carta', *Haskins Soc. Jnl* v, 1993, 99–109.

123  R.V. Turner, 'Changing Perceptions of the New Administrative Class in Anglo-Norman and Angevin England: the *Curiales* and their Conservative Critics', *JBS* xxix, 1990, 93–117. See also his *Men Raised from the Dust: Administrative Service and Upward Mobility in Angevin England*, Philadelphia 1988, and his 'Towards a Definition of the *Curialis*: Educated Court Cleric, Courtier, Administrator, or "New Man"?', *Medieval Prosopography* xv, 1994, 3–35.

124  R.V. Turner, 'The Reputation of Royal Judges under the Angevin Kings', *Albion* xi, 1979, 301–16. See also his 'Simon of Pattishall, Pioneer Professional Judge', *Albion* ix, 1977, 115–34. On the leading figures in the judiciary, see also E.A. Amt, 'Richard de Lucy, Henry II's Justiciar', *Medieval Prosopography* ix, 1988, 61–87; V. Oggins and R. Oggins, 'Richard of Ilchester's Inheritance: an Extended Family in Twelfth-Century England', *Medieval Prosopography* xii, 1991, 57–122.

century and the workings of their offices. However, Judith Everard reached the conclusion that two offices which were formerly thought to exist had no basis in reality. The historiographical existence of the 'seneschal of Brittany' and the 'justiciar of Ireland', she concluded, is largely the result of reliance upon literary sources, which gave exalted and official-sounding titles to men who, from the diplomatic sources, were simply leading royal agents.[125] The actual administrators of later twelfth-century England, and their family networks, have been the subject of several recent studies, including those by Richard Mortimer on that of Ranulf de Glanville;[126] by Emma Mason on the Mauduit chamberlains of the Exchequer;[127] by Richard Heiser on the households of the justiciars of Richard I;[128] and by Nicholas Vincent on Warin and Henry Fitz Gerold.[129] But while government was becoming increasingly shaped by bureaucracy and routine procedures, personal contacts maintained by potential litigants with influential members of the Exchequer, for instance, could still prove advantageous, as Emma Mason indicated.[130]

The officers who supervised the Forests were widely berated by their contemporaries in the royal administration. The forests had considerable economic potential for the king, as well as affording scope for his leisure activities. Emilie M. Amt follows Thomas K. Keefe in suggesting that the forests formed part of an 'administrative enclave'. They tended to cluster in those parts of England in which royal grants to *curiales* were most common, and where the majority of the *acta* of Henry II were issued.[131]

Economic considerations were taken seriously, and R.H. Britnell has demonstrated a growing royal interest, in the twelfth century, in regulating markets and fairs, and the franchises under which they operated.[132] Anglo-Norman and early Angevin government was sustained on the one hand by such practical means as tapping landed and commercial wealth, by the manipulation of patronage, and by the extension of royal justice, and on the other hand by the intangible aura which stemmed from anointing and coronation. Janet L. Nelson has drawn attention to the political significance of the king-making ritual,[133] and George Garnett has considered its implications for the Norman kings in their assertion of their right to the English throne.[134] The image of majesty was regularly displayed, both to 'the great and the good', and also, at a

---

[125] J. Everard, 'The "Justiciarship" in Brittany and Ireland under Henry II', *ANS* xxii, 1998, 87–105, at p. 105; idem, *Brittany and the Angevins*, Cambridge 2000, 147–9.

[126] R. Mortimer, 'The Family of Ranulf de Glanville', *BIHR* liv, 1981, 1–16.

[127] E. Mason, 'The Mauduits and their Chamberlainship of the Exchequer', *BIHR* xlix, 1976, 1–21; 'The King, the Chamberlain and Southwick Priory', *BIHR* liii, 1980, 1–10; 'Magnates, *Curiales* and the Wheel of Fortune', *ANS* ii, 1980, 118–40, 190–5.

[128] R. Heiser, 'The Households of the Justiciars of Richard I: an Inquiry into the Second Level of Medieval English Government', *Haskins Soc. Jnl* ii, 1990, 223–31. See also his 'The Royal *Familiares* of King Richard I', *Medieval Prosopography* x, 1989, 25–50.

[129] N. Vincent, 'Warin and Henry Fitz Gerald, the King's Chamberlains: the Origins of the Fitz Geralds Revisited', *ANS* xxi, 1999, 233–60.

[130] E. Mason, *Westminster Abbey and its People c. 1050 – c. 1216*, Woodbridge 1996, 147–61, 171–4.

[131] E.M. Amt, 'The Forest Regard of 1155', *Haskins Soc. Jnl* ii, 1990, 189–95.

[132] R.H. Britnell, *The Commercialisation of English Society 1000–1500*, 2nd edn, Manchester 1996, 110–26.

[133] J.L. Nelson, 'The Rites of the Conqueror', *ANS* iv, 1982, 117–32.

[134] G. Garnett, 'Coronation and Propaganda: Some Implications of the Norman Claim to the Throne of England in 1066', *TRHS* 5th ser. xxxvi, 1986, 91–116. See further P. Wormald, '*Quadripartitus*' (as note 87 above).

distance, to the urban populations of favoured centres, in the seasonal ritual of the crown-wearing, which Martin Biddle has traced from the reign of King Edward to the early years of Henry I.[135]

But royal government, inherently predatory, directed public relations exercises only towards those who were powerful enough to be disruptive if they thought that their interests were being damaged. Those who were too insignificant to be taken into account, or else too obtuse to grasp the political message inherent in such ceremonial, were constrained by the alternatives of the stick – of mutilation, in extreme cases[136] – or the carrot of occasional royal works of public benefit, such as the founding of hospitals and leper-houses.[137] A steady stream of royal grants to religious houses 'for the stability and security of the realm', seal-types which echoed imperial imagery, and the theocratic claim to be 'king by the grace of God', which first appeared in England on the seal of William Rufus, all served to reinforce a royal government which fully intended to govern.[138]

135 M. Biddle, 'Seasonal Festivals and Residence: Winchester, Westminster and Gloucester in the Tenth to the Twelfth Centuries', *ANS* viii, 1986, 51–72.
136 C.W. Hollister, 'Royal Acts of Mutilation: the Case against Henry I', *Albion* x, 1978, 330–40.
137 E.J. Kealey, 'Anglo-Norman Policy and the Public Welfare', *Albion* x, 1978, 341–51.
138 E. Mason, *Norman Kingship*, Bangor 1991, 1–19.

# 9

# The Anglo-Norman Church*

CHRISTOPHER HARPER-BILL

## The Papal Revolution

The history of the church in England in the late eleventh and early twelfth centuries was deeply influenced by the aftermath of two revolutionary events. The Norman Conquest was no less dramatic in its impact on ecclesiastical life than in the changes which it wrought in secular society.[1] The church, like the land, was under new management, and the new French élite introduced important organisational changes based on continental models. Even more significant than the Norman take-over of the Old English church, however, was the rise to power at Rome of a radical group who shattered age-old concepts of the relationship of religion and government within Christian society. This movement is known to historians as the papal reform, or the Gregorian or Hildebrandine reform, after its most dramatic exponent, the archdeacon Hildebrand, who from 1073 to 1085 pontificated over the western church as Pope Gregory VII.[2]

The reform movement at Rome falls into two distinct phases. From 1046 to 1057 the emphasis was placed on moral renewal. A succession of German popes, of whom the greatest was Leo IX (1048–54), with the full co-operation of the Emperor Henry III, mounted a determined attack on those clergy who had fallen from the ideals of the early church. The twin evils which they sought to eradicate were simony, or the purchase of ecclesiastical office from patrons, and nicolaitism, the keeping of wives, or in reforming eyes mistresses, by priests. Simony was regarded by hard-liners at Rome as heretical, for it involved trading in the gift of the Holy Spirit. The squalor of sexual relations could not be tolerated in those who celebrated the sacrament of the altar. Clerical marriage, moreover, created the likelihood of an hereditary priestly caste, passing on churches and bishoprics from father to son as family possessions. The papal reform movement was an attempt to recover the purity of the primitive church. It offended a great many vested interest, but it is remarkable how quickly its basic premises came to be accepted by Western Christendom. Neither cash transactions to acquire churches not the keeping of women by priests ceased overnight, but from the end of the eleventh century both activities became something to be hidden, a

---

* The text of this article is essentially that of my Headstart History Paper, Bangor 1992, and I am grateful to Mrs Judith Loades for allowing me to re-print it. The footnote references have, however, been revised to take account of more recent work.

[1]  R.A. Brown, *The Normans and the Norman Conquest*, 2nd edn, Woodbridge 1985, 216–25.

[2]  Among abundant literature, see C. Morris, *The Papal Monarchy: the Western Church from 1050 to 1250*, Oxford 1989, chs 4–5; G. Tellenbach, trans. T. Reuter, *The Church in Western Europe from the Tenth to the Early Twelfth Century*, Cambridge 1993, chs 5–8; H.E.J. Cowdrey, *Pope Gregory VII, 1073–1085*, Oxford 1998.

lapse from the newly-accepted norm. To take two English examples, in 1091 Herbert Losinga purchased the bishopric of East Anglia from William Rufus, but soon became troubled by the grave moral danger which he had incurred and, to the king's fury, surrendered his see into the hands of the pope who, recognising his merits, reinstated him.[3] Herbert, who proved to be an excellent bishop, had suddenly come to terms with a reforming ideology which was an innovation in his own lifetime. Around 1100 it was common form for the rich prebendal churches of St Paul's cathedral in London to pass from father to son; by 1150 it was extremely rare and noteworthy when such succession occurred.[4]

Within a decade of the Norman Conquest, however, the emphasis of the papal reform movement had shifted. Speculative theology combined with practical political considerations to convince the Roman reformers that the root cause of all evil within the church was lay domination of the clergy. Just as the local lord, whose ancestor had built a church on his estate, claimed much of its revenue and the right to appoint its priest, so at the highest level the king distributed bishoprics and abbeys to men who had given him good service and would continue so to do. In practical terms this might be seen as a sensible and just arrangement. The church held a high proportion of the landed wealth of Western Europe (some 25% in England, according to Domesday Book), and in return for this provided, in effect, the salaries of those educated men whose service was ever more essential in a world where written government was becoming increasingly the norm. In the first flush of enthusiasm in Rome, however, such practical considerations were forgotten. Gregory VII and his circle convinced themselves that if lay control of the church could be broken, moral reform would present no problem. The pope fulminated continually against investiture by the king of bishops and abbots with ring and staff, the badges of their spiritual office; but in fact investiture was only a symbol. What the reformers rejected was selection of the church's personnel by lay lords. The leaders of the church should be elected by the clergy or monks who would be committed to their charge, and the election should be scrutinised by higher ecclesiastical authority. In this selection process the king should have no part. This represented a doctrine of revolution; it was an assault on the custom of centuries. Yet, as Gregory VII sharply remarked, 'The Lord hath not said "I am custom", but He hath said "I am the truth".'[5] The papal circle honestly believed that in demanding the liberty of the church they were fulfilling God's plan for justice on earth. Naturally their plans met with the fiercest resistance from those whose customary rights were threatened, and the Investiture Contest was marked by prolonged intellectual and physical violence in Italy and Germany.[6] In the face of opposition the reformers' demands became ever more extreme. Their insistence on the freedom of the church was developed into an assertion that for the right order of society it was necessary that even kings should be subject to the clerical hierarchy,

---

3    For Herbert, see J.W. Alexander, 'Herbert of Norwich, 1091–1119: Studies in the History of Norman England', *Medieval and Renaissance History* vi, 1969, 115–232; I. Atherton *et al.*, eds, *Norwich Cathedral: Church, City and Diocese, 1096–1996*, London 1996, chs 2–3.
4    C.N.L. Brooke, 'Gregorian Reform in Action', in his *Medieval Church and Society*, London 1972, 94.
5    H.E.J. Cowdrey, ed., *The Epistolae Vagantes of Pope Gregory VII*, Oxford 1972, app. A no. 67.
6    For a convenient selection of key letters, see B. Tierney, *The Crisis of Church and State, 1050–1300*, Englewood Cliffs 1964, 45–73; for Gregory's correspondence, *The Register of Gregory VII, 1073–1085*, trans. H.E.J. Cowdrey, Oxford 2002; for extensive analysis, I.S. Robinson, *Authority and Resistance in the Investiture Contest*, Manchester 1978; J.H. Burns, ed., *The Cambridge History of Medieval Political Thought, c. 350 – c. 1450*, Cambridge 1988, chs 11–12.

culminating in the pope, since only the priesthood was qualified to interpret God's ordinance.

In the late eleventh century, therefore, two philosophies of world government came into conflict – the old order of an integrated church and society under the aegis of a sacerdotal king, ruling as God's deputy on earth, the world as it had been under the Emperor Constantine in the fourth century, under Charlemagne in the eighth and under the successors of Alfred in tenth-century England; and the projected new order of a united Christian commonwealth under the ultimate authority of the successor of St Peter at Rome. The history of the church in England in the century after the Conquest is, in one important sense, the development of a compromise between these two ideological systems, based on the realities of power and thus normally favouring the king, who was on the spot and who possessed the means of coercion by physical intimidation and persuasion by the exercise of his extensive patronage. The king, however, could never entirely ignore the new ideas emanating from Rome, and in moments of weakness, such as the uncertain successions of 1100 and 1135, the balance could tip the other way.

### The Late Old-English Church

The tenth century had been an heroic period in the history of the English church.[7] Religious life had been reconstructed after the devastation caused by the Viking invasions. This renewal had been accomplished by an alliance between the kings of Wessex and a group of outstanding monastic bishops who sought the regeneration of society by the application of principles expressed in the Rule of St Benedict. This alliance achieved its greatest triumphs in the reign of King Edgar (959–78), during which freedom from external attack was utilised as an opportunity both to consolidate the royal hold over an expanding realm and to reassert the moral influence of the Christian church. Whereas on the continent those intent on religious reform believed that this could best be achieved by the emancipation of the church from secular control (a programme symbolised by the foundation of Cluny in 911 as a monastery immune from all authority save that of St Peter), in England the strength of a king 'by God's authority, confirmed through the bishops and other servants of God',[8] was seen as the best guarantee of the spiritual welfare of the kingdom.

A century later William of Normandy advanced the degeneracy of the English church as a further justification for the invasion to secure his rights. Writing two generations after the Conquest the historian William of Malmesbury, himself of mixed parentage and deeply respectful of Anglo-Saxon Christian tradition, believed that religion had become totally moribund during the last years of the Old English

---

7  C.J. Godfrey, *The Church in Anglo-Saxon England*, Cambridge 1962, 294–309; M. Deanesley, *The Pre-Conquest Church in England*, London 1961, 276–327. For the immediate pre-Conquest period, R.R. Darlington, 'Ecclesiastical Reform in the Later Old-English Period', *EHR* li, 1936, 385–428; F. Barlow, *The English Church, 1000–1066: a Constitutional History*, London 1963; E. Mason, *St Wulfstan of Worcester, c. 1008–1095*, Oxford 1990, chs 1–5.

8  For Edgar's coronation and its significance, see P.H. Sawyer, *From Roman Britain to Norman England*, London 1978, 184–8.

kingdom and was revived by the Normans.[9] Was the decline as marked as the Conqueror's propaganda and the chronicler's judgement would suggest?

Much hinges on the view which is taken of Stigand, archbishop of Canterbury, who had been intruded into the primatial see, by the influence of the Godwin family, after the expulsion in 1052 of the Norman archbishop Robert of Jumièges, and who never resigned his former bishopric of Winchester.[10] Stigand's anomalous position is, in fact, a reflection of the way in which the leadership of the church had become enmeshed in the factional conflicts which characterised the last phase of the Old English state. Edward the Confessor himself, in the years of his greatest independence, had preferred household clerks to holy monks when filling bishoprics, and prelates other than Stigand where pluralists: Leofric abbot of Peterborough, for example, obtained the rule of four other monasteries. Even in the most blatant cases of irregularity, however, there is need for some qualification. Stigand himself was noted for his generosity to religious houses, despite the fact that his uncanonical position led English bishops to go to the continent for consecration. His colleague in the north, Ealdred, was noted as an advocate of reform who 'raised the see of York from its former rustic state'.[11] Leofgar bishop of Hereford was regarded with some suspicion because of his military enthusiasm, yet it should be remembered that in 1098 the papal legate personally commanded a division of the crusading army before Antioch.

To a great extent, the 'decline' was due to the failure of the English church, 'on the outer edge of the earth's extent',[12] to keep pace with the remarkable transformation of the Roman see. During the long eclipse of papal authority from the ninth to the early eleventh centuries, it had been English initiative which had maintained contact, by the payment of Peter's Pence (annual tribute originally levied from every household) and through the visits of archbishops to the apostolic see to receive their pallium, the symbol of their office. In 1047 papal permission was sought for the move of the bishopric of Crediton to Exeter, a transfer which foreshadowed the modernising site-changes accomplished after the Conquest. Despite the self-conscious loyalty of the English church to Rome, however, the reforming council held by Leo IX at Rheims in 1049 seems to have made more impact in Normandy than in the island kingdom, although nothing in fact was promulgated there that had not been foreshadowed in English royal legislation of the tenth and early eleventh centuries. It is perhaps significant that the foremost surviving advocates of reform in England, Wulfstan bishop of Worcester and Aethelwig abbot of Evesham, chose after 1066 to work in association with the Normans, even acting as William's local governmental agents, in much the same way as progressive Irish bishops after 1171 placed their trust in Henry II.[13] Yet if the spirit of reform generally was petering out in England just at the time when it was gathering force at Rome, and was eventually mediated through

9   *Gesta Regum* i, 458–61; *EHD* ii, 290–1.
10  For an unfavourable assessment, see N. Brooks, *The Early History of the Church of Canterbury*, Leicester 1984, 304–10; for a more favourable view, M.F. Smith, 'Archbishop Stigand and the Eye of the Needle', *ANS* xvi, 1994, 199–220.
11  For Ealdred, see J. Cooper, *The Last Four Anglo-Saxon Archbishops of York*, Borthwick Papers xxxviii, York 1970, 23–9; V. King, 'Ealdred, Archbishop of York: the Worcester Years', *ANS* xviii, 1996, 123–36.
12  For England as 'another world', see R.W. Southern, *Medieval Humanism and Other Studies*, Oxford 1970, 133.
13  J.A. Watt, *The Church and the Two Nations in Medieval Ireland*, Cambridge 1970, 39; see also M.T. Flanagan, *Irish Society, Anglo-Norman Settlers, Angevin Kingship*, Oxford 1989, ch. 1.

Rouen and Bec, it would be unjust to judge the state of the English church in the 1050s by the highest standards of the Gregorian papacy.

That the English church was not moribund is perhaps best illustrated by the strenuous efforts of missionaries from the island kingdom to evangelise Scandinavia.[14] Their campaign spans the Norman Conquest, beginning around 995 with those English priests who assisted King Olaf Trygvason in his forcible conversion of Norway. Sigfrid, a monk of Glastonbury, was the first missionary bishop in Sweden; another Englishman, Tursgot, around 1020 became the first Swedish diocesan bishop, and their work was continued by David, who died around 1080 and was subsequently canonised. During the reign of Cnut the Great, ruler of a double kingdom, English missionaries began to appear in Denmark and after the Conquest, in Rufus's reign, the great Danish monastery of Odense was founded from Evesham in Worcestershire.[15] The impetus continued well into the twelfth century, and in the 1150s the English St Henry of Finland initiated the conversion of the most remote area of Scandinavia. The total achievement falls not far short of that of St Boniface of Crediton in the eighth century.

*The Norman Model*

The contrast between the Norman and English churches in the quarter century before the Conquest can be explained in large measure by the consideration that the church in the duchy was undergoing then much the same experience as had that of the kingdom in Edgar's reign.[16] The need for the reconstruction of religion in Normandy had been even more urgent than in England, for the new rulers in the tenth century had been erstwhile pagan Vikings. Yet by the 1060s the Normans were noted throughout Christendom for their particularly militant brand of Christianity. For the duke and his greater vassals, the acceptance of the faith guaranteed their reception into the aristocratic community of Western Europe. The people followed their lead, encouraged no doubt by many incidents, such as those described by Bede in seventh-century England, when the magic of the Christian God proved more potent than that of the ancient Scandinavian pantheon. The transformation is easier to understand if it is remembered that the Christian religion did not become Christocentric until the twelfth century at the earliest; God was still very much the Old Testament tribal deity who favoured His chosen people and aided them in battle. Norman religion has been well described as 'a theology of armed action',[17] which was given practical expression as much in the conquest of England as in Southern Italy, Sicily, Spain and a few years later on the First Crusade.

As in tenth-century England, the reconstruction of Christianity in eleventh-century

14   L. Abrams, 'The Anglo-Saxons and the Christianisation of Scandinavia', *ASE* xxiv, 1995, 213–49; idem, 'Eleventh-Century Missions and the Early Stages of Ecclesiastical Organisation in Scandinavia', *ANS* xvii, 1995, 21–40; see also above, ch. 3.

15   P. King, 'English Influence on the Church at Odense in the Early Middle Ages', *JEH* xiii, 1962, 145–55.

16   For a survey of the church in pre-Conquest Normandy, see D. Bates, *Normandy before 1066*, London 1982, 189–235; and for an important reassessment of the monastic contribution, C. Potts, *Monastic Revival and Regional Identity in Early Normandy*, Woodbridge 1997.

17   D.C. Douglas, *The Norman Achievement*, London 1969, 101.

Normandy was the achievement of the ruling dynasty in alliance with zealous Benedictine missionaries. The monastic expansion, which resulted in the establishment between 1000 and 1070 of thirty-three religious houses, was assiduously furthered by the dukes as a means of fostering political unity, but by mid-century the secular aristocracy were also enthusiastic patrons of the monks. The second stage of Christianisation was marked by the re-establishment of defined dioceses, and over his bishops the duke also maintained firm control. William's agents on the episcopal bench were men of diverse character. Archbishop Maurilius at Rouen (1054–67) held the first effective reforming councils and issued the initial prohibition in the duchy of clerical marriage. Odo of Bayeux (c. 1049–97), half-brother of the duke, was immune to the moral strictures of the reformers and was intent on secular aggrandisement; he was, nevertheless, the creator of a well-organised diocese and of a cathedral chapter noted for its intellectual attainment.[18] By 1080 Duke William, through a mixture of conventional piety and political shrewdness, had created an episcopate noted for 'a professional quality which was outstanding in contemporary northern France'.[19] Clear contrary to the ideology of the Roman reformers, he presided in person over synods of the province of Rouen in which bishops and abbots met to promulgate measures which fostered both the observance of the faith and the consolidation of ducal authority. Most significantly, in 1047 the Truce of God was proclaimed in an attempt to curb internal violence which threatened both the peace of the church and the security of the duchy. It is noteworthy that lay investiture was never discussed at these meetings, and that at the Council of Lillebonne in 1080 it was decreed that if secular and ecclesiastical jurisdictions should clash, arbitration between them pertained to the duke.[20]

A recent historian of the duchy has passed a severe judgement on William's ecclesiastical policy. His control of the church was 'a carefully calculated operation' and his attitudes 'those of a proprietor, not a benefactor'.[21] This verdict is, perhaps, excessively harsh. If the Conqueror was prone initially to pillage churches associated with his enemies, both in north-western France and in England, contrition and piety combined to make him one of the great monastic patrons of an age noted for lavish benefaction. The papacy recognised him as an outstanding Christian prince and a champion of reform, albeit one not prepared to accept the most radical assertions of Roman supremacy over a united western Christendom. The Norman church was aggressively orthodox; duke and bishops accepted without question the doctrinal authority of the apostolic see and the desirability of those moral reforms which it advocated. Their implementation was attempted, however, within a self-contained ecclesiastical province in which papal legates intervened only at ducal invitation and outside which Norman prelates seldom ventured.

The same model of reform was to be applied in England after 1066. It must be emphasised, however, that reforming activity in the duchy reached its peak only in the 1060s and 1070s, and much remained to be done at home after the conquest of England. Orderic Vitalis commented on those priests of Danish extraction who, when

---

[18] D. Bates, 'The Character and Career of Odo, Bishop of Bayeux (1049/50–97)', *Speculum* l, 1975, 1–20.

[19] Bates, *Normandy before 1066*, 212.

[20] R. Foreville, 'The Synod of the Province of Rouen in the Eleventh and Twelfth Centuries', in *Church and Government in the Middle Ages*, ed. C.N.L. Brooke *et al.*, Cambridge 1976, 19–40.

[21] Bates, *Normandy before 1066*, 206–7.

confronted by the demand that they should abandon both their concubines and the pursuit of arms, were more ready to renounce their weapons than their women. In 1072 the bishop of Avranches was stoned by the priests of his diocese when he urged on them in synod the need for celibacy.[22] Equally significant, the plantation of Benedictine monasticism as an agency of reform and a vehicle of ducal authority was occurring in western Normandy at exactly the same time as in the north of England. Both areas had hitherto been immune to modern trends in religion and to centralised secular control; they felt simultaneously the impact of a reform movement which was papally inspired but monarchically directed.

### Domination and Accommodation

All over England, although particularly in outlying and border areas, the Normans used the church as an agent of colonisation. By the end of the Conqueror's reign the episcopate had been almost totally Normanised, most of the wealthy churches throughout the island had passed into the hands of influential clerics from north-western France, and the greater abbeys too were ruled by members of the conquering race.[23] The religious houses of the duchy received their share of the spoils by the grant of English estates – the place-name Tooting Bec, now in South London, is testimony to one such gift.[24] The foundation by William of Battle abbey on the site of his great victory is one symbol of the role of the church in the Conquest – a privileged royal church which served as a war-memorial;[25] as also, to take one example of many, are the Sussex town of Lewes and the Norfolk village of Acre, in both of which William de Warenne built great castles and planted colonies of French monks from the Burgundian abbey of Cluny.[26] The harrying of the North in 1069–70 was followed up by the foundation of numerous monasteries (of which there had been none north of Burton upon Trent in 1066) as well as by construction of motte and bailey fortifications. The new style of Romanesque architecture. ecclesiastical building on a scale never before seen in England, was itself a visual symbol of a new lordship, and if the historian concentrates on the great masterpieces at Durham, Winchester and St Albans, it should be remembered that the new dispensation was marked by the rebuilding of almost every parish and conventual church in England.[27]

Domination and ostentation were not, however, the only features of the Anglo-Norman church. At an early date there were clear signs of accommodation with the Old English past. There were, of course, isolated scandalous incidents, most famously the intimidation by the new abbot of Glastonbury of his native monastic congregation; but the culprit was removed from office by Lanfranc.[28] The archbishop himself was

---

22 *Orderic* iii, 121–3; ii, 201.

23 D.S. Spear, 'The Norman Empire and the Secular Clergy, 1066–1204', *JBS* xxi, 1982, 1–10.

24 D. Matthew, *The Norman Monasteries and their English Possessions*, Oxford 1962, 26–71; M. Morgan, *The English Lands of the Abbey of Bec*, Oxford 1946, part 1.

25 E.M. Hallam, 'Monasteries as "War Memorials": Battle Abbey and La Victoire', *SCH* xx, 1983, 47–57.

26 B. Golding, 'The Coming of the Cluniacs', *ANS* iii, 1981, 65–77, (notes) 208–10.

27 For a general survey of the Norman architectural impact, see E.C. Fernie, 'Architecture and the Effects of the Norman Conquest', in *England and Normandy*, 105–16; also ch. 11 below.

28 M.D. Knowles, *The Monastic Order in England*, Cambridge 1940, 114–15.

certainly dubious about the merits of undocumented Anglo-Saxon saints, whose veneration he regarded as a distraction from true religion, but once a case for sanctity was properly demonstrated, as in the case of St Alphege of Canterbury, he accepted and encouraged observance of the feast. The cults of Cuthbert at Durham, Edmund in his Suffolk borough and Etheldreda at Ely were eagerly taken up by the Normans; these saints were venerated for religious reasons, but also utilised for political purposes.[29] The great eighth-century historian Bede was a source of inspiration to Norman monks, historians and founders, while the abandoned site of St Hilda's abbey at Whitby prompted the conversion to religion of the knight Reinfrid, engaged on the devastation of the north, to which he returned with English monks from Evesham as a Benedictine pioneer.[30] In the early twelfth century Anglo-Saxon and Anglo-Scandinavian hermits such as Godric of Finchale, Wulfric of Haselbury and Christina of Markyate acted as intercessors and mediators between native populace and priests and their new ecclesiastical masters, but they were eagerly accepted by Norman religious communities as holy assets and spiritual capital.[31] The Norman aristocracy, too, soon came to terms with their new environment and abandoned their cross-Channel spiritual yearnings. Within a generation, the majority were choosing English rather than Norman burial-places, and there are instances of gifts to monasteries in the duchy being transferred to insular houses.[32] Conversely, surviving English landholders became benefactors of French foundations; an obscure native merchant, Ailwin Child, was the true founder of the Cluniac house at Bermondsey in 1089, and older Cumbrian families contributed to the endowments of monasteries founded by Anglo-Norman lords in the north-west.[33] The confraternity list of Rochester cathedral priory contains a healthy mixture of English and French names, united in their devotion and benefactions to St Andrew.[34]

The effect of the Conquest on the wealth of the English church is not a clear-cut matter.[35] Much of its landed endowment had been lost during the Viking invasions, and far from all the losses had been recovered during the tenth-century reformation, even before Scandinavian pressure resumed during Ethelred's reign. English monastic chronicles complained bitterly of Norman depredation, yet on occasion the diminution of a church's estates can be demonstrated to have pre-dated 1066. Christ Church Canterbury, for example, had suffered more from the misappropriations of Earl Godwin than of Odo of Bayeux, who was accused by Archbishop Lanfranc of detaching its lands. Domesday Book shows ecclesiastical losses to Norman lords to have been insubstantial, usually of outlying manors. The church did, however, suffer

---

[29] S.J. Ridyard, '*Condigna Veneratio*: Post-Conquest Attitudes to the Saints of the Anglo-Saxons', *ANS* ix, 1987, 179–206; idem, *The Royal Saints of Anglo-Saxon England*, Cambridge 1988.

[30] R.H.C. Davis, 'Bede after Bede', in *Studies . . . to Brown*, 103–16.

[31] H. Mayr-Harting, 'Functions of a Twelfth-Century Recluse', *History* lx, 1975, 227–52; C.J. Holdsworth, 'Hermits and the Power of the Frontier', in *Saints and Saints' Lives: Essays in Honour of D.H. Farmer*, Reading Medieval Studies xvi, 1990, 55–76.

[32] B. Golding, 'Anglo-Norman Knightly Burials', in *The Ideals and Practice of Medieval Knighthood* i, ed. C. Harper-Bill and R. Harvey, Woodbridge 1986, 35–48; E. Mason, 'English Tithe Income of Norman Religious Houses', *BIHR* xlviii, 1975, 91–4.

[33] D. Knowles and R.N. Hadcock, *Medieval Religious Houses, England and Wales*, 2nd edn, London 1971, 98; R.K. Rose, 'Cumbrian Society and the Anglo-Norman Church', *SCH* xviii, 1982, 119–35.

[34] H. Tsurushima, 'The Fraternity of Rochester Cathedral Priory about 1100', *ANS* xiv, 1992, 313–37.

[35] The following paragraph is based on A. Ayton and V. Davis, 'Ecclesiastical Wealth in England in 1086', *SCH* xxiv, 1987, 47–60.

through the Conqueror's imposition of knight service upon the bishoprics and greater abbeys. The land of England was listed at around £73,000 in 1086; of this, £18,400 was held by the ecclesiastical tenants-in-chief, but £3,500 of this was subinfeudated to provide for military obligations (and many knights, too, were still maintained in the households of bishops and abbots). Out of about 5,000 knights owed, 741½ were due from the church. Yet despite this substantial burden, there can be little doubt that ecclesiastical wealth did increase, except perhaps in the south of the country where the church had been so well endowed before the Conquest. In Lincolnshire, for example, the church's proportion of landed resources increased between 1065 and 1086 from 2% to 12%. Domesday Book, moreover, was produced a generation too early to reflect the real impact of the Conquest, for at least twenty-six Benedictine communities and six Cluniac houses were founded between 1086 and 1100, and thereafter Norman lords were extremely generous patrons of the new Augustinian and Cistercian orders. Domesday Book, moreover, hardly reflects the Norman ecclesiastical impact on the North.

In terms of organisation, the Conquest brought obvious changes to the English church. The institutions of the Old English church had been old-fashioned, and continental bishops were eager to modernise – although there was no need for the creation of territorial dioceses or the elimination of hereditary abbacies, as there would be when the reform movement permeated into Wales and Ireland. English sees were moved from rural sites to thriving centres of population – among others, Dorchester was transferred to Lincoln, Selsey to Chichester, Sherborne to Old Sarum (later Salisbury).[36] Within the secular cathedrals there was established the continental model of chapter, in which the responsibility for liturgy, education and financial administration was allocated to three major officers serving under the presidency of a dean, and in which the church's revenues were in large part divided between the prebendaries, senior and distinguished clerks, many of whom would be non-resident.[37] This was a retrograde step from Old English attempts to establish a communal life for cathedral clergy, but reflected the need of king and bishops to provide lucrative livings for valued administrators. Despite such practical considerations, however, the Normans greatly approved of the Anglo-Saxon monastic cathedrals, an institution unknown elsewhere in western Europe, and established new ones at Durham, Norwich and elsewhere.

Of more immediate significance to the great majority of English people was the reorganisation of the church's jurisdictional structure. The Anglo-Saxon bishop had sat as joint-president of the shire court, alongside earl or sheriff; there he administered royal law which, under the influence of the tenth-century monastic reformers, legislated as much against sin as against crime. Between 1072 and 1085 the Conqueror issued an ordinance which has traditionally been interpreted as separating lay and ecclesiastical jurisdiction and establishing independent church courts – a dichotomy which was to cause much dissension a century later. It has been convincingly argued, however, that the intention was not to remove the bishop from the shire court, but rather to allow him to hold his own courts as well, so that jurisdiction, and its profits, should now pertain in moral matters exclusively to the church.[38] Episcopal justice was

36 For one case, see D.M. Owen, 'The Norman Cathedral at Lincoln', *ANS* vi, 1983, 188–99.
37 D. Greenway, 'Orders and Rank in the Cathedral of Old Sarum', *SCH* xxvi, 1989, 55–63.
38 C. Morris, 'William I and the Church Courts', *EHR* lxxxii, 1967, 449–63; D.J.A. Matthew, *The Norman Conquest*, London 1966, 193–5.

henceforth exercised most publicly in synods, regular meetings of the clergy of the diocese, which served also to communicate to grass-roots level the legislation of provincial, and even papal, councils. There is evidence for a synod convened by Wulfstan of Worcester in 1092, and by the early twelfth century such were held in most, if not all, dioceses. Even more important, the archdeacon, newly introduced to England after 1066 as the bishop's judicial officer, should be able to hold his own courts, so that spiritual cases would no longer be decided in the local hundred courts, presided over by a sheriff. It was the establishment of a network of local ecclesiastical courts, held at regular meetings of the clergy of each rural deanery (a grouping of about twenty churches) under the presidency of the archdeacon, which allowed the application in the parishes of the new canon law introduced from the continent by Archbishop Lanfranc, a code which was rapidly evolving in the late eleventh and early twelfth centuries and which was increasingly Roman and universal rather than regional and dependent for enforcement on royal officers, as had been the case in Anglo-Scandinavian England.[39] The effectiveness of the archdeacons' courts in enforcing new norms of sexual morality and religious observance, most often by financial penalties, is indicated by the reputation for greed and extortion which these officials had already achieved by the mid-twelfth century.

## The Investiture Contest in England

The relationship between the papacy, the crown and the English church was complex.[40] In general terms there was quite remarkable cordiality between William the Conqueror and Rome.[41] In one sense the king was a disappointment to the pope, for in 1080 he conclusively rejected Gregory VII's demand that England should be held as a fief of the apostolic see, in the same way that the Norman duchies of southern Italy were theoretically dependent upon Rome. Yet despite this rejection Gregory recognised that William was a supporter of the programme of moral reform advocated by the papacy. In comparison with Henry IV of Germany he was a loyal son of the church, alongside Philip I of France he was a model of Christian morality. The Conqueror, confronted throughout his reign by challengers for his throne, and the pope, continually faced by imperial aggression, needed each other. The position of Archbishop Lanfranc was ambiguous. He came to Canterbury in 1070 as the favourite son of the papacy, the triumphant defender of doctrinal orthodoxy. Relations were soured by the failure of Rome to give whole-hearted support to Canterbury's claim for primacy over all churches of the British Isles, which was achieved, in the key matter of

---

[39] C.N.L. Brooke, 'The Archdeacon and the Norman Conquest', in D. Greenway *et al.*, eds, *Tradition and Change: Essays in Honour of Marjorie Chibnall*, Cambridge 1985, 1–20; J. Scammel, 'The Rural Chapter in England from the Eleventh to the Fourteenth Centuries', *EHR* lxxxvi, 1971, 1–21. M. Brett, 'Canon Law and Litigation: the Century before Gratian', in *Medieval Ecclesiastical Studies in Honour of Dorothy M. Owen*, ed. M.J. Franklin and C. Harper-Bill, Woodbridge 1995, 21–40, emphasises that the great advances in canon law in the late eleventh and early twelfth centuries were largely the result of local rather than Roman initiatives, even if the papal *curia* was the beneficiary.

[40] For general surveys, see C. Duggan, 'From the Conquest to the Reign of John', in *The English Church and the Papacy in the Middle Ages*, ed. C.H. Lawrence, London 1965, 63–116; F. Barlow, *The English Church, 1066–1154*, London 1979, ch. 7.

[41] H.E.J. Cowdrey, 'Pope Gregory VII and the Anglo-Norman Church and Kingdom', in his *Popes, Monks and Crusaders*, London 1984, ch. 9.

the relationship between the two English archbishoprics, and albeit ambiguously and temporarily, by the decision of a royal council rather than by papal decree. Lanfranc was an enthusiastic advocate of the reform programme initiated by Leo IX; by the 1080s he appears to have been cautious in the extreme in his support for Gregory VII's world-view.

Lanfranc's successor, Anselm, faced a very different situation.[42] He was appointed by William Rufus in 1093, after a long vacancy at Canterbury, only because the king thought himself at death's door. The new archbishop then insisted on recognising Urban II, rather than the rival imperial pope, before the king had announced his own decision. The king's attempt to rid himself of this aged and troublesome archbishop in return for royal recognition of Urban (which was a political necessity) misfired when the papal legate refused to keep his side of the bargain by deposing Anselm. The relationship between England and Rome therefore came, largely through Rufus's misjudgement, to centre stage, and this dispute, only superficially resolved, was the backdrop to the quarrel between king and archbishop in 1097 over the allegedly unsatisfactory discharge of the military obligations of the see of Canterbury. The altercation over the quality of the Canterbury knights led to Anselm's first exile, and it was his sojourn at the papal court, and his presence at the councils of Bari and Rome in 1098–99, where he heard Urban II condemn both lay investiture and the rendering of homage to laymen for the lands of the church, which brought the investiture controversy to England.

The new king, Henry I, despite his desire for reconciliation with the archbishop, could not afford to abandon homage for the extensive lands held by the church in England. Anselm now felt, as he had not before, bound to refuse that homage for the Canterbury estates, and so went into exile again in 1103. Eventually, when Henry was desperate for papal sanction of his conquest of Normandy from his eldest brother, a compromise was reached in 1106 at the abbey of Bec, which was ratified next year by the Council of Westminster. The king abandoned investiture with ring and staff, thus ceasing to intrude on the conferment of *spiritual* office, but was permitted to take the homage of bishops- and abbots-elect for their *temporalities* before their consecration. This, in effect, gave the crown power of veto, for ecclesiastical estates, accumulated over centuries and now burdened with military obligations, were in reality inseparable from any major church. This compromise ended the so-called 'investiture contest' in England, to which kingdom it had been late in coming, and it provided a model for the settlement in 1122 of the far more bitter struggle in the Empire. Pope Paschal II wrote to Anselm expressing the hope that the king would make further concessions, specifically the renunciation of homage, but in essentials the arrangements agreed in 1106 remained in force until the Reformation. Elections, it was agreed, should be free, but they were normally held in the royal chapel, with the cathedral chapter represented by a small delegation which could easily be persuaded, or intimidated, by the king. In terms of personnel, which was the key issue, the compromise changed little. Rufus had appointed Ranulf Flambard, his financial agent, and Robert Bloet, his chancellor, to bishoprics; after 1106 Henry I nominated his trusted servant William Warelwast to Exeter and his nephew Henry of Blois to Winchester.

---

[42] For Anselm, see R.W. Southern, *St Anselm and his Biographer*, Cambridge 1963, and his later treatment, *St Anselm: a Portrait in a Landscape*, Cambridge 1990; also S.N. Vaughn, *Anselm of Bec and Robert of Meulan: the Innocence of the Dove and the Wisdom of the Serpent*, Berkeley 1987.

*Lanfranc and Anselm*

The contrast between the cooperation which was the norm between 1070 and 1088 and the intermittent conflict which prevailed from 1093 to 1107 has often been viewed as a measure of the different characters and attitudes of Lanfranc and Anselm. The first post-Conquest archbishop of Canterbury acted in concert with William I to introduce moral reform of the church, yet sought to preserve the independence from Rome of an integrated Anglo-Norman church under the firm control of the king-duke. His successor not only had a more thorough approach to the reform of clergy, seeking to abolish clerical marriage instantly rather than allowing it to wither away; he also endeavoured to protect the independence of the English church from the secular ruler, rather than from the pope, in his obedience to whom he was unswerving. It has more recently been suggested, however, that there was in fact a strong element of continuity in the programmes of the two archbishops.[43] Lanfranc's reputation has been rather strangely diminished in some modern accounts.[44] He has been viewed as a derivative theologian and, as archbishop, passively acquiescent towards the king's wishes. A recent treatment of his career before 1063, however, seeks to restore his reputation as 'a major force in the political and intellectual life of his times', who was instrumental in establishing the Catholic doctrine of transubstantiation, whose views radiated outwards from his school at Bec which was the foremost educational institution of the age, and who did much to mould Duke William's attitudes towards reform.[45] For most of Lanfranc's archiepiscopate western Europe was racked by the most bitter phase of the investiture controversy. If in retrospect Gregory VII may be seen as the architect of the medieval papacy, during his lifetime his policies tore the church apart; from June 1080 there was genuine doubt as to whether he or the imperial 'anti-pope' Clement III was the rightful pontiff, and he died in exile deserted by most of his own cardinals. Lanfranc's ambiguous attitude to such a pope, who moreover had done nothing to support the primatial claims which were the birthright of the church of Canterbury, does not indicate mere subservience to the Conqueror. The archbishop as much as the king was unwilling that the governance of the Anglo-Norman church should be undermined by the intrusion of papal legates despatched from Rome, whose authority would override his own. He accepted without reservation the doctrinal supremacy of Rome, while eschewing aims which he felt impossible, such as the immediate deprivation of priests already, and in accordance with age-old custom, married. He did not feel bound to approach Rome for approval in all those jurisdictional or administrative matters in which the papacy increasingly claimed omnicompetence – the transfer of numerous sees, for example, was accomplished without reference to the curia. Lanfranc avoided conflict with a king who was himself an advocate of reform; he supervised the organisational changes which shaped the structure of the English

---

43  C.W. Hollister, 'St Anselm on Lay Investiture', *ANS* x, 1988, 145–58.

44  M. Gibson, *Lanfranc of Bec*, Oxford 1978; F. Barlow, 'A View of Archbishop Lanfranc', *JEH* xvi, 1965, 163–77, repr. in his *The Norman Conquest and Beyond*, London 1983, 223–38.

45  S.N. Vaughn, 'Lanfranc at Bec: a Reinterpretation', *Albion* xvii, 1985, 135–48. In the most recent review of his career H.E.J. Cowdrey ('The Enigma of Archbishop Lanfranc', *Haskins Soc. Jnl* vi, 1995, 129–52) emphasises Lanfranc's contacts with and support for reforming popes before Gregory VII, and his initial difficulties with William the Conqueror in England after 1070, but concludes that 'his greatness as an archbishop lay in his ability to respond to fresh situations as they developed'.

church until the Reformation;[46] and despite the primacy dispute and isolated conflicts with individual bishops, he was able to hold together an episcopal bench containing a mixture of Benedictine monks, royal clerks and Norman aristocrats, and to postpone the impact of the investiture controversy on England. It was no small achievement.

Anselm has often been viewed as a 'papalist' archbishop, bound by his monastic vow of obedience to follow unswervingly the dictates of Rome, and thus unable to tolerate that working arrangement with the king which Lanfranc regarded as the surest guarantee of gradual reform; twice he preferred exile to accommodation. There were, however, important differences in the conditions under which the two archbishops operated. The reputation of William Rufus has been considerably enhanced by recent studies,[47] yet there can be no doubt that he did ruthlessly exploit the church during the vacancy of bishoprics and abbeys and that the holding of reforming councils was suspended during his reign. The Conqueror, however tight his control over the church, had not resorted to such abuse or obstruction, which it is extremely unlikely that Lanfranc could have tolerated. There was, too, a substantial difference in the condition of the papacy. By the time of Anselm's first exile in 1097, Urban II had begun the reestablishment of the 'Gregorian line' of popes as the natural leaders of the western church, maintaining a firm line on reforming policies yet uniting the aristocracy of northern Europe by the launching of the First Crusade and seeking accommodation with former enemies within the ranks of the higher clergy. By 1099 'he had really made himself the head of the greater part of Christendom',[48] and after September 1100 there was no serious anti-pope to challenge his successor, Paschal II.

No more than Lanfranc was Anselm an uncompromising Gregorian. He was as adamant as his predecessor in his defence of Canterbury's primacy, which ran counter to papal policy favouring co-equal archbishoprics directly dependent on Rome, and he was firmly opposed to the entry into England of legates despatched directly by the pope. It is impossible that he should not have heard of earlier papal condemnations of lay investiture and the rendering of homage, especially that pronounced by Urban II at Clermont in 1095, yet he did not raise these issues in England. After he had personally heard the pope's decrees in 1098–99, however, he could not keep silent. By this time, moreover, he had first-hand experience of the aggressive nature of Rufus's ecclesiastical policy. It is instructive that, despite Anselm's stand, the investiture controversy never attained in England the same level of intensity as it did in Germany and northern Italy. It might have been avoided altogether, as it was in France, if Anselm had not been driven into his first exile by Rufus's intransigence.

Over Anselm's motivation in his relationship with the English crown there has recently been some disagreement between Sir Richard Southern and Professor Sally Vaughn.[49] It is perfectly possible to believe, with Southern, that Anselm did not desire the archbishopric, that his resistance to his appointment was no charade but rather 'the cry of an anguished soul who sees himself threatened with separation from his long

---

46 'It may be doubted whether of all the eminent men who filled the see of Canterbury between Augustine and Cranmer any individual, save only Theodore of Tarsus, had a greater share in organising the church in this country.' Knowles, *Monastic Order*, 143.

47 F. Barlow, *William Rufus*, London 1983; E. Mason, 'William Rufus and the Benedictine Order', *ANS* xxi, 1999, 113–42.

48 Morris, *Papal Monarchy* (as n. 2), 126.

49 See n. 42, and more specifically R.W. Southern, 'Sally Vaughn's Anselm: an Examination of the Foundations', and S.N. Vaughn, 'Anselm: Saint and Statesman', *Albion* xx, 181–220.

and intense struggle towards the knowledge of God', to reject utterly Vaughn's suggestion that he lingered deliberately in England in 1092–93 in the hope that Rufus would eventually advance him to Canterbury, and yet to consider that he was prepared to accept God's will when it was made manifest, to undertake a burden from which he had earnestly sought release, and thereafter to fulfil the obligations of his stewardship in every possible way. The Benedictine ideal most certainly lay at the heart of Anselm's endeavours in every field, but the monastic tradition did not encourage, for prelates at least, introspective withdrawal from the affairs of the world. Once he had unwillingly accepted the archbishopric, Anselm was obliged to capitalise on the friendship network which he had established with great and powerful men in the Anglo-Norman realm – and he had a remarkable gift for disinterested affection – to foster the welfare of the church in general and the see of Canterbury in particular. There was nothing dishonourable in this; indeed, to have failed to capitalise on his connections would have been a denial of his responsibilities to God and to the church. Vaughn's view of 'the philosopher-saint as politician' is unfortunate,[50] since the concept of ecclesiastical politics in the late eleventh century is anachronistic. Anselm, like all his contemporaries in religion, surely regarded the 'management' of his lay friends as a worthy activity if designed, as it always was, to further the advancement of God's kingdom on earth, the ultimate aim of all the reforming circle. Anselm sought the well-being (*utilitas*) of the church of Bec, the church of Canterbury and the church universal, and by this he meant spiritual well-being. Yet he was realistic enough to know that the church must exist in the world – his writings are permeated by the feudal images of his contemporary environment. As abbot he desired to extend the benefits of the monastic life to the countryside around Bec; so as archbishop he saw the Rule of St Benedict as an ideal for society as a whole. In this he was little different from St Dunstan in the tenth century or from his immediate predecessor, Lanfranc. He was certainly not like his contemporaries Henry I and Count Robert of Meulan, or even his own episcopal colleagues, in his vision of the church, for he was undoubtedly a spiritual genius; but neither was he incapable of entering into their world in the hope and expectation of transforming it to correspond more nearly to the divine model.

## The Predominance of Local Interests

Anselm's archiepiscopate witnessed the first episode in England of what is conventionally known as a 'crisis of church and state', which is one of the predominant themes of western European history between the late eleventh and early fourteenth centuries. Yet how meaningful is this concept? In speaking of a conflict between *regnum* and *sacerdotium* there must at least be many qualifications. The bishopric and the abbatial office had a dual nature, which the ardent reformers repudiated but which all practical men recognised. The bishop was not only father in God to those souls committed to his charge and judge of their moral behaviour; he was also a baron, a tenant-in-chief of the crown. He was responsible for the management of extensive estates; the value of the lordship of Canterbury was exceeded only by that of the royal

---

[50] S.N. Vaughn, 'St Anselm of Canterbury: the Philosopher-Saint as Politician', *JMH* i, 1975, 279–305.

demesne,[51] and the richer bishoprics were as valuable as any lay barony. Military service was owed on a scale commensurate with this wealth. The bishop of Lincoln was likely more at home in his castle at Sleaford than in his cathedral, the abbot of Bury St Edmunds was constantly occupied with the king's government in West Suffolk.[52] The saintly bishop Gundulf of Rochester appears in his biography as the type of the ideal monk and pastor, yet he was also the military architect who supervised the building of the Tower of London.[53] Even Anselm, despite his dispute with Rufus over the Canterbury knights, regarded it as his duty to superintend the defence of the south coast while the king campaigned in the north, where guarding the frontier was one of the paramount duties of the bishop of Durham.

When the conflict between Anselm and Rufus broke into the open in 1095 at the Council of Rockingham, the bishops almost to a man supported the king. The archbishop's backing came from the lay barons, resentful of the new and grasping style of kingship which threatened secular as well as ecclesiastical estates. This indicates the gross simplification in speaking of a conflict of church and state, but on reflection it is hardly surprising. Of Anselm's thirteen episcopal colleagues at the time he first went into exile, eight had been royal chaplains whose services, not only by prayer, had been rewarded with a bishopric; three of these men had been chancellor. They had been executors, in some cases perhaps the formulators, of royal policy, and it would have been unrealistic to expect that they would suddenly abandon the habits of a lifetime, risk the loss of royal favour and patronage and endanger the smooth running of the Anglo-Norman state for what must have seemed to them an inconsequential principle. This does not necessarily imply that they were hostile to reform. We tend, perhaps to see the ecclesiastical history of the twelfth century too much from the viewpoint of Anselm and Becket, to be influenced too easily by the semi-hagiographical accounts of Eadmer or John of Salisbury. We can easily forget that those who did not subscribe in full to the novel ideas of the Gregorian reform might be adequate, even admirable, bishops when judged by other standards. Osmund of Salisbury (1078–99), for example, royal chancellor before his elevation, enjoyed a reputation for sanctity and was eventually canonised,[54] and even the notorious Ranulf Flambard (1099–1128), instigator of Rufus's ecclesiastical policy, was remembered with great affection by the monks of his cathedral church of Durham.[55]

The majority of bishops, then, were drawn by background and circumspection towards the royal interpretation of the correct relationship between the secular power and the church. Most revealing of all, however, is the attitude adopted by William of St Calais, bishop of Durham. In 1088, arraigned on a charge of treason, he had

---

51  M. Brett, *The English Church under Henry I*, Oxford 1975, 69.

52  For military obligations, see H.M. Chew, *The English Ecclesiastical Tenants-in-Chief*, Oxford 1932; for Bury, A. Gransden, 'Baldwin, Abbot of Bury St Edmunds', *ANS* iv, 1982, 65–76, (notes) 187–95.

53  For Gundulf, see R.A.L. Smith, 'The Place of Gundulf in the Anglo-Norman Church', *EHR* lviii, 1943, 257–72, repr. in his *Collected Papers*, London 1947, 83–102; M. Ruud, 'Monks in the World: the Case of Gundulf of Rochester', *ANS* xi, 1989, 245–60; J. Potter, 'The *Vita Gundulfi* in its Historical Context', *Haskins Soc. Jnl* vii, 1997, 89–100; the *vita* is conveniently translated by the Nuns of Malling, *The Life of Gundulf*, Malling Abbey 1968.

54  D.H. Farmer, *The Oxford Dictionary of Saints*, Oxford 1978, 303–4.

55  R.W. Southern, 'Ranulf Flambard', in his *Medieval Humanism* (as n. 12), 55; see also H.S. Offler, 'Ranulf Flambard as Bishop of Durham (1099–1128)', *Durham University Journal* lxiv, 14–25; J.O. Prestwich, 'The Career of Ranulf Flambard', in *Anglo-Norman Durham, 1093–1193*, ed. D. Rollason *et al.*, Woodbridge 1994, 299–310.

attempted to appeal to the pope; reconciled to the king, he was at Rockingham Rufus's main spokesman, and castigated Anselm for his recognition of Pope Urban II without royal permission. In fact, even those bishops who were not bound to the king by ties of service had a rather different view of papal authority to that cherished at Rome. For them the papacy was a jurisdictional institution to be utilised when circumstances were propitious, to be denied when it threatened their own position or when it meddled overmuch in the complexities of feudal government.

The church in England, as in any other province of western Europe, seldom presented a united front. The papacy might envisage a great universal corporation acknowledging the leadership of Rome, in which national and feudal divisions were a mere administrative convenience. In practice, local and particular interests tended to prevail. The unity of the church in England was disfigured throughout the twelfth century and beyond by the bitter dispute over the primacy between Canterbury and York.[56] During Henry I's reign Bishop Urban of Llandaff spent the greater part of his episcopate of twenty-six years protesting and appealing against the alleged territorial incursions of his fellow-bishops of Hereford and St Davids.[57] The early twelfth century witnessed the growth of tension between the secular clergy and the monks; in 1123 the suffragan bishops of the province of Canterbury were prepared to go to almost any lengths to prevent the election of another Benedictine to the chair of St Augustine.[58] The great religious houses, wealthy and influential societies such as St Albans and Bury St Edmunds, were engaged in a perpetual struggle to free themselves from the jurisdiction, which they saw as domination, of diocesan bishops. Monasteries founded in close proximity quarrelled and litigated about the boundaries of their estates, secular priests competed for the choicest benefices. In all these conflicts churchmen were prepared to utilise whichever jurisdiction promised the best results, that of king or pope, and sought as far as possible to reject either when it failed to deliver a favourable verdict.

It has traditionally been thought that the Conqueror and his sons did everything possible to impede access to the papal curia, and that they erected around their dominions a 'ring-fence' or barrier which would prevent both the entry of papal legates and the exit of potential litigants bound for Rome.[59] The Anglo-Norman rulers were most certainly determined to resist papal jurisdictional claims when these presented a threat to their ancient rights as duke or king, or to the stability of the realm. When in 1082 Odo of Bayeux was accused of treason against his half-brother the king, he claimed that as a bishop he might be tried only by the pope. The reply, given by Lanfranc (and repeated in 1088 to William of St Calais), was that he was accused not as an ecclesiastic but as a tenant-in-chief, who was answerable in the *curia regis*. A far weaker king, Stephen, unsuccessfully forbade Archbishop Theobald to attend the papal council of Rheims in 1148, nominating three representatives of the entire English episcopate.[60] Throughout the period papal legates were allowed access to the

---

[56] D. Nicholl, *Thurstan, Archbishop of York*, York 1964, chs 2–4; D. Bethell, 'William of Corbeil and the Canterbury-York Dispute', *JEH* xix, 1968, 145–59.

[57] Brett, *The English Church under Henry I* (as n. 51), 52–5.

[58] D. Bethell, 'English Black Monks and Episcopal Elections in the 1120s', *EHR* lxxxiv, 1969, 673–98.

[59] The classic statement of this thesis is Z.N. Brooke, *The English Church and the Papacy from the Conquest to the Reign of John*, Cambridge 1931, especially ch. 9.

[60] R.H.C. Davis, *King Stephen*, 3rd edn, London 1990, 101–2.

kingdom only after long delays and to operate within parameters established by the king himself.

The various divisions and disputes within the English church, however, encouraged ecclesiastics to look to Rome for privileges which would safeguard the rights of their own sees or communities, and even for favourable judicial decisions.[61] And when the interests of the crown were not directly affected, recourse to the papal court was not hindered as a matter of principle. Henry I never attempted to impede the continual appeals of Bishop Urban of Landaff, since royal rights were in no way jeopardised by his internecine ecclesiastical quarrels; and despite a great deal of blustering by the king, the parties to the interminable primacy dispute between Canterbury and York eventually argued their cases in the papal curia, since northern separatism no longer presented the threat that it had in the Conqueror's reign. The resistance to papal legations came as much from Canterbury as from the king, for the archbishop habitually, and sometimes successfully, sought to exercise this office himself. In 1124, however, John of Crema was permitted by Henry I to fulfil this function, conducting a visitation of every bishopric and major abbey in England and in September 1125 presiding over a legatine council at Westminster. This was the first time since 1070 that a representative sent directly from Rome was able to exercise any real authority in England, and the legation made a great impression on contemporary writers.

Voluntary recourse to Rome was, however, more significant than legatine authority in accustoming English ecclesiastics to contact with the apostolic see. Papal justice increased in scope and volume in the course of the twelfth century for the same reasons as royal justice expanded under Henry I and Henry II. The exercise of centralised jurisdiction was an expression of authority, a prime factor in the creation of a united kingdom or a united Christendom, and justice to both popes and princes was a great source of profit. Rulers actively sought to increase their jurisdiction, but they were able to do so effectively only because of consumer demand. The science of canon law was in its infancy, the machinery for establishing the truth of allegations was rudimentary, but despite the difficulties caused by distance and by the subterfuge of litigants there was a marked tendency by 1135 to look to Rome as the ultimate tribunal in certain spheres of ecclesiastical justice. In 1100 the number of prelates known to have visited Rome can be counted on the fingers of one hand; by the end of Henry I's reign twelve out of fourteen bishops, nine of the greater abbots and a host of lesser clergy had made the journey, either on embassies or to participate in one of the *causes célèbres* of the reign. The episcopate and higher clergy were in the 1130s in no sense papalist, as against royalist, but even those bishops who had served their apprenticeship in the royal service recognised, as their predecessors fifty years before had not, that there were defined areas of ecclesiastical and religious life in which decisions were beyond royal competence. The king was no longer sacerdotal – that is, he was no longer regarded as God's deputy ruling over a unitary society in which there was no distinction between spiritual and temporal. The priestly function of kingship had been demolished by the Gregorian reform movement, and if in compensation the Anglo-Norman monarchy had created a superb administrative machine which retained control over the temporal aspects of the church, even as assertive a ruler as

---

61  An excellent survey of Anglo-Papal relations, on which the following is based, is in Brett, *The English Church under Henry I* (as n. 51), ch. 2.

Henry I did not attempt to maintain or implement the old-fashioned (and theologically unsound) doctrines of the Anglo-Norman Anonymous, who had argued in desperation that the king represented the divinity of Christ, the priest merely His humanity.[62]

## *The Secular Aristocracy and Reform*

Many historians, under the influence of contemporary monastic chroniclers, have viewed the western European aristocracy as enemies of reform, determined in general to maintain their stranglehold over the rich resources of the church. The two centuries before the Gregorian reform, indeed, have been described by two French experts as 'the church at the mercy of the laity'.[63] Yet in no region would the reform movement have made any progress without the support of a substantial number of lay lords.[64] It was the upper echelons of the laity who led the way in the lavish endowment of the church in Normandy and England in the late eleventh and early twelfth centuries, and it was from these ranks that the ecclesiastical hierarchy, not to mention the great majority of choir monks, were recruited.[65]

There was, of course, a lamentable record of depredation. Many of the 'new aristocracy' of Normandy carved out their position, in part at least, by the annexation in the 1040s of monastic estates; in the immediate post-Conquest years English houses did lose some land to their Norman neighbours, and again during the relative disorder of Stephen's reign they were vulnerable to the desperate acquisitiveness of powerful yet threatened lords seeking to compensate for losses elsewhere. The fortunes of the Montgomeries, made infamous by Orderic Vitalis as the type of aggressive feudal lordship, were based partially on the amputation of estates from Bernay, Fécamp and Jumièges, yet before 1066 Roger of Montgomery, now thoroughly established, was a benefactor of St Stephen's Caen, St Evroult and, outside the duchy, of Cluny; thereafter he founded St Nicholas, Arundel, as a dependency of his family monastery at Séez, established Shrewsbury as an independent abbey and re-founded Much Wenlock, centre of the Anglo-Saxon cult of St Milburga, as a Cluniac priory.[66] William de Warenne, Richard FitzGilbert of Clare and Picot the sheriff of Cambridge-shire were all regarded by the monks of Ely as rapacious enemies; viewed otherwise, they were the pious founders of houses in the vanguard of reform, respectively Cluniac, of the affiliation of Bec and Augustinian.[67] In a later generation Roger de Mowbray during the 'anarchy' made inroads on the estates of York Minster, but he was a benefactor, albeit at a price, to the new Cistercian abbeys of Byland and

---

[62] E.H. Kantorowicz, *The King's Two Bodies: a Study in Medieval Political Theology*, Princeton 1957, 42–60.

[63] E. Amann and A. Dumas, *L'Église au Pouvoir des Laïques, 888–1057*, Paris 1948.

[64] For an important survey, see J. Howe, 'The Nobility's Reform of the Medieval Church', *AHR* xciii, 1988, 317–39; for a case study, J.C. Ward, 'Fashions in Monastic Endowment: Foundations of the Clare Family, 1066–1314', *JEH* xxxii, 1981, 427–51.

[65] C. Harper-Bill, 'The Piety of the Anglo-Norman Knightly Class', *ANS* ii, 1980, 63–77, (notes) 173–7; C.J. Holdsworth, *The Piper and the Tune: Medieval Patrons and Monks*, Stenton Lecture 1990, Reading 1991; E. Cownie, *Religious Patronage in Anglo-Norman England, 1066–1135*, London 1998.

[66] J.F.A. Mason, 'Roger of Montgomery and his Sons (1067–1102)', *TRHS* 5th ser. xiii, 1963, 1–28.

[67] E.O. Blake, ed., *Liber Eliensis*, Camden Society 3rd ser. xcii, 1962, 188–9, 202–3, 210–12; Knowles and Hadcock (as n. 33), 75, 92, 98, 100, 146.

Rievaulx and to other northern houses.[68] At the lower end of the scale of donations stands Roger de Clinton, one of Henry I's most rapacious agents, who established an Augustinian community at Kenilworth in 1125 with property almost entirely misappropriated from others through legal chicanery;[69] at the higher end David king of Scots, son of an Anglo-Saxon princess and lord of a great English honour, has been termed 'a connoisseur of the religious orders' who revolutionised the church in his northern kingdom by the sponsorship of reforming religious congregations.[70]

The reason for this torrent of patronage was undoubtedly the conviction that the monastic order represented the ideal and the yardstick of Christian observance, and that the prayers of the monks for their founders and benefactors would ease their path to salvation. The early medieval church constantly emphasised the desirability of peace and condemned aggression – a penance was imposed on all those who had fought with William at Hastings, although the duke's campaign had been sanctioned by the papacy,[71] and it was not until after the First Crusade that knighthood, if practised in accordance with religious precepts, came to be regarded as a laudable vocation.[72] Princes, lords and knights therefore ardently desired to share in the spiritual benefits of monasticism. Many actually entered the cloister, if only on their death-beds; most made gifts, according to their means, to the religious, in return for their prayers and eventual burial within their precincts. There was nothing remotely cynical in this. Violence was at the same time essential for survival in this harsh competitive world, yet because of the church's strictures was deeply regretted. The monks were regarded as the knights of Christ, fighting the most important of all battles, against the Devil for men's souls, and long before William of Malmesbury described the new Cistercian order as 'the surest road to heaven',[73] the long-established Benedictines had been regarded in the same light. Whereas young Anselm, travelling northwards from Italy in search of a monastic home, would not be professed at Cluny because the constant round of masses allowed no time for study or contemplation,[74] it was precisely this incessant liturgy which appealed to the Norman warrior-lord William de Warenne, who after his visit founded the first Cluniac priory in England at Lewes in 1077.[75]

Over the next fifty years new forms of religious life evolved. breaking the Benedictine monopoly and challenging Cluny for the pinnacle of Christian observance.[76] Yet it was surely the same motivation which led Walter Espec, one of the greatest magnates of northern England in the 1130s, to found a house of Augustinian canons at

---

68 D.E. Greenway, ed., *Charters of the Honour of Mowbray, 1107–1191*, British Academy, 1972, nos 32–69, 117–48, 318, 322. For an overall view of northern monasticism, see J. Burton, *The Monastic Order in Yorkshire, 1069–1215*, Cambridge 1999.

69 R.W. Southern, 'King Henry I', in his *Medieval Humanism* (as n. 12), 216–17.

70 C.N.L. Brooke, 'King David I of Scotland as a Connoisseur of the Religious Orders', in *Medievalia Christiana xi^e – xiii^e siècles: homage à Raymonde Foreville*, ed. C.E. Viola, Paris 1989, 320–34; for the evidence, see G.W.S. Barrow, *The Charters of David I*, Woodbridge 1999.

71 H.E.J. Cowdrey, 'Ermenfrid of Sion and the Penitential Ordinance Following the Battle of Hastings', *JEH* x, 1969, 225–42.

72 C. Morris, '*Equestris Ordo*: Chivalry as a Vocation in the Twelfth Century', *SCH* xv, 87–96.

73 *Gesta Regum* i, 576–7; *EHD* ii, 694.

74 R.W. Southern, ed., *The Life of St Anselm, Archbishop of Canterbury, by Eadmer*, OMT, 1962, 9.

75 Golding, 'The Coming of the Cluniacs' (as n. 26), 65.

76 For the European context, see most conveniently J. Burton, *Monastic and Religious Orders in Britain, 1000–1300*, Cambridge 1994, ch. 4.

Kirkham and a Cistercian community at Rievaulx. From the late eleventh century to 1154 over ninety Augustinian houses were established in England and Wales, and from 1128 to 1152, when an ineffective ban on further expansion was imposed by the order's general chapter, over forty Cistercian foundations. In addition there were numerous nunneries, including nine communities of Gilbertines, the only native English congregation.[77] The military orders, the Templars and Hospitallers, had recently established their first English depots to further their war-effort in the crusading states. These new houses were generally far less well-endowed than the long-established Benedictine monasteries, but on the other hand their estates were seldom burdened with knight service, and their foundation *en masse* represents a quite remarkable investment by all levels of society, but primarily by the aristocracy and the knightly class.

### The Church's Ministry

In that aspect of the church's organisation which most closely touched the religious life of the English people as a whole, the provision of convenient sites of worship, continental influence, either Norman or Gregorian, had little direct effect. From the late tenth to the mid-twelfth centuries there was a tremendous proliferation of small, local churches in England.[78] This multiplication was one important aspect of the transformation of society as a whole. In the century and a half before 1066 there emerged a broadly-based class of thegns, who exercised, each in a very limited area, many of the rights formerly reserved to king and great nobles. At the same time there was a steady development of village communities, the result of population growth and improving agricultural techniques. 'As with villages and fields, so with the local church: there is probably no time at which it developed so rapidly and decisively as during the period between 1000 and 1150, for which the Domesday survey is the half-way mark.'[79]

Towards the end of the tenth century the predominant agency of pastoral care in England was the minster, a large church often sited in a royal manor, to which the population of an extensive area would come at great festivals, from which itinerant priests would venture forth to take the sacraments to outlying hamlets. This structure had been ideally suited to the missionary age – that of the initial conversion of the seventh century, or the period of reconversion after the first wave of Viking invasions. It used to be thought that the minsters suffered irreparably from these Scandinavian raids, but the few surviving tenth-century wills suggest that they remained at least until the 970s the normal focus of religious allegiance. Thereafter there was a building boom in these mother churches between c. 975 and 1080. Similar new institutions,

---

[77] Knowles and Hadcock (as n. 33), 124, 162; S. Thompson, *Women Religious*, Oxford 1991.

[78] For what follows, see R. Morris, *Churches in the Landscape*, London 1989, chs 4–5; J. Blair, ed., *Minsters and Parish Churches: the Local Church in Transition, 950–1200*, Oxford University Committee for Archaeology Monograph 17, Oxford 1988, especially Blair's introduction.

[79] J. Blair, 'Local Churches in Domesday Book and Before', in *Domesday Studies*, ed. J.C. Holt, Woodbridge 1986, 265–78, at pp. 265–6.

indeed, were founded on the eve of the Conquest, by Earl Aelfric at Clare in Suffolk around 1045 and by Harold Godwineson at Waltham Holy Cross in 1060.[80]

From the late tenth century, however, there was a marked shift of endowment towards small local churches. Some of these were established by the clergy of the minsters, one of whose priests might take up semi-permanent residence in a large centre of population within its extended parish. Others were founded by lords of manors, sometimes without reference and in opposition to the minster clergy, whose revenues and influence were thereby threatened. In the villages of East Anglia there are indications of communal initiative, with the inhabitants themselves combining to establish their own church. Such corporate effort was certainly the norm in the expanding towns of eleventh-century England.

Domesday Book is not uniform in its listing of village churches, but of the better documented areas, Suffolk in 1086 had at least 345 churches for 639 sites of population and Huntingdonshire fifty-three churches for eighty-three places named.[81] For Kent, Domesday lists only 175 churches, whereas it has been demonstrated that within a generation of the Conquest there were in fact at least 400.[82] By the beginning of the thirteenth century London had ninety-nine parish churches and Winchester fifty-seven; most of these had been established by c. 1150.[83] Between the tenth and twelfth centuries twelve churches were founded within a mile along the main road running through the small town of Cambridge.[84] The rural parishes varied greatly in size, those in towns were almost uniformly small – the average size in London was three and a half acres. This proliferation of small parish churches, most especially in towns, is not paralleled elsewhere in northern Europe, and the contrast with Italy is especially marked, for in the peninsula, while there were numerous private chapels, all babies from city and region were received into the faith not in a local church, but in a great baptistery such as those still standing in Florence and Pisa.

For a century after 1050 there was a tremendous upsurge in church building. Literally thousands of stone churches, at first very simple in form and style, by the mid-twelfth century increasingly sophisticated, rose from all over England. In the diocese of Canterbury, for example, in the fifty years after Lanfranc became archbishop almost every church was rebuilt and numerous new ones constructed, while Bishop Wulfstan was noted by his biographer to have dedicated numerous churches in Worcestershire and Gloucestershire. These newly permanent churches were given landed endowments, varying tremendously in extent but at least sufficient to provide sustenance for the village priest, who was becoming a normal member of every scattered rural community.

The old minsters, in many cases converted in the early twelfth century into houses of Augustinian canons, at first clung tenaciously to their ancient rights; yet if they succeeded in retaining, often for centuries, financial interests in the new parish

---

80  J. Blair, 'Secular Minster Churches in Domesday Book', in *Domesday Book: a Reassessment*, ed. P. Sawyer, London 1985, 104–42.

81  R. Lennard, *Rural England, 1086–1135*, Oxford 1959, ch. 10, 288.

82  Blair, ed., *Minsters and Parish Churches*, 105.

83  C.N.L. Brooke and G. Keir, *London 800–1216: the Shaping of a City*, London 1975, ch. 6; M. Biddle, ed., *Winchester in the Early Middle Ages: an Edition and Discussion of the Winton Domesday*, Oxford 1974, 329–36.

84  C.N.L. Brooke, 'The Churches of Medieval Cambridge', in *History, Society and the Churches: Essays in Honour of Owen Chadwick*, ed. D. Beales and G. Best, Cambridge 1985, 49–76 at p. 50.

churches, and particularly in burial-dues, the bishops of early twelfth century were universally convinced that every community was entitled to its own church. They never sought to suppress these new centres of worship and pastoral care. From the time of William Rufus, moreover, the minster clergy themselves increasingly recognised the realities of the new world by splitting their own territories into small parishes, centred on local churches in which one of their number had a personal financial interest.

By 1150, then, the English parochial system, of which the most obvious evidence is the multitude of medieval churches standing to this day all over England, had already in large measure been created by the joint efforts of Anglo-Saxon and Anglo-Scandinavian communities and new Norman lords, with the approval and often the cooperation of the bishops. In this endeavour at least all were united. The results of this proliferation of small, intimate parochial units were, in the long term, almost entirely beneficial. The close relationship between priest and people which resulted was surely a prime factor in the absence of those heresies which by the late twelfth century were endemic throughout much of continental Europe. Yet from the viewpoint of the reformed papacy there were dangerous drawbacks to this multiplication of independent parishes.

First, there was the risk that priests thoroughly integrated into their local communities, but isolated from centres of reforming activity, would continue, as had their predecessors in England and Normandy, to cohabit with women whom they regarded as wives. It is obvious that in the countryside of England Lanfranc's conciliar decree of 1075, that no married man should henceforth be ordained and that no priest should take a new wife, had little effect. In 1102 Archbishop Anselm took a harder line, demanding that all clerical 'marriage' should cease forthwith, and specifically ordering Bishop Herbert of Norwich to eject from their churches all priests who kept women. The bishop was more realistic in his view, that such dramatic action would leave his diocese devoid of pastoral care.[85] It was almost inevitable that married priests would seek to pass their churches on to their sons, and in England hereditary right to ecclesiastical livings was openly acknowledged a century and more after the initiation of the great campaign for clerical celibacy. Around 1150 the bishop of Norwich referred openly and without obvious disapproval to the custom of that city by which a parson held a church as had his ancestors, and in the same diocese monastic patrons, who had been envisaged as the guardians of reform, were prepared to condone the successions of sons to fathers in their parish churches.[86] Similar cases have been revealed on the other side of the country, in the diocese of Hereford, and were doubtless common elsewhere.[87] Not until the thirteenth century, at the earliest, was the battle against clerical 'immorality' won in the English parishes. Interestingly, however, there is no evidence of popular outcry against married priests, as there was on the continent, often orchestrated by the papacy itself.[88] Rather in England Henry I,

---

[85]  Brett, *The English Church under Henry I* (as n. 51), 219.

[86]  C. Harper-Bill, 'The Struggle for Benefices in Twelfth-Century East Anglia', *ANS* xi, 1989, 113–32, esp. pp. 126–8.

[87]  B.R. Kemp, 'Hereditary Benefices in the Medieval English Church: a Herefordshire Example', *BIHR* lx, 1987, 1–8.

[88]  R.I. Moore, *The Origins of European Dissent*, London 1977, ch. 3, esp. pp. 62–3.

and later John, cynically sought to exploit the situation by fining those priests found guilty of incontinence.[89]

The second, and perhaps more serious danger to reforming ideology was the strong possibility of lay domination and exploitation of small local churches. Historians have quite naturally focused primarily upon the great struggle of the papacy against emperors and kings for the freedom of the church at the highest level; but equally obnoxious was the local stranglehold of nobles and knights upon churches established by their ancestors on their estates. From the time of the Conquest, and increasingly in the first half of the twelfth century, lay rights in and profit from the proprietorship of churches were diminished. Ownership was gradually reduced to mere patronage, the right to nominate a priest, who must be suitable, to the bishop.[90] Once the rapidly evolving canon law and respectable public opinion rendered it impossible for lay lords to receive tithes and spiritual offerings, there emerged an increasing tendency to grant parish churches to monasteries. Materially much less was lost than by the gift of estates, spiritually the same dividend was acquired. Reformers sincerely believed that the transfer of local churches to monastic proprietorship would be a guarantee of their freedom. But the law of the church as much as the law of England treated a church as a piece of real estate, in which property rights transcended spiritual obligations. By the 1150s some monastic houses had already embarked upon a programme of financial exploitation designed to strip their parish churches of a great part of their revenues; such calculating policies were to become the norm in the second half of the century.[91] A new form of proprietary church was created alongside the relics of the old.

## The Reign of Stephen

The reign of King Stephen has conventionally been seen as a watershed in the history of the English church. It has been argued that now at last, with the breakdown of royal authority, the barrier erected by the Conqueror was breached, the English church for the first time enjoyed free intercourse with Rome and leading ecclesiastics absorbed novel views of the nature of Christian society which made them unwilling to submit any longer to royal control as it had previously been exercised.[92] Stephen, of course, was in a weaker position than his predecessors because there was an active and feasible rival claimant for his throne.[93] The concessions which he made to the church in the Oxford charter of liberties of April 1136 were more specific than those of Henry I's coronation charter, and there was greater expectation that he might he held to them. His arrest of Bishop Roger of Salisbury and his episcopal nephews in 1139 prompted a reaction, spearheaded by the king's brother Henry of Blois, bishop of Winchester and papal legate, which would have been unthinkable when Odo of Bayeux and

89 Brett, *The English Church under Henry I* (as n. 51), 220 n. 1.

90 B.R. Kemp, 'Monastic Possession of Parish Churches in the Twelfth Century', *JEH* xxxi, 1980, 133–59.

91 For an example, C. Harper-Bill, 'Battle Abbey and its East Anglian Churches', in *Studies . . . to Brown*, 159–72.

92 Z.N. Brooke, *The English Church and the Papacy* (as n. 59), 175–90.

93 H.A. Cronne, *The Reign of Stephen*, London 1970, ch. 4; K.J. Stringer, *The Reign of Stephen*, London 1993, ch. 5; C.J. Holdsworth, 'The Church', in *The Anarchy of King Stephen's Reign*, ed. E. King, Oxford 1994, 207–30.

William of St Calais had been imprisoned half a century earlier. When the two brothers, now reconciled, attempted to advance their nephew William FitzHerbert to the archbishopric of York, the northern Cistercians invoked the outraged fury of St Bernard of Clairvaux, who prevailed upon a Cistercian pope to quash the appointment.[94] For the first time in Stephen's reign there are indications of free elections to bishoprics, as at Norwich in 1144, and the see of Hereford was filled by agreement between pope and archbishop of Canterbury, who towards the end of the reign prevented the creation of a dynasty by their refusal to sanction the succession of Stephen's son.

It would be a fair judgement that Stephen's reign did not so much mark a watershed in the relationship between pope, king and English church, but rather that his problems and his need for ecclesiastical support accelerated the development of trends already apparent before 1135.[95] The chronicler Henry of Huntingdon believed, for example, that it was in the early years of the reign, during the legation of Henry of Blois (1139–43), that appeals were first made to Rome. This is not the case, for they had occurred under Henry I, but they now became far more frequent, and for the first time there is evidence of native ecclesiastical judges on the spot being commissioned by the pope to hear cases in England, administering a legal code which had achieved a new level of definition, albeit provisional, with the publication in 1140 of Gratian's *Concordance of Discordant Canons* (or *Decretum*), which provided the basis for the Romanisation and the rationalisation of the law of the church.[96] Englishmen at this crucial time became prominent in the papal curia – Robert Pullen became chancellor of the Roman church in 1144, and ten years later Cardinal Nicholas Breakspeare was elected as the only (to date) English pope, Adrian IV. Legatine authority in England became more pervasive than it had ever been before, whether exercised by special emissaries from the popes such as Alberic of Ostia in 1138–39 or by the king's brother. The strength of the English church in the mid-twelfth century is perhaps symbolised by the contrast between Henry of Blois, the prince-bishop, and Theobald, abbot of Bec, who in January 1139 became archbishop of Canterbury.[97] Henry was determined that not even his brother should trample underfoot the liberties of the church, Theobald less dramatically struggled to hold together his ecclesiastical province within a divided kingdom. Both of them looked to Rome for support and thus consolidated and perpetuated English participation in that expansion of papal jurisdiction which was a noteworthy feature of western European history in the first half of the twelfth century. Both Henry and Theobald recognised by 1154, however, that political weakness did not further the church's pastoral mission, and both were instrumental in the creation of that balance of power in the affairs of the English church which was only briefly interrupted by Becket's stand against Henry II.

---

94  M.D. Knowles, 'The Case of St William of York', in his *The Historian and Character*, Cambridge 1963, 76–97.

95  Duggan, 'From the Conquest to the Reign of John' (as n. 40), 84–7.

96  For early papal judges-delegate, see various cases in W.J. Millor, H.E. Butler and C.N.L. Brooke, eds, *The Letters of John of Salisbury*, I, *The Early Letters*, 2nd edn, OMT, 1986; for Gratian, see Morris, *The Papal Monarchy* (as n. 2), 400–3, 576–6.

97  For Theobald, see A. Saltman, *Theobald, Archbishop of Canterbury*, London 1955, repr. New York 1969. For Henry of Blois, see Knowles, *Monastic Order* (as n. 28); a new biography is promised by M.J. Franklin.

*Conclusion*

The main lines of development of the English church had, in fact, become clear by the death of Henry I in 1135. The lavish endowment of monasticism, which had been interrupted in the early eleventh century, had been resumed by the new Norman lords of the land, who both took to their hearts the ancient Benedictine foundations and were instrumental in the plantation of new communities of continental origin and diverse characteristics. These new orders soon attracted donations and recruits from surviving native landholders. The steady multiplication of parish churches, initiated by Old English lords and communities, continued unabated and was fostered by the Norman newcomers, although in all but the most richly endowed local churches the village priest was likely to be of Anglo-Saxon or Scandinavian descent. The status of the clerical order had in theory been raised by the Gregorian ideology, but in most English parishes the close affinity of priest and people was probably not affected. The higher clergy, on the other hand, were separated from their subordinates and from the people both by their racial origin (although by the mid-twelfth century the difference between French and English was already beginning to become blurred) and by the triumph of the ideal of celibacy. They had, moreover, become accustomed to contact with Rome, without believing that such links in any way diminished the role of a formidable king who, if he had abandoned the image of sacral kingship and surrendered the empty symbolism of investiture, retained real control over the personnel and estates of the church.

*Additonal Note on Sources*

Sources in translation are marked *.

Extensive materials for the governance of the Anglo-Norman church have become available in good modern editions, often with translations, in recent years. For councils, legislation and relations with the papacy, see D. Whitelock, M. Brett and C.N.L. Brooke, *Councils and Synods, with Other Documents Relating to the English Church, A.D. 871–1204*, part ii, *1066–1204*, Oxford 1981. For letters of Gregory VII relating to England, see *E. Emerton, *The Correspondence of Pope Gregory VII*, New York 1932, repr. Columbia University 1991; H.E.J. Cowdrey, *The Register of Pope Gregory VII, 1073–1085*, Oxford 2002; and *idem, *The Epistolae Vagantes of Pope Gregory VII*, OMT, 1972, nos 1, 16, 34, 57. For other papal documents, see W. Holtzmann, ed., *Papsturkunden in Anglia*, 3 vols, Göttingen 1935–52. For a cosmopolitan Anglo-Norman's view of the papal court, *M. Chibnall, ed., *The Historia Pontificalis of John of Salisbury*, London 1956.

Important episcopal letter collections are *H. Glover and M. Gibson, eds, *The Letters of Lanfranc, Archbishop of Canterbury*, OMT, 1979; *W. Fröhlich, trans., *The Letters of St Anselm of Canterbury*, 3 vols, Cistercian Studies Series 96–7, 145, Kalamazoo, Mich., 1990–94; *E.M. Goulburn and H. Symonds, *The Life, Letters and Sermons of Bishop Herbert de Losinga*, 2 vols, Oxford and London 1878; also the early letters in C.N.L. Brooke and A. Morey, eds, *Letters and Charters of Gilbert Foliot*, Cambridge 1967.

For increasing regulation by bishops of their dioceses, see the various volumes of

*English Episcopal Acta*, British Academy, 1980– : i, *Lincoln, 1067–1185*, ed. D.M. Smith, 1980; v, *York, 1070–1154*, ed. J. Burton, 1988; vi, *Norwich, 1070–1214*, ed. C. Harper-Bill, 1990; vii, *Hereford, 1079–1234*, ed. J. Barrow, 1993; viii, *Winchester, 1070–1204*, ed. M.J. Franklin, 1993; x, *Bath and Wells, 1061–1205*, ed. F.M.R. Ramsey, 1995; xi, *Exeter, 1046–1184*, ed. F. Barlow, 1996; xiv, *Coventry and Lichfield, 1072–1159*, ed. M.J. Franklin, 1997; xv, *London, 1075–1187*, ed. F. Neininger, 1999; xviii, *Salisbury, 1075–1207*, ed. B.R. Kemp, 2000; also A. Saltman, *Theobald, Archbishop of Canterbury*, London 1955, repr. New York 1969; H. Mayr-Harting, ed., *The Acta of the Bishops of Chichester, 1075–1207*, Canterbury and York Society, 1962; H.S. Offler, *Durham Episcopal Charters, 1071–1152*, Surtees Society clxxix, 1968.

For the lives of individual bishops, see *R.W. Southern, ed., *The Life of St Anselm, Archbishop of Canterbury*, OMT, 1962; R. Thomson, ed., *The Life of Gundulf, Bishop of Rochester*, Toronto 1977 (*the Nuns of Malling, trans., Malling Abbey 1968); R.R. Darlington, ed., *The Vita Wulfstani of William of Malmesbury*, Camden Society 3rd ser. xl, 1928 (*J.H.F. Peile, trans., Llanerch Publishers, Lampeter 1996).

For the lives of others, on the margins of the church, see J. Stevenson, ed., *Libellus de vita et miraculis Sancti Godrici* by Reginald of Durham, Surtees Society xx, 1845; M. Bell, ed., *Wulfric of Haselbury by John, Abbot of Ford*, Somerset Record Society xlvii, 1933; *C.H. Talbot, ed., *The Life of Christina of Markyate*, Oxford 1959.

For the histories of individual churches, see *S. Vaughn, *The Abbey of Bec and the Anglo-Norman Realm*, Woodbridge 1981; *D. Knowles, ed., *The Monastic Constitutions of Lanfranc*, London 1951, and *G. Bosanquet. trans., *Eadmer's History of Recent Events in England*, London 1964 (for Christ Church, Canterbury); *A.H. Davis, trans., *William Thorne's Chronicle of St Augustine's Abbey, Canterbury*, Oxford 1934; *D. Rollason, ed., *Symeon of Durham, Libellus de Exordio atque Procursu istius, hoc est Dunhelmensis*, OMT, 2000; E.O. Blake, ed., *Liber Eliensis* (as n. 67); *D. Greenway and L. Watkiss, eds, *The Book of the Foundation of Walden Monastery*, OMT, 1999; *C. Johnson, ed., *The History of the Church of York, 1066–1127*, rev. edn by M. Brett, C.N.L. Brooke and M. Winterbottom, OMT, 1990.

The relationship of individual churches with the lay society which sustained them is illustrated in numerous monastic cartularies, that is, registers containing copies of title deeds. Many of these have been published by local record societies. A list of manuscripts and printed editions is provided by G.R.C. Davis, *Medieval Cartularies of Great Britain*, London 1958, updated recently in *Monastic Research Bulletin* ii–v, Borthwick Institute of Historical Research, York 1996–99. Modern editions including much pre-1154 material include: U. Rees, ed., *The Cartulary of Shrewsbury Abbey*, 2 vols, Aberystwyth, National Library of Wales, 1975; B.R. Kemp. ed., *Reading Abbey Cartularies*, 2 vols, Royal Historical Society, Camden 4th ser. xxxi, 1986–87; C. Harper-Bill and R. Mortimer, *Stoke-by-Clare Priory Cartulary*, 3 vols, Suffolk Record Society, 1982–84; V. Brown, ed., *Eye Priory Cartulary and Charters*, 2 vols, Suffolk Record Society, 1992–94. An alternative approach is the collection of such charters by donor; for example, W. Farrer and C.T. Clay, eds, *Early Yorkshire Charters*, 12 vols, Yorkshire Archaeological Society Record Series, extra ser., 1914–65; D.E. Greenway, ed., *Charters of the Honour of Mowbray, 1107–1191* (as n. 68); R. Bearman, ed., *Charters of the Redvers Family and the Earldom of Devon, 1090–1217*, Devon and Cornwall Record Society xxxvii, 1994.

# 10

# Language and Literature

IAN SHORT

As Haskins in his now classic study of the Renaissance of the twelfth century reminds us, too close a focus on Latin obscures the fact that, over and above the revival of learning with which it is synonymous, the twelfth century was also 'an age of new creation in literature and art beyond the mere imitation of ancient models'.[1] Notwithstanding his own almost exclusive preoccupation with the achievements of the monastic and ecclesiastic intelligentsia, Haskins was well aware of how profoundly the secular world was also affected by the general broadening of horizons and the renewed intellectual vitality which characterised the twelfth century.

This is especially true of the field of literature. Here a whole series of innovations, generic, thematic and formal, laid the foundations for a written vernacular culture that was to flourish with ever-increasing creativity over the ensuing centuries. Such pervasive and durable concepts as chivalry, courtliness and Courtly Love, for example, trace their origins directly back to the lay world of the twelfth century.[2] More general developments of the time, such as increased historical consciousness and a more acute sense of the relevance of the past to the present, the 're-discovery' of the individual, the evolution of handwriting, book production and the decorative arts from Romanesque to Gothic modes, not to mention the political self-affirmation of the baronial classes or the growth of aristocratic patronage, are all reflected in one way or another in the pages of its secular texts.[3]

---

[1] C.H. Haskins, *The Renaissance of the Twelfth Century*, Cambridge Mass. 1927, 190; cf. R.L. Benson and G. Constable, eds, *Renaissance and Renewal in the Twelfth Century*, Cambridge Mass. 1982; C.N.L. Brooke, *The Twelfth-Century Renaissance*, London 1971; R.W. Southern, *Medieval Humanism and Other Studies*, Oxford 1970.

[2] M. Keen, *Chivalry*, New Haven/London 1984; J. Flori, *L'Essor de la chevalerie: XI^e–XII^e siècles*, Geneva 1986, also *La Chevalerie en France au Moyen Age*, Paris 1995; C.S. Jaeger, *The Origins of Courtliness: Civilizing Trends and the Formation of Courtly Ideals, 939–1210*, Philadelphia 1985 (who, however, traces the concept back to the German courtier class of the tenth and eleventh centuries); R. Boase, *The Origin and Meaning of Courtly Love*, Manchester 1977; cf. D. Burnley, '*Fine Amor*: its Meaning and Context', *Review of English Studies* ns xxxi, 1980, 129–48, and the same author's *Courtliness and Literature in Medieval England*, London 1998; R.H. Bloch, *Medieval Mysogyny and the Invention of Western Romantic Love*, Chicago 1991.

[3] Southern, *Medieval Humanism*, 135–80, also his 'The Sense of the Past', *TRHS* 6th ser. xxiii, 1973, 243–63; R.H.C. Davis, *The Normans and their Myth*, London 1976; N.F. Partner, *Serious Entertainments: the Writing of History in Twelfth-Century England*, Chicago 1977; C. Morris, *The Discovery of the Individual: 1050–1200*, London 1972; R.W. Hanning, *The Individual in Twelfth-Century Romance*, New Haven 1977; G. Zarnecki *et al.*, eds, *English Romanesque Art: 1066–1200*, London 1984; S. Macready and F. Thompson, eds, *Art and Patronage in the English Romanesque*, London 1986; G. Duby, *La Société chevaleresque: hommes et structures du moyen âge*, Paris 1988; D. Crouch, *The Image of Aristocracy in Britain, 1000–1300*, London 1992; W.F. Schirmer and U. Broich, *Studien zum literarischen Patronat im England des 12. Jahrhunderts*, Köln 1962.

Pride of place amongst the literary innovations of the century must go to the narrative genre of romance, one of whose founding fathers, Chrétien de Troyes, writing in French during the 1170s, explicitly links his own literary activity to the topos of the *translatio studii*.[4] There was, we are told, not only continuity of culture between the ancient world and his, but also a direct transfer of learning from one to the other – a cultural counterpart to the *translatio imperii* – from Greece to Rome and ultimately to the French-speaking world of the twelfth century.[5] Hand in hand with this appropriation of the written heritage of the past to the present goes a widening in the accessibility of knowledge, contemporary as well as ancient, as a whole new sector of society is brought within the purview of written culture.

The secular world, hitherto more or less excluded from the common fund of learning by virtue of the esoteric linguistic code in which it was transmitted, begins to have some sort of access to literacy when the language of everyday communication gains new status as an alternative medium of expression to Latin.[6] A new lay culture is born, operating in a parallel and symbiotic relationship to the learned. To the extent that this process entailed the breaking of the monopoly of Latin as the exclusive vehicle for the dissemination of knowledge, it can justifiably be described as a vernacularisation of culture. What thereby becomes available, in terms of our modern critical understanding of just how diverse and even contradictory the medieval outlook can be, are alternative voices to that of the ecclesiastical establishment. These are no less partial and distorting voices, perhaps, than that of the Church, but being less uniform and predictable, they are capable of throwing new light on events and, more importantly, on the value systems and the mentalities of a previously silent but powerful lay majority. Not so much a *vox populi*, no doubt, as a plurality of *voces communes*.[7]

What Haskins's deliberately internationalist and Latin vantage point over twelfth-century culture also prevented him from distinguishing clearly were the pioneering contributions that Britain, and particularly England, had to make to the Renaissance of the twelfth century. By concentrating on the roles played in intellectual history by such Insular luminaries as John of Salisbury and Adelard of Bath, Haskins was led to pass over in silence the more humble but no less far-reaching innovations made in the secular sphere by its vernacular writers and poets. Even though Gaimar, for example, and Layamon did not write in the same language (and John of

---

4   M.A. Freeman, *The Poetics of 'Translatio Studii' and 'Conjointure' in Chrétien de Troyes's 'Cligés'*, Lexington Kt 1979; cf. R.L. Krueger, ed., *The Cambridge Companion to Medieval Romance*, Cambridge 2000; A. Petit, *Naissance du roman: les techniques littéraires dans les romans antiques du XII^e siècle*, Paris 1985.

5   A. Micha, ed., *Les Romans de Chrétien de Troyes: Cligés*, Paris 1957, lines 28–34: 'Ce nos ont nostre livre apris Qu'an Grece ot de chevalerie Le premier los et de clergie. Puis vint chevalerie a Rome Et de la clergie la some, Qui or est an France venue. Dex doint qu'ele i soit maintenue . . .'; cf. D.D.R. Owen, trans., *Chrétien de Troyes: Arthurian Romances*, London 1987, 93; T. Hunt, 'Tradition and Originality in the Prologues of Chrestien de Troyes', *Forum for Modern Language Studies* viii, 1972, 320–44.

6   M.T. Clanchy, *From Memory to Written Record: England 1066–1307*, 2nd edn, Oxford 1993; R.V. Turner, 'The *miles literatus* in Twelfth- and Thirteenth-Century England: How Rare a Phenomenon?', *AHR* lxxxiii, 1978, 928–45; B. Stock, *The Implications of Literacy: Written Language and Models of Interpretation in the 11th and 12th Centuries*, Princeton 1983.

7   In the Provisions of Oxford, extracted from Henry III in 1258 by the barons, the latter refer to themselves as 'le commun de Engleterre'; W. Stubbs, *Select Charters . . .*, 5th edn, Oxford 1884, 388. Cf., for an illustration of the diversity of discursive voices, J.W. Baldwin, *The Language of Sex: Five Voices from Northern France around 1200*, Chicago 1994.

Salisbury, of course, chose to write in a different one again), they obviously belong together as part of the same cultural environment – as part of the same literature, indeed, whether we call it, loosely, English or, more accurately, Insular. The fact that most of the vernacular literature from twelfth-century England turns out to be in Anglo-Norman French draws attention to British society's most fundamental distinguishing feature, namely its ethnic plurality. And when we come to consider the inventiveness and the precociousness of the literature of England, it will be difficult to believe that this was not due in large measure to the multi-culturalism and multilingualism of the wider community of which it formed part.

As the primary vehicle of culture, language was a determining factor not only in the production of a remarkably wide range of works of literature but also in their reception and preservation. In addition to the five major dialects of English, the languages that were in use in twelfth-century Britain included Welsh, Cornish, Irish, Gaelic (not to mention Manx and a presumably moribund Cumbric), alongside the Anglo-Norman dialect of French imported in the wake of the Norman Conquest, and, of course, transcending them all, the Church's *lingua franca* of Latin.[8] Though not all of these languages necessarily produced significant literatures during the period with which we are concerned here, each must have contributed in different and often indirect ways to the rich variety of artistic production that makes twelfth-century Britain so distinctive. The geographical proximity of these same languages also facilitated the dissemination and transmission of the collective memories and written texts of particular groups to secondary audiences. This must sometimes have taken place through the intermediary of professional interpreters, or latimers, but more often than not was a natural result of the processes of practical bilingualism and cultural interchange.[9]

It was, of course, its political dominance which first and foremost gave England its privileged position within the cultural melting pot of Britain.[10] It was the meeting point of four different cultures in everyday contact: its own, the Celtic, the cross-Channel French and that of the international Latin tradition. It enjoyed in addition the practical advantages of a polyglot community of scholars, writers and poets, and an infrastructure of literary patronage provided not only by a leisured and intellectually curious nobility, but also by a religious establishment all too eager to embrace the vernacular as an effective medium of instruction. The stage was set, in other words, for innovation.

No single figure better illustrates the productive mix of England's pluralistic and trilingual society than the Anglo-Welshman Geoffrey of Monmouth. Drawing on his fertile imagination, his literary skill and Latin learning, and, one assumes, on a multiplicity of Celtic oral sources as well (perhaps) as 'a very ancient book in the Welsh tongue', this canon of Oxford succeeded in inventively re-writing British history.[11]

8   G. Price, *The Languages of Britain*, London 1984.
9   C. Bullock-Davies, *Professional Interpreters and the Matter of Britain*, Cardiff 1966; P. Sims-Williams, 'Did Itinerant Breton *conteurs* Transmit the *Matière de Bretagne*?', *Romania* cxvi, 1998, 72–111.
10  M. Chibnall, *Anglo-Norman England: 1066–1166*, Oxford 1986; A. Williams, *The English and the Norman Conquest*, Woodbridge 1995; M.T. Clanchy, *England and its Rulers, 1066–1272*, London 1983.
11  N. Wright, ed., *The Historia Regum Britannie of Geoffrey of Monmouth I: Bern Burgerbibliothek MS 568*, Cambridge 1984; L. Thorpe, trans., *Geoffrey of Monmouth: The History of the Kings of Britain*,

This he did around the semi-mythical figure of a sixth-century warrior chieftain, all but forgotten by the Latin chroniclers, who ended his life repelling the Saxon invader.[12] The function of King Arthur in Geoffrey's *Historia Regum Britanniae* was twofold: first to offer the native Celtic Britons a national hero whose past resistance against foreign domination would give them pride and hope for the future; and secondly to provide the Anglo-Norman knightly class with an idealised British king with whose chivalry they could identify and through whom they could come to integrate themselves into the history of a country that had become their adoptive homeland. Geoffrey was not only to exert, via his vernacular adaptor Wace, a profound influence on Continental French (and German) verse and prose romance, but also to leave, via Layamon and the *Gawain* poet amongst others, a lasting imprint on English literature from Malory through to Tennyson and beyond.[13] Only twelfth-century Britain with its interactive Celtic, English, French and Latin traditions could have provided the sort of breeding ground necessary for nurturing such a seminal conception as Geoffrey's.

The fate of other works from the literature of twelfth-century England is, naturally, less spectacular. While those composed in Latin or in Anglo-Norman form an impressive and voluminous corpus, those written in English are both thin on the ground and, with one exception, disappointingly undistinguished. One can only presume, however, that what survives represents an infinitesimal part of what was actually produced, orally or in written form, at the time, and that the picture we have today has been further distorted subsequently by the vagaries of manuscript survival. Numbers of medieval copies still extant rarely correlate with modern perceptions of the literary quality of the works they transmit. Only two manuscripts, for example, of the universally acclaimed *Owl and the Nightingale* have come down to us as against the seven which preserve the daunting *Poema Morale*, or the eight copies of the recondite *Ancrene Wisse*.[14] Even Latin literature shows startling discrepancies: Walter Map's entire opus survives in a single late fourteenth-century transcription, Orderic Vitalis' *Historia Ecclesiastica* in only two medieval copies, whereas the *Historia Regum Britanniae* counts today well over two hundred manuscripts, a significant number of which were copied in the course of the twelfth century alone.[15] The popularity of Geoffrey's best-seller, denounced as recently as 1986 as 'mendacious and intellectually dishonest' by a distinguished medieval historian, has much to tell us about real medieval attitudes to history.

Latin works would naturally have stood a better chance of survival than those in the vernacular, and French, given the social dominance of Anglo-Norman, would no doubt have been given precedence over English. But another important factor was

Harmondsworth 1966; J.S.P. Tatlock, *The Legendary History of Britain*, Berkeley 1950; R.W. Hanning, *The Vision of History in Early Britain*, New York 1966.

[12] E.K. Chambers, *Arthur of Britain*, London 1966; L. Alcock, *Arthur's Britain: History and Archaeology, AD 367–634*, Harmondsworth 1971; R. Bromwich *et al.*, eds, *The Arthur of the Welsh*, Cardiff 1991.

[13] R.S. Loomis, ed., *Arthurian Literature in the Middle Ages: a Collaborative History*, Oxford 1959; Norris Lacy *et al.*, eds, *The New Arthurian Encyclopedia*, New York 1996.

[14] J. Hall, ed., *Selections from Early Middle English, 1130–1250*, Oxford 1920, ii, 553, 312–13, 354–56. B. Dickens and R.M. Wilson, eds, *Early Middle English Texts*, London 1951.

[15] L. Thorpe, 'Walter Map and Gerald of Wales', *Medium Ævum* xlvii, 1978, 6–21; *Orderic*, i; J. Crick, *Historia Regum Britannie of Geoffrey of Monmouth, III: A Summary Catalogue of the Manuscripts*, Cambridge 1989.

patronage. This was not only a necessary condition for the production of medieval literature, but must also have had a rôle to play in its subsequent reception and transmission. Royal and monastic patronage, in other words, carried with it a different order of prestige and a greater potential for copying and preservation than did that of the less powerful and less wealthy secular courts, especially at a time when lay libraries and *scriptoria* were still very much in their infancy. Subsequent survival remained, of course, a question of accident, especially through the Dark Age of the Reformation and its systematic vandalism of the monasteries.

Given the virtual elimination of the native Anglo-Saxon aristocracy – the Normans had, in the poetic words of Adgar, 'sent them packing into the fields'[16] – it is clear that the principal factor determining the meagre production of literary texts in English during the twelfth century must have been lack of secular patronage. Among those texts that will inevitably have been lost are probably to be included the stories about Athelstan and Edgar known to William of Malmesbury, about Eadric the Wild and Godwine incorporated by Henry of Huntingdon into his Latin history, and perhaps about Havelok, Buern Bucecarl and Hereward used by Gaimar.[17] To what extent, however, these were specifically twelfth-century texts, and written rather than oral compositions (or, in the case of Gaimar, English rather than French) we cannot of course know. Written sources in English, unidentifiable today and in all likelihood spurious, were also claimed by the Anglo-Norman author of *Waldef* and by Marie in her French *Fables* towards the end of the twelfth century.[18] The English *Life of St Dunstan* survives only in the use made of it by Eadmer and Osbern.[19] The English version of the Hereward legend by Leofric is known only in a Latin reworking, as is the *Life of Wulfstan* by the Worcester monk Coleman, now preserved for posterity in William of Malmesbury's respectable Latin.[20]

All we have to fill the native literary vacuum, besides a poem on the death of Edward the Confessor incorporated into the *Anglo-Saxon Chronicle*, and another on the *Site of Durham*, both from the immediate post-Conquest period, is a handful of predominantly religious tracts – more specifically, some saints' lives, a few miscellaneous didactic texts, and a series of homiletic prose works in the Old English tradition, of which the *Lambeth Homilies* are a prime example.[21]

Outside the direct line of Anglo-Saxon descent are the versified sermons of the *Poema Morale*,[22] and the Gospel translations of the *Orrmulum* from around 1180 ('Þiss boc iss nemmned Orrmulum forrþi þatt Orrm itt wrohhte'), a spectacularly lengthy poem whose syllabic verse structure and unique spelling system are of more interest to the philologist than to the student of literature.[23] A somewhat more lyrical tradition is represented by the devotional treatise *The Wooing of Our Lord*, but the

---

16  P. Kunstmann, ed., *Adgar: Le Gracial*, Ottawa 1982, 215 (xxxi, 21–2): 'Li reis amat mult ses Normanz, Les Engleis enveia as chans.'

17  R.M. Wilson, *The Lost Literature of Medieval England*, 2nd edn, London 1972.

18  A.J. Holden, ed., *Le Roman de Waldef*, Cologny-Genève 1984, lines 33–86; H. Spiegel, ed. and trans., *Marie de France: Fables*, Toronto 1987, Epilogue lines 11–19 (256–8).

19  R.W. Southern, *St Anselm and his Biographer*, Cambridge 1963, 248–53.

20  Williams, *England*, 49, 170–1; E. Mason, *St Wulfstan of Worcester*, Oxford 1990.

21  R.M. Wilson, *Early Middle English Literature*, 3rd edn, London 1968, 7, 115–16; D. Wallace, ed., *The Cambridge History of Medieval English Literature*, Cambridge 1999, 61–91.

22  Hall, *Selections* i, 30–53.

23  M.B. Parkes, 'On the Presumed Date . . . of the MS of *Orrmulum*', in *Five Hundred Years of Words and Sounds: a Festschrift for Eric Dobson*, ed. E.G. Stanley and D. Gray, Cambridge 1983, 115–27; C.

strongly marked alliteration and the mysticism that characterise texts of this group anchor them firmly to the Anglo-Saxon past.[24] While the alliterative *Body and Soul Debate*, preserved within the *Worcester Fragments* corpus,[25] also remains largely uninfluenced by non-Insular traditions, *The Owl and the Nightingale* (c. 1189–1216)[26] is clearly indebted to French poetic techniques. Enthusiastically described by W.P. Ker as 'the most miraculous piece of writing . . . amongst the medieval English books', it is an ironic debate poem of considerable sophistication. Though it belongs ultimately to the learned tradition, the mastery it shows in the handling of the vernacular octosyllabic couplet is such that it must presumably have had English predecessors. Whoever its author was, he (or she) presumably shared the nightingale's preference for the south over the north:[27]

| | |
|---|---|
| Þat lond nis god, ne hit nis este, | Bad is that land and not well graced, |
| Ac wildernisse hit is & weste: | A wilderness it is and waste: |
| Knarres & cludes houentinge, | Skywards its crags and peaks do soar, |
| Snou & haȝel hom is genge; | It snows and hails for evermore; |
| Þat lond is grislich & unuele. | A fearful and repulsive place. |
| Þe men boþ wilde & unisele, | Its men both weird and wild of face, |
| Hi habbeþ noþer griþ ne sibbe. | No peace they know, no quarter give. |
| Hi ne reccheþ hu hi libbe: | They pay no heed to how they live: |
| Hi eteþ fihs an flehs unsode | They feed on fish, their meat is raw, |
| Suich wulues hit hadde tobrode . . . | Like wolves they tear at it and paw . . . |
| Hi goþ bitiȝt mid ruȝe uelle, | They dress in untanned hides as well |
| Riȝt suich hi comen ut of helle. | As if they come straight out of Hell. |

While the above works date from the last two decades of the twelfth century, two strictly syllabic hymns of praise to the Virgin, and another to St Nicholas, attributed to St Godric of Finchale pre-date, one assumes, the hermit's death in 1170.[28] Datable examples of English prose from earlier in the century include the continuations of the *Anglo-Saxon Chronicle* exemplar at Peterborough covering the period 1122–54,[29] Henry II's bilingual charter of 1155 for the monks of Christ Church Canterbury,[30] and parts of the trilingual *Eadwine Psalter* (1155–60), also originating from Christ Church.[31] The admixture in both Canterbury texts of features from Old (West Saxon standard) and Middle English illustrates how, as a result of the phonological and morphological changes of the eleventh century, English was at this time undergoing a process of radical transformation. The so-called tremulous hand of a scribe glossing a

   Cannon, 'Spelling Practice, the *Ormulum* and the Word', in *Forum for Modern Language Studies* xxxiii, 1997.

24  W. Meredith-Thompson, ed., *Þe Wohunge of Ure Laured*, EETS, London 1958.

25  Hall, *Selections* i, 1–4.

26  N. Cartlidge, 'The Date of *The Owl and the Nightingale*', *Medium Ævum* lxv, 1996, 230–47, argues that the poem could date from as late as 1272.

27  E.G. Stanley, ed., *The Owl and the Nightingale*, Manchester 1972, lines 999–1014 (my translation).

28  Hall, *Selections* ii, 241–5.

29  C. Clark, ed., *The Peterborough Chronicle 1070–1154*, 2nd edn, Oxford 1970; G.N. Garmonsway, trans., *The Anglo-Saxon Chronicle*, London 1972; *EHD* ii, 103–215.

30  J.C. Holt and R. Mortimer, eds, *Acta of Henry II and Richard I*, Cambridge 1986, no. 41 (facs. in N. Denholm-Young, *Handwriting in England and Wales*, 2nd edn, Cardiff 1964, pl. 9); cf. Hall, *Selections* i, 11–12; Pelteret, *Catalogue* (note 37 below), no. 51.

31  P. O'Neill in M. Gibson, T.A. Heslop and R.W. Pfaff, eds, *The Eadwine Psalter: Text, Image and Monastic Culture in Twelfth-Century Canterbury*, London 1992, 123–38.

series of Anglo-Saxon manuscripts in the library of Worcester Cathedral Priory in the early thirteenth century exemplifies continuing interest in the linguistic heritage of the past at a time when the gap between pre-Conquest and contemporary English was posing serious problems of comprehensibility.[32]

Women religious were the intended recipients of the so-called *Katherine Group* of texts, comprising translations of Latin lives of Saints Katherine, Margaret and Juliana in rhythmical prose, *Sawles Warde*, an allegorical homily, and *Hali Meiðhad*, a treatise on virginity. It is not, however, clear whether these texts, in which modern critics, particularly feminist, do not hesitate to find literary interest and value, fall within the twelfth century.[33] The *Ancrene Wisse*, closely allied dialectally to the *Katherine Group*, is a revision, from about 1225, of the earlier, presumably twelfth-century *Ancren Riwle*, originally written for three young aristocratic women to prepare them, in not only doctrinal but practical terms, for life as anchoresses:[34]

> 3e, mine leove sustren, bute 3ef neod ow drive ant ower meistre hit reade, ne schulen habbe na beast but cat ane. Ancre þe haveð ahte þuncheð bet husewif, ase Marthe wes; ne lihtliche ne mei ha nawt beo Marie, Marthe suster, wiðe griðfullnesse of heorte. For þenne mot ha þenchen of þe kues foddre, of heordemonne hure, olhnin þe heiward, wearien hwen he punt hire, ant 3elden, þa, þe hearmes . . . Nawt, deore dehtren, ne wite 3e in ower hus of oðer monne þinges, ne ahte ne claðes ne boistes ne chartres, scoren ne cyrograffes, ne þe chirch vestemenz ne þe calices bute neode oðer strengðe hit makie, oðer muchel eie. Of swuch witunge is muchel uvel ilumpen oftesiðen. Inwið ower wanes ne leote 3e na mon slepen.

> [You should not, my dear sisters, except when the need arises or on the advice of your spiritual director, keep any animals – with the exception of a cat. An anchoress with livestock begins to look like the sort of housewife Martha was, not easily able to be like her sister Mary and devote herself wholeheartedly to God. She would have to worry about finding fodder for her cow, paying the herdsman, first cajoling the hayward then cursing him when he impounds the cow and you have nevertheless to pay the damages . . . And do not, dear daughters, keep other people's things in your house: no personal possessions, clothes, boxes, charters, tallies or indentures, vestments or communion chalices, unless you need or are obliged or intimidated to do so. Much harm has often come from keeping objects of this sort around. Do not allow any man to sleep under your roof.]

Beyond its interest as a manual of spiritual instruction, the *Ancrene Wisse*, which is extant also in parallel French and Latin versions, is a lively social document with some particularly vivid character portrayals.

Romance as a literary genre emerges in England only in the early thirteenth century with *King Horn*, a re-writing of the Anglo-Norman original, and *Havelok the*

---

[32] C. Franzen, *The Tremulous Hand of Worcester: a Study of Old English in the Thirteenth Century*, Oxford 1991.

[33] B. Millett, 'Women in No Man's Land: English Recluses and the Development of Vernacular Literature in the Twelfth and Thirteenth Centuries', in *Women and Literature in Britain 1150–1500*, ed. C.M Meale, Cambridge 1993, 86–103 (93–7). Cf. B. Millet and J. Wogan-Browne, eds and trans., *Medieval English Prose for Women: Selections from the Katherine Group and Ancrene Wisse*, Oxford 1990.

[34] Hall, *Selections* i, 60 (my translation); cf. H. White, *Ancrene Wisse: Guide for Anchoresses*, London 1993; B. Millett, 'The Origins of the *Ancrene Wisse*: New Answers, New Questions', *Medium Ævum* lxi, 1992, 206–28; B. Millett, ed., *'Ancrene Wisse', the Katherine Group and the Wooing Group*, Cambridge 1996.

*Dane*.[35] To see Middle English romances such as these as catering exclusively for a lower class audience than their Anglo-Norman counterparts is misleading, since by this date Insular French speakers were already the new English and had been bilingual for several generations. Layamon's English version of Wace's *Roman de Brut*, itself a verse re-working of Geoffrey of Monmouth, falls in all probability outside the strict confines of the twelfth century.[36] It remains an isolated landmark on a somewhat desert landscape that stretches ahead to the 1370s and the Golden Age of Chaucer.

Also surviving as a testimony to the continued use of English as a language of written record in the twelfth century is a sizeable corpus of post-Conquest administrative documents.[37] The continuity of pre-Conquest law provides a further opportunity for the preservation of an Old English vernacular tradition into the Anglo-Norman era, as is illustrated, for example, by the *Textus Roffensis* (1122–23).[38] It is only later in the century that the practice of bilingual French/English glossing seems to become established, initially in Latin texts used for instruction and in medical recipes.[39]

The best known example of continuity with the British past is the Peterborough version of the *Anglo-Saxon Chronicle*. As an antidote, on occasion, to the pro-Norman bias of Latin historiography, it has documentary value, especially for the reign of Stephen, in addition to its modest literary qualities.[40] Some versions of the chronicle appear in Latin, but it was an archaic Old English text of its Northern Recension, from York or Peterborough perhaps, that Gaimar doggedly contrived to turn into Anglo-Norman rhyming couplets in 1136–37.[41] Like Geoffrey's *Historia* and the *Ancrene Wisse*, the *Anglo-Saxon Chronicle* exemplifies the permeability of England's trilingual culture and the interaction between its different elements.

It was, however, Latin that was the yardstick of literacy, and so it was to remain throughout the Middle Ages. To the high prestige which it enjoyed as the international language of Christian devotion and Curial politics, of theology, science and learning in general, of instruction in the Schools, of written administrative record, and of clerical literature and poetry, is to be added the kudos attached to its widespread use as an acquired spoken vernacular within monastic and ecclesiastical circles. St Godric's sudden mastery of it, resulting in his being able to join the learned conversation of the

---

[35] R.S. Allen, ed., *King Horn*, New York 1983; G.V. Smithers, ed., *Havelok*, Oxford 1987; S. Crane, *Insular Romance: Politics, Faith, and Culture in Anglo-Norman and Middle English Literature*, Berkeley 1986, 24–40 (*Horn*), 40–52 (*Havelok*); W.R.J. Barron, *English Medieval Romance*, London 1987, 65–74; T. Turville-Petre, *England the Nation: Language, Literature, and National Identity, 1290–1340*, Oxford 1996, 143–55.

[36] F. Le Saux, *Layamon's Brut: the Poem and its Sources*, Cambridge 1989; cf. Barron, *Romance*, 132–7; W.R.J. Barron and S.C. Weinberg (trans.), *Layamon's Arthur: the Arthurian Section of Layamon's 'Brut'*, London 1989.

[37] D.A.E. Pelteret, *Catalogue of English Post-Conquest Vernacular Documents*, Woodbridge 1990 (there are 148 entries); M. Laing, *Catalogue of Sources for 'A Linguistic Atlas of Early Medieval English'*, Cambridge 1993.

[38] P. Wormald, '*Laga Eadwardi*: the *Textus Roffensis* and its Context', *ANS* xvii, 1994, 243–66.

[39] T. Hunt, *Teaching and Learning Latin in Thirteenth-Century England* i, Cambridge 1991, 8–27; also 'The Old English Vocabularies in MS Oxford Bodley 730', *English Studies* lxii, 1981, 201–9, and 'The Trilingual Glossary in MS London BL Sloane 146 . . .', *English Studies* lxx, 1989, 289–310; cf. W. Rothwell, 'From Latin to Anglo-French and Middle English: the Role of the Multilingual Gloss', *Modern Language Review* lxxxviii, 1993, 581–99.

[40] See note 29 above; cf. R.H.C. Davis, *King Stephen*, 3rd edn, London 1990, 80, 147.

[41] I. Short, 'Gaimar's Epilogue and Geoffrey of Monmouth's *Liber vetustissimus*', *Speculum* lxix, 1994, 323–43 (330–3).

local monks visiting his cell, was hailed as miraculous by his biographer Reginald of Durham.[42] On the other hand, Gerald of Wales' scathing indictment of the latinity of some of his clerical colleagues probably represents a more realistic (if personally jaundiced) evaluation of its use:[43]

> Item exemplum de illo qui, clerico suo quaerenti quid esset *altera*, respondit quia piscis erat in partibus illis, quod et probavit per illud: "Mittite in dexteram navigii rete et invenietis altera . . ." Item exemplum de illo qui quaesivit a magistro Johanne de Cornubiensi quis esset *busillis*, putabat enim proprium nomen regis vel alicuius magni viri fuisse. Interroganti autem magistro Johanni ubinam hoc, et in qua scriptura inveniretur, respondit quoniam in missali; et currens propter librum suum, ostendit ei in fine columpnae paginae unius scriptum *in die*, in principio vero alterius columnae *bus illis*, quod recte facit *in diebus illis*.

> [There is the example of the priest who, when asked by his clerk the meaning of the word *altera*, replied that it meant some sort of foreign fish, which he proceeded to demonstrate by quoting [John 21,6]: 'Cast the net on the right side of the boat and you will find some . . .' Another example is of the priest who asked Master John of Cornwall what the word *busillis* meant; he thought it must have been a proper name, of a king or some important person or other. When asked by Master John where and in which book of the Scriptures the word was to be found, he replied that it was in the Missal. Running to fetch his book, he showed him, written at the foot of a column of one page *in die*, and at the head of the next column *bus illis*, which, properly arranged, gives *in diebus illis*.]

In view of which, it is hardly surprising to find Anglo-Norman being widely used as an alternative to Latin in church and cloister.[44]

The international character of Latin creates problems of classification and national demarcation. The writings of Lanfranc and of Anselm, for example, given their Italian origins, might be seen as not belonging to Anglo-Latin literature in the strict sense of the term, though it would be difficult to use the same argument in relation to Peter of Blois, whose twenty-six-year sojourn in England qualifies him – despite his curious inability to master any English during that time[45] – as a special case. The use of Latin across a wide gamut of writing also entails making arbitrary decisions on what should properly be included in the category of literature. By excluding historiography, one of the glories of the twelfth-century Renaissance in England, we exclude amongst others Orderic Vitalis and William of Malmesbury, both of mixed, Norman and English, parentage, Henry of Huntingdon, Florence and John of Worcester, Richard and John of Hexham, William of Newburgh, Jocelin of Brakelond and Gervase of Tilbury. Discounting theology, science and government leads to similar arbitrary omissions.[46]

Post-Conquest Anglo-Latin literature begins early with a prosimetrum *Life of Edward the Confessor*, subsequently re-written in 1138 by the Westminster monk

---

[42] J. Stephenson, ed., *Reginald of Durham: Libellus de vita et miraculis Sancti Godrici heremitae de Finchale*, Surtees Soc., London 1847, 179–80; cf. I. Short, 'On Bilingualism in Anglo-Norman England', *Romance Philology* xxxiii, 1979–80, 467–79 (475–6).

[43] *Gemma Ecclesiastica* in *Giraldi Cambrensis Opera*, ii, 341–3.

[44] M.D. Legge, *Anglo-Norman in the Cloisters*, Edinburgh 1950; M. Richter, *Sprache und Gesellschaft im Mittelalter: Untersuchungen zur mündlichen Kommunikation in England von der Mitte des elften bis zum Beginn des vierzehnten Jahrhunderts*, Stuttgart 1979, 54–94.

[45] 'Viginti sex annis in Anglia peregrinans linguam quam non noveram audivi' (Richter, *Sprache*, 67).

[46] A.G. Rigg, *A History of Anglo-Latin Literature, 1066–1422*, Cambridge 1992, 3–8; cf. K. Bate, 'La Littérature latine d'imagination à la cour d'Henri II d'Angleterre', *CCM* xxxiv, 1991, 3–21; D. Wallace, ed., *The Cambridge History of Medieval English Literature*, Cambridge 1999, 122–51.

Osbert of Clare, whose version was in its turn re-used by Ælred of Rievaulx for his *Vita Edwardi Regis* of 1161.[47] Other saints' lives were those of Malchus, in the form of a long verse epic by Reginald of Canterbury, French by birth and a monk at St Augustine's Canterbury, where he also wrote numerous incidental poems;[48] the prose lives of Wulfsige, Edith, Wulfhild, Ivo, Mildred and St Augustine of Canterbury by Goscelin, also at Canterbury following a stay at Sherborne until 1078, and likewise an adoptive Anglo-Norman, this time a Fleming; and the lives of Dunstan and Elphege by Osbern, again of Canterbury.[49] Eadmer's *Vita Anselmi* (1122) also belongs to the same productive hagiographic circle of Canterbury.[50] One of the more remarkable features of the Normans' gift for cultural assimilation was the willingness with which they came to accept and indeed revere Anglo-Saxon saints.[51]

The *Carmen de Hastingae Proelio*, whose date and provenance have both been the subject of controversy, uses elegiac couplets to paint a dramatic picture of the Norman Conquest in epic colours.[52] The *Disciplina Clericalis*, a collection of moral tales by Petrus Alfonsi, a converted Spanish Jew who was physician to Henry I, was later to become a popular source for sermons. It was also translated into Anglo-Norman.[53] In addition to the *Historia Regum Brittaniae* (1138), the wide repercussions of which we have already discussed, mention needs also to be made of Geoffrey of Monmouth's *Prophetiae Merlini*, which he extracted from his as yet unfinished *Historia* and published separately in 1135. He dedicated it to Alexander, bishop of Lincoln, a patron he shared with Henry of Huntingdon.[54] Geoffrey's *Vita Merlini*, a long poem in unrhymed hexameters addressed to Alexander's successor, Robert Chesney, in 1148, is an individualistic celebration of magic, steeped in Celtic folklore.[55]

Henry, archdeacon of Huntingdon, intersperses numerous poems into his *Historia Anglorum* (1132–54), which also proves to owe a particular debt to Sallust and Lucan as well as to classical rhetoric.[56] Henry's epigrams have earned him the recent accolade of a 'versatile and imaginative poet'.[57] Lawrence, prior of Durham, (d. 1154) enjoys an even higher reputation as a poet, in particular for his *Dialogi* in which he appears to use his own personal experience as a moral exemplum.[58] Ælred of Rievaulx (d. 1167), as well as being a hagiographer and historiographer (he composed a verse account of the Battle of the Standard of 1138, in addition to a prose *Genealogia*

---

47  *Vita Aedwardi.*
48  L.R. Lind, ed., *Vita Sancti Malchi*, Urbana Ill. 1942; Rigg, *Anglo-Latin*, 24–30.
49  Rigg, *Anglo-Latin*, 20–1.
50  R.W. Southern, *The Life of St Anselm . . . by Eadmer*, Oxford 1962; also *St Anselm and his Biographer*, Cambridge 1963.
51  S. Ridyard, *The Royal Saints of Anglo-Saxon England*, Cambridge 1988; also '*Condigna veneratio*: Post-Conquest Attitudes to English Saints', *ANS* ix, 1987, 179–206.
52  *Carmen*; R.H.C. Davis, 'The *Carmen de Hastingae Proelio*', *EHR* xciii, 1978, 241–61; also with L.J. Engels, 'The *Carmen* . . .: a Discussion', *ANS* ii, 1979, 1–20; E. van Houts, 'Latin Poetry and the Anglo-Norman Court 1066–35: the *Carmen de Hastingae Proelio*', *JMH* xv, 1989, 39–62.
53  A. Hilka and W. Söderhjelm, eds, *Petri Alfonsi Disciplina Clericalis* iii, Helsingfors 1922, 79–158; Rigg, *Anglo-Latin*, 31.
54  Wright, *Historia Regum Britannie* (note 11 above), x–xii.
55  B. Clarke, ed. and trans., *Life of Merlin. Geoffrey of Monmouth: Vita Merlini*, Cardiff 1973.
56  *Huntingdon*, xxxiv–xxxviii.
57  Rigg, *Anglo-Latin*, 40, also 'Henry of Huntingdon's Metrical Experiments', *Journal of Medieval Latin* i, 1991, 60–72; *Huntingdon*, cvii–cxii.
58  J. Raine, ed., *Dialogi Laurentii Dunelmensis monachi et prioris*, Surtees Soc., Durham 1880; cf. Rigg, *Anglo-Latin*, 54–61.

*Regum Anglorum* addressed to the newly crowned Henry II), was also an important figure in the field of devotional literature, and the earliest of the English Cistercian writers.[59] Walter Daniel wrote a life of Ælred which treads the narrow line between hagiography and biography.[60]

John of Salisbury, one of the figureheads of the twelfth-century Renaissance, has a place in literature principally by virtue of his letters, the *Metalogicon* and his *Entheticus*, an anti-*moderni* satire in praise of traditional learning, written around 1159 in elegiacs and addressed, like his more famous *Policraticus*, to Thomas Becket.[61] John also wrote a prose life of Becket after the archbishop's assasination, swelling the hagiographic ranks of, amongst others, Herbert of Bosham, William of Canterbury, Benedict of Peterborough, William fitz Stephen and Edward Grim.[62] The polish and sophistication of his epistolary style can be gauged from the opening of his letter to the abbot of Celle:[63]

> Cum haec scriberem, notario risum mouit praemissa salutationis inscriptio, cuius causam inquisitus, ridiculum me salutatorem monuit loqui consultius et, ne amara uel insipida dulcibus misceam, temperare; ait enim te sicut *salutem* acceptare oblatam, sic aspernari quod subiungitur *et seipsum*, forte quia amarum, quia insipidum, praesertim domi suae dulcioribus habundanti. Ego autem quid ad ista?

> [As I was writing this letter, my secretary was moved to laugh aloud at the greeting with which I began it. On my asking him the reason, he replied that he found it an absurd opening, and advised me to choose my words more carefully. I should, he said, avoid mixing anything bitter or tasteless with something sweet, explaining that just as you might be willing to accept the *sincerely* that I offer, so you will certainly reject the *yours* with which I follow it. Perhaps because I am a bitter person, or a tasteless one, but more likely because I am addressing someone whose household is overflowing with sweetness. What can I possibly say to this?]

The exact extent of the poetic output of Peter of Blois (c. 1135–1212), who with Walter of Châtillon and Walter Map famously frequented the court of Henry II, is controversial. Assuming Pierre de Blois to have been a convenient pseudonym of his rather than that of an unrelated namesake, it is possible to credit him with a large and sophisticated corpus of frequently amatory or erotic verse which places him firmly within the *Carmina Burana* tradition.[64] Peter was also the author of over two hundred letters which survive to show the depth of his learning, the breadth of his interest in contemporary life, his gift for intellectual provocation, and his finely wrought Latin.

---

59 R. Howlett, ed., *Relatio de Standardo*, in *Chronicles of the Reigns of Stephen* . . ., RS, iii, London 1886, 181–99; R. Twysden, ed., in *Historiae Anglicanae Scriptores X*, London 1652, 347–70 (*Genealogia*); A. Hoste, *Bibliotheca Ælrediana* . . ., Steenbrugge 1962.

60 F.M. Powicke, ed. and trans., *The Life of Ailred of Rievaulx by Walter Daniel*, Oxford 1950.

61 J. van Laarhoven, ed., *John of Salisbury's Entheticus Maior and Minor*, Leiden 1987; cf. Rigg, *Anglo-Latin*, 73–6.

62 A. Gransden, *Historical Writing in England, c. 550 to c. 1307*, London 1974, 296–307.

63 W.J. Mellor, H.E. Butler and C.N.L. Brooke, eds and trans., *The Letters of John of Salisbury* i, London 1955, 183 (cf. xlvii–l; my translation).

64 P Dronke, 'Peter of Blois and Poetry at the Court of Henry II', *Medieval Studies* xxxviii, 1976, 185–235; cf. Southern, *Medieval Humanism*, 105–32; also 'The Necessity for Two Peters of Blois', in *Intellectual Life in the Middle Ages: Essays Presented to Margaret Gibson*, ed. L. Smith and B. Ward, London 1992, 103–18.

Here we see him in his rôle as a poet debating the conflicting demands of the spirit and the flesh:[65]

| | |
|---|---|
| Grata est in senio | Age finds consolation |
| religio, | embracing religion; |
| iuveni non congruit; | the young this suits less well. |
| carnis desiderio | To yearning for passion |
| consencio, | I give my permission: |
| nullus enim odio | no one feels revulsion |
| carnem suam habuit. | at his own flesh's will. |
| Neminem ab inferis | None have we ever seen |
| revertentem vidimus – | from Hell's jaws returning – |
| certa non reliquimus | we shan't stop believing |
| ob dubia; | and live life in doubt; |
| sompniator animus | those given to dreaming |
| respuens presencia | from life's toil should opt out |
| gaudeat inanibus – | and waste their time idling. |
| quibus si credideris, | If on vain hope you lean, |
| expectare poteris | join the British who dream |
| Arturum cum Britonibus. | of Arthur returning. |

Nigel Wireker (Whiteacre) is best known as a brilliantly mordant satirist. He was of mixed French and English blood, a monk of Christ Church Canterbury and author of the *Speculum Stultorum*, written in elegiacs in the course of the 1180s. Its hero, an ass called Burnellus, following a series of ever more grotesque adventures, comes into contact with the medical profession and the universities (after seven years at Paris he has learnt only to say 'hee-haw'), after which, having rejected a career in the Church, he opts to become a monk. Finding all of the existing orders wanting, he is forced to establish a new one, to which he gives his own name ('qui meus ordo meo nomen de nomine sumat') – presumably the Asinines.[66]

The *Poetria Nova* of Geoffrey of Vinsauf, who taught at Northampton, comes within the category of School texts, and *Babio*, a play in the *commediae* style with a humour that is largely linguistic, may well belong to the same category.[67] So also do the *Proverbs* of the Cistercian Serlo of Wilton and Alexander Neckam's *De Nominibus Utensilium*, a widely used pedagogical text that came ready equipped with extensive French glosses.[68] Both were also poets, the latter a particularly prolific and versatile one. Joseph of Exeter's *Ylias* (c. 1185) is a full-scale epic on Troy in unrhymed hexameters of highly polished Latin.[69] Sometime between 1179 and 1181 Henry of Saltrey wrote an account of *St Patrick's Purgatory*, which was the source of the French *Espurgatoire* by Marie, identified by some with the author of the *Lais*.[70]

---

65  Dronke, 'Peter of Blois', 208 (my translation).

66  J.H. Mozley and R.R. Rymo, eds, *Speculum Stultorum*, Berkeley 1960; cf. Rigg, *Anglo-Latin*, 84–7.

67  Rigg, *Anglo-Latin*, 108–11, 113–14; M.W. Walsh, '*Babio*: Towards a Performance Reconstruction of Secular Farce in Twelfth-Century England', in *England in the Twelfth Century: Proceedings of the 1988 Harlaxton Symposium*, ed. D. Williams, Woodbridge 1990, 219–40; cf. M.M. Brennan, trans., *Babio: a 12th-Century Profane Comedy*, Charleston Vi. 1968.

68  Rigg, *Anglo-Latin*, 70–2, 117–22; T. Hunt, 'Les Gloses en langue vulgaire dans les manuscrits du *De Nominibus Utensilium* d'Alexandre Nequam', *Revue de linguistique romane* xliii, 1979, 235–62.

69  L. Gompf, ed., *Joseph Iscanus: Werke und Briefe*, Leiden 1970; A.K. Bate, trans., *Joseph of Exeter: Trojan War I–III*, Warminster 1986; cf. Rigg, *Anglo-Latin*, 99–102.

70  Y. de Pontfarcy, ed., *Marie de France: L'Espurgatoire seint Patriz*, Louvain 1995 (contains an edition of the Latin text).

Walter Map was, like Geoffrey of Monmouth before him, Anglo-Welsh, and arch-deacon of Oxford, although he had also been a courtier of Henry II and was renowned as one of the sharpest wits and most accomplished liars of his time. 'I am unversed in the art of lying on my own', wrote the Anglo-Norman poet Hue de Rotelande from Hereford, 'but Walter Map is a past master in it'.[71] Walter's *De Nugis Curialium* (1181–93) is highly individualistic: a bewildering farrago of macabre Welsh legends of demons, ghosts and fairies, lengthy anecdotes and stories, much of them seemingly inconsequential. The text is studded with learned allusions, flashes of black humour, and there are extended passages of satire on the royal court ('I speak of the court, but God alone knows what the court actually is; I certainly don't'),[72] monks, particularly the Cistercians and the Templars, and women. It is rounded off by a résumé of English history in which Eleanor is singled out for outspoken treatment:[73]

Cui successit Henricus Matildis filius, in quem iniecit oculos incestos Alienor Francorum regina, Lodouici piissimi coniux, et iniustum machinata diuorcium nupsit ei, cum tamen haberetur in fama priuata quod Gaufrido patri suo lectum Lodouici participasset. Presumitur autem inde quod eorum soboles in excelsis suis intercepta deuenit ad nichilum.

[Henry son of Matilda succeeded to the throne, but Eleanor, queen of the French and wife of the exceedingly pious Louis, cast her lascivious eyes on him. Having contrived a ques-tionable divorce, she married Henry despite rumours circulating to the effect that she had already shared Louis's bed with Geoffrey, Henry's father. This, one supposes, is why her progeny, sullied as their origins were, finally came to naught.]

Walter's pungent anti-matrimonial views circulated separately under the title of the *Epistola Valerii ad Ruffinum*.[74] The attribution to him of a large number of satirii Latin poems probably tells us more about his reputation than his actual output. His name also came to be attached to the corpus of French Arthurian prose romance, and the authorship of 'maistre Gautier Map qui fu clers au roy Henri' is claimed for *La Quête du Saint-Graal* and *La Mort le roi Artu*, written in France two decades or so after Walter's death.[75]

Another palpable personality and flamboyant Anglo-Welshman was Walter's contemporary Gerald of Wales (more accurately Gerald de Barri, commonly Giraldus Cambrensis). A vain, acerbic observer and critic of society, Gerald has an appealingly quirky judgement, often stimulated by prejudice and/or frustrated personal ambi-tion.[76] He was pro-Norman or pro-Welsh as the whim took him and personal advan-tage dictated. His output is truly impressive: his *Topographia Hiberniae* and *Expugnatio Hibernica* (both 1180), the *Itinerarium Kambriae* (1191) and *Descriptio Kambriae* (1194) reveal his gifts for learning, elegant synthesis, telling anecdotes and vivid description, and an abiding interest in social customs and natural history, folk-lore and marvels. His *Gemma Ecclesiastica* (1197) is a manual of instruction for the

---

71  A.J. Holden, ed., *Ipomedon: poème de Hue de Rotelande . . .*, Paris 1979, lines 7185–6: 'Sul ne sai pas de mentir l'art, Walter Map reset ben sa part.'
72  M.R. James, C.N.L. Brooke and R.A.B. Mynors, eds and trans., *Walter Map: De Nugis Curialium . . .*, Oxford 1983, 2: 'De curia loquor et nescio, Deus scit, quid sit curia'.
73  *De Nugis*, 474–6 (my translation).
74  *De Nugis*, xlviii.
75  E. Baumgartner, 'Figures du destinateur: Salomon, Arthur, le roi Henri d'Angleterre', in *Anglo-Norman Anniversay Essays*, ed. Ian Short, London 1993, 1–10.
76  R. Bartlett, *Gerald of Wales*, Oxford 1982.

Welsh clergy, his *De Principis Instructione* (1218) largely a critical account of the reign of Henry II. His *Speculum Duorum* (1208–16) is a splendidly immoderate invective against a wayward nephew, 'so thick-skinned, so thick-skulled and such an oaf'.[77] The *Speculum Ecclesiae* of 1220 is his last and most satirical work, with an anti-Cistercian bias that is reminiscent of Walter Map. He also wrote saints' lives and much else besides. Some of his views on the Irish give the flavour of his prose:[78]

> Laneis quoque utuntur seu braccis caligatis, seu caligis braccatis . . . Est autem gens haec gens silvestris, gens inhospita, gens ex bestiis solum et bestialiter vivens . . . In musicis solum instrumentis commendabilem invenio gentis istius diligentiam. In quibus prae omni natione quam vidimus incomparabiliter instructa est . . . Mirum quod in tanta tam praecipiti digitorum rapacitate musica servatur proportio, et arte per omnia indemni . . . consona redditur et completur melodia.
>
> [They wear woollen trousers that also serve as boots, or are they boots that are at the same time trousers? . . . They are a savage and unwelcoming people who live on animals alone and themselves live like animals . . . The only praiseworthy feature I find in them is their diligence in playing musical instruments, and in this they are incomparably more skilled than any other people I have encountered . . . What is remarkable is how, despite the frenzied speed of their fingering, they contrive to maintain a sense of musical balance . . . The consonance is preserved and the melody rendered without a note being lost, with a skill that remains consummate throughout.]

As his frequent word plays and linguistic jokes show, and his penchant for quoting popular proverbs confirms, Gerald's own vernacular was French.[79] He also claims proficiency in Welsh as well as English and Latin, and there seems indeed no reason to deny him access to the exalted company of other well-attested clerical polyglots such as Odo of Battle, Ralph Flambard, Herbert Losinga, Samson of Bury, Gilbert Foliot and Stephen Langton.[80] Having himself studied at Paris, Gerald was particularly scornful in his dismissal of the Insular variety of French that we today call Anglo-Norman: he dubs it gutter French, a turgid and inelegant distortion of what should be the proper French of France, thereby echoing, with characteristic hyperbole, earlier descriptions of it, from the 1160s, as false or unauthentic French. The more sardonic Walter Map termed it Marlborough French.[81]

However it may have been perceived in relation to the Continental norm, Anglo-Norman or, as it might more accurately be called, Insular French, was the socially and politically dominant idiolect of the descendants of the Conqueror and his followers who governed twelfth-century Britain as a powerful aristocratic élite. As early as the 1130s, however, these Norman incomers are found referring to themselves as Englishmen, and there is evidence that they were not only naturally bilingual from a very early stage, but that, by the 1170s at the latest, their mother tongue had in fact become English.[82] They were, on the other hand, to persist in preserving the colo-

[77]  Y. Lefèvre *et al.*, eds and trans., *Giraldus Cambrensis: Speculum Duorum*, Cardiff 1973, 60: 'tam cervicosum tam indiscretum et tam indomitum' (adapted from editors' translation).

[78]  *Topographia Hiberniae*, in *Giraldi Cambrensis Opera* v, 150–3 (my translation); cf. J.J. O'Meara, trans., *Gerald of Wales: The History and Topography of Ireland*, Harmondsworth 1982, 101–3.

[79]  Richter, *Sprache* (note 44 above), 87–94.

[80]  R.M. Wilson, 'English and French in England, 1100–1300', *History* xxviii, 1943, 37–60 (46–7).

[81]  Short, *Bilingualism* (note 42 above), 470–3.

[82]  I. Short, '*Tam Angli quam Franci*: Self-Definition in Anglo-Norman England', *ANS* xviii, 1996, 153–75.

nial language of their ancestors, in an increasingly anachronistic gesture of separate identity and cultural distinctiveness, well beyond its natural lifespan into the fifteenth century and later. The first English-speaking king of England after the Conquest is reputed to have been Henry IV, who acceded in 1399. Law French survived into the seventeenth century, when Milton, castigating the legal profession, wrote of 'that old entanglement of iniquity, their gibberish laws'.[83] Some of its formulae can still be heard today, *mutatis mutandis*, in the Houses of Parliament.

The high status enjoyed by Insular French in post-Conquest England was out of all proportion to the numbers – but not, of course, the power – of those who spoke it as their first language. Using the data of the Domesday Survey of 1086, we can estimate the number of French-speaking incomers at the start of the twelfth century at something in the region of 15,000 (William's invading army had been half that number), which would represent less than 1% of the total population of some 1.75 million.[84] This is the principal reason why they were destined to remain an ethnolinguistic minority – and why Anglo-Norman French is not today the spoken language of England (or Danish or Norse that of Normandy). Social adaptability, especially through intermarriage, was, moreover, one of the Normans' most consistent accomplishments. There was no question of Insular French ever displacing English, and in the twelfth century it failed to make any significant inroads at all into the English-speaking majority, which, from vicar to villein, remained stoutly monoglot. French forenames, however, rapidly became fashionable, especially among women.[85] One assumes that the vogue for Thomas, Richard and Henry (Dick and Harry were respectively sixteenth- and fourteenth-century developments) must have come later in the century. There is no evidence of the newcomers attempting to impose their language; the myth of the Norman Yoke was the invention of a later age.[86] Anglo-Norman might well, on the other hand, have been, initially at least, a predominantly urban phenomenon.[87] The implications of the incomers' progressive bilingualism would be that, while their own literature remained inaccessible to non-French-speakers, and was in this sense class-exclusive, the new Anglo-Norman English would increasingly have had access to texts delivered and written in English, which would thereby become a class-inclusive language.

As well as a vernacular, Anglo-Norman was a language of law and of record, an acceptable alternative to Latin in the cloister, and a literary language in its own right. Rapidly developing dialectal characteristics of its own, which include lexical borrowing from English, literary Anglo-Norman formed a natural bridge with Continental vernacular culture while at the same time retaining its linguistic distinctiveness from Norman and other French dialects. The dialectal colouring in Anglo-Norman literary texts, as distinct from their orthography, is variable: Hue de Rotelande, for

83  J. Milton, *The Tenure of Kings and Magistrates*, London 1649, 3; cf. W. Rothwell, 'The Problem of Law French', *French Studies* xlvi, 1992, 257–71.

84  J. Moore, '*Quot homines?* The Population of Domesday England', *ANS* xix, 1997, 307–34; cf. C.M. Gillmor, 'Naval Logistics of the Cross-Channel Operation 1066', *ANS* vii, 1985, 105–31.

85  C. Clark, 'People and Languages in Post-Conquest Canterbury', *JMH* ii, 1976, 1–33, also 'Women's Names in Post-Conquest England: Observations and Speculations', *Speculum* liii, 1978, 223–51 (both now repr. in *Words, Names and History: Selected Writings of Cecily Clark*, ed. P. Jackson, Cambridge 1995, 179–206, 117–43).

86  Turville-Petre, *England* (note 35 above), 91–8.

87  Wilson, 'English and French', 54; in the fourteenth century the urban bias was very pronounced (Richter, *Sprache*, 173–201).

example, uses a French only marginally different from its Continental equivalent. This poses the methodological problem of how valid Anglo-Norman literature is as a discrete category, more specifically whether dialectal difference alone is a sufficient criterion for admittance to the canon. If so, in what relationship does this body of literature stand to its Continental counterparts, and how far do strict distinctions need to be made between, on the one hand, indigenous production and, on the other, Insular patronage and conservation of literary works in Continental, and specifically Norman, French? To adopt an inclusive approach would seem the most convenient and practical answer to such intractable questions.

However one might explain the three decades of literary silence between the Conquest and the accession of Henry I, Anglo-Norman literature, when it does get under way, immediately lays claim to an impressive series of precocious developments via-à-vis the Continent: the earliest appearance in French literature of the rhymed chronicle (Gaimar), of eyewitness historiography (Jordan Fantosme), of the Celtic-inspired narrative (Benedeit), of scientific (Philippe de Thaon), scholastic (Sanson de Nantuil), Biblical and administrative prose, of monastic rules, the earliest named patrons of literature and women writers.[88]

Whatever its ultimate origins – and they can hardly be other than Celtic – the legend of Tristan and Yseut rivals that of Arthur in terms of breadth of diffusion throughout Europe. Only a quarter or so of what must originally have been a 13,000-line *Romance of Tristan* (c. 1160–90) by Thomas survives today.[89] Incomplete though it is, this poem is regarded by many as the finest achievement of Anglo-Norman literature. A pervading sense of human imperfection and necessary suffering is counterbalanced by a wealth of psychological observation and analysis of love. Thomas's analytical control and narrative concision give the impression of being effortless, as a recently discovered new fragment describing Tristan and Yseut's first falling in love illustrates:[90]

| | |
|---|---|
| Delitablë est le deport | Love-making is a true delight |
| Qui de sa doulur ad confort, | To comfort sufferers in their plight, |
| Car cë est custome d'amur | For love is wont to repay pain |
| De joie aveir aprés dolur. | By bringing pleasure in its train. |
| Pus quë il se sunt descovert, | Those who love's ways together choose, |
| Qui plus s'astient e plus i pert. | The more they wait, the more they lose. |
| Vont s'en a joie li amant | The joyful lovers now proceed |
| La haute mer a plein siglant | Over the open sea and speed |
| Vers Engleterre a plein tref. | To England's shore with full sail spread. |
| Tere ont vëu cil de la nef . . . | The mariners spied land ahead . . . |

88  I. Short, 'Patrons and Polyglots: French Literature in Twelfth-Century England', *ANS* xiv, 1992, 229–49; M.D. Legge, *Anglo-Norman Literaure and its Background*, Oxford 1963; also 'La Précocité de la littérature anglo-normande', *CCM* viii, 1965, 327–49; S. Crane, 'Anglo-Norman Cultures in England: 1066–1460', in D. Wallace, ed., *The Cambridge History of Medieval English Literature*, Cambridge 1999, 35–60.

89  F. Lecoy, ed., *Le Roman de Tristan par Thomas*, Paris 1991. There is a facing English translation in S. Gregory, ed. and trans., *Thomas of Britain: Tristan*, New York 1991. In the thirteenth century Thomas's text was adapted into German and Norse; see C. Marchello-Nizia et al., eds, *Tristan et Yseut: les premières versions européennes*, Paris 1995.

90  M. Benskin, T. Hunt and I. Short, 'Un nouveau Fragment du *Tristan* de Thomas', *Romania* cxiii, 1992–95, 289–319, lines 85–94 (my translation).

*Amadas et Ydoine* is a counter-text to the Tristan story in that it proposes a model of ideal, socially integrated love. Among the shorter narratives, *Le Donnei des Amanz* also uses the Tristan legend as its point of literary reference, while *La Folie Tristan* is a résumé of a version of it close to Thomas's.[91] Le *Lai del desiré* is a fairy-mistress story set in Scotland, and Robert Biket's *Lai du Cor* a parodic Arthurian variation on the theme of chastity-testing.[92] The most widely known exponent of the Breton (= British) Lay genre is Marie. A skilful and learned Continental poet at the court of Henry II or the Young King, she wrote a series of short lyrical narratives around the theme of courtly love, for some of which she claims oral Celtic sources. Though her French is not distinctively Anglo-Norman, Insular culture inspires and pervades her work.[93] A collection of fables, the *Esope*, and an *Espurgatoire seint Patriz* are also attributed to her.

Love occupies a less prominent rôle in the *Romance of Horn* (c. 1170) by Thomas, the central theme of which is the hero's pursuit of his birthright and of dynastic justice. Set in a remote, archaic past reminiscent of the Danish invasions, its epic-flavoured narrative contains a plethora of contemporary social detail. The *Lai d'Haveloc* offers close thematic parallels with *Horn*.[94] Both were to be adapted into Middle English. Influence of epic discourse is very much in evidence also in Thomas of Kent's *Roman de toute chevalerie* (c. 1175), an independent version of the Alexander legend.[95] Although no Anglo-Norman *chanson de geste* survives from the twelfth century, the copying in England of the Oxford *Chanson de Roland* and of the sole-surviving texts of the *Voyage (Pèlerinage) de Charlemagne*, the *Chanson de Guillaume* and *Gormont et Isembart* are additional indications that French epic poetry was known and appreciated in Insular circles.

Hue de Rotelande's *Ipomedon* (c. 1180), a romance of love and chivalry within the courtly tradition, shows a well developed sense of literary irony and parody, though this tends to be swamped by a prolix narrative. *Protheselaus* (c. 1190), written for Gilbert FitzBaderon, is less successful, but its recipe of a runaway plot around a basic theme of disinheritance and reinstatement was clearly popular.[96] It becomes the staple diet of Anglo-Norman adventure romances such as the interminable *Roman de Waldef*, which probably falls outside the twelfth century, and of the influential *Gui de Warewic* (of which there are two English versions), which certainly does. Though not a romance in the generic sense, the *Voyage of St Brendan* by Benedeit is French literature's earliest octosyllabic adventure narrative from Celtic sources. Dedicated to the successive wives of Henry I, it is a vividly written adaptation of the Irish *Navigatio Sancti Brendani*, tightly stuctured and resolutely monastic in perspective.[97] While an Anglo-Norman origin has been claimed for the oldest surviving drama wholly in French, the *Jeu (Mystère) d'Adam* (c. 1150–60?), Insular provenance is assured for *La*

---

[91] Legge, *Anglo-Norman Literature*, 109–15, 121–32; Crane, *Insular Romance*, 181–8. The *Folie Tristan* is translated in J. Weiss, *The Birth of Romance, an Anthology: Four Twelfth-Century Anglo-Norman Romances*, London 1992.

[92] Legge, *Anglo-Norman Literature*, 132–4.

[93] G.S. Burgess and K. Busby, *The Lais of Marie de France*, Harmondsworth 1986.

[94] English translations in Weiss, *Birth of Romance*, 1–120 (*Horn*), 141–58 (*Haveloc*).

[95] B. Foster, ed., *The Anglo-Norman Alexander . . .*, ANTS, London 1976–77.

[96] Both romances are edited by A.J. Holden: *Ipomedon*, Paris 1979; *Protheselaus*, ANTS, London 1991–93; cf. Crane, *Insular Romance*, 158–74.

[97] I. Short and B. Merrilees, eds, *Benedeit: the Anglo-Norman Voyage of St Brendan*, Manchester 1979.

*Seinte Resureccion* (c. 1200), whose fluent dialogue and well sustained dramatic tempo are notable.[98]

Biblical translation is a particular speciality of Anglo-Norman literature, and at least five different vernacular texts of the Psalms, two of which were re-cycled for use in the *Eadwine Psalter*, have survived from the twelfth century.[99] *Li Quatre Livre des Reis* is distinguished by the quality of its rhythmical, poetic prose. The Book of Judges was also translated for the Templars, and at Temple Bruer Henri d'Arci was the dedicatee of four Anglo-Norman verse translations of pious texts. The Hospitallers' Rule was turned into rhyming Insular octosyllables in 1181–85, and a prose versions of the Benedictine Rule also survives.[100] Other religious verse includes French literature's first scholastic text, Sanson de Nantuil's translation and gloss of Proverbs made under the secular patronage of Alice, wife of Robert de Condet towards 1150.[101] Adgar's *Gracial* is a rhymed collection of Miracles of the Virgin. At the end of the century Simund de Freine, a canon of Hereford and friend of Gerald de Barri, wrote a verse vulgarisation of Boethius entitled *Le Roman de Philosophie*.[102]

To the first of the Anglo-Norman poets, Philippe de Thaon, we owe the *Bestiaire* (1121–39; dedicated to Queen Adeliza), *Le Livre de Sibile*, and the *Comput* (1113), the earliest example of scientific French, of which the prologue can serve as a cautionary foretaste:[103]

| | |
|---|---|
| Philippe de Thaün | This text Philip de Thaon |
| Ad fait une raisun | Has composed and set down |
| Pur pruveires guarnir | So no priest should ignore |
| De la lei maintenir. | How to safeguard God's law. |
| A sun uncle l'enveiet | To his uncle he'll send |
| Quë amender la deiet | It so he can amend |
| Si rien i ad mesdit | Any faults he may find |
| Ne en fait ne en escrit, | Of fact or other kind: |
| A Unfrei de Thaün, | He's chaplain to Eudo, |
| Le chapelein Yhun | Dapifer to the Crown, |
| E seneschal lu rei. | Uncle Humphrey de Thaon. |

There are early examples of the use of the vernacular as a language of record and the law, and of the glossing in French of Latin texts.[104]

The field of vernacular hagiography was intensely cultivated in Anglo-Norman. The much praised *Vie de saint Alexis* is preserved in its oldest form as an addition to the *St Albans' Psalter* (1120–30), though the text is probably of Norman origin. To the nun Clemence of Barking, who composed *La Vie de sainte Catherine* in the last quarter of the century, goes the credit of being French literature's earliest named woman author. Her octosyllabic poem is distinguished by the elaborate integration of

---

98  Wolfgang van Emden's edition of *Le Jeu d'Adam*, Edinburgh 1996, has a facing English translation. *La Seinte Resureccion*, ed. T. Atkinson Jenkins et al., ANTS, Oxford 1943, is translated into English in R. Axton and J. Stevens, *Medieval French Plays*, Oxford 1971, which also has a modern version of the *Adam*.

99  See note 31 above, and, for the detail, Short, 'Patrons' (note 88 above), 233.

100  K.V. Sinclair, ed., *The Hospitallers' Riwle*, ANTS, London 1984; cf. 'Patrons', 234–5.

101  C. Isoz, ed., *Les Proverbes de Salemon by Sanson de Nantuil*, ANTS, London 1988–94.

102  'Patrons', 236, 241; cf. Rigg, *Anglo-Latin*, 96.

103  I. Short, ed., *Philippe de Thaon: Comput*, ANTS, London 1983, lines 1–11 (my translation); cf. 'Patrons', 237, 241–2.

104  'Patrons', 242–3, and note 39 above.

the terminology of *fin' amor* into its pious narrative.[105] Clemence may have been the same person as the anonymous Nun of Barking who composed her *Vie d'Edouard le Confesseur*, based on Ælred's *Vita*, in the 1160s. The murder of Becket gave rise to a vernacular *Life* by Beneit, monk of St Albans (c. 1184), who wrote in six-line tail-rhyme stanzas. Other monks composed saints' lives in French: Denis Pyramus, a Benedictine of Bury (St Edmund), and, also from Bury, Simon of Walsingham (St Faith). By the end of the century, the choirs of Anglo-Norman hagiography had been further augmented by lives of Nicholas and Margaret (both Wace), Edmund, Modwenna, Lawrence, Giles by the gifted Guillaume de Berneville, George by Simund de Freine, Josaphat by Chardri.[106]

Anglo-Norman literature is perhaps most widely known for its early and innovative achievements in historiography. Wace, Norman by birth but Anglo-Norman by adoption, completed his adaptation of Geoffrey of Monmouth's *Historia*, *Le Roman de Brut*, in 1155. He stopped writing his *Roman de Rou* (= Rollo) in 1174, when Henry II withdrew his patronage in favour of Benoît de Sainte-Maure, whose vast *Chronique des ducs de Normandie* was left incomplete sometime during the 1180s.[107]

But the scene had already been set by Geffrei Gaimar's octosyllabic *Estoire des Engleis*, written between 1136 and 1137 for Constance, wife of Ralph FitzGilbert. This is all that survives of a much longer and more ambitious chronicle which had originally opened with the mythical Trojan origins of British history, and which closes with the death of William Rufus. Gaimar used Latin, French and English sources, and translates long stretches of the *Anglo-Saxon Chronicle*, which he is one of the first to link with King Alfred and Winchester:[108]

| | |
|---|---|
| Cronike ad nun, un livre grant, | It's called Chronicle, a large book, outsized, |
| Engleis l'alerent asemblant. | Which English compilers made and devised. |
| Ore est issi auctorizéd | Now it is housed with due authority |
| Que a Vincestre a l'evesquiéd | At Winchester within the bishop's see. |
| La est des reis la dreite estoire | Here is to be found the true history |
| E les vies e la memoire. | Of the kings and their lives in memory. |
| Li reis Elvred l'ot en demeine, | Its owner was King Alfred in times past, |
| Fermer i fist une chaeine; | Who had a chain attached to make it fast: |
| Qui lire i volt, bien i gardast | You could, should you wish to read in it, look |
| Mais de sun liu nel remuast. | But never from its shelf remove this book. |

Firmly secular in outlook, Gaimar celebrates kingship, courtliness and chivalry, painting positive pictures of Cnut and Rufus, and portraying Hereward as a freedom fighter against Norman oppression. Not averse to taking liberties with chronology to make his point, he is a pioneer in French vernacular chronicle writing, setting the

---

105 J. Wogan-Browne and G.S. Burgess, trans., *Virgin Lives and Holy Deaths: Two Exemplary Biographies for Anglo-Norman Women, The Life of St Catherine, The Life of St Lawrence*, London 1996.
106 J. Wogan-Browne, '*Clerc u lai, muine u dame*: Women and Anglo-Norman Hagiography in the Twelfth and Thirteenth Centuries', in *Women and Literature*, ed. Meale, (note 33 above), 61–85.
107 J. Blacker, *The Faces of Time: Portrayal of the Past in Old French and Latin Historical Narrative of the Anglo-Norman Regnum*, Austin Tx 1994; P. Damian-Grint, *The New Historians of the Twelfth-Century Renaissance*, Woodbridge 1999.
108 A. Bell, ed., *L'Estoire des Engleis by Geffrei Gaimar*, ANTS, Oxford 1960, lines 2327–36 (my translation). There is an English translation, of sorts, in Hardy and Martin's edition for the RS, ii, London 1888. Cf. J. Gillingham, 'Kingship, Chivalry and Love . . . Gaimar's *Estoire des Engleis*', in *The English in the Twelfth Century*, Woodbridge 2000, 233–58.

pattern for popular narratives that are neither history nor romance, but inseparable amalgams of both.[109]

Jordan Fantosme wrote a largely eyewitness account of the rebellion of the Young King in 1173–74. His mixed-prosody poem, which offers a more or less orthodox providential view of history, borrows from the epic style and maintains a good narrative pace.[110] The poet responsible for the *Song of Dermot and the Earl*, a rhymed history of the Conquest of Ireland between 1152 and and 1175, also looked to the epic for inspiration, but singularly failed to find it.[111]

While its expansion into Ireland following Strongbow's expedition reminds us of the rôle of Anglo-Norman as a language of colonialisation, it had from the start of the twelfth century rapidly evolved into a language of literature, channelling the Matter of Britain to the Continent and, on the home front, providing the new Anglo-Norman English with access to a broad range of texts whose function was as much to 'prodesse' as to 'delectare'. As well as being a widely used adjunct to Latin, it was also the vehicle of an extensive corpus of purely secular literature. To trace its remarkable longevity on British soil would take us well beyond the confines of the twelfth into the fifteenth century.

What gives the literary context of twelfth-century England its unique character is the coming together of three social processes: intellectual renewal, cultural symbiosis and vernacularisation of learning. England was the linguistic crossroads of several co-existing cultures, of which the predominant one, the Norman, had, since the Conquest, been bringing its society and institutions more closely within the ambit of Continental Europe. The Latin, revived also by Norman-inspired reforms within the Church, had always flourished in an environment that transcended the strictly national. The Celtic, despite (or perhaps because of) the political repression to which it was continually subjected, always contrived to maintain a strong and inventive identity and project it outwards towards its neighbours.[112]

As for the English, the production of indigenous vernacular literature had been arrested in its natural evolution by the arrival and consolidation of the ruling French-speaking élite and the consequent loss of the patronage necessary for its survival. At the end of the twelfth century it was only slowly beginning to recover its impetus, apparently catering for the needs of a new female public. Its principal achievement is to be found in its ensuring some measure of continuity with its Anglo-Saxon past while at the same time accommodating to new forms and new functions. It may well be also that native traditions in the use of the vernacular as a

---

[109] Cf. R. Field, 'Romance as History, History as Romance', in *Romance in Medieval England*, ed. M. Mills, J. Fellows and C.M. Meale, Cambridge 1991, 163–73.

[110] R.C. Johnston, ed. and trans., *Jordan Fantosme's Chronicle*, Oxford 1981; M. Strickland, 'Arms and the Men: War, Loyalty and Lordship in Jordan Fantosme's Chronicle', in *Medieval Knighthood, IV: Papers from the Fifth Strawberry Hill Conference 1990*, ed. C. Harper-Bill and R. Harvey, Woodbridge 1992, 187–220.

[111] G.H. Orpen, ed. and trans., *The Song of Dermot and the Earl . . .*, Oxford 1892; cf. E. Mullally, 'Hiberno-Norman Literature and its Public', in *Settlement and Society in Medieval Ireland*, ed. J. Bradley, Kilkenny 1988, 327–43; R. Frame, '*Les Engleys nees en Irlande*: the English Political Identity in Ireland', *TRHS* 6th ser. iii, 1993, 83–103.

[112] R.R. Davies, *Domination and Conquest: the Experience of Ireland, Scotland and Wales, 1100–1300*, Cambridge 1990; R. Bartlett, *The Making of Europe: Colonialisation and Cultural Change, 950–1350*, London 1993.

language of instruction and the Old English cultivation of literary prose exerted some indirect influence on Anglo-Norman literature. The influence of French traditions on English literature, on the other hand, is clear not only in the formal sphere of rhyme and syllabic prosody, but also in matters of literary technique and themes. Such influence was to continue through the reign of Henry III, when it was regenerated by fresh crosss-Channel links, and thence to Chaucer and beyond.[113]

From the early decades of the century, Anglo-Norman French literature exhibits both a vigour and a capacity for innovation which far outstrip anything achieved at the same time in Normandy or northern France – at least to judge from what survives today. In terms of its precociousness, volume and variety, Anglo-Norman literary production clearly benefitted from social conditions both specific and favourable enough to foster its rapid growth. These included a religious community long used to including the vernacular amongst its means of communication, enlightened French-speaking secular patrons, polyglot poets and writers, and, above all, the presence of different cultural traditions interacting together. Literature in French assumed the function of articulating questions of cultural identity and responding to the needs of those whose assimilation gave rise to them. It could also act as a substitute for Latin.

The extent of Continental influence on Insular French literature is difficult to assess, though the importation from Normandy of the *Vie de saint Alexis* and the copying of French epic texts would, for instance, lead us to believe that cultural interchange was a routine feature of cross-Channel life. Whether or not Hue de Rotelande, for example, would have written as he did without knowing the spirit and tone of Chrétien de Troyes' romances, with which he often seems to be in dialogue, must remain an open question. Marie de France and Guernes de Pont-Sainte-Maxence both came from the Continent to find their literary fortunes in England. Benoît de Sainte-Maure, like the Norman-born Wace, was also of Continental (Touraine) origin, and he had presumably already written his *Roman de Troie* before his installation at Henry II's court as historiographer.[114] Although we need to be cautious in evaluating the personal rôles played by Henry II and especially by Eleanor in directly patronising vernacular literature, there can be no doubt that the environment of the itinerant Angevin court was particularly propitious to literature.[115] Troubadours were unlikely otherwise to have been attracted to it.[116]

It would, however, be misleading to view developments in vernacular literatures in isolation from the Latin culture with which they co-existed and of which they formed part. There is no automatic correlation to be made between the vernacular and the secular when it comes to assessing which particular publics were the intended recipients of works in French or English and under whose patronage they were produced. The vernacular texts of the *Eadwine Psalter* had manifestly nothing to do with lay

---

113  E. Salter, *English and International: Studies in the Literature, Art and Patronage of Medieval England*, ed. D. Pearsall and N. Zeeman, Cambridge 1988, 1–100.

114  G.A. Beckmann, *Trojaroman und Normannenchronik: die Identität der beiden Benoît . . .*, Munich 1965.

115  K.M. Broadhurst, 'Henry II of England and Eleanor of Aquitaine: Patrons of Literature in French?', *Viator* xxvii, 1996, 53–84; cf. C.W. Hollister, 'Courtly Culture and Courtly Style in the Anglo-Norman World', *Albion* xx, 1988, 2–17; R.R. Bezzola, *Les Origines et la formation de la littérature courtoise . . .*, Paris 1958–63, ii/2 391–548, iii/1 3–311.

116  Bertrand de Born, Bernart de Ventadorn and Marcabru are reputed to have visited Henry's court; see J. Audiau, *Les Troubadours et l'Angleterre*, Tulle 1927.

readers or commissions. A moment's reflection also will suffice to realise that adaptation and translation from Latin sources account for a large number of the surviving monuments of twelfth-century vernacular literature. This is part of a secondary phase, as it were, of the more general phenomenon of *translatio studii*, and a process of vulgarisation which opens up access to learning to a wider secular community.

It was inevitable that the influence of Anglo-Norman historiography in Latin, which Southern describes as twelfth-century England's 'greatest intellectual achievement', should have made itself felt on secular writers. Gaimar, whose history shares its title with Henry of Huntingdon's *Historia Anglorum*, was in this sense a collaborator in a wider historiographic enterprise. This also true, of course, of Wace who, as well as adapting Geoffrey of Monmouth, made free use, in his *Roman de Rou*, of Norman historical texts such as Dudo of Saint-Quentin, William of Jumièges, William of Poitiers, not to mention those of Orderic Vitalis and William of Malmesbury. Benoît likewise exploits Dudo and William of Jumièges for his *Histoire des ducs de Normandie*. All three were clerics, and particularly scholarly ones at that, who chose to write in vernacular rhyme to cater for the needs of those previously excluded from Latin culture.

While some specific works, particularly the historical and didactic ones, are obviously responses to needs peculiar to English society, it is much less easy to discern any significant Insular specificity within the broader totality of the literary texts produced in twelfth-century England. Both French and Latin, it must be remembered, were international languages, and all literature produced in them belongs to a wider cultural hegemony. In the case of Anglo-Norman, it is as an integral part of French literature as a whole, not as an essentially national sub-culture, that it can most profitably be understood and evaluated. To seek to explain Anglo-Norman romance, for example, by supposing either parochial ancestral concerns or wider and more amorphous political preoccupations, is to subordinate the world of literature to the ultimately conjectural meta-construct of 'real life'.[117] Similarly in the case of Latin, where internationalism is of a greater order still, one searches in vain for any identifiable Englishness in Anglo-Angevin poetry and literature of the twelfth century.[118]

But a hundred years is a long time in literature, and between the reigns of Henry I and John the general picture changes. While the glories of Middle English literature were still a long way off, production does seem, by the closing decades of the century, to be resuming after the ominous silence which had descended on it since the Conquest. Insular French literature, on the other hand, after its early and auspicious start, was, by the 1180s or so, already being overtaken in terms of production, originality and artistry by Continental poetry. It would, nonetheless, be only a slight exaggeration to conclude that, for a short space of history, the courts of Henry I and Henry II and the Anglo-Norman baronage and Church had presided over a literary and intellectual efflorescence of remarkable brightness, a sort of Halley's Comet illuminating its brief passage across the Insular sky. The traces left behind them, however, by these thriving literary communities were significantly longer-lived.

The fact that it was French and not English that shared centre-stage with Latin brings us back to the Anglo-Norman English – be they direct descendants of the

---

117  Legge, *Anglo-Norman Literature*, ch. vii: 'The Ancestral Romance'; Crane, *Insular Romance*, esp. 14–18.

118  Rigg, *Anglo-Latin*, 5, 62–3, 153–4.

Conqueror, of mixed Norman and English blood like William of Malmesbury and Adgar, people who were English by birth and Norman by adoption like Orderic Vitalis, Anglo-Welshmen such as Geoffrey of Monmouth and Gerald de Barri, French exiles in England like Peter of Blois, cross-Channel magnates, or even representatives of the native stock such as Ælred of Rievaulx. There seems little doubt that it was their cohabitation and interaction which, more than any other single factor, explains the emergence of England from the Insular backwaters of the tenth and eleventh centuries into the Continental mainstream of the twelfth.

Viewed by certain of our Victorian ancestors as hardly more than a foreign belch, even though an unforgivable one, at the high table of British history,[119] the Norman Conquest is now by general consensus seen as a decisive and productive turning point in the cultural as well as the political history of our nation. While the different rôles played in the Renaissance of the twelfth century by Anglo-Norman and Anglo-Angevin builders, scribes and artists, and by Anglo-Latin historiographers, intellectuals and writers, are well appreciated and widely recognised, the accomplishments of their more modest vernacular compatriots are a no less important part of the total picture. These, as we have seen, frequently fulfilled the rôle of literary intermediaries, and, through a complex process of inter-cultural exchange, made a real and lasting contributuion to the variety of medieval literature, not only Latin and French, but English also. More originally still, they were directly instrumental in what one might be forgiven for calling the democratisation of the culture of the twelfth century and of the past.

But what the twelfth century witnessed above and beyond this was the start of a long linguistic process (sporadically visible as early as the *Anglo-Saxon Chronicle*, still hesitant in *The Owl and the Nightingale*, but more assertive in the *Ancrene Wisse*) which was, over the next century, profoundly to alter the development of English and immeasurably to enrich its lexical resources.[120] While the assimilation of English words into Anglo-Norman remained local and limited, that of Anglo-Norman into English was to be wholesale, systematic and profound – so much so that there is scarcely (hardly) a sentence (string of words) in current (everyday) English that does not indicate (show), or is testimony (bears witness) to, the profound (deep) and enduring (lasting) imprint from Anglo-Norman that has remained (stayed) a feature (the hallmark) of our language (tongue) since the end of the twelfth century. It is in this particularly rich and expressive quality of English – now a world language shared by over 300 million native speakers and, at the very least, an equal number of second-language speakers[121] – that twelfth-century vernacular culture surely left its most far-reaching and indelible trace on posterity. On which note, it may be as well to conclude that the ultimate victor, thus far at least, of the Battle of Hastings was English.

---

119  E.g. E.A. Freeman, *The History of the Norman Conquest of England . . .* v, Oxford 1876, 547: 'So strong a hold have the intruders taken on our soil that we cannot even tell the tale of their coming without their help. This abiding corruption of our language I believe to have been the one result of the Norman Conquest which has been purely evil.'

120  D. Burnley in N. Blake, ed., *The Cambridge History of the English Language, ii: 1066–1476*, Cambridge 1992, 423–32.

121  D. Crystal, *English, a Global Language*, Cambridge 1997.

# 11

# Ecclesiastical Architecture, c. 1050 to c. 1200

## RICHARD PLANT

The one hundred and fifty years, from about 1050 to 1200, which will be briefly reviewed here was a period of intense architectural activity and change, from the pre-romanesque of Anglo-Saxon England, to the developed gothic styles of c. 1200. While the architecture of Normandy followed a relatively stable course through this period, that of England was convulsed in 1066, one of the clearest signs we have of the profound cultural change brought about by the Conquest. While the conquering Normans imported a style developed in the duchy, they also brought England into the wider orbit of European architecture, and the architectures of England and Normandy followed surprisingly different courses from the late eleventh century onwards.

Romanesque, as with many *post facto* style labels, is resistant to convenient definition. The term is used to describe the predominant style of architecture in western Europe in the eleventh and first half of the twelfth centuries, which was characterised by clearly articulated spaces, well-cut masonry, and decorative schemes subordinated to the overall architectural conception. This was accompanied in some areas by a renewed interest in vaulting techniques and the adoption of a number of Roman architectural forms, for example Corinthian capitals. The style, such as it was, varied markedly in different regions of Europe, and in a fashion which did not always closely follow either contemporary political boundaries or modern ones. It also developed at an uneven pace across the continent, and while Normandy in 1066 appears to have been somewhere near the leading edge of developments in Europe, the picture in the Anglo-Saxon world is far more murky.[1]

Discussion of late Anglo-Saxon architecture is made difficult by the destruction of most of the great churches, and the doubtful dating of many smaller monuments. Indeed, the methodology of periodisation has been the subject of lively scholarly debate; the question is not purely an academic one, either, as the direction, if any, taken by Anglo-Saxon architecture in the mid-eleventh century depends on the body of buildings which are taken to precede the Conquest. Much the most comprehensive coverage is provided by Harold and Joan Taylor's three volume *Anglo-Saxon Architecture*,[2] which tends to be generous in is assessment of the number of buildings completed under the Anglo-Saxons, and credits them with developing features others prefer to see as imported from elsewhere. The problem of what, if anything, is owed by Anglo-Saxon architecture to sources outside of England is dealt with more fully by

---

1   For a recent attempt to define the romanesque style in architecture see R. Stalley, *Early Medieval Architecture*, Oxford 1999, 191–211.
2   H. Taylor and J. Taylor, *Anglo-Saxon Architecture*, 3 vols, Cambridge 1965, 1965 and 1978.

Eric Fernie, but despite his discussion of 'Anglo-Saxon romanesque'[3] it is clear that around 1050 England was far from being the most vigorous region of Europe in terms of architectural production, despite high levels of proficiency in other fields of artistic endeavour. By way of explanation for the lack of building in earlier eleventh-century England, Richard Gem has proposed the widely accepted notion that there was a recession in building in the first half of that century, caused in part by the economic strains caused by the Danish wars and the exaction of Danegeld.[4] This should not be taken to indicate that there was no late Anglo-Saxon architecture – Gem himself notes that architectural production started to pick up around the middle of the century – but it is hard, from what we know of the the architectural remains, to establish a consistent stylistic trend, or to see that England was wholeheartedly joining in the architectural experiments taking place elsewhere in Europe, even if some of the more negative assessments of Anglo-Saxon architectural production are overstated.

Other reasons for the seemingly backward state of late Anglo-Saxon architecture might be offered, of which the liturgy of the late Anglo-Saxon church is one. One of the best preserved churches from this period is that at Deerhurst, which has a bewildering array of small chapels tacked on at different heights to the body of the church. These chapels were used by the clergy both for private worship and stational liturgy, as laid down in the *Regularis Concordia*, a tenth-century codification of liturgical practice.[5] These practices did not encourage the unification of architectural space which is a characteristic of romanesque architecture. Another factor may have been a strand of cultural conservatism among the late Anglo-Saxon clergy. The respect in which the Anglo-Saxons held their old buildings has often been mentioned; there appears indeed to have been a feeling of reverence towards buildings erected or used by the saints of the Anglo-Saxon past, which discouraged wholesale destruction and reconstruction.[6]

What we have discovered of the buildings of the Anglo-Saxons in the past forty years has, however, at least in part undermined the notion that their ecclesiastical structures were meanly proportioned. The Old Minster at Winchester, for example, though dwarfed by its Norman replacement, was built on substantial if largely additive lines; while the cathedral of Canterbury was, on the eve of the Conquest, of approximately the same size as the Norman building which replaced it. Both the Old Minster and Canterbury cathedral seem to have displayed quite close affinities to architecture of the Holy Roman Empire, particularly at their west ends, where Winchester had what seems to be a westwork in the tradition of Corvey, and Canterbury had a western choir. A late Anglo-Saxon building, the cathedral at Sherborne, rebuilt after 1045,[7] also had what would appear to have been a western liturgical complex. While these buildings may have been in their fashion very grand, there is no suggestion that at this period English architecture as a whole was moving towards the coherently articulated and unified spaces of Norman, or indeed any other, roman-

---

3  E. Fernie, *The Architecture of the Anglo-Saxons*, London 1983.

4  R. Gem 'A Recession in English Architecture during the Early Eleventh Century and its Effect on the Development of the Romanesque Style', *JBAA* 3rd ser. xxxviii, 1975, 28–49.

5  A. Klukas, 'Liturgy and Architecture: Deerhurst Priory as an Expression of the *Regularis Concordia*', *Viator* xv, 1984, 81–106, and D. Parsons, *Liturgy and Architecture in the Middle Ages*, Deerhurst 1989.

6  R. Gem, 'England and the Resistance to Romanesque Architecture', in *Studies . . . to Brown*, 129–140.

7  J. Gibb, 'The Anglo-Saxon Cathedral at Sherborne', with an appendix by R. Gem, *Arch. Jnl* cxxxii, 1975, 71–110.

esque. Of the last phase of building in England we have only tantalising, and rather contradictory, glimpses. Apart from Sherborne, a new cathedral was built at Hereford some time before 1056, but we know nothing of its form, and can only guess at its position. Edward the Confessor and his queen built churches at Wilton and Westminster; Wilton was dedicated the sooner, but of its architecture we know nothing. We know precious little of Westminster; there are fragmentary remains of foundations and bases, a schematic image in the Bayeux Tapestry and an ambiguous poetic description, on which a superstructure, largely following that of Jumièges, has, perhaps somewhat overconfidently, been built.[8] Bases found at the east of the church have long been interpreted as similar to bases at Jumièges, and the discovery in the nave of alternating square and cruciform pier foundations has suggested to most (but by no means all) that the nave, like that of Jumièges, had alternating columns and cruciform piers.[9] Evidently Edward the Confessor was looking to the land where he was brought up for architectural models, though another possible connection is through Robert of Jumièges, a former abbot, who became bishop of London and archbishop of Canterbury. One commentator, Richard Gem, has gone so far as to suggest that the relationship between the two buildings should, in part, be reversed; in this view Robert, who was expelled from England, returned to Jumièges to find no nave, and copied the design he he had seen in England.

If the remains of Westminster abbey suggest that English architecture was moving towards a more continental, and specifically Norman, model, other late pre-Conquest buildings suggest otherwise. Harold's foundation at Waltham, perhaps begun in the 1060s, had one of the more bizarre plans of the eleventh century, with a continuous transept and a tiny axial apse, a form which suggests once more some connection with the Holy Roman Empire, where the continuous transept, a form first developed at Old St Peter's in Rome in the fourth century, was in use in the high middle ages. An exact parallel for the plan at Waltham has, however, been impossible to find.[10] In the small village of Great Paxton the three bay arcade and the crossing survive of what is the closest thing to an 'Anglo-Saxon romanesque' church that we have. The pier forms are highly elaborate, both in the nave and in the crossing, with series of shafts divided by small rolls or pointed arrises.[11] The closest comparisons for these piers seem to be in the western part of the Holy Roman Empire, where the form of the transepts, once evidently lower than the nave, was also most commonly found. One final piece of pre-Conquest rebuilding is worth considering; from 1049 onwards two of the complex of abbey churches at St Augustine's Canterbury were linked by a polygonal structure, the form of which has been associated with buildings in the tradition of the palatine chapel at Aachen, or the abbey church at Charroux, but it appears never to

8   E. Fernie, 'Enclosed Apses at Edward's Church at Westminster', *Archaeologia* civ, 1972, 235–60; E. Fernie, 'Reconstructing Edward's Abbey at Westminster', in *Romanesque and Gothic: Essays for George Zarnecki*, ed. N. Stratford, Woodbridge 1987, 63–7; R. Gem, 'The Romanesque Rebuilding of Westminster Abbey', ANS iii, 1981, 33–60; R. Gem, 'The Origins of the Abbey', in *Westminster Abbey*, ed. C. Wilson, London 1986, 6–21.

9   A. Clapham and L.G. Tanner, 'Recent Discoveries in the Nave of Westminster Abbey', *Archaeologia* lxxxiii, 1933, 227–36, denied that the 'weak' supports could be columns; Gem, 'Romanesque Rebuilding of Westminster Abbey'. For Jumièges see below.

10  P.J. Huggins and K.N. Bascombe, 'Excavations at Waltham Abbey, 1985–91: Three Pre-Conquest Churches and Norman Evidence', *Arch. Jnl* cxlix, 1992, 282–343.

11  Fernie, *Architecture of the Anglo-Saxons*, 129–34.

have been finished, and the juxtaposition of contrasting architectural spaces was an experiment abandoned in English architecture for some time to come.[12]

This brief survey of pre-Conquest architecture could be expanded to include other buildings, but the picture, of an idiosyncratic architecture, would not be altered. There are one or two oddities of late (and not so late) Anglo-Saxon architecture worth noting, however. The first is what is known as the salient crossing, when the area where the four arms of the church meet is wider than any of those arms as, for example, at Stow in Lincolnshire. The second is the manner of decoration of the buildings, with strips of masonry. This stripwork, used to surround architectural features such as arches, or as a pattern on towers, does not respond to any structural requirements and adds an air of charming illogic to the flat surfaces of some later Anglo-Saxon churches, such as that at Barnack.[13] Despite relations with continental architectural ideas, there does not seem to be a consistent underlying trend in Anglo-Saxon building design, and it is hard to see what direction Anglo-Saxon architecture would have taken had the Battle of Hastings turned out differently. The Conquest was to change everything.

In contrast to the rather chaotic picture of the architectural scene in England in 1066, romanesque architecture in Normandy is usually presented as developing in a logical and coherent fashion.[14] From about 1020 onwards there was a wave of building, secular as well as ecclesiastical, in the duchy, and though many of the monuments are lost it is possible to trace, through a series of buildings, how Norman romanesque came to be formulated.[15] These buildings are the abbey churches of Bernay, Mont-Saint-Michel, Jumièges, and St Etienne, and to a lesser extent La Trinité, in Caen. As will be immediately clear this list includes no cathedrals, not because none were rebuilt, but because the remains, if any, are exiguous in the extreme. This should warn us against too straightforward a reading of the development of architecture in the duchy leading up to the Conquest, especially as, while certain features of Norman romanesque are consistent, the buildings themselves are quite varied in appearance. Of the 'lost' buildings, perhaps the most revealing is the crypt of Rouen cathedral.[16] begun in the 1020s with an apse-ambulatory and radiating chapels, similar, in some ways to the more or less contemporary work at Chartres. This scheme, whereby the aisles run round the exterior of the apse at the east end of the church, usually serving a set of subsidiary chapels which themselves were apsidal, was one of the standard plans of romanesque Europe (the scheme is shown in Fig. 1 as used at St Augustine's, Canterbury, after the Conquest). In the other main scheme, often known as an apse echelon plan, the central vessel and aisles all terminate in apses, with the those of the aisles ending further back than the main vessel, as at St Etienne's abbey in Caen (Fig. 2).

The first known appearance in Normandy of this latter scheme is at the abbey church of Bernay, now partially reconstructed and the earliest substantially surviving

[12] R. Gem, *The English Heritage Book of St Augustines*, London 1997; Fernie, *Architecture of the Anglo-Saxons*, 157–9, who argues that it was an attempt to provide some kind of romanesque order.

[13] For the salient crossing see Fernie, *Architecture of the Anglo-Saxons*, 124–9.

[14] Two works are particularly useful for Norman romanesque: R. Liess, *Der frühromanische Kirchenbau des 11. Jahrhunderts in der Normandie*, Munich 1967, and the two volumes of *L'architecture normande au moyen âge*, ed. M. Baylé, Caen 1997.

[15] For architecture in Normandy before this date see M. Baylé, 'Norman Architecture around the Year 1000: Its Place in the Art of North-Western Europe', *ANS* xxii, 1999, 1–28.

[16] J. Le Maho, 'Rouen Méconnu', in *Les amis des monuments rouennais*, 1995–96, 62–83.

romanesque church in Normandy.[17] It was founded between 1008 and 1017 by Judith, duchess of Normandy, at the prompting of William of Volpiano, who had been brought from Burgundy to assist in the reform of the Norman church. In this church, unlike contemporary English structures, the liturgical spaces are disposed of in a regular fashion. Apart from the choir, the church has transepts with apsidal chapels on their east walls, a regular crossing, with arches to all main vessels of equal height, and a nave with aisles and a three storey elevation. Above the arcade level, there is a low intermediate storey, known as a triforium, with paired openings into the roof space alternating with blind arches, and above this the window storey, or clerestory. In the nave the piers of the arcades are longer on an east-west axis than north-south, with stretches of plain wall between each opening, recalling the simple arcades of the Carolingian era which appear to be cut through a plain wall. However, on the inner faces of the piers are half shafts, an important element of romanesque decoration, and these support a roll on the lower face of the arch itself, known as the soffit. There is some debate as to whether these half shafts were built with the piers themselves, or added during construction, and if so how late they were added, as the stones of the half shafts do not always course regularly with the piers; but this still marks their first appearance in Norman architecture. In the choir, the bays are divided by half shafts which run up the middle of the piers, again another sign of awareness of the roman-esque aesthetic which stressed bay division. As important for the future of Norman romanesque is the appearance of a passage, in the thickness of the wall, running between the staircase at the end of the south transept and the crossing tower. This functional passage, providing access to high levels of the tower, was to have a great future in Norman and English architecture.[18] There have been some disagreements about when the building was commenced, but it is generally considered that it was complete by 1050, by which time the second building under consideration, the abbey church of Jumièges, was underway.

Unlike Bernay, Jumièges had once an apse ambulatory plan, unusually in this case built without chapels. Jumièges seems to have been begun in 1040 by Abbot Robert, who later came to England.[19] The romanesque choir is destroyed, and has been partly uncovered through excavation, but large parts of the transepts, the nave and the western block survive. The nave, which is now roofless, has an alternating system of supports, cruciform piers with simple columns, though the scheme at Jumièges differs from many previous buildings with this arrangement in that the piers are not joined by a blind arch, the system generally used at buildings in the Holy Roman Empire such as Echternach; rather there were bay-dividing shafts on the piers, and the nave was divided at the middle by a single diaphragm arch running between the two arcade walls.[20] The elevation of the nave above these alternating piers was otherwise uniform, with a large vaulted middle storey, known as a gallery, opening to the nave

17  J. Decaëns, 'La datation de l'abbatiale de Bernay: quelques observations architecturales et résultats des fouilles récentes', *ANS* v, 1982, 97–120; Baylé, *L'architecture normande* ii, 27–31.
18  J. Bony, 'La technique Normande du mur épais', *Bulletin Monumental* xcviii, 1939, 153–88. For antecedents and other continental parallels see P. Héliot, 'Les antécédents et les débuts des coursières anglo-normands et rhenanes', *CCM* ii, 1959, 429–43.
19  Liess, *Frühromanischen Kirchenbau*, 215–16; Baylé, *L'architecture normande* ii, 32–6.
20  Gem, 'Romanesque Rebuilding of Westminster Abbey', discusses earlier churches with pier alterna-tion. On the diaphragm arch see James Morgenstern, 'Reading Medieval Buildings: the Question of Diaphragm Arches at Notre-Dame de Jumièges', in *Architectural Studies in Memory of Richard Krautheimer*, ed. C. Striker, Mainz 1996, 123–5. Older literature claims there were more than one.

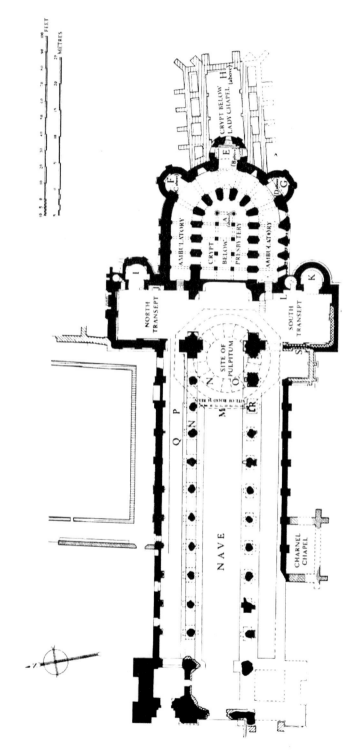

1. Plan of St Augustine's abbey, Canterbury, after 1070
(Crown copyright)

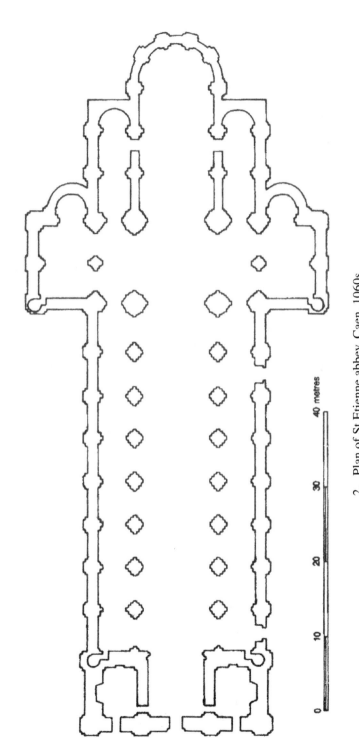

2. Plan of St Etienne abbey, Caen, 1060s
(Dean and Chapter of Canterbury Cathedral and the Canterbury Archaeological Trust)

through a triple arcade, and a clerestory. The proportion of height to width at Jumièges is unusually great. Some commentators, however, have detected signs of slight hesitations and alterations of plan at the east end of the nave, at the junction with the crossing, and a shift from elaborate capitals to simple ones. This has led to speculation that there was a change of design at this point and prompted Richard Gem to explore the idea that the nave of Westminster, usually seen as a derivative of Jumièges, in fact provided the model for that of the Norman abbey, a proposition which has been vigorously denied.[21] If the nave scheme were copied from Westminster, the west end was not; where the English church had a relatively simple two towered arrangement, Jumièges has a more complex western block. This consists of a gallery facing into the church over a deep porch, both of which form a projection in front of a pair of towers. This arrangement seems to have been derived from an earlier church at the site, Saint Pierre, though it also bears a superficial resemblance to some western liturgical arrangements in the Holy Roman Empire, such as the west end of St Pantaleon in Cologne. This latter is almost a western transept, and regarded as such it has another feature shared with Jumièges, since the transepts in the eastern part at Jumièges were filled with galleries as are those at St Pantaleon. This element of the design was repeated in a number of later churches, both in the duchy and, after the Conquest, in England, and it is sometimes explained as providing space for choirs to sing contrapuntally over the (liturgical) choir.[22] The western block is also remarkable for the large blind arches in the walls, which, with the towers, give a sense of massiveness to the building. The masonry is better cut and of considerably smaller blocks than the large stones used at Bernay.

The abbey church of Mont St-Michel was probably begun before Jumièges, as it was initiated by Abbot Hildebert, who died in 1024.[23] However, the earliest part of the church, the choir, has been destroyed and is only known from excavation. It was on an apse ambulatory plan, like Jumièges without chapels; indeed since the absence of chapels at Mont-Saint-Michel was probably conditioned by its location, it may have served as the model for Jumièges. The transepts are supported on individual vaulted crypts, again probably as a result of the geography of the site, although they do contain chapels. The transepts above are barrel vaulted, which is relatively unusual in Normandy at this time and has suggested to Baylé the presence of a designer from Burgundy or Italy, while sculptural similarities to work at Bernay suggest that masons came with Abbot Raoul who arrived in 1048.[24] The presence of vaults in the transepts renders it almost certain that there were vaults in the choir, as when vaults are not used throughout a building they tend to be confined to its most liturgically important parts. The nave, begun after 1058, is more ornate still, though unvaulted, with moulded arches around the low middle storey, and a giant arch, running from ground level to

---

[21] Gem, 'Romanesque Rebuilding of Westminster Abbey', 53–5, disputed by E. Fernie, *The Architecture of Norman England*, Oxford 2000, 94–6, where he denies that there was a change of plan at the east end of the nave.

[22] For a discussion of the liturgical uses of the upper levels of churches see A. Klukas, '*Altaria Superiora*: the Function and Significance of the Tribune in Anglo-Norman Romanesque', Ph.D. thesis, University of Pittsburgh 1978.

[23] The most recent extended treatment is again by Maylis Baylé: *Le Mont-Saint-Michel: Histoire et Imaginaire*, Paris 1998, 101–32.

[24] Baylé, *Le Mont-Saint-Michel*, 106–8.

above clerestory level, possibly borrowed from a similar motif at Speyer cathedral in Germany.[25]

The two abbey churches in Caen, La Trinité and St Etienne, were built by William the Conqueror and his wife Matilda, in part perhaps in order to expiate the consanguinity of their marriage. Vows were taken to build the new houses in 1059, but work seems to have begun on Matilda's nunnery, La Trinité, before St Etienne. Each was destined to be the last resting place of its respective founder, and there is perhaps a sense in which these foundations were intended as the counterparts of Wilton and Westminster, founded by the English monarchs, and reflect the aspirations of the duke and his wife. The presence of the two abbeys cemented the attempt to make Caen an administrative centre in that part of Normandy. What can be reconstructed of the original form of La Trinité seems now archaic compared to the slightly later St Etienne, and this was perhaps apparent even at the time, since the building was heavily remodelled in the later eleventh and twelfth centuries, making the original form of the building hard to reconstruct.[26] The building has an apse echelon choir with a crypt underneath, though the choir walls are solid between the main vessel of the choir and the aisles, and a west front in which a porch, which was originally open on three sides, supports two towers. The building appears to have had a great deal of superficial chip carved ornament but little architectural elaboration. The nave supports were simple cruciform piers with a half shaft on each face; there was no alternation. While most of the buildings we have considered have their aisle walls articulated in line with the the the piers opposite, where an architectural member, a half shaft or pilaster, known as a respond, faces the pier and often receives the transverse arch of the aisle vault, La Trinité has nothing.[27] This perhaps indicates that vaults were not originally planned for the aisles. All the crossing arches were lower than the vessel into which they led, creating a boxed-in effect for the central area: the east and west arches were later heightened. The choir was rebuilt, in stages, starting sometime before 1100, and the nave and transepts were remodelled in the first half of the twelfth century, partly in association with the introduction of vaults. Even the oldest-seeming part of the building, the crypt, may have been an adjunct of the later eleventh century.[28] Indeed much of the attention in this first phase of building, which is now substantially refaced, if not rebuilt, seems to have been concentrated on the carving of capitals.

Precisely the opposite is true of St Etienne, which was perhaps not begun until 1066, and the dissimilarities between two buildings, so close in time, geography and patronage, call into question the idea of a unified romanesque style in Normandy at the time of the Conquest.[29] St Etienne was built on an apse echelon plan, with a two bay choir, which has been replaced, and an eight bay nave (Fig. 2). The transepts have

25  P. Heliot, 'L'ordre colossal et les arcades murales dans les églises romanes', *Bulletin Monumental* cxv, 1957, 241–61.

26  M. Baylé, *La Trinité de Caen: sa place dans l'histoire de l'architecture et du décor romans*, Geneva 1979, provides a thorough analysis of the building, including the complex restorations.

27  For the articulation of vaults in Anglo-Norman buildings see Larry Hoey, 'A Problem in Romanesque Aesthetics: the Articulation of Groin and Early Rib Vaults in the Larger Churches of England and Normandy', *Gesta* xxxv, 1996, 156–76.

28  This at least is the opinion of Baylé, *La Trinité*, 38–40, based both on an interpretation of an excavation report from the nineteenth century and stylistic considerations, contested by George Zarnecki in his review, *Burlington Magazine* cxxii, 1980, 259–60.

29  L. Wood Breese, 'Early Normandy and the Emergence of Norman Romanesque Architecture', *JMH* xiv, 1988, 203–16, explores this notion.

galleries.[30] At the west end are a pair of towers, more or less completely cut off from the body of the church on the inside, but appearing from the exterior to rise out of the last bays of the aisles, which perhaps form the earliest example of the two towered *facade harmonique*.[31]

On the interior the supports in the nave are, as at La Trinité, essentially cruciform, but there is a subtle alternation between supports where the bay dividing half shaft is backed by a pilaster, and those where it is not (Fig. 3). The arches of the arcade and gallery, which are of approximately equal height, are of two orders, and each of the orders is supported by its own shaft. This clear articulation of parts is one of the characteristics of St Etienne, as is the absence of superflous decoration: the arches are decorated with an angle roll, and no more, and the capitals of the earliest phase of the building are a fairly uniform sub-corinthian type. The most complex decoration, a series of rolls and hollows, is found on the inner faces of the crossing arches. Three aspects of the gallery are worth noting: it is vaulted, and the implication of this may be that the choir was once vaulted too; the openings to the gallery are slightly wider that those of the arcade, giving the building a spacious feel; and the gallery arcades are thicker than those of the main arcade below, a technique known as oversailing which was exploited in the gothic era. At St Etienne it was used to provide for a thicker wall at clerestory level allowing for a passage. This was perhaps the most significant innovation at St Etienne, as it took the passages in the thickness of the wall, previously confined to the transepts at Bernay and Jumièges, and employed them in a full circuit of the building at the upper level. Originally there were continuous arcades in front of them, broken only by shafts rising to the ceiling. This is the thick wall, or hollow wall, technique which was to be the hallmark of Norman architecture and its derivatives in England for the next one hundred and fifty years. Indeed, playing with the mass of the wall was to be a principal preoccupation for English and Norman architects for centuries to come.[32]

The construction of St Etienne is a good moment to pause and consider general factors in Norman romanesque. Stone preparation had improved markedly; the large unwieldy blocks at Bernay were replaced by more manageable pieces of stone, at least in the more prestigious buildings, and the quality of masonry by the 1060s was generally excellent. The Normans were adept at the use of vaults, but generally used them only over aisles and galleries and over the more important of the main spaces of the building – chapels and the choir. Partly as a result of this sparing use of stone vaulting, a number of churches were revaulted in the twelfth century. The Norman thick wall was excellently suited to the addition of vaults, even if it was not always the

---

[30] The fullest survey is E.G. Carlson, 'The Abbey Church of Saint-Etienne at Caen in the Eleventh and Early Twelfth Centuries', Ph.D. thesis, Yale University 1968; for the choir, E.G. Carlson, 'Excavations at Saint Etienne, Caen (1969)', *Gesta* x, 1971, 23–30.

[31] There is also the possibility that the facades of Westminster and Canterbury pre-date that at St Etienne, which appears to have been finished quite slowly. The completion date at Westminster is uncertain, but certainly post-Conquest, while Canterbury may have been finished by 1077. For the towers at St Etienne see Carlson, 'The Abbey Church', 264–94; for Westminster see Gem, 'The Origins of the Abbey'; for Canterbury below. On the *facade harmonique* in general in English romanesque see J.P. McAleer, 'Romanesque England and the Development of the *Facade Harmonique*', *Gesta* xxiii, 1984, 87–106.

[32] The principal article remains Bony, 'Mur épais', but see also L. Hoey, 'The Design of Romanesque Clerestories with Wall Passages in Normandy and England', *Gesta* xxviii, 1989, 78–101.

3.  St Etienne, Caen, nave

original intention to roof in stone.[33] Norman architecture seems to have picked up forms from neighbouring areas, and indeed regions futher afield such as Burgundy, the Empire and in its sculpture from Anglo-Saxon England and Italy.[34] In the construction of St Etienne these influences were subsumed into the production of one of the most harmonious buildings of the romanesque era, obeying a strict visual logic.

The position of St Etienne as the supreme monument of Norman romanesque is secured by several factors, some of them not intrinsic to the building itself. In the first place, it appears to be a summation of all the earlier experiments in church building in Normandy; secondly, as will become apparent, it served as a model for many of the romanesque buildings the Normans constructed in England after the Conquest, and many of the succeeding buildings in Normandy which remain appear to resemble it. However, this view is somewhat distorted by the lack of evidence for other Norman great churches contemporary with the construction with St Etienne, and the destruction of most of what was built later at the major establishments. Comparative material therefore comes from buildings of lesser status.

Turning to contemporary buildings first, Bayeux retains part of the west front and crypt of the church consecrated in 1077, but was otherwise rebuilt from the twelfth century.[35] The form of the east end is unknown, but the crypt has no ambulatory, so perhaps had an apse echelon plan. There were platform galleries in the transepts, and, it was discovered during nineteenth-century restorations, galleries in the nave. The thickness of the walls even suggests the possibility that a clerestory passage ran round the building, though there can be no certainty of this, and there is a danger of simply reading features backwards from St Etienne and creating Bayeux as a source for these features. The surviving capitals in the crypt, however, suggest high-quality workmanship. The romanesque cathedral of Coutances was remodelled rather than rebuilt in the thirteenth century, but the eleventh-century building is still pretty thoroughly disguised; it had galleries, but they were unlit, and compound piers.[36] Of the eleventh-century cathedrals of Sées, Evreux, and Lisieux nothing remains; of Avranches little is known apart from an unusual plan of uncertain date in which round and square chapels alternated round an ambulatory, and therefore it is likely to be contemporary with the late eleventh-century rebuilding of Fécamp of the same form.

The best preserved later buildings are from foundations of the second rank: Ouisterham, Cerisy la Forêt, Lessay, and St Georges de Boscherville, while all are elegant enough in their way, are not groundbreaking. In the latter three, as well as the rebuilt choir of La Trinité in Caen, the romanesque apses are preserved, with superposed levels of windows, and in some cases passages, a particularly satisfying

---

[33] M. Baylé, 'Structures murales et voûtements dans l'architecture romane de Normandie', in Baylé, *L'architecture normande* i, 49–78. Vaults, specifically barrel vaults, have been proposed as intended, or indeed built and destroyed, at many of the buildings considered here in U. Bangert *et al.*, *Die romanische Kirchenbaukunst der Normandie – ein entwicklungsgeschichtlicher Versuch*, Freiburg im Breisgau 1982. The ideas therein have not gained wide acceptance, or indeed dissemination, in discussions of Norman architecture in Engand and in France.

[34] C. Heitz, 'Influences carolingiens et ottoniennes sur l'architecture religieuse normande', in Baylé, *L'architecture normande* i, 37–48; M. Baylé, *Les origines et les premiers développements de la sculpture romane en Normandie*, Caen 1991.

[35] Liess, *Frühromanischen Kirchenbau*, 139–48; Baylé, *L'architecture normande* i, 38–9.

[36] J. Herschman, 'The Eleventh-Century Nave of the Cathedral of Coutances: a New Reconstruction', *Gesta* xxii, 1983, 121–34.

composition which bathes the area of the altar in light. Of these smaller scale buildings only Cerisy had the full gallery favoured at St Etienne. Lessay has attracted most
attention for the use of rib vaults, which are argued by some to date from before 1098,
when the son of the founder was buried in the choir, though others point to the use of
the multi-scallop capital, otherwise unknown in Normandy until twenty years later, as
indicating a later date.[37] Cerisy, from the last twenty years of the eleventh century, is
generally credited with introducing chevron ornament to Anglo-Norman architecture
– a motif with a great future.[38] Ouisterham has alternating compound and columnar
piers, which appear to be derived from England, and a number of other churches
appear to pick up their decorative repertoire from the kingdom.[39] The trade in stone
from Caen to England also promoted some contact between the two areas, and at a
time when the two countries were drifting apart architecturally, it seems that a single
sculptural workshop produced works for both Canterbury and La Trinité in Caen.[40]

Fécamp was rebuilt around the end of the eleventh century, with the same ambulatory and alternating round and square chapels as Avranches, and what remains, a thin
wedge of the apse and attendant chapels, is rather plain in appearance. Precisely the
reverse is true of the remaining nave arcade spandrels of Bayeux cathedral,
sandwiched between gothic piers and clerestory. These were built after a fire in 1105
but how long after is a source of some debate, dates as early as 1120 and as late as
1160 having been suggested. The former seems a little early for the decorative repertoire, elements of which seem to owe something to developments in England, though
others are more exotic. The arcades are a riot of decoration; the spandrels have fields
of decoration, rather like a fabric, and over each pier sits a framed carving, some
human, some (mythical) beasts. Each arch has a different type of decoration. It is the
building in which one regrets most the absence of the paint that would have covered
most of the buildings considered in this chapter, yet not one in which one can detect
any great architectural developments.

Despite the fragmentary state of most of the later romanesque work in Normandy,
it remains something of a disappointment. Some building activity went into the
updating of existing churches – both the Caen churches were rib-vaulted, for example.
It is made clear, however, that the heroic efforts of the middle years of the eleventh
century were not continued into the twelfth, by the dilatory reconstruction of the
churches damaged by Henry I. The cathedral of Evreux, for example, damaged in
1119, was not finished until after the middle of the century, and the earlier phases
reveal a structure that was thinly decorated, but one which seems to have been built in
preparation for a high quadripartite rib vault. The building had 'thin walls', that is to
say it had no clerestory passage, and here we are perhaps seeing the groundwork for
the development of gothic, and its affiliations are in part in areas outside this discussion. Viewed as such the building is interesting, as late romanesque it is a little

---

[37] For an early date, Baylé, 'Structures et voûtements', 56–8; against, R. Plant, 'English Romanesque
   Architecture and the Holy Roman Empire', Ph.D. thesis, University of London 1998, 67–9.

[38] For Cerisy-la-Forêt see Baylé, *L'architecture normande* ii, 65–8; for chevron, A. Borg, 'The Development of Chevron Ornament', *JBAA* 3rd ser. xxx, 1967, 122–40.

[39] For Ouistreham see Baylé, *L'architecture normande* ii, 78–81; for connections with England, J.F.
   King, 'Possible West Country Influences on Twelfth-Century Architecture and its Decoration in Normandy before 1150', *JBAA* cxxxix, 1986, 22–39.

[40] D. Kahn, *Canterbury Cathedral and its Romanesque Sculpture*, London 1991, 117–23.

feeble.[41] It is also, perhaps, disappointing in comparison with what the Normans produced in the same period in England.

This corpus, the romanesque architecture of England from 1070 to 1150, is much the largest body of material in this short survey, and no buildings can be discussed in the detail they deserve. Some themes, however, can be addressed.[42] The first thing to emphasise is that all major Anglo-Saxon churches were replaced, if not immediately, then within a half century of the Conquest, with one conspicuous exception.[43] This was Westminster abbey, which may have been retained either because it accorded aesthetically with the Normans' expectations of what a great church should look like, or for the political importance which was attached to it as a physical link with the reign of Edward the Confessor, whose true heir the Conqueror claimed to be. Whatever the reason, Westminster was, in the view of the twelfth-century historian William of Malmesbury, a prototype for later Norman architectural patronage. Of Westminster abbey, he notes that the church which Edward the Confessor built was the 'first of its type of design in England, which all now try to emulate at great expense'.[44]

At first glance the earliest post-Conquest churches in England seem to adopt Norman models in a quite straightforward fashion. Battle abbey, founded on the site of the Conqueror's victory, and St Augustine's in Canterbury are built on an ambulatory plan; the latter also had a crypt, making it somewhat similar to Rouen cathedral (Fig. 1). Canterbury cathedral, rebuilt in its entirety from 1070, seems to follow quite closely the former church of the new archbishop Lanfranc, St Etienne in Caen, having the same number of bays in the nave, being of roughly the same size, with a similar elevation (the gallery was perhaps somewhat smaller), a choir of the same form, galleries in the transepts and so on.[45]

These buildings, however, are known in only a very fragmentary form, and even some of those fragments point to architectural sources outside Normandy. Both Canterbury churches employed a capital type unknown in the duchy, the cushion capital, which appears to derive from the Holy Roman Empire, and became, with its derivative the scallop capital, the standard form used in Anglo-Norman churches. Both also had crypts; that at the cathedral distinguished it from its model in Caen, and,

[41] L. Grant, 'Architectural Relationships between England and Normandy, 1100–1204', in *England and Normandy*, 117–29, at p. 125, and L. Grant 'Early Gothic Architecture in Normandy c. 1150 – c. 1250', Ph.D. thesis, University of London 1987, 52–4.

[42] The standard treatment of the subject was for many years A.W. Clapham, *English Romanesque Architecture after the Conquest*, Oxford 1934. Its successsor is very recent: E. Fernie, *The Architecture of Norman England*, Oxford 2000, with an extensive bibliography. This can be consulted for all the buildings covered in this section and will only be footnoted when a particular point is raised therein.

[43] For the destruction of the Anglo-Saxon great churches, with a strong emphasis on the cultural obliteration it entailed, see E. Fernie, 'Architecture and the Effects of the Norman Conquest', in *England and Normandy*, 105–16, esp. 105–9.

[44] '[ecclesiam] quam ipse illo compositionis genere primus in Anglia aedificaverat, quod nunc pene cuncti sumptuosis aemulantur expensis', *Gesta Regum* i, 418–19.

[45] Among the more important recent contributions on Lanfranc's Canterbury are K. Blockley, M. Sparks and T. Tatton-Brown, *Canterbury Cathedral Nave: Archaeology, History and Architecture*, Canterbury 1997; R. Gem, 'The Significance of the Eleventh-Century Rebuilding of Christchurch and St Augustine's, Canterbury', *BAA Conference Trans.: Medieval Art and Architecture at Canterbury before 1220*, Leeds 1982, 1–19; H.J. Strik, 'Remains of the Lanfranc Building in the Great Central Tower and the North-West Choir/Transept Area', *BAA Conference Trans.: Medieval Art and Architecture at Canterbury before 1220*, Leeds 1982, 20–5; and F. Woodman, *The Architectural History of Canterbury Cathedral*, London 1981, especially 23–45; for St Augustine's see Gem, 'Significance', and R. Gem, *The English Heritage Book of St Augustine's*, London 1997.

4. Winchester cathedral, begun 1079, transept

while the two west towers of the cathedral seem to have beeen modelled on St Etienne, they may have been completed earlier (the cathedral was apparently finished in seven years), and were open to the aisles in a way which integrated them into the body of the nave more completely than at St Etienne.

In the buildings which followed a number of elements appear which make it clear that Norman architectural patrons, or their architects, were seeking to rival the most prestigious architecture in Europe, while using (for the most part) the architectural framework derived from the duchy. This is most conspicuous in the size of the buildings constructed; Winchester cathedral, mausoleum of Anglo-Saxon kings and site of the royal treasury until well into the twelfth century, was built, seemingly, with the proportions of Old St Peter's in Rome in mind, and when it was designed was the largest church built since antiquity.[46] The building of the late eleventh century survives in the crypt and to its full height in the transepts (Fig. 4), while the late gothic piers in the nave are in part a recut earlier fabric. The west end, which lay to the west of the current west front, has beeen excavated, and, while its form is unclear, it was of considerable mass. While other English churches did not quite match the scale of Winchester, many, particularly on the eastern side of the country, came close.[47] This outburst of architectural gigantism was limited both chronologically and geographi-

---

[46] R. Gem, 'The Romanesque Cathedral of Winchester: Patron and Design in the Eleventh Century', *BAA Conference Trans.: Medieval Art and Architecture at Winchester Cathedral*, Leeds 1983, 1–12; J. Crook, 'Bishop Walkelin's Cathedral', in *Winchester Cathedral: 900 Years*, ed. J. Crook, Chichester 1993, 21–36.

[47] See Fernie, *Architecture of Norman England*, appendix 1, 304–6, for a table of dimensions of larger Anglo-Norman churches.

cally. All the buildings over 120 metres were begun after Winchester in 1079 and before 1100; the exception, Peterborough, was begun as a comparatively modest structure and extended during construction.[48] The second limit, the geographical one, extends, as we shall see, to more than just size, since the architecture of the western side of England differs in many respects from that of the east.

The reason for the size of these buildings, at Ely, London, Norwich, Durham and Bury St Edmunds, can hardly be functional, and the motive may be sought in the aspirations of the patrons. Reference, direct or indirect, to Old St Peter's aside, the area of Europe which had previously boasted the most substantial churches, Mainz, Worms and Speyer, was the homeland of the German Emperors, and it may be that the Norman rulers, ecclesiastical and secular, wished to emphasise their new position in the world. Certainly William Rufus impressed observers, if not always favourably, with his new hall at Westminster, the largest of its kind in Europe.[49]

Size apart, a number of other strands can be picked out from the cathedral at Winchester. The elevation of the church is three-storied, as were nearly all major romanesque churches in England, with a clerestory with passage and a substantial gallery. In this it follows Canterbury, and before that St Etienne.[50] The clerestory that survives in the transept at Winchester has been altered in its form, partly to provide support for the replaced crossing tower, and partly to accommodate the transept facade towers which will be discussed shortly, but it is clear that in principle the structure that screened the passage towards the main vessel had three openings per bay, a large opening in front of the window, flanked by twin lower ones, the type that was to become standard in Anglo-Norman romanesque, and which appeared for the first time either here or in a remodelled part of the choir at La Trinité.[51] The design, which was inventively treated by later masons, adds an elegant touch to an otherwise very austere structure.

As at Winchester, most galleries in England were unvaulted. This is not to say that they were not functional spaces; in most of the major churches the gallery had windows. Winchester has an aisle on the east and west side of its transepts, another feature of some architectural pretension, which has been used to connect it to the major pilgrimage churches of southern Europe. Above the eastern aisle the gallery has provision for altars, and in this the gallery replaces the two-storied chapels at Canterbury. The galleried elevation was much the more common of the three storied elevations; Gloucester abbey, however, has galleries (with chapels) in the east arm, but a triforium in its nave (Fig. 6), as did Tewkesbury abbey and a few other churches, predominantly in the west. The end bays of the transepts at Winchester have galleries, another feature borrowed from Canterbury, but their deployment was of limited duration; apart from Winchester, Lincoln, Worcester and Christchurch (Dorset) had galleries in the transepts, as did Ely, though these were reduced in size sometime early in the twelfth century. Other churches, beginning perhaps with St Albans in 1077, ran passages round the transept at both clerestory and at triforium levels. In some later romanesque churches, this lower passage was treated almost like a lower clerestory,

[48]  L. Reilly, *An Architectural History of Peterborough Cathedral*, Oxford 1997, 89–90.

[49]  Fernie, *Architecture of Norman England*, 84–7.

[50]  Though there is some suggestion that there was no clerestory passage at Canterbury; see Fernie, *Architecture of Norman England*, 104–6

[51]  Hoey, 'Design of Romanesque Clerestories', 78–101.

and the reduction in wall mass and increase in light into the building, most visible now at Peterborough, begun in 1118, was an important step in the development of gothic.

Winchester also appears to have had a number of towers over the extremities of the building. Although not planned at the outset, and probably never completed, pairs of small towers were intended to flank the transept facades, an arrangement only known at one earlier building, the destroyed abbey of St Trond, now in Belgium,[52] though it is found in later gothic structures. This was not the full extent of towers at Winchester; along with the crossing tower, which collapsed early in the twelfth century, and whatever stood over the western block[53] there also appear to have been some sort of towers at the east end, and Winchester may thus stand at the beginning of a small group of English churches, including Durham, Canterbury as rebuilt after 1096, Hereford cathedral and St John's Chester, which had eastern towers, some much more substantial than those of Winchester. At Winchester, as later at Canterbury, these towers stood over the radiating chapels in a church with an apse ambulatory plan. At Durham and Hereford they stood over the eastern ends of the aisles with an apse echelon plan. These towers have generally been taken as a feature imported from the Holy Roman Empire, but the distribution of eastern towers in Europe seems to have been relatively wide, even if none are attested in Normandy.[54]

The west end of Winchester is something of a mystery; a large rectangular foundation has been revealed, but it is clear that it was not a two-towered facade of the St Etienne or Canterbury type. Facades in England are surprisingly diverse, and generally very showy. While some churches followed the two tower model (Durham and Southwell, for instance), there were also two west transepts, at Ely and Bury St Edmunds, which have been interpreted as providing buttressing for west towers, or as additional liturgical space and an impressive public face to the church.[55] West transepts are otherwise almost exclusively found in the Holy Roman Empire at this time. There is also a type of expansive facade, known as a screen facade,[56] and several one-offs. The most impressive of these is Lincoln, where a huge western block with three deep niches has been associated with St Mark's in Venice, or alternatively identified as a fortified bishop's palace or a free standing military structure.[57] At Tewkes-

---

[52] J. Crook and Y. Kusaba, 'The Transepts of Winchester Cathedral: Archaeological Evidence, Problems of Design, and Sequence of Construction', *Jnl of the Society of Architectural Historians* l, 1991, 293–310.

[53] For a conjectural reconstruction see J.P. McAleer, 'The Romanesque Facade of Winchester Cathedral', *Proceedings of the Hampshire Field Club and Archaeology Society* xlix, 1993, 129–42, and l, 1994, 153–68.

[54] J. Crook, 'The Romanesque East Arm and Crypt of Winchester Cathedral', *JBAA* cxlii, 1989, 1–36; more generally on eastern towers, M.G. Jarrett and H. Mason, ' "Greater and More Splendid": Some Aspects of Romanesque Durham Cathedral', *Antiqs Jnl* lxxv, 1995, 189–233; Plant, 'English Romanesque and the Empire', 183–99.

[55] J.P. McAleer, 'Le problem du transept occidental en Grande-Bretagne', *CCM* xxxiv, 1991, 349–56; Plant, 'English Romanesque and the Empire', 218–33.

[56] J.P. McAleer, 'Particularly English? Screen Facades of the Type of Salisbury and Wells Cathedral', *JBAA* cxli, 1988, 124–58.

[57] St Mark's: F. Saxl, 'Lincoln Cathedral: the Eleventh Century Design for the West Front', *Arch. Jnl* ciii, 1946, 105–18; disputed by J.P. McAleer, 'The Eleventh-Century Facade of Lincoln Cathedral: Saxl's Theory of Byzantine Influence Reconsidered', *Architectura* xiv, 1984, 1–19; Palace: R. Gem, 'Lincoln Minster: *Ecclesia Pulchra, Ecclesia Fortis*', *BAA Conference Trans.: Medieval Art and Architecture at Lincoln Cathedral*, Leeds 1986, 9–28; freestanding: D. Stocker and A. Vince, 'The Early Norman Castle at Lincoln and a Re-evaluation of the Original West Tower of Lincoln Cathedral', *Medieval Archaeology* xli, 1997, 223–33.

5.  Norwich cathedral, begun 1096, choir

bury the facade has a huge niche, rising nearly the height of the building, perhaps derived at some remove from Charlemagne's palace chapel at Aachen.[58]

Winchester had an ambulatory which served chapels, but instead of radiating from the centre of the apse, they faced due east and were square ended. Variations on the standard plan types appeared in Normandy, at Fécamp for example, as has been noted, but the variations were far greater in England. This has been seen as part of the progressive drifting apart of Norman and English architecture, but Winchester is an early building, as is Rochester, which was in use by 1083. This building had a long aisled choir with a square end from which projected a small axial chapel, though both the form and the date of the choir have been disputed.[59] Square east ends and chapels set at odd angles had quite a future in England; the latter are found at Canterbury in the choir rebuilt after 1096 and at Norwich cathedral, begun in the same year, and in both cases the radiating chapels have subsidiary apses which are angled towards the axis of the church. At Romsey and at the cathedral of Old Sarum from the 1120s, the ambulatory runs round an 'apse' which is square.[60] There is a parallel development in echelon churches, where the apses at the east end are separated from the main vessel by a square wall; this remains at Hereford, and was once at St John's in Chester, where there is evidence for a screen running between the easternmost piers to provide a kind of furniture ambulatory. In general the east end is the least well preserved part of the surviving romanesque churches in England; changes in liturgical fashion, ambition or emulation saw many of them altered, before the Reformation destroyed many more. The best preserved are probably those of Norwich cathedral and Peterborough, where despite the addition or alteration of vaults the best sense of the spatial effects of the English romanesque great church can be gauged (Fig. 5).

These effects often differed between the nave and the choir; for example, St Augustine's probably had columns in the choir and compound piers in the nave; and varying pier design, whether to indicate change in liturgical status or for purely aesthetic purposes, was a forte of church designers in the eastern part of the country. To indicate liturgical distinctions different pier types could be used in the eastern arm and the nave, as was the case at St Augustine's and indeed Winchester, where alternating columns and compound piers were used in the choir and solely compound piers in the nave. Other points could be marked by a single support which differed from all others. For example, there is a single columnar pier at the east end of the nave of Romsey abbey, and two pairs of columns decorated with spirals at the east end of the nave at Norwich, which probably marked out the choir screen and the nave altar dedicated to the Holy Cross.[61] Spiral columns often seem to have marked areas of partic-

58  There was a building claimed as a copy of Aachen in nearby Hereford. Whether this was the bishop's chapel destroyed in the eighteenth century – which had a western niche – or another building has been the subject of some debate recently: R. Gem, 'The Bishop's Chapel at Hereford: the Roles of Patron and Craftsman', in *Art and Patronage in the English Romanesque*, ed. S. Macready and F.H. Thompson, London 1986, 87–96; H. Böker, 'The Bishop's Chapel at Hereford Cathedral and the Question of Architectural Copies in the Middle Ages', *Gesta* xxxvii, 1998, 44–54.

59  Fernie, *Architecture of Norman England*, 115–17; J.P. McAleer, *Rochester Cathedral 604–1540: an Architectural History*, Toronto 1999, 35–7, is the most recent to doubt this reconstruction.

60  M.F. Hearn, 'The Rectangular Ambulatory in English Medieval Architecture', *Jnl of the Society of Architectural Historians* xxx, 1971, 187–208; Plant, 'English Romanesque and the Empire', 201–12; Fernie, *Architecture of Norman England*, 251–2.

61  E. Fernie, 'The Use of Varied Nave Supports in Romanesque and Early Gothic Churches', *Gesta* xxiii, 1984, 107–17.

6.  Gloucester abbey, now cathedral, begun 1089, nave
(Conway Library, Courtauld Institute of Art)

ular importance, the choir and shrine of St Cuthbert in Durham for example, and this may be related to their use at the shrine of St Peter in Rome.[62]

At Durham the spiral columns form part of an alternating system with compound piers; in the nave, although the columns are decorated, none of them have spirals. Alternation of pier types was a common way for masons in the eastern part of England to vary the design of a church. Sometimes, as at Westminster, simple columns and compound piers were used, but increasingly the alternation was between two sorts of compound pier, one often incorporating a columnar element, or, following the second choir at Canterbury, alternation between round and polygonal columns. Later examples of compound piers in England became increasingly complex, and a sort of bizarre climax to this tendency was reached at Castle Acre priory in the twelfth century, where the piers were designed so that the east and west faces would match the face of the pier on the other side of the bay, not the other side of the pier itself.[63] It is this variety of pier forms which chiefly sets apart the architecture of eastern and western England. In the west uniform columnar arcades tend to be the norm; in the naves of Gloucester and Tewkesbury abbeys, the columns were of extraordinary height (Fig. 6). The use of columns often meant that above the arcade level there were no bay dividing shafts, and the pronounced horizontal division of these churches was to remain a strand in English church design until well after the period under consideration here.

With Gloucester and Tewkesbury we move away from the eastern English style; not only do these buildings have uniform columnar supports, but they use – in the nave at least – triforia rather than galleries. They are both (comparatively) modest in size. Both have choirs which are, though somewhat remodelled, polygonal in plan. This plan is perhaps derived from Worcester, the most important see in the region, the cathedral of which had been rebuilt by Bishop Wulfstan, the only Anglo-Saxon bishop who survived for long after the Conquest. Gloucester was begun by Abbot Serlo, who had come from Mont St-Michel, and it may be the example of that house which suggested the use of a triforium, though a variety of other influences, from Burgundy, or indeed from the bishop's chapel in Hereford, have been suggested.[64] Tewkesbury was begun at around the same time as Gloucester – the latter begun in 1089, the former after 1087, though exactly when is uncertain. It had barrel vaults – unusual in an English context – possibly including a barrel vault in the nave which sat above the triforium, leaving the building without a clerestory. The east end was more sharply polygonal than Gloucester, and contained a feature which was to be occasionally imitated in later English romanesque, a giant order, in which a column rises through two (or more) storeys of the elevation unbroken; in the case of Tewkesbury with a gallery springing from the rear part of the columns in the choir. Something like this is described in Vitruvius, and Vitruvius has been cited as a possible inspiration, as

62  E. Fernie, 'The Spiral Piers of Durham Cathedral', *BAA Conference Trans.: Medieval Art and Architecture at Durham Cathedral*, Leeds 1980, 49–58; E. Fernie, 'St Anselm's Crypt', *BAA Conference Trans.: Medieval Art and Architecture at Canterbury Cathedral before 1220*, Leeds 1982, 27–38.

63  L. Hoey, 'Pier Form and Vertical Wall Articulation in English Romanesque Architecture', *Jnl of the Society of Architectural Historians* xliii, 1984, 258–83; B. Cherry, 'Romanesque Architecture in Eastern England', *JBAA* cxxxi, 1978, 1–29.

64  C. Wilson, 'Abbot Serlo's Church at Gloucester (1089–1100): its Place in Romanesque Architecture', *BAA Conference Trans.: Medieval Art and Architecture at Gloucester and Tewkesbury*, Leeds 1985, 52–83.

indeed have different areas of France for various elements that make up the abbey church.[65]

One building that fits with neither eastern nor western groups is the cathedral of York, built by the first Norman archbishop, Thomas of Bayeux. The Norman building has (almost) entirely disappeared above ground, but was thoroughly excavated when the present cathedral needed underpinning. The cathedral that was revealed was aisleless, with elaborate foundations, and an extremely long choir in comparison to its nave. There was a persistent dispute, beginning shortly after the Conquest, between the archbishops of Canterbury and York, and Thomas's cathedral may have been designed to be as unlike the standard Canterbury type of building as possible. Besides its unusual plan, it had an archaic rectangular ring crypt, and both this and the long choir are perhaps most easily paralleled in the Holy Roman Empire, while sources in the Empire and western France have been suggested for the aisleless form.[66]

The Norman replacement of the major Anglo-Saxon churches represents an almost clean break; very little was retained that would have been familiar from an Anglo-Saxon context, though some have seen attempts to revive Anglo-Saxon elements in later buildings. This stylistic break is perhaps the more telling as in smaller buildings Anglo-Saxon building techniques, and some decorative motifs, persisisted much longer, in buildings which are generally described as 'overlap'.[67] It should by now be apparent, however, that the architecture that developed in England was not wholly dependent on Normandy.[68] There was a fairly steady divergence of interests, especially noticeable with the buildings begun in the 1090s, Durham and Norwich cathedrals, and the rebuilding of the choir of Canterbury cathedral. Canterbury survives only in part, at crypt level and in some of the aisle walls, but this is enough to show that it was a remarkable building. The new choir that was built from c. 1096 was the same length as the nave, and had a second, eastern, transept, an idea that may have come from the third abbey church at Cluny. The plan, however, has been connected to the church of St Maria im Kapitol in Cologne. The crypt, which extends under all parts of this new eastern arm, was of unparalleled size for an Anglo-Norman crypt, and had, moreover, an elaborately arranged set of decorated columns, and carved capitals.[69] In the choir itself a number of window openings survive, and are comparable in size to early gothic windows. Though the supports have disappeared, they were perhaps alternating round and polygonal columns; however, a better sense of the growing sophistication of pier design in England is given by Norwich cathedral, where the piers alternate, and the inner order of the arcade is supported alternately by

[65]  M. Thurlby, 'The Elevations of the Romanesque Abbey Churches of St Mary at Tewkesbury and St Peter at Gloucester', *Medieval Art and Architecture at Gloucester and Tewkesbury*, 36–51 (western France); R. Halsey, 'Tewkesbury Abbey: Some Recent Observations', ibid., 16–35 (Maine); P. Kidson, 'The Abbey Church of St Mary at Tewkesbury in the Eleventh and Twelfth Centuries', ibid., 6–15 (Vitruvius); Fernie, *Architecture of Norman England*, 160–5.

[66]  D. Phillips, *Excavations at York Minster, ii: the Cathedral of Thomas of Bayeux at York*, London 1985; Fernie, *Architecture of Norman England*, 122–4.

[67]  Fernie, *Architecture of the Anglo-Saxons*, 162–77; Fernie, *Architecture of Norman England*, 208–19; for an argument in favour of a revival of Anglo-Saxon architectural forms, L. Reilly, 'The Emergence of Anglo-Norman Architecture: Durham Cathedral', *ANS* xix, 1996, 335–51.

[68]  Exotic elements summarised in E. Fernie, 'Architecture and the Effects of the Norman Conquest'; relations, or lack of them, in the later period are discussed in L. Grant, 'Architectural Relationships between England and Normandy, 1100–1204', in *England and Normandy*, 117–29.

[69]  Fernie, 'St Anselm's Crypt'.

7. Norwich cathedral, nave

triple shafts and a section of a column embedded in a compound pier (Fig. 7).[70] At Durham cathedral the arcades themselves are richly moulded, in the eastern part by a series of rolls and hollows, further west with chevron ornament (Fig. 8). The elaboration of the Durham arches is not entirely new – it had previously been found on the St Etienne crossing arches – but until this stage church building in England had, for some reason, largely eschewed ornamentation; later English romanesque embraced it wholeheartedly. Mention has already been made of the spiral piers at Durham, but outside the liturgical foci other types of incised decoration were used on the columnar supports, and these too gained a following at other churches, such as Waltham abbey. The aisle walls are decorated by intersecting arcading, another design that would become common in later English romanesque. Durham is often seen as the high water mark of Anglo-Norman romanesque, a judgement influenced, perhaps, by the role Durham is perceived to have played in the development of rib vaults. Various questions have arisen around these vaults, which Sir Alfred Clapham could claim were 'prior to any important surviving competitor in France by fifteen years or more'.[71] This view has been substantially modified in recent years, as has the view that the arches in the nave gallery, apparently to support the roofs, were prototypical flying buttresses.[72] Investigation of the fabric at Durham has done much to recover the orig-

[70]  E. Fernie, *An Architectural History of Norwich Cathedral*, Oxford 1993; S. Heywood, 'The Romanesque Building', in *Norwich Cathedral: Church, City and Diocese, 1096–1996*, ed. I. Atherton *et al.*, London and Rio Grande 1996, 73–115.

[71]  Clapham, *English Romanesque Architecture*, 57.

[72]  For earlier vaults see P. Kidson, 'The Mariakerk at Utrecht, Speyer and Italy', in *BAA Conference Trans.: Utrecht: Britain and the Continent, Archaeology, Art and Architecture*, Leeds 1996, 123–36; on the galleries, S. Gardner, 'The Nave Gallery of Durham Cathedral', *Art Bulletin* lxiv, 1982, 564–79.

8.  Durham cathedral, begun 1093, nave

inal form of the choir vault, which was rebuilt in the thirteenth century. There has also been an extended debate on the question of how much of the building was originally intended to be vaulted, and on the reasons for the use of ribs. Recent years have seen a notable shift of emphasis from structural interpretations of ribs to iconographic ones, seeing them as a marker for locations of particular sanctity.[73] Curiously, however, vaulting does not seem to have been as much of a priority in England as in some other areas of Europe; the new choir of Canterbury, for example, had a splendid wooden roof.

Architecture after Durham is less well known; in part this is an accident of survival, and in part because the project of replacing the Anglo-Saxon great churches was coming to a close. Exeter and Hereford cathedrals and Peterborough abbey were begun in the early years of the twelfth century, but the buildings that really excite scholars are the rebuilding of Old Sarum cathedral, probably underway around 1120, and the new foundation of Henry I at Reading, both of which survive principally as magnificent fragments.[74] Both these buildings are fairly thoroughly destroyed, but the remains suggest a new (for England) readiness to use decorative sculpture, a trend also demonstrated in the reworkings of Lincoln cathedral in the mid twelfth century.[75] The other major new foundation of the middle years of the century, King Stephen's monastery at Faversham, is less well known than the other two buildings, but may have been one of the first buildings to use polished purbeck limestone.[76] It also, like the rebuilt Old Sarum, had a rectangular east end, a feature shared with Romsey abbey, one of the most exquisite survivals of late romanesque in England, and a building with a very mannered decorative repertoire. One or two of these late buildings employ pointed arches – Durham does for geometrical reasons in its vaults, but the nave at Malmesbury has a conspicuously pointed arcade in an essentially romanesque context.

There were a number of new foundations which were affiliated to monastic or other reformed orders from outside England. William the Conqueror's own foundation at Battle was one such, colonised from Marmoutier. Of greater importance were the houses dependent on Cluny, of which the first was at Lewes in Sussex, and one of which, Lenton, followed the pattern of the great abbey church of Cluny III (and Canterbury cathedral) and had an eastern transept.[77] More pervasive were the Augustinians, who attracted patronage from the royal family, especially for their largest

---

73 See the clutch of articles by Malcolm Thurlby: 'The Romanesque and Early Gothic Fabric of Durham Cathedral', in *Durham Cathedral: a Celebration*, ed. D. Pocock, Durham 1993, 15–35; 'The Purpose of the Rib in the Romanesque Vaults of Durham Cathedral', in *Engineering a Cathedral*, ed. M. Jackson, London 1993, 64–76; 'The Romanesque High Vaults of Durham Cathedral', in *Engineering a Cathedral*, 43–63; 'The Roles of Patron and Master Mason in the First Design of the Romanesque Cathedral of Durham', in *Anglo-Norman Durham 1093–1193*, ed. D. Rollason, M. Harvey and M. Prestwich, Woodbridge 1994, 161–84; Fernie, *Architecture of Norman England*, 131–40.

74 For Old Sarum, R. Stalley, 'A Twelfth-Century Patron of Architecture: a Study of the Buildings Erected by Roger, Bishop of Salisbury, 1102–1139', *JBAA* 3rd ser. xxxiv, 1971, 62–83; J. King, 'Sources, Iconography and Context of the Old Sarum Master's Sculpture', *BAA Conference Trans.: Medieval Art and Architecture at Salisbury*, Leeds 1996, 79–84.

75 G. Zarnecki, *Romanesque Lincoln: the Sculpture of the Cathedral*, Lincoln 1986, though some of the sculpture has been the subject of lively discussion about its dating.

76 Fernie, *Architecture of Norman England*, 178–9.

77 For Lenton see R.H. Elliott and A.E. Berbank, 'Lenton Priory: Excavations 1943–1951', *Transactions of the Thoroton Society* lvi, 1952, 41–53.

house in England, Holy Trinity Aldgate, in London.[78] This survives now only as a fragment, but was once a building of the greatest elaboration. In contrast, London's other Augustinian house, St Bartholomew's, seems almost self-consciously plain, which could have been the result either of the poor financial state of the house, or of a desire for austerity. Certainly some of the early churches of the Augustinians, like that at Portchester, seem to have been relatively plain. Others, however, tended to the ornate, the west front of St Botolph's priory in Colchester, the earliest house of the Augustinians in England, being covered in blind arcading despite being made from brick. A number of Augustinian churches also have giant orders, as at Dunstable and Oxford cathedral, and perhaps at St Mary Overy, Southwark, and Holy Trinity, Aldgate,[79] but the Oxford scheme is perhaps more plausibly related to imitation of local examples such as Reading.[80] The last great Augustinian church of our period was the (now destroyed) extension to Waltham, built at the instigation of Henry II in the 1170s.[81]

There were other reformed orders in the twelfth century; two even originated in the Anglo-Norman realm, though little has survived of their architecture. One peculiarity of the Gilbertines was that their houses contained both canons and nuns, entailing complex arrangements of buildings for both communities.[82] The Savignacs were a Norman order founded in 1112 who flourished, particularly in the duchy, in the earlier part of the century, but after a slight decline were subsumed into the Cistercian order in 1147. Very little Savignac architecture survives, and in fact much of the little that is known of the church architecture has to be inferred from fragments and excavations in England, above all at Furness, where parts of the Savignac church survive amidst the later Cistercian rebuildings.[83]

By far the most successful of the reformed orders of the twelfth century, spiritually, politically and architecturally, were the Cistercians.[84] The order was founded at the end of the eleventh century, partly inspired by an ascetic reaction to the artistic and liturgical excesses of Cluniac monasticism. The first Cistercian house in England was at Waverley, founded in 1128, and there were over thirty by the middle of the century, including the recently converted Savignac houses. As part of their desire for a simple

---

[78]  The Augustinians have perhaps not received the treatment they deserve from architectural historians: see J.C. Dickinson, 'Les premières constructions des chanoines réguliers en Angleterre', *CCM* x, 1967, 179–98.

[79]  For Southwark see B. Cherry and N. Pevsner, *The Buildings of England: London 2, South*, Harmondsworth 1994, 566; research on Holy Trinity by Richard Lea and John Schofield will be published shortly.

[80]  R. Halsey, 'The 12th-Century Church of St Frideswide's Priory', *Saint Frideswide's Monastery at Oxford: Archaeological and Architectural Studies*, ed. J. Blair, Oxford 1990, 115–68, at 155–60.

[81]  P.J. Huggins, K.N. Bascombe and R.M. Huggins, 'Excavations of the Collegiate and Augustinian Churches, Waltham Abbey, Essex, 1984–87', *Arch. Jnl* cxlvi, 1989, 477–537.

[82]  W. St J. Hope, 'The Gilbertine Priory of Watton, in the East Riding of Yorkshire', *Arch. Jnl* lviii, 1901, 1–34.

[83]  L. Grant, 'The Architecture of the Early Savignacs and Cistercians in Normandy', *ANS* x, 111–43.

[84]  They have also been most successful in attracting the attention of architectural historians; recent general works on Cistercian architecture in England include P. Fergusson, *Architecture of Solitude: Cistercian Abbeys in Twelfth-Century England*, Princeton 1984; R. Halsey, 'The Earliest Architecture of the Cistercians in England', in *Cistercian Art and Architecture in the British Isles*, ed. C. Norton and D. Park, Cambridge 1986, 65–85; and *The Cistercian Abbeys of Britain: Far from the Concourse of Men*, ed. D. Robinson, London 1998, especially the essay by N. Coldstream, 'The Cistercians as Builders', 35–61. Both the first and last of these works contain gazetteers.

life the Cistercians chose unpopulated and relatively unpropitious locations, which sometimes resulted in the need for rapid relocation as the site proved uninhabitable.[85] This, however, has had the advantage of leaving the sites of the monasteries relatively undisturbed in the years since they were dissolved and therefore susceptible to archaeological investigation and Romantic contemplation. The Cistercians were enjoined in their architecture to build simply, and the maintenance of architectural propriety and observation of architectural models were aided by an annual meeting of all the abbots at Cîteaux in Burgundy, and by the visitation of each abbey by the abbot of its founding house. A great deal of uniformity has been discerned in early Cistercian architecture: the plans of the earliest stone churches in England are extremely similar – simple aisleless naves, square chancels and stubby transepts somewhat separated from the main vessel of the church.[86]

Expansion of the order led, fairly rapidly, to an expansion of the churches, and a number of English monasteries, including the three important Yorkshire houses of Fountains, Rievaulx and Kirkstall, were rebuilt along the lines of what has become known as the Bernardine plan, with a square aisleless chancel, with transepts with square ended chapels. The plan is so called after the church built at St Bernard's house at Clairvaux in Burgundy, and other aspects of the Burgundian romanesque also seem to have been employed at the English churches. The elevation of all three was of two storeys, rather than the standard Anglo-Norman three, and at Rievaulx and Fountains the aisles were vaulted with pointed barrel vaults at right angles to the main vessel. Rievaulx, begun soon after 1147, is mostly destroyed, but appears to have been closer to Burgundian simplicity than Fountains, from the 1150s, where cylindrical piers with scallop capitals and multiply-ordered arches, familiar from Anglo-Norman romanesque, are employed.[87] The next major church for which we have evidence, Kirkstall, introduces still more complex elements: rib vaults for the aisles, and piers composed of multiple shafts. The sources for these have been variously identified in Burgundy, northern France or from an earlier English romanesque tradition.[88]

The third quarter of the twelfth century, in greater churches at least, brought the transition from romanesque to gothic. Treatment of the advent of the new French style has, however, been uneven. In England both national sentiment and the marked idiosyncrasy of the buildings have provoked extended debate on the reception of gothic, while Norman early gothic has been less extensively discussed. The subject is complicated in both cases by the obvious debts which gothic architecture, as formulated in the French royal demesne in the mid twelfth century, owed to Anglo-Norman precedent.[89] Rib vaults are an obvious example and in some case early gothic buildings in Normandy appear to be a be a continuation of romanesque predecessors. As has been noted, the cathedral of Evreux, which was destroyed by fire by Henry I in 1119, retains some of the romanesque west bays of the nave from the rebuilding which

85  Fergusson, *Architecture of Solitude*, 173–4, provides a list.

86  See plans on p. 40 of Coldstream, 'The Cistercians as Builders'.

87  P. Fergusson and S. Harrison, *Rievaulx Abbey: Community, Architecture, Memory*, New Haven and London 1999, 69–81.

88  M. Thurlby, 'Some Design Aspects of Kirkstall Abbey', *BAA Conference Trans.: Yorkshire Monasticism: Archaeology, Art and Architecture*, Leeds 1995, 62–72.

89  A matter discussed at length in J. Bony, *French Gothic Architecture of the 12th and 13th Centuries*, Berkeley 1983, and R. Branner, 'Gothic Architecture 1160–1180 and its Romanesque Sources', *Studies in Western Art: Acts of the 20th International Congress of the History of Art* i, Princeton 1963, 92–104.

followed the fire. These appear, along with the now destroyed choir, to have been rib-vaulted. Thereafter the duchy appears to have been peripheral to what is generally regarded as the central thrust of the development of French gothic.[90] The earliest gothic in Normandy provides a convenient pair of churches which display the slightly ambivalent feelings which Norman patrons displayed to gothic innovations. The abbey of Fécamp and the cathedral of Lisieux present the 'Norman' and the 'French' alternative interpretations of the new style at approximately the same period. The cathedral of Lisieux (Fig. 9), begun around 1170, displays intimate knowledge of the latest French trends, with columnar supports and foliate capitals. The vaults are supported on tubular triple shafts which rest on top of the arcade capitals. The whole thing looks like a scaled-down version of Laon cathedral, though there is only a three storey elevation to Laon's four, with a large middle storey. The nave has flying buttresses, possibly derived from Mantes, and the upper walls are thin.[91] The rebuilding of the abbey of Fécamp, begun after a fire in 1168, preserves in a small section of the choir the romanesque elevation, discussed above. Despite later remodelling, it is clear that this was reworked to fit the gothic elevation, and cannot be said to condition the form of the church. However, the capital forms of the new work west of the romanesque bay are close to romanesque capital types, and a sense of conservatism, based on the traditions of a house intimately connected to the earliest dukes of Normandy, and artistic links to England may have encouraged the very Norman interpretation of French style. The piers are compound, the middle storey is a vaulted gallery, and there is a passage at the level of the clerestory windows. The transept terminal walls look in some respects like those of Peterborough, though with the pointed arch used throughout. There appears to have been a thwarted desire to build a double ambulatory around the east end of the church.[92]

We have lost a number of other important buildings in Normandy, the greater part of the Cistercian abbey of Mortemer for example, but it seems that the model of Fécamp prevailed, at least for a while, at churches like that at Eu, where the gothic of the duchy was imbued with a strong admixture of Norman traditionalism. The rebuilding of the choir of Caen, on the other hand (Fig. 10), displays a number of features derived from the Paris region, such as the large oculus windows lighting the gallery; indeed the very form of the choir may have been derived from St Denis. However, it also shows strong affinities with the choir of Canterbury cathedral as rebuilt after 1174, often in the kinds of small detail which display intimate knowledge of one building by the builders of another; the form of the clerestory, for example, appears to be derived from the transepts of the English cathedral. For this and other reasons the date and construction campaigns of the building, once assumed to be early thirteenth-century and marked by a clear break in the design between plan and elevation, have been convincingly combined into a single campaign probably starting in the

---

[90] See for example the scanty treatment in Bony *French Gothic Architecture*. The most recent, though very brief, overview of the subject is A. Erlande-Brandenburg, 'Architecture gothique normande', in Baylé, *L'architecture normande* i, 127–36; much more substantial is L. Grant, 'Gothic Architecture in Normandy, 1150–1250', Ph.D. thesis, University of London 1987.

[91] Grant, 'Gothic Achitecture', 74–83; W. Clarke in Baylé, *L'architecture normande* ii, 168–77.

[92] Grant, 'Gothic Architecture', 61–3, 66–9; M. Baylé, 'La première sculpture gothique à la Trinité de Fécamp', in *Pierre, lumière couleur: Études d'histoire de l'art du Moyen Âge*, ed. F. Joubert and D. Sandron, Paris 1999, 89–101.

9.  Lisieux cathedral, begun 1170, nave

10.  St Etienne abbey, Caen, late twelfth-century, choir

1180s.[93] The turning bays of the choir stand on paired columns of unequal size, which probably had narrow shafts betwen them; the piers in the straight bays are compound. It has, like the romanesque work to which it is joined, a vaulted gallery and a clerestory with a passage. The decorative repertoire, however, is much more elborate; there are foiled recesses in the spandrels, and a variety of geometric ornament used on the various architectural members. The decoration gets subtly richer in the turning bays by the chapels; the pier between the chapels have *en délit* shafts, that is, long stone monoliths set against the grain, while the shafts on the straight bays are coursed with the body of the pier. The exterior is superb, the chapels are contained under a single continuous roof, two sets of flying buttresses reach up to support the vaults, and two pairs ot turrets mark the springing of the apse. It is one of the most satisfying gothic choirs of whatever region, and its appeal was obviously felt by those who designed the choirs of Bayeux, Lisieux and Coutances cathedrals in the first half of the thirteenth century, who produced elaborated versions of the Caen type.

It is curious that Normandy seems to have played little part in the transmission of gothic to England. Discussion of early English gothic architecture has tended to centre on the 'hows' and 'wheres' of transmission of the style from its homeland in France to England.[94] The question is complicated by a number of factors; one, as in Normandy, is the role of Anglo-Norman romanesque in the development of gothic. There are, indeed, a number of buildings in which some features which appear 'French' and 'gothic' are grafted onto buildings which are in general conception more English and romanesque. St Frideswide's, Oxford, and Winchester Holy Cross are the clearest examples. At Oxford gothic capital types and a reduction in ornament contrast with an elevation of giant order columns and round arches, and at St Cross, which uses a number of gothic features, rather French looking vault shafts are combined with a traditional English thick wall structure.[95] A further factor is the appearance, at similar times, of three quite diverse approaches to the use of gothic in different parts of England. Roughly speaking, these areas can be defined as the west, where Wells cathedral, begun c. 1180, stands as the best example; the north, epitomised by Ripon and some of the Cistercian houses; and the south-east, for which Canterbury is the obvious exemplar.

In the north the debates about the advent of gothic have centred to an unusual degree on the role played by the Cistercians, and that of the now destroyed rebuilding of the choir of York Minster. This is in part due to the disproportionately high percentage of great churches being built, or rebuilt, by the Cistercians at that time.[96] The first use of gothic motifs in Cistercian architecture in England appears to have been in monastic buildings, rather than the churches themselves. It is a feature of early

93  L. Grant, 'The Choir of St Etienne in Caen', in *Medieval Architecture and its Intellectual Context: Studies in Honour of Peter Kidson*, ed. E. Fernie and P. Crossley, London 1990, 113–25.

94  The fundamental article is J. Bony, 'French Influences on the Origin of English Gothic Architecture', *Jnl of the Warburg and Courtauld Institutes* xii, 1949, 1–15; more recently P. Draper, 'Recherches récentes sur l'architecture dans les Iles Britanniques à la fin de l'époque romane et au début du gothique', *Bulletin Monumentale* cxliv, 1986, 305–28, provides an overview of the literature on the subject; the only other recent overview is in G. Kowa, *Architektur der englischer Gotik*, Köln 1990.

95  R. Halsey, 'St Frideswide's Priory'; Y. Kusaba, 'The Architectural History of the Church of the Hospital of St Cross and its Place in the Development of English Gothic Architecture', Ph.D. thesis, Indiana University 1983.

96  C. Wilson, 'The Cistercians as "Missionaries of Gothic" ', in *Cistercian Art and Architecture in the British Isles*, 88–116.

Cistercian architecture that more elaboration was allowed in the chapter house than elsewhere, and the conventual buildings of Fountains and Rievaulx, from the late 1140s and 1150s, seem to have employed a number of gothic features, or perhaps it is fairer to say features which were later to become staples of north British gothic.[97]

The transformation of Cistercian church architecture is apparent in a number of ways, such as the addition of a third storey to the elevation, and the change of piers from the simple supports found at Fountains to the sets of bundled shafts – fasciculted piers – intimated at Kirkstall. This was a form that was to become common in the north, and which seems to have been derived from north-eastern France, and perhaps before that Burgundy. Transept chapels, which previously had been divided from each other by a solid wall, were opened up. All these features are found at Furness, in the alterations to the formerly Savignac church from about 1160, though even here a certain amount of romanesque detailing was retained, and for some commentators the solidity of the structures renders it less than fully gothic.[98] At Roche, from c. 1170, the building was fully rib vaulted, comparatively rare in the north at this time, with a middle storey which was blind rather than isolated openings into roof space. The building has, however, shafts which articulate the bays into clear compartments.[99]

If these buildings are not the earliest gothic structures in the north of England, they may at least show some of the processes by which the new style became assimilated. Of the (partially) remaining buildings, there has been much debate about the precedence of the Cistercian church at Byland over the minster at Ripon, or *vice versa*, which recent investigations have partially clarified. Ripon has been dated as early as the 1160s, but examination of a charter to the church indicates that work may still have been underway on the choir in 1180.[100] On the other hand, work at Byland has found an earlier church, which suggests the current building would not necessarily have been begun before 1177, when the monks occupied the site.[101] The designs of the two buildings are closely related, though, surprisingly, the Cistercian house is the more richly ornamented. It is often suggested that the design of Ripon was heavily influenced by the rebuilding of the choir of York Minster, begun sometime after 1154 when Roger of Pont l'Evêque, who later supported the rebuilding of Ripon, became archbishop. The choir of York has disappeared, and the remaining fragments have yet to be fully analysed and published, but it is clear that above an ornate late romanesque crypt, albeit one with some stylistic affinities to the Burgundian romanesque out of which Cistercian architecture grew, was a choir with some northern French early gothic features.[102] It has been argued that these gothic/Cistercian elements were first found in north-eastern France, and were first employed in English Cistercian churches, though the destruction of many of the buildings in France, such as Dommartin, and indeed of York itself, makes the exact process of transmission hard to track.

Ripon has survived much better that any of the other buildings we have been

97   Fergusson, *Architecture of Solitude*, 50–1, 54–5.
98   Fergusson, *Architecture of Solitude*, 55–61; Coldstream, 'Cistercians as Builders', 45–7.
99   Fergusson, *Architecture of Solitude*, 62–6.
100  S. Harrison and P. Barker, 'Ripon Minster: an Archaeological Analysis and Reconstruction of the 12th-Century Church', *JBAA* clii, 1999, 49–78.
101  S. Harrison, *Byland Abbey*, London 1999.
102  Much the fullest account of Roger's choir at York and its place in northern British gothic is in Wilson, 'Cistercians'.

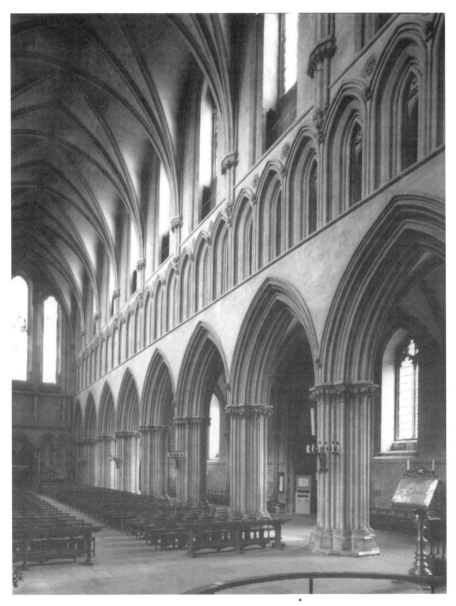

11. Wells cathedral, late twelfth-century, nave
(Conway Library, Courtauld Institute of Art)

discussing, in as much as its choir survives for most of its height. It is an unmistakeably gothic church,[103] vertical in its emphasis, the linear qualities of all its elements being stressed by their slenderness. Above the bundled piers, the bays are emphatically divided by groups of five shafts, which sit, in a French fashion, immediately on top of the abacus of the piers. The walls appear thinner than buildings of the Anglo-Norman tradition, an effect partly acheived by having the upper walls oversail the aisles. However, the upper stages of the choir were less French. The clerestory has a passage running through it, and the plan to vault was abandoned, the shafts intended to support the vault stop at the clerestory sill, giving a horizontal aspect to the upper elevation. Byland has a still more English air to it,[104] in part because the articulation of the building is richer. It was also never intended to have a stone vault, though there were slim shafts dividing the bays, the building was probably covered by a wooden barrel. Byland also has a plan which is suspected for York and Ripon, with an aisle running around the square east end of the building, in a manner similar to Romsey, though this scheme also appears in continental Cistercian houses.

There are many questions about the ways in which northern English gothic, which in itself should not be seen in isolation from contemporary developments in Scotland, related and continued to relate to French. It is difficult to construct a watertight lineage when so many buildings, not only in England but also in France, have been destroyed. It also seems that northern English gothic used its source material in rather different ways to its French models. Although bundled or fasciculated piers were used in French building, they were, at least as far as we can tell, relatively unusual, and tended in any case to be used in less important buildings than the church itself. Likewise, northern gothic abandoned stone vaults. Ripon was planned for them, but for some reason, perhaps financial, they were not built. Thereafter, at Byland, wooden vaults were used.

The west country also has a Cistercian building with early gothic tendencies, Abbey Dore, which itself has caused argument as to the contribution made by English, French and Cistercian traditions. In the west of England, however, Cistercian architectural values seem to have made less of an impact, and at Dore itself French gothic-derived features in the transepts and east end coexisted with a columnar nave in the tradition of west-country romanesque.[105]

The principal twelfth-century gothic church in the west country, Wells cathedral, is an extraordinary building, and some extraordinary claims have been made for it. It has been claimed by some as the first fully gothic building anywhere (including France),[106] while others might see it as hardly gothic at all, having a marked sense of

---

[103] The fullest discussion of Ripon is in M.F. Hearn, *Ripon Minster: the Beginning of the Gothic Style in Northern England*, Transactions of the American Philosophical Society lxxiii/6, Philadelphia 1983, who claims it, as the title suggests, as the first gothic building in northern England, designed in part by a mason who had worked at Laon; but see also Harrison and Barker, 'Ripon Minster'.

[104] Wilson, 'Cistercians', 112–15, argues it is a copy of Ripon; Harrison and Barker claim the two buildings were in part designed together, perhaps by the same masons (75 and n. 46). See also Harrison, *Byland Abbey*; P. Fergusson, 'The South Transept Elevation of Byland Abbey', *JBAA* 3rd ser. xxxviii, 1975, 155–76, who believed the church derived much of its vocabulary directly from France; and Fergusson, *Architecture of Solitude*, 69–90.

[105] The most recent contribution on Abbey Dore is S. Harrison and M. Thurlby, 'An Architectural History', in *A Definitive History of Dore Abbey*, ed. R. Shoesmith and R. Richardson, Wootan Almely 1997, 45–62.

[106] J. Harvey, 'The Building of Wells Cathedral, 1: 1175–1307', in *Wells Cathedral, a History*, ed. L.S.

horizontality and a traditional thick wall. Indeed, one of the very aspects that is most gothic at Wells, the multitude of fine shafts, also emphasises the solidity of the structure beneath. Much of the banded effect which one finds in the Wells nave (Fig. 11) is the result of an alteration to the design of the transept. The number of arches in the triforium was increased from two to three, and the shafts which support the high vaults spring from the spandrels of the triforium, instead of its sill, thereby rendering the arcade and triforium as almost independent horizontal storeys. It is clear that Wells belongs also in a tradition of design, or at least decoration, of buildings in the west country, which stretches back into the romanesque period.[107] This is most apparent in the prevalence of arches with no capitals, and the habit of placing two arches of the same curvature, one within the other. The only surface ornamentation in what is otherwise a curiously modern-feeling building is decorative rosettes placed in sunken circles, another motif related to earlier west-country buildings. The building has comparatively recently been shown to date from around 1180, and its position in the evolution, if that is the right word, of west-country gothic has been reassessed

Wells was not the model for other west-country gothic buildings. The best extant predecessor on the road to gothic in the west is provided by the west bays of Worcester cathedral, after 1175, which are in many respects an elongated version of a romanesque elevation, though a number of the architectural elements are starved into gothic slenderness. A few miles away from Wells, masons working in the same tradition, and probably beginning somewhat later, after 1184, were producing the Lady Chapel at Glastonbury, in a fashion which, while it takes certain up-to-date architectural motifs, does so in a style which is defiantly romanesque. Shortly after this the abbey church at Glastonbury was also rebuilt, and in this case the the building is gothic in its general outlines, but employs romanesque ornament, and indeed the giant order which had first been employed at Tewkesbury nearly a century before. Explanation of the differing styles of these buildings have been diverse, from the character of the masons to the differing nature of the institutions which commissioned them.[108]

The future of English gothic, however, did not belong with Wells, but with the choir of Canterbury cathedral (Fig. 12), begun after a fire in 1174.[109] Canterbury is responsible for popularising many of the elements of later English gothic, notably the use of coloured polished limestone for piers and shafts, second eastern transepts and, perhaps, the use of a spacious retrochoir. The gothic rebuilding was, however, not the

---

Colchester, Shepton Mallet 1982, 53; it is notable that Jean Bony, who thought that the church was begun later than has subsequently been shown to be the case, believed it in a period beyond the reach of French influence, Bony, 'French Influence', 13.

107  H. Brakspear, 'A West Country School of Masons', *Archaeologia* lxxxi, 1931, 1–18, was the first to identify this phenomenon, claiming Malmesbury as the first building to display these characteristics; C. Wilson, 'The Sources of the Late Twelfth-Century Work at Worcester Cathedral', *BAA Conference Trans.: Medieval Art and Architecture at Worcester Cathedral*, Leeds 1978, noted other features stretching back to Gloucester, and noted a number of Burgundian features at Malmesbury, though see M. Thurlby, 'Hereford Cathedral: the Romanesque Fabric', *BAA Conference Trans.: Medieval Art and Architecture at Hereford Cathedral*, Leeds 1995, 20, for earlier English examples of decorative paterae. Wilson points to a number of convincing Ile de France parallels for some of the more gothic elements of Worcester and Keynsham.

108  For the former, Harvey, 'Building of Wells'; for the latter, P. Draper, 'Interpreting the Architecture of Wells Cathedral', in *Artistic Integration in Gothic Buildings*, ed. V. Chieffo Raguin, K. Brush and P. Draper, Toronto 1996, 114–30.

109  The most extended recent treatment of the new choir is in Woodman, *Architectural History of Canterbury Cathedral*, 87–130.

12.  Canterbury cathedral, choir, after 1174
(Conway Library, Courtauld Institute of Art)

originator of any of these. The most popular polished limestone, purbeck, was used, for example at Faversham and the Temple church, London, which may have predated the rebuilding of Canterbury by a decade or more.[110] The romanesque second choir of Canterbury, of course, provided the model for the eastern transepts, and a building along the lines of the current western galilee was planned for the east end of Durham cathedral.

This romanesque choir was damaged in a fire in 1174, a few years after the shocking murder in the north transept of Archbishop Thomas Becket. The need to accommodate the cult of the sainted archbishop was one factor which conditioned the reconstruction of the cathdral, as was the decision, seemingly at the insistence of the monks, that large parts of the old structure be preserved. A third was the choice of a French architect, William of Sens, who was evidently well acquainted with many recent trends in gothic architecture in northern France. One other factor which has proved very important in discussion of the rebuilding is an account, written by a monk called Gervase, which purports at least to give a year by year account of the rebuilding of the church, and in a fashion which seems surprisingly close to the terms in which modern architectural historians discuss buildings.[111] The precise dates which this account gives for sections of the building has allowed us to see how Canterbury cathedral marched in step with some of the great French gothic cathedrals. Some of the architectural affiliations are surprising, with churches further east than other areas related to English gothic, at Arras, Valenciennes and Cambrai, though this may relate to earlier cross-channel cultural connection at Canterbury. The choir capitals can be quite closely related to French examples, many at the great Ile-de-France cathedrals then in construction at Laon and Paris.[112] Our historian also gives us the interesting information that the master, William of Sens, fell off the scaffolding in 1179, and that the work was continued by an English William. Much discussion of the artistic personalities of the two Williams has ensued, with claims advanced that the English William was more 'French' in his style than the William of Sens.[113]

The decision to retain the outer walls of the old church, and its crypt, and seemingly even the form of the piers in the western part of the choir, dictated a number of the curiosities of the church. However, exactly how the choir was to be terminated beyond the lines of the romanesque work evidently caused some problems to the builders, and at a certain point a number of small but telling changes in plan have generated a lengthy literature as to what was originally intended.[114] The question is ultimately impossible to resolve, though some form of polygonal structure, of a type

110  Wilson, *The Gothic Cathedral*, London 1990, 82.

111  A translation of some of the text is supplied by Woodman, *Architectural History of Canterbury Cathedral*, 91–8.

112  R. Mair, 'The Choir Capitals of Canterbury Cathedral, 1174–84', *BAA Conference Trans.: Medieval Art and Architecture at Canterbury before 1220*, Leeds 1982, 56–66.

113  Woodman, *Architectural History of Canterbury Cathedral*, 125; or that all his innovations were derived from the Frenchman's work: P. Draper, 'William of Sens and the Original Design of the Choir Termination of Canterbury Cathedral 1175–1179', *Jnl of the Society of Architectural Historians* xlii, 1983, 238–48; P. Draper, 'Interpretations of the Rebuilding of Canterbury Cathedral, 1174–1186: Archaeological and Historical Evidence', *Jnl of the Society of Architectural Historians* lvi, 1997, 184–203.

114  Draper, 'William of Sens'; Draper, 'Interpretations of the Rebuilding'; P. Kidson, 'Gervase, Becket and William of Sens', *Speculum* lxviii, 1994, 969–91; M.F. Hearn, 'Canterbury Cathedral and the Cult of Becket', *Art Bulletin* lxxvi, 1994, 19–51; and a judicious review article, L. Hoey, 'New Studies at Canterbury Cathedral', *Avista Forum* ix, 1995, 6–9.

ultimately traceable to the Holy Sepulchre, but widely dispersed in the earlier middle ages, seems quite plausible. The effect that the dramatic events of the last thirty years of the twelfth century may have had on the cathedral fabric has also excited much discussion in recent years. Kidson, for example, has proposed that the fire which destroyed the old choir was started deliberately by the monks, while Hearn has postulated a complex set of plan alterations during the course of building, dictated by the attitude of monarch and community to the cult of Becket.

Leaving aside hypothetical reconstructions and historical circumstances, the new choir of Canterbury was the clear inspiration for much of what followed in the next forty years of English architecture. In the monks' choir, the westernmost part, the form of the piers from the romanesque church was retained, alternating polygonal and columnar supports. The arcade was, however, heightened, and above it is a low tribune with polished limestone shafts. The clerestory has polished limestone shafts too, but also a passage, unlike any gothic great church in the French royal demesne. The vaults were supported by clusters of shafts which sit above the capitals of the columns in an authentically French fashion. The columns themselves take up an unusual amount of the elevation, the leggy effect this once must have had being now masked by the screen around the choir. Beyond the liturgical choir is the eastern crossing, with the piers which define it caged in *en délit* coloured marble shafts. In the area beyond, the presbytery, the pier forms vary from bay to bay, and there are indications, moreover, that they were altered during construction. Beyond this, and raised above it, is the Trinity Chapel, destination of the relics of Thomas Becket. This section of the church, completed by William the Englishman, and the round axial chapel at the eastern extremity, achieve extremes of structural delicacy; as the aisle rises the inner skin of the wall is hollowed away into a passage with the windows brought down close to floor level. The pier types in the Trinity Chapel are paired columns, made from stones of varied colours. The effect of the glass (this is the earliest ensemble of glass to have substantially survived in England) and coloured stone creates a richness that would have provided an appropriate setting for the shrine.

A number of features from Canterbury recur in later English architecture, and they are rarely the orthodox French features. It was important in the popularisation of eastern transepts, found later at Lincoln and Salisbury, and may have helped inspire the alternation of piers in later English gothic.[115] The presence of a disorderly series of supports also perhaps helped to legitimise the varied and sometimes bizarre forms in later buildings,[116] though both of these features have romanesque precedents. *En délit* polished shafts spread rapidly, to Chichester, Rochester and Lincoln cathedrals. Finally Canterbury may have been instrumental in promoting the use of retrochoirs, separate architectural spaces behind the altar, sometimes, as at Canterbury, used for shrines.[117]

English gothic never broke with revolutionary force over the architectural scene in

---

[115] L. Hoey, 'Pier Alternation in Early English Gothic Architecture', *JBAA* cxxxvi, 1986, 45–67.

[116] For gothic variety, R. Stalley, 'Choice and Consistency: the Early Gothic Architecture of Selby Abbey', *Architectural History* xxxviii, 1995, 2–24.

[117] P. Draper, 'Architecture and Liturgy', in *The Age of Chivalry*, ed. J. Alexander and P. Binski, London 1987, 83–91, presents a case for understanding retrochoirs in association with relics; N. Coldstream, 'Cui Bono? The Saint, the Clergy and the New Work at St Albans', in *Medieval Architecture and its Intellectual Context, Studies in Honour of Peter Kidson*, ed. E. Fernie and P. Crossley, London 1990, 143–57, presents a counter example.

the way it did in France. Evidently it was not inability to produce a French gothic building that stopped the style from becoming adopted as a whole. Ripon provides a fairly convincing, though idiosyncratic, impersonation of a French building, and Canterbury was in part built by a French architect. Reasons for the rejection of what has been seen as the most advanced form of gothic, that of the Ile-de-France, have been sought by recent scholars. Peter Draper has examined parallels with the emergence of a sense of English identity, and increasing distinctions between the culture of France and the (still French speaking) culture of England. Larry Hoey emphasised that English patrons seem to have had other priorities in their designs than those in France, such as complex pier designs which made impossible the simple, 'logical' articulation of buildings found in France.[118]

The beginning of our period saw England in something of a backwater and Normandy at the forefront of architectural developments in Europe. At St Etienne in Caen the Normans produced, on the eve of the Conquest, one of the most consummate statements in romanesque architecture, and it is unsurprising that it formed the model for much of what followed, especially as it had the added appeal of being a ducal, later royal, foundation. However, the occupation of England, with the access to greater wealth and opportunities for building which that entailed, seems to have encouraged Norman patrons to aim for buildings of a size and diversity hard to parallel elsewhere in Europe. While this architecture was firmly rooted in the Norman tradition, the architecture of the two areas drifted apart somewhat, that in England in particular developing a high degree of architectural richness. The divorce was not absolute, however; certain common preoccupations survived into the gothic era, notably an interest in thick-walled structures, which resulted in highly individualistic interpretations of the new French style in both duchy and kingdom.

[118] P. Draper, 'English with a French Accent: Architectural *Franglais* in Late Twelfth-Century England', in *Architecture and Language: Constructing Identity in European Architecture c. 1000 – c. 1650*, ed. G. Clarke and P. Crossley, Cambridge 2000, 12–35; L. Hoey, 'Pier versus Vault Shafts in Early English Gothic Architecture', *Jnl of the Society of Architectural Historians* xlvi, 1987, 241–64.

# Further Reading

What follows is a selection of the vast and growing literature on the history of the Anglo-Norman realm in the widest sense.

## Basic Bibliographies and Collections of Articles

From 1978 specialist papers on all aspects have appeared in *Anglo-Norman Studies: the Proceedings of the Battle Conference*, and from 1989 in *The Haskins Society Journal*. A comprehensive annual bibliography on all matters pertaining to Normandy is published in the *Annales de Normandie* (i 1952, continuing) and to Anglo-Saxon history in *Anglo-Saxon England* (i 1971, continuing). Extremely useful is the bibliography by Simon Keynes, *Anglo-Saxon History: a Select Bibliography*, Old English Newsletter subsidia xiii, Michigan 1998, 3rd revised edn, and its electronic version on the Internet at:
http://www.wmich.edu/medieval/rawl/keynes1/index.html

## The Normans and Angevins

Useful surveys of the history of the Normans in general are the classics: C.H. Haskins, *The Normans in European History*, New York 1915; D.C. Douglas, *The Norman Achievement 1050–1100*, London 1969, and *The Norman Fate 1100–1150*, London 1976. For a modern and compelling narrative, see Marjorie Chibnall, *The Normans*, The Peoples of Europe, Oxford 2000; this can profitably be used in conjunction with the collection of sources *The Normans in Europe*, translated and edited by Elisabeth van Houts, Manchester Medieval Sources, Manchester 2000. R.H.C. Davis, *The Normans and their Myth*, London 1976, concentrates on the historiographical 'myth making'. An important collection of conference papers was published by the Italian Centre of Early Medieval Studies at Spoleto: *I Normanni e la loro espansione in Europa nell' alto medioevo*, Settimane di studio del centro italiano di studi sull' alto medioevo xvi, Spoleto 1969. A splendid catalogue of a recent exhibition on the Normans organised in Rome, *I Normanni: popolo d' Europa 1030–1200*, ed. M. d' Onofrio, Venice 1994, provides ample visual material for the history of the Normans in Europe.

The best overall introduction for the Angevin period is the second edition of John Gillingham's *The Angevin Empire*, London 2001. Still good, though somewhat dated, is John Le Patourel's 'The Plantagenet Dominions', *History* l, 1965, 289–308, supplemented by his collected essays, *Feudal Empires: Norman and Plantagenet*, London 1984. Thought-provoking discussions can also be found in R.V. Turner, 'The Problem of Survival for the Angevin "Empire"', *AHR* c, 1995, 78–96, and R. Mortimer, *Angevin England 1154–1258*, Oxford 1994.

*Early Normandy*

The essential studies are David Bates, *Normandy before 1066*, London 1982 (a new revised edition is forthcoming); E. Searle, *Predatory Kinship and the Creation of Norman Power, 840–1066*, Berkeley 1988; and Cassandra Potts, *Monastic Revival and Regional Identity in Early Normandy*, Woodbridge 1997. For the Frankish context, see also David Bates, 'West Francia: the Northern Principalities', in *The New Cambridge Medieval History, iii: c. 900 – c. 1024*, ed. T. Reuter, Cambridge 1999, 398–419, and 'Britain and France and the Year Thousand', *Journal of the British Institute in Paris* xxviii, 1999, 5–22.

For the administrative and institutional history of Normandy, C.H. Haskins, *Norman Institutions*, New York 1918, remains the classic study, but it should be complemented by others, for example J. Yver, 'Les premières institutions du duché de Normandie', *I Normanni e la loro espansione*, 299–366; K.F. Werner, 'Quelques observations au sujet des débuts du "duché" de Normandie', *Droit privé et institutions régionales: Études historiques offertes à Jean Yver*, Paris 1976, 691–709; and the vast *oeuvre* of Lucien Musset. For a selection of his papers, see *Autour du pouvoir ducal normand Xe–XIIe siècles*, ed. L. Musset *et al.*, Cahier des Annales de Normandie, xvii, Caen 1985 and *Aspects de la société et de l'économie dans la Normandie médiévale (Xe–XIIIe siècles)*, Cahier des Annales de Normandie xxii, Caen 1988. For legal history, E.Z. Tabuteau, *Transfers of Property in Eleventh-Century Norman Law*, Chapel Hill 1988, is essential.

The Norman ducal charters can be found in *Recueil des actes des ducs de Normandie de 911 à 1066*, ed. M. Fauroux, Caen 1961, and for the period 1066–87 in *Regesta Regum Anglo-Normannorum. The Acta of William I (1066–1087)*, ed. D. Bates, Oxford 1998. For the chroniclers, see the introductions to the following works: *Dudo of St Quentin, History of the Normans*, trans. E. Christiansen, Woodbridge 1998, viii–xxxvii; *The Gesta Normannorum Ducum of William of Jumièges, Orderic Vitalis and Robert of Torigni*, ed. and trans. E.M.C. van Houts, 2 vols, Oxford 1992–95, i, pp. xix–cxxxiii; *The Gesta Guillelmi of William of Poitiers*, ed. and trans. R.H.C. Davis and M. Chibnall, Oxford 1998, xv–xlvii; and *The Ecclesiastical History of Orderic Vitalis*, ed. and trans. M. Chibnall, 6 vols, Oxford 1969–80, as well as M. Chibnall, *The World of Orderic Vitalis*, Oxford 1984. Modern interpretations of the medieval historiography of the Normans are L. Shopkow, *History and Community: Norman Historical Writing in the Eleventh and Twelfth Centuries*, Washington 1997, and E. Albu, *The Normans in their Histories*, Woodbridge 2001.

*Later Normandy*

A general introduction is provided by David Bates, 'The Rise and Fall of Normandy, c. 911–1204', in *England and Normandy in the Middle Ages*, ed. D. Bates and A. Curry, London 1994, 19–36. A wider French context is given by J. Martindale, 'Succession and Politics in the Romance-Speaking World, c. 1000–1140', in *England and her Neighbours 1066–1453: Essays in Honour of Pierre Chaplais*, ed. M. Jones and M. Vale, London 1989, 19–41, and for the Angevin period by Daniel Power, 'What Did the Frontier of Angevin Normandy Comprise?', *ANS* xvii, 1995, 181–202, and 'French and Norman Frontiers in the Central Middle Ages', in *Frontiers in Question: Eurasian Borderlands 700–1700*, ed. D. Power and N. Standen, London 1999. For the southern border of Normandy, see G. Louise, *La seigneurie de Bellême Xe–XIIe siècles*, Le Pays Bas-normand lxxxiii–lxxxiv for 1990–91, 2 vols, Flers 1992–93; and K. Thompson, *Power and Border Lordship: the County of Perche 1000–1226*, Woodbridge 2002. For the relationship between Normandy and France, see C.W. Hollister, 'Normandy, France and the Anglo-Norman "Regnum" ', in his *Monarchy, Magnates and Institutions in the Anglo-Norman World*, London 1986, 17–58, but see the comments of D. Bates, 'Normandy and England after 1066', *EHR* civ, 1989, 851–80. Also important is M. Chibnall, 'Anglo-French Relations in the Work of Orderic Vitalis', in *Documenting the Past: Essays in Medieval History Presented to George Peddy Cuttino*, ed. J.S. Hamilton and P.J. Bradley, Woodbridge 1989, 5–20. The problem of the Vexin as border area is discussed by J.A. Green, 'Lords of the Norman Vexin', in *War and Government in the Middle Ages*, ed. J. Gillingham and J.C. Holt, Woodbridge 1984, 47–61. For the late Norman nobility, see M. Billoré, 'La noblesse normande dans l'entourage de Richard I', *La cour Plantagenêt (1154–1204)*, Civilisation Médiévale viii, Poitiers 2000, 151–64.

### Later Anglo-Saxon England

The classic study remains the useful overview by F.M. Stenton, *Anglo-Saxon England*, 3rd edn, Oxford 1971. Other good introductions are H.R. Loyn, *The Making of the English Nation: From the Anglo-Saxons to Edward I*, London 1991, and his *The Governance of Anglo-Saxon England 500–1087*, London 1984. Excellent collections of papers by James Campbell highlight aspects of government and administration; see his *Essays in Anglo-Saxon History*, London 1986, and *The Anglo-Saxon State*, London 2000. For the late tenth and eleventh centuries an important study is P. Stafford, *Unification and Conquest: a Political and Social History of England in the Tenth and Eleventh Centuries*, London 1989. An interesting study comparing England under Kings Cnut and William I is R. Fleming, *Kings and Lords in Conquest England*, Cambridge 1991. For individual kings, see S. Keynes, *The Diplomas of King Aethelred the Unready, 978–1016*, Cambridge 1980; M.K. Lawson, *Cnut: the Danes in England in the Early Eleventh Century*, London 1993; *The Reign of Cnut, King of England, Denmark and Norway*, ed. A.R. Rumble, London 1994; and F. Barlow, *Edward the Confessor*, London 1970. For eleventh-century queenship, see now P. Stafford, *Queen Emma and Queen Edith: Queenship and Womens' Power in Eleventh-Century England*, Oxford 1997.

An indispensable collection of sources can be found in *English Historical Documents*, vol. 1 *(500–1042)*, ed. D. Whitelock, 2nd edn, London 1996.

### The Norman Conquest of England

The literature on this topic is vast. For a useful recent guide to the debates on the Norman Conquest and its various effects, see M. Chibnall, *The Debate on the Norman Conquest*, Manchester 1999, chapters of which include topics like feudalism and lordship, 79–96, law and the family, 97–114, empire and colonisation, 115–24, peoples and frontiers, 125–38 and the church and economy, 139–54, as well as a comprehensive modern bibliography. *The Blackwell Encyclopaedia of Anglo-Saxon England*, ed. M. Lapidge, J. Blair, S. Keynes and D. Scragg, Oxford 1998, contains many entries pertinent to the Conquest period as well.

The classic but now outdated study of the Norman Conquest is E.A. Freeman, *History of the Norman Conquest*, 6 vols, Oxford 1867–79; 2nd edn of vols 1–4, 1870–76; 3rd edn of vols 1–2, 1877. Excellent narratives of the main events of the Conquest are R.A. Brown, *The Normans and the Norman Conquest*, 2nd rev. edn, Woodbridge 1985, and A. Williams, *The English and the Norman Conquest*, Woodbridge 1995. For Anglo-Norman annals, chronicles and saints' lives, see the invaluable survey by A. Gransden, *Historical Writing in England c. 550 to c. 1307*, London 1974, as well as commentaries in E.M.C. van Houts, *History and Family Traditions in England and the Continent, 1000–1200*, Variorum Collected Studies Series, Aldershot 1999; no. VIII therein contains her 'The Norman Conquest through European Eyes', which analyses the non English and non-Norman reactions to the Conquest.

The post-Conquest charters of William the Conqueror can now be consulted in the *Regesta Regum Anglo-Normannorum. The Acta of William I (1066–1087)*, ed. D. Bates, Oxford 1998, the introduction of which provides a good guide to the continuity of English practices after 1066 and to a comparison between diplomatic styles in Normandy and England. Later acta are registered in *Regesta Regum Anglo-Normannorum*, ed. H.W.C. Davis *et al.*, 4 vols, Oxford 1913–69. The change of land ownership in 1066 and the ensuing litigation is a fruitful area of research into the effects of the Conquest. This is made easier by a modern English translation of all judicial cases in *Domesday Book* provided by R. Fleming, *Domesday Book and the Law*, Cambridge 1998. The effects of the Conquest on English feudalism have been scrutinised with a fresh eye by David Bates; see his *Re-ordering the Past and Negotiating the Present in Stenton's "First Century"*, The Stenton Lecture 1999, Reading 2000, and 'England and the "Feudal Revolution" ', *Il feudalesimo nell'alto medioevo, 8–12 aprile 1999*, Settimane di studio del centro italiano di studi sull'alto medioevo xlvii, 2 vols, Spoleto 2000, ii, 611–49.

Prosopographical studies have illuminated the origins of the continental landholders in post-Conquest England; see K.S.B. Keats-Rohan, *Domesday People. A Prosopography of Persons Occurring in English Documents 1066–1166, I: Domesday Book*; *II: Domesday Descendants*, Woodbridge 1999–2002.

*Anglo-Norman England*

J. Le Patourel, *The Norman Empire*, Oxford 1976, remains an inspiring study for the period up to 1154. Other excellent introductions are M. Chibnall, *Anglo-Norman England, 1066–1166*, Oxford 1986, and M. Clanchy, *England and its Rulers, 1066–1272*, 2nd edn, London 2002. R. Bartlett's *England under the Norman and Angevin Kings, 1075–1225*, Oxford 2000, provides the latest synthesis. Useful biographies or studies by ruler are David Bates, *William the Conqueror*, 2nd edn, Stroud 2001, which corrects in many places David Douglas, *William the Conqueror*, London 1964. For William's sons, see F. Barlow, *William Rufus*, London 1983, and C. Warren Hollister, edited and completed by A. Clark Frost, *Henry I*, Yale 2001. For administrative matters, Judith Green, *The Government of England under Henry I*, Cambridge 1986, is still unsurpassed. Stephen's reign has received attention from R.H.C. Davis, *King Stephen, 1135–1154*, London 1977; from K.J. Stringer, *The Reign of Stephen: Kingship, Warfare and Government in Twelfth-Century England*, London 1993; and from David Crouch, *King Stephen*, London 2000. The collection of papers on his reign, *The Anarchy of King Stephen's Reign*, ed. E. King, Oxford 1994, is also very useful. Queenship is an important area of new research; see Lois Huneycutt on Queen Matilda II, 'The Ideal of a Perfect Princess: the *Life of St Margaret* in the Reign of Matilda II (1100–1118)', *ANS* xii, 1990, 81–97, and 'Images of Queenship in the High Middle Ages', *Haskins Soc. Jnl* i, 1989, 61–71. Matilda's successor Adeliza of Louvain, who was much less politically active, is portrayed by L. Wertheimer, 'Adeliza of Louvain and Anglo-Norman Queenship', *Haskins Soc. Jnl* vii, 1995, 101–16. Although never a queen in her own right, Empress Matilda came close to that position in the early 1140s; see M. Chibnall, *The Empress Matilda: Queen Consort, Queen Mother and Lady of the English*, Oxford 1991, as well as her study of Matilda's charters in *Law and Government in Medieval England and Normandy: Essays in Honour of Sir James Holt*, ed. G. Garnett and J. Hudson, Cambridge 1994, 276–98.

The aristocracy of the Anglo-Norman period has been studied by D. Crouch, *The Image of Aristocracy in Britain, 1000–1300*, London 1992, and, more recently with special emphasis on England, by Judith Green, *The Aristocracy of Norman England*, Cambridge 1997. Both books have excellent bibliographies for works on individual families.

*Angevin England*

For the later Angevin period see R. Mortimer, *Angevin England 1154–1258*, Oxford 1994; M.T. Clanchy, *England and its Rulers, 1066–1272*, 2nd edn, London 2002. Excellent introductions with special reference to the Celtic lands of Ireland, Wales and Scotland are R. Frame, *The Political Development of the British Isles*, Oxford 1990; R.R. Davies, *The First English Empire*, Oxford 2000, and his *Domination and Conquest: the Experience of Ireland, Scotland and Wales, 1100–1300*, Oxford 1990. The most important biographical studies of King Henry II are W.L. Warren, *Henry II*, London 1973, and focusing on his early reign, E. Amt, *The Accession of Henry II in England: Royal Government Restored, 1149–1159*, Woodbridge 1993, and G.J. White, *Restoration and Reform, 1153–1165: Recovery from Civil War in England*, Cambridge 2000. Henry II's rule in Brittany has been explored by J. Everard, *Brittany and the Angevins: Province and Empire, 1158–1203*, Cambridge 2000. For Richard I see J. Gillingham, *Richard I*, London 1999, and *Richard Coeur de Lion in History* and Myth, ed. J. Nelson, London 1992. A stimulating collection of studies on King John is *King John: New Interpretations*, ed. S. Church, Woodbridge 1999, although the older works remain valuable: see S. Painter, *The Reign of King John*, Baltimore 1949, and J.E.A. Jolliffe, *Angevin Kingship*, London 1955, as well as W.L. Warren, *King John*, London 1961. J.C. Holt's work on John's reign is indispensable; see his *The Northeners*, London 1961, and, most importantly, *Magna Carta*, 2nd edn, Cambridge 1992. There is also the more recent narrative by R.V. Turner, *King John*, London 1994. For queenship in this period, invaluable are J. Martindale's study of the later years of Eleanor of Aquitaine, and N. Vincent, 'Isabella of Angoulême: John's Jezebel', both in *King John*, ed. S. Church, 137–64 and 165–218.

*Relations with Scandinavia*

For general Scandinavian matters, *Medieval Scandinavia: an Encyclopedia*, ed. P. Pulsiano, New York and London 1993, is essential. An excellent narrative is B. and P. Sawyer, *Medieval Scandinavia: from Conversion to Reformation, circa 800–1500*, Minneapolis and London 1993. For Normandy and Scandinavia, see especially L. Musset, 'Relations et échanges d'influences dans l'Europe du Nord-Ouest (Xe–XIe siècles)', *CCM* i, 1958, 63–82, and his collected essays, *Nordica et Normannica: Recueil d'études sur la Scandinavie ancienne et médiévale, les expansions des vikings et la fondation de la Normandie*, Paris 1997. For the literary contacts, see E. van Houts, 'Scandinavian Influence in Norman Literature of the Eleventh Century', *ANS* xii, 1990, 107–21 (reprinted in Van Houts, *History and Family Traditions*, no. II), and L.W. Breese, 'The Persistence of Scandinavian Connections in Normandy in the Tenth and Early Eleventh Centuries', *Viator* viii, 1977, 47–61. For Anglo-Scandinavian relations, see now primarily L. Abrams, 'The Anglo-Saxons and the Christianization of Scandinavia', *ASE* xxiv, 1995, 213–49, and her 'Eleventh-Century Missions and the Early Stages of Ecclesiastical Organisation in Scandinavia', *ANS* xvii, 1995, 21–40. For more political matters, see S. Körner, *The Battle of Hastings, England and Europe 1035–1066*, Lund 1964. For trading contacts, see P. Sawyer, 'Anglo-Scandinavian Trade in the Viking Age and After', in *Anglo-Saxon Monetary History: Essays in Memory of Michael Dolley*, ed. M.A.S. Blackburn, Leicester 1986, 185–99.

*The Church*

Good introductory studies for England are the two volumes by F. Barlow, *The English Church 1000–1066*, 2nd edn, London 1979, and *The English Church 1066–1154*, London 1979, as well as the classic Z.N. Brooke, *The English Church and the Papacy: from the Conquest to the Reign of John*, rev. edn by C. Brooke, Cambridge 1989, and M. Brett, *The English Church under Henry I*, Oxford 1975. Amongst studies of hagiography particularly recommended are S. Ridyard, *The Royal Saints of Anglo-Saxon England: a Study of West Saxon and East Anglian Cults*, Cambridge 1988, and D.W. Rollason, *Saints and Relics in Anglo-Saxon England*, Oxford 1989. For female monasticism, see the magnificent work by S. Foot, *Veiled Women and the Disappearance of Nuns from Anglo-Saxon England*, 2 vols, Aldershot 2000; and for the post-Conquest period, S. Thompson, *Women Religious: the Founding of English Nunneries after the Norman Conquest*, Oxford 1991. The development of parishes is discussed in *Minsters and Parish Churches: the Local Church in Transition 950–1200*, ed. J. Blair, Oxford University Committee for Archaeology, Monograph xvii, Oxford 1988. For Anglo-Norman England, studies of several individual ecclesiastics are invaluable, for instance M. Gibson, *Lanfranc of Bec*, Oxford 1978; R.W. Southern, *Saint Anselm: a Portrait in a Landscape*, Cambridge 1990; S.N. Vaughn, *Anselm of Bec and Robert of Meulan: the Innocence of the Dove and the Wisdom of the Serpent*, Berkeley 1987; A. Saltman, *Theobald, Archbishop of Canterbury*, London 1956; F. Barlow, *Thomas Becket*, London 1986; and *The World of John of Salisbury*, ed. M. Wilks, SCH, Subsidia iii, London 1984. It is worth pointing out the existence of the series English Episcopal Acta, published by the British Academy, Oxford 1980, which aims to publish the medieval episcopal charters of all English dioceses; thus far more than twenty-three volumes have seen the light. Among the studies of particular institutions can be recommended W.M. Aird, *St Cuthbert and the Normans: the Church of Durham 1071–1153*, Woodbridge 1998; *Canterbury and the Norman Conquest: Churches, Saints and Scholars 1066–1109*, ed. R. Eales and R. Sharpe, London 1995; and for Normandy A. Porée, *Histoire de l'abbaye du Bec*, 2 vols, Evreux 1901. Aristocratic patronage of churches and monasteries in England is the subject of E. Cownie, *Religious Patronage in Anglo-Norman England 1066–1135*, London 1998. For bishops and saints in Normandy, see the proceedings of conferences at Cerisy-la-Salle: *Les évêques normands du XIe siècle*, ed. P. Bouet and F. Neveux, Colloque de Cerisy-la-Salle, Caen 1995, and *Les saints dans la Normandie médiévale*, ed. P. Bouet and F. Neveux, Colloque de Cerisy-la-Salle, Caen 2000. For monastic life, see C. Potts, *Monastic Revival and Regional Identity in Early Normandy*, Woodbridge 1997; and for canons, *Des clercs au service de la réforme: Études et documents sur les chanoines réguliers de la province de Rouen*, ed. M. Arnoux, Bibliotheca Victoriana xi, Turnholt 2000.

*Culture*

On architecture and sculpture, see especially E. Fernie, *The Architecture of the Anglo-Saxons*, London 1983, and his inaugural lecture at the Courtauld Institute of Art, London, *Art-Historical Theory and English Romanesque Architecture*, London 1996. See also R.D.H. Gem, 'England and the Resistance to Romanesque Architecture', in *Studies . . . to Brown*, 129–40; G. Zarnecki, *English Romanesque Sculpture*, London 1951, and his *Later English Romanesque Sculpture*, London 1953. Norman architecture can now be most profitably approached in the comprehensive volume edited by M. Baylé, *L'Architecture Normande au Moyen Age*, Colloque de Cerisy-la-Salle, 2 vols, Caen 1997. For art and precious objects the most lavishly published works remain *The Golden Age of Anglo-Saxon Art: Catalogue of the Exhibition at the British Museum*, ed. J. Backhouse *et al.*, London 1984, and *English Romanesque Art, 1066–1200: Catalogue of the Exhibition at the Hayward Gallery*, ed. G. Zarnecki *et al.*, London 1984. A beautifully illustrated catalogue of an important exhibition, *Trésors des abbayes normandes*, was published by the Musée des Antiquités at Rouen in 1979. For the Bayeux Tapestry, see *The Bayeux Tapestry*, ed. F. Stenton, London 1957; *The Bayeux Tapestry*, ed. D.M. Wilson, London 1985; and *La Tapisserie de Bayeux*, ed. F. Neveux and B. Levy, Colloque de Cerisy-la-Salle, Caen 2002 (forthcoming). For manuscripts and illumination, see C.R. Dodwell, *The Canterbury School of Illumination 1066–1200*, Cambridge 1954; J.J.G. Alexander, *Norman Illumination at Mont St Michel 966–1100*, Oxford 1970. For a recent inventory, see R. Gameson, *The Manuscripts of Early Norman England, c. 1066–1130*, Oxford 1999. A splendidly illustrated collection of articles is *Manuscrits et enluminures dans le monde normand (Xe–XVe siècles)*, ed. P. Bouet and M. Dosdat, Colloque de Cerisy-la-Salle, Caen 1999.

*Law*

The starting point must always be F. Pollock and F.M. Maitland, *The History of English Law before the Time of Edward I*, 2nd edn with a new introduction by S.F.C. Milsom, Cambridge 1968. The magisterial survey by P. Wormald, *The Making of English Law: King Alfred to the Twelfth Century*, Oxford 1999, constitutes the first volume of a two-volume history of early medieval English Law. His collected essays are published as P. Wormald, *Legal Culture in the Early Medieval West: Law as Text, Image and Experience*, London 1999. A concise and clear introduction to the survival of Anglo-Saxon law after 1066 can be found in B. O'Brien, *God's Peace and King's Peace: the Laws of Edward the Confessor*, Philadelphia 1999. For *Domesday Book* as a mine of legal material, see R. Fleming, *Domesday Book and the Law: Society and Legal Custom in Early Medieval England*, Cambridge 1998. For the Common Law, indispensable are S.F.C. Milsom, *The Historical Foundations of the Common Law*, London 1966; R.C. van Caenegem, *The Birth of the Common Law*, 2nd edn, Cambridge 1988; and, by far the most accessible, John Hudson, *The Formation of the English Common Law: Law and Society in England from the Norman Conquest to Magna Carta*, London 1996. For the immediate post-Conquest period, see the important study of legal identities by G. Garnett, '*Franci et Angli*: the Legal Distinctions between Peoples after the Conquest', *ANS* viii, 1986, 109–37. For the links with France, see P. Hyams, 'The Common Law and the French Connection', *ANS* iv, 1982, 77–92, 196–202. On the development of the justice system, see the classic study by D.M. Stenton, *English Justice between the Norman Conquest and the Great Charter, 1066–1215*, Philadelphia 1964, and the more recent excellent studies by P. Brand, *The Origins of the English Legal Profession*, Oxford 1992, and some of his collected work in *The Making of the Common Law*, London 1992. For Magna Carta the fundamental work remains J.C. Holt, *Magna Carta*, 2nd edn, Cambridge 1992.

*Nationality and Identity*

This is a relatively new and fruitful angle from which to approach matters of conquest, colonisation and cultural identities. A stimulating introductory book is now available in the shape of J. Gillingham, *The English in the Twelfth Century*, Woodbridge 2000. For language and national identities, see I. Short, '*Tam Angli quam Franci*: Self-Definition in Anglo-Norman England', *ANS* xviii, 1996, 153–76. For Anglo-Norman literature, and historiography in particular, see P. Damian-Grint, *The New Historians of the Twelfth-Century Renaissance: Inventing Vernacular Authority*, Woodbridge 1999. The link with the so-called Twelfth-Century Renaissance is also exploited in *Anglo-Norman Political Culture and the Twelfth-Century Renaissance*, ed. C. Warren Hollister, Woodbridge 1997. For the role of women in vernacular literature and the forging of national identities in Anglo-Norman England, see J. Wogan-Browne, *Saints' Lives and Literary Culture: Virginity and its Authorizations*, Oxford 2001. For early Normandy, see C. Potts, '*Atque unum ex diversis gentibus populum effecit*: Historical Tradition and the Norman Identity', *ANS* xviii, 1996, 139–52.

*War and Chivalry*

The fundamental study is M. Strickland, *War and Chivalry: the Conduct and Perception of War in England and Normandy, 1066–1217*, Cambridge 1996. This can profitably be supplemented by the thought-provoking chapters 12 and 13 in Gillingham's *The English in the Twelfth Century*, which deal specifically with attitudes to warfare, violence and clemency.

For technical aspects of the conduct of war, see the comprehensive survey by J. France, 'Historiographical Essay: Recent Writing on Medieval Warfare from the Fall of Rome to c. 1300', *The Journal of Military History* lxv, 2001, 441–73. For sieges and siege engines, see the stimulating study of J. Bradbury, *The Medieval Siege*, Woodbridge 1992. For Anglo-Saxon England, see in particular R. Abels, *Lordship and Military Obligation in Anglo-Saxon England*, London 1988, and M. Strickland, 'Military Technology and Conquest: the Anomaly of Anglo-Saxon England', *ANS* xix, 1997, 353–82. For the later period, see the still invaluable C.W. Hollister, *The Military Organisation of Norman England*, Oxford 1965. An excellent modern study is M. Prestwich, *Armies and Warfare in the Middle Ages: the English Experience*, New Haven 1996, as well as S. Morillo, *Warfare under the Anglo-Norman Kings 1066–1135*, Woodbridge 1994. For castles in England, see J.G. Pounds, *The Medieval Castle in England and Wales: a Social and Political History*, Cambridge 1990, and R.A. Brown, *English Castles*, London 1976. For a useful update, see C. Coulson, 'Cultural Realities and Reappraisals in English Castle Study', *JMH* xxii, 1996, 171–207. Most welcome also is the forthcoming volume of essays, ed. R. Liddiard, Woodbridge 2002.

*The Normans in the South*

Excellent recent introductions are G.A. Loud, *The Age of Robert Guiscard: Southern Italy and the Norman Conquest*, Harlow 2000, or for a compact survey M. Chibnall, *The Normans*, Oxford 2000, especially 'Part III: The Normans in the South', and in French, J.-M. Martin, *Italies normandes, XIe–XIIe siècles*, La vie quotidienne, civilisations et sociétés, Paris 1994. The fundamental study, however, remains F. Chalandon, *Histoire de la domination normande en Italie et en Sicile*, 2 vols, Paris 1907, while J.J. Norwich, *The Normans in the South, 1016–1130*, London 1967, is the classic, but now somewhat dated, standard work in English. The main chroniclers of the Norman period in Italy are the subject of K.B. Wolf, *Making History: the Normans and their Historians in Eleventh-Century Italy*, Philadelphia 1995. For the historiographical traditions of the arrival of the Normans in Italy, see E. Joranson, 'The Inception of the Career of the Normans in Italy: Legend and History', *Speculum* xxiii, 1948, 353–96, and J. France, 'The Occasion of the Coming of the Normans to Southern Italy', *JMH* xvii, 1991, 185–205.

For the Norman origin of the majority of immigrants, see L.R. Ménager, *Hommes et institutions de l'Italie normande*, Variorum Collected Studies Series, London 1981, no. IV, 189–214, and G.A. Loud, *Conquerors and Churchmen in Norman Italy*, Variorum Collected Studies Series, Aldershot 1999, where no. II deals with the question 'How "Norman" was the Norman Conquest of Southern Italy?'

For the conquest of southern Italy important studies are H. Hoffmann, 'Die Anfänge der Normannen in Süditalien', *Quellen und Forschungen aus italienischen*

*Archiven und Bibliotheken* xlix, 1969, 95–144. Graham Loud's case study of Campania provides a stimulating study on 'Continuity and Change in Norman Italy', in his *Conquerors and Churchmen*, no. V. For the church, see G.A. Loud, *Church and Society in the Norman Principality of Capua, 1058–1197*, Oxford 1985, and his collected essays, *Montecassino and Benevento in the Middle Ages*, Variorum Collected Studies Series, Aldershot 2000. For the papacy and the Normans in the eleventh century, see J. Déer, *Papsttum und Normannen: Untersuchungen zu ihren lehnsrechtlichen und kirchenpolitischen Beziehungen*, Cologne 1972, and H.E.J. Cowdrey, *The Age of Abbot Desiderius: Montecassino, the Papacy and the Normans in the Eleventh and Early Twelfth Centuries*, Oxford 1983. Essential studies on government and administration are V. von Valkenhausen, 'I ceti dirigenti prenormanni al tempo della costituzione degli stati normanni nell'Italia meridionale e in Sicilia', in *Forme di potere e struttura sociale in Italia nel Medioevo*, ed. G. Rossetti, Bologna 1977, 321–77, and W. Jahn, *Untersuchungen zur normannischen Herrschaft in Süditalien (1040–1100)*, Europäischen Hochschulschriften, Reihe 3, Bd 401, Frankfurt am Main 1989. The charters of the early Norman dukes can be consulted in *Recueil des actes des ducs normands d'Italie (1046–1127)*, vol. 1: *Les premiers ducs (1046–87)*, ed. L.R. Ménager, Società di storia patria per la Puglia, Documenti e monografie xlv, Bari 1980.

A stimulating discussion of the role of women in southern Italian society can be found in the work of P. Skinner; see her 'Disputes and Disparity: Women in Court in Medieval Southern Italy', *Reading Medieval Studies* xxii, 1996, 85–104, and ' "Halt! Be Men": Sikelgaita of Salerno, Gender and the Norman Conquest of Southern Italy', *Gender and History* xii, 2000, 622–41.

Two French collections of essays, *Les Normands en Méditerranée*, ed. P. Bouet and F. Neveux, Colloque de Cerisy-la-Salle, Caen 1994, and *Frédéric II (1194–1250) et l'héritage normand de Sicile*, ed. A.M. Héricher-Flambard, Colloque de Cerisy-la-Salle, Caen 2000, are particularly good for military architecture and fortification in southern Italy. For the conquest of Sicily, see D. Matthew, *The Norman Kingdom of Sicily*, Cambridge 1992; H. Houben, *Roger II of Sicily: A Ruler between East and West*, Cambridge 2002. For government and administration in Sicily, see E. Jamison, *Admiral Eugenius of Sicily*, London 1957, and E. Jamison, *Studies in the History of Medieval Sicily and South Italy*, ed. D. Clementi and T. Kölzer, Aalen 1992. More recent and eclectic is H. Takayama, *The Administration of the Norman Kingdom of Sicily*, Leiden 1993.

The fundamental studies for the Normans in Byzantium are J. Shepard, 'The Uses of the Franks in Eleventh-Century Byzantium', *ANS* xv, 1993, 275–305, and E.M.C. van Houts, 'Normandy and Byzantium', *Byzantion* lv, 1985, 544–59.

The early arrival of the Normans in Spain is discussed by M. Defourneaux, *Les Français en Espagne au XIe et XIIe siècle*, Paris 1949; and for the later settlement at Tarragona, see L.J. McCrank, 'Norman Crusaders in the Catalan Reconquest: Robert Burdet and the Principality of Tarragona, 1129–55', *JMH* vii, 1981, 67–82.

The Norman and Norman Italian origin of the crusaders is the subject of A.V. Murray's, 'How Norman was the Principality of Antioch? Prolegomena to a Study of the Origins of the Nobility of a Crusader State', in *Family Trees and the Roots of Politics: the Prosopography of Britain and France from the Tenth to the Twelfth Century*, ed. K.S.B. Keats-Rohan, Woodbridge 1997, 349–60. Less emphasis on the Normans is found in T.S. Asbridge, *The Creation of the Principality of Antioch, 1098–1130*, Woodbridge 2000. An interesting source in translation is *Walter the Chancellor's The*

*Antiochene Wars*, trans. T.A. Asbridge and S.B. Edgington, Aldershot 1999. An excellent, but dated, discussion of Robert Curthose and his Norman followers on the First Crusade is C.W. David, *Robert Curthose, Duke of Normandy*, Cambridge, Mass., 1920; a new study is promised by W.M. Aird.

# Genealogies

## 1. *Anglo-Saxon Kings 871–1066*

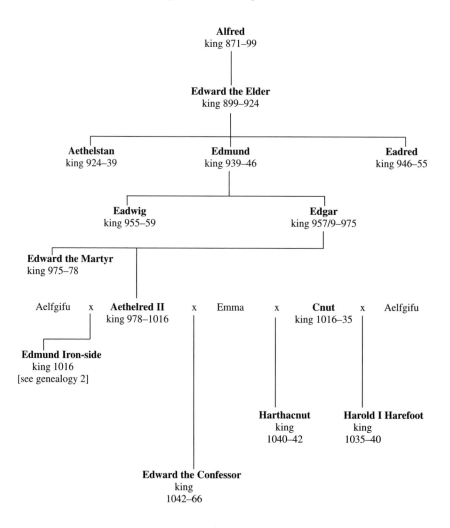

**Alfred**
king 871–99

**Edward the Elder**
king 899–924

**Aethelstan**
king 924–39

**Edmund**
king 939–46

**Eadred**
king 946–55

**Eadwig**
king 955–59

**Edgar**
king 957/9–975

**Edward the Martyr**
king 975–78

Aelfgifu   x   **Aethelred II**
king 978–1016   x   Emma   x   **Cnut**
king 1016–35   x   Aelfgifu

**Edmund Iron-side**
king 1016
[see genealogy 2]

**Harthacnut**
king
1040–42

**Harold I Harefoot**
king
1035–40

**Edward the Confessor**
king
1042–66

## 2. Anglo-Saxon Kings and Descendants 1016–1189

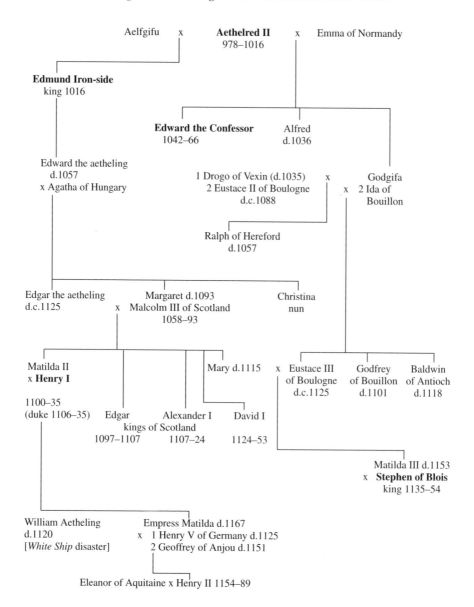

## 3. *Kings of England and Dukes of Normandy 1066–1216*

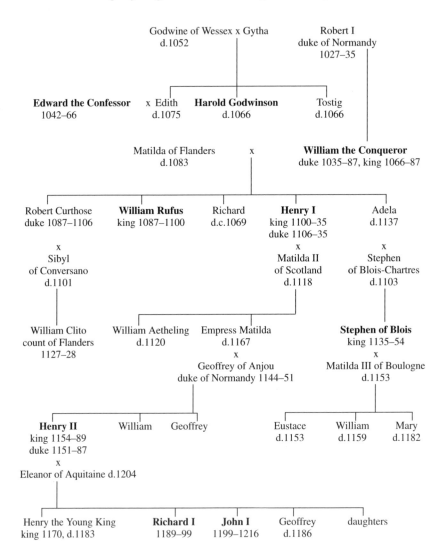

## 4. *Counts of Rouen and Dukes of Normandy c. 911–996*

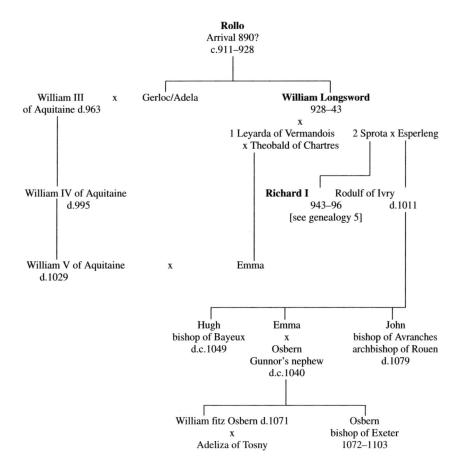

**Rollo**
Arrival 890?
c.911–928

William III        x        Gerloc/Adela                **William Longsword**
of Aquitaine d.963                                                     928–43

x

1 Leyarda of Vermandois        2 Sprota x Esperleng
x Theobald of Chartres

William IV of Aquitaine                                **Richard I**        Rodulf of Ivry
d.995                                                           943–96            d.1011

[see genealogy 5]

William V of Aquitaine        x        Emma
d.1029

Hugh                        Emma                        John
bishop of Bayeux              x                  bishop of Avranches
d.c.1049                    Osbern               archbishop of Rouen
                       Gunnor's nephew                  d.1079
                          d.c.1040

William fitz Osbern d.1071                  Osbern
x                         bishop of Exeter
Adeliza of Tosny                    1072–1103

# 5. Dukes of Normandy 943–1087

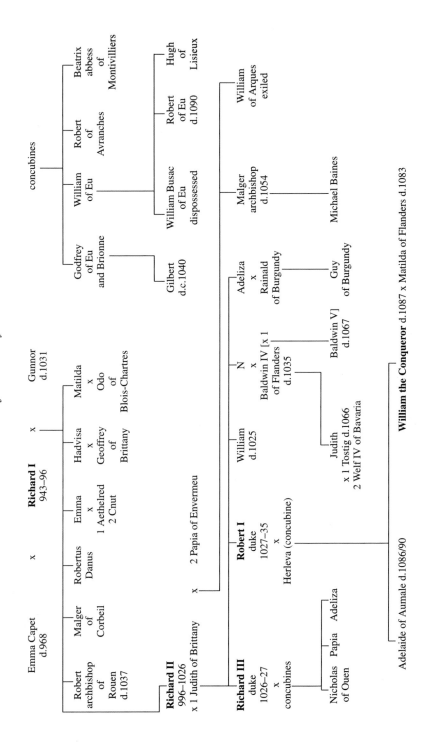

## 6. The Hauteville Dynasty and the Norman Rulers of Southern Italy and Antioch

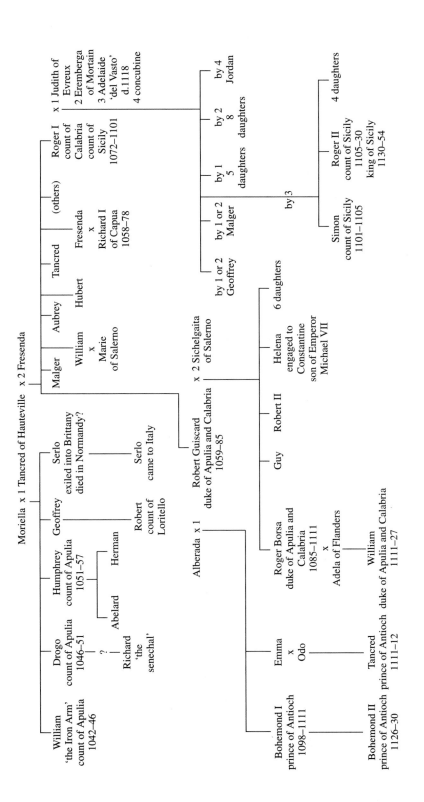

# Time Lines

## 1. *Kings in North-West Europe and Dukes of Normandy*

|  | France | Normandy | England | Denmark | Norway |
|---|---|---|---|---|---|
| 900–950 | **Charles the Simple** 893–922 (d. 929) **Robert I** 922–3 **Ralph of Burgundy** 923–36 **Louis IV** 936–54 | **Rollo** arrives 890? c.911–c.928 **William Longsword** c.928–943 | **Edward the Elder** 899–924 **Athelstan** 924–39 **Edmund** 939–46 **Eadred** 946–55 | **Harold Bluetooth** c.930–c.988 | **Harald Fairhair** c.872–c.930 **Eric Bloodaxe** c.930–c.935 **Hakon I** c.935–961 |
| 950–1000 | **Lothar** 954–86 **Louis V** 986–7 **Hugh Capet** 987–996 | **Richard I** 943–996 | **Eadwig** 955–9 **Edgar** 957/9–75 **Edward the Martyr** 975–8 **Aethelred II** 978–1013/16 | **Svein Forkbeard** c.988–1014 | Petty rulers 960–975 **Hakon Sigurdsson** 975–95 **Olaf Tryggvason** 995–1000 |
| 1000–1050 | **Robert the Pious** 996–1031 **Henry I** 1031–60 | **Richard II** 996–1026 **Richard III** 1026–7 **Robert I** 1027–1035 **William I** 1035–1087 | **Svein Forkbeard** 1013–14 **Edmund Ironside** 1016 **Cnut I** 1016–35 **Harold I** 1035/7–40 **Harthacnut** 1040–42 **Edward the Confessor** 1042–66 | **Harald** 1014–c.1018 **Cnut I** 1016–35 **Harthacnut** 1035–42 **Svein Estristhson** 1042/7–74 | **Eric and Svein Hakonson** 1000–15 **Olaf (St) Haraldsson** c.1015–30 **Svein Alfifason** [= son of Cnut I] 1030–35 **Magnus I** 1035–47 |
| 1050–1100 | **Philip I** 1060–1108 | **Robert Curthose** 1087–1106 | **Harold II Godwinson** 1066 **William I** 1066–87 **William Rufus** 1087–1100 | **Harald Hen** 1074–80 **Cnut II** 1080–6 **Olaf** 1086–1095 **Erik** 1095–1103/4 | **Harald Hardrada** 1047–66 **Magnus II** 1066–69 **Olaf Haraldsson** 1067–93 |

| | France | Normandy | England | Denmark | Norway |
|---|---|---|---|---|---|
| 1100–1150 | **Louis VI** 1108–37 | **Henry I** 1106–35 | **Henry I** 1100–35 | **Niels** 1104–34 | **Magnus III** 1093–1103 **Eynstein and Sigurd** 1103–23/30 |
| | **Louis VII** 1137–80 | **Stephen of Blois** 1135–44 **Geoffrey of Anjou** 1144–51 | **Stephen of Blois** 1135–54 | **Cnut III and Svein III** civil strife 1140s–57 | **Olaf Magnusson** 1103–1115 **Harold and Magnus IV** 1130–35 **Inga and Sigurd** 1136–55/61 **Eynstein Haraldsson** 1142–57 |
| 1150–1200 | **Philip Augustus** 1180–1223 | **Henry II** 1150–89 | **Henry II** 1154–89 | **Valdemar I** 1157–82 | **Hakon Eynsteinsson** 1157–62 **Magnus Erlingsson** 1161–84 |
| | | **Richard I** 1189–99 **John I** 1199–1204 | **Richard I** 1189–99 **John I** 1199–1216 | **Cnut IV** 1182–1202 | |

## 2. *Popes, Emperors of Byzantium and Norman Rulers in Italy*

| | Popes | Byzantium | Apulia Calabria | Sicily |
|---|---|---|---|---|
| 1000–1050 | **Sylvester II** 999–1003 **John XVII** 10003 **John XVIII** 1004–9 **Serge IV** 1009–12 **Benedict VIII** 1012–24 **John XIX** 1024–32 **Benedict IX** 1032–44 **Sylvester III** 1045 **Gregory VI** 1045–6 **Clement II** 1046–7 **Damasius II** 1048 **Leo IX** 1049–54 | **Basil II** 976–1025 **Constantine VIII** 1025–28 **Romanus III** 1028–34 **Michael IV** 1034–41 **Michael V** 1041–42 **Zoe and Theodora** 1042 **Constantine IX** 1042–55 | **William Iron-Arm** 1042–6 **Drogo** 1046–51 | |

| | Popes | Byzantium | Apulia Calabria | Sicily |
|---|---|---|---|---|
| 1050–1100 | **Victor II** 1055–7 | **Theodora** 1055–6 | **Humphrey** 1051–7 | **Roger I** 1061–1101 |
| | **Stephen IX** 1057–8 | **Michael VI** 1056–7 | **Robert Guiscard** 1057–85 | |
| | **Benedict X** 1058–9 | **Isaac I** 1057–9 | | |
| | **Nicholas II** 1059–61 | **Constantine X** 1059–67 | | |
| | **Alexander II** 1061–73 | **Romanus IV** 1068–71 | | |
| | **Gregory VII** 1073–85 | **Michael VII** 1071–8 | | |
| | **Victor III** 1086–7 | **Nicephorus III** 1078–81 | **Roger Borsa** 1085–1111 | |
| | **Urban II** 1088–99 | **Alexius I** 1081–1118 | | |
| 1100–1150 | **Pascal II** 1099–1118 | **John II** 1118–43 | **William** 1111–27 | **Simon** 1101–5 |
| | **Gelasius II** 1118–19 | | | **Roger II** 1105–54 |
| | **Calixtus II** 1119–24 | | | |
| | **Honorius II** 1124–30 | | | |
| | **Innocent II** 1130–43 | | | |
| | **Celestine II** 1143–44 | | | |
| | **Lucius II** 1144–5 | | | |
| | **Eugenius III** 1145–53 | **Manuel I** 1143–80 | | |
| 1150–1200 | **Anastatius IV** 1153–4 | **Alexius II** 1180–3 | | **William I** 1154–66 |
| | **Adrian IV** 1154–9 | **Andronicus I** 1183–5 | | **William II** 1166–89 |
| | **Alexander III** 1159–81 | **Isaac II** 1185–95 | | **Tancred** 1190–94 |
| | **Lucius III** 1181–5 | **Alexius III** 1195–1203 | | **William III** 1194 |
| | **Urban III** 1185–7 | | | **Henry VI** 1194–7 |
| | **Gregory VIII** 1187 | | | **Frederick II** 1198–1250 |
| | **Clement III** 1187–91 | | | |
| | **Celestine III** 1191–8 | | | |
| | **Innocent III** 1198–1216 | | | |

# Index